The gifted
in
socioeducational
perspective

T. ERNEST NEWLAND
Professor Emeritus, Educational Psychology
University of Illinois, Urbana

PRENTICE-HALL, INC., ENGLEWOOD CLIFFS, NEW JERSEY

Library of Congress Cataloging in Publication Data

NEWLAND, T. ERNEST.
   The gifted in socioeducational perspective.

   Bibliography: p. 391-400.
   Includes index.
   1. Gifted children—Education.   I. Title.
LC3993.N54   371.9'5   75-15729
ISBN 0-13-356287-5 lib. bdg.

*To Dot, Mary, and Theryl
who have done so well
in adjusting to
an individual difference*

PRENTICE-HALL SERIES IN SPECIAL EDUCATION
William M. Cruickshank, *Editor*

10 9 8 7 6 5 4 3 2 1

Printed in the United States of America

PRENTICE-HALL INTERNATIONAL, INC., *London*
PRENTICE-HALL OF AUSTRALIA, PTY. LTD., *Sydney*
PRENTICE-HALL OF CANADA, LTD., *Toronto*
PRENTICE-HALL OF INDIA PRIVATE LIMITED, *New Delhi*
PRENTICE-HALL OF JAPAN, INC., *Tokyo*
PRENTICE-HALL OF SOUTHEAST ASIA (PTE.) LTD., *Singapore*

Contents

Foreword

Dr. Newland is an established scholar recognized for both his research and his wealth of experience in educational affairs. Both forms of wisdom appear in this book, but it is more than a report on research and experience: it is a personal document enlivened by the perspectives and enthusiasms of the author.

Synthesis is always a personal act reflecting the knowledge, commitments and feelings of the synthesizer. Personal attributes have significant effect in educational thought, which is an inexact amalgam of several fields brought together with some view of influencing others. The facts are created or changed by the philosophy that presides at the joining of intuition and analysis. Systematized studies are essential if we are to avoid endless repetitions or simple sentimentality. Nevertheless, a rigorously empirical approach leaves out too much, achieving accuracy with sacrifice of

meaning. Invarying dependence on particularism and operational specificity helps reduce murky thoughts but results in overcultivation of arid ideas. Throughout this work, Dr. Newland links scientific research and everyday observations with a vigorous point of view.

The purpose is to offer a resource for thinking without a list of either ideational ingredients or pedagogic recipes. These observations are consistent with the heightened individuality characteristic of gifted children and with the fact that specific behavior or speech may contribute to good teaching, but the real issue is in the accompanying mental events.

The text is both philosophic and practical. There are special treatments of early admissions, administrative arrangements, testing, program evaluation, and probable costs. There are descriptions of programs and cases, of personnel requirements, and an unusual and detailed treatment of the role, selection, and development of consultants.

The distinctive theme of this work is struck in the title *The Gifted in Socioeducational Perspective*. Not in a special section but persistently, Dr. Newland places society at the center of support and nonsupport of high potential. Education is not compartmentalized and confined in formal courses and schools, nor can education for the gifted be separated from society's general attitude toward education. Restrictions on growth come from adult values, student apathy, and ungenerous social conditions as readily as from inadequate instruction or paucity of facts.

Among children who dislike school or have no relation with school achievement there are many undeveloped gifts. Some are angry and alienated; others are politely adjusted to popular stereotypes and values. Special concern must go to those who are deprived of relevant experience, stimulation, the joys of learning, or the rewards of accomplishment. Head Start and other programs have been directed to overcoming environmental drabness and modifying ineffec-

tive intellectual strategies, but little has been done for children who accomplish average or superior work while being significantly retarded below their potential.

Societal, ethnic, and racial differences are not just differences in level or mean IQ. The professional must ask: Does the same score say different things about different children? Why do boys dominate girls in most gifted samples but girls outnumber boys in gifted black groups? Do gifted lower-class children need more classroom structure than others? Must visual style be replaced by an auditory one as a prelude to intellectual accomplishment? Probably there is no placid road to high intellectual achievement, but the easiest road is available to those children whose parents either have arrived at or are mobile in moving into the successful class. How may teachers work with noninvolved and estranged parents? These are but a sample of questions, perhaps enough to suggest a need to read and think.

Maurice F. Freehill
Professor and Chairman
Educational Psychology Department
University of Washington

Preface

Every study involves some degree of frustration. On the one hand, one needs to identify and isolate the factors that are operative or that require consideration. On the other hand, one must recognize that these various factors interact—and these interactions often are such as to cause these seemingly separate factors to appear grossly oversimplified by virtue of being treated as separates. In considering the gifted within our society we must remember that, while components necessarily are described separately, the interaction of those components is of prime importance.

It is important that we know whom we mean when we say "gifted children," that we explore the nature of society's concern with respect to the gifted, that we understand the psychoeducational and personality characteristics of such children, that we examine the educational philosophy which has or should characterize their educational milieu, and that we consider the kinds of educational provisions that have been or should be made for them. Relatively discrete treatments of these facets of the total problem can have some value, yet each to be understood must be related to the others. How the needs of society are perceived has affected how gifted children are defined as well as what has been done for them. Educational provisions for the gifted have varied in terms of both the philosophy underlying educational effort and the clarity with which these children have been identified. Implementing educational philosophy for the gifted has depended on just how the gifted were identified, how effective administrators and teachers have been, and the degrees of resistance operative.

In this book, therefore, we shall consider not only the major components of the psychoeducational problem of the gifted but also many of the interactions among those components which make society's meeting the needs of the gifted such a challenge—and at times such a frustrating one. We shall limit our concern for the most part to social, psychological, and educational aspects of providing for the gifted from early age until, essentially, the college level. Rather than delineate fully and explore in depth specific educational methods and materials, we shall use them primarily to illustrate the concepts and principles which must underlie actualizing the gifted.

The truly extensive published research on the gifted and on their education has been used selectively to illustrate matters of major import—particularly in terms of the use of the findings rather than their production by research. In the course of such discussion, major research dimensions and research needs have been identified.

The emphasis is on programmatic aspects of facilitating school learning by the gifted, illustrated with episodes from the author's experiences during some forty years in working with individual gifted youngsters. In all these real-life cases, ranging from the most pleasant to the most depressing and frustrating, the educators involved have played primary roles. (The names of the children are,

of course, fictitious.) The underlying commitment, both programmatic and personal, has been twofold: that the gifted (and all children for that matter) should be helped to be self-fulfilled and self-actualized, and that they should be helped to learn that they can contribute to society to a degree that is in harmony with their superior potentials. To this end, the book discusses the importance and nature of psychological factors such as motivation, reinforcement through success in learning to learn, concept development, and the nurturance of creativity.

This book has its share not only of the author's convictions and contentions but also of his overt professions of ignorance of what is or should be. It is hoped that some readers, encountering the latter, will be motivated to research such problems or their offshoots. Included, as illustrative rather than exhaustive, is a series of topics (Chapter 14) for consideration which the reader might profitably examine before reading the text. This should dispose him toward a critical reading of the text, sensitize him to issues that the text does not adequately resolve, and prompt him to do important correlative reading and to collect additional information.

T. ERNEST NEWLAND

1

The gifted as an area of concern

Logically, society's concern for the gifted should involve their full age range, including the preschool period; the school period, (extending through the level of advanced graduate work); the employment period; and the postemployment, or gerontological, period.

Least attention has been paid to the needs of, and society's needs for, the gifted "senior citizen." To a certain extent, the gifted in this age group may appear to have taken care of themselves. Such certainly is the case of those who, with or without the help of the school or other agencies of society, have established themselves as jurists, musicians, researchers, medical specialists, teachers, religionists, legislators, labor and other social leaders, writers, actors, and the like. Having found their niches, demonstrated competence, and acquired status in their activities, they have tended to continue to function in terms of the habits they

have acquired and the social expectations they have fulfilled. But there probably is a residual area of concern for those older gifted who may not have made *Who's Who* but who still can make significant contributions to society. Much needs to be done here—both in research and in program development.

More consideration needs to be given to the preschool gifted. Accounts of early manifestations of giftedness have abounded, but primarily as aiding our understanding of older gifted children rather than as an area of primary scientific inquiry. Since the 1930s, the magic age of six years as the time of school entry has been pushed down. One reason has been an increasing recognition of the vital importance of starting earlier to educate handicapped children, particularly the visually impaired, the auditorially impaired, and the orthopedically disabled. Another has been an increasing

1

recognition of the importance of early and systematic psychological nurturance of the cognitive development of the non-handicapped, as in the case of the "disadvantaged." Perhaps, as educators and the rest of society move further from laissez faire and elitism, the "preschool" delineation will shift further downward. Since no formal social institution exists for providing specifically for the preschool gifted, it is understandable that what comes to be known scientifically about them should be a part of the larger concern for early child development. As this takes place, the importance of societal programs of nurturance—social, physical, and intellectual—should be recognized.

Considerable study has been made of the gifted and talented in the employment period. Some attempt has been made to relate the findings of such studies to those of the school period in terms of its predictive and preparation possibilities. The scope of activities of gifted school children, however, is much narrower than that of gifted adults. Children in school are primarily the responsibility of a single function of society; adults are "scattered to the winds," working as laborers or lawyers—teachers or technicians—mayors or manufacturers—artists or architects—musicians or medical doctors. Such diversity has mitigated against much research that is possible within the educational structure.

The primary focus here will be on the gifted in the school period—for two reasons. First, in this period a social institution—the school—is at least implicitly charged with the major responsibility for helping the gifted ultimately to become meaningful contributors to society. Second, during this particularly significant period, the gifted are forming habits of functioning—and it is here that later ineffective functioning can best be prevented. The problems of the gifted at the college level will be dealt with

only as they represent major extensions or implications of those considered more intensively below that level. Our major concern will be with the preschool and elementary school levels.

PURPOSES OF AMERICAN EDUCATION

Few have denied—and many have cited authoritatively—the four major purposes of education set forth by the Educational Policies Commission in 1938: the attainment of self-realization, the cultivation of effective human relationships, the acquisition of economic efficiency, and the learning to assume civic responsibility. Bennis (1970), in discussing social change and social demands, or expectations, noted certain important shifts in cultural values:

From	Toward
Achievement	Self-actualization
Self-control	Self-expression
Independence	Interdependence
Endurance of stress	Capacity for job
Full employment	Full lives

These shifts, taking place in America over a long period, generally incorporate the aims of education as stated by the Educational Policies Commission. "Self-realization" and "self-actualization" clearly must constitute the background in terms of which the gifted should be perceived in the school period—emphasizing not only each individual's "need" and social "right" to attain to the fullest of his potential but also the importance of his contribution to society's present effectiveness and future growth.

THE RETARDED BRIGHT CHILDREN

As far back as the 1920s, Pintner observed that the most retarded children in the schools were the bright ones. He based this conclusion upon the frequency and extent to which the educational achievements of bright children were below their capacities to achieve. As part of the post-Sputnik spurt of interest in the gifted, numerous studies of underachieving bright children were made, revealing that the problem identified by Pintner some thirty years earlier had only lain dormant. Psychoeducational clinic files bulge with cases of bright children who are regarded as "maladjusted," a major percentage of these maladaptive behaviors ensuing from the failure of society, largely through the schools, to enable these bright children to function more nearly in harmony with their potentials.

This disharmony between potential and opportunity to function more nearly in terms of that high potential does not afflict *all* bright children, but the condition is encountered dishearteningly often. In such instances both the bright individual and society are the losers. Those who fail in this form of self-realization often come most vigorously and frustratingly to the attention of parents, teachers, school psychologists, counselors, and clinicians. The following instances, all real, illustrate the all-too-common condition.

Arnold was reading comprehendingly at third-grade level when he entered school at the conventional age six. His first-grade teacher, believing in "peerness" and togetherness, not only started all her children off with reading readiness instruction but continued to keep all the children together in their reading work. The parents, observing the child's loss of interest in reading at home, sought to motivate him to continue in his voluntary and largely independent reading. When he told them what the situation was at school, they suggested that he seek an opportunity to go to the school library and read more interesting materials. Such permission was denied the child, and he was told to read the assigned first-grade material—which he

had read, at least a year before, two or three times in order to "become more familiar with it." His behavior in school became increasingly maladaptive until he had to be sent to the principal on account of his aggressive nonconformity. Because of his increasing aggressive behavior at home, the parents took him to a competent school psychologist. After examining the situation, the psychologist helped the school personnel work out an educational adjustment, and within two months the child became much happier and better adjusted both in school and at home.

Bertha was failing in her fifth-grade work, in fact had already failed one whole grade. She was grossly aggressive toward others, both children and adults, and was actually destructive of property at school and at home. Evaluation of this child revealed that she was intellectually capable of doing ninth-grade work. A major educational readjustment was effected for her, providing both for her acquiring some necessary relevant educational skills and for her being challenged with learning opportunities that were more in harmony with her educational and intellectual potentials. Within six months she was working happily at the eighth-grade level and adjusting well to others in her environment.

Charles barely squeezed through his academic work in the first semester of his freshman year at college and was threatened with complete failure in his work for the second semester. (He hadn't wanted to go to college, but his parents were requiring him to "get an education.") His high school academic performance had been essentially of only a passing quality, although most of his teachers had reported that, while he "seemed to have much promise," he probably was working below his capacity. He had started with much promise and enthusiasm in the first grade but did increasingly less well as he progressed through the grades. Both his parents and teachers had insisted he be kept with his "peers." Even with some compensatory efforts at providing him with remedial education and help in how to study, he failed to complete the second semester's work well enough to remain in college. He not only had not been helped to acquire good habits of learning, from the first grade up, but, by virtue of his barely eking his way through school work in spite of his (and others') awareness of his superior potential, he had become conditioned against the act (and joy) of learning. He *did* graduate to heroin.

Underachievement and Maladaptive Behavior

Not all failure is due to an absence or neglect of self-realization. Not all who fail to achieve adequate self-realization fail; many learn to get by and settle for only partial utilization of their potential —often at a demonstrable price. Two pioneer studies tested the validity of the following generalization with respect to elementary school children: The greater the disparity between well-measured learning potential ("intelligence") and measured educational achievement (and expectation as implied by grade placement), the greater is the frequency of teacher-reported pupil maladaptive behavior (Grubb, 1969; Whitehurst, 1968). The findings have sufficiently supported the hypothesis to warrant continued objective exploration of this important phenomenon.

Facilitating the self-realization of the gifted can do much for society, but it can do more for the gifted themselves. Not only will they achieve more satisfaction in their own lives, but also they will thereby come to a clearer understanding of the importance of self-realization in the lives of others.

SOCIETY'S NEED FOR THE GIFTED

We must also recognize society's continuing need for superior contributions by the gifted. Whatever the efforts of educators may be to facilitate the effective learning and adjustment of the gifted, the fundamental decision as to what should be done for or with them must be made in terms of their potential roles in society. To what extent does society want, or need, the gifted to function effectively? Should society, not just the educational portion of it, systematically seek out its gifted and prepare them to assume their appropriate contributive (major influential) roles in it, or should society just take it for granted that its future leaders gradually and naturally will emerge from the mass and move by some kind of social sifting into roles of major social influence and responsibility?

Obviously, the expectations any society has regarding its gifted depend upon the nature of that society. The roles which (largely implicitly) the gifted are expected to play differ, for instance, between people in the United States and those in Russia, or between those in Indian and Black segments within larger societies. They differ, also within any given social group from time to time. The manner in which and the extent to which the gifted have been recognized as important to this country's society were discernibly different, both explicitly and implicitly, in early colonial days, in the early industrialization era, and just after the flight of the first Sputnik. They were accorded a status in Czarist Russia that was quite different from that under the Communist regime.

Selection and Emergence of the Gifted

Society's perceptions of the gifted have varied with the ways in which it perceives its needs. At times, no "help wanted" signs are apparent. When a society is evolving in a "natural" state, in the absence of social planning, its leaders emerge in terms of the implicit needs of the moment—whether they involve geographic frontier exploration and settlement, the planning and execution of military strategy, the establishment of formal bases of government, or

teaching, or medicine. At other times—
even while, for instance, labor leaders
are "emerging"—society may formally
study its needs, identify its potential
leaders, and systematically prepare them
for roles in which they are needed. Immediately after the Russians' orbiting of
Sputnik, for instance, the United States
addressed itself vigorously to a study of
its needs for scientists and technologists;
consequently, programs were mounted
for the identification of promising students in these areas and programs were
expanded to prepare those for whom an
abundance of scholarship funds quickly
had been provided. (Major curricular
innovations in mathematics and science,
some conceived before Sputnik, bur-
geoned, as did criticisms of educational
practices, under society's heightened
sense of educational need.) For a number of social and economic reasons, this
was but a spurt in our educational history, so far as the gifted were concerned,
being followed by a reversion to earlier
conditions with respect to the identification of leaders, or potential leaders, in
higher education, racial, and peace movements. The United States has not committed itself as fully to a policy of formal selection of its leaders as have (for
instance) England and Russia.

EDUCATIONAL PROVISIONS
FOR THE GIFTED

Our consideration of the gifted must also
concern itself with the nature of the
educational provisions made for them.
The schools have been regarded as the
primary agency for meeting the basic
needs of society. The first major commitment of the schools is to enable the
members of society to communicate—
and in particular to read—understandingly. The 1970 commitment of the U.S.
Office of Education to enable "everyone
to read" exemplifies high awareness of
such a need. But for the gifted, particu-

larly, more is needed. Education, as an
agency of society, has the responsibility
of facilitating their drawing of generalizations, their identifying and employing
of abstract ideas or concepts, their seeing
relationships among those concepts,
thereby arriving at still higher-level conceptualizations, and their being innovative and creative in the light of that
kind of learning and development. Such
ways of behaving must consistently be
recognized as involving abstractions in
more than the areas of economics, law,
philosophy, science, and the arts; similar
abstractions are important in government, organizational planning and manipulation in industry, in education
itself, in labor, in politics, and even in
organized crime. Leaders in social movements, much more so than the rank and
file, necessarily operate in terms of major
abstractions which are called policies,
theories, and principles.

Philosophical and Psychological
Undergirdings

Educational provisions for the gifted
must themselves be based on discernible
general principles both of philosophy
and of psychology. All too often, such
provisions have been made in a philosophical near-vacuum and/or with an
inadequate or distorted psychological
orientation. The school administrator
who decides in May to start a special
class for the gifted the following September because he has learned that some
financial assistance can be obtained for
such a class, or because a nearby, competing school district superintendent has
done so, rarely acts on the basis of sound
educational philosophy. The teacher suddenly given a "fast" section to teach
often lacks adequate educational or psychological orientation to the unique intellectual characteristics and needs of
her children. She tends to do pretty
much what she has been doing all along
—and thereby contributes to a failure

in the undertaking. A state department that uses hastily provided funds "for the education of the gifted" to introduce a variety of "experimental" programs, yet fails to make sure that the school administrators are philosophically oriented to the goals of such an undertaking and that the teachers involved understand and can operate in terms of the relevant psychological facts and principles, quickly finds an outlet for its funds but does little fundamentally for the gifted.

Any undertaking in the name of the gifted that lacks sound philosophical undergirdings, particularly in the case of the administrator, and that is not executed in terms of sound psychology must be regarded only as so much window dressing. In fact, the pernicious effect of such undertakings can deter the promotion and inauguration of a sound program for the gifted. Ill-founded attempts tend to be short-lived, especially when the stimulus of special funding is removed, but their lack of perceptible accomplishments—or their all-too-evident harmful effects—are remembered and held against *any* program for the gifted.

Division of Responsibility

Educational provisions for the gifted are of two kinds—those which are essentially administrative, and those which involve actual classroom practices. Decisions to employ a consultant, to introduce special classes or other special groups, to provide for acceleration, and to provide for some kind of released time are the responsibilities (and opportunities) of school administrators. Activities within the classroom to facilitate the learning of ("teaching") the gifted are the responsibilities (and opportunities) of the teachers. Administrative actions unaccompanied by appropriate adjustments in the teaching process can mean failure. Similarly, the introduction by the teacher of

even sound instructional provisions without administrative philosophical support and authorization is hazardous.

OTHER FACTORS AFFECTING THE GIFTED

A full exploration of a concern for the gifted would include factors not dealt with here. A humanistic social philosophy is important to the self-realization orientation. Economic factors have a bearing upon society's perception of its needs for the contributions of the gifted as well as upon its ability or willingness to provide funds. The kind of preparation required of administrators and teachers, the criteria for employing them, and the kinds of status accorded them by society influence the quality and extent of educational provisions they make for the gifted. The periodic shrinking of employment opportunities for certain scientists, the part played by the school in keeping young people out of the employment market, the shifting perceptions regarding justifiable expenditures in society—these and many other considerations affect society's reaction to its gifted.

We have singled out three major orientations for separate discussion: the needs of the gifted for self-actualization, society's need for their contributions, and the educational provisions that should be made for them. Other factors also have been mentioned. We must recognize, however, the continuous interaction among all of them. A rope is not merely the strands that make it up; it is also the interaction among them.

Having blithely used terms such as the "gifted" and the "bright," we must now delineate more precisely those with whom we are concerned. Here, too, the necessity of "defining" them in terms of a social context will be apparent.

2

Definition
of the gifted

Doris' third-grade teacher, who knew that the child was a "quick learner" with a Binet IQ of 141, asked her fourth-grade teacher why the girl had not been placed in the district's "gifted program." Almost disdainfully she was informed that only children with "IQs above 150" were gifted. Because a research project in that district had been concerned only with children who had Binet IQs of 150 and above, teachers had generalized their perceptions of the gifted in terms of the 150-plus definition.

In the 1930s, a superintendent of schools in a moderate-sized city, prodded by a staffer of the state education department, made a study of whether his district had any gifted and found, much to his surprise, that there were none. Having read about Leta Hollingworth's 1926 study of gifted children, particularly that portion concerning children above Binet IQ 180, he was using the 180 definition.

He had defined himself out of responsibility.

A teacher who had a very verbal child in her class spoke of this child as "gifted," although the conceptualization level of the roughly appropriate words the child used so freely did not suggest superior general learning aptitude. Other children who have outstanding competencies, say in spelling, or in dance, or even in getting along quite well with other children and adults, often are characterized as "gifted" even though they actually lack more inclusive basic capability. Others—parents and educators—have used the word "gifted" to denote children (or adults) who have a single outstanding competency, such as demonstrated skill in lettering, or an impressive voice quality.

How tall must a fifteen-year-old girl be to be regarded as "tall"? Probably no one would disagree that six feet six inches would suffice. Most, probably, would regard six feet as "tall." Fewer might agree that a girl five feet nine would qualify. In any group and on any trait, the further out from the average the cutoff point is, the more easily agreement is reached that a subgroup can be identified. Unlike height, however, giftedness is a very complex characteristic, even if the major component in it can be identified, and defining it in terms of a single dimension is a problem even before we consider cutoff points. For many educators, moreover, the act of defining giftedness has threatening implications; it menaces the familiar, comfortable practices geared to the average and based upon lockstep, uniform assignments to all members of a given class or grade.

DEFINITIONS
AND CONFUSION

One author of a text on the gifted has declared: "We can no longer afford to get bogged down in definitions and confusion" (Abraham, 1958). However, this book will define and characterize gifted children in order to improve precision in communication.

The condition against which Abraham, in effect, was protesting started with the pioneer Binet IQ characterization, which had considerable psychoeducational validity (as we shall see later). Subsequent characterizations were shaped by personal and social·biases, often tending to be functions more of personal and professional enthusiasms than of logic or psychological grounding.

Early IQ Limits

Stedman, in describing her experimental class for the gifted, begun in 1918, reflected Terman's thinking in setting a Binet IQ of 125 as her lower limit, al-

though four years later she raised this to 140. Terman began his extensive study of gifted children in 1921 using a Binet IQ of 130 as his lower limit. His famous *Genetic Studies of Genius* was concerned with children whose Binet IQs were 135 and above, although the bulk of his subjects were 140 and above. Subsequent serious researchers, at least prior to the 1950s, tended not only to define their gifted in terms of Binet IQs of 120 to 125 (or their validated equivalents) and above, but also to characterize them as particularly capable of learning, especially in the verbal area, and of superior abilities in generalization and conceptualization. Such characterizations were, in effect, redundant or only elaborative, since these kinds of behavior tended to be observable in children who had earned such Binet IQs.

An analysis by the author of the characterizations employed in 126 research studies on the "gifted" over a 23-year period showed that 99 of the research populations were denoted in terms of psychological test performance superiority (two with an IQ cutoff point of 110 on some unspecified test), 19 populations were identified only in terms of some kind of educational superiority ("accelerated," "Phi Beta Kappa"), and eight studies were concerned with "talented," "eminent," and other social characterizations.

Non-Binet Criteria

However, the relatively simplistic state of affairs of characterizing the gifted in terms of Binet IQs (or their validated equivalents) was influenced by two kinds of developments. One was the appearance, largely for use in the schools, of a large number of group, and a few individual, tests purporting to measure "intelligence." By virtue of the diversity of the behaviors sampled and of the standardization procedures used, measures called IQs or MAs tended both to contaminate and to seem to disagree with the original meaning of the Binet IQ. This condition stimulated a questioning, on the part of the technically less well informed, of the validity of the Binet IQ as a criterion cutoff for giftedness. A second observation was also disconcerting: some individuals who did outstanding things in society, such as creative writing, singing, painting, acting, and exerting social leadership, appeared gifted even though they might not have met the Binet IQ criterion. In large part, this type of person came to be regarded as "talented."

As a social climate developed which was antagonistic to testing and as abuses of the Binet (or its prototypes) with the "disadvantaged" became increasingly apparent, an overgeneralized aversion to Binet-type IQ thinking developed. Such a composite of forces helped to contribute to the kind of thinking about the gifted later reflected in educators' definitions. Further distracting were the results of some highly publicized research which suggested that some "creative" children had Binet IQs below the range of 120–130. Some school systems, owing to the actions of certain social pressure groups and to an inadequacy of properly trained school personnel, ceased the "intelligence" testing of their pupils; great confusion can result if any interest in the gifted is shown in such systems.

In a symposium chaired by Havighurst, a broad definition was proposed: "The gifted or talented child is one who shows consistently remarkable performance in any worthwhile line of endeavor" (Henry, 1958, p. 19). This definition has two extremely significant inherent weaknesses. First, it is a *post hoc* definition—the child has to have already demonstrated his giftedness in his performance, which means that he can be identified only at a later phase in his school career. Second, what consti-

tutes "any worthwhile line of endeavor" can be quite debatable.

The Top *x* Percent

The impact of social agitation, during the late 1950s and early 1960s, to make education more effective for more children had a still different effect on the defining of the gifted. DeHaan (1957) contended that the top 16 percent of any class or school population should be regarded as gifted and/or talented. DeHaan's figure stems from his and Havighurst's experience in the Quincy, Illinois, Youth Development Project, in which they found that when they took the top 10 percent in general intellectual ability (as measured by DeHaan's procedures), the top 10 percent in leadership, and the top 2 percent in drawing ability, the combined group represented 16 percent of their total population. When they included children who were in the top 10 percent in music, dramatic abilities, creative writing, and mechanical ability, they included the top 20–25 percent of the total school population (DeHaan and Havighurst, 1957). In summarizing research on the gifted and talented over a six-year period, Fliegler and Bish (1959) took the position that

> The term *gifted* encompasses those children who possess a superior intellectual potential and functional ability to achieve academically in the top 15 to 20 percent of the school population; and/or talent of high order in such special areas as mathematics, science, expressive arts, creative writing, music, and social leadership; and a unique creative ability to deal with their environment (p. 409).

Even though "the school population" refers to the *total* school population— *all* the school children in the United States—it was advocated by some that giftedness should include the top sixth in *any* school district. This criterion is insensitive to the fact that in some schools, and even in some school districts, there would be a much larger or a much smaller percentage who could be so identified. To accommodate differences among schools or school districts, a recommendation was made that "every school must seek to include within its gifted student program all those students for whom, because of their special abilities, the regular curriculum is not sufficiently challenging" (*Administrative Procedures and School Practices for the Academically Talented Student*, 1960, p. 33).

One passing "expert" declared unequivocally that the top sixth of *any* class should be educated as gifted. When confronted with a real-life situation in which the brightest of eighteen children had, at best, average book-learning potential, as ascertained by sound psychological assessment (not just testing), he insisted that those two should be educated as "gifted". It did not concern him that these two children had not given, and probably would not give, any evidence of any high-level generalization and conceptualization ability and probably would have serious difficulty working with materials making more than conventional learning demands.

The "Talented"

The term "educationally talented" has been used by many educators in preference to "gifted," perhaps because the latter was regarded as too restrictive, and in preference to "mentally superior," probably because of negative connotations regarding the children not so characterized. This new term was taken to denote both those children who had achieved outstandingly and those whose actual achievements were not as great as the evidence of learning potential suggested they might be—the "under-

achievers." However, the term "academically talented" was used also to include the different kinds of outstanding performances or potential performances incorporated in the Fliegler-Bish definition. Partly a euphemism to avoid socially disturbing connotations of "mental superiority" and any explicit anchorage to "intelligence" testing, the term also reflected the educators' bewilderment with the vast array of tests, many of which did not yield Binet-type evidence on learning aptitude.

FACTORS AFFECTING PERCEPTION OF THE GIFTED

As all of the foregoing illustrates, just how the gifted are defined depends upon the interaction of a variety of factors: the extent of humanitarian commitment to giving each individual the opportunity to realize his potential; the general philosophy of the society to which the schools were expected to contribute; the philosophy and practices of educators, presumably reflecting the first two factors; compulsory school attendance laws and their enforcement, reflecting society's perception of the needs of its children as well as the relation of school attendance to the labor market; and, particularly, the availability of sound procedures by which to assess the potentialities of its embryonic citizens. At different times these factors have interacted in different ways to affect attitudes—particularly those of educators—toward the gifted.

During the first quarter of this century, for instance, schools were committed to relatively narrow perceptions of children's academic learning. Enforced school attendance contributed less heavily, then, to the size and heterogeneity of the school-attending population.

Terman's 1916 revision of the Binet measured fairly well the potential necessary for the kinds of learning the schools then expected. In fact, it was the major instrument available for such measurement; only later were group testing devices adapted from military to school use with elementary and high school children. Within this pattern of interacting factors, the relatively simple Binet IQ served as a relevant and reasonably objective criterion in terms of which giftedness could be perceived.

Within the next generation, along with the increased size and heterogeneity of their population, the schools increasingly incorporated other than the strictly academic kinds of learning opportunities, in response to society's needs for wider diversification in the preparation of children. Not only was there a burgeoning growth of "intelligence" tests, particularly for younger children, and of a variety of aptitude tests, such as reading readiness and specific subject-matter area aptitude tests, but the Binet was being found not to yield equally valid predictive information for the various new areas of learning activity, such as music, drawing, and different vocational training areas at the secondary level. Such factors combined to limit the general utility and relevance of the older Binet-type criterion of giftedness. Add to these, later, society's growing aversion to testing of all types and its increased concern for the "disadvantaged," misuses and abuses of "intelligence" testing, a growing interest in leadership qualities (accompanied by an almost studied unawareness of the results of research on social leadership manifested by the gifted), a growth of research on adult creativity combined with Guilford's delineation of divergent thinking as a psychological basis of educators' interest in creativity in children, and you have the social-psychological-educational mi-

lieu for the evolving characterization of the gifted—from the early, admittedly simple, Binet-type definition to the later multiple characterizations.

REDEFINING THE GIFTED

The distracting array of terminology used in regard to the gifted must be set in order. Too often, as we have seen, educators have defined the gifted in dubious ways. In conventional prescientific fashion they have let the gifted identify themselves by demonstrating superior achievement. Or they have specified that some percentage of *any* class should be educated as gifted. Or they have chosen to identify the gifted in terms of both learning capability and achievement, capitalizing on those children whose achievements have been more in harmony with their potentials and ignoring those who have high potential but, for one reason or another, low achievement.

A Sound Rationale

A sound rational for determining the magnitude of the school's job in educating the gifted must incorporate three components:

1. Society itself should provide a sound first approximation of how many are needed to carry out its high-level operations. This will provide a quantitative statement of the magnitude of the school's responsibility.
2. The identification of the important conditions which differentiate those with top-level responsibilities from those with lower-level responsibilities is the responsibility of psychologists. They thus delineate those behavioral characteristics which individuals must have to meet their high-level responsibilities.
3. The schools then have the job of locating that portion of the school population

which is large enough to meet the needs of society and which has the essential psychological characteristics.

This reasoning applies only to how the school *identifies* those who are to be educated as gifted. As we shall see later, just how it should go about *educating* the gifted involves a commitment to a socio-educational philosophy, an understanding of the educational significance of the psychological characteristics of the gifted, and the employment of appropriate educational policies and procedures.

A Socially Based Definition

The definition of the gifted is necessarily a sociopsychological responsibility. Society both explicitly and implicitly makes apparent the extent to which it needs the gifted. Studies of the numbers of physicians, teachers, lawyers, judges, scientists, and social and industrial organizational personnel required reflect quite overtly the magnitude of its needs for top-level individuals. However, these needs vary with social conditions. In the later 1950s and early 1960s, major needs for scientists, teachers, and physicians were clearly identified; by the early 1970s certain of these needs (as reflected in the number of positions available) had abated markedly, whereas well-specified needs for medical, legal, and social personnel were continuing to be sharply felt.

Many of society's "needs," however, are implicit. Persons of high capacity are needed, albeit in an emergent evolutionary sense, in agriculture, in industry, and in roles of social organizational responsibility at the local, state, national, and international levels, and in the areas of social welfare, labor and consumer activity, and governmental operation. The fact that superior persons do "find their way" to positions of great responsibility requiring major leadership and organizational competencies reflects a very real societal need. It can be argued that society also has latent needs in the arts areas—creative writers, painters, musicians, and creators and interpreters in the theater. While the field of sports presents a picture of mixed needs for physical superiority and for intellectual acumen, certain of the more commercialized sports make unmistakable demands for persons of superior mental capability.

Percentages of Leaders Needed

Taking the point of view that society in general needs some of its members to play major contributive roles, the author sought to ascertain the percentages of the total working population who were so functioning. Implicit in this approach was the assumption that if x percent of the present (U.S.) working population were involved in high-level roles, the schools were obligated to regard at least that percentage of the general school population as needing to be prepared to fulfill those kinds of roles. Since there would probably be some loss between the percentages so ascertained and the percentages who fulfilled the expectancies for them, as well as some error in identifying those who should be so prepared, an additional percentage (y) should be added to the pool of candidates for high roles. The total candidate pool thus would need to be the socially identified percentage (x) plus the "insurance" factor (y). Since high capability in learning was expected to be the major component in preparatory learning and in later functioning, the assumption was made that this x-plus-y percentage could be identified by moving down from the top of the distribution of learning capability to that point that would mark off the total percentage sought.

Taking the numbers of persons reported engaged in the 51 occupations for 1950 (as listed in the *Statistical Abstracts of the United States*) in the top three occupational groups of the United States, managerial through professional, 147 persons—largely teachers in graduate education courses—made judgments regarding the percentages of persons within each occupational category who would need to operate at a high conceptualization level. These judgments, when synthesized, suggested that 5 percent of the working population would be so regarded. If an additional 3 percent are included, to provide for possible "slippage" or error, we would regard 8 percent of our population as essential to society's high-level responsibilities. Applying this to the normal IQ distribution, we find the gifted of social concern to be those who earn Binet-type IQs above 120 to 125 (Newland, 1963). We shall not, at this point, explore the sociopsychological validity of IQs; rather, we are concerned with a procedure for arriving at a first, but objective, approximation of the *magnitude* of the need of society for those who are to meet its major needs.

Limitations and Dangers

One might argue that such an approach could be used in any totalitarian society. It could be regarded as highly deterministic and potentially antithetical to the self-realization criterion. While it would be possible to identify a promising six-year-old as a candidate for preparation for a specific social role (say, lawyer)—a highly deterministic manner of thinking —it is equally possible, and much more defensible, that such a youngster might need particular consideration to help him toward self-realization without specifying his future role. He could be regarded as having high potential for a general kind of later social involvement. His role would be identified much later in his educational and developmental picture, and in terms much more inclusive than that of only his basic poten-

tial for learning. The concepts of meeting the anticipated needs of society and of self-realization are reconcilable, if one posits the recognition of a fluid and changing (but still definable) society, a flexible and socially and psychologically sensitive educational system, and a philosophy that incorporates a high regard for the rights of the individual.

Two possible dangers in this approach need to be recognized. First, the data used here reflect an assessment at a particular period in our society. If such an analysis were made, say, 20 or 50 years later, it might reflect a greater or lesser social need for high-level social involvement. (One would guess, however, that no great shift would be found.) Second, the approach may be regarded as highly deterministic. Since it might be found that x percent were involved in occupation A, y percent in occupation B, z percent in occupation C, and so on, it might be assumed that such specific percentages of children will need to be educated to function later socially in those specific occupations. The glaring fallacy in that, while general superior learning potential is detectable by means of competent psychological assessment at first-grade level, other more specialized aptitudes generally do not emerge until later. As we shall see when we discuss educational provisions for the gifted, the implementation of programs discernibly related to specific areas of future social contribution should come later in the education of the gifted than in the case of the nongifted.

Procedural Sequence

While society, in one way or other, must tell us how many it needs to have educated as gifted, psychology is uniquely qualified to help us understand who the gifted are. Once we know how many society needs to play major roles and what they are like, it then becomes the responsibility of educators to identify whatever that number, or percentage, is and to provide them with an education that is suitable both to the focal characteristics which psychology has identified and to the anticipated general or specific kinds of participation in which they will engage.

GENERALIZATION
AND SYMBOL ACQUISITION
IN THE GIFTED

Fundamentally, the gifted are particularly capable of quick and generally accurate generalization. All learning, "bookish" or otherwise, involves generalization. With no formal training, the young child first learns to respond, usually positively, to other persons in his immediate environment; he then generalizes, on the basis of these reactions, to others in his expanding environment. He acquires means of communication, whether it be crying, gesturing, or language, by virtue of his capacity to generalize. Practices learned with respect to crossing one street generalize to the crossings of other streets. He generalizes his likes or dislikes of persons he knows well to others he knows less well (his teachers, the scoutmaster, athletes, Baptists etc.) —and similarly with pets, dangers, subject-matter areas, school, "authority," justice. While all children (and adults) generalize in the process of their learning, the gifted do so more quickly on the basis of fewer encounters and instances, and also to a greater degree of complexity—as illustrated by "understanding" and/or discovering general principles, complicated interrelationships, and abstractions. It is not, then, that the gifted just generalize, because all animals do; their primary differentness is that they generalize much more quickly, effectively, and extensively than do the non-

gifted. They differ not in kind, but in degree.

The capacity to generalize should be much more broadly recognized as a potentiality, as something that may be nurtured and helped to become manifest and effective. It is a "given" of the act of living in a society that such behavior "just naturally" is helped to take place, and, usually, to continue to function. It is contributive to the existence of any society that such generalization be nurtured, encouraged, reinforced. Tribal mores, customs, laws, interpersonal and intergroup relationships, tribal cohesiveness and international relationships—all are generalizations which have been nurtured as contributive to the good of the group. Some of this nurturance of generalizing is formally provided for in any society, but much of it is seemingly informally and unsystematically nurtured. The child generalizes as he makes rules for his games; the adult codifies rules of personal or institutional behavior.

Hidden Potentials
for Generalization

But within any society there are segments, or subcultures, which do not so consistently or systematically nurture generalizability. Starting in the 1960s, our society became aware, as never before, that in some of its segments such reinforcement—even unintentional—was either lacking or discernibly different. The learnings that were nurtured and reinforced in these segments came to be recognized as noncontributive to larger social effectiveness. While some portion of these segments had at least above-average potentials for superior generalization, they were not nurtured by their relatively simple environments and the value systems prevalent there. Too often, educators assumed that such potentials did not exist in such minority groups, or they made inadequate attempts to identify and nurture them.

Acquisition of Symbols

The biological predisposition of the organism to behave in the way called generalizing is the basis for the child's capacity to acquire symbols. Symbols themselves can be regarded as generalizations. As such, they facilitate communication. Symbols are used to denote things or classes of things, conditions, complexes of phenomena relationships, or patterns of relationships. It is much more convenient and feasible to use the symbol "elephant" than to present the animal itself when reacting to, or about, it. The symbol "dog" may denote a specific object or animal, or it may denote a class of animals, depending not only upon the experiential background of the person using or hearing it but also upon his capacity to generalize with respect to dogs. The symbol pattern, "I'm happy" (a pattern because it involves not only three or four symbols but also an interrelationship among them) denotes a condition. The use of the symbol "$\pm$" enables its user to indicate a specified uncertainty about some condition. Instead of guessing a woman's age as just 35 years, we can guess it as 35 ± 5, or somewhere between 30 and 40 years. The symbol "evolution" denotes a complex of phenomena, each of which involves other phenomena (and symbols). The symbol pattern "$r = .41$" denotes a particular pattern of relationship between phenomena, the understanding of which necessitates the "knowledge" of other symbols.

While generalizing properly can be regarded as learning, there is learning without generalizing. Children may be confronted with a task such as learning the number combinations $3 + 7, 4 + 5, 7 + 3, 5 + 4$, and so on. As was discovered in the 1920s, some children learned them as separates, as discrete learnings. However, a few generalized quickly that $4 + 5$ yielded the same result as $5 + 4$. In effect, even though they may not have so verbalized it, they "discovered" that if $x + y = z$, then $y + x = z$, a form of statement early introduced in the "new mathematics." Even within these statements, generalizing is involved, since x was learned as a symbol for some number and y as a symbol for some other number. Abstract symbols have been learned to be usable in the place of concrete numbers. There is a progression from the concrete to the abstract and also a progression from the less complex to the more complex. Complexity may denote either the interaction of a number of relatively simple variables (length $\times$ width $\times$ depth = volume) or the interaction of variables each of which is quite complex (position/time/velocity/point of entry into the atmosphere).

Differences among individuals

Differences among individuals in their capacities to acquire symbols can be perceived in three ways. Individuals differ in the *speed* with which they acquire symbols of the same order of complexity: cat-dog, multiplication-division, acceleration-accumulation, evolution-emergence. Individuals differ in the *degree of abstractness* of the symbols which they can learn: animal, building, precipitation, osmosis, justice. And individuals differ in regard to the *complexity* of the relationships among the symbols which they can comprehend: balance, deduction, parity.

Memory

Importantly, though in a secondary way, two variables can contribute to the effectiveness with which this overall capacity operates: memory and motivation.

The behavior called remembering appears in different manners:

1. Fear of dogs (a sequel to prior negative conditioning with respect to a dog or dogs); fear of failure (a sequel to negative conditioning due to lack of success); swimming, or riding a bicycle; recognizing a person whose name is not recalled; retracing a route previously traveled without being able to tell others how to follow that route; playing a musical selection—all of these may be nonverbalized remembering
2. Reproducing previously presented visual designs, patterns, or maps, with or without verbalizing
3. Reproducing number series, or words, or sentences, or selections—often called rote memory (and often a major educational demand in some "teaching")
4. Reproducing the main ideas in passages read or heard (paraphrasing involves more than memory)
5. Recalling facts formally or incidentally encountered

With respect to the last kind in particular, while some feebleminded individuals appear to remember certain things very well and some very bright persons seem disconcertingly forgetful, bright individuals tend to remember more things than do the less-bright. In fact, while it is not psychologically their special forte, bright persons manifest a disconcertingly superior "intellectual adhesiveness." Such remembering is highly contributive to symbol acquisition—the number of things remembered providing a wider and potentially sounder basis for generalization. Also, remembering more and being able to make more generalizations probably provide a richer apperceptive mass to which newly encountered data can be related, this in itself being facilitative to remembering.

Motivation

The phenomenon of motivation plays an important role in the functioning of the capacity to acquire symbols. More

fully to understand this, it will help to recognize the basic predisposition of the human organism, or of any organism for that matter, to push out into its environment. From the infant's reaching out to the schoolchild's information-seeking "Why?," the organism is acquiring specifics which serve as bases for generalizing and later acquiring symbols. This contributes to his survival and, later, to his social effectiveness. The ways in which the child's significant others react to this behavior, of course, crucially affect the extent and the manner in which this behavior continues to be manifest. Usually such outgoingness, or pressing into one's environment, is encouraged, rewarded, and positively reinforced. Yet in some cases it is not nurtured fruitfully and at times is curbed with disturbing consistency by the adult—parent or educator—who fails to respond productively to the child who actually is seeking information (as contrasted with the child who seeks thus to obtain or hold adult attention).

In certain portions of our society there are no inherent demands nurturant to the acquisition of a broad experience base for ultimate symbol acquisition. Many of the "disadvantaged" are so reared. True, they generalize and acquire symbols, but their motivation generally is born more of immediate social needs than of response to the nurturance of the kind of "inherent intellectual inquiry" that has been suggested, and, as a result, the symbols they acquire are of limited utility in the broad social scene. The school's role in compensating for this is particularly important with respect to the "disadvantaged" and especially the gifted among them.

In general, though, the gifted basically appear more avid in seeking out learning opportunities—both in the number of things to be learned and in the discovery and understanding of relationships. The satisfaction of learning and discovering reinforces this avid "drive for knowledge" and enhances motivation.

Science and Technology

We have seen that a sound definition of the gifted must be developed first in terms of how many such individuals will be needed to perform the various tasks that call for their particular kinds of capability. The proper execution of such responsibility requires primarily the capacity to think, plan, and act in terms of generalizations—such as the general principles of law and government, the underlying theories of history, economics, science, music, education, and social welfare, the major conceptualizations of mathematics, the generalizations of philosophy and religion, the general principles of organization in commerce, industry, labor, and the generalized sensitivities in the areas of creative composition. To a lesser degree, but still involving at least the capability of understanding, if not expanding, the underlying generalizations, rather similar basic potential is required in the growing area of technology, as in the case of data processing, nonresearch medicine, highly skilled mechanical work, program implementation, agricultural management, and the like.

Those in the first category discover new relationships (principles, laws) or conceptualizations, or synthesize (see new relationships among) existing facts and phenomena, checking on specifics only to test the validities of the generalities that should incorporate them. Those in the second category, while they must understand general principles and concepts in the different areas, at least in an elementary way, are concerned primarily with application, the taking of action in specific instances in the light of known generalizations, rather than with producing new or more inclusive ones. (This parallels, roughly, the differentiation between science and technology, between

research and professional application.) While the two categories are logically separable, no sharp line demarcates them.

At both levels, however, a great deal has to be learned by means of symbols, and what is learned can be quite complex. We might think in terms of a continuum: at one end the primary work demand requires the discovery and development of general principles by means of highly conceptual thinking; at the other end the work activity is the least "thought-provoking," the most routinized and motor-habituated. The more social responsibilities were assigned toward the first end, the more giftedness would be called for; and the more such responsibilities were assigned toward the other end, the less giftedness (as described thus far) would be necessary. In both kinds of activity, however, a great deal needs to be learned and understood by means of symbols, and what has to be learned can be quite complex.

THE TASK OF THE PSYCHOLOGIST

As we have seen, the schools are obligated to regard roughly the top 8 percent of the generalized school population as needing to be educated such that they can assume major social responsibility as adults. Their tasks will necessitate their being able, for example, to perform in terms of abstractions, generalizations, and principles in the sense of dealing with specific situations in terms of general principles, as in the area of law; in the sense of identifying new principles in terms of which to understand nature, as in the area of science; or in the sense of identifying or developing new relationships among existing phenomena, as in the areas of science and creative endeavor. This being the case, the task of the psychologist is twofold. He has the responsibility of identifying, by means of careful research, those traits and characteristics which persons must possess if they are to discover, integrate, and apply the generalizations essential to the maintenance and improvement of society. Having identified such traits and characteristics, he has also the responsibility of developing objective procedures by means of which educators can validly ascertain both the presence and amounts of those traits or characteristics in school children. The earlier these characteristics can be identified and nurtured, the more society is likely to benefit and the greater can be the self-realization of the "gifted" individuals.

Behavior That Indicates Giftedness

Terman (1925, p. 280) listed the following parental indications of early manifestations of superior ability in 282 boys and 237 girls:

Behavior Reported	Frequency	
	Boys	Girls
Grasps and understands new ideas quickly	50	40
Desire for knowledge	31	31
Retentive memory	21	21
Intelligent conversation	20	15
Rapid progress at school	16	16
Keen general interests	22	9
Range of general information	15	12
Reasoning ability	13	13
Early speech	11	14
Asking intelligent questions	14	11
Ability in accomplishing difficult things	14	11
Keen observation	13	10
Unusual vocabulary	8	12
Originality	3	12

Heavily overlapping these are the characteristics of such children listed by Witty in 1955:

The early use of a large vocabulary, accurately employed

Language proficiency—the use of phrases and entire sentences at a very early age, and the ability to tell or reproduce a story at an early age

Keen observation and retention of information about things observed

Interest in or liking for books—later employment of atlases, dictionaries, and encyclopedias

Early interest in calendars and clocks

Ability to attend or concentrate for a longer period than is typical of most children

Demonstration of proficiency in drawing, music, and other art forms

Early discovery of cause-and-effect relationships

Early development of ability to read

Development of early interests

The post-Sputnik spate of publications dealing with the gifted, particularly those intended for teachers and parents, included many comparable listings of observations.

For fundamental understanding, there appears to be merit in collapsing such characterizations in terms of fundamental psychological concepts. Bear in mind that any analysis of a group of variables such as these into discernibly different components should not imply that these components are psychologically discrete; logically separable elements may, and often do, interact psychologically. Bear in mind, too, the probability that the parents queried were not representative of the full socioeconomic range.

Five different kinds of behaving would seem to incorporate the seemingly wide variety of characterizations of the gifted:

1. Pressing or pushing into the environment —both physically and symbolically
2. Discovering relationships among things experienced
3. Remembering what has been experienced, facilitated undoubtedly by perceiving relationships within which things could be remembered

4. Being motivated (the rewarding effect of discovery)

5. Focusing or concentrating upon a particular line of behavior

The tendency of an organism to push out into its environment, variously characterized as, "drive," "exploration," or "curiosity," is more obviously relevant to our concern when manifested as a wanting to know about things, as reflected in asking questions and, later, reading to acquire relevant information (at the symbolic level). Typical of the gifted is a breadth of interest, seemingly "self-motivated" and extending over a wide range of phenomena, free of "flightiness" or easy distractibility. The gifted also manifest a "depth" of interest, fed by their capacity to perceive relations among things related to the focus of interest. They tend not only to see relationships between things but also, given the relationship, to identify other things or phenomena which are in harmony with that relationship—further reflecting their tendency to generalize.

Defining and Measuring Traits

It is essential to understand how psychology distinguishes the gifted from the nongifted. The psychologist starts off with the recognition that gifted children are, first of all, children. Children eat, sleep, are active, ask questions, have height and weight, have the capability of learning, interact with other children and adults, can become adjusted or maladjusted, and the like. Any characteristic is possessed by all children, but not to the same extent or degree by all of them. In a sense, then, the psychologist's primary responsibility is not just of identifying the unique basic or predominant trait, but also of ascertaining the extent to which the gifted possess that trait.

A grossly oversimplified analogy would

be the task of arriving at a definition of tallness (if that be the focal trait). When is a six-year-old to be regarded as "tall" for his age? Six-year-old boys have been found to range in height from 40 to 54 inches (Martin, 1955). Where, along this range in height, does tallness begin? Certainly the six-year-old boy who measured 53 inches would be regarded as tall. How about one 50 inches tall? One way to specify tallness would be to regard the top 16 percent as tall; this is analogous to one manner of defining the gifted, as we have seen. This would mean that any six-year-old boy who was 47 or more inches in height would be regarded as "tall."

So, to sum up, the psychologist has to identify the trait that is focal to the gifted's playing the roles society "says" are necessary, has to work out ways to measure that trait, and then has to decide how much of it is needed.

We have thus far developed a rough idea of the nature of the trait that plays the major role in the meeting of those responsibilities—the capability to generalize, to conceptualize, to acquire and use symbols effectively, and to deal with abstractions and general principles. The psychologist is responsible for developing procedures to identify that trait in children, and later in the gifted—procedures that (1) can be used by less technically trained persons, such as teachers, to locate candidates for the category of the gifted, and (2) can be used by specialists for the more definitive determination of giftedness. It is like using screening procedures to locate children who may have impairments in hearing or seeing and then following up by having such children more thoroughly examined by otologists or ophthamologists. We shall consider both of these aspects of the psychologist's responsibility.

Although a number of characteristics must be evaluated in identifying and understanding gifted children, there has to be a primary focus or point of initial consideration. Emotional, social, motivational, and physical as well as intellective or cognitive characteristics all are important. Because of their interaction and because of society's implicit demands, the determination of giftedness cannot be based entirely upon any one of these. Yet the characteristic that is of primary importance (stated above) is not unique to the gifted; they just possess it to a greater degree. While this characteristic can logically be dealt with separately, psychologically it may be affected by one or more of the other important characteristics. The functioning of high cognitive capability can be enhanced by good emotional adjustment or grossly impaired by emotional maladjustment. Social and motivational factors may facilitate effective cognitive functioning (as for a child in a family with healthily high achievement aspirations), or they may be intellectually debilitating (as for a child of high capability who has acquired an attitude of despair and frustration). The physically healthy bright child can function intellectually more effectively, whereas the child who may have been born with superior potentiality can have this superior promise impaired by poor early nutrition or, if he has some physical impairment, by how the adults in his environment see him. And these are only one-to-one interactions; more complex interactions also may have either nurturant or deleterious effects or both. The essential problem in identifying the gifted, then, is one of ascertaining the extent to which children possess this cognitive capability, with a view to regarding the top 8 percent of them as gifted.

Product-Process Aspects

The point has been developed that symbols figure predominantly in learning, in communication, and in thinking or rea-

soning. Thus, the task of the psychologist is one of ascertaining either, or both, of two things (1) the extent to which children have symbols and how effectively they can use them, and (2) the extent to which children have the capability of acquiring and using symbols. The first of these may be misleading, because the possession of symbols contributes to the acquisition of symbols. But an individual must also be able to see relationships among them in order to acquire other symbols, even of the same order of conceptual difficulty. Take, for example, a child who knows the meaning of the symbol "addition." He can, if he is educationally lucky, learn that the symbol "multiplication" means, basically, repetitive adding. Suppose now that the child is learning the meaning of the symbol "evolution." Here, he not only must know the meanings of the symbols for the various elements in some kind of progression but also he must be able to perceive the overall relationship among them. In a sense, then, symbols serve to beget symbols *if* the relationship among them also can be perceived. Again, the importance of discovering relationships and generalizing is apparent.

But what about children who have not acquired even the "normal" supply of symbols because they have been reared in experientially deprived situations or have been living with those whose attitudes toward learning do not foster such normal, everyday learning? Some of these children may have superior capability for symbol acquisition but have not picked up preschool or out-of-school learnings (especially of the symbolic kind) because of the limiting effects of the environments in which they have been growing up. Many such children have been missed by conventional procedures. The proper identification of the gifted children in this group is a social necessity, an educational responsibility, and a special psychological task.

Inference from Achievement

Since the beginning of group intelligence testing, this assumption has been forthrightly stated: *capacity to achieve can be inferred from the extent to which achievement is found to be present.* Because group testing of intelligence filtered down from the testing of adults, in World War I, to the upper grades and then slowly to the lower grades, this was a reasonably defensible assumption. Another assumption was implicit: *the experiential backgrounds (acculturation) of the individuals tested were roughly comparable, though not necessarily identical.* The basic characteristic being thus indirectly measured was the disposition to benefit from both incidental and formal learning experiences, which was more nearly relatable to "book learning" capability than to "intelligence" in its larger sense. For our purposes this capability was (or was very closely related to) the capacity of the individual to acquire symbols, as that term has been used here. Therefore, the psychologist's measuring the extent to which children possess symbols as an indication of their potential for learning can be seen to have some validity.

But the assumptions underlying this approach have been increasingly challenged. As younger and younger children were tested, the measuring of their achievements—usually kinds of learning which were predominantly verbal in nature—as a basis for inferring capacity to achieve became more difficult. Further, school-entering children come from the most diverse acculturation backgrounds, a fact that heavily taxes the assumption of comparable opportunity to achieve. Moreover, particularly during the 1960s, society became increasingly concerned with the "disadvantaged" and informed about the heterogeneity of their cultural backgrounds. The new viewpoint can be generalized: *the more heterogeneous the acculturation backgrounds of individuals, the less defensible, or valid, is the inferring of capacity to achieve from what has been achieved.*

Group Learning Aptitude Tests

The psychologist, then, must get objective evidence of the capacity to achieve in some way other than by measuring achievement. As a result, group learning aptitude ("intelligence") tests came increasingly to be published with separate verbal and nonverbal, or language and nonlanguage, sections, and those issued for use with younger children came to have an increasing number of items (behavior samplings) which did not make verbal demands.

Spearman's approach

Spearman (1927) maintained that intelligence is manifested in two ways: the educing (discovering) of relationships between correlates; and the educing (identifying) of correlates, given a relationship. His thinking was reflected in test items such as: "Boy is to father as girl is to (1) aunt (2) mother (3) female (4) woman." Here, it was presumed that the person being tested knew all the words and was able to read (achievement), but the "psychological demand" of the item was to identify the correct correlate. On the basis of the relationship identified between "boy" and "father" (the correlates), the task was to find that word (the correlate) which would satisfy the established relationship of parentness. The role played by achievement could be brought increasingly to bear on the "demand" of the item, as in items such as these: "Feather is to bird as (1) bark (2) tail (3) size (4) fur is to dog"; "Which of the following numbers comes next in this series? 1—2—6—15— (1) 24 (2) 31 (3) 38

(4) 45"; and "NEA is to educators as (1) AMA (2) CIO (3) APA (4) NASA is to doctors." The assumption of the comparability of opportunity to achieve (acculturation) would be most tenable with respect to the first of these three examples, but would be decreasingly tenable as one progressed to the second and the third.

Nonreading tests

The same kind of psychological operation can be sampled, though, without requiring the child (or adult) to read—without substantially involving achievement. We might, for example, ask the child, without expecting or requiring him to read, or even to verbalize his response: "Which one of these is different? (1) ○ (2) ● (3) ○ (4) ○ "; or we could use the response elements (1) □ (2) △ (3) □ (4) ○ ; or we could instruct him to "Cross out the one that doesn't belong: in groups such as (1) ⌊ (2) ⌉ (3) > (4) ⌋ or (1) ○ (2) □ (3) □ (4) □ or (1) ☺ (2) ☹ (3) ☺ (4) ☺ . A considerable variety of test items, of greater difficulty, with either verbal or nonverbal content, can be used to get evidence regarding the cognitive capability of children (and adults). Tests consisting, at least in part, of items such as those in the paragraph above have greater validity when used with children who have a more conventional acculturation, whereas tests involving items such as those in this paragraph are more appropriately used with children from culturally less nurturant environments. We shall regard these items or tests which sample predominantly what has been learned or achieved as reflecting learning aptitude in terms of *product;* those which sample predominantly the psychological operations which make such acquisition possible, as reflecting learning aptitude in terms of *process* (Newland, 1971, 1972).

A Rationale for Testing

Historically, the gifted were psychometrically identified only in terms of a glob called "intelligence," made up of some unspecified mix of samples of what the individual has picked up (product) and of the ways in which he did or could go about picking up (process). Much current testing continues in the same vein. However, it is now possible, in fact crucial, to accomplish this in a more differentiated manner. The necessary measures of "intelligence," better thought of as learning aptitude, need to be analyzed in terms of the light they throw on both product and process, and the relative importance of each must be considered in terms of the background and age of each child. The more deviant the child and his acculturation, the more such an approach is essential. Later, we will consider this more fully.

The foregoing should help us understand the rationale of psychologists who have developed devices to illuminate the capacities of children to acquire verbal symbols and see relationships among them. The ascertainment of the capabilities of children, as a basis for deciding whether or not they are to be educated as gifted, is basically the psychologist's responsibility, and he should be thoroughly familiar with procedures and devices that can properly be employed. It is not just a matter of "IQ"! The psychologist should know and help others understand not only the limitations of his findings and of the devices that might be employed, but also the special assessment approaches required in certain situations, particularly if physically impaired and other disadvantaged children are involved.

ASCERTAINING
COGNITIVE CAPABILITIES

Both the psychologist and the educator need to be alert to a number of facts and principles in the ascertainment of cognitive capabilities:

1. The first step in deciding whether a child needs to be educated as gifted is to find out whether he has sufficient learning aptitude (cognitive capability, learning potential) to qualify. Judging in terms of how well the child has done, academically or otherwise, has to be based on knowing how well he has responded after being provided with nuturance and education. Such evaluation tends to come later in the child's life and must reflect a sensitivity to the fact that a significant percentage (perhaps some 20 percent) of school-aged children come from less-than-desirable acculturation backgrounds. Although a few children do learn to read before they enter school, some unknown percentage have a capability sufficient to acquire this skill but are not reared in social situations that are conducive, or nurturant, to their doing so.

2. There are marked differences among learning aptitude ("intelligence") tests just as there are among children. The IQs or other measures earned on the Peabody Picture Vocabulary Test, on the 1960 Stanford-Binet Intelligence Test, and on the Wechsler Intelligence Scale for Children "say" quite different things about children. This is true even with respect to the WISC Verbal IQ and the Binet IQ. Group tests of learning aptitude differ in their values as screening tests; and even the same group test may differ in validity from one age or grade level to another.

3. The possible uses of group and individual learning aptitude tests must be considered carefully in terms of the children on whom they may be used. The results obtained can, and often do, mean quite different things when used on disadvantaged and nondisadvantaged children.

4. Learning aptitude tests consisting totally or predominantly of either verbal or nonverbal items, where reading or nonreading by the children is involved, are neither totally preferable nor totally undesirable. Here, sensitivity to children's acculturation backgrounds and age levels is crucial. *Both* kinds of behavior sampling are needed—not only to find children who have not learned because they have lived in nonnurturant environments as well as children who have learned "in spite of" such environments, but also to help the educator understand how to provide properly for either type of child.

5. While evidence regarding the child's cognitive capability is of primary importance, his "total psychological picture" must be obtained. This means a full evaluation of the roles played in the child's development and present functioning by emotional, social, motivational, and physical factors. The bright ten-year-old with a sustained bed-wetting history would need to be helped emotionally, or possibly physically, before he would be a good risk in a program for the gifted, whereas the bright six-year-old with a history of maladaptive behavior since entering school might learn quickly to adjust in the right kind of third grade.

Early Evaluation

The first, admittedly coarse, screening for gifted children should be carried out by the proper use of appropriate group tests. However, the view was promulgated, and quickly accepted by most educators and some psychologists, that this approach could not properly be employed below the fourth-grade level. This contention was understandable; the organization making such a statement was in the process of shifting its concern with group testing downward from the college level, and it was considering the problem of group testing of learning aptitude by means of tests that heavily involved reading—an orientation that long had been quite generally held by test makers and test users. But the nature of group testing devices has changed, and the merits of early identification are being recognized —especially by those seriously concerned with providing the gifted with appropriate educational opportunities.

In 1940—as an illustration—the following group device was used to yield some early understanding of children's learning capabilities. Since the children's physical condition had to be ascertained before the school would accept them, it was believed that their learning aptitude deserved equal consideration. The school psychologist trained three first-grade teachers in the administration of the Kuhlmann-Anderson Intelligence Test (Fourth Edition) and the children in groups of four or five took the group test. The teachers had been alerted to important aspects of the children's behavior before, during, and after the group testing. Those children who performed far enough above or below "the average" were then evaluated individually by the school psychologist. Thus, not only were the potentially "fast" and "slow" learners identified, but their teachers were provided with important information which they could use in helping such children. While this school system did not have a highly publicized "program for the gifted," the philosophy of the administrator and the commitments of the teachers were such that the pupils' self-realization was accorded a realistic recognition.

Procedures and problems in the individual evaluation of gifted children will be discussed later.

The "Talented"

We have not as yet considered the "talented"—a term that has been used in confusing ways. At times, educators have used "academically talented" as a euphemism for "mentally superior" or "gifted," because they believed the latter might be regarded as derogatory of those not so characterized. Some have used "talent" or "talented" to characterize individuals who have demonstrated superior skill. Such was the case when Anastasi and Levee (1960) reported an "adult male mental defective" (Stanford-Binet IQ of 67, WAIS Full Scale IQ of 73, Verbal IQ of 82, and Performance IQ of 52) who was accorded Carnegie Hall privileges for a piano concert. Numerous ways of contributing to our society require high-level skill without demanding much capacity to generalize or conceptualize.

A differentiation between the talented and the gifted is most difficult. In some kinds of social functioning the giftedness thus far described seems to be the primary factor—as in the judiciary, science and philosophy, engineering, musical composition, creative and even much reportorial writing, organizational operation, and policymaking for a large variety of society activities. Insofar as general principles have to be applied and bits of action "geared into" a general theme or scheme, as in the theater, creative painting, sculpting, and the like, giftedness as described here is the major factor, even though research evidence is lacking. Yet people make other recognized contributions to society that cause them to be characterized as "talented." This attribution becomes increasingly tenuous as the contributions they make are dominated more by emotion or physique than by intellective activities. It is proposed here that those children whose anticipated superior social contribution is primarily a function of their superior conceptualization capacity be regarded as gifted and that those whose promise is not primarily so based be regarded as talented. However, most truly talented persons are also gifted, in the sense developed here.

The Skillful

Certain individuals do make outstanding social contributions in ways that do not appear to involve superior cognitive capability. Although composers and certain improvisators necessarily operate at a high conceptual level, highly competent vocalists and instrumentalists can receive much social acclaim even though functioning strictly at a skill level. Many persons are quite competent in effecting social action and movements toward social organization, although all major social leaders comprehend general principles and theories. Outstanding sports and military performances are possible without accompanying major conceptualizations. Strategy, as contrasted with tactics, always requires the operation of major conceptualization.

Society can and should cultivate, nurture, and act to enhance the acquisition of high-level skills. But the position is taken here that only to the extent that a high ability to conceptualize is involved is social nurturance of the gifted relevant. When the term "talented" is used to denote both the highly skilled and the high conceptualizers, the consequence is confusion in social and educational planning for the gifted.

THE GIFTED
IN TERMS OF IQ RANGE

The point has been made that the schools must recognize their special responsibility for 8 percent of the total school population in order that society can execute its high-level functions. It is necessary to translate this into terms that can have meaning for educational planners. Keep in mind that we shall be thinking in terms of a *total* population, and not in terms of Chickenfoot Crossing or Midas City; particular school districts may have populations that are not typical of the whole country. Also, while we shall identify the gifted in terms of those who fall above some specific point on the total distribution of learning aptitude, it is necessary to regard such a point as, in effect, a small range around that point.

Administrative decisions tend to be made in terms of absolutes. For example, children are requried to be x years old when they enter school. This may be dealt with in the sense that a child must have attained x years of age on or before the first day of school, or in the sense that he must have attained that age, or be capable of attaining it, within two, three, or six months of that day. But a child who would miss that deadline by one hour, or by half an hour, just wouldn't be accepted. In like manner, minimal eligibility for participation in school programs for the gifted tends to be stated, at least in part, in terms of IQ. From an administrative point of view, then, our problem is one of identifying that point (or small range) on the distribution of IQs that will mark off the top 8 percent of the general population. Because even the same number on different "intelligence" tests can mean quite different things, we shall use the intelligence quotient on the 1960 Stanford-Binet Intelligence Scale as our frame of reference. (Bear in mind that our consideration will be in terms of the total population rather than of any single school system.)

Populationwide Distribution of Intelligence

Since we shall be thinking in terms of how "intelligence" is distributed among the total population, Figure 2.1 will be helpful. The curve reflects the assumption that what is measured by tests such as the 1960 Binet is "normally" distributed in the general population. While few collections of such data have shown precisely this distribution, many have approximated it closely enough to qualify it as a reasonable generalization.

It can be seen that some 16 percent of the population falls above the point marked off one standard deviation unit above the mean. This is the point at which a 1960 Binet IQ of 116 falls (and

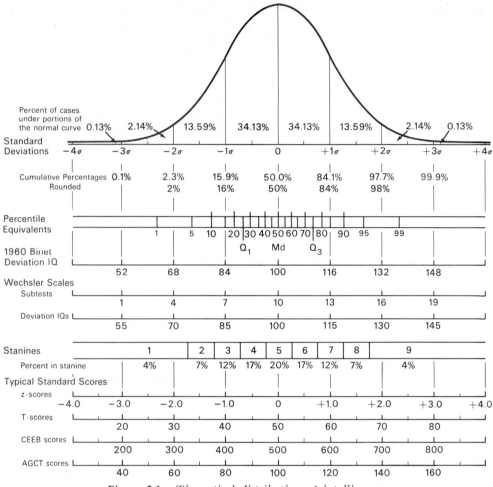

Figure 2.1. *Theoretical distribution of intelligence.*

(Adapted from Test Service Bulletin No. 48, **The Psychological Corporation**, January 1955.)

at which a Wechsler IQ of 115 falls). A bit more than 2 percent would be expected to earn Binet IQs of 132 or more. Now, if we move down from the upper limit of the 1960 Binet IQ distribution to that point which will mark off the top 8 percent, we find that the 1960 Binet IQ of 120–125 will be the lower limit for the population we shall call gifted. (This would be technically a bit different for the Verbal IQ on the Wechsler Intelligence Scale for Children —a measure which is psychologically

more meaningful in predicting ease of school learning than the Performance IQ or the Full Scale IQ of that test. But this difference—of some two points— would be of more interest to the psychometrician than to the psychologist or educator.)

Differences among the Gifted

The temptation is very strong to stop at this point in attempting precisely to characterize this population of children in terms of their learning capability. But some points need particular consideration. First, our benchmark is the 1960 Binet, and the point has been stressed that different tests yield different numbers on the same children, whether tested at the same or different times. Therefore, if gifted children are to be searched for by means of other learning aptitude tests, it is necessary to know for certain just how closely the results on a given test numerically approximate those on the Binet (and correlation coefficients will not necessarily tell you this; IQs on two tests may correlate highly, but the mental levels of the children who earned them may differ distractingly). Second, while our population has been identified as those earning 1960 Binet IQs of 120–125 and above, we still have identified a very heterogeneous group, even on this one measurement. In the early days of working with and writing about the gifted, Binet IQs in the 200 area were obtained and clinically estimated. Leta Hollingworth observed: "In the case of discovering six hundred and forty-three children testing above 140, Terman found fifteen who tested at or above 180 IQ" (1926, p. 223). This involved the use of the 1916 Binet and the use of computed IQs. But the highest deviation IQ obtainable on the 1960 Binet is 172. Thus, even "the Binet" can yield different IQs. But our gifted group still must

be regarded as quite heterogeneous, and we shall see later that the differences within this group, even in this one characteristic of learning aptitude, call for different educational and, probably, social provisions because of demonstrable differences in secondary traits.

Different categories of the gifted have been identified in order to emphasize the differences among the gifted, but they have been highly arbitrarily determined and may misleadingly suggest that some sort of firm demarcation separates one category from others. While we have identified our population as those who can learn school work more easily than the rest of the population, and we know that the 125er probably can learn discernibly more easily than can the 110er, we need to recognize that the child with a Binet IQ of 150 or 165 presents a still different learning picture than does the one with 125. To make clearer the nature of the population we are thinking of, let us take an imaginary population of 10,000 randomly selected children. Some 800, then, would constitute our gifted population. Some 225 of these would be likely to have 1960 Binet IQs of 132 and above; some 14 could be expected to earn 1960 Binet IQs of 148 and above; and one could be expected to fall at or above 164. By checking Figure 2.1, you can see how these estimates were arrived at.

3

Social

considerations

Social concern for the gifted is manifested by two interacting groups—those who depend upon the competencies of high-level personnel for the maintenance of society and those whose responsibility it is to help the gifted develop or acquire the competencies needed in society. Education is the agency charged with so helping children that they can assume effective roles in society, both as it is and as it will be. While education is thus responsible for all children, it can be regarded as having a particular commitment to those who will play major roles in society. Whether it seeks, in effect, not to stand in the way of those who will attain such responsibility, or whether it actively seeks out and helps those who are capable of becoming leaders, long has been at issue.

SOCIAL NEED
FOR THE GIFTED

To what extent does society have identifiable needs for high-level personnel? Should society's need for such individuals serve as the primary basis for deciding whom to regard as "gifted"? What kinds of factors have mitigated against education's more forthrightly dealing with this kind of social need? These and related matters are the concern of this chapter.

Society needs its gifted, not only its adults of superior capability who presently are fulfilling current roles but also its children of superior promise who, with proper nurturance, later will be able to contribute in the light of their capacity. Some may challenge this premise because of their interpretation of the term "need." "Society" may be construed to denote a relatively small interacting group of individuals, such as a tribe, or a larger group, such as a nation, or a still larger group, such as the world. The frame of reference employed here is, for the most part and for convenience, the United States.

Our society is perceived here as evolving, as emerging. Generally, and especially in the early stages of such evolution, those factors or conditions which affect the evolutionary process just "occur." A society per se does not thoughtfully plan for the creation of the altered condition—"good" or "bad"—any more than one's whole body "plans" for dealing with some chemical deficiency or excess. As a society becomes more sophisticated, members or subgroups of that society may undertake to introduce, modify, or otherwise control the presence or operation of certain factors or conditions, just as the interaction of certain functions and tissues causes the individual to "decide" he needs a drink of water. In both kinds of situations there exists a "need." In the primitive society there may exist some factors or conditions that, if introduced into the society, could "improve" it, but the society is not aware of the nature or effects of those factors or conditions. A more sophisticated society, or some subgroup of it, may believe or know that the introduction (or removal) of a given factor or condition could "improve" it. Although our society is made up of "thinking" beings, there exist both recognized and unrecognized needs. One of these, more often professed in public pronouncements than effectively recognized and acted upon, is the need for a fuller and more forthright capitalization upon the potentials of the more able.

SOCIAL EXPRESSION OF NEED— A BRIEF HISTORY

Historically, society's need for the gifted has been largely implicit, the major exception being manifested by patrons of the arts who provided funds, housing, and other encouragement to enable specific painters, sculptors, musicians, and others to engage in their creative activities. It is interesting to note that the creations so produced generally did not require those who enjoyed or took pride in them to read—since few among the consumer population could do so. Even where playwrights, dramatists, and court poets were financially supported, their productions were more listened to than read. Whether the writings in the area of philosophy or in science were financially nurtured by patrons is less clear. Certainly, in the middle ages, the church provided nurturance as well as specific motivation for writing by its more capable members, mainly in the area of religion and philosophy, although even some of these wrote in the area of science (Mendel). But the tradition of the "writer in the attic" and the emergence of socially important contributions in spite of both economic and physical adversity persists.

"Medieval" Definition of the Gifted

Two aspects of this situation are especially relevant. First, those who were so supported in their creative endeavors had to have accomplished something in the past that suggested the probability of later, and perhaps greater, contribution. This is the "medieval" definition of the gifted as those who have shown "consistently remarkable performance in any worthwhile line of endeavor." During the period when patron support figured largely, a view of the gifted in terms of *potential* rather than observed production was not the rule, since the psychologist and the psychological viewpoint had not become a part of the social scene and made their contributions to the identification of the gifted. Second, high-level contributors had to *emerge*, largely by virtue of their own superior capability (and adventitious circumstances), and in effect thus had to identify themselves, rather than being sought out early in their lives and systematically nurtured. This condition is reflected in the observation that the gifted must force their way up through the concrete of education. The contention that society thus far has managed to pursue its progressively evolutionary course by means of such essentially unnurtured emergent contributors still is operative (at least implicitly) in society's slowness and lack of consistency in mounting any significant program for early identification and educational nurturance of the gifted.

The Literature Since 1927

Since 1927, technical literature reflecting consideration of the gifted and related groups has varied from the infinitesimal to the minute. Studying the extents to which "genius," "distinction," "eminence," "fame," "creative ability," "giftedness," and "gifted children" have been the focus of concern in psychologi-

cal literature, Albert (1969) found that in *Psychological Abstracts* from 1927 through 1965 such references varied from one tenth of one percent to 1.2 percent of the annual volume. In all, 1318 such references were located for the 38-year period. Allowing a one-year lag for an article to be abstracted after it had appeared in the literature and recognizing that it usually took two years for an accepted article or book to appear in print, it is interesting to note that 95 percent of the 202 abstracts on "giftedness" and 55 percent of the 306 abstracts on "gifted children" appeared after 1951, and 81 percent of the 618 abstracts on "creative ability" appeared after 1949. The impact of Sputnik is reflected in the

Figure 3.1. *Abstracted literature in the area of the gifted, 1927–1965.*

(Adapted from Albert, 1969.)

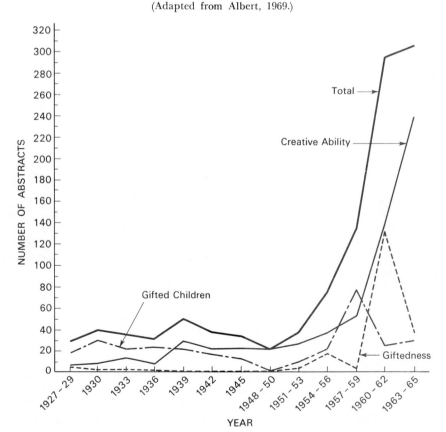

fact that 83 percent of the abstracted articles on "giftedness," 37 percent of those on "gifted children," and 65 percent of those on "creative ability" appeared after 1958. And Guilford and others had started writing considerably about divergent thinking and creativity by 1954. Of course, these were only abstracted articles or books in the "scientific" domain. A larger number of articles, books, and newspaper items appeared in lay and professional outlets, probably distributed over these years in much the same manner. After 1965–1970, the frequency of such scientific, professional, and lay publications fell off, though not quite to the lows of the 1930s and 1940s.

Education for the Gifted in America

American society has come quite slowly and spottily to recognize the importance of providing for the education of the gifted. While not so planned, early education, particularly higher education, provided relatively more for those who were likely to be bright than for other children. Early secondary schools at first were largely committed to the preparation of pupils for colleges and universities, and these were essentially geared to the education of their students for entry into the professions and the sciences. This pattern, by virtue of the high academic demands, thus tended to educate those in the group we have designated as gifted. The costs of education engendered still greater selectivity. As education became increasingly a state rather than a church, city, or private responsibility,[1] as the nature of our society

changed from agrarian to urban-industrial, and as compulsory attendance laws were enacted, the heterogeneity of our school population increased greatly and educational offerings became somewhat more diverse. Many regarded the retention of a college preparatory curriculum as adequate opportunity for the more capable pupils. Yet this still did not constitute a formal program geared specifically to meeting the needs of children of superior learning potential.

Action at the state level

At the state level the public schools began to make formal provisions for the special education of handicapped children during the first fifth of the twentieth century. Legislation was worded in terms of the physically handicapped and seriously retarded (the latter generally defined as those who educationally were retarded two or more years). Social concern for the gifted, as reflected in state-level legislation regarding their education, came much later. Early action in the interests of the gifted resulted from the concern of individuals working in local school districts.

Reports on the establishment of special classes for the gifted, other than multiple tracking, began to appear in the educational literature by 1916 (Race, 1918; Specht, 1919; Gosling, 1919; and Cleveland, 1920). By 1924 Stedman had described the operation of an experimental program for gifted children (1916 Binet IQs from 125 to 167) started in 1918 as an "opportunity" room under the auspices of the (then) training department of the Los Angeles State Normal School. On the basis of his five years of experience as consultant to the program, Goddard (1928) described a special class program for the gifted started in Cleveland in 1922, with which he had served five years as consultant. (This program was written up, in lay style, by Hall in 1956.) As early as 1866, in Eliza-

---

[1] Note the dates of these first continuing state superintendents of schools: New York, 1812; Kentucky and Michigan, 1837; Vermont, 1845; Louisiana, 1854; Pennsylvania, 1857; and Tennessee, 1867; by 1870 only 28 cities had city superintendents of schools (Cubberley, 1922, pp. 377–379).

beth, N.J., and 1871, in St. Louis, multiple-track plans were introduced into the public schools to provide more meaningfully for both the gifted and the slow pupils (Witty, 1951). As interesting and suggestive as these and many other early undertakings were, they reflected only local, not formally legislated, efforts to meet the needs of the gifted.

By the 1930s a unit in the U.S. Office of Education, long headed by Dr. Elise H. Martens, was concerned with the gifted as a subgroup of exceptional children. The International Council for Exceptional Children at that time regarded the gifted as one of its areas of concern. In 1940 Pennsylvania included its gifted in legal provisions for special education; this was accomplished by substituting the term "exceptional" for "physically handicapped and seriously retarded" and incorporating, logically, the gifted within the exceptional category. A few years later Pennsylvania dropped these provisions for the gifted, then reintroduced them. This vacillation, reflecting the contrasting philosophies of shifting department personnel, was not peculiar to Pennsylvania. Although society's needs for the gifted might not vacillate, peoples' perceptions of them did. After Sputnik in 1957, however, legislation in favor of the gifted began to appear at the state level. Still, in 1964,

Rhode Island Representative Fogarty was obliged to observe with respect to the gifted: "Here the Congress and the educational community still have their homework to do to arrive at specific proposals defining the role of the Federal Government (1964, p. 3)."

The relative surge during the mid-60s in educational provisions for the gifted is shown in Table 3.1. (The data were obtained from an unpublished U.S. Office of Education survey of "Special Education for Exceptional Children"; the numbers for 1966 were U.S. Office of Education estimates.) Both the actual numbers and the percentages are interesting. If one assumes that the U.S. population was 200 million at that time, that one-fourth of them were children of school age, and that 15 percent of those children were exceptional, some 7,500,000 children would be exceptional. Of these, not less than 2 million children would fall in the gifted category (if we regard only 4 percent of the school-age population as gifted).

THE GIFTED AS EXCEPTIONAL

Both logically and historically the "exceptional" include the gifted. Whereas in the 1940s it was regarded as logically

Table 3.1. Increase in total local public school special education enrollment.

Category	1963	1966	Increase	Percentage increase
Visually handicapped	13,962	15,400	1,438	10
Deaf and hard of hearing	28,551	32,700	4,149	14
Speech impaired	802,197	989,500	187,303	22
Crippled and special health problems	64,842	69,400	4,558	7
Emotionally and socially maladjusted	30,871	32,200	1,329	4
Mentally retarded	393,237	495,100	101,863	26
Other handicapping conditions	22,039	32,500	10,461	47
Gifted	214,671	312,100	97,429	45
TOTAL	1,570,370	1,978,900	408,530	26

Source: 1963 and 1966 data from Renotzky and Greene, 1970, Table 43, p. 69.

appropriate for both the gifted and the handicapped to be provided with state-authorized special education services and programs under the general rubric of "special education," in the 1960s the gifted were increasingly regarded as falling outside this domain—for a number of reasons.

First, since state legislative provisions for the special education of the handicapped had been in effect for so long, the number of children thus provided for has been considerable and the number of people prepared to work specifically with and in the interests of the handicapped has been large. Those so prepared and experienced are just not properly equipped to work effectively in the gifted area. At the administrative level, many who were involved with the special education of the handicapped, for which they were receiving sizable state appropriations, were fearful that requests for additional funds would be regarded by their legislators more as attempts just to increase their budgets than as necessities for new work with the gifted—a group on whom the legislators were not nearly as well "sold" as they were on the handicapped. Many special education administrators believed, and pragmatically so, that funds for the special education of the two groups should be quite separate. Perhaps, too many special educators of the handicapped were not equally committed to the goal of effective education of the gifted.

Second, society itself responds differently to the handicapped than to the gifted. The handicapped are more "photogenic" and evoke more emotion or sympathy. For promotional purposes, pictures of children who are handicapped, such as the crippled and the blind, clearly communicate the child's impaired condition, whereas the gifted or bright pupil in a photograph does not appear discernibly different from other children. He looks like a child who ought to be able to get along on his own, without special consideration. A gifted child has to be posed in front of a stack of books, or some laboratory equipment, or a chalkboard on which some complicated formula has been written in order to suggest to the viewer that the child is bright and in some way "deserving." Also, society tends to feel more compassionately toward a disabled child than toward a nondisabled child.

A further psychological factor may contribute to educators' reluctance to exert themselves as fully for the gifted as for the handicapped. Handicapped children need special provisions that generally have been highly tangible—large-print reading materials, compensatory hearing equipment, transportation, physical therapy equipment, simplified learning materials, and specially equipped rooms with tools and cooking facilities. The gifted, on the other hand, while they might require extra reading and laboratory facilities (apparently just more of the same kind of facilities as provided for all children), are in need of cognitive nurturance—a matter more of how available materials are used than one of just more physical things. Generalization and conceptualization are much more difficult to perceive than are aprons and bookends. The phenomenon of society's reacting primarily to the tangible is pervasive.

Perhaps, too, a larger portion of our population than we should like to admit still operates on the assumption that "Genius will out": if the gifted really are gifted, they will manifest their giftedness in surmounting any reluctance or obstacles they may encounter, in school or elsewhere, in accomplishing more or better things. Their self-realization thus depends on whether they "have what it takes," leaving society without responsibility for nurturing superior potential. This vestigial attitude is not confined to laymen; many educators entertain and openly affirm it.

FLUCTUATING DEMAND
FOR THE GIFTED

Emergencies can heighten society's interest in capitalizing upon the superior potential of the gifted. World War I did not greatly increase demand for high technical skill or major scientific competence. In World War II, however, major scientific advances had profound consequences in military action, making society highly aware of its need for scientists and other high-level personnel as well as of the competing advances made in science and technology in other countries. As a result, both lay and scientific literature teemed with reports of shortages in a variety of high-level endeavors, and graduate school enrollments surged upward. Between the fall of 1960 and the fall of 1967 enrollment for master's and doctorate degrees increased nearly 107 percent. February 1963 and February 1966 the numbers of children reported as being educated as gifted went from 214,671 to 312,100—an increase of 46 percent (see Table 3.1). Society began to examine its pool of high-level potential, school curriculums were examined with respect to their social relevance, and the ideas of scholarship programs and modified educational programs for the gifted were accepted as never before.

But society is complex. What seemed to be an insatiable demand for highly trained scientists and technologists fell victim to a shifting pattern of social needs. By 1970, not only had the demand for highly qualified personnel dropped off, but significant numbers of those already employed had to be let go. Graduate enrollments dropped because of the changed job market as well as the curtailment of scholarship funds. Rising prices increased the cost of education generally, and taxpayers became increasingly reluctant to approve added funds for education. At the same time, society grew more sensitive to the needs of the "disadvantaged," and public funds were diverted to develop compensatory programs. Both in the schools and in higher education—where, during the mid-1960s, teaching positions were hard to fill—there occurred a surplus of qualified persons.

But other kinds of social involvement began to create new needs for high-level personnel. Aspects of computer development and usage, work to be done in ecology, new needs in the area of urban development and communication, the development and creation of social welfare programs, involvement in the growing area of work with and for "senior citizens," and the delivery of legal and health services to disadvantaged segments of society—these and others constitute new demands by society for contributions by its more capable members. While a given scientist may find it personally distressing to be unemployable in his speciality or even in any of the newly emerging social-need areas, the fact of social need, in the broader sense, represents a continuing demand for the highly capable. This shift regarding the education of the gifted is highly significant, as we shall see. Anticipating a bit, the more specifically a person is trained or prepared for a job, the less flexible or adaptable he is if a need for change arises. In psychological terms, the more perceptual education is, the less adaptable is the person so educated; the more conceptual his education is, the more adaptable he is when social changes occur.

THE PROBLEM
OF ELITISM

Not only lay persons but some school personnel as well contend that providing educational programs specially for the gifted will contribute to the establishment of an intellectual elitism and, thereby, the creation of a nonelite of second-class citizens. Whether this claim be regarded as a rationalization for insensitivity to interest in the gifted or in terms of fearful recollection of the malevolence of certain elitist groups in history, it needs to be explored in terms of its emotional component and psychological facts.

The fact of individual differences remains with us: there always have been some persons who can do some things better than some others. Some can repair cars better than others, some can get out more votes than others, some can do better at raising money for causes than others, some dentists can fill teeth better than others, some can see relationships among phenomena better than others, and so on. It is doubtful that the fact of individual differences per se is at the heart of this aversion to doing something special for the gifted. Most of those who express such concern about "second-class" citizenship accept unhesitatingly and uncritically the fact of first teams in sports, or the fact that some youngsters "make" the band or orchestra, or become first violins in orchestras, or come in first in races, art contests, or in competitions in essay writing about our democracy. Attempting to put this phenomenon into perspective, Friedenberg (1962) observed: "It is possible that students respect an elite of athletes because good athletes are encouraged to be proud of themselves for being as good as they can, and that these are the only people left on campus with anything in particular to be proud of."

A fundamental psychological principle seems to be operating. Aside from the secondary factor of financial motivation, those areas of behavior in which there is forthright acknowledgment of firstness all involve some clearly observable or tangible performance. The gifted, on the other hand, while they often do outstandingly well in many areas, are regarded as having some ill-defined, difficult-to-understand characteristic by means of which they behave in much less tangible or observable ways in generalizing and in discovering new relationships among phenomena. Man tends to fear the unknown, and the more intangible it is the more it is likely to be feared. The possibility exists too, that some persons, perhaps wishfully ignoring the fact of individual differences, have overgeneralized regarding the equipotentiality of all members of the social group.

Arguments against Special Provisions

Special educational provisions for the gifted have been opposed by some on the grounds that they would be inimical to education in a democracy. Three different arguments are entailed:

1. Special education of the gifted would contribute to intellectual snobbishness.
2. The gifted themselves would be deprived of benefiting socially from association with the nongifted.
3. Nongifted children would be deprived of the experience of learning from the gifted —the stimulus to learn more, and the picking up of the gifted's learning styles.

These arguments might have some validity if the gifted were educated in separate schools, but this is seldom advocated for the gifted, at least in the United States. Sound research evidence concerning the last two contentions just does not exist, although there are a few hints. Therefore, they must be evaluated from logical and psychological points of view.

The arguments above have been used to oppose special classes for the gifted. Generally, it is assumed that the children spend all their school time in these classes—a condition seldom advocated by their proponents. Usually such special classes are established for the "academic" areas of learning, the gifted being assimilated into the total heterogeneous group for "nonacademic" educational activity. What needs to be explored is the effect of the special classes generally recommended. Unfortunately, research evidence is lacking.

Besides multiple tracking, many special education provisions for the gifted can be made within the regular class programs—early admission and other forms of educational acceleration, bona fide individualized instruction, the cultivation of individual interest activities and special interest groups, the capitalization on other extraschool community facilities, and other special adjustments on up to the use of college courses as adjunctive to high school programs. Some observers condemn all of these as contributive to the much-feared elitist attitude.

Those who use the aforementioned three arguments must recognize that their obverse is presumed to be true of the "regular" educational program—namely, that the gifted do not become snobbish when kept in heterogeneous classes, that the gifted do become better socialized (democratized) in such classes, and that the slower children are better motivated to learn and do benefit by picking up learning techniques and styles by being in classes with the gifted. To many, such presumptions are clearly "common sense." But such "common sense" needs to be checked out both in terms of whatever research evidence is available and in terms of "the psychology" of the situation.

Snobbishness

Available research evidence suggests that negative interpersonal perception, both on the part of the gifted and on the part of others, is neither typical of nor clearly relatable to special educational provisions made for the gifted. However,

definitive research findings on whether the gifted regard others in a negative, derogatory manner, or are perceived by their significant others (adults and schoolmates) as so behaving, is limited.

In order for the "snobbishness" contention to be fully researched, it would need to be studied in terms of its two major facets: the educational provision made for the gifted and the interpersonal perceptions observed (rather than inferred). The kinds of educational placements of the gifted should range from special schools, through full-time special classes in regular schools, through part-time special classes in regular schools, through one or more kinds of regular classes in which individual adjustments were provided, to regular classes in which nothing special was done for them. At least two aspects of interpersonal perception would need to be studied: the perceptions of others by the gifted and the perceptions of the gifted by others. To be properly encompassing, at least these additional variables would have to be given due consideration:

1. Inclusion of classmates and/or schoolmates among the "others"
2. The grade level at which the study was made
3. The time of placement in the special provisions
4. The duration of such placement
5. The uniformity of definition of the behavior being studied and the manner in which it was observed
6. The socioeconomic and sex constitution of the groups studied

It is quite possible, too, that the teachers' competencies could be significant.

A seemingly simple problem thus has many aspects. Of major importance is just how the presence or absence of the attitude of snobbishness, and the perception by others of such behavior in the gifted, is to be defined and ascertained. A distinction needs to be made, for instance, between the behavior of the bright child who quickly and easily arrives at the correct responses to questions and problems, may be a bit impatient with others who proceed more slowly and laboriously, and who manifests, overtly or covertly, no derogation of the response speed or accuracy of other pupils, as contrasted with such a child who is openly contemptuous of his less effective classmates. Some observation and measurement techniques may classify as snobbish first kind of gifted youngster; others, only the latter kind. It is necessary to distinguish between legitimate self-confidence and pride and the conceit which underlies snobbishness. The insecure often resentfully perceive what is only self-confidence or pride in others as snobbishness. And, more importantly, the manner in which others—teachers, parents, and even some other children in the gifted child's environment—react to his performing more effectively than the others itself determines the way in which such a child comes to perceive his successful performances. By tone of voice, by manner of speaking, by what is said, even by unverbalized communication, the superior performances of children may be evaluated as a worthwhile contribution to the end toward which his group is working, or only as being better than some other youngster's performance.

*Personality
and social adjustment
of the gifted*

Research evidence on the personality and social adjustment of the gifted throws considerable light on our problem. Because the systematic study started by Terman and pursued by others is the most complete one we have, we shall first examine those findings, recognizing that they apply not just to the ten-year-olds he started with but cover a 35-year time span in their lives.

The generally more desirable personal characteristics and social adjustment found to hold for the initial group apparently contributed to their taking on (or being accorded) leadership roles in both their later school and community activities. Hobson (1948), comparing children who had been admitted to school early on the basis of Binet mental age with those admitted at conventional school-entering age, found that the accelerated group held significantly more extracurricular offices at the high school level. Klausmeier, Goodwin, and Ronda (1968) found that children who had been accelerated when they were in the second and third grades manifested "normal sociability and social development" when they were in the ninth grade.

Representative of comparisons of gifted children in special classes with their equivalents in regular classes are two studies by Bell (1958) and Grupe (1961). Both studies involved fifth graders who had Binet IQs of 125 or more. Bell, using 30 matched pairs of such children, observed: "The gifted revealed an ability to adjust himself that was equal to or better than that of the normal child, regardless of his classroom group. Homogeneity (of classes) appeared to have no real effect upon personality traits of self-adjustment." Grupe, using 50 matched pairs, concerned herself also with the extent to which the bright elementary school youngsters were accepted by their classmates. Her finding that the gifted in the regular classes were more highly accepted than their equivalents in the special classes is particularly interesting because, in special classes, the choices had to be spread among the other gifted children, whereas in the regular classes the brighter children were in the minority but still were more highly accepted than those of lower IQs. In the regular classes, 89 percent of the bright children either were highly accepted or accepted, and 10 percent were "tolerated." Gallagher (1958), using the "best-friends" nominations approach in grades two through five in an elementary school, found that the 29 boys and 25 girls with Binet IQs of 150 and above were "highly popular" and were so nominated by classmates at all IQ levels. The fact that this school was in a university community and was involved, at the time, in a larger study of supra-150 children may have affected the magnitude of Gallagher's findings, but their tenor is in harmony with other such research. In another study in the same general setting he and Crowder (1957) found much the same condition, half of the gifted group falling in the top fourth of all such nominations.

Taking Terman's findings regarding the characteristics of his gifted group, two researchers in effect reversed the approach and ascertained which children in regular classes were perceived by their classmates as possessing those traits or characteristics. Boyd (1958), using 565 children in 20 representative elementary-level classes in a mid-America school system in which there were 88 children with Binet IQs of 120 and above, found that the proportion of such bright children exceeded that of the sub-120 Binet IQ group in having the characteristics "helps me" and "is bright or good in school work." Pielstick (1963) made a "Guess Who" type of test with 14 of Terman's traits and gave it to fourth-, fifth-, and sixth-grade children in regular classes. He had 60 children in what he termed the "high superior" group (Binet IQ of 140 and over) and 158 in the "low superior" (Binet IQ equivalents of 130 to 139). Both groups were identified as having, significantly beyond chance expectancy, the characteristics Terman had observed. The high superior children who attended schools in the lower socioeconomic areas of the school district

were relatively more often identified than were those in the high socioeconomic-area schools. Not only were the high superior youngsters recognized by their classmates as different, but they were regarded as favored models.

Although the representative research findings cited shed no light directly on whether the gifted, when special educational provisions are made for them, are perceived as being "snobbish," the preponderance of favorable perceptions of the gifted by their classmates, in whatever educational setting, suggests strongly that the gifted are perceived favorably, thus casting considerable doubt on the validity of the snobbishness contention.

The psychology of snobbishness

Because of its relevance to the total social climate in which the gifted must do their learning we need to examine "the psychology" of snobbishness—both how such behavior patterns may develop in the gifted and how others may perceive it in them when, in fact, it may not be present. As we proceed, let us keep in mind several possibilities: the gifted are inherently predisposed to be snobbish; the gifted are more likely than other children to learn to be snobbish; snobbishness may occur in any children; and snobbishness may be in the perceiver and not in the perceived.

In any social group—political party, church denomination, student body, Scout troop, school class, or neighborhood play group—some individuals tend to stand out noticeably from the rest. Quite understandably, subgroups tend to occur, in part because those who differ believe they have more in common with each other than with the larger group, although in times of threat (either to themselves or to the larger group) they tend to abandon their separateness and revert to the larger group structure. Such a "different" individual, or group of such individuals, may coexist with the larger group without displaying or evoking either positive or negative feelings (attitudes)—essentially a nonthreatening situation to either the subgroup or the larger group. But let the subgroup behave in certain ways toward the larger group, or, just as importantly, let the subgroup be perceived by the larger group (with or without discernible "justification") as behaving in ways regarded as inimical to the interests or integrity of the larger group, and aversive attitudes are nurtured and generated in both groups. On the other hand, positive attitudes will be manifested at least by the large group, if the behavior of those in the subgroup is perceived to be contributive to the welfare of the large group. Add to this the fact that attitudes manifested by the members of one group toward the members of another group, or toward another group as an entity, tend to evoke comparable attitudes in the other group: the attitudes of those who are perceived tend to reflect, or mirror, the attitudes of those who are doing the perceiving.

We must recognize two facts regarding social interaction: (1) Subgroups inevitably will emerge within any larger group. They last a while, then either dissipate, recombine into new and larger subgroups, or merge back into the larger group. A seemingly endless variety of social subgroups exists, often with considerable overlapping in membership; for example, a white, Methodist, male, Republican teacher has five subgroup identifications. More importantly, the bases for the constitution of subgroups vary along a continuum from the highly intangible (such as the sophists and the humanists) to the increasingly apparent and more easily discriminable (such as the gifted, the Democrats, the truck drivers, the Weight Watchers, and the cerebral palsied). It is quite probable that the less tangible the basis on which any subgroup is constituted, or perceived to be constituted, the less that subgroup tends to be "understood" and/or tolerated by the larger group.

(2) Intergroup attitudes—either positive or negative—may or may not exist, depending upon many factors. Threat to or promise of power or status, employment opportunities or demands, moral commitment—such conditions provide the bases for attitudes by and toward any group as well as the way members of any group may come to perceive (suspect, fear, project, hope for) actually nonexistent attitudes in any other group.

Intergroup attitudes between the gifted and the nongifted, then, are learned, just as misperceptions of attitudes may be learned. Snobbishness (taken here to be reflective of an attitude) on the part of the gifted is learned just as apprehension on the part of the nongifted that the gifted might be snobbish is learned—just as intergroup attitudes between the well-to-do and the not-so-well-to-do, or between the better "educated" and the not-so-well "educated," are learned. That such attitudes can develop and have at times developed is granted; that they will or must develop is debatable. But the development of particular intergroup attitudes does not have the same inevitability as does the emergence of subgroups within a larger group.

Democratization

The concern that the provision of special educational adjustments for the gifted may alienate the gifted from the rest of the children, or vice versa, overlaps a bit the fear of snobbishness. On the assumption that things would be better all around if we all understood each other and that commingling contributes to such understanding, heterogeneous grouping of children for the purposes of education often is preferred to homogeneous groupings. The desideratum is a mix of sharing and understanding of social values by the gifted and nongifted.

Research evidence on this condition, though mostly indirect, clearly indicates that the gifted, as a group, tend to be perceived favorably by their classmates, whether in special class or regular class settings, and tend, with demonstrably greater relative frequency, to be accorded or elected to leadership roles. This being so consistently the case, it is difficult to support the contention that the gifted have, or are likely to have, lost "the common touch." The research evidence reviewed above is in part supportive to this conclusion.

"Intelligence," of course, is not the sole determinant in such socially complex situations, as illustrated in the findings of Janson and Gallagher (1966). Studying the sociometric choices of 100 gifted disadvantaged children in four classes at the intermediate grade level, they found "substantial" cross-racial choices being made, with factors such as sex and racial proportions in the classes appearing to influence the nature and kind of choices that pupils made. As they observed, "When the range of ability is reduced by the type of ability grouping practiced as part of the current project, intelligence ceases to be a major factor in social choices" (p. 225). Mann (1957) explored the nature of the friendships of gifted and "typical" children in a program of partial segregation. On the basis of a sociometric inquiry (Have near you, Help you with school work, and Be on your side when playing games) of 281 children in grades four, five, and six, of whom 67 were regarded as gifted, it was observed that "the heterogeneous class experiences did not actually produce relationships significant enough to be classified as friendships." The import

was taken to be "the fallacy of believing that because we group children together we have trained them to accept each other for what they are" (p. 206). Democratization is not achieved merely by putting children together; it is, rather, a function of the quality of the psychological interactions among the members of the group.

Recognizing the social value in children's cultivating and maintaining a sensitivity to and an understanding of the value systems and needs of others in the schools, we must beware of overgeneralizing to the point of engendering overall conformity, thus washing out socially valuable individual strengths and weaknesses. The gifted, just as any other child, or group of children, have both a need for and a right to the opportunity to "be alone" at times. Further, subgroups have interests and characteristics which mitigate against an all-pervading homogenization. What, for instance, is the nature and frequency of social interaction between the teamsters' union and Phi Beta Kappa, between the custodians' union and the associations of college professors, of teachers, of ministers? In this country, having lived "together" for quite some time, how well have those on "one side of the track" become informed of and sensitive to living conditions, value systems, other cultural patterns, or even the communication systems of those on the "other" side? At times differences between individuals, as well as between groups, need to be recognized and respected, just as at other times such differences have to yield to certain overriding considerations. The danger lies in overgeneralization regarding either of these kinds of social conditions. The slogan "to be a part of and not apart from" has validity only insofar as it is anchored in social and psychological facts.

The contention that the gifted need democratization, then, implies that they are deprived of it when special educational provisions are made for them; but the facts appear to be otherwise. Perhaps some such concern needs to be felt, but not to alarmist proportions. The fact that the gifted, as a group, for years have been favorably perceived socially by their schoolmates suggests strongly that, in view of the principle of reciprocal attitudinal interaction, they entertain similar perceptions in their social relationships.

"Osmotic" Learning

The claim that the nongifted will benefit by being in the same learning situations as the gifted cannot yet be either proved or disproved, since relevant research evidence is lacking. This benefit can be thought of in two ways: that gifted youngsters can directly help the nongifted in their learnings, and that the nongifted can "pick up" learning styles and concepts from the gifted and thereby be further motivated to learn.

Some teachers have told of successfully using brighter children to work individually with some of their slower classmates. The brighter youngsters have communicated learning approaches, restructured the learning demands, or analyzed the learning act in ways helpful to the slower youngsters. Usually such learning tips are not those which the teacher has utilized, but children sometimes will employ learning approaches suggested to them by classmates after they have failed to "hear" the very same suggestions made by their teachers. Important in such learning situations is the enhancement of interpersonal relationships—particularly as regards the slower and perhaps more frustrated youngster. The factors of one-to-one relationship (often lacking when teachers "teach" *classes*) and of social peerness, or even of being recognized by the brighter youngster, can be conducive to a positive learning atmosphere. Such conditions need not be precluded when special educational provisions are made for the gifted.

Potential, curiosity, interest, competency

The expectation that slower youngsters will, on their own, catch on to the how and what of the learning of brighter youngsters calls for serious examination in the light of the psychological facts. To what extent has watching and even studying, on one's own, a high jumper make a seven-foot jump, or an outstanding musician perform, or a good politician or labor organizer operate, or a scientist benefit from serendipity been helpful to those who lack the underlying relevant potentials and competencies? Important distinctions among competency, potential, interest, and curiosity must be noted. As used here, curiosity is an information-seeking form of approach behavior that may or may not imply overt reaction to that about which one is "curious." Interest denotes a more extensive reaction to the condition or phenomenon. It is more than incipient reaction; in fact, to be "interested" in something, one usually has to have had some modicum of successful relationship with it. More generally, interest is an approach behavior tendency which results from a psychological sum of successful experiences in some area of activity, multiplied by the individual's capability of understanding, or comprehending, the components to which he is reacting (and the relationships among them), divided by the psychological sum of his unsuccessful experiences in such involvement. One may be curious about the playing of bridge or chess, or the repairing of a carburetor, or the use of formulas in communication. But to become interested in any of these he must have the capability of comprehending their various elements and the relationships among them, and he must have had more successful than unsuccessful experiences in the area. Competency denotes typically successful performance, occurs after the manifestation of curiosity and interest, and depends on the individual's capability or potential relevant to the activity. Understanding—taken here to be the ability of the individual to verbalize his performance—usually accompanies competency; you block a man out in football by doing thus and so, you assemble a carburetor by putting its parts together in such and such relationships, you use a given formula in such and such a situation because of the presence or absence of certain variables in that situation, and so on.

Central to the matter of the nongifted's "picking up" the gifted's learnings or strategies is his basic capacity to do so. The story is told of the girl who expressed considerable frustration in finding out what "x" was equal to; she said she had kept a full record of the different numbers she had found for "x," and they didn't agree at all! Hers was a failure of conceptualization. For one to learn "osmotically" from any group, he must possess an adequate armamentarium of whatever symbols (words, signs, and other notations) are contributive to that learning, must be able to abstract and generalize, and must be capable of seeing less-frequently recognized and understood relationships that are involved in that learning. This, of course, is the forte of the gifted—the characteristics that most clearly differentiate them from their slower-learning classmates.

Motivation and outcomes

That the presence of the gifted in a heterogeneous class can motivate learning by their less capable classmates should be regarded more as an expression of hope than as a statement of psychological probability. This hope hinges primarily upon the meaning attached to the term motivation, and somewhat upon the nature of the learning outcomes that may be expected. Later, we shall consider more intensively the nature of motivation, but here it will denote relatively "self-sustained" application to a task to achieve some personally or socially acceptable outcome. In more explicit behavioral terms, child A sees (or is caused by his teacher to see) that child B is (or has been) working productively on some learning task. With or without prompting, child A addresses himself to the task, continuing to do so until he completes it or until his teacher stops him with praise for "really trying," or ostensibly continuing at the task with great apparent effort (furrowed brow and all that) until the teacher, ready to move the class on to something different, "springs" him from such pseudo-application. If the educational tasks primarily involve rote memory (learning the multiplication table, the capitals of the states, simple definitions of pieces of laboratory equipment, life dates of artists or historical personages, boundary states, and the like) or copying out of dictionaries definitions of words for no particular use (called "enrichment" by one teacher), such a motivational setting may yield some benefit. If, on the other hand, the learning tasks necessitate the acquisition of concepts, the perceiving and discovery of abstractions, and the drawing of generalizations, fruitful returns from such motivation of the less able are less likely. In fact, in the latter situation the less capable child actually may be further frustrated.

In sum, the three arguments often used against special educational provisions in the schools for gifted children seem to reflect an underlying aversion to such action rather than of an understanding of available research evidence or sound psychological expectations. Such aversion may spring from an apprehensiveness regarding the possible roles of the gifted in our society. Although in some instances the worst fears have been horribly justified, they have been the exceptions. Insofar as such negative contentions are psychologically invalid and, further, based on unsound motives, we are obliged to challenge them.

THE GIFTED
IN THE SOCIAL SCENE

Often over the ages society has been called upon to identify those with leadership capabilities—even to identify them early in order to plan their formal education programs. Most utopias differentiate among their members in terms of leadership and followership roles, or in terms of planners and participators. And even in egalitarian societies (as noted in Orwell's *Animal Farm*) some turn out to be "more equal" than others.

Although crises have prompted American society to extra effort to identify, nurture, and make special uses of certain of its more capable members, these episodes have been short-lived and, until the early 1970s, had resulted in no systematic governmental programming to that end. State and federal programs in the United States tend to be much more habilitative, rehabilitative, or correctional than preventive or long-range constructive—particularly as regards education at the lower educational levels. Witness the funding, both state and federal, of special services for the handicapped, for children with learning disabilities, and for vocational rehabilitation for those of public school age. It can be argued that the funding of programs for the disadvantaged and even for Head Start is committed as much to correction or compensation for the absence of conventional cultural nurturance as to the prevention of later learning difficulties attendant on extraschool experiential im-

poverishment. In other words, governmental agencies tend not to act but to *react.*

SCHOLARSHIPS

With the exception of state senatorial scholarships (often modest recognition gestures rather than bona fide supportive scholarships), financial encouragement and support for the more capable typically have been the function of extragovernmental agencies. Undergraduate college-level scholarships have been provided for the demonstrably more capable since the early 1930s by colleges and universities, by business firms (largely, at first, for employee's children and partly because, on account of income tax computations, $100 of scholarship money actually cost the company only a fraction of that amount), by foundations, and by some state governments. In the early 1940s Westinghouse started supporting a Science Talent Search, in which top-level high school students competed to obtain scholarships in colleges and universities of their choice (Edgerton and Britt, 1943). In 1951 the Ford Foundation instituted a scholarship program for superior students capable of entering college before they had completed high school.[2] A still broader base for the screening of candidates and the awarding of scholarships was accomplished by the creation, in the mid-1950s, of the National Merit Scholarship Organization, originally funded by the Ford Foundation and the Carnegie Foundation and later augmented by funds from business and industrial firms.

[2] This and three other programs germane to the education of the gifted at the high school and college levels are described in the Fund for the Advancement of Education's publication, "Bridging the Gap between School and College" (1953). The Fund's "They Went to College Early" (1957) describes the follow-up of the program.

As early as 1940, New York and Pennsylvania had some limited funds for scholarship purposes. In response to Sputnik several more states appropriated scholarship money. In 1961, for instance, New York appropriated funds for a program that granted over 16,000 scholarships in its first year of operation. Funds for stipends and assistantships, tantamount to scholarship support, have been provided by the National Science Foundation, the National Institutes of Health, and other governmental and nongovernmental national organizations, both to further the education of the more capable at the graduate level and to improve the quality and quantity of scientific and professional personnel. At both the national and state levels the increasing difficulty in raising money, along with a shifting pattern of social needs, led in the 1970s to a decrease in such funds.

The Scholarship-Awarding Process

It is important, in thinking about the gifted, that we examine the scholarship-awarding process in society and its social-psychoeducational implications, with a view to the possibility of modifying or extending it.

Superior capability should be discovered early in the lives of individuals, both to capitalize upon superior potential and to facilitate the self-realization of the gifted, which in turn can help them become greater social contributors. Understandably, and for a long time necessarily (before psychology made earlier identification possible), scholarships have been awarded to those who *have* produced—reflective of the post hoc definition of giftedness. Given the absence of good predictive devices and procedures or the existence of only moderately effective ones, scholarships were awarded to those who had achieved well in society's educational programs and whose

future performance was thereby reasonably well predictable. This principle will continue to be operative, but we can improve the performances of the gifted not only by means of psychologically strengthened early identification devices and procedures but also by shaping educational provisions more to the needs of the gifted, some of whom now are being overlooked and deprived of the right of self-fulfillment. Not only has it been demonstrated repeatedly from the early 1920s that, in terms of their basic capability, the most underachieving children in the schools are the bright youngsters but also, particularly since the 1960s, concern has been expressed about the extent to which gifted youngsters among the disadvantaged populations have not been identified by conventional testing approaches and/or have not been motivated to achieve to an extent more in harmony with their latent or even their demonstrated superior learning capability. This latter condition needs further examination with respect to scholarship-awarding practices.

Research by means of conventional group and individual learning aptitude tests consistently has shown a higher percentage of the gifted to be in the higher socioeconomic levels than in the lower levels. In Terman's monolithic study of the top one percent in tested "intelligence," 31 percent of the parents were in the top (professional) level, 50 percent were in the semiprofessional and business level, 12 percent were skilled laborers, and some 7 percent were in the semiskilled or unskilled group. Such findings have caused great concern among those who believe that "high intelligence" should be found either equally or more equitably distributed among the different socioeconomic levels. Havighurst, for instance, contended in the 1950s that we should expect the percentages represented by the gifted to be essentially the same for all levels. It was maintained that those in the lower levels who might be of superior capability were not as highly motivated to do their best on tests and in school as were those in the upper classes. It has also been contended that the content of most of the tests used was culturally biased in favor of those in the upper classes. That both factors have been contributive to locating lower percentages of gifted among the lower socioeconomic class is granted, but to what extent has not been clearly demonstrated. It is the author's contention (unsupported by hard research evidence and without suggesting any genetic implications) that a higher percentage of gifted can be found among the socioeconomically or culturally disadvantaged than has been found, but that, even at earliest entry into public education programs, there will continue to be some disparity among the percentages of the gifted in such different groups. Whatever the facts or one's hopes may be, some people are distressed that a higher proportion of higher education scholarships are awarded to children in the upper socioeconomic classes than to those in the lower classes.

Policy on adjusting the amounts of such financial assistance to the recipients' financial needs has varied. For a time in the 1930s, when scholarships were beginning to be granted in earnest, some colleges and universities proceeded in the light of the philosophy that any pupil with sufficiently high achievement and promise, regardless of his financial status, should be granted a scholarship. More recent policy is to adjust the magnitude of scholarship assistance to the student's financial needs and to his family's ability to pay. In some instances a certificate of merit—a dollarless scholarship—is awarded to any candidate who has performed well enough in the screening process to be awarded a bona fide scholarship but whose parents are regarded as capable of financing his continuing edu-

cation. When the concept of need is thus brought into play, scholarship monies can enable larger numbers to obtain higher education.

The Disadvantaged Gifted

Scholarships historically have been granted only to pupils who have completed high school and are serious candidates for higher education. Yet, from 10 to 25 percent of college-capable pupils have failed to seek acceptance as college students, some of them primarily for financial reasons, and there has been a failure to extend scholarship help to these pupils at the high school level. Although public high schools do not charge tuition, the book rental and other fees and added expenses, or the pressure to become income-producers for needy families, constitute financially restricting demands on more capable disadvantaged high school students and their families. Grossly inadequate, too, is the breadth of thinking as to how the financial assistance which might be provided by such "scholarships" could be used by such promising high school students. The use of scholarship grants to defray the students' necessary, nontuitional high school expenses and, possibly, even to provide some moderate partial financial support for his family could contribute much both to his sense of personal worth and social aspiration and toward a more favorable attitude on the part of his family regarding his continuing his education. Thinking of this sort was expressed in the 1960s by a Harvard educator but evoked little significant response. And yet such assistance could do much to help nurture legitimate educational and social aspirations by high school students of superior promise who believe it is socially "unreal" even to aspire to continue their education.

This idea may be extended further. Society has seen fit not only to reimburse extra expenses incurred in the education of the handicapped but also to lower the age limit of eligibility. In view of mounting evidence concerning the importance of lowering the age limit in order to provide early nurturant learning experiences for the gifted, constructive social thinking will need to go beyond the confines of the school plant and into the very homes of children. While some school districts have, from time to time, allocated $25, $50, or even $75 per gifted pupil per year for special facilities needed in their education, the practice is by no means typical. One school district, reluctantly agreeing to admit qualified gifted children early, required the parents of such children to have their children psychologically evaluated, at costs varying from $50 to $100, before such children would even be considered for early admission —clearly a blatantly undemocratic procedure. It would seem that social thinking regarding the gifted must be considerably extended, probably to the point of providing for such things as special training for parents and preschool personnel, the necessary special learning materials, transportation, and day-care maintenance, as the needs of the situation may dictate.

It is easy, as well as unrealistic, to say that higher education scholarships should be awarded forthwith to those disadvantaged who are known to be properly high in learning potential but who have not shown proportionally high academic achievement. (The discussion here pertains only to helping the gifted among the disadvantaged, and not to the practice, started in the 1960s, of using special funds to induce or help the disadvantaged generally to enter upon and continue in higher education. Some of the points to be considered are, however, quite relevant to that larger group.) If the standards of achievement during the higher education period are maintained, those admitted under such scholarships are put in an unfair or stressful situation —even if compensatory educational adjustments are made for them—for two reasons. (1) For a student to enter upon higher education with a reasonable chance of just succeeding, let alone doing very well in it, he must "bring with him" not only a superior capability to learn but also a certain fund of prior learnings. To the extent that the learning demands are academic in nature, as contrasted with those of technical or trade school, if he lacks them the odds are high against his even getting through. This is particularly true if no effective "remedial" education program is provided. (2) There may be a pattern of prior learning experiences in which the student, though basically capable, has been underachieving or achieving only halfheartedly at the elementary and high school levels. Generally, such a gifted youngster gets along passably well during his first semester in college but then progressively falls behind and loses out— having, in effect, tried to cross a desert with only a partially filled canteen of water. He may bring with him a fund of learning, usually acquired incidental to his regular school program, but he has accomplished it so casually and easily that he has failed to develop the study skills and habits essential to later success. Most such youngsters have had a four- to eight-year vacation from serious work, so that they just aren't accustomed to the sustained and systematic application (which even the gifted need to acquire) that is needed for even passable success in higher education. The gifted underachiever has, in fact, formed habits of nonwork. Further, he has failed to acquire a joy of learning. And in college the pattern of learning shifts from the frequent tests and recitations over smaller units of learning customary in high schools to that of less demanding recitations and less frequent tests over larger units of learning, thus demanding greater personal responsibility in performing the educational tasks. The college-entering student with high basic learning aptitude but no more than an average high school achievement record has a very low probability of doing above-average work in college.

The awarding of scholarships to candidates who have high basic learning potential but low academic performance may help assuage social guilt but may not be as fruitful of high-level social leadership and participation as many may expect. Probably a higher percentage of the disadvantaged need and can benefit from scholarships in education, but they (especially) also need more effective earlier education.

This problem has deep social and psychological roots. It will be helpful if we first consider important characteristics of the disadvantaged, examine what takes place in their early learning, and see what important implications emerge.

CHARACTERISTICS OF THE DISADVANTAGED

The term "disadvantaged" is taken here to denote those segments of our society whose style of life is discernibly less nurturant to conventional learning than the average of the total society. Most commonly, they are found in the lower socio-economic groups and constitute relatively intact subgroups, such as certain white mountain folk, the blacks, the Puerto Ricans, the American Indians, and those of Mexican backgrounds, who have moved into the general culture of our country. As a rule, they tend to maintain their group integrity, maintaining their own lifestyles, communication systems (patois or foreign language), and value systems. For some, this behavior is a compensatory, defensive response to the larger society which (itself perhaps defensively) perceives the disadvantaged

as unable to strive for higher and more secure status in society. The minority group tend to perceive themselves as the majority group perceive them. The disadvantaged often tend to be bilingual, speaking their original language, or patois, in the home, and yet often having to learn another in order to communicate with the larger society. (Note that the deaf, especially those born deaf, are socially and psychologically a disadvantaged group.)

Unequal Distribution of the Gifted

Concern has been expressed that proportionately higher percentages of gifted have been found among the more advantaged portions of our society than among the disadvantaged. It has been suggested that something is wrong with identification procedures that thus violate the presumption of a more equitable distribution of giftedness among the several classes of society. Much of the adverse criticism of "intelligence testing" of the 1960s and 1970s has stemmed from such thinking. It is important to consider this problem a bit before going on.

Bias in testing

The problem is much more basic (again ignoring possible genetic probabilities) than the claimed prejudicial cultural bias in the "testing of intelligence." Let us consider briefly the matter of bias in testing, then get back to some things every bit as fundamental psychologically. We start from the fact that repeatedly, on a variety of tests of learning aptitude, it has been reported that the average IQs of the different socioeconomic classes tend to increase from the lower to the upper ones—or to reflect on the minorities less favorably than on the majority. The test critics then point out that certain items in the tests most generally used sample information which is quite alien to the culture of the disadvantaged. Yet no research evidence is advanced to show that where the disadvantaged "fail" on certain test items owing to their cultural bias or "unfairness," the loss in average score due to such failure is sufficient to account for the difference between the disadvantaged and other groups tested. Suppose the average of group A is less than that of group B, and there are culturally "unfair" items in the test which both groups took; was the number of potentially failable items (due to cultural unfamiliarity) sufficient to account for the difference found between the average scores? Keep in mind two things here: (1) Our thinking has been in terms of the tests most generally used on six-year-olds, on nine-year-olds, and on twelve-year-olds (and involving "general information"), and not in terms of different groups of specially educated adults. (2) Our thinking has been in terms of a difference between the *averages* of two groups, and not what happened in the case of some specific child.

Aside from such psychometric considerations, there are important psychological facets to the problem of the impact of different kinds of acculturation. One of these is a procedural matter—involving the administration of the test, group or individual, by a member of the majority group to a minority class or child. It is contended that prior interclass attitudes operate to depress the scores earned by minority-group members, owing to certain characteristics of the majority-group test administrator, such as the operation of middle- or upper-class expectancies and explicit demands in the testing situation, or even in his manner of communicating the tasks of the test, or the operation of previously acquired attitudes on the part of the disadvantaged children toward the class of which the administrator is a member, whether they be of negativism, of despair, or of futil-

ity, or some combination of these, or even the unconscious operation of bias in scoring responses to test items. Research evidence on this problem is not at all clearcut, some researchers finding evidence of such biasing influences, others not. That some such conditions can and do affect the outcomes of individual testing in the cases of specific children is known, as illustrated in the case of one seven-year-old who earned a Binet IQ of 135 with one tester but a week later earned a WISC Verbal IQ of 105 (Full Scale IQ of 108). The second test was administered by a person of the same sex as that of the child's parent against whom the child had strong negative feelings. Even the quality of the child's responses in the second testing was discernibly poorer than in the first testing. (All three participants in this were of the same socioeconomic class and of the same race.) But one swallow doesn't make a summer.

Unfavorable psychological conditions

More fundamental psychological conditions can, however, operate to depress the test scores of the disadvantaged. It will help if we consider how children get started in their learning life—before they enter school. We have posited a behavior tendency which was termed "outgoingness" in all infants and children. While its degree or extent varies, it is manifested in the young child's reacting to and interacting with the things and persons in his environment. As he grows older, and if he is fortunate, his reactions and interactions are "enriched" and reinforced. This has the effect of causing him at least to continue, if not to increase his outgoingness. The objects in the infant's environment are manipulated by others in his environment so as to "attract and sustain his attention." The adults (and others) utter words—

"ball," "pretty," "doll," "baby," "bath," "water," "soap," "warm," and such acts not only enable the infant to associate such sounds with objects and phenomena but also reinforce his tendency to react to them. But such an acculturation atmosphere includes more than such verbalized nurturance; there is present also, and nonverbally communicated to the child, what may be termed a quality of the interactive process, a tenseness or relaxedness in the personal interaction, a staccato or smooth-flowing characteristic, or a merely tolerant one as contrasted with an encouraging reaction on the part of the others in the environment. Both the what and the how of the interactive process are important in the nurturance of the infant and child.

Now let's look at the child by, say, the conventional school-entering age of five or six. What he brings to school psychologically are the results of two things. If his acculturation has been "normal," he has had a very large number of cognitive learnings, many of them largely incidental in nature. To the extent that his experiencing has been limited, he will be entering upon the school learning situation with a less-than-expected experiential background, and this may cause him to have some difficulties in his school learning; to the extent that his experiencing has been wide and fruitful, he enters with an "educational plus." It is well here to think of acculturation as a continuum which ranges from deprivation through "normal" or average nurturance to a condition we may call "hothousing." Deprivation may result from living in an environment of things and people that is just not as "rich," as stimulating, as full of things and people to react to, or not as reinforcing to the child's responses as is generally the case. An overprotective person in the child's environment actually can deprive a growing child of his "normal" experiencings. Physical impairment, especially deaf-

ness, can be equally deprivational. At the other end of the continuum, significant others in the child's environment may, perhaps because of their own need to compensate, so confront the growing child with a multiplicity of things to be reacted to that the child is overwhelmed and either self-protectively withdraws or else reacts in only a superficial manner. Effective nurturance and acculturation (the former more a matter of intentional acculturation by significant others, the latter more characterized by the child's incidental learnings) depend on the child's readiness and capacity to benefit from them.

Perhaps even more important than cognitive learnings are affective and attitudinal learnings. In a sense, these are products of the emotional climate in which the child engages in his early cognitive learnings. Here the seeds are planted which will result in the child's doing his later learning (which he seems to "want" to do) because it evokes pleasurable responses on the part of the significant others in his environment or in his gradually coming to like to learn just because it is "fun" or self-fulfilling. The two conditions are not completely separable, and the second can grow out of the first, but they are discriminable. In a sense, the psychological cards are stacked in favor of the child's progressing toward the second stage—as witness the experiences adults have when children openly resent their intrusions into something they wish to do for themselves.

Now let us relate this discussion to our basic problem here—that of the depressing effect of the limited acculturation of the disadvantaged on scores of conventional tests of learning aptitude. Imagine for the moment two kinds of acculturational backgrounds—the one characterized by a "healthy" (not stultifying) wealth of experience-acquiring opportunities plus an attitudinal milieu which is conducive to acquiring the joy of learning to learn, the other opposite in nature. A product of the second not only is handicapped by his smaller supply of incidental learnings but also is impaired by his unverbalized attitude of having to be "taught" and/or of learning only to please some adults, itself an attitude shared by the adults from whom the child learns to react passively to learning motivation. Recognize, too, that other attitudes among the adults in the second kind of condition may be those of despair over a lack of (or a perceived lack of) opportunity to advance themselves socioeconomically, of resentment against what is perceived to be a nonaccepting social system, and/or of futility regarding odds to be overcome. Add to this the fact that, either by virtue of a long-standing ethnic pattern of behavior or as a result of such attitudes, certain subgroups just are not disposed to respond positively under time pressures which most of our society accept as "normal"— a condition that is explicitly an integral part of many of our testing procedures, as well as of many classroom practices. Maybe, too, some of them have learned not to tackle something new and therefore threatening because if they don't try it they will not fail.

Psychologically sound testing

So far as effective, psychologically sound test identification of the gifted among the disadvantaged is concerned, then, the major, but not the sole, emphasis should be placed upon ascertaining responses to demands which tap rather directly the children's basic learning potential (process) rather than the actual learnings they have acquired (product). The more heterogeneous the experiential backgrounds of children, the more this statement holds true. Envision, for example, all the one-year-olds in this country and recognize that their experiential backgrounds differ among

themselves now more than they ever will later. As these children grow older, the differences among their backgrounds will tend to decrease, at least as long as they attend school. Note, though, that while schooling tends to reduce this heterogeneity of experiential background, it by no means eliminates it—something which our society began to take in earnest in the 1950s. "Individual differences" remain, not only in experiential backgrounds and attitudinal predispositions to learning but also in variability of basic learning capacity.

Effects
of Early Acculturation

Two points need to be borne in mind here—one psychoeducational and one psychological. Important as it is to ascertain the extent to which children differ in having the fundamental psychological processes with which they can learn, it is necessary also to discover the extents to which they have benefited from their opportunities to learn, whether incidentally or formally. Let us limit our consideration here to children of school-entering age and assume that no other contaminating emotional conditions are present in them. That child who enters upon school learning with the most effectively operating basic learning processes and who also has benefited maximally from a good acculturation background will have the highest probability of learning easily and well in school. On the other hand, if the child has superior basic psychological processes by means of which he could learn well if provided the opportunity but has not had good acculturation background, he will have more difficulty in school learning. The second kind of child, with his superior or adequate basic "promise," will need, and will be likely to benefit from, an educational program that at first compensates for his limited acculturation and then progresses to "normal" learning nurturance. Particularly important, especially for the disadvantaged, will be effort toward the inculcation of attitudes which are conducive to learning, helping the child to learn the joy of learning.

Psychologically, we have characterized the gifted child as one who tends more than other children to interact with his environment, to learn more from fewer instances and repetitions, and to abstract and generalize. What about this kind of child in below-average levels of acculturation? While he may benefit somewhat from his opportunities, he still cannot compensate for a serious lack of acculturative stimulation. He will fail to get his "fair share" not only of experiential learnings but also of reinforcement to his tendencies to react, to abstract, to generalize. Much like a deaf child, he may be experientially deprived, poorly reinforced, and unmotivated—yet have hidden promise. In those uncommon instances where gifted adults appear to have emerged, largely on their own, out of disadvantaged classes, there invariably has been some influence which has caused (and probably partly enabled) them as children to start to compensate for their environmental limitations. Generally, high achievement aspirations and success-oriented value systems on the part of significant others in their environs struck the responsive chord.

The higher-education scholarship candidate from a disadvantaged background need not have less than adequate educational achievement; this situation can be prevented by the early inauguration of psychologically sensitive educational programs. Their aim should be to compensate for deprived extraschool experiential backgrounds, to nurture the psychological processes which make learning possible, and to nourish positive attitudes toward learning. The awarding of scholarships to high-potential, low-achieve-

ment candidates is unlikely to be productive in preparing such persons to assume major social roles, particularly of a highly cognitive nature (Raph, Goldberg, and Passow, 1966).

There are probably more gifted children among the disadvantaged than has been recognized by conventional identification procedures—by self-identification, by being recognized by teachers and other adults, or by the kinds of testing and evaluative procedures generally used. A more definitive psychological assessment procedure can make possible early identification of particularly disadvantaged scholarship candidates in order better to qualify them for such support. This procedure must involve a greater sensitivity to the psychological operations by means of which such children do their learning without ignoring their prior learnings, and to the impact their attitudinal milieu may have had upon the functioning of their basic potential.

SOCIAL PERCEPTION OF THE GIFTED

In the main, the United States socially and educationally continues to tolerate a Darwinian perception of the gifted—a tacit belief that a sufficient number and kind of socially responsible leaders will come to the fore in our "normal" social evolution. The contest between those who would let nature take its course and those who advocate facilitating social evolution continues, perhaps at a somewhat heightened tempo. The former take comfort in the belief that man appears on his own to have improved his lot, pointing out that new efforts, particularly in the area of early and more objective identification of potential leaders, are plagued with pitfalls, and comfortably ignoring the errors and loss in that which they wish to perpetuate. The social facilitators, on the other hand, have tended to be impetuous and overgeneralizing in their practices and their claims for the contributions of psychology. Interwoven with this has been a clamor for "the social good" with little concern for the self-fulfillment of the individual, ignoring the fact that the two are related.

Educators, meanwhile, repeatedly rediscover early philosophical and methodological orientations and cloak them in new terms, often seeming to seek just the "new" rather than the socially relevant and psychologically sound. Sensitivity to social needs often has resulted in preparing youngsters in school and college for social involvements that, at best, had half-lives of no more than five or ten years. The tendency to think and act in terms of a dichotomy—of either one or the other of the various possibilities instead of how much of which when—has caused needless contention and a socially inadequate program for the gifted.

The Gifted
as National Resources

While concern for the more effective education of the more capable in this country was aroused by the appearance of Sputnik, the concern was not a new one. As a result of shortages of highly trained specialists during World War II, the Conference Board of Associated Research Councils (American Council of Learned Societies, American Council on Education, National Research Council, and the Social Science Research Council) obtained Ford Foundation funds to determine the practicability of studying objectively the extent to which those who were capable of benefiting from high-level training for such specialized roles in society were being so helped. As a result, the Commission on Human Resources and Advanced Training was created to make such a study, the contribution to that end by the Ford Foundation being $240,000. The results were compiled by Wolfle in his volume, *America's Resources of Specialized Talent* (1954). (The study actually pertained only to the United States, and the term "talented" denoted the population herein designated as gifted.) Even though Wolfle's presentation is geared primarily to those concerned with higher education, particularly at the college and university level, the implications support the general thesis of this book—that the gifted child should be identified early and effectively educated early.

Wolfle observes in his introduction:

A nation with as complex an economy, as important a role in world affairs, and as tangled a web of social, economic, military, and technological problems as confront the United States is peculiarly dependent for its future welfare upon those of its citizens who are competent to work effectively with ideas. The development of new weapons, the conduct of government and statesmanship, the discovery and development of means to improve health, increase productivity, and add to human welfare, the ability to bring all these forces to the benefit of the less fortunate peoples of the world, and the ability to use them effectively to counteract the influences of totalitarianism all depend primarily upon those of the nation's workers who labor chiefly with their heads instead of with their hands.

It is therefore with a special segment of the total population that this study is concerned: with those persons who are educated, intelligent, able to work with ideas, and qualified to plan and understand and direct the nation's complex web of industrial, technological, social, scientific, and governmental institutions and problems. This limited portion of the population is easier to illustrate than to define. It includes the engineers and doctors, the philosophers and historians, the scientists and teachers, the business executives, and all the other people who have mastered some appropriate portion of the great and growing body of knowledge upon which the nation's ever more complex industrial, military, scientific, and social machinery is based. It includes, too, those who have gone beyond knowledge of engineering, law, or some other specialty and have acquired the broad vision and wide knowledge that give them the capacity for leadership in industry, labor, government, or education . . . .

It is easy to misinterpret an emphasis upon these groups and the roles they play in national and world affairs as special pleading for an intellectual elite. Any such charge misses the point. The democratic ideal is one of equal opportunity; within that ideal it is both individually advantageous and socially desirable for each person to make the best possible use of his talents. But equal opportunity does not mean equal accomplishment or identical use. Some men have greater ability than others and can accomplish things which are beyond the powers of men of lesser endowment. Along with moral and legal and political equality goes respect for the proper use of excellence. And this too is part of the American tradition, a tradition that has been proud of Benjamin Franklin, Booker T. Washington, and Babe Ruth, and is proud of the right of other men of humble origin to develop their talents and use them for the good of society.

The nation needs to make effective use of its intellectual resources. To do so means to use well its brightest people whether they come from farm or city, from the slum section or from the country-club area, regardless of color or religious or economic differences, but not regardless of ability. Democracy at its best gives each child access to the education and opportunities which will enable him to develop his potentialities. Each can then progress to the highest level which his abilities and interests allow. The United States stands in too vital need of the high abilities of its ablest sons and daughters to adopt any lesser goal.

What the specialists have in common is trained intelligence. The scientists and ministers, the doctors and philosophers, the engineers and management experts, and all other specialists who work at comparable levels possess the ability to use their heads, the capacity for abstract thought which takes them beyond the self-evident. Since the time of the Greeks, the search for truth has been a deep and persistent value in the culture of western civilization. "It is good to know, even if just for the knowing." But it is also good to know because of the benefits which flow from knowing. And now it may be that survival of the free world will depend upon knowledge, for the capacity for abstract thought becomes of steadily increasing importance as our lives grow in interdependence with those of other peoples, as technology increases the complexity of our industrial and economic lives, as communication and transportation shrink time and distance, as everyday occurrences must be interpreted against a background of many unseen relationships. As men become more and more dependent upon each other, for their jobs, their food, their enjoyment, and their security, they must depend more and more upon the best utilization of the abilities of each. The state of the world for some centuries to come may hinge largely upon the effectiveness with which the United States employs her intellectual resources (pp. 5–7, reprinted with permission from the publisher, Harper & Row).

Waste of College Potential

An analysis of certain of Wolfle's data reveals considerable support for some of our contentions. First, however, the following points must be made clear:

1. His baseline data are for those children who were 14 years old as of 1949, "who have or are expected to have entered high school, graduated from high school, entered college, and graduated from college," and are based upon estimates themselves based upon other studies made by or available to the Commission (p. 31). They therefore reflect neither the situa-

tion resulting from the upsurge in birth rates following World War II nor the results of the extra social and educational efforts following the impact of Sputnik.

2. Only the data from his total population of 2,193,000 are used.

3. The "IQs" in Figure 3.2 are really IQ equivalents to scores on the Army General Classification Test which served as the common denominator throughout his report (p. 143).

As far as the total population was concerned, 78.8 percent entered and 57 percent graduated from high school. However, only 20 percent entered and 11.9 percent graduated from college. Of the top 8.4 percent of the population with which he was concerned, 99.3 percent entered and 97.5 percent graduated from high school; 50.8 percent entered and 44.5 percent graduated from college.

If we concern ourselves only with those in Wolfle's study who were reported to have "IQs" of 128 and above, we have a total group of 184,080, or slightly more than $8\frac{1}{3}$ percent of this group—approximating the percentage of public school children included in our socially based definition of the gifted—and some very interesting conditions became apparent. (Bear in mind the 1954 publication date of his study; we don't know what a comparable updated study would show.)

Of this top (roughly) $8\frac{1}{2}$ percent, 99.3 percent entered and 97.5 percent graduated from high school; but only 50.8 percent of the top $8\frac{1}{2}$ percent entered college, 44.5 percent graduating. Note that nearly half of the ostensibly college-capable group did not even enter college. Sensitivity to this condition, similarly reported in other studies, undoubtedly played a part in subsequent decisions to increase scholarship funds.

Figure 3.2 reflects interesting facts on high school entering, high school graduation, college entering and college graduation in terms of the different "IQ" levels at the time of the study. Characteristi-

cally, this group entered and graduated from high school. Gifted dropouts were not a major factor in this 1949 population (Curve A, in the figure). However, the loss to society is strongly suggested by Curve B: while 48 percent of the 130 "IQ" group and 70 percent of the 165 group entered college, the percentage for the total gifted group who entered college was only 50.8. Those who entered college (Curve C) tended pretty well to graduate from college (Curve D), but the fact remains that only 44.5 percent of this college-capable group obtained bachelor's degrees. Thus, roughly half of the college potential was unrealized.

Bear in mind the nature of the social milieu when this study was made. In large, society was in the process of returning to "business as usual." Guidance practices had been operative in the high schools for almost a generation, yet many very bright youngsters were not going on for higher education. Society was regarding education favorably: the Council on Basic Education was only getting ready to launch its attack on popular education; Conant's report of his study of the American high school, with some highly relevant recommendations, was five years away; and overt expressions of dissatisfaction with education was some fifteen years in the future. Wolfle's report, perhaps understandably, was focused upon society's need for the potential contributions of the gifted without emphasizing self-fulfillment. College graduation was explicitly the criterion of adequate preparation, because college and university work was regarded as promising the highest probability of nurturing the capacity to deal effectively with the multitude of facts, principles, generalizations, and theories needed in professional and highly technical work.

In his book *The Uses of Talent* (1971) Wolfle considered the roles of the gifted in terms less of specific needs than of the fact of a changing society, the dy-

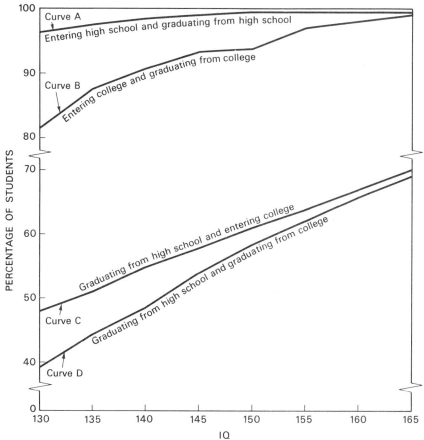

Figure 3.2. *Percentages of students entering and graduating from high school and college for different IQ groups in the top 8½ percent.*

(Adapted from Wolfle, 1954, p. 304.)

namic complex of the needs and capabilities of the gifted themselves, and the interactions among and the emergence of new roles which the gifted must be expected to play in society.

Less intensively, but in one sense more updatingly, Taubman and Wales (1972) studied college-entering populations. They analyzed a number of major studies, a number of them statewide (Iowa, Kansas, and Minnesota), and Project TALENT, in order to ascertain the relationship between mental ability level and college entering from 1925 to 1962. The percentages of college-entering stu-dents who were of average mental ability or below varied over the period from about one-third to one-half. Of those scoring at a point better than three-fourths of their population, slightly more than 50 percent entered college over the 1925–1950 period; in the 1960s, 72 percent of this group entered college. The authors summarized their findings about the more capable group—the top 10 per-cent—thus: "In the 1920s only about 60 percent of the most able high school graduates entered college, whereas by the 1960s the corresponding figure was about 90 percent" (p. 19).

SUMMARY

Basically the effective education of the gifted is a social issue. Whether the schools are only implicitly charged with that responsibility, as appears to have been the case historically in the United States, or, as more recently, specifically obligated to give consideration to the gifted, or the handicapped, or the disadvantaged, or differing ethnic groups, the responsibility rests primarily with education. It has been largely assumed that social leaders will, on their own, emerge to take the responsible roles in society; the more capable benefit as they will from whatever education has to offer, some of them being helped in the process by those few personally and socially committed teachers who have sensed their promise. If, on the other hand, education is specifically charged with this responsibility, or if it of its own social insight perceives this need, it will provide systematically for early identification of the gifted, for appropriate nurturance of their learning, and for the mix of a sense of self-fulfillment and of social responsibility and opportunity that will facilitate their assuming responsible social roles.

While there were a few local efforts early in this century to establish special classes for the gifted, it was not until after Sputnik in 1957 that efforts in the interest of the gifted assumed material proportions. But such developments represented the concern of the few rather than the convictions of the many. The Darwinian attitude that those who were gifted would, on their own, emerge was reflected in defining the gifted as those who had demonstrated superiority. This tended to absolve educators from the responsibilities of identifying the gifted early in their school lives and of making special educational provisions for them. The condition of giftedness, being essen-tially intangible in nature, was ill perceived, and aversions to providing specially for them were cloaked in claims both psychologically unfounded and unsupported by research findings.

In contrast with post hoc and other intuitive definitions of the "gifted," it seems logical and socially relevant to regard as gifted a percentage of the total school population comparable to the percentage of the adult population who assume major, high-level roles in society's functioning. With the inclusion of an "insurance factor" this appears to be 8 percent. In psychometric terminology, gifted children could be defined as those whose valid Binet IQs were 120 to 125 and above, or psychological equivalents thereof.

Owing to the post hoc perception of the gifted, the most plausible adjustment seemed to be the provision of scholarships for them. Research during and after World War II, however, showed clearly that society was failing to capital-ize properly upon the superior capabilities of its more promising members. The advent of Sputnik prompted further study of this sort, which even more sharply delineated society's need for high-level personnel. Later, concern developed that gifted individuals among the disadvantaged were not being identified and provided for. Ultimately, two needs were recognized: (1) the need to improve psychological approaches in identifying the gifted among the disadvantaged, and (2) the need to perceive much more broadly the nature of scholarships or financial assistance for the gifted.

Important as such developments were in sharpening certain sensitivities, education fell far short of acting programmatically in the interests of the gifted. It became even more apparent that the improvement or inauguration of practices for the gifted did not constitute the implementation of a program for them.

4

Psychological
considerations

In this chapter we shall examine the intellectual, socioemotional, and educational characteristics of gifted children. We shall look closely at the concept of peerness, because allusion to the "peers" of the gifted so often is either ambiguous or psychologically misleading. Because communication is so important in the development and functioning of the gifted, we shall explore some important psychological aspects of that area. Since much of the treatment of the motivation of the gifted has been more admonitory than enlightening, we shall analyze this behavioral area in terms of its fundamental psychological nature and its social and educational importance.

It is, of course, psychologically and educationally unreal to divorce any consideration of the gifted from their social milieus, past and present. It can be helpful if we look specifically at the effects of social situations upon certain psychological characteristics of the gifted. While the environment may tend to depress "the IQ," other conditions also heavily influence the functioning of the gifted.

What will be presented here as a picture of the gifted as a group may not hold at all for a particular gifted child. The characterization of any group tends to be either in terms of the average for that group (average height, weight, family size, income, and so on) or in terms of what predominantly exists with respect to that group (a group may be characterized as "having a high energy level"—meaning that anywhere from 51 to 100 percent of the group can be so perceived). However, although gifted children tend to be taller than nongifted children of the same age, George was considerably shorter than his five-year-old agemates—and his parents both were

57

very much shorter than average adults. Whereas the gifted, as a group, tend to be better adjusted emotionally than the nongifted, ten-year-old Leo was a physiologically unjustified bedwetter.

Valid generalizations are useful as bases for general expectations; the fact that the gifted tend to learn certain kinds of things much more easily than do the nongifted should predispose educators toward making certain kinds of educational provisions. Social and educational policy for gifted children and program planning for them have to be decided on in terms of generalizations. Program execution, on the other hand, requires a pervading awareness of the fact that certain youngsters within the group will differ from the generality. As an oversimplified example, gifted children, as a group, tend to achieve educationally in a manner superior to that of their agemates, but some children, even though they have definitely superior learning potential, achieve less well than even the average of their agemates. Once such a general orientation has been accepted, we must be constantly alert to the fact that certain gifted children may not perform in the generally expected manner for any of a number of reasons —such as the poor quality of nurturant preschool experiences, ineffective stimulation and motivation in the school learning situation, negative, or lack of positive attitudes toward learning, extra-school demands, and the like. Disparity between group and individual characterization may exist when only two variables—learning potential and academic achievement—are involved. However, more variables always are involved— socioemotional adjustment, health and physique, learning styles, particular strengths and (relative) weaknesses in certain learning areas, creative capability, and the like—and their interrelated roles in the total behavior of any gifted child must be recognized.

CHARACTERISTICS OF THE GIFTED

Early Findings

Much that will be presented here can be attributed to Terman's surpassingly significant research first reported in 1925. Although the 1,528 ten- and eleven-year-old subjects (857 boys and 671 girls) whom he identified as having earned Binet IQs of 140 and above came from larger and medium-sized urban areas in California, and although the socioeconomic class distribution of their families, even then, was not representative of that of the United States (31 percent were professional, 50 percent semiprofessional and business, 12 percent skilled laborers, and less than 7 percent were semiskilled or unskilled)—two aspects that have caused many to regard his sample as untypical of the gifted—he did maintain that whatever socioeconomic and ethnic groups were in the general population were represented also in his gifted group. Subsequent studies of this group by Terman and his co-workers, Barbara S. Burks, Dortha Jensen, and Melita H. Oden, made possible not only the essential verification of his 1925 findings but also the further examination of the characteristics and social contributions of the group forty years later (Oden, 1968). Even in 1960 he received replies to his Information Blank from 664 men and 524 women who were in his original group.

Many subsequent studies of the gifted have tended to validate or to delineate more sharply what the research of Terman and his fellow workers had revealed. Kincaid (1969), for instance, reported his findings on 331 boys and 230 girls in the Los Angeles elementary schools (1960 Binet IQ of 150 and above): one-half were first-born; the average number of siblings was 1.7; reading was most popular among the girls, arithmetic among the boys; girls expressed anticipated careers in areas of social service and art, boys in science, social service, and "mechanical" involvement; one-half had fathers working at the professional level; less than 5 percent of the fathers had not completed high school; and underachievement was most marked, for both sexes, in courses in science, arithmetic, and social studies. Other studies, aided by improvements in psychological measurement and growth in psychological perceptions of children, pressed on into areas of major concern—cognitive styles, personal and social adjustment, sharper delineations of capacities, achievement and underachievement, and divergent or creative thinking.

Research on the effectiveness of educational methods and procedures for the gifted must be regarded, particularly as of the 1920s but also currently, as at best exploratory rather than definitive, owing in part to narrow perceptions of the populations involved, in part to variations in the statements of the goals to be attained (and their adequate measurement) and to the artificiality of the "experimental" situations studied. Probably another major consideration is that fortunate, well-motivated gifted youngsters can do considerable learning in whatever situations they find themselves.

Effects of Social Change

In considering research findings on the gifted, we should bear in mind four major changes in the social scene from the 1920s to the 1960s. (1) The percentages as well as the numbers of children attending school and continuing into college have increased materially. (2) Women have become increasingly involved in responsible social roles outside the home. This is in part related to the further fact that (3) the range of occupational opportunities has changed significantly, coming to include data processing, social service, educational and medical adjunctive services, and a myriad of technological and parascientific involvements. (4) There has been a marked increase in the concern for the "disadvantaged" in our society. The extent to which this will affect the magnitude of society's obligation to the gifted remains to be seen. However, it is highly doubtful that all these changes will alter the fundamental psychological picture of the gifted. Much more likely to be influential are such matters as the effective early nurturance of the gifted, the educational treatment we accord them in the light of the increasingly ephemeral nature of "facts" in substantive areas of learning and the changing patterns of important roles in society, and society's concern for the wastage of important human potential and the attendant personal maladjustment.

It has quite properly been asked whether the findings of Terman and other researchers on groups of gifted children should be regarded as characteristic of *the* gifted. The fact that his and other groups of gifted children have tended to come from populations that were not socioeconomically representative of the United States has been taken as a basis for challenging the findings. The fact that some children believed to be "bright" on the basis of nonschool learning behavior have not scored commensurably higher on good "intelligence" tests has caused some to wonder if *the* gifted really are what research has indicated them to be. The contention that there are bright children among the disadvantaged groups and among certain subcultures who have not and cannot score high enough on conventional, but still good tests of learning aptitude has cast doubt on our picture of the gifted.

Such questioning—so long as it is born of objective curiosity rather than psychological myopia—merits serious consideration and calls for much more definitive research. The countervailing question is whether such additional information would in fact greatly alter the basic psychological picture of the gifted. Even so, there is a continuing need for more objective validation of the procedures for identifying them. There is a rational—rather than emotional—need for a much broader social concern for both the potentially gifted (the undiscovereds, the unrealized) and the known gifted,—including objective ascertainment of the roles played by nutrition, diet, and other health practices; preschool psychological nurturance procedures; greatly modified educational curricula and methods; and the cultivation of at least a more tolerant social attitude toward the gifted. What we do know about populations of the gifted must be regarded as a minimal picture— and even with respect to this minimum, education in particular and society in general still seem uninformed.

The characteristics of the gifted (as demonstrated by research) may be thought of roughly as of two different types: those which learning has little affected, such as intellectual and physical characteristics (although certain kinds of physical and psychological nurturance may have had deleterious effects), and those in the socioemotional and educational areas, which more clearly result from the interaction between the biologically determined traits of the gifted and conditions in their social environments. While we shall consider these separately, their probable interaction must be kept in mind.

INTELLECTUAL CHARACTERISTICS

The primary basis on which children have been identified as gifted has been their superiority in the intellectual area. Much has been contributed to society, of course, by those in the performing,

expressive, and graphic arts, but an important distinction needs to be made here between performance or potential that involves *high conceptualization* and that which does not. We have limited the term "talented" to skilled performers in the latter category. High intellectual potential—a superior capability to make and work on the basis of abstractions, to grasp and use complex relationships, and to generalize meaningfully—is taken to be the primary ingredient in giftedness.

Although a "high IQ" (on a good test, properly administered) may be nicely symptomatic of a superior capacity to function well in a symbolic learning situation as well as suggestive of later superior social contribution, it reflects only part of the intellectual picture. If we were to identify five or ten gifted ten-year-olds who had exactly the same Binet IQ, their cognitive styles—the ways in which they would function intellectually—probably would be discernibly different. As Martinson and many others have pointed out, "One may find persons who respond and function rapidly, those who are deliberate and contemplative, those who are logical and direct, or those who are exploratory and circuitous. The quality of the end product may be excellent (and different) from any of these." Whether the manner of the child's responding or functioning— whether quick or deliberate, logical or "intuitive"—is a result primarily of his "natural" disposition or of the nature of his acculturation is not known.

Children who have been identified as gifted tend to continue to score relatively high within the general population, as shown not only in the Terman studies but also in those of Bayley (1970) and others. Terman's subjects tended to maintain their own levels relatively well, half of the original group continuing to score above Binet IQ 130 after seven years. In 1940, 527 men and 427 women, and in the 1950–1952 follow-up, 551 men and 453 women, in his original group were retested by means of Terman's Concept Mastery Test—a test he developed in order to provide for more discrimination among his top 1 percent. "A comparison of the CMT scores of the gifted subjects with those obtained for five groups of college graduates, most of whom had obtained or were candidates for advanced degrees, shows that the Terman group, regardless of amount of schooling, far outdistanced all other groups in mean score" (Oden, 1968, p. 11). In the 40-year follow-up, the results of testing the children of Terman's subjects were reported. The 813 males and 758 females earned respective average Binet IQs of 133.3 and 133.1. Only about one-fifth of these children earned Binet IQs below 120, in contrast with some 90 percent of the general population. Counting 14 untested children who had been institutionalized as feebleminded and assuming that they would have earned Binet IQs of less than 100, only 3.2 percent of the offspring tested below 100, and only 1.3 percent fell below IQ 80.

This essentially positive picture must be considered in terms of certain conditions:

1. In studies such as these, observations are made primarily in terms of group averages rather than the inevitable variations around the averages.

2. Gifted children, just like any others, have spurts and plateaus in their developmental curves—intellectual and otherwise.

3. The kinds of measures made can determine the nature of the intellectual developmental picture obtained. Tests which measure in terms of speed of response, or of performance within time limits, can yield results different from those based upon power, or difficulty; this probably accounts in part for Miles' (1954) observation regarding some of Terman's findings that precocity due to overtraining may regress to a mean of mediocrity.

4. When one thinks of degrees of giftedness, whether it be supported by high test scores or by some nontest superior performance having a major intellective component, one must bear in mind the extent to which motivational patterns and other cultural determiners may have influenced performance. This applies with regard both to those who have scored high enough to be so regarded and to those who have not.

5. Even though the gifted are discernible as a group, there remain wide diversities within this group.

6. Factors contributing to the statistical phenomenon of regression toward the mean need to be considered. Since Terman's original group consisted of the top 1 percent of the total population, there were more conditions operating to lower their subsequent scores than there were to maintain or raise them.

Such factors can be of particular relevance with respect to giftedness among minority groups. Deutsch and Brown (1964), in studying high intelligence among Negro elementary school children in five schools in a metropolitan area, found that 73 percent of those with superior intelligence were in the primary grades, whereas only 27 percent were in the upper elementary grades. They found, as have many others, that the relative frequency of high tested intelligence increased as socioeconomic level increased.

Interests

While the curiosity of the gifted is wide-ranging—unless it has become stultified by an impoverished environment and/or by adults who are annoyed or thwarted by its manifestation—sharper focusings of endeavor take on the nature of interests. (Refer to the distinction between curiosity and interest, p. 41.) The interests of the gifted are like those of other children in two ways. First, they are nurturable—in the sense that, while at times they seem to spring out of nowhere, they constitute positive approaches to elements or situations in the child's environs. Once such behavior is apparent, it can be helped along by the adults' providing relevant experiences or materials. A child who has manifested some interest in, say, ants may be helped to learn about different kinds of ants, their social behavior, their habitats, their places in ecology and in the insect world. Effective nurturance can be achieved by maintaining a delicate balance among the "strengths" of the child's interests, the amount of adult "teaching" introduced, opportunities for successful involvement as well as legitimate challenge, and the provision of appropriate opportunities for the child to employ his own discovery procedures.

Second, children's interests are determined more by their levels of mental development than by their chronological ages. A six-year-old of below-average capability is likely to be satiated with a relatively small number of quite specific facts about ants, whereas a bright six-year-old probably would concern himself with relationships among such specifics. Further, the bright child, since he is so much more capable of symbolic learning, may pursue his interest, perhaps with surprisingly little help, by the use of a child's encyclopedia, a children's dictionary, and/or children's books written for his level of verbal capability. In the area of play interests, the less capable child is more likely to be effective, and therefore happy, as a bat boy or score-keeper, whereas the more capable child is more likely to perform effectively, and therefore to "like" it, as a manager or as a coach at third base. The more complex and symbolic the activities in any interest or play activity, the more they are likely to attract the bright child.

In some ways, however, the interests of the gifted differ from those of the nongifted. From Terman on, they have been found to be both more varied and more numerous than those of their age-mates, and, although they often change over time, each such interest tends to involve relatively intensive commitment. One bright eleven-year-old, for example, in two years' time delved surprisingly deeply into archeology, astronomy, and mathematics. For the gifted child the intensive pursuit of an interest tends to be self-satisfying and self-rewarding ("He seems just to want to know") rather than a means of pleasing significant others in his life space.

The pattern of interest differences between Terman's gifted and nongifted groups has been identified consistently in research: over the age range 10–13, interests of an intellectual nature have been most contrasting, those of a social nature next, then those involving activities (music, dramatics, arts, and various kinds of handwork). Environmental influences are, of course, operative. Interests can suggest future kinds of occupational susceptibility. Stewart (1959) analyzed the responses of 842 National Merit Scholarship winners and runners-up to the Strong Vocational Interest Blank and concluded that, rather than manifesting strongly focused interests, these bright youngsters "have a large number of interests which are spread over different areas" (p. 138).

On the other hand, a smaller percentage—those who fall in the talented or genius groups—often quite early manifest strong interests which later become their areas of major social contribution.[1] Roe (1952) found in her study

---

[1] The use of the terms "talented" and "genius" often clutters communication rather than clarifies it. Ignoring usages in lay writings, at least a partial differentiation is involved here. A distinction already has been made between individuals who are highly skilled and those who are talented, the position being that high-level conceptualization is an essential component or contributing factor in the functioning of the talented. The talented and the genius are taken to have comparable high-level conceptualization ability, the possibility being that the media of

of eminent scientists that as children they had made serious collections and performed experiments. The literature on the gifted is replete with illustrations of early, deep, and productive involvement, manifested more intensively than the less-enduring interests we mentioned earlier (Cox, 1926; Lehman, 1953). Handel was composing by the age of 11, Mozart at 4, and Mendelssohn at 9. By the age of 8, John Stuart Mill had read Xenophon, Herodotus, and Plato. Alexander Pope had published poems by the age of 12, Robert Burns by the age of 14, and Milton at 15. Pascal wrote a treatise on acoustics at age 12. Galileo made his famous observations of the swinging lamp when he was 17. Carl

Gauss, one of the most creative mathematicians in history, was doing research at age 15. Henry Ford started as a watch repairman at such an early age that his employer found it better for him not to be seen at work. William Cullen Bryant completed *Thanatopsis* when he was 18. These and many other gifted persons, perhaps exceptions to the gifted group as a whole, early manifested an intensity of and a perseverance in interests which culminated in their own self-realization and in their major social contributions. Pressey (1955) observed, "Superior original capacity, *growing under a favorable concomitance of circumstances,* develops into genius."

Such early manifestations of talent and genius—cited almost routinely in writing about the gifted—should be perceived in the light of two conditions. First, much has been made by Lehman and others of the fact that genius or talent quite early manifested itself. (This perhaps contributed to the early defining of giftedness in terms of outstanding achievement.) Some, however, have been concerned about the relationship between such early manifestation and the social and cultural situations in which it occurred. To what extent, for instance, was such early manifestation a function of contemporary educational practices? Educational facilities and services were less generally available and less forced upon youngsters and parents in those earlier times. Generally, children moved into responsible adulthood earlier than now. The "world of knowledge" then was much simpler. Some wonder why we seem to have to go back so far in history to find citable examples of such early manifestation of genius and talent. Do we have fewer of such outstanding individuals, or do we keep them under wraps for longer portions of their lives? Some even fear that our schools, and perhaps other agencies of society, actually may have a stultifying effect. Cer-

---

their expressions are different. An orientation in terms of a continuum can help here. Given the total continuum of general "intelligence," the gifted are perceived as falling along the higher range. Within this range and toward its upper end would fall those properly termed talented and genius. Any specification of some "IQ" point above which they would fall is purely speculative; perhaps the Binet-type IQ of 180 or 185 could be justified as such a point, but, owing to a disconcerting variety of measurement problems, this may need to be pushed back into the 165 area. It might help if the extreme upper range of our "intelligence" continuum could be regarded as trifurcating in order to help differentiate among those whose giftedness is manifested particularly in the arts (music, dance, graphic arts), in science (theory development and amplification, higher mathematics, philosophy), and in literature (verbally expressive, as in poetry and other literature and descriptive writing). Having made such a differentiation, we must not regard these areas as completely discrete. Musical composition involves both superior theoretical and mathematical competence. Developing a philosophical point of view involves very high verbally expressive capability, but one which can be differentiated from that of the novelist. Such a delineation could help sharpen communication regarding the gifted, since many writers and researchers in the field have shown little sensitivity to the need to define or describe precisely the subpopulations with which they have been concerned. Two other proposed differentiations are cited in Chapter 13 (p. 365).

tainly, both the forces in our society which contribute to a delay in the attaining of responsible adulthood and the tremendous acceleration in the discovery of new facts and the development of new concepts have combined to delay the apparentness of genius. Perhaps performance in music is an exception, but even here time is needed to separate the merely highly skilled from the truly talented.

Second, the social contributions of those early manifesting their genius or talent have had to stand the test of time. Often they conflicted with the beliefs, expectations, and practices of contemporary societies. That formal education has had a stultifying effect on the most capable is illustrated, for instance, in the cases of Edison, Lindbergh, and Einstein, and others who found formal education frustrating. While Einstein rebelled particularly against the drillmaster atmosphere of German education and found the relatively permissive educational condition of Switzerland more tolerable while taking work in mathematics, physics, and astronomy, he unofficially supplemented his educational diet with extra work in anthropology, geology, business, politics, literature, and philosophy (Clark, 1971).

Remembering

The remembering behavior of the gifted is distractingly mercurial. Most children recall seemingly isolated events and facts for no apparent rhyme or reason, but the gifted manifest more of this, causing some to regard "intelligence" as a kind of intellectual adhesiveness. (Such incidental rememberings by the gifted tend to be both more numerous and more vivid or detailed.) Generally, rote memory is not their forte, and they are less likely to master quickly the memorizing of number combinations, as in the case of rote computational problems or the

multiplication tables. When, however, they see the relationships underlying them and when such knowledge helps in the solving of problems, the gifted learn them very quickly.

Gifted youngsters generally tend to perform much better in arithmetic reasoning problems than they do on simple arithmetic computation. As a general principle, where there is some general structure, some intellectual schema, some developing concept, bits of information related to such tend quickly to be assimilated and remembered. (While this is particularly important in the case of the gifted, it is, of course, contributive to learning by other children.) If, for example, we assume that a child has "learned" ten unrelated bits of information, any new possible learnings he may experience can have only those ten possible "anchorages" or associations which can help him in the new learnings. If, on the other hand, he has many more, the possibility of his relating new learnings is thus increased. Further, if there are meaningful relationships among his earlier learnings, the new learnings can fit into or be related to both the bits of information earlier acquired and the relationships perceived as existing among them. In this sense, the gifted may be perceived as "having better memories," since they tend to have more such potential anchorages and to have identified more relationships.

But the field of "memory" is little researched and too often is dealt with in an undifferentiated manner. What about motor memory—as in riding a bicycle, playing a musical instrument, driving a car, and the like? What about auditory memory—as in the area of music? Recognizing a pictured object as an accordion is quite different from recalling it and defining it; the former involves remembering and recognition, but the latter also requires effective verbal production.

The gifted do remember better, but they remember better when they see relationships among the things to be remembered. But what child doesn't?

Creative Thinking

Creativity, or the capacity for and the act of behaving creatively, is a cognitive style regarded by many as an intellectual characteristic of the gifted. It has been treated with such logical abandon, however, that we shall take time to delineate its connotation and to describe the general background in terms of which it needs to be perceived.

The point of view taken here is that "being creative," "creativity," and "creative thinking" denote a kind of behavior, the primary component of which is a degree of conceptualization that contributes toward some identified objective. Unique to such activity is the identification, delineation, or specification of some new relationship among given elements —new at least so far as the individual is concerned and often so far as a given society is concerned. The elements involved may be either identifiable prior learnings or their analogues or modifications.

Creative thinking, then, is an intellective process. It must, of course, be perceived in terms of the age of the individual in whom it is observed—whether a young child, an older one, or an adult. Random expressive behaviors may be only that, or they may be manifestations of incipient creative behavior.

To what extent is creativity involved in the graphic arts, the theater, music, and literature? We may answer as follows: to the extent that any production —picture, statue, play, composition, or writing—is a resultant primarily or solely of emotion or feeling (primarily visceral functioning) rather than of conceptualization (primarily intellective functioning), it is noncreative. Innovational, per-haps, but not creative in our sense. To the extent that the production has an integrative theme, or overriding conceptualization, to that extent it is "creative" or the result of creative behavior. This is not to imply that viscerally based behavior necessarily is devoid of intellective accompaniments or that intellective behavior necessarily is devoid of visceral accompaniments. A continuum is implied here, ranging from productions that emanate from purely emotional expression to those that embody conceptual structure or theme. The opportunity for disagreement in interpretation increases, of course, as any production approaches the midpoint on the continuum. As indicated above, improvisation upon the purely representational can still retain the basic theme or schema, as in the cases of certain modernistic (bi- or multi-perspective) art, in jazz, or in the free-associational style of writing where the major thesis still provides the overriding structure. The use of lighting effects or colors in the theater may be only innovative (and not creative), but their use to create or convey mood (to contribute to theme development) would be creative. It seems necessary thus to delineate "creativity" if it is to be regarded as a cognitive style.

Cognitive style

We shall first define cognitive style and then identify certain important determiners of it. The term "cognitive style" is used to denote the manner in which an individual intellectually processes or employs, rather than simply reacts to, information, or stimuli, in his own ruminations relating to those stimuli and/or in a context of social communication regarding those stimuli. In certain subcultures monosyllabic, gestural, and postural responses can be perceived as components of cognitive style, but we are concerned here with verbally and symbolically—and hence conceptually—richer kinds. For example, ask a number of adults what they think about the current economic situation. Some will respond in terms of what it costs them to live and how much they earn, or don't earn—entirely self- and perceptually oriented—and some will respond conceptually in terms of the nature of national policies. Some will proceed to analyze logically the relevant factors involved in the total social situation; and some will respond with, "Yes, it's a real problem, isn't it?" and immediately proceed to discuss how their favorite team or orchestra performed the last time out. Ask a group of twelve-year-olds what they think about education, and their responses will be of a similar diverse nature.

What determines the nature of one's responses? Certainly, the social situation in which the individual has been reared, or in which he is caused to respond, is a major factor. Many adults who work with children, because of factors such as time, their own level of intellectual operation, or their perceptions of children, reinforce short, "shallow," self-oriented, even only semi-relevant responses in children—thus, in effect, teaching them to respond in such ways. Others expect and press for fuller, more involved, more highly conceptual responses, hence contributing to that type of response habit formation. Certainly, the child's capability of responding—whether he has the conceptualization ability and/or a supply of relevant concepts—is important. But it is the interaction of these two conditions—the social setting and the individual's basic capability—that accounts for the response style of any given individual.

Illustratively, let us take some simplified behavior samples—in this case responses to an imaginary "intelligence" test item—and examine their implications. To the item: "In what way are a chair and a table alike?" Ed and Irma,

both eleven-year-olds, respond, "They both have legs." Harry, a nine-year-old, says, "They are both pieces of furniture." The latter response is of a higher conceptual level than the former, the concept of "furniture" being regarded by Harry as capable of including the specifics of chair and table. If this were typical of his responses to such questions, we would say he had a higher learning capability than the other two children. While their response reflects some idea of "leggedness" as a class, it does not suggest higher-level intellective functioning. The conceptual capabilities of these children would be important determiners of their conceptual styles.

At first (if this type of response were typical) both Ed and Irma might be regarded as having less-than-average learning potential. In Ed's case, the rest of his test behavior and other behaviors in his learning situation strongly suggest that he *is* below average in basic learning capacity. On the other hand, Irma's other test and learning behaviors suggest that she is capable of a higher level of conceptual operation. It was observed that her parents, too, operated at this lower level. When both children were put in a training situation focused upon the nurturance and use of higher-level conceptualization, Ed showed no improvement, just seemed unable to identify higher-level categories, whereas Irma, after only a few practice items, quickly identified higher-level conceptualizations for novel elements, which still were within her experience. In other words, Irma had a higher level of learning potential but her social situation, including her schooling, had not adequately nurtured her basic learning aptitude. Irma's earlier cognitive style involved the operation of a lower conceptualization process, even though she was capable of higher-level functioning; after only a little training, her cognitive style was different.

Cognitive styles can be functions of

individuals' developmental levels, emotionality, and neurological conditions. Maturation can be a primary determiner. The ways in which average six-year-olds process their information will be different from those of average twelve-year-olds because the six-year-olds, still operating pretty much at a perceptual level (and probably self-oriented), haven't yet matured to the twelve-year level, which is much more likely to be conceptual. As shown by the work of Witkin (1962), Barron (1968), and others, emotional factors can influence cognitive style. Certain differences in cognitive style have been found also among certain cerebral palsied individuals (though not typical of all of them) and in certain others known to have some kinds of brain injury.

As we have defined it, kinds of cognitive style can be regarded as falling somewhere on a continuum from simple perception to high-level conceptualization, as illustrated in our example of the behaviors of the three children. Styles also can be perceived in terms of the developmental levels of children, as in the contrast between six-year-olds and twelve-year-olds. Or they could be thought of in terms of Piaget's developmental progression from the sensory-personal to the most mature level. They could also be considered in terms of an intuitive-deliberative continuum. Guilford's (1967) "operations," especially his divergent thinking, convergent thinking, and evaluative thinking, could be so regarded.

Variations in style

It will help us to look at the more clearly differentiated cognitive styles of gifted adults and then see or imagine them in gifted children who may be in the process of forming such major habit patterns. Let us imagine a group of adults who are very highly intelligent (in the broad sense). While this group is highly homogeneous with respect to this general trait, its members will manifest widely varying typical manners of intellectual functioning. Some will operate most effectively in devising experimental means (devices, procedures) for discovering new phenomena. Some will be particularly adept in discovering new relationships among phenomena which others have discovered; their forte is the ability to synthesize at high levels of abstraction. Some will be especially capable in writing descriptions of the experimental approaches developed by others, in describing the resultant syntheses or even the process of synthesizing. Some will be less skillful in all of these, but will have superior ability in effecting an organization which can make all the other contributions possible. In these and other kinds of high-level contributions, persons of high-level intelligence and of high degrees of sophistication (at least in the given field of endeavor) will be cooperatively and productively involved. While each will be contributing by virtue of his most effective means of functioning intellectually, all will have superior competence in the general area in which they are working. Such kinds of cognitive styles may be discoverable and discernible among gifted children, and can be nurtured.

Within the general superior capability of the gifted there are discernibly different kinds of actual or potential cognitive style, reflected in behaviors such as the following:

1. *Discovering:* locating and/or identifying data, phenomena, and/or interrelationships of a relatively minor conceptual magnitude among phenomena—the "bits and pieces" (relatively) of which our world is constituted. Probably we should include here the recognizing of relationships among such givens or "discovereds," the integrations and principles which are necessary to but not of the same inclusiveness as a science, or the "subthemes" in musical productions. This kind of behaving can

be related to Guilford's "cognition" kind of intellectual operation.

2. *Organizing*, of both ideational and social phenomena: as in effecting a well-integrated research undertaking; in effecting structure to implement some form of social welfare, union, or (even) criminal program; in structuring a philosophy or a philosophy of science, a major work in music or in the theater. In terms of social outcome, this well may be superordinate to the function of discovering and recognizing conceptual structures, although equally "high intelligence" is essential to both.

3. *Describing:* setting forth what has been discovered, how the discovery was made, and/or how the organization was effected. Given the productions of 1 and 2 above, there is a need to communicate them verbally to lay persons or to other specialists in the same or other, possibly related, fields. This is essentially an expository function but necessitates high-level comprehension and high verbal skill.

4. *Evaluating:* determining whether elements or structures (probably provided by other persons as described above) are new, different, relevant, or contributive. This is a necessary adjunct to the other manners of functioning. It obviously is related to Guilford's "evaluative thinking."

5. *Creating:* the manipulating of givens, whether symbolic or physical, with a view to producing something that is new, productive, and relevant to some goal or objective. This kind of functioning is apparent in producing novel relationships among words (literature), sounds (music), ideas (science, philosophy, religion), and operations among components of a social or mechanical structure (new welfare and educational programs, new motors, or whatever).

Even though these behaviors have been listed and described separately, they do not just coexist; they interact—more obviously at some times than at others. The describer organizes and evaluates as he produces; the creator does at least

this and more. Certain individuals tend to operate predominantly in one way, but not to the exclusion of the other ways. The major educational implication is that teachers (and other adults) are responsible for nurturing all of these different kinds of functioning and should be ever ready to capitalize upon the particular strengths of different children in different kinds of learning situations.

Studies of "creative ability"

As noted in the preceding chapter, publications pertaining to "creative ability" have outnumbered those pertaining to gifted children and giftedness every year, except 1957, since 1939. The confluence of Guilford's (1956) promulgation of his *Structure of Intellect* and the appearance of Sputnik sharply heightened educators' professed concern for the gifted. Guilford's identification of "divergent thinking" as one of his intellectual operations and educators' quick substitution of "creative thinking" for his term (a liberty which he more than tolerated) provided a "new front" for educators, who were under no little fire from rebels against rote and other relatively sterile classroom activities. Here again, the fact that the results of creative thinking usually are more easily observable than the results of other kinds of functioning may help account for the relatively greater attention generally accorded "creativity."

Earlier studies of "creativity" were much concerned with adults who tended also to be regarded as gifted, predisposing readers to the assumption that creativity and giftedness were closely associated in children. But the parallel was too easily drawn. The creative productions of adults had, at least to a considerable degree, to meet the criterion of social applicability or acceptance. The creative productions of the architect, the engineer, or even the scientist had to serve social purpose in some better and/or esthetically more pleasing manner. The productions of the creative artist or author, whatever his medium of expression, were expected to meet some kind of expectations or standard. Stated or implicit expectations of this sort generally were not set for children whose creativity was being explored, nurtured, or measured; in large part they were to be encouraged to respond, or produce, in any way they say fit, almost studiously unconventionally—much as connoted by Guilford's term "divergent thinking." Also, most of the attribution of giftedness to adult creativity was nebulous and literary, whereas for children the characteristic of creativity was heavily test-anchored.

A concatenation of conditions contributed to confusion about the relationship between creativity and giftedness:

1. Many writers, especially technically untrained ones, presumed a close relationship, if not an identity, between giftedness and creative behavior, such that if the individual was creative (and particularly if adult) he was presumed also to be highly intelligent.

2. Many persons—both qualified and unqualified—held oversimplified or unjustified expectations about the information which even good "intelligence" tests could yield about children.

3. This was potentially tempered by Guilford's identification, as kinds of cognitive operations in his *Structure of Intellect,* of evaluative thinking, convergent thinking, and divergent thinking.

4. There was a growing social unrest with respect to any testing, let alone that of "intelligence."

5. There was a growing dissatisfaction with the social and intellectual effectiveness and relevance of contemporary education.

6. There was an easy and uncritical equating of the psychologist's concept of divergent thinking and the educator's perception of creative thinking.

As a result, the relationship between creativity and giftedness in children became a focus of much curiosity. Simply put, questions like these called for answers: To what extent are those who have been identified as gifted (by various means, but most often by means of "intelligence" tests) also creative? To what extent are those who have been identified as creative (again, by varying means) also gifted? Also being researched, but not so extensively, was the extent to which creativity was found among the whole child population—not just among the gifted. The reasoning here was that, if creativity is a trait, in the psychological sense, it should be present in varying degrees in all members of a representative population—children, adults; males, and females.

As simple and as straightforward as these questions may have been, the answering of them has been far from unambiguous and satisfying. Even with the assumption (often highly gratuitous) that it was relatively easy to identify a population of children as highly gifted, the identification of those who were to be regarded as creative, or as having the capacity to be creative, has been most sticky. For adults, whose creative productions could be regarded in terms of some social criterion, the definition or identification of the criterion group, the creatives, was relatively simple. But for children much of this was not feasible, although artists, musicians, authors, and scientists have been used as judges of the creative productions of gifted children. Guilford had identified divergent thinking on the basis of tests given to highly selected, highly capable adults. Most of his tests therefore had little direct applicability to children, especially young ones. Tests developed along the lines of

Guilford's were adapted or developed for use with children, but their validity as measures of creativity in children, or of creative thinking (as contrasted with divergent thinking), remained to be demonstrated. Against what criterion could, or should, they be validated? Granting that some children could be identified as creative, to what extent would they be creative as adults? A study of this would involve ascertaining the extents to which such children would, ten, fifteen, or more years later, manifest creative behavior. Quite an array of intervening variables could affect such outcomes.

Much was made of the publicized implications of the findings (Getzels and Jackson, 1961; Torrance, 1962) that children who scored high on "intelligence" tests did not score comparably high on tests of divergent thinking—usually called "creativity" or creative thinking—and that high scores on divergent-thinking tests were found among children who did not score high enough on the "intelligence" tests to be regarded as gifted. Those who did much in catalyzing educators' interests in "creativity" did so on the basis of children's performances on tests of divergent thinking, playing down the fact that such measures tended to correlate with test-measured "intelligence" in the 30s. Wallach (1970), after an intensive analysis of such research, concluded that a reliable index of general "intelligence" predicts virtually all practical abilities as well as does a measure of any more specific thinking characteristics within the general "intelligence" area.

Still, the defensible position remains that if children are to be identified objectively as gifted, the use of a good test of learning aptitude should play a major role, and if children are to be identified as creative, valid tests of that characteristic should be an important part of that procedure, caution being exercised with

respect to any presumed identity between tests of divergent thinking and tests (or other manifestations) of creativity. In other words, even though height and weight are positively correlated in children, height should be measured by one scale and weight by another, care being taken that the device measuring each is properly validated.

But the area of creativity includes more than test manifestation of divergent thinking, although tested variables of flexibility of ideation, fluidity of ideation, uniqueness of ideation, and the like may play important parts in behaving creatively. Highly relevant but almost of different worlds are the performances of children in writing stories and poems (for which verbal competency is required), in producing drawings, paintings, sculptures, and musical compositions, and in identifying improvements in toys, tools, and machinery (Welch, 1964). Such can be "measured" by means of special-area experts' judgments regarding the creativeness which such behavior reflects.

As diversified and as divergent and creative as behaviors may be, and as important as they are socially, psychologically, and educationally, it is understandable that the behavioral scientist will be trying to identify valid and fruitful commonalities among them. Divergent thinking, still to be differentiated from creative thinking, probably is a significant substratum.

Creativity in the gifted must be evaluated in the light of all the foregoing. Rather than meticulously or compulsively review even those studies which merit serious consideration, we shall consider here only representative findings—enough, it is hoped, to cast the gifted in a meaningful divergent- or creative-thinking light which will be relevant to the later discussion of educational and other nurturant treatment of the gifted. We shall note first some findings regarding original thinking in adults, then a few studies of "creative" behavior in children, and finally consider in fuller detail an intensive and fruitfully suggestive study of the creativity-intelligence problem in some fifth-graders.

Barron's studies of originality

Barron (1968, 1969) has intensively studied originality in thinking among college students and other adults. In one study of 105 captains in the U.S. Air Force, he derived a composite score of originality and then examined the characteristics of the highest 25 in contrast to those of the lowest 25. The high scorers were found to be "intelligent, widely informed, concerned with basic problems, clever and imaginative, socially effective and personally dominant, verbally fluent, and possessed of initiative." The low scorers, on the other hand, were "conforming, rigid and stereotyped, uninsightful, commonplace, apathetic, and dull." Such contrasts remained after the possible contributing factor of intelligence (performance on the Concept Mastery Test) was statistically controlled. His observations, resulting from intensive personality assessments of each person in his study, are highly suggestive with respect to the treatment and understanding of original thinkers: (1) "Originality flourishes when suppression is at a minimum and when some measure of disintegration is tolerable in the interests of a higher level of integration which may yet be reached." Einstein's behavior illustrated this nicely: even as a youngster in school, he was intellectually chafing at his inability to identify relationships among phenomena, yet he held a firm conviction that such relationships could be discovered. The creative thinker is baffled—Barron's "disintegration"—by sensing relationships which he firmly believes exist, doesn't brush such

frustrations aside, and perseveres until he discovers what he long has suspected must be there. (2) This, understandably affects the ways in which the original thinker affects his associates, who tend to perceive him as rebellious, disorderly, and exhibitionistic (which latter characteristic we shall explore later as part of the communication problem of the gifted). He also is characterized as independent in judgment, free in his expression, and insightful and novel in his perceptions of things, persons, and self. (3) Barron puts the characterization of the "creative genius" together in a paradoxical picture that can be perplexing at first glance: "(He) may be at once more naive and knowledgeable, being at home equally to primitive symbolism and to rigorous logic. He is both primitive and more cultured, more destructive and more constructive, occasionally crazier and yet adamantly saner than the average person."

Criteria for creativity

Creativity in, or the creative behavior of, gifted children can be reflected in the things they produce—poems, stories, news reporting, drawings, paintings, sculptures, musical compositions, clothing stylings, recipes, scientific apparatus, conceptual schemes, mechanical improvisations, social organizational activities, and the like—or in terms of test-elicited behaviors. Approaches such as Barron's contribute by identifying personality characteristics which are closely associated with the characteristic of creativity. From the time of Terman, the fact that gifted children do produce unusual and creative things has been consistently recognized. With the advent of the concept of divergent thinking, the bulk of the research on creativity shifted to the exploration of the extent to which gifted children identified new or unusual phenomena and relationships among phenomena. Such behaviors were evaluated in terms of one or more criteria:

1. *The low frequency of response.* If a number of children responded in the same way to a test item, the response was regarded as evidencing convergent thinking; if a child responded in a way which differed from the responses of all the other children, or from those of a large percentage of his age group, it was regarded as reflecting divergent thinking.

2. *The quality of response.* If a response was judged to be of high or unusual quality, it was taken to indicate divergent thinking.

3. *The use of multiple frames of reference in responding.* The giving of only one response to a question or problem was regarded as evidence of less flexibility in thinking than the giving of two or more responses. To the orally presented (imaginary) question, "What does spade mean?", one child might respond only, "What you dig with," whereas the more "flexible" child would respond, "What you dig with. Or one of those things you see on cards. Or what is done to dogs to keep them from having pups. Or the name of a detective."

4. *The number of responses made to a question or problem.*

Given the identification of such variables as important in or constituting creativity, the curiosity of many was piqued as to the possibility of improving them by training.

Training in thinking skills

Guilford shares with Bartlett (1958) the belief that thinking skills are trainable. This admits of three possible interpretations. It could mean that the basic relevant neural characteristics of the organism can be improved. It could mean that, while no basic neural change can be effected, whatever is there can be helped to function more effectively, as

when basically capable individuals are trained in the essential processes of logical thinking. Or it could mean that such functioning of individuals can be enabled to operate more effectively and productively because of improved emotional, motivational, or other social conditions. Perhaps some combination of the three kinds of conditions could be beneficial. Such possibilities of interpretation must be borne in mind with respect to the illustrative findings now to be presented (for which we shall not consider the magnitudes of measurement error in the testing instruments and the procedures used to reflect the results).

Johnson (1969), working with eleven boys and six girls (Binet IQ 135–150) in a third grade, endeavored to train them in creative thinking, verbal intelligence, and creative writing ability. She reported significant improvement in verbal intelligence and claimed some improvability in creative writing. Bachtold (1970) submitted 17 fifth- and sixth-graders ("WISC IQ" 129 and up) to an eight-month training program on Guilford's five operations (cognition, memory, divergent thinking, convergent thinking, and evaluative thinking). Using Torrance's Minnesota Tests of Creativity as pre- and post-tests, she claimed significant differences on the tests of product improvement, unusual ideas, and evaluation of consequences—these being scored both for fluency and flexibility. O'Rourke (1969) submitted academically talented high school pupils to a special curriculum incorporating emphasis on independent, creative thinking; he reported significant gains in creative thinking over a two-year interval. Cartledge and Krauser (1963) trained first-graders for five twenty-minute sessions on thinking about how to improve toys and found that they improved in scores for fluency, flexibility, and originality. The youngsters who were motivated for increased quantity of responses improved about as much as did those who were motivated to improve the quality of their responses. Rusch, Denny, and Ives (1965) taught sixth-graders "creatively" for a school year and found that they improved significantly in five of seven tests of divergent thinking. Torrance and others (1960), using ten elementary school teachers and their children, trained half of the teachers to teach "creatively" and gave the other half no such training. The specially trained and the regular teachers taught their respective groups of children for four weeks. The experimental group showed gains superior to those of the control group in originality and elaboration in four of the six grades, in fluency in three of the grades, and in flexibility in two of the grades. Note, however, these variables in the "experiment": The authors believed that "nearly one-third" of the experimental teachers did not grasp adequately the principles they were to follow in their teaching. These teachers tended to be authoritarian, defensive, dominated by time schedules, insensitive to their pupils' intellectual and emotional needs, preoccupied with disciplinary problems, and unwilling to give much of themselves. The following principles were involved in teaching "creatively":

1. Treat pupils' questions with respect.
2. Treat imaginative ideas with respect.
3. Show pupils that their ideas have value.
4. Permit pupils to do some things "for practice" without threat of evaluation.
5. Tie evaluation in with cause and consequences.

Creativity and intelligence

Wallach and Kogan (1965) made a very enlightening study in an attempt to delineate relationships between creativity and intelligence. They used all the fifth-grade pupils (70 boys and 81 girls) in an all-white, middle or upper-middle socioeconomic level, suburban New England public school system. All the children were tested for intelligence and creativity, the latter being measured by means of devices which the authors developed and which correlated low, though still essentially positively, with tested intelligence. However, they sought religiously to follow their principle that the samplings of creative behavior should not resemble tests, either in being timed or in creating a testlike situation in which the samples were taken, thus providing for a relaxed, nondemanding evocation of "creative" responses. (These researchers objected to extant tests of divergent thinking as being either explicitly or implicitly timed tests and as being perceived by the children as tests.) Personality assessments of the children also were made.

The researchers compared the pupils who scored above with those who scored below the median in both intelligence and creativity, thus defining four populations—the high intelligence-high creativity group, the high intelligence-low creativity group, the low intelligence-high creative group, and the low intelligence-low creative group. They proceeded to describe the youngsters in each of the four groups in terms of their personality characteristics. Tables 4.1 and 4.2 give their descriptions of the boys and girls.

This is not a sharp picture of just the gifted or of just the creative; rather, it reflects the interaction of the presence and absence of these two characteristics in children. It is a comparative picture of the upper and lower halves of a group for which we do not have the median scores, especially in the intelligence area. However, some gifted and some creative youngsters were in all probability among the top halves. These clinical descriptions help us perceive more sharply how such children behave—not only those who were relatively high in both areas but also those who were relatively higher

Table 4.1.   Personality characteristics of fifth-grade boys scoring high and low in intelligence and high and low in creativity.

| | Intelligence | |
	Above median	Below median
Creativity Above median	Acute sense of interpersonal sensitivity.... Sharp awareness of one's own identity and integrity in the midst of adults and peers.... A simultaneous awareness of adult and peer-group frames of reference and a capacity to maintain contact with both.	Give impression of being engaged in a battle against others and/or values.
Below median	Overriding concern with academic success.	Simple avoidance, resignation to a sour fate as far as academic activities are concerned.... Blustering hypersensitivity.... Basic sense of bewilderment, seeking comfort by melting into peer group, through protection from sympathetic adults, and through mischief.

Source: Adapted from Wallach and Kogan, 1965, pp. 269-270.

in one area than they were in the other.

That these children were regarded as behaving in these ways is one thing; how they "got that way" is another. Such behaviors were not results just of what had happened to the children in school, although the school had played a major role in how they learned to behave, and probably should play an even larger role. The contributive influence of extra-school factors, especially the value systems operative in their environments, also must be recognized.

As helpful and suggestive as this study is, one would strongly wish for a comparable analysis of similar kinds of data on children of a comparable grade level but of discernibly different—higher and lower—socioeconomic levels. And, even at the one socioeconomic level, the population studied was fifth-graders who already were products of four years of school exposure and eleven years of extraschool social nurturance. What would be the picture five or ten years later? That the personality patterns, already becoming habituated at the fifth-grade level, continue along much the same lines is suggested.

SOCIOEMOTIONAL CHARACTERISTICS

From a psychological point of view, the social and emotional characteristics of the gifted, or of any child or adult, require joint consideration. Logically, it is possible to differentiate between them, social characteristics being those discernible in the interactions between or among individuals, emotional characteristics those which are intraindividual. Yet, in the human being, characteristics which are logically differentiable always are interacting—how one feels affects how he thinks about and reacts to others. And individuals exist in a constantly interactive world—they learn from others how to love, hate, be happy or sad, be retiring, competitive, or dominant, and even, to some extent, to show curiosity. Even though each child has his own outgoingness and psychological integrity, so much happens to him, impinges upon him, and influences him that what he becomes must be regarded as a resultant both of such interaction and of his basic constitution or disposition. While it may at times be clinically possible and appropriate to isolate for consideration the emotional aspect or area of a child's be-havior, it always has to be considered in the context of social interaction, both how others react to him and how he reacts to others. Thus the "personality" of the gifted, their total social stimulus value, will be considered, and so too will their "adjustment"—how they get along with themselves and how, as a result, they function in relation to others.

Observations by Researchers

First, we shall consider Terman's findings, noteworthy because they have so consistently been reaffirmed in subsequent studies and because they incorporate the 40-year follow-up of his original population of gifted children. Evidence

Table 4.2. Personality characteristics of fifth-grade girls scoring high and low in intelligence and high and low in creativity.

		Intelligence	
		Above median	Below median
Creativity	Above median	Ability to range freely and imaginatively with rich affect and enthusiastic involvement.... Much social awareness and sensitivity to emotional expression in others.	Appear to be reacting negatively to school pressure.... Regressive bitterness and/or mischief in response to academic demands.... Social shyness.... Free and wild imaginings which seem to reveal themselves most strongly in a nurturant adult environment that does not invoke sanctions of academic failure and success.
	Below median	A rather mechanical use of academic achievement as a means of attaining status and success, with the impression that such achievement has for these girls more the meaning of reducing pain than of increasing pleasure.... Holding themselves carefully within bounds.... Terribly important to them to do well in school, and they concomitantly seem to inhibit themselves emotionally.	Seem not to know how to cope successfully with academic work, and at best resort to stimulating the surface behaviors that reflect successful coping by others. One result of the frustration is the use of relatively infantile defenses such as being aggressive toward others, being passive or unresponsive, or developing psychosomatic complaints.

Source: Adapted from Wallach and Kogan, 1965, pp. 283-285.

regarding the social and emotional characteristics of the gifted generally has been obtained in three ways:

1. In terms of how others have perceived them
2. In terms of how they have seen others, which reflects their own sensitivities and value systems
3. In terms of how they see themselves, as reflected in tests they have taken and things they do

We shall note also how some of these characteristics have been related to their intellectual levels and to their socioeconomic status. Adjustmental characteristics identified as related to differing kinds of special educational provisions for the gifted will be discussed later.

Terman's findings

The category of "Terman's findings" has become a broad one. Originally denoting what he and his co-workers reported in the 1925 volume of his *Genetic Studies of Genius,* it has come to denote also the findings reported by others, under his direct stimulation, and at subsequent times on his population (Volume III, 1930, *The Promise of Youth;* Volume IV, 1947, *The Gifted Child Grows Up;* Volume V, 1959, *The Gifted Group at Mid-Life;* and Oden's 1968 report of the 40-year follow-up). Catherine Cox Miles' chapter on gifted children in Carmichael's 1954 *Manual of Child Psychology* summarized the literature that had appeared up to the 1940s. Others, such as Hollingworth and Witty, directly influenced by the early Terman studies, conducted research which both essentially reaffirmed the findings of the Terman group and provided supportive elaborations of them. Again illustratively rather than exhaustively, we shall review early evidence and then progress to later findings of educational and social significance.

Terman (1940), reporting on a 16-year follow-up, observed that his group "are not as a group characterized by intellectual one-sidedness, emotional instability, lack of sociality, or other types of maladjusted personality. . . . Indeed, in practically every personality and character trait such children average much better than the general population. . . . In social intelligence rating, social interest, and play activities, gifted children are either normal or superior" (p. 68). Such observations were based not only on how his gifted group performed on tests, as compared with the nongifted, but also on observations of their activities. Considering the earlier evidence in the light of still later findings, Miles (1954) observed:

1. Exceptionally high IQs proved to be neither peculiar nor one-sidedly intellectual.
2. Personally and socially the gifted tend to differ characteristically and favorably from unselected children.
3. The gifted are by no means characterized by studious reclusiveness—as shown by their social and leadership ratings and in their community activities.
4. The special problems of adjustment of the gifted are not, as was at one time supposed, primarily due to an essential instability.

Here again, both performances on tests and everyday behavioral evidence provide the basis for such generalizations.

In the 1947 report, *The Gifted Child Grows Up,* the top and bottom fifths of those in the original study group were identified in terms of their vocational success. The top group, designated the "A" group, consisted of the 150 most successful; the bottom group, designated the "C" group, were the 150 least successful. While many comparisons were drawn between the two groups, of particular interest here is the conclusion that the top group excelled in integration toward goals, perseverance, and self-confidence, undertook more extracurricular and leadership activity in school, and did superior work in high school. It should be noted that these two groups were equivalent in intelligence. The traits in which the A group excelled would have contributed to their becoming members of that group.

The report of the 40-year follow-up (Oden, 1968) made two points regarding the identification of the A and C groups. "The most important consideration was the extent to which a man made use of his superior intelligence in his life work, both in his choice of vocation and in the attainment of a position of importance and responsibility in an area calling for a high degree of intellectual ability" (p. 52). Second, "Most of the C men equal or excel the average of unselected white men of comparable age in vocational status" (p. 53).[2]

Judgments had been obtained from parents, teachers, and medical examiners regarding the quality of adjustments of the study population in 1922 and in 1928. Judgments based on all the data available, hospitalization, employment and other activities, marriage and divorce, and the like, were made in 1960. Table 4.3 shows the results for the two groups over the time range.

The 1960 follow-up data on marriage and divorce reflect certain aspects of social and emotional adjustment. Of the 755 men, 94.3 percent were, or had been, married, as was the case for 90.8 percent of the 607 women. Of the men, 23.3 percent of those married had been divorced,

---

2 It is interesting to note the phenomenally high degree of follow-up in this study. To a four-page Information Blank distributed in 1960 to the study population, 87 percent of the 1,398 subjects still living replied, and information was obtained from other sources on an additional 5 percent. Terman's ability and willingness to maintain a close relationship with those in his original group have been unique in the field of such research.

Table 4.3 Percentages of A and C groups making "satisfactory adjustment."

Year	Group A	C
1922	96	86
1928	95	83
1960	81	46

Source: Adapted from Oden, 1968, pp. 65, 78.

as compared with 22.5 percent of the women. Of the 166 divorced men, 83 percent had remarried; of the 124 divorced women, 70 percent had remarried. In the A-C group comparison, however, 16 percent of those in the A group who had been married were divorced, as contrasted with 41.5 percent of the C group. The operation of some emotional factors in the C group is clearly suggested.

The total group characteristically was involved in one or more avocational activities. Only 6 percent of the men and 7 percent of the women reported no avocational involvements. Understandably, 78 percent of the A group expressed deep satisfaction with their present occupation, sharply contrasting with the 22 percent of those in the C group; only 2 percent of the A group expressed dissatisfaction, whereas 17 percent of the C group reported that they were dissatisfied with their vocations. This condition can be cast into a social and attitudinal context in terms of the data in Table 4.4.

The respondents' recollections of the parts played by their parents in motivating them in school are shown in Table 4.5.

Several things should be kept in mind in interpreting this information. The evaluations in Table 4.4 must be seen in terms of our society as of or before 1960. The recollections indicated in Table 4.5 must be recognized as just that—subject to forgetting, halo effect, and the like— and must be perceived in terms of our

Table 4.4. Percentages of A and C groups deriving the greatest satisfaction from different aspects of life.

| | Group | |
	A	C
Work itself	91.4	62.3
Children*	82.8	58.4
Marriage*	81.7	61.7
Avocational activities	51.6	59.7
Recognition for accomplishments	47.3	28.6
Income	44.1	20.8
Social contacts	25.8	32.5
Community service activities	17.2	13.0
Religion	14.0	19.5
Other	5.4	5.2

Source: Adapted from Oden, 1968, Table 45, p. 89, 1960 data.

*100 percent of the A group were, or had been, married; 18 percent of the C group were single.

Table 4.5. Percentages of A and C groups receiving different types of parent motivation.

| | Group | |
	A	C
Parents encouraged child to forge ahead in school	59.3	39.3
Parents demanded high marks	15.1	5.7
Parents encouraged high marks	73.3	52.9
Parents encouraged college attendance	96.5	62.3

Source: Adapted from Oden, 1968, p. 83.

society as of the 1930s and 1940s. The typicality of Terman's study population must be questioned. Even though it was described as incorporating representatives of different ethnic groups, certain of the findings probably would not be representative of similar phenomena among, for instance, the disadvantaged. Certainly, the nature of parental motivation regarding education and attendant social milieu factors among the disadvantaged would be different from Terman's findings whenever such data were collected. It would seem much safer to generalize over time from such findings in terms of their *direction* rather than their *magnitude*. The findings of Terman and his co-workers still throw much valuable light upon the characteristics and social and educational needs of the gifted, suggesting an essentially favorable picture of their emotional and social adjustment as a group.

Self-Reports

How the gifted perceive themselves can throw light on how they are likely to relate to others and to react to educational programs. Groth and Holbert (1969) had 281 gifted youngsters, 10 to 14 years old, write out their wishes. The 402 wishes then were analyzed in terms of the "needs" which such wishes were taken to suggest. As a group, the paramount need was that of self-actualization. This was true more of the girls than of the boys who, interestingly, were judged to express greater concern for what the authors regarded as security and as self-esteem. Torrance and Dauw (1966), comparing the responses of 115 "creatively gifted" high school seniors with those of 100 job applicants, found the gifted to be discernibly more experimental-minded, intuitive, and resistant to social pressures. The gifted manifested greater needs for freedom, achievement, and recognition, and also a higher disposition toward anxiety. Bachtold (1968), on the other hand, administered a Survey of Interpersonal Values to gifted youngsters, 12 to 14 years of age, and found that the boys attached less than average value to "recognition," whereas the girls evaluated "independence" more highly than did the average. Such contrasts can be due to differences among the populations studied, to the use of different devices and procedures to obtain the information, to any of the many unaccounted-for differences among the settings in which the information was obtained, or to any combination of these and other factors. Yet a residual pattern can be discerned: the expressions of bright youngsters are interpreted as reflecting paramount needs for self-realization and independence and a perfectly legitimate need for recognition—certainly needs that are not unique to the gifted.

Use of standardized devices

Sometimes generally standardized devices are used with the gifted to ascertain the quality of their adjustment, thus making it possible to compare the average scores earned by the gifted with those of normative populations of different ages or grades, as in the following illustrative studies. Lessinger and Martinson (1961) administered the California Psychological Inventory to gifted eighth-graders and found that their average scores were much like those of average twelfth-graders—not at all an atypical finding. (It is one thing to note that the score of a thirteen-year-old, or the average score of a group of thirteen-year-olds, falls among the top 4 percent of all thirteen-year-olds; it is much more meaningful socially to characterize such a performance in terms of its comparability to that of average sixteen- or seventeen-year-olds.) Hollingworth and Rust (1937) gave the Bernreuter Personality Inventory to 36 male and 19 female highly gifted adolescents (Binet IQ 135–190; all but four Jewish) and found them less neurotic, more self-sufficient, and less submissive than the average. This pattern was more pronounced for the boys than for the girls. Warren and Heist (1960) reported the performances of 918 National Merit Scholarship winners and runners-up (mean estimated IQ, 150; minimum, 130) who as college freshmen (659 males and 259 females) had taken the Omnibus Personality Inventory and

the Allport-Vernon-Lindzey Study of Values. Both sexes were characterized as "independent, confident, and generally mature in their interactions with the external world, and also as manifesting a stronger esthetic orientation than is commonly found." Smith (1962) compared the social and personal adjustment of gifted adolescents (95th centile and above on the California Test of Mental Maturity) with that of average adolescents (scoring between the 25th and 75th centiles on the CTMM). The data on 42 matched pairs of Syracuse, N.Y., youngsters (24 boys, 18 girls; all white) consisted of teacher and classmate evaluations and self-report responses. He observed significant contrasts in Leary's (1957) Independent-Dominant domain, the gifted demonstrating more dominant, forceful, independent, and competitive types of behavior.

Such findings illustrate the psychologically favorable picture of the gifted which so long has been a matter of record. Some have questioned the validity of the self-information which responding to such inventories yields. It has been contended that the gifted are more likely to know the "right" responses to the questions or statements which make up such devices and so are better able to earn scores which reflect themselves in a favorable light. To some extent this may be true, as it could be with anyone taking such a device, but the psychological evaluations of the behavior of the gifted by others consistently support the essential validity of the general picture which the gifted present of themselves.

Inference from Interests

Further light on the social and emotional picture of the gifted is shed by the long-observed interests which they manifest in others. Martinson (1961) noted this in her extensive study of gifted children in a special education program, concluding,

"The other-mindedness of the gifted, as compared with the average, and their significantly more frequent idealization of humanitarianism rather than personal contribution revealed a maturity of social concern beyond that of their age-mates." In support of this, she observed that "problems of morality, religion, and world peace may be troublesome at a very early age. Interest in problems besetting society is common even in elementary age children." This general phenomenon is clearly relatable to the capacity of the gifted earlier to operate at a higher conceptual level than can average children, as evidenced in their responding to generalized conditions rather than just to the specific problems of specific individuals.

The social adjustment of the gifted is reflected also in their play activities and interests. The characteristics of Terman's findings have persevered, although the specifics may have changed with time: Canasta, Monopoly, three-dimensional chess, chemistry sets, and the like have come upon the scene. Terman's average gifted child at the age of nine had acquired more factual information about plays and games than the average child twelve years of age. His gifted youngsters preferred games typically played by older children and engaged in the same number of play activities—findings reported also by Witty (1940). There was one qualitative difference, though: the gifted tended to engage in more sedentary and less socially interactive kinds of play activities. Some have suggested that this should be attributed to the fact that the gifted child is more self-sufficient and thus more able to amuse himself. This "play syndrome"—knowing more about games and tending toward less socially involved play—has important implications regarding "peerness" and communication, as we shall see later.

The breadth of interest found early by Terman continued. At mid-life "More than four-fifths of the subjects reported an interest in two or more avocational pursuits and more than one-half reported three or more. . . . Many of the special abilities that had been evidenced by the subjects in their youth found expression in hobbies and avocations at mid-life. . . . The group has displayed an interest in and responsibility for the community and civil welfare through participation in a wide variety of activities such as organizations concerned with youth, help programs, civic betterment projects, and similar plans" (Terman and Oden, 1959, pp. 117–118). Note that this broad concern and participation clearly antedated subsequent, more generally promoted social action efforts.

Such activities—whether the extra-school activities and interests or the avocational ones of later life—reflect the value systems of the gifted. These, in turn, are resultants of the kinds of social stimulation which the gifted have received, effectualized jointly by their special capabilities and successful experiences in such undertakings. Note that whereas such a combination of learning and capacity is productive of social contributions of these kinds, a similar combination, but with different accompanying patterns of values, can lead to less desirable social outcomes. This latter is illustrated by (though not peculiar to) some happenings in a study by Haggard (1957). He made a seven-year study of 76 bright children, starting when they were in grade three in the Laboratory School of the University of Chicago. He was particularly interested in the interaction of socialization and achievement, contending that "superior performance on intelligence tests is in large part a function of the same socialization factors which were found to be related to the high general academic achievement" (p. 401). One suspects the operation of "excessive socialization processes" as contributory to his observation that "by

Grade VII the high general achievers seemed to have become over-intellectualized, almost to the exclusion of other interests and activities. In arriving at this point, they had become somewhat disdainful of adults and hostile toward, and competitive with, their peers in order to maintain the position of intellectual superiority in the group" (p. 406). Bearing in mind the fact that Haggard's group of youngsters were bright, certain similarities between his characterization and those of Wallach and Kogan (pp. 73–74, above) are apparent.

Perception by one's fellows

Our understanding of the gifted is furthered by the examination of how others —fellow pupils, teachers, parents, and psychologists—have perceived them. (Again, our citations will be illustrative, not exhaustive.) Liddle (1958), using all the 1,015 children in the fourth and sixth grades in a school system, obtained nominations from teachers and fellow students by means of a Guess Who approach and a Behavior Description List. From his analysis of the results on the top 10 percent of the group he concluded, "Children who were highly gifted in one of the three talent areas (intellectual, leadership, artistic) were quite likely to be talented in other areas, and quite unlikely to be seen as highly maladjusted by their teachers and classmates" (pp. 222–223). Here, the possibility of a generalized halo effect (seen high on one trait, therefore likely to be seen high on others) must be recognized, but the trend of the findings would suggest that this was not a major determining factor. Mueller and Rothney (1960) compared descriptive and predictive statements of 78 ninth-grade superior pupils, their parents, and their teachers. The statements pertained to nervousness, social-mindedness, open-mindedness, influence, acceptance by peers, academic performance,

responsibility, and acceptance of peers. Interestingly, these researchers observed that only the parents predicted accurately how the pupils would describe themselves, the pupils were able to predict accurately only the teachers' responses to them, and the youngsters expected a much less enhancing characterization by their parents than they actually received.

Pervading the research literature on the gifted is another kind of evidence indicative of their social acceptability, and, therefore, of their favorable social adjustment: the gifted consistently have been found to hold many more elective offices in school activities than their low frequency in the total school population would lead one to expect. This is understandable not only in terms of their generally superior social adjustment, which causes them to be perceived favorably by others, but also because the quality of their school work is such as to make them eligible for such consideration, because they have more time available for such activity since they learn so easily and quickly, and because their ability to deal with the generalities of social organization and interpersonal relationships contributes materially to their capable functioning in such social roles. That the gifted are thus positively perceived not only by their classmates but also by the school staff is illustrated in the complaint of a high school principal. A number of the bright youngsters in his school were being given the opportunity to complete their high school programs at an accelerated pace and also to devote part of their high school attendance time to taking courses in colleges in their community. Under this kind of motivating educational arrangement, they were able to leave high school earlier than usual and to get an early start with their college work. While this high school principal did not actually oppose such an arrangement, he did complain about it, rather seriously, because such an accelerative arrangement in effect deprived him of the services rendered by such bright pupils not only in helping him with administrative chores but also in running, with considerable degrees of independence, the school newspapers and other important extracurricular activities. His complaint was shared by other principals in the area who, in the 1950s, were inaugurating this type of educational acceleration.

Composite Impression

In an overall sense, then, the social-emotional picture of the gifted—in childhood and in adulthood—is, to put it minimally, essentially favorable. In summarizing studies in this area for the U.S. Department of Health, Education, and Welfare (Marland, 1971), Martinson wrote: "The composite impression . . . is of a population which values independence, which is more task- and contribution-oriented than recognition-oriented, which prizes integrity and independent judgment in decision-making, which rejects conformity for its own sake, and which possesses unusually high social ideals and values." Unfortunately, the inevitable unusualness of the behavior of a few gifted individuals tends to get a bigger play in the public press and in the conversations of some apprehensive parents and educators than does the generality of the social contributions of the typical gifted.

Intragroup Variations

It has been and will repeatedly be brought out that within the gifted group there can be important differences, even in the area of socioemotional adjustment. Illustrative is the observation by Hollingworth (1942) to the effect that, in gifted children having Binet IQs between 135 and 150, there are traits which give these children certain advantages, such as su-

perior size, strength, and "beauty," along with emotional balance, self-control, good character, and ability to win the confidence of their contemporaries and thus contribute to their assuming leadership roles. But she pointed out that certainly above Binet 160 they deviate so greatly, not only from the total population but also from the other gifted, that their difference predisposes to "isolation and alienation." As a result of her early study of gifted children (1924) she identified four categories of possible maladjustment:

1. Problems associated with physique—being weaker and smaller than their classmates with whom they may be placed
2. Problems associated with "adjustment to occupation"—due to their preferring self-direction
3. Problems involved in "suffering fools gladly"—having difficulty in accepting the dogmatism of lesser intellects
4. Problems associated with the tendency to be isolated in interests and goals

As will be seen later, the latter two must be perceived in terms of the problems of "peerness" and communication.

Socioeconomic Correlates

It seems plausible that the interests of the gifted, their value systems, and the nature of their educational and social motivation could be considerably influenced, or even heavily determined, by the nature of their socioeconomic backgrounds. Whether their social and emotional characteristics would be similarly affected can only be guessed at. The relationship between variables such as these and socioeconomic levels just has not been studied systematically—partly because of the magnitude of the problem. Our discussion here will suggest not only the problem's major research dimensions but also the limited generalizability of what has been learned.

Assume that whatever trait we want to study in the gifted, say their consideration for others, is to be examined in terms of socioeconomic level. But the degrees to which this trait is present will vary also by the age levels of those in whom it is to be studied. And it may vary also from community to community. If we take only these three conditions as possible determiners of the overall situation, we can represent the total problem by means of Figure 4.1. The major dimensions (parameters) have been simplified: only three socioeconomic levels are identified; only four age levels or age groups are indicated; and communities A to Y have been specified. To facilitate communication in terms of this structure, let us designate each of the vertical columns as A-6, A-10, and so on (for age); the three socioeconomic levels as SEH, SEM, SEL; and the communities (vertical slices, front to back) as C-A through C-Y. Thus, a study of the gifted's consideration for others among six-year-olds at a lower socioeconomic level in New York City would yield a "chunk" of information denoted by A-6/SEL/CA. (Where in this structure would fall such research on children with whom you work?) "The" picture of consideration for others, by the gifted, would have to be made up not only of the "chunks" of information in each of the 36 (or more) portions of the research structure but also of the natures of the relationships between and among such "chunks." As complex as this may seem, it still represents a highly simplified structuring of the essential research domain for this type of problem. (This type of thinking about the structuring of research is generalizable to other problems.)

Illustrative within this research structure are two studies bearing upon possible differences among the gifted in terms of socioeconomic level. Nichols and Davis (1964) compared National Merit Scholarship winners with other college seniors and found that the advanced psychological maturity (attitudes, interests, and career plans) of the Schol-

Figure 4.1. Simplified research domain involving age, socioeconomic level, and community.

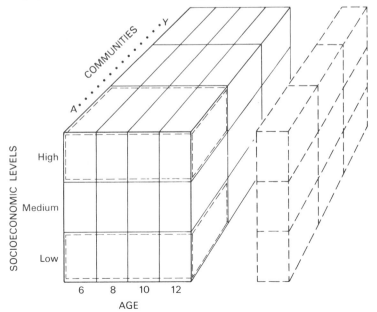

ars was superior even when socioeconomic variability was controlled. (The scope of this study would be represented by the dotted-line portion at the right in Figure 4.1.) Frierson (1965) made a more intensive comparison of gifted and "average" children in two socioeconomic levels—"upper" and "lower." He made his study in Cleveland, historically noted for its program of relatively early identification of the gifted and special classes for them. He divided the elementary level children (age and sex distribution not specified) into four groups:

1. Upper socioeconomic status—gifted (88 children, average Kuhlmann-Anderson IQ 133.2)
2. Lower socioeconomic status—gifted (56 children, average KAIQ 132.1)
3. Upper socioeconomic status—average (86 children, average KAIQ 102.9)
4. Lower socioeconomic status—average (55 children, average KAIQ 96.8)

Within this structuring, the groups were "matched on the basis of sex, age, ethnic background, and school experience." On the basis of the data he collected, Frierson drew the following conclusions:

1. Statistically significant differences (.05 level) were found in the areas of interest and activity. The gifted upper-class children had higher educational aspirations and read more; the lower-class children did not like school, did not achieve so well, and preferred sports activity to reading.
2. On the Minnesota Tests of Creative Thinking the upper-class children scored significantly higher than did the lower-class children.
3. The gifted children were taller and heavier than the average children, but not statistically significantly so.
4. None of the differences on 14 personality traits (Cattell's Children's Personality Questionnaire) was statistically significant, although "the personality patterns of the upper-status gifted children and lower-

status gifted children were slightly more similar than were the personality patterns of lower-status gifted children and lower-status average children" (p. 89).

Frierson's summarization is relevant to our area of concern: "The data clearly indicate that several differences between groups of gifted children are associated with differences in the socioeconomic backgrounds of the children. It is equally clear from the data that many differences between gifted children and average children exist regardless of the socioeconomic backgrounds of the children" (p. 89). Frierson's portion of the total research field is represented in the heavily lined components of Figure 4.1.

PHYSICAL CHARACTERISTICS

General Superiority

Generally, the gifted present a more favorable physical picture than do the general population of comparable age. Terman's subjects ranked above the average of their agemates. They were characterized as having a higher energy level, this undoubtedly associated with their above-average physical condition. The 40-year follow-up was essentially supportive to the earlier picture, the evidence indicating a more favorable mortality rate and a continued typical range of activities in the light of the higher energy level (Oden, 1968). Frierson's findings (above) are typically in support of Terman's early findings. Laycock and Caylor (1964), for example, made 81 physical comparisons between gifted children and their less gifted siblings and found no significant differences—a condition attributable to intrafamily comparisons.

Any further elaboration of the essentially favorable physical picture of the gifted is not essential to the intent of this book. No amassing of such evidence has seemed adequate to allay the unwarranted assumption on the part of the few that the gifted child or adult is runty, weak, or in ill health. Some undoubtedly have misinterpreted the tendency of some gifted children to prefer more sedentary types of play activity as symptomatic of physical limitation, but the fundamental reason for this is more psychological than physical.

Physically, the gifted reflect the generality that correlation, not compensation, is the law of nature. Sometimes social situations are created or arise which may cause the casual observer to forget this generality. For instance, if a very bright nine-year-old is, for some reason or other, placed with seventh- or eighth-graders, he well may be smaller than they are even though he may be larger than his agemates. The bright four-year-old may play, or want to play, with six- or seven-year-olds because his interests and intellectual capability are more like theirs, but he may be inconveniently smaller and less coordinated than they, although his own physical condition may be superior to that of average four-year-olds. In some instances, temporary growth spurts may be conducive to periods of poor coordination. The clumsiness of the ten-year-old boy with a Binet mental age of 18 and a physical age of 14 generally is relatively short-lived.

The contentions of novelists that for a genius to be truly productive he must have some physical malfunctioning, as Mann has claimed in regard to Dostoevski, are born only of overgeneralization from specific cases. Beethoven's creative work in music was not compensatory; he had started his work in music before the onset of his deafness. As attention-getting as such instances are, they do not constitute the generality any more than would the naval officer with six toes on one foot.

Explanations of Superiority

That such differences between the gifted and the general child population exist is one thing; what they mean or imply may be quite another. Some contend that the gifted, being genetically of superior biological stock, are above the average of the general population primarily due to such genetic determiners. Others maintain that the gifted, tending to have parents who are "brighter" than the general population, tend to benefit from better health attention—diet and medical services—and therefore become better physically. Each school of thought has its ardent proponents; factors of both kinds probably are contributive. Regardless of the causation, the situation is such that overall positive rather than compensatory planning is warranted.

Physique and health are such complex conditions that, while the more favorable picture of the gifted may be valid, reverse reasoning in regard to an individual may be most misleading. The fact that child A is tall for his age and healthy does not warrant his being regarded as gifted. And a gifted child who is notably shorter than the average of his agemates may have parents both of whom are considerably shorter than average adults. Adequate research evidence, in any event, does not yet warrant firm or sweeping conclusions regarding the physical characteristics of the gifted as compared to the generality of the population. Frierson's study most nearly approaches adequacy in this regard. The criticisms of Terman's possible selective population cannot be ignored. The scope of an adequate study of this sort is suggested in Figure 4.1. The principles of correlation, suggested above, might very well lead to an expectation that the gifted group would equal if not surpass the average of the general population in physical characteristics. But, in thinking about and planning for the effective education of the gifted, these physical characteristics are not of primary concern.

EDUCATIONAL CHARACTERISTICS

We shall refer first to two Terman-motivated studies that illustrate early objective studies with educational implications, and we shall note certain of Terman's observations. We shall illustrate the typicality and sharpening of his observations by citing the findings of a major California study. The results of an Iowa study of the dropout picture will be presented as both illustrative and suggestive; the problem area of under-achievement, a major focus of later studies, also will be explored. Educational characteristics more relatable to differing kinds of educational provisions will be discussed later. The findings presented here have been selected to be representative and to contribute to later philosophical and educational considerations.

Early Findings

In 1918, Race reported findings on 10 boys and 11 girls with Binet IQs 120 to 168 (median, 137.4) who ranged in age from "7.7 to 9.8" years. This study yielded the following correlations between Binet IQs and scores on different tests:

with Thorndike Reading	.494
with Kelly Reading	.39
with Trabue Language	.509
with Starch Reasoning (arith.)	.48
with Woody Addition	.14
with Courtis Addition	.09

These results are of particular interest because they reflected so early a phenomenon that has remained relatively stable: Binet IQ (not as good as Binet MA) correlates more closely with educational performances which involve higher mental processes than with those depending more on rote learning.

Specht's study (1919) was of a different nature, reflecting the tenor of Terman's early admonitions. She studied the educational performances of a group of bright children (Binet IQ 120 and up) who compared in age with average children in grades 4B through 6B. The teacher for this class was very carefully selected, being chosen from a group of 84 elementary level teachers. Specht observed that during the first six months of their work in the special class the average measured educational progress was two and two-thirds grades. During the second six months the average progress was observed to be at least an additional two grades. In accounting for this phenomenal progress, we must keep in mind the status of educational test standardization at that time. Discounting the possible impreciseness of the evaluation of educational growth, there still is reflected here the discernibly superior educational potential of such children which has been observed so consistently over time. This study is cited here primarily to illustrate the pioneering efforts of Terman and of those whom he early influenced—before starting his early study—to show objectively that bright children could progress educationally more rapidly than the conventional one grade per year. On the other hand, the phenomenal "growth" reported in this study cannot be regarded as typical, although in the cases of certain very bright children, usually higher than Binet 120, educational improvements of this magnitude have been found.

Later Findings

Terman's early educational findings were found repeatedly over succeeding years: The gifted tended to learn to read, without formal instruction, before entering school at age 6, with an appreciable number reading by the age of 4. . . . The superior school achievement of his group was maintained over succeeding years, even though they had been accelerated a year in their progress through school. . . . In their scholastic interests, gifted girls resembled gifted boys more clearly than they resembled control girls. . . . In terms of (Binet) mental ages and total educational achievement, the gifted group were far below their appropriate grade placements.

This general picture is both confirmed and sharpened, typically, in the following observations by Martinson on her 1961 California study—prepared for and somewhat condensed in the Department of Health, Education, and Welfare report to the Congress (Marland, 1971).

> In a statewide study which included more than 1,000 gifted children at all grade levels, the kindergarten group *on the average* performed at a level comparable to that of second grade children in reading and mathematics. The *average* for fourth- and fifth-grade gifted children in all curriculum areas was beyond that of the average seventh-grade pupils. Nearly three-fourths of the gifted eighth-grade pupils made *average* scores equal to or beyond the average of twelfth-grade students on a test battery in six curriculum areas. Three-fourths of the tenth- and eleventh-grade gifted exceeded the average of college sophomores. . . . As a special test to determine true potential, a representative sample of gifted high school seniors took the Graduate Record Examination in social sciences, humanities, and natural sciences. In all of the tests, the randomly selected gifted high school seniors made an *average* group score which surpassed the average for college seniors. In the social sciences the high school seniors surpassed the average of college students with majors in that field. In the statewide study cited earlier, the highest level of performance by a first-grade pupil was at the eighth-grade level. The upper

one-fourth of the fourth- and fifth-grade students rated beyond the *average* for high school sophomores on a comprehensive battery of achievement, while one-fourth of the eighth-grade gifted were at or beyond the level of college freshmen (Section II, p. 2).

Example:
A Gifted Eight-Year-Old

To the point here is the following representation of the psychoeducational findings obtained on one gifted eight-year-old. Bear in mind that gifted children's "scoring high" on achievement tests can be misinterpreted if one assumes that they are generally high in all the areas measured. Few children, gifted or otherwise, produce "flat" profiles on such multiarea tests; often there are peaks and dips, whether the child has a high or low overall score. Taking the case of the gifted child whose performances are shown in Figure 4.2, if we compute his "overall" performance by finding the average of his separate test standings, he would be characterized as having earned an "achievement grade status" of 5.3, or to have performed much as an average child at the third month of the fifth grade (6.0 + 5.7 + 5.6 + 3.9, ÷ 4). True, he would be perceived as doing very well, his average being two years above the grade in which he is sitting. But to stop there, as too many educators do, is to lose valuable information: that he scored as well as an average beginning sixth-grader in reading comprehension, but scored as low as an average child nine months into the third grade on arithmetic computation. A profile such as this is not unusual of the gifted in two senses: many bright children do less well in rote computation than they do in arithmetic reasoning or in verbal measures, and, even more importantly, their performances tend to vary in different learning areas. Terman and Oden (1959) observed in this regard,

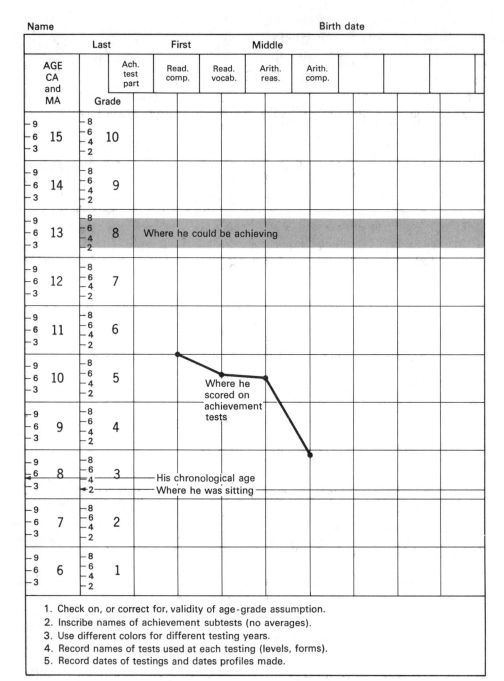

Name _____   Birth date _____

			Ach. test part	Read. comp.	Read. vocab.	Arith. reas.	Arith. comp.			
AGE CA and MA		**Grade**								
9 6 3	15	8 6 4 2	10							
9 6 3	14	8 6 4 2	9							
9 6 3	13	8 6 4 2	8	Where he could be achieving						
9 6 3	12	8 6 4 2	7							
9 6 3	11	8 6 4 2	6							
9 6 3	10	8 6 4 2	5		Where he scored on achievement tests					
9 6 3	9	8 6 4 2	4							
9 6 3	8	8 6 4 2	3	His chronological age Where he was sitting						
9 6 3	7	8 6 4 2	2							
9 6 3	6	8 6 4 2	1							

1. Check on, or correct for, validity of age-grade assumption.
2. Inscribe names of achievement subtests (no averages).
3. Use different colors for different testing years.
4. Record names of tests used at each testing (levels, forms).
5. Record dates of testings and dates profiles made.

Figure 4.2. Psychoeducational profile of a gifted third-grader.

"The amount of unevenness in subject matter profiles of the gifted does not differ significantly from that shown by unselected children" (p. 9). And do not forget that the weakest area in a gifted child's profile still can be higher than the performances of the nongifted of the same age or grade in that area.

Some further information about this child will be helpful. He was brought to the attention of a school psychologist, the mother reporting that, while he had started in school happily and with much pleasurable anticipation, he had become progressively unhappy during the first and second grades and had reached the point of having to be forced to go to school. The second- and third-grade teachers described him as highly distractible, inattentive, belligerent, emotionally immature, and even at times overtly aggressive in his behavior. (Some, of course, were sure he was "brain damaged"!) As shown in Figure 4.2, he was eight years three months old and was sitting in the third grade. His teacher and principal regarded him as being with his "peers." The school psychologist gave him four sections of the Stanford Achievement Test, converting his scores to the grade equivalents shown in the figure; we can see that he was achieving in a manner generally perceived as superior to his classmates. He also was tested by means of the 1960 Binet and the Wechsler Intelligence Scales for Children (WISC). Emotional evaluation of the child revealed no underlying problem. The results of the two learning

aptitude tests were clinically reconciled (not averaged) in order to get some idea of his school learning potential level. This was regarded as being much like that of an average eighth-grader, suggesting a mental age of about $13\frac{1}{2}$ years. In order to communicate this fact to the child's parents and his teacher, he was characterized as being capable of learning school work, assuming that he had the relevant basic skills, pretty much in the 8.3 to 8.9 grade range. Thus, while in an overall sense he was achieving academically better than an average third-grader, he was underachieving in terms of his own potential by at least two years. No wonder the child was unhappy. But he was still fighting!

Underachievement

Gifted dropouts

Numerous studies have been made to ascertain the extent to which the gifted are among high school dropouts. Most often these studies have been made only in single school districts. Green's (1962) analysis of 1957 data on all high school dropouts in Iowa reflects a more general condition. Identifying 735 high school dropouts, he found that 29 of them had earned IQs (on some test or tests) of 120 or more; he characterized these as "talented." His overall results are presented in Table 4.6. His "talented" group constituted 3.5 percent of all of the dropouts and represented nearly one-fifth (17.6 percent) of all the "talented"

Table 4.6. The "talented" among Iowa high school dropouts and persisters.

| | "Talented" | | | | Student Body | |
	Male	Female	Total	Percentage	Total	Percentage "Talented"
Dropouts	10	19	29	17.6	735	3.5
Persisters	68	68	136	82.4	917	14.8
TOTAL	78	87	165	100.0	1652	10.0

Source: Adapted from Green, 1962.

Table 4.7. Comparison of Iowa dropouts and persisters.

	Dropouts	*Persisters*	*Significance of differences*
High school grade point average	2.18	3.25	.01
Composite score, Iowa Tests of Educational Development	15.6	17.0	N.S.
Absence ratio	.0771	.0265	.01
Extracurricular activities	1.2	3.2	.01
Father's occupational level	4.47	4.57	N.S.

Source: Adapted from Green, 1962.

in the population studied. More important, though, is his analysis of possibly related factors or conditions, as shown in Table 4.7. The averages here are based upon data on 21 matched pairs of dropouts and persisters. Understandably, the dropouts had lower grade point averages, more absences, and engaged in fewer extracurricular activities, but, interestingly, the composite scores on the achievement tests and the levels of fathers' occupations did not differentiate significantly between the two groups.

Underaspiration

What bright high school youngsters say about their plans for further education was revealed in Project Talent (Flanagan, 1964), a longitudinal study of 400,000 high school pupils (grades 9–12) made in 1960. These youngsters were also followed up one and five years after graduation. While relatively many more gifted than average pupils did enter college, some 13 percent of them planned either not to go to college or to enter upon some kind of terminal educational vocational training which involved less than a bachelor's degree—intentions which were essentially validated one year after high school graduation. Slightly less than one-fifth of the parents of the college-capable pupils had higher educational aspirations for their youngsters that were in harmony with the children's capabilities. Contrast this with the infor-

mation (Table 4.5) on the extent of parental motivation regarding college attendance, but keep in mind the influence which the knowledge that their children were the subjects of a study of the gifted might have had on such parental aspirations.

The lack of a socially and emotionally fruitful combination of parental aspirations for their gifted children, the gifted youngsters' motivation for furthering their education, and the provision of effectively individualized educational programs for them has been an abiding and distressing phenomenon. Shaffer (1936) commented on the adjustmental implications of such a concatenation of influences in one of the most widely used books in the area of mental hygiene:

> The pupil of superior intelligence is also educationally maladjusted in the conventional school, for he is kept from progressing up to the potentialities of his ability. Bright children are appreciably less likely to develop serious conduct problems from this situation than are the dull, but some maldevelopments of personality traits occur. Compelled to sit through lessons that are boresome to him, the gifted pupil may resort to daydreaming and develop habits of seeking unreal satisfactions. The lack of necessity for effort leads to slipshod habits of work which prove embarrassing in later years when concentration is demanded. Some bright pupils devote their spare time to mischief and thus get a

reputation for bad conduct, even though no real maladjustment exists (p. 509).

Supporting at least part of Shaffer's observation is the fact that Terman's subjects, on the Supplementary Biographical Data blanks they filled out in 1951–1952, observed in connection with failures in college that in high school they found it so easy to make high marks that they underestimated the amount of study necessary in college (Terman and Oden, 1959, p. 68).

New concern with underachievement

It is understandable, then, that the problem of underachievement in the gifted would become a matter of serious concern. The term "underachievement" is used to denote an individual's performing less well than reasonably can be expected. Usually, both how well the child performs and how well he is capable of performing are objectively ascertained, the use of well-standardized and valid measuring devices or procedures being presumed. Usually, also, the disparity between measured performance and measured capacity to perform is arbitrarily set at a magnitude sufficient to offset measurement errors in the two areas. Logically, any slow, average, or bright youngster may be an underachiever, though underachievement is most obvious in the case of the gifted and has been observed more in the academic area. Obviously, there can be underachievement in areas other than the academic. The mentally retarded, especially some of the trainable children in that group, have come increasingly to be recognized as underachievers in the area of social behavior. The youngster whose data are plotted in Figure 4.2 was an underachiever.

The near-typical underachievement of the gifted is not news; Terman com-

mented on it repeatedly in the early stages of his studies. But a combination of factors—the revival of interest in the education of the gifted, the arousal of general concern regarding the effectiveness of education, and the improved status and widespread use of objective tests—contributed to make underachievement in the gifted a focus of much concern and research. In one annotated bibliography on the gifted (Gowan, 1961) 82 references pertaining to underachievement were included for the years 1951–1961, 57 of them being for 1957–1961. In contrast, only 47 references for that period pertained to "creativity." No attempt will be made here to summarize such studies. Many only echoed what long had been known. Many suggested no fruitful generalizable preventive directions. Most described only the condition per se. Some sought to identify concomitant conditions; others, concurrent corrective treatments. Those few which will be cited were chosen for their implications regarding social and educational strategies for the gifted.

Reflective of the overall magnitude of the problem is the finding of Miner (1957) that 54.6 percent of 251 highly gifted students were working below the levels of which they were intellectually capable, and that the majority were at least four grade levels below where they could be working. Obviously, the magnitude of this "educational lag" increases as one goes up the educational ladder. The truly important task is to identify where underachievement begins in order that corrective steps can be taken at that time—or, even better, that preventive steps can be taken before that time.

Shaw and McCuen (1960) studied the onset of underachievement in bright children. They studied the records of eleventh- and twelfth-graders in one school system, all of whom had taken the Pintner General Ability Test (of learning aptitude), taking the top 25 percent of those populations on this measure as the "bright" children. In this manner they identified 36 male achievers, 36 male underachievers, 45 female achievers, and 17 female underachievers —the achievers being defined as those who earned marks that were regarded essentially in harmony with their relatively high learning aptitude scores. The grade point averages of these youngsters were examined over the range of eleven grades. For the males, the average marks of the underachievers were below those of the achievers even in the first and second grades, although the differences were not statistically significant then. By grade 3 the differences had become statistically significant, this condition increasing up to grade 10. Interestingly, those girls who were regarded as underachievers at grades 11 and 12 actually had higher average grades than did the achievers in grades 1 through 5. Starting at grade 6, the female underachievers' grades fell below those of the achievers, and were statistically significantly so from grade 9 through grade 11.

Barrett (1957) made the same kind of study, though less intensively, examining the educational records of 32 high school pupils who had earned Henmon-Nelson IQs of 130 and above. He found that the pattern of underachievement was apparent as far back as the fifth grade, and that the low achievers tended to be "less gifted" in numerical and abstract reasoning as measured by the Differential Aptitude Tests. Two of his observations were déjà vu in nature: those achieving "high" in elementary school continued to do so at the secondary level, and those who were weak at the elementary level did even more poorly in high school. Barrett concerned himself also with the parents of the underachievers, finding them to be inconsistent and either apathetic or overanxious.

One of the major reasons for advocating suitable educational provisions for the gifted was the belief that doing so would contribute to their self-fulfillment, and self-fulfilled individuals are more likely to be socially contributive than those who, for one reason or other, are not operating at their respective efficiency levels. The self-fulfilled tends to be the achiever; the non-self-fulfilled is the underachiever—at least academically, although he may be quite an achiever in creating disruptions in the school, home, or community, accomplishing things quite alien to the academic realm.

Adjustments and maladjustments: Some examples

Gifted academic underachievers constitute a homogeneous group only with respect to the characteristic of underachieving. They differ among themselves in many ways. Some react to the attending frustration by withdrawing. Some react to their frustration by open, but often blind, aggression.

Eight-year-old *Mary*, sitting in the second grade, was brought to the clinic because she "couldn't read," attacked other children, had talked also to her teacher, and even "maliciously broke up materials" in the classroom. On the Binet she was found to have an IQ of 152, with a mental age of about 12 years. She refused to read second-grade materials in the clinic setting, but read fifth-grade materials quite comprehendingly. No aggressive behavior was manifested in the clinic setting, probably in part because of the nature of the setting but more probably because she was worked with as though she were at least a fifth-grader. When she was returned to school, her different teacher worked with her as though she were a sixth-grader and her behavior became increasingly that of a well-behaved child. With the accompanying cooperation and understanding of her parents, she became a happy child, thoroughly enjoying the more appropriate learning opportunities that were being provided.

Mary was an incipient underachiever, but her energy level and motivation were such that she rebelled against the intellectual stifling to which she was being subjected. It is possible that her psychological picture was more complex than this—as many of them are. The extent to which her having received a perfectly understandable psychological nurturance in her home may have contributed to her being dissatisfied with her being expected to "learn to read" first- and second-grade materials, some of which she already had read before starting to school. Her rebellion helped save her intellectual life.

The parents of five-year-old *Norman* tried to enter him in public school because he already was reading children's books and captions in magazines and newspapers and was enjoying finding out for himself relationships among numbers, but the school authorities refused to let him enter because he wouldn't be with his "peers." When he finally did get into school, everything he was confronted with was a "breeze," which resulted in his having much free time. (One ingenious teacher, in order to capitalize upon his seeming excess of energy and to "enrich his learning experiences," had him run errands for her, which he did skippingly.) While he earned high marks in the lower elementary grades, he began to receive failing marks by the time he was in junior high school. At this time he was found to have a Binet IQ of 166, but that apparently suggested nothing to his teachers (who even then were participating in a much publicized "experimental" program of individualized instruction). His teachers agreed that he was "just plain lazy." His academic performance became still worse in high school, as a result of which he not only dropped out of school but also ran away. (One of his high school counselors—he had had several—was heard to observe that his running away might be "just what the doctor ordered, because he needed to do some emotional maturing.") The school personnel had known, since Norman was in the upper elementary grades, that there was considerable emotional tension in his home, of which he

was not the focus, but firmly maintained that such was not their proper concern. Sketchy subsequent reports revealed that he was carrying on his sampling of drugs (which he had started in high school), that he had stopped just short of becoming addicted, that he had gotten married and was living in a "commune." As of the age of 25 he was marginally subsisting by running a natural foods grocery for his friends; he still had not turned out to be the socially productive person he had been capable of becoming.

Norman in effect succumbed to his intellectual starvation diet. As a preschooler, he had shown a lively curiosity about things, volunteering, for instance, that he "could count by every other number" and doing so effectively. He related outgoingly to the other children in his kindergarten group and was perceived generally as a "happy child." But his psychological assets of curiosity, vivacity, and relating to other children were dried up in the educational setting. He had been taught to be an underachiever of the first magnitude.

Seven-year-old *Oscar* had been validly found to have a Binet mental age of at least an average eleven-year-old. Instead of his being promoted to the second grade, he was placed in a third-grade room. He was the tallest boy in his grade. Objective educational achievement test results indicated that in arithmetic he was a bit better than the average third-grader and in reading he performed quite like an average sixth-grader. Because he was so low, relatively, in arithmetic and because he wouldn't "stay with his group in reading," his teacher had recommended that he be put back into the second grade "where he belonged." His behavior in class had become increasingly disruptive. He "flew off the handle" at the slightest annoyance, at times physically attacking some of his classmates, at other times acting very much put out when, for instance, a paper did not tear as evenly as he wished, and at other times simply sulking. At home he did not give way to so many or such violent outbursts, although his mother did observe that he had, over the past two or three months, become increasingly "itchy."

On the basis of an evaluation of his total psychoeducational picture, he was placed with a fourth-grade teacher who had him work with fifth- and sixth-grade verbal materials and got him involved in quantitative learning situations which motivated him to acquire in a very short time arithmetic computational skills at a fifth-grade level. Since his aggressive behavior pattern had not yet become habituated and since his educational life had become appropriately challenging, his maladaptive behavior no longer occurred.

Here, again is an example of aggressive behavior appearing after, or along with, frustration. Fortunately for Oscar, his parents—interested but not driving—had sought psychoeducational help outside the school situation and corrective recommendations were followed. Another underachiever was "headed off at the pass."

A common denominator to these three cases, and to many others, is the fact that preventive, rather than corrective, steps could have been taken by the teachers and other school personnel. The supporting strengths of bridges are determined before vehicles are allowed to cross them. Below the heavyweight level, boxers are weighed carefully in order that no boxer will be at a major disadvantage for that reason. Generally, the physical conditions of school-entering children are ascertained in order that children will not enter upon their schooling experiences with that kind of handicap. All too slowly schools are coming to see any merit in "weighing in" children intellectually. When this *is* done, it tends to be done unjustifiably late in the children's school lives. To a socially unjustifiable extent, schools cause or allow problems in children to happen rather than endeavoring systematically to prevent the development of such problems.

The variables which contribute to underachievement in gifted (and other) children are numerous and, generally, knowable. Figure 4.3 gives a simplified

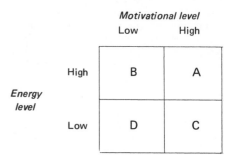

Figure 4.3. *A perspective of gifted underachievers.*

representation of gifted underachievers. Although other factors also are important, only two dimensions are shown here. Motivational level is used to denote the strength of the drive to achieve, which has resulted from the operation of social and academic value systems in the child's total environment—the community, the home, the school (usually in some combination)—and from success experiences in learning. Energy level denotes also its accompaniment, outgoingness. Mary would be illustrative of the condition in space A in the figure, as would, to a lesser extent, Oscar. Norman would fall in C or D, depending upon the time in his life when his condition was being studied. Those falling in B would be the bright, generally outgoing kind of youngster coming from situations lacking in positive motivational impact, where the adults apparently did not know what was wrong or what to do. Many of the "disadvantaged" probably would fall in D. This view of underachievement can be related to the findings of Wallach and Kogan and the observations of Haggard (above).

Remedial efforts

Given the fact of underachievement, what do we do about it? The answer depends in part upon the age levels of the underachievers. Raph, Goldberg, and Passow (1966), after an intensive study at the high school level, concluded that remedial efforts were of little value. Numerous studies of the counseling of underachievers have shown no consistent positive benefits. When confronted with the facts in Oscar's situation (above), school counselors in several mental hygiene classes understandably suggested that he should be "counseled," yet a simple manipulation of educational factors in his case quickly yielded highly positive results. This was true, too, in Mary's case.

Yet in some instances counseling—at least of a certain kind—can be helpful, as illustrated in the case of Oliver, a junior high school son of an atomic scientist, who, in spite of his very high capability, was failing in a course of general science. When asked about his poor performances on course tests, he replied that the tests were either wrong or scored incorrectly. Pressed for elaboration, he presented texts—more up-to-date than the one used in his class—by means of which he clearly demonstrated that at least certain content in the tests was not valid. Although he knew what his course text said, he just couldn't agree with it in the light of his other, rather extensive reading in the field. The counselor helped Oliver handle his problem: Oliver agreed to answer questions in his tests in terms of the basic course text, even though he didn't regard the answers as valid. He was then to star those items which were at variance with his other knowledge and indicate in a general footnote on the test paper that he was not in agreement with the answers given because of what was presented in other sources. He conformed, but with his fingers crossed. Fortunately, he had a teacher who could operate under those conditions and who himself may have learned something about the field as he checked Oliver's reasons for his disclaimers.

Underachievement often can be corrected or ameliorated by early intervention, as it was for Mary and Oscar. But when educational provisions for the gifted begin only with the sixth grade, or later—as so often is the case—the habits of underachievement already have been formed. As with tooth decay, pollution, and national inadequacy in reading, the best strategy is prevention. Even with improved effectiveness in prevention, there still will be need for some remediation, but that need can be greatly reduced.

Learning to underachieve

Underachievement cannot be attributed entirely to "poor teaching." Underachievement can occur if parents or teachers have not made effective adjustments for children who have moved to new school districts or whose schooling has been interrupted by poor health. Some gifted children underachieve because the value systems in their extra-school environments are at variance with those of the school: "Wassa matta? Ya wanna learn that stuff an be a sissy?" Family attitudes that are passive or neutral as regards school achievement are nonreinforcing to the process of learning. Underachievement patterns of bright children often spring from emotional conditions, which themselves at times result from protest against the quality and/or quantity of motivation employed by significant adults in their environs. Some gifted children underachieve as a protest against some of their elders. Despite all this, a few observers (generally unheeded) maintain that the properly effective teacher accepts his or her responsibility to be fully informed about the whole psychosocial educational picture of each child and structures each child's learning opportunities accordingly. In any event the complex picture of underachievement requires detailed analysis.

Let us examine a simplified example of a gifted ten-year-old who is underachieving. Let us assume that (1) there is no clash between the value systems of home and school, (2) he has been in an educational situation in school in which most other gifted youngsters have been reasonably effective in their achieving, (3) there is no valid evidence of "brain injury," and (4) he has or has had no physically debilitating condition which may have been contributive. Two kinds of histories of the development of the present underachievement can be conceived.

First, the child may have "stumbled" in his earlier learning, so that he did poorly academically, and as a consequence his parents and/or his teachers may show great concern about his progress. Two further possibilities now present themselves: he may find that he gets more attention by his failure than he did by doing well, or he may find that some of the adults in his world are being frustrated by his underachieving and, because of the quality of his prior relationship to them, he continues to be-

have in an underachieving manner because he feels aggressive toward them. As Haggard (1957) observed, "A child who develops marked learning problems also provides himself with an ingenious means of self-defense and of frustrating and embarrassing his parents and teachers—particularly if they place primary emphasis on intellectual achievement" (p. 403).

Another possible history of the development of underachievement, perhaps overlapping somewhat the kind just discussed, can involve an orderly progression of psychological phenomena. The underachieving child could have responded to the kind or quantity of efforts exerted by his parents or teachers to get him to achieve more effectively. He may have come to perceive his doing well as a means of satisfying the adult(s) rather than as a source of enjoyment and self-fulfillment. Or—and the two possibilities often are both operative—he may have been subjected to such incessant urging that he rebelled against what he perceived as "nagging."

Figure 4.4 may help make clear the

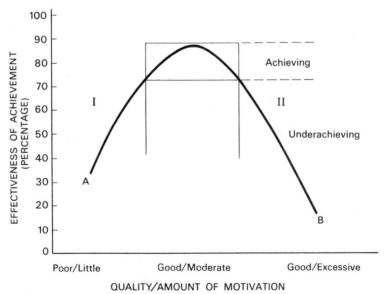

Figure 4.4. Posited interaction between motivation and achievement.

general condition we are considering. This represents only a hypothetical relationship between the effectiveness of achievement and the nature of the operative motivation. Empirical research is needed to ascertain the validity of this perception. The Y axis represents the degree of effective achievement, ranging from some probably unreal 0 percent up to an almost imaginary 100 percent. The two horizontal lines intersecting the curve AB mark off a zone representing reasonably effective achievement somewhere between 80 and 90–95 percent. The X axis represents, in effect, two continua—one for the quality of operative motivation and ranging from very poor to good, the other for the amount of operative motivation and ranging from none or very little up to excessive (nagging). The ends of the curve AB also are imaginary, points A and B being placed so as to suggest that under poor quality and little motivation more achievement may take place than under excessive motivation even of good quality. Keep in mind that what the motivator may perceive as good quality and adequate amount may be perceived by the motivatee as absurd and excessive. Even though the perceptual frame of reference is not specified or defined and the measures of amount and quality of motivation are ill delineated, Figure 4.4 does suggest one way of looking at the relationship between achievement and motivation in a molar sense.

The area designated as I denotes the kind of underachievement that was represented in cells B and D in Figure 4.3. The area designated as II denotes what we have just described—what might be designated "protest underachievement." It is important to keep in mind the psychological probability that a gifted youngster, having discovered some protest value in underachievement, may continue in his underachieving ways, thus further habituating this form of behavior.

To understand the foregoing, let us start with an imaginary youngster who, for some reason or other, is just learning to be an underachiever. He is a fourth-grader whose underachievement in reading has been identified by his conscientious teacher, Miss X. She tries everything she knows to help him become a reasonably adequate achiever, but with no success—which, of course, can be frustrating to her. His lack of recovery from his underachievement condition becomes additionally frustrating to him, either because he has become more aware of his low efficiency in reading or because her working so intensively with him has caused him to believe that he is losing status with his classmates, or both. This can affect him in two ways. He may become negatively conditioned to the subject-matter area of reading because of his lack of success in it and/or he may become negatively conditioned to Miss X because he perceives her as pestering him so much (or so ineffectively). Further generalization may then occur: he may develop a generalized aversion to other subjects and/or other teachers. The former can generalize still further to an aversion to all school learning activities, particularly those of a verbal nature; the latter may generalize still further to an aversion to all persons in an authority (or teaching) relationship to him. Such generalized aversion often occurs without the individual's being aware of what is happening.

This is not just armchair theorizing; real-life instances reveal clearly the development of this kind of progression. Fortunately, such extremes constitute a minority. Research is lacking, but clinical experience with children so "afflicted" is abundant. A generalization, supported both theoretically and experientially, is suggested: to the extent that the learner is successful in his learning experiences, to that extent he is positively conditioned to (favorably disposed toward) the area of learning activity with which such success is experienced and the person manipulating those successful learning experiences. Put more concisely, the child (or adult) who is successful in his learning tends to like what he has learned and probably will increase in his liking of the teacher who made it possible for him to succeed in learning. While the development of this idea of "attitudinal spread" has been simplified considerably here by the omission of some factors which usually are involved, the essential description is valid. Of course, what has been said applies to all children (and adults), but especially to the gifted, since so often the responsibility for their learning in the school is so largely placed upon them.

Our primary concern here has not been a review of the bits and pieces of research on the pervading phenomenon of underachievement in the gifted. Rather, the aim has been to help the reader understand the concept of underachievement—its contributing conditions, psychological components and accompaniments, and its growth history. It is particularly important to recognize that underachieving is learned and must be dealt with much the same as any learned behavior. Preventive procedures, as important and necessary as they are, can reduce the frequency and magnitude of underachievement but, human nature and society being what they are, probably won't eliminate the condition. Certainly, school personnel can be more effective by acting in the light of knowledge of the total child and the forces operating in both his intra- and extra-school life.

THE GIFTED:
A GENERAL PERSPECTIVE

The research evidence supports the conclusion that the gifted, compared as a group with the generality of the population, clearly excel in socioemotional, are at least equal in physical, and are superior in educational characteristics. Put in statistical terms, the averages of the characteristics in these areas are at least equal or superior to those for such characteristics of the general population of comparable ages—in the sense that the distributions of measures of these characteristics overlap with the distributions of such measures on the nongifted, even when the differences between the averages are significant. Such differences, found in Terman's early study of his ten- and eleven-year-olds, continue into adulthood. Possibly, because Terman's population and certain of the others may have been more selective than the total population of the gifted, the differences between the gifted and the nongifted may have been somewhat magnified, although findings regarding different subpopulations of gifted suggest clearly that the fact of such differences holds.

There remain, of course, differences among the gifted in each of the areas. Hollingworth early called attention to the fact that certain adjustmental problems could arise more frequently among the very highly gifted. Oden's contrast (1968) of the most successful and the least successful adult performances reflected differences within Terman's gifted group, although the lower group—the C group —still performed better than the generality of the adult population.

Miles (1954) suggested the caution necessary in thinking about this most capable group:

> No single responsible element in the picture has been found to block accomplishment in the gifted if a sufficient number of others are favorable. Similarly, no single favorable element has proved sufficient to insure the realization of potential ability along the many possible lines of gifted accomplishment or even along a single line (p. 1027).

The U.S. Commissioner of Education's report to the Congress in *Education of the Gifted and Talented* (Marland, 1971) observed:

> Of all human groups, the gifted and talented are the least likely to form stereotypes. Their traits, interests, capacities, and alternatives present limitless possibilities for expression; the chief impression one draws from studying groups, at either the child or adult level, is of their almost unlimited versatility, multiple talents, and countless ways of effective expression at their command (Section II, p. 4).

This sense of diversity among the gifted was expressed by Miles (1954):

> Only acquaintance with individual gifted children can create the appropriate lively sense of unduplicated human personalities, differing even in the patterns and expressions of their exceptional intellects and in other traits covering the whole wide range of constitutional and functional potentialities. . . . Thus the scientific, analytically ingenious, inventive child differs from the literary, generalizing, verbally expressive and retentive, interpretative child (p. 1022).

PEERNESS

Traditional View of "Peers"

A surprisingly large percentage of educators contend that children should be educated with their "peers." Usually this has meant that children of comparable life ages should be grouped together in order to be "taught" effectively. Interestingly, educational practice has been socially effective enough under this kind of thinking that it has been difficult to challenge. The practice of setting the age of six as the school-entering age has "worked" for the statistical reason that, since book-learning aptitude reasonably approximates a normal distribution, the large majority of the population of a given age fell closely enough around the average for that group that no general harm resulted and the "greatest good" was served.

From Figure 2.1 you can derive facts that will support this. Assuming a minimal school-entering age of 6 years 0 months, the *average* age of school-entering children will be higher than that. Let us assume, then, that this average is 6 years 3 months. The average child 6 years 3 months old will have a Binet mental age pretty close to 6 years 3 months, his Binet IQ being 100. Using Figure 2.1, you will observe that some 84 percent of a representative population will have Binet IQs of 84 or above. The approximated Binet mental age of a child 6 years 3 months old and having an IQ of 84 would be nearly 4 years 6 months. Since research has shown that children with Binet mental ages of 4 years 6 months have a pretty decent chance of engaging profitably in reading readiness activities, even those at the bottom limit of this general population of school-entering children would have a reasonable probability of benefitting discernibly from schooling.

Interestingly, educators who hold to this idea of peerness are more willing that children who give evidence of slowness to learn start their schooling a year or so later than "normal" than they are to accept fast learners a year or so early. In the case of the slow-learning youngster, some sensitivity to capacity to learn has become a factor in determining school-entering peerness; in the case of the bright youngster, chronological age has been adhered to tenaciously.

The abuse of the term "peers" in education can be attributed to two conditions. First, those loosely using it have themselves failed to recognize the need to communicate more precisely—to differentiate meaningfully in their communication. Even in much of our professional literature, the term "peers" is used when "classmates" or "agemates" would more precisely characterize the appropriate frames of reference, especially when the children under primary consideration were gifted. Second, and probably even more pervadingly, the adult decides on his own who a given child's peers are, rather than reaching such a decision on sounder psychological grounds by finding out from the child whom he perceives as his peers. Usually, the adult projects himself into the child's perceptual field—puts himself in the child's place—and this projection is at variance with what the child himself thinks or believes. Time and again, educators advise parents (who tend to agree, since they are products of the educational process) that their six-year-old with a Binet mental age of nine should be kept with his "peers," meaning other six-year-olds, even though this child may be as large, as well adjusted, as advanced in his learning, and have the same play interests as average eight-year-olds.

Relativity of Peerness

Peerness should be regarded as a highly relative concept; it varies, or should vary, with the frame of reference relative to the behavior being considered. Peerness in track events does not encompass all males and females of a given age or stature, but, rather, those whose prior performances in the respective events are within such a range as will make the competition reasonable. Peers in violin playing in an orchestra are not those who are only strong enough to handle a violin but those who have demonstrated a certain level of competency and promise in prior playing of the violin. But too often in the school classroom the primary criterion has been chronological age.

Actually, who a child's peers in school are depends upon the situation. They may be one group in art, another in physical education, another in music, and still another for academic learning

—all with some overlapping. Even in academic learning, there may, and often should be, a further differentiation in terms of reading, arithmetic, English, social studies, science, and the like, again with probable overlapping. To the extent that verbal symbol learning is the major component in any learning area, the *primary* basis for determining peerness should be level of basic learning aptitude (not IQ, unless all members of the group are of essentially the same chronological age). Once this is properly determined, the picture needs to be sharpened further in terms of relevant educational skills. Still further consideration should include characteristics such as emotionality, social adjustment, and physique. In social situations, also, mental level is an important factor.

Who were Mary's learning peers? Certainly not the younger children whom she so violently rejected. Ignoring the psychoeducational crime being perpetrated by his current teacher, were the second-graders with whom Oscar was recommended to be placed his peers? Hardly physically, since he appeared to be larger than average third-graders. Certainly not, with his reading competency at or near the sixth-grade level. Or take this youngster: a ten-year-old in the eighth grade, in a two-teacher elementary school, who had a Binet mental age of 18 and who was as large as an average fourteen-year-old. Who would be his effective peers physically, educationally, and socially? Terman early set the stage regarding the importance of mental level in pointing out that generally the interests and attitudes of those in his gifted group were more related to mental age than to chronological age, although there were differences within and between gifted youngsters. The gifted child's peers must be identified in terms of at least reasonable comparability in potential and skill in performing whatever task is to be undertaken, in compatibility of interests relevant to that task, and in emotional accommodation.

The determination of psychologically meaningful peerness is not a one-time thing, nor can it be presumed to hold across all situations, as illustrated in Peter's situation. When he was brought in at age seven by his principal, his second-grade teacher, and his parents, a question was raised as to the appropriateness of his being promoted to the third grade. His teacher thought he was a bright youngster and wondered if any special planning should be considered for him. He was comparable in size to an average third-grader. However, his teacher reported that, during recess and other free time, he played with somewhat larger youngsters who were in the fourth and fifth grades, with whom his healthily cocky and self-confident manner seemed to enable him to hold his own. Emotionally, Peter was essentially on an even keel, although he was slowly recovering from the trauma of his older brother's accidental death. Since Peter's mother was quite involved in bowling circles and his father, because he ran a tavern, didn't get home until past midnight, Peter spent much time with high school sitters—from whom, he said, he was learning "a lot."

On examination, Peter's learning aptitude level was much like that of an average eleven-year-old, and his performances on important parts of the Stanford Achievement Test were quite like those of average fifth- and sixth-graders. Since the attitudes and practices of a teacher can "make or break" the suitability of such an educational placement, the strengths and weaknesses of the teachers in the third, fourth, and fifth grades were gone over carefully with the principal. After all the factors were evaluated, it was recommended that he be placed with a fourth-grade teacher who, the principal had said, would make it possible for him to work on fifth- and sixth-grade ma-

terials with two other bright youngsters she would have. While these three youngsters did a great deal of their work as a small group, after they had done all the work required of the other fourth graders, they also participated in activities involving the whole class, contributing much enrichment. The three, on the iniative of Peter, constituted themselves, for one year, as a "map company" and made special maps for use in their and other classes—one of them a series of superimposable transparencies showing the changing cartography of Europe for five centuries.

The meaning of peerness for Peter was similarly redetermined for each of the five succeeding years. He entered the state university at age fifteen, planning to major in mathematics, and started off there by being on the honor roll.

COMMUNICATION

Peerness as a Basis

Psychologically determined peerness plays a significant role in communication. With the exception of interchanges such as "Nice day, isn't it?", "How are you?", and the like, communication takes place on a sustained basis between persons who have interests and experiences in common. These tend to be functions of the intellectual levels of those who are communicating. Communication about economics is difficult to maintain if one person can deal with it only in terms of how much it costs him to live and the other is concerned more with federal economic policies. Adults tend to gravitate into groups which communicate among themselves at mutually understandable levels. Many teachers gain much from discussions of the specifics of the methods they employ or hear about; others are less "interested" in such specifics and prefer discussions of the philosophies underlying methods. Some persons would be more "interested" in talking about the development and improvement of the gadgetry necessary to some field of science and would be completely lost, or "uninterested" in the development of formulae by means of which to describe basic phenomena in that area. As pointed out earlier, one is "interested" in an area to the extent that he is competent in it.

A parallel condition exists with respect to children. With the exception of play activities in which there is primarily a physical component—riding a scooter, running, or wrestling, for instance—the play activities in which they engage and the youngsters with whom they play are heavily determined by their levels of mental development. Young bright children tend to play with older average children, if they have the opportunity, because they are more nearly at the same mental levels. Older, mentally slow, children tend to play with younger children, unless they accept some supportive role, because of the comparability of their mental levels. In leisure reading, such differences are even more apparent.

Communication among the Gifted

It is important to consider the phenomenon of communication with respect to the gifted from two interrelated points of view. First, the bulk of sustained communication between and among persons —children or adults—tends to occur between or among individuals who are comparable intellectually—who have comparable symbol supplies and abilities to manipulate those symbols. There is no justification in regarding this observation as snobbish; it is only a statement of psychosocial fact. Generally, the underlying idea is cloaked in terms of peoples' common interests, but these interests, as has

been pointed out, are themselves determined by conceptual capabilities.

A second aspect of communication with respect to the gifted involves a premise not yet stated: a primary factor in determining the adjustment of an individual is his positive interpersonal relationships. "Maladjustment" is accompanied by impairment of such relationships, the most extreme form of which involves the complete withdrawal of the individual from personal interaction; "therapy" involves the reestablishment of positive interpersonal relationships, first between the maladjusted person and his therapist and later, by the process of generalization, between the less maladjusted person and others in his environment. Communication is the primary ingredient in interpersonal relationships, whether in the form of gestures, signs, or postures (more at a perceptual or low-conceptual level) or in the form of verbal or other symbols which are facilitative to higher-level conceptual interchange. Put more simply, the socioemotional adjustment of the gifted is helped by their being able, but not necessarily at all times confined, to communicate meaningfully with others of comparable, but not identical, kind.

A very real danger in thinking and acting in terms of this principle is that it may be overgeneralized—construed in such a manner as to grossly alienate the gifted from the rest of society. Such fear generally is involved when persons oppose any grouping of bright youngsters for educational purposes, their contention being that the gifted will lose the common touch. Such has not been the typical outcome of such educational arrangements, although some communication gaps actually have been created by teachers and parents, almost as if intentionally. When schools generally fail to identify and provide effectively for their gifted children and then do make some special provision for only an occasional bright child who has, in some manner or other, made himself visible, they are very effectively forcing such an outstanding child into isolation. Unless compensatory efforts are well exerted, the communication gap between such a child and his classmates can be increased.

Isolation of the Gifted

Two factors have helped deprive the gifted of nurturant communication possibilities. First, the gifted themselves constitute only a small percentage of the total population, and the brighter they are, the fewer there are of them. The ten-year-old with a Binet IQ which is one out of 1000 could be the only one that bright in an entire elementary school; often he has only a few others with mental ages of 15 (his learning capability peers) with whom he could, if permitted, interact conceptually. If, second, the school makes little or no provision for such fruitful interaction among the gifted or between them and their schoolmates, further alienation tends to result. In such cases, such a bright child can withdraw, sit back on his intellectual haunches, perhaps proceed with his learning to be an underachiever, just bide his time in school until he gets home where he can do the things in which he is interested. Or else he can openly, and usually blindly, rebel against a system that is making intellectual life unfruitful for him.

Relevant behaviors of the gifted often have been described, but the pattern of such noncommunication has been little researched. Roe (1952), in her intensive study of outstanding scientists, observed, "These men indicated that they had quite specific and strong feelings of personal isolation as children. They felt different or apart in some way." As two of her scientists observed, "I have always

felt like a minority member" and "I was always lonesome." Social scientists saw their problem thus: "The family was essentially ostracized" and "We developed forms of living which were different from those around us."

Clark's (1971) description of Einstein's early behavior also is illustrative. Einstein did not speak fluently until the age of nine. Was the reason slow development—or was it a lack of adequate rewarding communication experiences? The rigid educational procedures he encountered in the Gymnasium at Luitpold contributed to his deep antagonism to educational authority in particular, later generalizing to a general challenging of accepted belief. In reminiscing, he regarded that educational experience as a "negation of the human being." He found some escape in relating to Max Talmey, a young Jewish medical student. He was expelled from his Gymnasium with the observation, "Your presence in the class is disruptive and affects the other students." After going to Berne, at the age of 23, he and two of his students formed a small group, the "Olympian Academy," which provided informally the opportunities for explorations and discussions in the area of physics and mathematics, which he so much wanted. It is not unreasonable to assume that the communication gap between Einstein and most of those with whom he studied and worked was the basis for the observation about him, "Prickly arrogance appears increasingly throughout his student years." Even his free-flowing hair style was recognized as a manifestation of his rebellion against his fellow students and most of his instructors, with whom he was unable to communicate and who therefore perceived him as arrogant.

If we think of communication in the general context which has been presented, we can understand Hollingworth's (1942) observation that gifted children in the Binet IQ range of 130 to 150 have better possibilities of relating to the group, since there are more of them and they are less different from their agemates, whereas, as the IQs increase, assuming the same chronological ages, the possibilities for impaired communication increase. Her two categories of maladjustment—"suffering fools gladly" and tending to be isolated in interests and goals, should seem quite comprehensible in terms of the communication phenomenon. It takes considerable accommodation to establish a harmony between the walking pattern of a five-foot-tall youngster and that of his three-and-a-half-foot agemate. If the five-footer does not adapt his pace to that of his shorter friend, he soon is out far ahead, at least spatially alienated; if he does adapt to his shorter friend's pace, he must restrain himself, thereby being able to go less far. Bright children whose communication channels are restricted or grossly impaired because of a lack of reasonable reciprocity of conceptual levels have the social and educational cards stacked against them. The implications of the communication phenomenon are of major educational import.

MOTIVATION

This section will examine the nature of the phenomenon called motivation, first as regards all children, and then indicating aspects of particular importance to the gifted. An understanding of the nature of motivation can contribute much not only to the social effectiveness and self-fulfillment of the gifted but also to an awareness of the nature of society's responsibility in nurturing and capitalizing upon it. We shall concern ourselves with motivation primarily in children, recognizing that motivation in adults is the result of further elaboration along the lines established in childhood.

Teachers and parents comment that their children are "motivated" to do well in school, are not so "motivated," or that some children are "motivated" in some areas but not in others. Some adults reach the point of throwing up their hands in despair, saying "I just can't get anywhere with him because he just doesn't want to do anything." How did such a child get that way? Is this state of affairs the fault of the child or is it the result of how his adults have handled his learning experiences, or "taught" him, or both? To anticipate a bit, the "fault" lies fundamentally and primarily with the significant others in the child's environment.

"Inner Drives"

One encounters in the literature, particularly that of the novelists, allusions to "inner drives" and the roles they are presumed to play in determining the individual's pursuit of some line of endeavor. Many regard the early manifestations of interest and sustained activity along specific lines, especially in the cases of gifted children, as attributable to such inner drives. Karl Witte was proficient in several languages at the age of nine. Haydn has been reported as playing and composing at the age of six. William Cullen Bryant was writing poetry by the age of eight. By the age of five, Einstein was challenged by the action of the needle in the compass which his father had given him, and at the age of seven he became interested in playing the violin. Since the antecedents to such early manifestation of interest and sustained involvements have been little studied and are essentially unknown, it is understandable that such behavior would be attributed to some sort of inner drive.

It seems reasonable to regard such behavior as manifestations of the tendency of the organism initially to be outgoing —to press into its environment and thus to react to the stimuli there—a basic characteristic of organisms described earlier. Whether the direction this outgoingness takes is due more to some biologically determined condition or to the nature of environmental stimulation is not known, but the position is taken here that the latter should be accorded the greater weight. This basic tendency of the organism to be outgoing—to press into its environment rather than just "wait" to be stimulated—seems to be the initial "given." The particular patterns of behavior which ensue are determined by the nature of the positively reinforcing stimuli that impinge upon the organism.

If one takes the position that motivation is basically inner-determined, it can be perceived as a manifestation of this initial amorphous outgoingness. Some do this, in large part totally absolving themselves, or society, of responsibility for its cultivation or nurturance. Motivation thus came to be regarded as an autonomous, self-initiating, and self-maintaining drive for which some inherent biological condition was presumed. Such reasoning, however comforting it may be to the adults who encounter children who have "no motivation" to learn, either generally or specifically, omits from consideration certain important psychological variables and principles. In order to bring these into proper perspective, we shall now look more closely at motivation.

What Motivation Is

Motivation is taken to denote the operation of conditions, either outside or within the individual, which are conducive to his responding in certain ways, or which dispose him to react in certain ways. Usually, motivation is regarded as getting the individual to "want" to do something, as when therapists try to cause seriously maladjusted clients to "want" to relate to other persons, or when teachers try to get their pupils to "want" to do better academically, to "want" to learn. Granting even the basic tendency of the individual to be outgoing, two kinds of conditions need to be identified here: (1) those in which stimuli are brought to bear on the individual in order to get him to "employ" that outgoingness in responding in a certain way—his response being mostly or entirely a reaction to such externally applied stimuli, and (2) those in which the individual, on his own and largely or totally in the absence of such external motivating stimuli, reacts in the desired manner. In this latter case, the conditions immediately predisposing to such action are regarded as residing within the individual.

Implicit, under either kind of motivation, is the individual's evaluating what he has done. In the former kind the individual—child or adult—does his evaluating in terms of the expectations, or standards, of the others whom he desires to please. In the latter kind, the individual either has learned (internalized) the standards of others or he himself perceives the task to be well done—the arithmetic problem checks, his drawing is regarded by him as sufficiently representative or symbolic of his model, the elements of the situation interrelate so as to make a logically intact concept or functioning whole, and the like.

Extrinsic motivation

The first kind of condition is denoted by the term "extrinsic motivation." Note its operation in the following instances. The five-year-old firmly refuses to accompany the examiner into a testing room when his mother suggests that he "go with the man and play some games." However, when she gives him a nickel, he does so with alacrity. A child is proud of her spelling paper with 100 percent marked on it when her mother praises her for getting a higher mark than did a neighbor's child. A child is proud of his high average in school, or ashamed of his low average, primarily because of the reaction of his parents to such marks. A student wants to do well in college primarily because his parents will be pleased with such a performance. The major common element in these situations is that the child attempts to do well as a means of achieving favorable recognition from others—his parents, his teachers, his classmates. The mechanic does a good job primarily because his boss demands it, and not because of his pride in workmanship.

Intrinsic motivation

The second kind of condition is denoted by the term "intrinsic motivation." Here, the individual does well, or tries to do well, primarily because he enjoys the activity in which he is engaged. He learns and knows as he goes along when he is doing well—the problem checks out, the paragraph "makes sense," the motor functions properly. In the words of some, he has internalized standards for acceptable performance. The major component here is his own enjoyment in performing; that others look with favor upon his performing well is secondary in, though not necessarily absent from, his system of values. The more he succeeds in performing, whether in terms of verification processes inherent in his act (the problem checks out) or in terms of some external criterion (someone says the task is well done), the more such successful behavior is positively reinforcing to his self-motivated performance and the more it conduces to later similar self-valued

performance. Whether he continues with an identified interest or branches out into some area about which he is curious, his behavior is as though it is self-determined or self-directed, and it becomes increasingly autonomous in nature.

Since it is so desirable that the members of our society—children and adults —function in terms of intrinsic motivation and since many do not, it is necessary to consider how intrinsic motivation comes about, how children and adults learn to be self-motivated. Intrinsic motivation must be regarded as essentially an end-product of learning, the initial ingredient of which is the organism's original tendency to be outgoing, this then being shaped by reinforcement, which in turn leads to extrinsic motivation. In the learning progression, extrinsic motivation precedes intrinsic motivation but by no means assures it. The psychological phenomenon of generalization figures importantly in this progression from outgoing behavior to intrinsically motivated behavior, and the social and educational implications of this progression and interaction are of great importance.

We must back up briefly to the early manifestation of outgoingness and recognize that it may be encouraged or reinforced by means of positive stimulation, or responses having a positive effect on the infant, or it may be discouraged by the infant's having negative or unpleasant experiences when it is manifested. Continuing to be outgoing or becoming more so or less so—these seem to be the infant's range of reactions to his environment. Fortunately, our society is such and/or the nature of the infant is such that the overall picture of infants and young children is one of generally sustained outgoingness. As the child grows, he learns which of his behaviors evoke positive responses to himself from the significant others in his environment. In this process, his behavior is being extrinsically motivated. Most parents and teachers make apparent to their children that the children's behaviors have been pleasing to the adults, thus reinforcing such adult-pleasing behaviors.

It is interesting—and perhaps disturbing to some—to note that young children generally express desires to do things for themselves, thus giving early evidence of the operation of an intrinsic motivational tendency. This is manifested in regard to specific acts, as distinct from an amorphous outgoingness. However, society tends generally to restrain or curb such expressions of independence and almost to force the young child to go through the stage of extrinsic motivation before he can return, if he is lucky, to that of intrinsic motivation.

Bear in mind that such generalization can take place without being put into words. Very young children don't have either the words or the concepts by means of which "consciously" to verbalize their generalizations. Older persons often generalize behaviorally without being "aware"—without verbalizing—that they are doing so. Children, in learning to do things to please their significant others, thus may generalize "unconsciously" so that behaving in that manner becomes a typically other-oriented way of life. This can become a dominant factor in their value systems. The child who consistently does only the ten assigned problems or who draws the map only to please the teacher, and the skilled workman—carpenter, plumber, electrician—who does his work typically only to satisfy his foreman or to get by, are of a kind.

But some parents and teachers recognize the psychologically cramping and crippling effect of such a generalized behavior pattern and seek as early as they can and in whatever ways they can to get children to do things on their own, to "set their own standards," to be self-critical of their performances. This involves the adults' accepting the inevitability of the stage of extrinsic motivation and moving at every plausible opportunity from that antecedent condition to one in which the child seems to do things "on his own," to do things for himself, to enjoy the act of doing. Generalization is taking place as he moves toward internalizing standards in terms of which he evaluates what he has done or is doing. To the extent that generalization takes place in this type of situation, the child becomes intrinsically motivated. The child who, on his own, reads the extra essay, newspaper item, or story because he is "interested" in it and likes doing it, and the skilled motor repairman who adjusts the engine so that it runs just right because he takes pride in his work, are of a kind.

Generalization of Motivation

Some illustrations should help make clear that two kinds of generalization are discernible with respect to the acquisition of both extrinsic and intrinsic motivational tendencies. Let us assume that child A does predominantly well, receiving a preponderance of positive over negative reinforcement from his significant others for doing so. This can occur, for instance, in some academic area (reading, arithmetic, English, handwriting) or in the self-care and maintenance area (feeding, washing, bathing, cleaning his teeth, keeping his room clean), or in behaving in a socially acceptable manner in his relations to others (children, neighbors, parents, teachers, strangers). The generalization, whether in terms of trying to please others by doing well or later in terms of the intrinsic enjoyment of doing well, may occur in regard to only one such kind of behavior, leading to characterizations such as: "He's such a well-behaved child, even though he seems not to like school," or "He works like a beaver in English, but he certainly isn't interested in arithmetic," or "She turns out the best handwriting in the class, but just doesn't seem motivated in reading." Such a child has generalized *within* types of situations. Some children may be highly intrinsically motivated in certain kinds of behavior and also be badly in need of some simple extrinsic motivation in other learning areas (probably thereby reflecting the value systems in their environs). Then let us assume that we have child B who does a variety of things well under either extrinsic or intrinsic motivation. He washes his face acceptably, he cleans up his room adequately, he writes legibly, he pets the dog instead of kicking it, and he does his work well in all (or most of) his school subjects. This child has generalized *across* situations, either in terms of sustained "need" for extrinsic motivation or in terms of a disposition to function under intrinsic motivation.

Still recognizing that we are thinking in terms of either extrinsic or intrinsic motivation, the generalization(s) in the case of child B are broader, encompassing or operative in a number of areas of behavior rather than being limited to a single area of behavior, as in the case of child A. In the cases of both children, the generalizations are results of learning, even though most of the "teaching" may have been incidental or unwitting. The gifted will be disposed to generalize across situations.

Transition to Intrinsic Motivation

The learning transition from extrinsic to intrinsic motivation is neither smooth nor rapid and easily observable. It is one to which increasingly subtle positive reinforcement needs to be applied at psychologically opportune moments. But the transition should be an ever-present objective. Nothing is so positively reinforcing as experience of success in learning. To say of elementary school children that they are "academically motivated" may mean either that they are responding adaptively to certain kinds of extrinsic motivation or that they are having successful learning experiences and are beginning to operate under intrinsic motivation. To say that certain elementary school children just aren't "motivated" to learn is to admit psychoeducational defeat or unproductivity because the youngsters haven't had a preponderance of successful learning experiences over their unsuccessful school experiences and haven't been helped to make this important transition.

Some tests purport to measure the generalized "need" to achieve, or motivation. This characteristic usually is represented by "n-Ach" in the research literature, and the measure is construed to reflect the individual's overall strength of motivation—not being limited to the strength of motivation in the academic area. Used mainly with respect to older pupils and college students, a high n-Ach score indicates only that the individual has said that he does or will work hard to achieve his goals; it does not necessarily differentiate between the individual's being extrinsically or intrinsically motivated. While what the majority of persons say they do or will do reasonably well agrees with what they actually do, or will do, some persons paint better-than-real pictures of themselves—an interesting manifestation of extrinsic motivation.

Care must be exercised to differentiate between evidences of energy and other external manifestations and what is validly reflective of motivation. Some youngsters pursue their lines of interest with quite evident physical activity, even to the extent of giving the adults in their environment, who themselves may not be actively disposed, an impression of hyperactivity, even though there may be no physiological condition conducive to such excessive physical activity. The concern of such adults actually may reinforce such activity to such an extent that it becomes grossly disruptive to the child's effective functioning as well as to those around him. Other youngsters may have learned that such behavior, and even squinting and brow-furrowing ("intellectual grunting"), may have been interpreted by adults as indicative of intensive commitment to tasks. As a result, such children manifest such behaviors in order to create the impression that they are highly motivated in their work. Some adults, unfortunately, construe such evidence of extrinsic motivation to indicate intrinsic motivation.

The concept of motivation has been dealt with as being either extrinsic or intrinsic. It should be clear that the individual—child or adult—does not always behave only the one way or the other. Even when the individual reaches the stage at which he generally is perceived as intrinsically motivated, there remains some residual sensitivity to extrinsic motivation. The child who attains high status on an academic honor role primarily as a result of his intrinsic motivation still is sensitive to his being highly regarded by the significant others in his milieu, although in some instances he may manifest disdain for such status as a means of retaining social acceptance by his classmates or his agemates—itself evidence of some extrinsic motivation. The musician, sculptor, or scientist who has been completely immersed in the self-realizing activity of achieving a major accomplishment is not totally insensitive to the public acclaim it later may receive. The relative roles played by extrinsic and intrinsic motivation vary with the situation. The public official may take stands that he believes will get him votes (extrinsic motivation) or he may take stands that are based primarily upon his fundamental philosophy or social convictions regardless of their vote-getting possibilities (intrinsic motivation), and he may in his personal life be primarily extrinsically or intrinsically motivated.

Motivation of the Gifted

Motivation has been considered at such length partly to set the psychological stage but mostly because it is so contributive to the self-fulfillment and social effectiveness of the gifted. Certain aspects have particular significance. We just don't know, in spite of the novelists, whether very young gifted children early manifest marked intrinsic motivation as the result of some inherent characteristic, or whether they merely learn very quickly to progress from extrinsic to intrinsic motivation, or whether their parents only accede more fully when they independently undertake some line of endeavor. We just don't know whether the particular foci of their highly motivated behavior (music, graphic art, scientific bent) result from any genetic predisposition, from some particular kind and quality of nurturance, or from some interaction of the two. That a few very early have performed outstandingly is a matter of record, for which we can at least be grateful. But for the bulk of the gifted population it seems reasonable psychologically to proceed in terms of the kind of developmental picture described here.

Two things are crystal clear regarding the gifted's learning to be motivated. The characteristic that most clearly differentiates the gifted from the nongifted is their relatively superior capacity to abstract, see relationships, and generalize. This being the case, one would expect the gifted to generalize more quickly, whether with respect to a susceptibility to and use of extrinsic motivation or with respect to a disposition toward and enjoyment of intrinsic motivation. Add to this the fact that the gifted need fewer instances on the basis of which to generalize and the fact that they tend to respond to, see relationships among, and generalize on the basis of more subtle cues, or stimuli, and you have a population that one would expect to be quite responsive to the nurturance of either kind of motivation. The tendency of the gifted to be impatient with perceptual "loose ends," to press consistently toward fuller "psychological packaging" or the amplification and rounding out of conceptual structures or entities, should contribute toward their being basically more disposed toward the acquisition of intrinsic motivational tendencies than toward being satisfied with extrinsic motivation. Yet many gifted underachievers, especially the older ones, have, in effect, been arrested at the extrinsic motivation stage.

While part of our problem involves gifted youngsters who have learned, under one kind or other of motivation, to achieve, it seems that the larger problem, if we will but face it, lies with the gifted who have learned not to achieve, whose motivational picture has been unproductive educationally and socially. Certainly, to the extent that the self-fulfillment of the gifted is accepted as a goal for our endeavors for them, intrinsic motivation should be a major component in their educational pictures. Whether the gifted generalize quickly in terms of extrinsic motivation or of intrinsic motivation must be recognized as the responsibility of the significant others in their lives, and thus a major responsibility of the school personnel with whom they do so much of their learning. The problem of their much-researched underachievement in school must be perceived in this light. Whether the gifted perceive the others in their lives as ones *for* whom they perform in order to be accepted or as ones *with* whom they enjoy working because they find such activity self-rewarding will determine to a large degree the effectiveness of the social roles they will play as adults. That we aspire for them a condition of highly autonomous, intrinsically motivated performance need not imply that they are being socially alienated, because for the most part there remain residuals of extrinsic motivation. For some very few of the gifted, however, perhaps even this residual should not be encouraged or demanded because such a sensitivity of itself may be restrictive of their production or creativity.

SUMMARY

Defined as the top 5 to 8 percent of the total public school population in terms of learning aptitude, the gifted clearly excel also in the adequacy of their social-emotional adjustment and educational performance, and evidence in the area of physical characteristics suggests the possibility of some superiority here too. Compared with the average of their age-mates in childhood and adulthood, the gifted have more and wider-ranging interests. Although the kinds of cognitive styles discernible in their behavior may be universal, they manifest them to greater degrees and in richer ways, owing largely to the nature of the major component in giftedness. Their creative behavior has had a particular and re-awakened appeal to educators. Both in perceptions by others and in their self-perceptions, their social and emotional adjustments are of a superior quality, although exceptions to this generality are highly publicized.

Some have questioned evidence that the gifted also are superior physically, owing to a lack of sound comparative studies. Yet the fact that they are taller and heavier than the norms for their agemates cannot be ignored. Whether their superiority in general health is attributable primarily to genetic determiners, to a superior capability of their parents and of themselves, or to some combination of these conditions is not clear.

In spite of their being the relatively most educationally retarded group, their absolute educational superiority essentially has been apparent. However, their relative underachievement—the fact that many of them tend to perform noticeably below their individual capabilities, with an attendant failure of self-fulfillment and ultimate social loss—calls for preventive efforts on the part of the schools and an understanding of the importance of this condition by parents.

Three conditions play major roles in influencing the psychological characteristics of the gifted. The *perception of peerness* by most educators, and by many parents who themselves are products of education, calls for psychological evaluation, because it is in terms of chronological peerness rather than developmental level peerness and is adult-projected rather than child-determined. *Problems of communication,* among the gifted as well as between the gifted and the nongifted, have tended to be ignored and/or misperceived. *Motivational factors* have been either superficially recognized or faultily dealt with in helping the gifted progress from dependent, other-oriented extrinsic motivation to autonomous intrinsic motivation.

The overall psychological picture of the gifted is fundamentally one of great social promise. The general superior potential which characterizes them must not, however, blind us to the considerable differences among individuals within the group. The special problems which such differences between the gifted and the nongifted pose call not for forcing the gifted into the mold of the average but for socially wise and psychologically sound differential treatment in the light of such differences. What is promise also is challenge, and the primary social agencies responsible for meeting that challenge are the school and the home.

5

Philosophical considerations

The bulk of the literature regarding the gifted has been concerned with the description of educational provisions being tried for them and with the recounting of research findings on them, little consideration being given to the relationship between such manifestations of interest and action and any philosophy of education. The indexes of seven representative texts on the gifted, for instance, carry no references to the term "philosophy": Bentley (1937), Witty (1951), De Haan and Havighurst (1957), Abraham (1958), Durr (1964), Gallagher (1964), and Hildreth (1966). Freehill's (1961) text discusses it briefly in connection with his fuller treatment of curriculum and educational methods. Everett (1961) has two chapters—one by himself and one by Kilpatrick—addressed to the matter, while French's (1964) book of 43 readings includes one reading bearing rather directly on philosophic aspects and one implicitly relevant. Ward (1961), however, devoted his book specifically to implications of educational philosophy with respect to learning by the gifted.

Crucial to planning for, introduction of, and operation of any sound educational provisions or program for the gifted is a full realization of the importance of the philosophical undergirdings of such effort. Time and again, "programs" for the gifted have been concocted and imposed in schools or school systems, and some even have been "democratically" developed and inaugurated by school personnel and parents, which have failed quickly because of an absence, or impoverishment, of valid and relevant philosophic essence. Like faultily nurtured, hothoused plants, even though they attracted attention at the moment, they withered and died in the outdoor weather of educational and social reality. One easily could contend that potentially fruitful efforts at making special provisions for the gifted have failed more because of faulty or inadequate philosophic grounding than because of inadequate funding.

This chapter will explore the area of educational philosophy as the backdrop for any sound planning for the education of the gifted. Then—after defining "education"—we shall consider whether there is, or need be, an educational philosophy for the gifted. Certain overriding generalizations regarding society and the individual which must be recognized in making education effective will be discussed briefly. Such a background will help us later to evaluate certain educational considerations in terms of the extent to which they are philosophically tenable.

A PHILOSOPHY OF EDUCATION

Essentially, an educational philosophy is a superordinate integrated system of principles in terms of which education can be perceived, its aims or goals identified or specified, and on the basis of which the natures of learning experiences can be identified and actualized. It is a studied integration of social ideals and aspirations and of current knowledge. Thus it is, or should be, reflective of sensitivities both to political, social, and economic aspects or conditions of the environment and to the biological and psychological natures of individuals. While it has integrity as of any given period of time, it must, if it is to be viable, be subject to ongoing modification to meet the inevitably changing situations to which it is presumed to be applicable. The more truly superordinate the principles within such a system

are, the less susceptible to such changes they tend to be.

The paramount purpose of a philosophy of education is to identify the conceptual setting in which education is expected to occur. Progressing from such a general characterization to more specific purposes, such philosophy makes possible the identification of the goals of the educative process. We can then define education in terms of these two stages in the progression. Certain less general principles of education, presumed to be conducive to the attaining of these goals, are then derived. Moving to the still more specific, and at least implicitly in harmony with the principles of education, we can delineate what the content of education should be and identify the methods which are relevant to those principles and contributive to the attainment of the identified goals.

Dewey's (1916) characterization of education as a reconstruction or reorganization of experience which adds to the meaning of experience and which increases ability to direct the course of subsequent experiences has been widely recognized. Elaborated as a process of continuous reconstruction of experience with the purpose of widening and deepening its social content, at the same time enabling the individual to gain control of the methods involved, it identifies the major perpectives in terms of which Dewey perceived education to involve ongoingness, social orientation, and learning to learn. The last aspect is reflected nicely in Henry James' observation: "What one knows is, in youth, of little moment: They know enough who know how to learn."

If we take as an imaginary "principle" the statement, "Children have a right to be reared in good health," we have a generality which could be contributive to the definition of the role of some agency in society. Social action in the light of such a general commitment would necessitate an adaptation or sharpening of the statement in terms of current knowledge about nutrition and in regard to possible differences between boys and girls, between four-year-olds and fifteen-year-olds, between Orientals and Occidentals, among socioeconomic levels, and the like. Adaptations, or sharpened specifications, still within the general context of such a principle, may be needed for different individuals. At such points as these, we begin to move into the implementation area of methods. Putting this kind of thinking into an educational perspective, whether Johnny is praised or punished for his learning performance is a matter of method, although the use of either method may be justified on the basis of some principle regarding the use of reinforcement in connection with the learning process. Statements concerning implementation are not philosophy, although they should stem from philosophy.

Dewey's characterization of learning can, in fact, be regarded as just as applicable in a totalitarian society as in a democratic society, requiring only the properly adaptive definition or delineation of key words in the statement. In the United States we are committed to a democratic perspective. Such being the case, we need to take care, as Burton (1934, p. 172) pointed out, lest we confuse the term democracy "with egalitarianism, with majority rule, with social conformity, with individualism, and even with paternalism or socialism."

Certain "givens" associated with a philosophy of education warrant consideration. We have noted that it must reflect a sensitivity both to the facts of the social milieu within which it is to be operative and to what is known about the individual in terms of whose interests it is to be perceived. Given the sensitivity to the total situation, there necessarily is some ensuing indication of what is desired both for the society and for the individual.

Some Seeming Paradoxes

The statement of a philosophy of education usually results in the identification of certain seeming paradoxes which must be resolved in its implementation. At least the following five constitute such challenges.

Generality–specificity

The statement of a philosophy is general, yet it must at least connote specifics. It must be global, yet it must be sensitive—or provide for a sensitivity—both to geographically provincial conditions (as regards factors such as rural-urban, advantaged-disadvantaged, and different ethnic needs) and to conceptually "provincial" conditions (as regards such specific matters as motivation, learning demands in specific learning areas, and unique problems/needs at different developmental levels). While philosophy is by its very nature necessarily most general, in its ramifications and implications greater specificity is manifested.

Social focus–individual concern

A philosophy of education is necessarily developed and promulgated in terms of what is perceived to be "the good of society"; a philosophy of education must be stated in terms of, or even committed to, the good of the individual. Should education be perceived primarily in terms of social good, or should its pressing concern or focus be the individual?

Basically, educational philosophizing occurs within a total social milieu which involves some combination of a more encompassing philosophizing regarding what is "good for man" and political philosophizing regarding the role which man should play in determining the nature of the society in which he is to live. Even committed as we are to a democratic position, the question arises as to the primacy of concern—whether one's first thought should be "Is it good for society?" or "Is it good for the individual?" Usually this is reconciled by taking the view that if individuals are "educated" in certain ways, the end result will be a bettered society. Is it good for society, and therefore good for each individual, for each child to have learned certain multiplication tables by eight o'clock on Wednesday? Is it good for society, and therefore good for each child, that he be required to march quietly in line into the school building at the opening of school or after recess? After all, some contend, that's the way traffic operates on streets and highways.

Control–freedom

Related to the society-individual "dilemma" is the concern about the relative values to be attached to control and to freedom. To many, in order that a society be "good" (meaning develop and progress in the manner they prefer), control of those in it must be exercised. This is anathema to those who contend that the components of society—individuals, organizations, institutions—should be allowed complete freedom to progress or develop in their own socially emergent manners because, these advocates maintain, whatever "society" results under such conditions will be the "good society." We see these views reflected politically, claimed economically, and preached educationally in our country. On the one hand, some states and school districts prescribe rather precisely the educational content, practices, and methods to be followed, whereas others tolerate and may even encourage their subunits in making their own decisions

and following their own procedures on such matters.

Included here, too, is the problem of the extent to which the learnings of children are to be controlled—whether the adult, who "knows best," should determine what is to be learned and when it is to be learned, or whether such responsibility—or opportunity—should rest with the child. On the one hand, the child is seen as being expected to learn "the wisdom of the race," usually construed to be limited to the acquisition or mastery of whatever content adults have identified. By contrast, others contend that the child himself should do what learning he wants to do, in whatever sequence he sees fit. Those opposing this latter position make the point that children in their relatively short life spans, even into adulthood, will be unable to discover for themselves what the human race has taken so long to learn. Subsumable under this kind of thinking are the contrasting contentions that the adult is responsible for seeing to it that the self-realization goal for children has to be controlled—planned for, programmed, and implemented—by the adults, as contrasted with the belief that children, on their own, will grow and develop in such a manner that self-realization will result.

The contrast between the poles of social conformity-personal freedom is most sharply seen in terms of the extremes in which the holders of the one position characterize the educational and social products of the other. The anti-conformity advocates fear a horrifyingly planned world—either as represented in *Brave New World,* which provides, in its own way, for differences among individuals, or as represented by the kind of social conformity exemplified and implied in *The Organization Man.* On the other hand, the social conformists quake at the social chaos that they envision as possible, if not inevitable, if each person is completely free to determine his lines of action, since the concept of complete freedom logically admits of no sensitivity to the rights of others in the group. In effect, then, patterned performance is contrasted with pandemonium.

Stability–change

Philosophically, education must be conceived in terms of its contributing to social stability, yet a full sensitivity to the inevitability of change must be incorporated. While man's progress over the ages has given evidence of some change, over relatively long periods of time it has been characterized more by constancy. Therefore, education has been regarded by many as a preparation for a status quo. Opponents of this view contend that such education is unreal, since it tends to make for a rigid, nonadaptive kind of living and fails to recognize that the only thing that is constant is change. The spirit of this condition is reflected in the cartoon below.

Predictability–unpredictability

Somewhat relatable conceptually to the above is the seeming paradox of predictability–unpredictability. At one extreme is the conviction that children should be educated so as to be aware that events are predictable, given an adequate delineation of the antecedents of those events. Oversimplified, this has been taken to mean that, given the condition or phenomenon A, B will follow. This resulted, for instance, in the conviction that stimulus A would evoke response B, which later became liberalized by the recognition that response B was evoked by some combination of stimuli rather than by a single stimulus. But there remained the seeming one-to-one relationship which served as the basis for prediction. Early science rested upon such an assumption. Man went forward backward on the basis of such reasoning; older historians advocated the study of their field in order that man could discover that conditions A, B, C, and so on followed, and therefore were caused

TODAY'S AVANT IS TOMORROW'S PASSE

"It's the one thing that sustains him."

(Drawing by Dana Fradon; © 1971 The New Yorker Magazine, Inc.)

by, their antecedent conditions, thus enabling man, when he discovered such conditions in his society, to predict the outcomes and therefore to take steps either to further such sequencing or to prevent it. On closer examination of phenomena, however, such precise predictability was found not to be possible, leading to the initial generalization that nothing was predictable (except death and taxes, as Benjamin Franklin pointed out in 1789).

Earlier the concept of predictability was perceived and used in an absolutistic sense. Then predictability came to connote probability rather than inevitability. As the complexity of phenomena came increasingly to be recognized in both the "causes" and the "effects," the term predictability came to denote "the chances are" that some B will follow some A, and the relationship designated by the words "tends to," as in the statement, "Children tend to learn better under positive motivation than under negative motivation." The words "tends to" suggested a range of likelihood, from the expectancy that B was more likely than not to follow A to the expectancy that B was highly likely to follow A. Other developments contributed to the attenuation of the absolutistic position: the disconcerting discovery of the ephemeral nature of "facts,"[1] the increasing use of probabalistic statistical approaches in describing relationships among phenomena, and the development of the phenomenological view which placed emphasis on "reality" as that which the individual perceived it to be—a highly relativistic position.

There remains a too-common tendency to proceed simplistically with respect to such seeming impasses—some firmly holding to the one extreme, others to the other. Such persons operate as though these possibilities were dichotomies, as though they were black and white. This kind of perceptual thinking is discernibly different from a more meaningful conceptualization of the extreme positions in the paradoxes which were mentioned in terms of their being ends of continua. (There is a probability that acceptance of the first-mentioned in any of the pairs that have been identified would be accompanied by acceptance of the first-mentioned of the other pairs, and vice versa.) A commitment to any of the extremes would be grossly undesirable, but the history of education in this country is replete with examples of the taking of such extreme positions. It would be only perceptual and sophomoric to attempt to decide which of the extremes of any of the pairs is the better or more desirable. Education well can be thought of in the light of both extremes, in each case, but with some kind of accommodation. More tenable would be the recognition that what is called for is the decision as to how much of which, where, and when—realizing that the nature of the "mix" very well may need to vary from situation to situation.

Unfortunately, educators—and they are not alone in this regard—have demonstrated a disturbing tendency to commit themselves to only one point of view at a time, reflecting an almost total unawareness, the while, of other equally meritorious points of view. Witness such all-out commitments to such as these: the teaching of the "fundamentals," the teaching of the "whole child," practices in grouping pupils for instructional purposes, the teaching for "adjustment," the

---

[1] The story is told of the graduate student who appreciatively and adoringly told his major professor how indebted he felt for his having been taught so much in the professor's class. The professor sought to tone things down a bit by pointing out that half of what the student had been taught already had been found not to be true. The student insisted on expressing his appreciation by saying that he had gained at least that much. The professor sighed and replied, "Yes, but I don't know which half is true."

use of the "discovery" method, remedial reading, group testing, the phonetic teaching of reading, and many others. Each of these had inherent merit, but failure to consider them seriously in the light of a unifying philosophy of education which was sensitive to social conditions and to individual characteristics, and to act in terms of such philosophy, resulted in their inevitably becoming overgeneralized and faddish, only later to be rejected when something "new" or "experimental" was promulgated. Those educators who were eclectic—who employed or advocated whatever educational strategy and tactics seemed soundly relevant to a given kind of learning activity in a given child, or kind of child—often were regarded by their impetuous brethren as not having taken a discernible "position" on the nature of the educational process.

DEFINING EDUCATION

It has been indicated that there is a logical sequence within which the defining of education falls. First, there is the statement or delineation of the philosophy which is regarded as appropriate. Given this, the defining of education is possible. On the one hand, the goals of education either may be incorporated in a definition of education or they may be clearly implied in it. On the other hand, goals of education may be stated, with the definition of education being implied, this being the more common practice in educational literature pertaining to the gifted. Logically, any definition of education or statement of goals should apply in regard to all children.

By way of recapitulation and integration, then, Dewey's characterization of education is accepted: *the reconstruction or reorganization of experience which adds to the meaning of experience and which increases ability to direct the course of subsequent experience.* This is such that it can accommodate, within an overall social commitment to a democracy, the major paradoxical purpose of education in terms of its involving both the processes which will contribute to the kind of society we favor and the provision for the development of an acceptable degree of individuality. The four objectives of education stated by the Educational Policies Commission in 1938—attainment of self-realization, cultivation of effective human relationships, acquisition of economic efficiency, and learning to assume civic responsibility—can be regarded as specific commitments which can be taken as elaborations of the basic definition. While these are reflective of what is needed in terms of a broad social outlook, Bennis' (1970) discussion of a shift in value systems must be perceived in terms of individuals' expressions of what they regard as personally significant—self-actualization, self-expression, recognition of the fact of interdependence among individuals, personal adequacy in terms of employment, and the experiencing of "full lives"—recognizing some redundancy in such expressions. Understandably, the social goals and the expressed personal values are essentially comparable, although the economic self-sufficiency objective is not as fully reflected in Bennis' list. The two primary foci of commitment of this text—self-fulfillment and social contribution—are in harmony with both the basic definition of education and the derived educational goals.

A PHILOSOPHY
OF EDUCATION
OF THE GIFTED?

As the idea of a philosophy of education has been presented here—admittedly sketchily, it is not justifiable to think in terms of a philosophy unique to the gifted, so far as the nature of educational provisions made for them is concerned. The general philosophy which should underlie all education would seem to hold with respect to educational principles applicable in the cases of all children—gifted, the retarded, the "disadvantaged," the "normal," and all other subgroups. At most, only a sharper delineation of the principles relevant to the education of the gifted would appear to be needed.

The inauguration or implementation of special educational provisions for the gifted all too often has taken place in school situations seemingly devoid of anchorage in relevant educational philosophy. The oft-expressed admonition, "In case of doubt do *something*," too often has resulted in the implementation of philosophically and psychologically unsound and unwarranted provisions for the gifted. Especially in the late 50s and during the 60s, educational changes, intended to be in the interests of the gifted, were effected more under pressure than as a result of a deep and abiding philosophical comprehension of the potential contributive value of such provisions. Many bright youngsters undoubtedly benefited from such innovations. Some enjoyed the sampling of new and temporarily rewarding learning experiences, getting a taste of what could have been and what could be, but having such experiences only while they were "in season." Some enjoyed such innovations not because they constituted valid and appropriate learning experiences but primarily because they constituted a temporary diversion from other essentially boring and unproductive educational experiences. But such innovations were, in large part, only that, and were not educational changes conceptualized out of a deep and abiding educational philosophy that included sound philosophical concern for and valid psychological understanding of the gifted and their potential roles in society.

The implementation of a philosophy

of education in the interests of the gifted, while expected within education as an agency or function of society, must take place in the philosophical milieu of the total society. As will be seen later, there has been and apparently still is a frustratingly pervasive absence of sensitivity on the part of educators to the fact that the gifted need and are entitled to some kind of provisions tailored to their—and society's—needs. Such a condition has obtained among educators in spite of their publicly professed commitments to the importance of "meeting the needs of the children." This gap between profession and performance must be attributed to the fact that society itself has, at least implicitly, a philosophy that either is insensitive to the presence and needs of the gifted or even is studiously negligent in their regard. To ask what is society's philosophy of educating the gifted is to ask the wrong question; the fundamental question must be, "What is society's philosophy of education?"— because a socially adequate response to this should be applicable to all kinds of children who are to be educated.

To only a limited extent and in only the most general sense has the non-educator component of society expressed an overriding philosophical commitment to the education of its children. In the majority of instances in which this has occurred, the phrasings of the contentions of educators have been used. Expressions regarding "inalienable rights" have come closest to providing any philosophical basis for educators' role in society. If, however, we "look at the record," we find extensive evidence of the operation of a laissez faire attitude which has allowed those gifted who, for one reason or other, have made places for themselves in society only to act in terms of the status and recognition to which their accomplishments entitled them. As pointed out earlier, this seems to have been adequate to enable society to progress as it has. How much better it might have emerged if there had been a fuller sensitivity to providing for more effective participation in and contribution to society by the gifted is something for which only the social-educational idealist can contend. If our measure be the extent to which society, especially at the governmental level, specifically has provided for its subgroups (with view to the greater social good), the record shows that society has tended generally to react rather than to act, and this in terms of the more tangible social problems presented by subgroups, as in the cases of the physically disabled, the mentally retarded, the brain injured, and the like. But, as pointed out in Chapter 3, specific broad-based social consideration for the gifted has been constantly difficult to obtain and to sustain. As a society, we have settled for muddling through rather than for broad social planning. In terms of our paradox of control-freedom, we have almost studiously avoided getting involved in the vicissitudes inevitably associated with a type of control that unified and systematic planning would entail and have proceeded with an assumed pride in letting individual states, school systems, and even schools do as they pleased, especially if they called it "experimental."

Recapitulation

The intent thus far has not been to present formally "a philosophy" of education but, rather, to identify components or aspects which are believed to be of major import as they pertain to the effective education of children and, therefore, to the gifted. A definition of education either can be shown to emerge from a statement of a philosophy of education or it may be so worded as, in effect, to suggest rather clearly the philosophy implied in it. The statement of the goals of education may emerge from the definition of education or, as seems more generally the case, may be

construed as reflecting such a definition. What was developed was regarded as supportive to the dual and equipotential orientation of this text: the self-fulfillment of the gifted child and the potentiality of the social contribution by the gifted, recognizing the interactive relationship between the two. Any such philosophical orientation must be continuously sensitive to and reflective of both the social milieu in which the gifted live and the biological and psychological characteristics of the gifted. The fundamental prerequisite for the establishment of any sound program for the gifted is the sound and abiding comprehension of an encompassing democratic philosophy of education.

The position is taken here that if any individual—school administrator, teacher, or parent—understands and accepts the meaning and ramifications of a democratic philosophy of education, and if he is conversant with and understands the findings—the facts and general principles—of the psychology of the gifted, and if he is able to operate in terms of such attitudes and facts, he can hardly avoid recognizing and acting in terms of the necessity of working in the interests of both the gifted and of society. Acting in the absence either of a relevant philosophy of education or of the psychological evidence regarding the gifted will, with high probability, result in the establishment of ill-conceived and potentially harmful provisions for the education of the gifted.

GENERALIZATIONS REGARDING SOCIETY

As has been stated, what society at large is doing or should do for the gifted must be perceived as but one facet of its overall responsibility for or commitment to all of those of its various subgroups which have received special consideration—its physically disabled, its mentally retarded, its juvenile delinquents, its "mentally ill," its "disadvantaged," its "learning disabled," and many other conceivable subgroups. It is not logically tenable to maintain that, over time, any such subgroup, including the gifted, is more deserving of such special consideration than is any other. Against the grossly obvious, tangible, relatively immediate, clearly economic needs of some of them would be pitted the much more subtle, intangible needs of the gifted. Pervading all of this would be the source of personal worth that would attend their being more fully self-realized which could result from the implementation of effective programs for them.

Society tends more to react with respect to what it regards as crises rather than to act to prevent the occurrence of crises. Most of the subgroups such as those mentioned have come to be perceived as presenting problems which have economic and humanitarian aspects. Whatever initiative society might take in regard to its gifted—systematically seeking them out early in order that they can more effectively be educated, providing sound and stable scholarship programs for them throughout as much of their school lives as is necessary, providing for their involvement in important social roles after their formal schooling—requires a recognition of the gifted as positively and constructively contributive to society, as contrasted with the necessarily habilitative and rehabilitative perceptions of most of its other subgroups.

Education, as a function of society, necessarily reflects the society's perceptions of its obligations to its members. While education has the obligation to make it possible for the members of society to function effectively within the society as it is, it also is regarded as having the opportunity, if not the responsibility, so to educate its members as to effect improvement in society. On the one hand, education has been charged implicitly with, in effect, maintaining a tolerable status quo. Yet in the 1960s its members rediscovered the fact, reflected in major studies since early in the century, that it wasn't doing a very good job at even that, as shown by the educational skill levels of its products. On the other hand, those in the area of education who do seek to enhance the contributions of the schools to the possible improvement of society do so against a pervading inertia, the growing problems of financing education, and a constantly varying array of often-resistant social pressures. In view of the fact that, nationally, education is trying to meet the needs of not more than 40 percent of its handicapped children, optimism regarding education's effectively meeting the needs of the gifted can be, at best, restrained. Congress' recent imposition on the U.S. Office of Education of an obligation to give more constructive consideration to the gifted can augur well, providing what is undertaken in their interests is soundly based psychologically and philosophically.

In this section, we shall consider first some broad generalizations that should be relevant to the implementation of a philosophy of education for all children and later consider certain generalizations more specifically relevant to the education of the gifted. There will, of course, be instances of conceptual overlapping, since many of the specifics regarding the gifted will, in effect, be but applicable extensions or elaborations.

The point has been made that the nature of the social milieu in which children live and grow should be taken into consideration in planning for their education. We shall consider the nature of this environment from four perspectives: our basic political commitment, the changing nature of society, the inconstancy of our substantive world, and changes in the nature of our social relationships. Again, it should be borne in mind that while such facets may be logically separable, each is both a resultant of the others and at the same time influences them. Each element or component in any field of forces is both cause and effect.

Our Political Commitment

As a nation, we are committed to the maintenance and furtherance of a democratic society. This necessitates the education of the individual in such a manner and to such an end that he comes to perceive his role in society both as legitimately unique and as contributive to a society constituted of others who have been educated to perceive themselves in like manner. For every right which the individual believes himself to have he is obligated to recognize and act in the light of paralleling social responsibilities. He must learn not only to recognize the social validity of majority opinion but also be able to work in the light of the fact that, once such a majority opinion is attained, by that very fact it is out of date and is conducive to stagnation, since social growth results only from the progression of valid minority conceptions into majority opinion. A minority of opinion of yesterday becomes a majority opinion of today after having been validated by the acid test of a composite of emerging interacting social conditions. For us, the overriding value determination of the appropriateness and acceptability of any such emergent minority opinion is that it be contributive to a democratic society as we see it.

Our Changing Society

There is an interesting parallel between the nature of the developmental pattern of the individual and that of society. Generally, this phenomenon in the individual is referred to as growth; in society

it is more cautiously referred to as evolution. Differences exist among individuals and societies in the rates of such changes. In both, there are periods when the rate of growth or change seems particularly accelerated, and there are times when there seems to be no discernible growth or change. Yet the aphorism that the only thing that is constant is change applies to both.

While an overall orientation toward democracy is presumed and maintained, the particular format of our society changes over time, as does the interpretation of even the nature of democracy. New substructures emerge—political parties, unions, professional and lay organizations, scientific organizations, and governmental structurings—but they continue to interact within a predominantly democratic superstructure, and individuals continue to contribute to society in and through such structurings. Any once-amorphous group tends to organize into a social group in which subcomponents and their interrelationships are defined. There follows an inevitable and seemingly endless social mitosis—a splitting into subgroups. After these proliferate, some tend to disappear and others form new combinations for more effective social action. Such a structural patterning and life-flow is characteristic of our democratic society.

Such social phenomena are of particular significance as regards the gifted. The need for a subgroup having a particular social function may be perceived originally by one of the brighter members of the larger society because of some conceptualization he has. Or, members of a society may identify specific conditions which they regard as desirable or undesirable (essentially at a perceptual or low conceptual level) and then a gifted member of the society expresses a conceptualization which incorporates, in terms of general concepts and principles, a generalized need and, perhaps, ways of meeting such a need in the light of the attendant or a newly proposed policy. In both kinds of situations, the social change results from the conceptual functioning of the brighter members of the society—those who have generalized regarding some idea pertaining to the functioning of society as contrasted with reacting to some idea or need that is only personally oriented, or perceptual in nature.

It is necessary to recognize that such thinking about the restructuring of segments within a total society in a manner reflecting conceptualization on the part of the instigator or integrator must be independent of any value system which may be associated with such structuring. The Ku Klux Klan, an organization conceptualized with view to exerting a certain kind of social pressure, and the Mafia, or Mafia-like, organization conceptualized with view to acquiring wealth and political clout, are just as much results of generalized planning by a gifted few as are the conceptualizations which resulted in the development of programs of legal aid for the poor, or programs addressed to the expansion of economic opportunities, or programs for the habilitation-rehabilitation of the handicapped, and the like, although the latter illustrations reflect more the value systems of most of us than do the former ones. The recognition by some student, teacher, or school administrator of the desirability of having some generalized pattern or system of awarding varying amounts of recognition merits, school participation credits, or academic credits would be a manifestation of a conceptualization of a problem or problem situation, as contrasted with the perceptual activity which would be operative in deciding for each child, as the occasion arose, just how his participation in an extracurricular activity should be recognized or evaluated in the absence of any general policy for the making of such

decisions. The bright individual is more likely to see more elements in a situation and also more possible interrelationships among those elements, as contrasted with others who live lives of specifics which, more often than not, tend to be only personally relevant or of very limited applicability.

Generally social leaders have emerged from the social mass not because society has sought, in any forthright and systematic way, to make their emergence possible. Such emergence may be, at best, only tolerated. A social leader, or a potential one, may promote a conceptualization of considerable integrity only to have it strike no positive responsive chord because his society was not ready for it. The same conceptualization, or the essence of it, may be promulgated at another time or place and be accepted because of a differing constellation of social factors. The concepts of the League of Nations and of the United Nations are cases in point, as is the contrast between educators' acceptance and action on Dewey's early educational pronouncements and Bruner's and Guilford's later advocacies regarding teaching methods and "creativity." It is only within the last few decades that portions of our society have taken any systematic initiative in cultivating and encouraging those with leadership potential to emerge more quickly and effectively. Such efforts have pertained largely to management rather than to leadership in the broader sense. Fortunately, we hear from time to time of isolated instances where educators have had the capacity and willingness to identify and nurture potential leaders in the light on the needs of society, but there are not a few who firmly believe that the school, as an agent of society, has not functioned in a manner which reflected such a sense of obligation to the gifted and to society. Whatever restructurings may occur within our democratic society, it is inevitable that persons operating at a high conceptual level will tend to play outstanding parts.

Trend toward centralization

Our children must be educated in the light of the fact that, by virtue largely of changes in communication in our culture, the society in which they are and will be living is changing from one of widespread, marked autonomy to one of increasing centralization—a phenomenon that can be contributive to an increasing concern lest the individual be lost in the transition. While this centralization is perceived initially in terms of its beneficial organizational and integrative possibilities, the extent to which control aspects will come increasingly to the fore give concern to many. In regard to education, matters such as school financing, curriculum determination, school athletics, and transportation constitute foci of both promise and concern. Paralleling the problem of the privileges and role of the individual in society is that of the individual school district, or the county educational unit, or even of the state educational unit in relation to whatever larger educational organization may be involved. Parallels exist also in the governmental, political, and economic areas. Pervading the whole social transition is the problem of how to effect the inevitable shift toward greater centralization, on the assumption that overall improvement will result, and still avoid impairing local and individual initiative and responsibility. Since this necessitates the conceptualization essential to policy development, the acumen of the gifted in such social action can be of great value.

Increasing humanitarianism

The American scene has reflected a discernible shift in some components of its value system. From the start, the "in-alienable rights" of the individual were forthrightly proclaimed. In our early pioneer days, this provided an understandable basis for the manifestation of rugged individualism, whether in the discovery and settlement of new areas or in the development of trade. As the industrial evolution took place, this commitment to rugged individualism came to be applied more to the employer than to the employee. This primary focus of concern for the employer so dominated the scene that child labor laws, "sweatshop" regulations, and unionization by the employees developed as a means of protecting the lot of the employee. Even now, such unionization is infiltrating the professional areas of our society. While these developments have resulted largely in an adversary system of employer-employee, there has been a growing manifestation of concern for the individual and for subgroups within our society—for example, the "disadvantaged."

Even though much of this concern can be ascribed to the increasing recognition of the importance and legitimacy of a right to self-fulfillment on the part of all members of society, no small portion can be attributed to increasing the individual's productivity for his employer. No small part of the motivation thus to enhance the individual's self-perception must be attributed also to economic facets of the phenomenon. Granted that such minority members—the trainable, the educable mentally retarded, the physically disabled, the culturally disadvantaged—can be provided for more adequately by means of special education, rehabilitation programs, and compensatory and maybe corrective education programs for the economically and ethnically disadvantaged, thus presumably contributing to their improved self-regard, such social action also can contribute toward their being able at least to contribute toward their economic self-sufficiency, or even enable them to contribute on a larger scale to the economy of their society. Regardless of the part played by such economic contribution, the importance of social thinking in terms of the self-fulfillment of such individuals and subgroups has come increasingly to the fore as an expression of part of our value system.

Rural-urban shift

The population of our country is becoming increasingly urban. In 1790, 95 percent of our population was rural—defined generally as living in communities of less than 2500; in 1890, some 65 percent was rural; and in 1960, the rural population of our country constituted only 30 percent of the total (*Statistical Abstract of the United States,* 1966). By 1970, 73 percent of the population was urban. And the growth of population centers continues such that the concept of the megalopolis is coming to be regarded as more appropriate, economically and culturally, than that of the large city. According to the 1970 census, 73.5 percent of the U.S. population was living on 15.3 percent of the land.

This shifting of population dispersion has widening implications for education. On the one hand, it has major implications regarding the content of education as it bears upon the mounting interdependence of components in our society, as contrasted with their relative independence in the colonial days and regarding the kinds of social and technological skills important in the learnings of children. On the other hand, major implications regarding the support and administration of the public schools are emerging and becoming much more complex—as in areas such as the development of consolidated school districts and the related fiscal support and transportation problems. In fact, already the

schedule for the regular busing of school children figures largely in determining the length of the school day and the extent of the curriculum.

Age, employment, and educational change

Owing to a composite of factors, the average age of our population is increasing. In 1820 the average age was 16.7 years. A century later it was 25.3 years, and in 1960 it was 29.6 years (*Statistical Abstract of the United States,* 1966). Not only is the teenage population becoming a major target group for the sale of goods—thus having significant implications regarding consumer education in the schools—but our "senior citizens" are coming to constitute a major group so far as need for social services is concerned, this also having major economic and sociological implications for the content of education. Educating in long-range anticipation of retirement and providing educational activities for those who have retired are as yet little recognized and less acted upon by public school educators.

Even within our own national spectrum, a new pattern of social conditions is developing which can serve as a basis for further challenging the social relevance of the schooling being provided. The length of youths' dependency upon parents and on public funds for their education is increasing. Not only are more of those employed reaching mandatory retirement ages but more of them are being encouraged to retire before reaching those ages. The age range of employability thus is being shortened at both the earlier and later age levels. Inevitably, new technological employment opportunities are being identified, and other employment opportunities in the area of rendering services also have begun to emerge with possibilities yet only vaguely imagined. But, along with these developments is the increasing introduction of the shortened work week, which increases the need for education for leisure, whether after retirement or before it. This shifting pattern of social needs makes at least implicit demands on the nature of the education of all children and adults and can present unique opportunities for social involvement and contribution by the gifted.

Any attempt thus to describe, even as of a given period of time, the complex interactions of factors or conditions in our society induces frustration because of oversimplification, which tends to necessitate the identification and description of single factors and to treat inadequately the changing interactions among them. The passage of compulsory school attendance laws, for instance, can be perceived as having been influenced by the expression of humanitarian concern for working children, but it served also to keep the children longer off the labor market, thus making for more jobs for older persons. Improved technology led to increasing simplification of jobs, as on an assembly line, which led to an increased mechanization of jobs, which has led to the shortened work week, helped, of course, by the expected increased production resulting from the increased mechanization of assembly jobs. The aproned grocery clerk of yore needed sufficient schooling to enable him to write down orders, compute costs, total the bill, make change, and, at times, to find his way about town in order to deliver the groceries. With increasing urbanization, the growing availability of large markets, and the development of cash registers that not only add up the bill but also determine and make the customer's change, to say nothing of their being so tied in with the automated record of stock that a constant inventory is maintained, the nature of even the new cashier's job has changed—with atten-

dant implications regarding what his schooling should consist of.

Still other factors mitigate against any simplified consideration of the social scene. The self-protective interests of trade unions and professional groups, for instance, curtail the numbers of entering workers, although the needs for their services tend to exceed the ability to provide them. Educators tend to proclaim loudly, and to have their claims echoed by employers, that completion of high school and/or college is necessary for the young to be employed. This involves a kind of dignified hypocrisy, probably contributing more to keeping the labor market down than to enhancing the social relevance of the offerings of the schools. The employers, by setting such standards of employability, are implicitly supporting the increasingly questioned view that the completion of education constitutes a valid aptitude testing for any such employment, instead of developing their own valid employability criteria. In the views of an increasing number, the match between the realities of the society for which the children are being "prepared" and the social relevance of the experiences which are contended to be contributive to that end is somewhat less than perfect even for the nongifted.

Education, constantly alluded to as "the hope of our society," has, in effect, been sluggish in adapting its curriculum to the needs of even current society. Too often, many school personnel have sought to make adaptive modifications in schooling only to be opposed by parents (and some educators) who believe that their children should be "educated" the way they themselves were. In the early part of this century, when a youngster "went to college," this had a relatively clear and unitary meaning: he either was going to prepare for work in one of the professions or the sciences, or he was going on in a general liberal arts program. In the

1920s the junior college movement was started, essentially as a means of continuing general education beyond the high school. By the 1960s the junior college became a widespread component of public education, but had a double goal—the continuation of general education, usually of a liberal arts nature, and the provision of training opportunities in technological areas. The latter tended to be regarded as terminal and of such a nature that those who finished such a program could be immediately employable. This development, plus the fact that many colleges and universities introduced technological training into their curricula, has resulted in a blurring of the meaning of "college attendance," an important matter when thinking about the gifted's continuing their education.

With this in mind, and remembering that in 1930 only some three percent of the school-going population were in colleges and universities, the data in Table 5.1 support the view that the school-attending population have been increasing their educational exposure. While the increases from the 1930 three percent are noteworthy, more significant is the decreasing disparity between the percentages attending high school and those attending college. Again, the condition is partly contributed to by the shift in the meaning of college education. Certainly more are not likely to be immediately on the employment market, a fact that can

be supportive to the already mentioned lengthening of the economic dependency of the young, and the attending questions that can be raised regarding the nature of the education to which they will be exposed.

Changing role of the home

The home continues to be the basic focus of much professed consideration, although many of the responsibilities of the family for its children are being relegated to, or taken over by, other agencies or institutions in society. While the schools generally require parents to have their children examined physically, at least before the children enter upon their schooling, other agencies in society may provide for more thorough physical examinations, and the school itself is coming increasingly to make periodic evaluations of the children's hearing and vision. As more and more mothers work, part-time or full-time, facilities for the care of the children of such mothers are becoming an integral part of our social scene. Whereas the children routinely have provided for the care of their parents and grandparents, this responsibility is shifting increasingly to agencies and institutions in our society, owing, at least in part, to decreasing size of family living facilities, this in part being due to the crowding of our population into increasingly impacted urban living. Changing economic conditions and altering value

Table 5.1. Actual and projected school enrollment (in millions).

	1970		1980		1985	
	Number	Percentage	Number	Percentage	Number	Percentage
Kindergarten and elementary school	36.7	62	33	57	36	60
High school	14.7	25	15	26	14	23
College	7.4	13	10	16	10	17
TOTAL	58.8		58		60	

Source: Adapted from *Projections of School and College Enrollments: 1971-2000,* U.S. Department of Commerce, Series P-25, No. 473, Jan. 1972.

systems also are contributive to this emerging role of the family unit.

Basically, the school is implicitly charged with the responsibility for doing for children what the family can't do, can't do as well, or won't do. The school probably does better than parents in general can do in helping children to learn to read and compute, in the area of driver education, and even in the area of training for many of the jobs in society. Some school personnel are strongly convinced that the school can, and should, play a major role in cultivating broader and more integrative social value systems and take a more meaningful role in facilitating the effective social and emotional adjustment of its charges. In fact, many schools provide special services addressed specifically to helping maladjusted youngsters, on the premise that maladjustment interferes with effective learning regardless of where that maladjustment is learned. In perhaps too few instances, specialized school personnel work intensively with the parents of such children in order to help them work more effectively and soundly with their own children, thus contributing even more to the school-based services provided.

Our society has changed, is changing, and will change. In the light of this, the school is obligated to demonstrate convincingly that, in educating its charges, it has been meaningfully aware of the past, effectively functional in terms of the present, and adaptively sensitive to what will be. The learning experiences of the nongifted and of the gifted justifiably will have certain commonalities between them, but significant differences will stem largely from the superior capacity of the gifted in symbolic functioning to deal more deeply, more comprehendingly, and more conceptually with the realities and the possibilities inherent in such change.

Our Substantive World

What was fantasy yesterday may be fact today; what is fact today tomorrow may seem like fiction. The merit of such a statement inheres in its communicating the reality of the changeability of what, over time, is taken to be factual, or in its suggesting the evanescence of factness. The danger inhering in such a statement is its possible contribution to the impression that, within a person's life span, nothing is of sufficient certainty to warrant learning about it or taking any action on the basis of it. Yet the overall impact of such a statement can be salutary in that it can cause one to give serious consideration to the nature of the "facts" which children may be expected to learn. So far as the vast majority of people at one time were concerned, it was a "fact" that the earth was flat, and some died because they did not accept the statement as fact. An engineer regarded it as a "plain fact," from his point of view, that bees just couldn't fly, although they did. To most people, the sum of two and two is four, but only because they operate in terms of the same number base. To a given individual, it is a "fact" that he hears voices which others don't hear, or that he is the only one who believes that he is being spied upon. A historian writes a text on American history, supporting his several points factually, but the overall stance is one of considered opinion. Yet many children may be expected by their teachers to accept the opinion as fact.

The salutary import of the opening statement inheres in the querying of the factness of "fact" and in the implicit questioning of the extent to which formal education should presume the mastery of facts or "facts," as contrasted with the process of learning how to deal with what later may be regarded as fact— "how to think." But thinking thus of formal schooling, generally called "education," is too simplistic, since different kinds of learning are appropriate to different intellectual developmental levels or stages. The younger the individual, the more likely he is to "think" in terms of the simple dichotomies of black-white, good-bad, true-false. Only later, as he progresses from the mass stage of intellectual development to the differentiated stage, is he capable of recognizing the phenomenon of in-betweenness, or grayness, of tolerableness, of relative truth or falsity.

Implications of the nature of the phenomenon of factness in regard to individual differences in the learning capacities of children can be drawn a bit more clearly if we conceptualize factness as being identifiable along a continuum from absolutism to complete indeterminacy. Keep in mind that the fundamental difference between the nongifted and the gifted is one of degree of capacity to understand, to "reason," and, therefore, to act in terms of symbols and generalizations. At the absolutism end of the continuum, things are or they aren't, they are facts or they are not facts, and they tend therefore to be perceptual, or low conceptual, in nature. High intellectual ability, for instance, may be believed to be due to genetic determination *or* to nurture. Indeterminacy is a concept itself of no mean magnitude. At the indeterminacy end of the continuum, whether something is a "fact" depends upon some contingency, such as the frame of reference in terms of which it is being perceived or dealt with. Something may be a fact, or valid, only in terms of when it was conceptualized, or in terms of the conceptual frame of reference of the individual who identified it or was dealing with it.

Further, orientation at, or near the indeterminacy end of the continuum involves a recognition of the provisional nature of "fact"—the recognition that the "fact" under consideration may be only partially relevant or valid because it may be attenuated by other facilitating or inhibiting "facts." Functioning at this end of the continuum necessitates thinking in terms of two or more interacting phenomena or conditions which are necessary to account for a given situation or condition. Often, those who so operate are accused of "double talking"—of refusing to take one stand or another (absolutistic). High intellectual ability, for instance, is due to *both* genetic factors and nurturance, the manner and degree of their interaction varying with other contributing conditions. The brighter the individual, the more capable he is of functioning at or near the indeterminacy end of the continuum.

The last statement must be interpreted in terms of the level of intellectual development of the individual—this itself being a manifestation of operating toward the indeterminacy end of the continuum. The bright four-year-old with a mental level of six would not be as capable of understanding and thinking in terms of some complex interaction as would a bright ten-year-old with a mental level of fifteen. But both would be more capable, even at such ages, of indeterminacy thinking than would children of average intellectual ability at those respective age levels.

The simpler the phenomenon involved the more limited the frames of reference employed, and the lower the level of conceptualization involved the greater the possibility of "facts" being facts—a statement which implies a continuum from fact to "fact." This is tantamount to saying that the earlier the individual is in his intellectual development the more necessarily he lives a life in which "facts" are facts; the more advanced the mental level attained by the individual, the more capable he is likely to be of living a life in which facts are "facts." The young child learns at first that he is never to start to cross the street if he sees a car coming; the older child learns to attenuate that factually based admonition by so reacting only if the oncoming car is within some still-being-defined, actually threatening distance. The young child learns to reply unhesitatingly that the sum of five and three is eight; the older child may reply that the sum is eight providing one assumes a number base of ten.

This slight disquisition on the factness of "facts" is highly relevant to the determination of the kinds of cognitive learning which are regarded as essential in education. Such learning cannot be presumed to be confined to the acquisition of facts. The table of chemical elements in the 1970s is different from that of the 1930s. The areas of physics and chemistry, once studied as discrete entities, now consist of significant overlapping concepts. If the emphasis in education is to be on helping children to learn to think ("reason"), even this would entail children's acquiring certain "facts," since thinking is not done in a factual vacuum.

Overriding all this must be the cultivation of differentiated thinking, appropriate to the intellectual developmental levels of children, regarding the nature of "fact." In the first place, children need to learn to think in terms of facts, opinions, and beliefs, recognizing that facts are those phenomena, at any given point in time, about which there exists objectively verifiable evidence. Before the time of Columbus, the predominance of "evidence" supported the factness of the earth's being flat; now such is not the case. Opinions can be of two kinds: those which result from some careful evaluation of evidence and which can be regarded as considered opinions, and those which are more hastily pronounced, less

deliberately arrived-at opinions. Beliefs are based on even less demonstrable evidence; it was the biblically based belief that man was created literally in the image of God that constituted the basis for some state laws which prohibited teaching reflecting the acceptance or tolerance of Darwinian evolutionary theory.

But there also are different kinds of facts. Certain facts are truly ephemeral, as witness the now-specified distance from the Earth to the Moon, professed to be accurate within twenty feet. There are what may be called conditional facts or contingency facts—phenomena or conditions which have been reasonably well verified *so long as* certain attending conditions are met and which could be different if certain of those attending conditions were altered. Given certain conditions, positive reinforcement is more facilitative to learning than is negative reinforcement; given other conditions, the reverse may be true. Perhaps more importantly, facts should be perceived probabilistically rather than absolutistically, a kind of indeterministic thinking. There are phenomenological facts, which figure largely in interpersonal relationships. A child, or a principal, or a parent may, in terms of his own personal experiences, regard a given teacher as "good" or "bad," and this, for that person, is a psychological fact.

The recognition of the evanescence of "fact" should be an essential component in education as long as education is regarded as facilitative to the adjustment of the individual. Education for a changing world must contribute to effective operation not only in the present with whatever may be regarded then as factual but also in the future as a wealth of new information becomes available. And it is highly probable that the fruitfulness of efforts in this direction is directly relatable to the intellectual capabilities of children.

Our Social Relationships

From intra- to inter-

At least some of what already has been said can be regarded as reflecting the fact that the self-sufficiency of our colonial, agrarian era has been in the process of being replaced by a large pattern of interdependency in our urban, increasingly industrialized period. In our colonial days, individuals learned, largely in their own homes, most of the occupational competencies for which there was a relatively stable social demand, learned how to produce their own food, how to make their own implements, how to make their own clothes. From this, we have changed into a social condition in which individuals have had to learn, largely outside the home, increasingly fractionated and specialized competencies by means of which each tends to share the responsibility for doing what is needed in society, and, by means of the returns from such participatory labor, they purchase from each other, directly or indirectly, the food, implements, and clothing they need. From an era of rugged individualism we have changed into one of pronounced interrelated social competencies, the functioning of any one of which depends upon the functioning of the others. Just how, for instance, the highly skilled electronics technician functions depends upon how the engineer designed the equipment on which and with which the technician will work. Whether either will work depends upon the demands for his services, which can depend upon the economy, itself a highly interlocking and interacting pattern of factors which, in turn, has come to depend upon highly interdependent factors in the international situation. Thus, what was once a relatively simple, localized pattern of competencies and responsibilities has assumed a truly international scope and complexity.

Communications and travel

Accompanying this technologically and economically caused shift to an enlarged arena in which individuals must learn how to function has been a highly significant and, in part, contributory change in the communication area. Changes in communication have significantly reduced the insularity of individuals, segments within our society, and of countries. News that once was spread slowly by word of mouth now reaches many simultaneously by radio and television, even within hours after the newsworthy event. We are in an era in which we learn from our news media the essence of forthcoming pronouncements even before they are formally made.

Not only have the radio and television decreased the psychological space separating segments of our country and separating our country from other countries, but changes in travel facilities also have contributed to the reduction of insularity. The transition from the horse and buggy to the automobile, from the sailing vessel to the steamship and to the airplane, has contributed to our awareness of this interrelatedness, if not also a sense of interdependence, among people. We can fly from New York to Los Angeles in less time than our pioneering forefathers needed to go from Columbus to Cleveland. In a sense, we have seen a shift from a kind of provincial perception of segments of our society to the possibility of, and a need for, an international conceptualization of man and needs. The implications of this shift from a molehill view to a mountaintop panorama must bear heavily on at least the content of education. And the attendant increase in the need for high-level conceptualization of such interrelationships, as contrasted with what used to be relatively lower-level conceptualizations of social needs, can present conceptualization possibilities having major implications regarding the education of all, and especially of the gifted.

Historical perspective

Yet the nature of the society from which we have been moving needs to be known, both so that we can understand some of the vestigial traces we still have and so that we can deal meaningfully with that which is becoming and that which will become. Knowing the facts and conditions specifically about points A and B in our society's history requires essentially perceptual or low conceptual capabilities in school children; knowing such specifics *plus* understanding the relationships between them necessitates higher-level conceptualization and generalization abilities.

A philosophy of education must reflect a pervading sensitivity to the society in which the child is doing his learning and in which he will go on learning. It must be fully sensitive to the fact that societies change. Knowledge of what conditions did exist and what conditions presently exist is important, but a comprehension of the phenomenon of change is of equal importance.

Certain generalizations regarding the nature of the individual who is to do such learning also call for consideration. We shall turn now to a consideration of what appear to be major biological and psychological characterizations of the individual.

GENERALIZATIONS REGARDING THE INDIVIDUAL

Biological Characterizations

Two biologically oriented observations are fundamental to a sound conceptualization of a philosophy of education—one pertaining to the fact of individual differences, and the other to the matter of the genetic basis of such differences. We shall concern ourselves with these only so far as they bear on the matter of the verbal symbol learning of children.

Individual differences

Individuals differ in many ways, but we are primarily concerned here with their capacities to do abstract thinking and with the ways they function psychologically which are conducive to such behavior. Such differences are discernible from the time of birth, from the infant's early, relatively simple reactions to external and internal stimuli to the later "reasoning" behavior. It is important to keep in mind that decisions as to the presence and magnitude of such differences in capacity to learn symbolically are based upon inferences. A child responds to some (preferably) systematic pattern of stimuli. On the basis of the behavior he manifests, and taking into consideration how other children of comparable acculturation behave, the behavior is evaluated—it is better than, the same as, or poorer than that of his general age population. An inference then is drawn that this child is "brighter" than the average, as "bright" as the average, or less "bright" than the average. While some inferences regarding children's learning potential are drawn irresponsibly by unqualified persons, the inferences with which we are here concerned are those which are drawn by qualified persons on statistically supported grounds.

The fact remains that some two-year-olds (or younger) will manifest behaviors normally expected of three-year-olds and some three-year-olds will not behave like three-year-olds until they are four years old (or older). Some seven-year-olds give evidence that they can learn as easily and as well as average twelve-year-old youngsters, and some are more like five-year-olds in that regard. A bright ten-year-old can conceptualize as well as an average eighteen-year-old; another, only as well as an average six-year-old. Parallels to such diversity exist, of course, at all age levels of children, a fact yet to be taken adequately into consideration by many educators and parents.

Genetic determination

Fundamentally, such individual differences in behaviors result from differences in what individuals inherit biologically. The term "inherit" must be taken in its scientific sense—in this context, the functioning nervous systems with which individuals are born and which mature physically in terms of conditions inherent in the organism, as contrasted with "social inheritance," which denotes the conditions into which individuals are born. Both are important, but they require thoughtful differentiation.

The precise role played by genetic determination of individual differences has not been identified, hence the perennial hassle regarding the relative contributive roles of nature and nurture. Recent research suggests that between 60 and 80 percent of such differences are attributable to genetic influence. Considered opinions—some of them promulgated as "facts"—regarding the magnitude of the role played by genetic determination have varied over time. During most of this century, genetic factors have been accorded the major role in determining the basic capacity in which we are particularly interested.

To accept such a position is not to deny the important contributive role played by environmental factors. Observing that "normal" nurturance—the more-or-less conventional impingement of environmental conditions upon individuals—makes possible, or contributes to, or even determines "normal" development of behavior called "mental" or intellec-

tual says both much and little. On the one hand, it merely states the generalization that, given the run-of-mine concatenation of conditions impinging upon some presumably normally heterogeneous group, the average development of that group has been observed to be such and such, this average then being characterized as "normal." If, on the other hand, one or more of the impinging conditions, or some interaction among them, is discernibly different—absent, reduced, or exaggerated—and if the average of the development of the group is different from that which was found to be "normal," the difference in the development is attributed to the difference in that which impinged upon the group.

In more specific behavioral terms, if one subgroup of a culture performs less well in oral and/or written communication than does the generality of the larger culture and if the subgroup is known to have been reared in and living in a subculture in which single-word utterances or simple phrases serve within that subculture as socially acceptable communication, and if both culture samples are known or believed to possess equal or comparable basic capabilities, the impingement of a simplified communication style tends to be recognized as having had an adverse effect on that subculture. In such a situation, that communication development attained by the majority group is regarded as "normal" and that of the subculture group as "retarded," "inadequate," or "subnormal." That such differences in acculturation can and do contribute to developments in subculture groups that are different from the development in the larger culture is coming increasingly to be recognized. The past two decades have seen numerous attempts on the part of the larger component in our society to attempt to compensate for what are regarded as inadequacies in acculturation in subcultures.

Just what really does happen with respect to the inherent learning potentials of individuals who are reared in subcultures that are less psychologically nurturant than in the larger cultures has been the focus of much argument; it merits examination here because it bears upon the identification of the gifted among disadvantaged groups. Valid consideration of this problem necessitates the use of the concepts of process and product in testing learning aptitude—already dealt with somewhat on pages 50–51. The nature of our examination of this kind of situation usually is regarded by the psychometrician as of secondary importance or even as inconsequential because he tends to be concerned with average scores for groups, but for the psychoeducational diagnostician, who usually is concerned with the performances of individuals within the psychometrist's groups, such differential psychological evaluation has major psychological, educational, and social potential value.

Let us imagine a population originally normally heterogeneous as regards their genetic backgrounds. In order to keep the situation relatively simple, let us assume, further, that they all have been tested by the age of six. Let us assume then that this original population was divided at birth into two subpopulations, A and B, each of which was also normally heterogeneous on the variable in which we are primarily interested. Imagine subpopulation A to have been reared under conditions generally considered to be psychologically nurturant and subpopulation B to have been reared under conditions generally considered to be disadvantaged, the difference between the nurturance of the two groups to have been essentially one of the extent to which verbal symbols have been used in intragroup communication. If both groups were tested at age six by means of the Binet (or by means of any good

current group test of "intelligence") and the total score used, the average of group B would be lower than that of group A because such tests heavily tap product. The differential verbal nurturance of the two groups would be contributive to and reflected in such test performances. If they were tested by means of tests which tapped primarily process, there would be discernibly less difference between the averages.

Here, two conditions need to be recognized. First, the absence of verbal sampling, or the sampling of behavior in a verbal manner, makes possible the testing of the two groups in a less culturally biased manner, thus contributing to the possibility that no significant difference between the averages would be found. Second, and this has the greater probability, *some* difference would be found (though less than if product samplings of behavior were made in the testing), because the phenomenon of verbal-style communication which was less nurturant in group B did not cause the members of that group to use as fully as did those in group A the basic psychological processes with which they presumably started. Such nonuse and nonreinforcement of those processes would cause the members of group B to perform even on process-dominant tests less well than their original potential might have made possible. Still, a "truer" picture of the learning potential of group B could be obtained by process sampling than by product sampling. Operating in the light of this thus can make possible an improved identification of the gifted among the "disadvantaged."

Factors other than acculturation are believed to exercise deleterious effects upon the realization of genetically determined potential. One important and plausible factor is that of malnutrition. In a review of research on the relationship between nutrition and learning, Eichenwald and Fry (1969) report the following findings, among others, regarding malnutrition and intellectual functioning:

> . . . Inadequate protein nutrition, or synthesis, or both, during brain development could result in changes of function and, if the degree of deprivation were sufficiently severe and prolonged, the changes in function might be permanent. Other experimental observations do in fact indicate that insufficient intake of protein during early neural development affects mentation, and the intellectual attainments of children who have recovered from a clinically severe episode of protein-calorie malnutrition are consistently lower than those of individuals with adequate nutrition during infancy (pp. 645–646).

The direction of the implications regarding the deleterious effect of malnutrition on the basic learning capacity of young children seems clearly indicated. But what about the aftereffect of malnutrition upon unborn children? The findings in one relevant study are at hand, and have very interesting implications. This study (Susser et al., 1971), in fact, was so unusual that it warrants at least limited description. In the Netherlands, from November 1944 into May 1945, there were clearly circumscribed areas in which famine was suffered and others where it was not. At eighteen, the age of induction into military service, all males were medically examined and psychologically tested. Some 98 percent of such males surviving and living in the Netherlands were tested by means of the Raven's Progressive Matrices, yielding a total of 20,000 who had been exposed to famine through maternal starvation, when official food rations fell as low as 450 calories per day—a quarter of the minimum standard, with a concurrent and equally serious drop in fats, carbohydrates, and protein. In such a general setting it was possible to identify the following kinds of populations among

those males: those conceived and born prior to the famine, those conceived prior to the famine but born during it, those conceived during and born during the famine, those conceived during the famine and born after it, and those conceived and born after the famine.

The authors drew three conclusions: (1) "Variations in nutrition during pregnancy had no detectable effect on the adult mental performance of surviving male offspring; (2) mental performance of surviving adult males from a total population had no clear association with the known decline in mean birthweight in a selected sample of that population," and, since data had been analyzed separately for those who were born of "manual workers" and for those who were of "non-manual workers" parentage, (3) the results "emphasize the powerful association of social class with mental performance," the offspring of the "manual workers" having scored lower than did those of the other class (p. 14). In regard to their latter finding, as well as in the case of similar findings in this country of differences between performances of members of differing socioeconomic classes, the extent to which such differences can be attributed to underlying genetic differences and to differences in acculturation has not been firmly ascertained. Yet, the Stein findings strongly support the underlying contribution of genetic factors.

Supportive to the earlier statement regarding the possible or probable extent to which the individual differences in which we are interested are genetically determined are the conclusions of researchers in this country from the 1930s, when the nature-nurture controversy peaked (Shuttleworth, 1935), to Jensen (1969), as well as those who have done related research on populations in other countries (for example, Vernon, 1969). But the position that genetic factors play the larger part in determining the basic school learning aptitudes of children does not mean that cultural factors play an inconsequential role. Responsible researchers in this area consistently have called attention to the fact that the quality of the acculturation to which individuals are exposed may, and probably does, play a facilitative role, making possible the manifestation of the basic capacities which exist, or that they very well can have a deleterious effect on such capacities either by not nurturing latent capacities or by having a clearly depressive effect upon their manifestation, expression, or "release."

Psychological Characterizations

Many components already have been touched upon—the phenomenon of motivation, the recognition of learning as a social phenomenon as well as a matter of individual behavior, the recognition that the child (or adult) is an active learner—has to do his own learning rather than just being an individual who is to be "taught"—the nature of the variety of evidence of the learning potentials of children, and the like. It does seem appropriate in this context to identify five generalizations that seem fundamental in thinking about a philosophy of education. That some of them are somewhat duplicative of or overlapping with certain of the earlier psychological considerations seems warranted in view of their fundamental importance in thinking about the larger dimensions of our educational commitment and opportunity. It still should be remembered that these generalizations hold for all children, of whom the gifted are but one kind.

Outgoingness

Assuming reasonably normal physique and physiological functioning, from at least birth onward the individual behaves in a way referred to as "pressing into its environment." Later, this kind of behavior is characterized by statements such as "being curious," "showing curiosity," "being interested in something (or things)," manifesting "curiosity," and even being "nosey." The pervasiveness of this phenomenon is shown by the fact that even lower animals being studied under experimental conditions have been described by careful observers as "seeking stimulation" from sources other than those to which they had been habituated.

While it is important to recognize the "normality" of such a behavior tendency and to capitalize upon it as fully as possible, it is even more important to recognize the relative diminution of this kind of behavior. A most important study, probably leading to some most interesting social and educational implications, is needed which would identify the (probably waning) relationship between the relative amounts of "curiosity" behavior among children of increasing age, taking into account probable marked differences among cultural subgroups. The decreasing relative frequency with which children, as they get older, engage in question-asking behavior is hardly likely to be primarily attributable to their increasing acquisition of the answers. Such behavior on the part of children can be very threatening to adults who presume that they should be the repository of all that children need to know instead of being only a partial repository for facts and a larger source of information about procedures and sources by means of which answers can be sought out.

Homeostasis

The basic concept here is that any field of force, of which the human is only one, tends to maintain its integrity. In the physical world, the impingement of any force, or pattern of forces, on a field of forces, results in a realignment of all the components within it such that a new pattern of interacting forces results which accommodates the intruding force or pattern of forces. It may seem like a big jump from this to observe that the individual tends to maintain his integrity, adapting to whatever pattern of stimuli impinge upon him. The child who doesn't ("can't") read well or doesn't "like" reading tends to avoid situations where this competence is called for. He may succeed in not getting so involved or he may compensate by acquiring some other skill or skills (academic, motor, or social) in which he can perform well and thereby, perhaps, divert others from confronting him with expectations and demands in the area in which he is deficient. The child who reads effectively three, four, or more years in advance of his agemates or classmates and whose competence is not adequately provided for socially and educationally may hit upon other behaviors which contribute to the social status he legitimately seeks as part of his own, probably "unconscious," integrity. The possibility that the gifted may have more compensatory avenues open to them, or may be more clever in utilizing them, should not be capitalized upon, even unwittingly, by putting them in social and educational situations where such compensatory behavior is necessary to the maintenance of their integrity. The self-fulfilled youngster has little need for such adjustive behavior.

Hereditary-cultural determination of behavior

The manner in which the individual performs in society is a result of the interaction between the nature of the nervous system with which he is born and the kind of stimulation he receives and has received from his environment.

The amount and quality of the physical nurturance he is provided can be a further contributive factor. Any degree of inherent capability which is accompanied by limited nurturance and stimulation will result in a lower level of functioning than if it were accompanied by more adequate nurturance and stimulation. But even optimal nurturance and stimulation will not cause a neurologically defective organism to function as though it were not so impaired. Being increasingly recognized is the fact that a disconcertingly large percentage of our population is not being caused or allowed to function more nearly in harmony with their potentials because of the lack of proper early nurturance. Many of those regarded as mentally retarded can function much more effectively than is currently the case. Many of those regarded as "average" can function much more effectively than at present. And the literature teems with evidence of the tolerated underachievement of the gifted.

Reinforcement

While there are kinds of situations in which some individuals' learning can be facilitated by negative reinforcement and reprimand, in large part individuals tend to learn better under conditions involving positive reinforcement in learning. Success is more conducive to further learning than is failure. This is one of the major favorable components in programmed learning developments. Yet a pattern that consists only of inevitable positive reinforcement of each successful performance is less effective than one which, while still predominantly positive, is employed intermittently.

Other facts reflect clearly the importance of individual differences in learning potential in regard to the effectiveness of motivational techniques such as praise and blame and tangibility of reward and punishment. While there is an overall prevailing merit in positive over negative treatments (as perceived by the child), the learning of less capable children is more consistently positively affected by praise and more consistently negatively affected by blame, whereas, while the more capable children still need a predominance of positive reinforcement, they do respond more positively to criticism than do their less capable classmates. This, however, must be interpreted in the sense of warranting occasional use of negative reinforcement with the more capable rather than in the sense of justifying a predominantly negative (and sometimes emotionally based) motivational setting.

As regards the tangibility and timing of the positive and negative reinforcers, the roles of more tangible and less tangible are more clearly differentiable, and for good psychological reasons. This generalization is tenable here: the less capable children are, in the kind of learning aptitude with which we are concerned, the more tangible, or concrete, and the more immediate the reward or penalty should be; the more capable children are in this regard, the less tangible and the more removed in time the reward or penalty can be. Because of the important psychological variable involved, the age level of the child is of significance. Tangibility and immediacy of reward or penalty requires little, if any, abstract thinking, or dealing with symbols. A pat on the head, a smile, encouraging words, or even a gold star on a good paper can be immediately discerned by the child. For a child to perceive as rewarding a gold star (or other evidence of approval) after he has done well, say, five or more times in a row or within a given time period, he may be able to work in terms of such a delay in manifestation of approval, and this requires him to deal with the reward system in a more abstract man-

ner. The same kind of psychological phenomenon is involved in reacting to an immediate and tangible reward, such as the proverbial M and M candy, as contrasted with accumulating, say, free play time for use at the end of a week or month. However, even the more capable have to learn, and they must be at a developmental level at which they can learn to move from the concrete and immediate to the less tangible and more remote in time. The manual worker tends to want his raise in the here and now; the professional worker or scientist can work toward a considerably delayed and less tangible attainment of achievement or status.

Particularly important in regard to the whole matter of reinforcement are the dynamics of the situation in which it, whatever its form, is employed. Two interactive aspects are involved. One can be called the emotional focus of the adult utilizing the reinforcement—whether positive or negative. The fundamental decision to be made in this regard is the extent to which the reinforcing manipulation was primarily a function of the adult's pleasure or displeasure as contrasted with its being primarily a function of the child's success or failure in the learning act. Too often, the application of a negative reinforcement is predominantly a function of the adult's being frustrated by the failure of the child to perform satisfactorily in some learning. This, of course, is one of the merits of programmed learning techniques: whatever negative or positive reinforcement occurs is inherent in the learning act and thus, so far as the learning situation is concerned, is emotionally neutral. The second aspect, inescapably interactive with the one just mentioned, is the matter of how the child perceives the reinforcement—whatever its nature. On the one hand, the child who succeeds or fails in the learning act may perceive his behavior as a means of pleasing the adult who administers the reinforcement rather than as inherently relevant to progress in the learning. On the other hand, the child may not perceive the reinforcement as related to or inherent in the learning act, even though the adult may believe (project) that the child will perceive it as even related to, let alone inherent in, the learning act. This is but another elaboration of the difference between extrinsic and intrinsic motivation and the importance of helping the child learn the necessary transition from the former to the latter, as discussed earlier.

The social setting of learning

While the individual must do his own learning—as contrasted with his being "taught"—his learning takes place in a highly contributive social milieu which involves the resultants and concomitants of interactions between and among the learner and his significant others. Some educators have expressed a healthy and at times critical concern regarding the extent to which formal schooling is responsible for what children learn. Children do much "teaching" of each other outside the school structure, in both academic and social areas. Children bring to school the value systems which they have acquired before starting school and even some they learn concomitant to their formal school exposure. These are clearly related to, if not highly determinative of, their motivation to achieve. From the kindergarten through college, many of the learning experiences provided by the school seem to the learners to bear no discernibly meaningful relation to the learnings and experiences of their out-of-school lives.

The individual—child or adult—tends to function primarily in terms of his system of values. Children's value systems, having gotten their start before formal schooling begins, tend, at least

during the early school years, to be more strongly habituated than any differing ones they may encounter in the school and which they may be expected quickly to acquire. When the preschool value systems are not in harmony with those which the child encounters in school, the more strongly habituated ones tend to be the dominant ones.

When the value system of one group differs from that of another group, those values expressed by the minority tend to be regarded by the members of the majority group as disadvantaged, savage, sinful, or criminal—depending upon the time and the matters about which these values are expressed. In our times, different majority components of our society tend rather quickly to regard as "disadvantaged" any minority group whose value system differs discernibly, particularly as regards the value attached to striving to achieve and to succeed. Care should be exercised in order not to confuse the facts of differentness with value-laden perceptions of disadvantageness.

Let us, for example, regard the whole of the United States as a culture. Within this, there are subcultures. One of these subcultures is identifiable as the majority, or "dominant," subculture. This we shall denote as subculture A. There is discernible a multitude of minorities, such as lefthanders, those who have to order oversize clothing, preschoolers, the disabled, and the like, and these function more or less obviously as subcultures. Certain of these subcultures have come to figure more largely in current social and educational concern: the blacks (which we shall designate as subculture B), the Indians (subculture I), the Mexican-Americans (S), the Puerto Ricans (P), those living in Appalachia (Ap), and so on. Each subculture is discernibly different from the others in terms of racial, economic, and attitudinal history and characteristics. Each has objectively demonstrable unique characteristics—they may look different, they may talk differently, they may have differing motivations, they may present differing employment pictures, and so on. While all subcultures are differentiable in terms of some characteristics, they have many characteristics in common—either those which apply to all subcultures (they eat, love, reproduce, and die), or those which are more pronounced in two or more subcultures than in the others. Most Mexican-Americans and some Indian tribes, for instance, appear not as achievement-motivated as are, for instance, the Jews and the Japanese. Differentness itself among subcultures is a value-neutral condition.

When, however, subculture A regards the characteristics of any of the other subcultures in terms of how members of those subcultures perform when commingling or competing with itself, some subcultures may be regarded by members of A as being "disadvantaged." This means that members of one or more of the subcultures may be considered by the members of A as less motivated to perform along with the members of A, less competent in doing things done by the members of A (reading, computing, writing, and/or work skills, and so on), generally less successful in being assimilated into the A culture. From the standpoint of the standards, demands, requirements, and opportunities existing in A, the members of the other subcultures tend to be judged in terms of the characteristics of the A subculture as lacking in one or more of the components—and therefore "disadvantaged." So long as the members of any subculture, X, are operating only within their own culture, however "effectively," they are only different from the members of subculture A. When, however, the members of subculture X move into subculture A, whether because they want to be a part of subculture A or because the members

of A believe that they should do so, the value characterization is applied to those in X by those in A (or at least by some of those in A).

Two aspects of this social situation should be noted. Much of the thinking about disadvantaged subcultures has progressed on the assumption that the members of a given subculture should or will commingle, cooperate, and/or compete with the members of the majority subculture A. Our society being as mobile as it is and the phenomena of communication being what they are, such commingling is inevitable, at least to a degree, although all the characteristics of the minority subculture need not be wiped out by such commingling. But the demands of subculture A will be highly determinative of the degree and nature of the disadvantageness of the minority subculture so long as and to the extent that such commingling is expected or exists. Disadvantageness is highly probable so long as there is a commingling of a minority and a majority social culture. A second aspect of the situation probably is even more important. The phenomena of subcultures have tended predominantly to be perceived in terms of racial differences, whereas increasingly it is becoming apparent that differentness in terms of socioeconomic levels calls for primary consideration.

Disadvantageness has tended to be perceived perceptually—as of the particular subcultures of B, S, I, and so on. It must be perceived conceptually—as a phenomenon common to at least certain subcultures. The socioeconomic perspective would seem to be much more sound socially and educationally, since characteristics such as poor reading performance and lower drive to succeed are shared by different subcultures and are, at the same time, essential foci of concern in endeavoring to facilitate the success of members of subcultures in commingling with the majority culture.

Certainly, gifted youngsters exist among all subcultures, even though we do not know the extent to which such is true.

SUMMARY

Our philosophy of education reflects our commitment to a democratic orientation. We are living in a social situation which seems to be characterized by an accelerated rate of change from a colonial-agrarian condition to one that is industrial-urban. It being true that the only thing that is constant is change, we must try to avoid either of two extremes—that of committing ourselves entirely in terms of what has been and that of focusing entirely upon what is now or what is to be. A total commitment to the tried, and therefore the "true," can be crippling in a changing society. General principles have a greater probability of viability than do much of educational content and considerable method, as in rote learning. Any addition of the "new," which is often the case, is just that. There is, unfortunately, a general presumption not only of the invalidity of "the old" but also of the inherent merit of whatever seems to be new, or "experimental." Too often, the "new" is poorly anchored in sound social and educational philosophy, is based upon only sketchily demonstrated "facts," and suggests more a dissatisfaction with the old relatively ineffective practices than a sound grasp of the realities of the total emerging social-psychological-educational picture.

The biological generalities regarding the individual have retained essential general validity for this century at least. The generalities regarding the psychological aspects of the individual, at least those which we have considered, have shown relative stability over this period; mounting research evidence has tended more to shape them rather than to identify new, equally basic generalities.

All too many of those working in the interests of the gifted tend either to be unaware of the nature of the social and philosophical groundings which such efforts should have or to be insensitive to the necessity of directing their efforts in terms of a full philosophical consideration of their problem and opportunities. A conviction expressed earlier bears repeating: more "programs" for the gifted have failed for lack of sound philosophical grounding than for lack of adequate financing. Hence this chapter has attempted to suggest, admittedly sketchily, important facets of a sound philosophy of education of all children, of whom the gifted are but a part. In the next chapter, we shall examine certain areas of the gifted's educational picture upon which the philosophical orientations which have been suggested in this chapter should bear heavily.

6

Some specific philosophical impingements

Before we identify specific philosophical implications for the gifted, it is well that we review certain of the "givens" which determine the frames of reference within which, or in respect to which, such implications should be perceived.

THE "GIVENS"

The School Population

We start with the most obvious—the fact that the population of school children with whom we are particularly concerned is one with relatively greater abstract learning potential than the general school population. While even in this one characteristic they differ quite significantly among themselves, they present an array of differences in other respects. Some may come from rich and highly nurturant experiential backgrounds, others from backgrounds that

have left them experientially impoverished. Some will come out of, and still be in, social situations that have caused them to be highly motivated—to be "off and running" insofar as wanting to learn is concerned; others, coming from less favorable backgrounds, will have only latent possibilities to acquire even "normal" motivation. The gifted, as a group, present constellations of differing capabilities in combination with their symbolic learning capability; generally, these other areas of promise are not compensatory for lack of basic learning potential, but constitute the "something extras" on which education can capitalize, and from which society can benefit.

School Settings

Another important category of givens is the condition of widely varying differences among the school settings in which the gifted are to do their learning. Marked personal and professional differences exist among school superintendents, principals, teachers, and other educational personnel. Some superintendents, seemingly devoid of an educational philosophy that is sensitive to the realities of society, will do anything in their power to keep from rocking the educational boat which they have firmly anchored in the past; others not only tolerate but may actually encourage their staffs' seriously concerned efforts to improve the quality of their educational programs. Some school personnel pride themselves in confining the learning by their children in a lockstep mold; others seek assiduously to individualize their educational programs. By virtue of their differences in professional training and preparation, their own personality characteristics, their responsiveness to lay pressures and professional advocacy, and their astuteness in utilizing effectively the facilities at hand— to mention only a few of the kinds of predisposing or contributing factors—those in positions of key responsibility differ tremendously in the kinds of educational programs which they administer. Factors such as these contribute to a wide range of administrative and teaching climates in which the philosophy of any program for the gifted may be potentially fruitful.

Accompanying such a variation in professional competence and orientation is the disconcertingly wide range of the physical conditions in which learning is expected to take place and the variety of instructional materials available to help learning occur. While the provision of attractive modern school plants and an abundance of instructional materials no more guarantees that the children using them will learn than studying in the light of a fireplace precludes learning, and while there is a growing tendency to create larger centralized school districts on the assumption that a richer learning environment thereby can be created, there remain many poorly constructed and equipped school buildings and classrooms which, along with attendant conditions, mitigate against effective learning by the children in them. And sprinkled among them are gifted youngsters whose need for superior opportunities to learn is just as great, if not greater, than that of more advantageously located gifted youngsters. Paralleling this diversity is the wide variety of communities in which the schools are located—some of them potentially rich in learning-enhancing facilities (colleges, theaters, libraries) and many of them not reachable even by traveling libraries. And, of course, the parental and community climate, to which the schools must be regarded as having contributed, can determine the realizability or the implementability of a philosophy of educating the gifted. Educational philosophy is never implemented in a social or attitudinal vacuum.

Use of Funds and Resources

Among the givens must be included the phenomena which attend the expectation, allocation, and effective utilization of extra funding by means of which to implement and operate educational programs and practices which can be facilitative to the education of the gifted. It is quite possible that what will be said here may be construed by some as tantamount to the questioning of motherhood, but the points need to be made. It was well that the Congress saw fit, in response to no small amount of lobbying, to incorporate in the Elementary and Secondary Education Amendments of 1969 an expression of concern for the "gifted and talented" and thus provided a basis on which the U.S. Office of Education would seek funds to be used in their interests. It is true that extra funds can be facilitative, although it is interesting that those same adults who expect their children to "do right" without being paid to do so because that's the way things should be are also the ones who wait to be granted funds to be used to initiate practices in the interests of the gifted when such practices long should have been integral parts of their regular educational programs. But there were identifiable needs for some extra funds: some classes were excessively large, teachers (and their supervisors) did need extra amounts and different kinds of special preparation in order to work effectively in the interests of brighter children, there was—and still is—a dearth of reading, laboratory, and supplementary instructional materials, and, not to exhaust the list, there was a need for certain important extras—transportation costs, school psychological services, specialist involvements, financial aid for pupils, and the like. Whether such needs are *extra* is, however, debatable.

Granting all of these legitimate needs, however, it probably could be demonstrated quite objectively that there already exist more sources and facilities that are latent or dormant in many schools and communities and which do not require special funding than have been utilized constructively in the interests of the gifted. Competent and effective teaching, not just of the gifted, is less a function of the amount of money spent to that end than it is of the interest, motivation, commitment, ingenuity, energy, and overall content competency of those teaching. These comments must not be taken to imply that extra funding of special efforts in the interests of the gifted is not needed; rather, they are intended to point out that many educators have failed to capitalize well even upon what has been at hand. By virtue of such extra funding, much more can be done for the gifted than has been done; without it, however, more could have been done than was done.

Applicability to the Gifted

Just as the discussion of philosophy of education in general had inevitable implications with respect to the gifted, just so do the generalizations to be discussed with specific regard to them have varying degrees of relevance to the education of all children. Any unique applicability to the gifted is a function of the ways, or degrees, in which the gifted differ from the generality of the school population. Whether the generalizations can be regarded as philosophy or only as stemming from philosophy is not important here. They do, however, constitute foci requiring particular philosophical sensitivity. These include the major program objective, the gifted pupil, his teacher, teaching methods, his curriculum, and the administration of the educational program as it relates to him.

PROGRAM OBJECTIVE

The overriding objective of any educational program that is desirable for the gifted is fundamentally the same for all children. It has two major facets—to contribute to the self-fulfillment of each child and to help him learn with a view to his contributing to society in a manner and to a degree in harmony with his capability to do so. By virtue of our knowledge of the superior learning potential of the gifted, we are justified in expecting them, with the help of education, to make superior contributions to society in one or more areas of major social significance.

The probability that any self-fulfilled individual is more likely to be a socially contributive individual than not is presumed. The two characteristics are interactive, and can interact either positively or negatively. The self-fulfilled individual is a "happy" individual, and therefore is less likely to be at odds with the social setting within which he is functioning. The individual who is not functioning in harmony with his capabilities, whether he be bright, average, or dull, passes through a stage where his homeostasis is disturbed, often without his being aware of the cause or nature of his problem, to a stage where he adapts to such a condition in either of two ways. He may just learn to adapt to marching to a tempo slower than the one for which he originally was suited, becoming a conforming underachiever. Or he may learn one or more behavior patterns that are compensatory for the disparity between his level of potential and the level of accepted—and therefore expected—performance. Whether the nature of his compensatory behavior is socially contributive, as in the cases of Einstein, Edison, and Lindbergh, or is socially noncontributive, as in the cases of many high-level criminals, depends upon the nature of the system of social values under which he has been reared and is operating.

While each person can be socially contributive in his own way (rather than passive or parasitic), both the capabilities of the gifted and the needs and demands of important segments of our society (law, science, government, social services, and the like) combine to make legitimate our expectations of their contributions in such areas. The implications of such expectations are relevant to the learnings by the gifted from the time they enter upon formal schooling—or even before, throughout their involvement in the educational process.

THE GIFTED PUPIL

Integration and Isolation

The gifted, on the one hand relatively homogeneous as regards their greater potential for ease and extent of learning, yet manifesting a demanding diversity of patterns of promise and needs in other areas, face the social task of effectively reconciling the unique paradox of developing and maintaining positive interpersonal relationships and of being able to enjoy their need for and right to significant, and probably varying, degrees of "splendid isolation." Affecting the gifted's understanding of both the general principles underlying interpersonal and intergroup relationships and their own personal relationships with others is the quality of their own socioemotional adjustment. That this is not a major problem for the gifted has been indicated clearly by research, but, again, differences within the group need to be recognized.

That the gifted should themselves relate effectively to the others in their lives is, generally, a warranted expectation, but it should not be construed to mean that they should be reduced to a back-slapping, slogan-uttering conformity. Each person, gifted or not, has both a need to commingle with others and a right to privacy. As pointed out earlier, the communication gap between a few of the gifted and those in their environs may be so great as to justify their being regarded as entitled to what many might perceive as an excess of aloofness. Two aspects of this are of importance: such isolation should not be imposed, wittingly or unwittingly, upon the gifted by their associates or adults, and the aloofness must not be primarily of the nature of emotional withdrawal. For the educator, and parent, of the gifted, the task in this regard is that of helping the child to develop and maintain the important and sometimes delicate balance between the appropriateness of interacting socially and the legitimacy of behaving self-sufficiently, recognizing that the relative emphasis on each must depend upon both the nature of the situation and the characteristics of the given child.

Social adjustment, however, is not a one-way street; in its simplest form it is the result of an interaction between two persons. It is disturbingly interesting that, when the social adjustment of the gifted is discussed, the facet of the matter that receives by far the greater consideration is that of the gifted's adjustment to others in their environs. (It well might be that this condition results from a fear or apprehension, on the part of the nongifted, of the gifted.) However, deserving equal consideration is the matter of the nongifted's adjustment to the gifted. Those not identified in society as gifted have not only the right to expect at least tolerable social interaction with at least the large majority of the gifted but also the obligation to at least certain of the gifted to accord them the right to such psychologically healthy separateness as may be legitimately contributive to their development and creative endeavors.

Fundamentally, adjustment or nonadjustment is in the eyes of the perceiver. Given the fact of differentness in an individual, or in a group of individuals, the others who usually constitute a majority tend to generalize that such individuals are different also in other respects. Individuals possessing an outstanding "good" characteristic tend to be perceived by others as being equally "good" in other respects; conversely, individuals regarded as having a given "bad" characteristic tend to be regarded by others as equally "bad" in other respects. Feelings of fear and insecurity are conducive to negative generalizations; feelings of security and positive regard are conducive to positive generalizations. Later in the educational-maturational growth, sounder and more integrative social perception can occur. The role and responsibility of teachers and parents in this regard are clearly suggested.

Roles and Involvements

While the gifted as a group differ most from the nongifted in their capacity to do "abstract reasoning" and they differ also in the number, range, and depths of their interests, thinking in terms of such averages can lead to neglect of the fact that they, as individuals, present widely varying constellations of these and other characteristics—other socially significant special aptitudes, differing cognitive styles, and the like. With all the important individual differences among the gifted, the matter of their coming to focus with respect to their anticipated or probable adult roles in society merits consideration. Even though some quite early in their lives have become committed to given lines or areas of involvement, as in the areas of music, art, and science, and have persevered in those areas, generally delayed commitment is to be expected, or even encouraged. Whereas it may be relatively early in their lives that involvement in some general area can be anticipated for the gifted (verbal, quantitative, music, art), it can be generalized that the brighter the individual the later his decision regarding the specific area of commitment should be made. He may, for instance, appear to have the qualities which might contribute to his becoming a scientist, but whether he will, or should, move into, say, biology, chemistry, physics, mathematics, or physiology properly can become apparent considerably later.

The gifted come from highly varying kinds of social milieu. Because of their particular competence in the acquisition and use of symbols, largely verbal in nature, the gifted are particularly capable of comprehending, thinking about, and understanding the world which is beyond their immediate experience. By means of this capacity to learn to know about the world vicariously, by means of concepts, instead of having to rely solely or so heavily upon more limited perceptions of the immediate world, their range of social awareness and sensitivity can be highly extensible. While the immediacy of their present environment initially has major educational implications, the possibilities of the remote constitute potentially fruitful educational frontiers. Particularly for the gifted, the experiences in their immediate world constitute but stepping stones to the universe.

THE TEACHER
OF THE GIFTED

The generalization to be developed here, perhaps not very definitive as it stands, is that the teacher of the gifted must possess in abundance those characteristics which can be particularly contributive to the learning to be done by the gifted. Ward (1961) advocated that teachers of the gifted "should be among those of the greatest general excellence to be found in the profession" (p. 109) and that they "should be deviant with respect to those qualities common to the gifted group" (p. 115).

Having identified 109 successful high school teachers of the gifted and on the basis of intensive interviews of 30 of them, Bishop (1968) characterized them as having vocational interests which were intellectual in nature, expressing high achievement needs, wanting to teach to enhance the intellectual growth of their pupils, having democratic attitudes toward their pupils, being more systematic, orderly, and businesslike in classroom approach, being intellectually among the top 3 percent of the adult population, and being enthusiastic about their subject-matter areas—thus creating interest on the part of their pupils. The 204 respondents, nationally visible in the edu-

cation of the gifted, in the U.S. Office of Education's Advocate Survey (1971) regarded the successful teacher of the gifted as one interested in learning and possessing a rich academic background. They agreed that, since teaching of the gifted required a different approach, the successful teacher must have a high level of self-reliance. Martinson, in preparing material for Marland's report to the Congress on the education of the gifted and talented (1971), observed that studies have shown that teachers with the highest ability and accompanying performance tend to be the most accepting and understanding of the gifted and that the characteristics of high intelligence, intellectual curiosity, and love of learning were seen as more important more often with the gifted.

First, however, it is necessary to reiterate a view that already has been expressed. The underlying premise is that a teacher is a person who is skilled in helping children to learn. Especially in regard to the gifted, this needs to be amplified to communicate the idea that the teacher of the gifted is a person who is skilled in helping the gifted to learn in order that they, in the process of learning, will learn how to learn. To say that a teacher "teaches" children tends to contribute to unfortunate perceptions of the teacher: that he/she is a drillmaster (and too many of them are only that); that the focus of the learning activity is the teacher rather than the pupil; and that the teacher is *the* source of information (and too many of them so perceive their role).

To say that the teacher's job is to help children to learn in no way removes him/her from a position of importance in the learning act. The teacher's first task, after acquiring a full comprehension of her pupils' important characteristics, is fundamentally to so manipulate the stimuli which impinge upon the children that they respond in a way called learning. This varies in degree of complexity and obviousness from directing practice in, say, handwriting, to the use of flash-card drills for word recognition or drill in arithmetic, to spelling contests, to "mental" arithmetic, to practice in dictionary and encyclopedia usage, to activities such as the identification and evaluation of conditions related to periods of economic strife, or understanding the relationships between rainfall pattern and location of deserts, and, more importantly, the generalizing on the basis of the relationships among any such set of conditions or factors. Generally later in the learning process, the teacher's second task consists of helping the children to learn to identify and use sources of information and to integrate the information, thus helping them to learn to learn. The importance of the teacher in relation to the learning act is in no way denigrated; it is only modified in order that the teacher can contribute more to long-time practices in the lives of the children.

While somewhat more applicable to teachers of older children and probably more appropriate to some kinds of learning situations than to others, one of Ward's characterizations of teachers of the gifted is particularly appropriate here. (He writes generically, of course!)

> Men who think as they talk, rather than recall; who speak from the wealth that they have learned, rather than from what they have been taught; who argue with a clear recognition and sensitive acknowledgment of the position from which they argue; men who differentiate faith from fact, and label each accordingly; men who in one breath state not only the conviction, but its reasoned base—such are the teachers for youth who are critically and analytically disposed (p. 113).

Understanding is better than knowing.

While the following kinds of charac-teristics should not be regarded as unique to teachers of the gifted, their degree or quality can be of particular importance when considering the teacher's role in helping the gifted to learn. It must be recognized that these characteristics contribute interactingly. [An earlier and more detailed listing of qualifications believed to be essential to teachers of the gifted will be found in an article by Newland (1962).]

Intelligence

The intellectual capability of teachers of the gifted should be appropriate to the educational level of their pupils. This is crucial for three principal and somewhat overlapping reasons. First, it is important that no intellectually based communication gap exist between the gifted child and his teacher. The teacher must be capable of understanding the vocabulary and concepts employed by the child in his learning, and the teacher should not typically communicate with the child by means of a vocabulary or in terms of concepts which are either disconcertingly frustratingly higher or unnurturantly lower than the level of the child's capability. Second, the teacher must be intellectually capable of understanding relatively fully the concepts essential to the learning of the gifted child. Third, the teacher of the gifted must be sufficiently psychologically insightful and intellectually competent to understand and work with such children in their necessary progress from behavior that is essentially perceptual, or low-level conceptual, to behavior that involves higher-level conceptualization.

Thinking along such lines can lead to absurd and nonrealistic expectancies. Considering not just the teacher but also others who can work directly in the interests of gifted pupils, since our discussion of desirable characteristics will be applicable to both the classroom teacher of the gifted and to the specialist, consultant, supervisor, or other specifically designated worker in the interests of the gifted, the following situation is apropos. One school superintendent, pressed by some parents to "do something for the gifted" and acting out of a dearth of social awareness and relevant information, accepted and got his Board of Education to accept the recommendation that the district employ a specialist on the gifted. At his suggestion, one of the criteria for this person was that she should be a "genius," assuming that such a person should "have an IQ" at least as high as the brightest child likely to be encountered. (Such a criterion could, of course, be at best a mixed blessing with respect to the relationships between the person so employed and the school staff and the community!) Assuming adequate relevant preparation and teaching experience, such a person should, in the light of what has been said, be bright. But, assuming such a person to have the equivalent of a Binet mental age of 16, most of the elementary-level gifted children would have mental ages not in excess of that. Further, the competence of such a person in the content areas would be such as to accommodate the conceptual levels of those in whose interests she would be working. She, like many others working successfully with gifted pupils, clearly would be not equally conversant in all the substantive areas, but she would have sufficient insight into her own capabilities and be emotionally secure enough to be able to help the brightest in the group to get access to those who were more basically capable themselves and/or more conversant with the higher-level conceptualizations in the particular fields of intellectual interest of such children.

While the teacher of the gifted, or others working in their interests, needs more than above-average "raw intelligence," it probably is necessary to suggest at least a minimum level in that area. Very crudely, and assuming a valid measurement of verbal and quantitative capabilities, it is a considered opinion that the teacher or worker at the elementary level should be in at least the top 10 percent of the adult population, with the criterion of the top 5 percent being applied with respect to those working in substantive areas at the junior-senior high school level. Such would seem necessary in the light of the potential problem of effective verbal symbol communication between pupil and teacher, the adult's capacity to have acquired appropriate substantive orientation, and the comprehension of major psychological concepts which are of central importance in the learnings of the gifted. Whether such an opinion would be equally valid with respect to teachers in the areas of art, music, and expressive activities may be open to some question, because somewhat different capabilities may be of primary relevance there. Since definitive and sound research in this area is lacking, only a judgment which incorporates due consideration of the important variable can be rendered.

Emotional Adjustment

Above all, teachers of the gifted should be sufficiently well adjusted emotionally that they can relate effectively to their youngsters. Bright children, being, at least originally, highly curious and motivated to learn and doing much of this learning outside the school setting, can behave in ways that are very threatening to insecure teachers. (One youngster in a class that was learning how to extract square root asked his teacher if she would like to see another way it could be done. She replied that they didn't have time for that, and he was "rewarded" by being required to do ten additional extraction problems by her method although he already had given evidence of having mastered it!) Given a feeling of emotional insecurity on the part of the teacher, especially when he or she operates on the assumption that the teacher and his/her textbook possess all the needed facts to be learned by (or "taught" to) the child, any intellectual excursion by a bright child whose motivation hasn't yet been killed off can constitute a very real threat to such a teacher—just as divergent methodological approaches by teachers can be threatening to insecure principals.

The emotionally secure teacher may be quiet and seemingly unruffled, deliberate, or quick to react. Whether he is truly placid or compensatorily smug may be difficult to ascertain on short acquaintance. He has no need to be conceited, but has every right to be (preferably quietly) aware of his capabilities. Being confident, he knows his limitations and unhesitatingly turns to others or directs his students to others for help as appropriate. His personal and professional integrity is such that he has no need to be a social or professional leech. By virtue of this characteristic he is particularly able to cultivate and maintain a classroom atmosphere in which learning is perceived as an activity shared by pupils and their teacher.

Substantive Adequacy

Teachers of the gifted must be thoroughly grounded in their subject-matter areas if they are to work effectively in helping their children learn. A teacher so qualified is in a position to earn the healthy respect, as contrasted with a crippling awe, of bright youngsters who are likely to find "the" text a meager diet. Breadth and depth in the teacher's intellectual background—as distinguished from any broad familiarity he or she may have with educational methodology—is of importance at all educational levels, although the quality and scope of such background can vary somewhat at the different levels. Bright chil-

dren in particular respond most positively to the teacher's enthusiastic and unassuming manifestation of a true scholarship, based upon a broad and deep familiarity with and understanding of not only the subject matter at hand but also of the many rewarding interrelationships among differing areas.

Curiosity

Teachers of the gifted must be capable of sharing with their youngsters a healthy, sincere, abiding, and wide-ranging curiosity. One of the characteristics with which all children start out in life, and the gifted in particular, is that of an outgoingness that quickly becomes curiosity. It is the responsibility of education to nurture rather than to stifle such behavior. If the child's curiosity has been stifled before he enters school, the teacher must seek to rearouse it, starting by capitalizing upon situations that arise rather than creating social, psychological, and educational situations or conditions that are initially grossly foreign to the child. Curiosity about the familiar can generalize into curiosity about the unfamiliar, and the superior capacity of the gifted to learn and deal with abstractions can be highly facilitative to this progression.

Granting that certain "answers" have to be learned at times in order for us to function appropriately in our society, from the elementary school level on up, curiosity can be whetted as to whether things might be done differently (How may ways can you use to find out if two plus two equals four? How else can the problem be computed, thus checking on an answer? Why do automobiles need to be purchased by individuals?), why things are as they are (Why is St. Louis located where it is? Why does the sunset seem red at times? Why do countries seek to have favorable trade balances?), or the validity of generalizations (Does moss always grow on the north side of trees? Are dogs smarter than cats? Does the spending of more money on schooling increase the quality of education?). The cultivation of a more educationally contributive curiosity can bear directly on the youngster's learning to learn (Where else could you turn to in order to get the views of others on the Indians, on the "causes" of the War between the States? on the merits and dangers of inflation?). The utilization of such approaches, plus the use of the question stem, "How many different ways can you discover or think of that might account for . . . ?" can be contributive also to the operation called "creative thinking."

Remember, though, that the manifestation of curiosity is inversely related to feelings of insecurity, and this holds for both pupils and teachers. One should be alert also to the fact that such question-asking behavior on the part of the child may be a manifestation either of valid curiosity—the child really seeking information—or of pseudo-curiosity—the asking of questions as a means of getting attention (although that can serve as a starter) or of maintaining a dependency relationship between the one asking the questions and the one of whom the questions are asked (a phenomenon that suggests a need for considered emotional weaning).

Enthusiasm for Learning

Another characteristic which the gifted have a right to expect to share with their teachers is an insatiable and enthusiastic drive to learn more. While enthusiasm and drive for further learning have their psychological roots in the basic outgoingness (and, later, curiosity) of the individual, the role of learning in its cultivation must be recognized. Like any acquired drive, its learning history inevitably includes some succession of episodes which have included the

rewarding experiences either of learning more about what the individual was curious about or is interested in, or the enjoyment of learning something new. Each such experience is reinforcing to liking and wanting to learn. The teacher's honest enjoyment of being engaged in learning experiences is both one of the important intangible returns to him or her for being engaged in helping children learn and something that is contagious to the children with whom he or she is working. The superior teacher syndrome expands: curiosity and enthusiasm in learning are mutually facilitative, and they are increasingly possible in one who is emotionally secure and who has the capability to enjoy and comprehend a potential cascade of new experiences.

Probably not unique to the gifted, though more apparent in them, owing to their superior ease and depth of learning, is their enjoyment of just learning. Quite analogous to the mountain climber who wants to climb, or climbs, the mountain "just because it's there," unstunted gifted youngsters frequently undertake to learn about something just for its own sake rather than as a means to some identified end. The adept teacher can nurture this tendency by subtly throwing out lures rather than by formally requiring such undertakings.

Skill

Keeping in mind that the teacher is charged with the responsibility of so manipulating the learning environments of children that their learning is thereby facilitated, the teacher must be thoroughly conversant with the wide range of procedures, materials, and sources of information that can be contributive to that end. He or she needs to understand and act in terms of the readiness and backgrounds of the youngsters, to know what learning experiences can be regarded as reinforcing to each child in his learning, and to anticipate in a realistic and supportive manner those learning needs of which the child may not at the moment be aware. While the gifted child generally does not need to be "drilled" much in the learnings the nature of which he understands, there may be certain skills, such as handwriting, spelling, and typewriting, in which properly motivated drill may be appropriate. The important point is that the drill not become the sustained, dominating characteristic of the classroom activity. The teacher who was mentioned earlier as limiting practice in the use of the dictionary merely to looking up words and copying down the definitions without having the children use such words in their communication is a negative case in point. All such drill must be clearly perceived by the child as contributive to some larger goal and must, as quickly as possible, lead in to the larger, functional behavior in that goal. Again, while what has been said is generally relevant in regard to the learnings of all children, it is doubly true in the case of gifted youngsters.

Nurturing conceptualization

Paramount in importance in regard to the skill of the teacher of the gifted, and definitely related fundamentally to his or her own intellectual capability and professional preparation, are, first, the capacity to discern when the child's learning activity reflects perceptual or low-level conceptualization, and when it gives evidence of higher-level conceptualization, and, second, the ability to cause the child, according to his level of capability, to progress from the lower levels of such behavior to the higher level, recognizing the while that there are differing kinds of higher-level conceptualizations. This important progression, probably insufficiently recognized and dealt with as regards many children, is of particular significance in the case of the gifted, since such a progression is of especial importance in the proper nurturance of their development. It is, of course, true that children, on their own, do tend to generalize—just as animals tend to generalize in responding to white-coated veterinarians. Children do respond to the classness of things or phenomena, and it is the extending, sharpening, deepening, and enriching of such categorizing behavior that is referred to here.

The young child who says a plum is "something" is categorizing, but not very definitively. The older child properly observes that a peach and a plum are round, or have seeds in them. This is somewhat more definitive, but not as sharply as if he were to categorize them as fruit. A child may learn that the Mojave and the Sahara are deserts, an essentially perceptual response, or may characterize them both as having sand and little water—a move in the direction of low-level conceptualization. But when he comes to understand desertness as a geographic-climatic phenomenon having certain unique causes and characteristics, he has arrived at a higher stage of conceptualization. Rain and snow have the commonality of wetness, but the concept of precipitation can be much more inclusive and definitive. The child who pointed only to a certain picture of a necktie when he was given that word to respond to operated at a perceptual level; in failing to identify neckties on persons in his environs, he showed clearly that he did not have the concept of necktieness. The child who is honest only in his relations with his parents operates only at a perceptual or low conceptual level; for him to be honest in varying social situations he must have acquired the concept of honesty. The child who operates, even relatively effectively, in terms of addition, subtraction, multiplication, and division as quite discrete manipulations operates at a relatively low conceptual level; at a higher conceptual level he sees and understands the interrelatedness of them. Depending upon their levels of mental development, the gifted have capabilities of higher-level conceptualization, and the teachers of the gifted need the capability and the understanding appropriate to the nurturance of conceptualization.

More than passing recognition is given here to this matter of nurturing conceptualization, especially among the gifted, because, unfortunately, this matter has generally been dealt with only superficially in the literature of educational psychology and teaching methods. Any child who is not helped to develop conceptually to a degree appropriate to his capability is a disadvantaged child; any gifted child who is not so nurtured is doubly disadvantaged—first, because he is being in effect deprived of abstractions useful and necessary in his understanding and thinking, and second, because his basic capacity for such abstracting is not being reinforced or caused to function.

As has been pointed out, children generalize without being "taught" to do so. The four-year-old who cried that another child "hitted" him was illustrative of this. Yet, especially in regard to the gifted who can generalize even more, the existence of this inherent capability can provide no assurance that he will effectively "utilize" this capacity, because it is highly probable that the child (or adult) will tend to generalize only to the extent that he thereby attains a communication competence that is appropriate to his milieu. Clinical experience clearly indicates two things: bright children, capable of functioning at a higher conceptual level, have been found to be functioning at a lower conceptual level because the significant others in their environs—parents and teachers—so function, and such

children respond quickly and effectively to nurturant experiences which help them to progress to higher-level conceptual functioning. It is therefore incumbent upon teachers of the gifted to see to it that the gifted function conceptually appropriate to their mental levels—a matter of self-fulfillment as well as of social value.

The conceptualization of plum and peach as fruit is possible for younger children, whereas anger and fear are more likely to be conceptualizable as emotions by older bright children. One reason for the latter is that anger, fear, and emotion are abstractions themselves which tend to become comprehensible at a later (10- to 12-year) mental level. The nurturance of conceptual thinking is not the sort of activity that should be scheduled for the first fifteen minutes of the school day, or for the third period on Wednesdays. It is, rather, characterizable as a persistent readiness on the part of the teacher to incorporate this kind of stimulation at whatever time and in whatever learning activity it is relevant. More often than not, it should involve only individual pupils, although there can be valid opportunities to involve small groups of children or even, occasionally, class activity in conceptualization activity appropriate to their levels of mental development.

TEACHING METHODS AND THE GIFTED

Teaching methods employed with the gifted (1) should focus upon helping them to learn to learn, (2) should be appropriate (a) to the level of the intellectual and social development of the child and (b) to the varying kinds of demands and opportunities inherent in the different kinds of learning situations encountered by the child, (3) should reflect a dominant and consistent, though not sole, nurturance of the relatively high capacity of the gifted in the cognitive area, and (4) should reflect persistently a sensitivity to the importance of the progression from the perceptual or low conceptual level to the higher conceptual kinds of cognitive operation.

There is no teaching method uniquely appropriate to the needs of the gifted. What is a good teaching method, and not as regards just the gifted, depends upon the particular constellation of factors at any given time: the nature of the social situation in which the learning is occurring or is to occur, a composite of the characteristics of the teacher (his/her experience and skill, the nature of his/her interpersonal relationships, and so on), a composite of the characteristics of the pupils doing the learning (what they bring to the learning task in terms of their potentialities, their prior learnings, their motivation, and their social-emotional adjustments, and the nature of the learning which the children are expected to experience—skill acquisition, content acquisition, appreciation, creative thinking, and so forth). Hence it is meaningful only to identify important characteristics, most of which could characterize any good method. Inescapably, some of these already have been touched upon in relation to important characteristics of the gifted and of their teachers. Some will be recast briefly, others amplified a bit. Again, all apply to some degree to the teaching of all children, but some merit unique emphasis as regards the gifted.

Any teaching method should be regarded fundamentally as a means of helping children to learn. It is, perhaps, particularly important in connection with the gifted that this be accomplished with the major end in mind of helping them to learn to learn. As Ward (1961) has stated, the education of the gifted child and youth should emphasize "enduring methods and sources of learning, as opposed to a terminal emphasis upon present states of knowledge" (p. 156).

Even the gifted must start in their learning. Therefore it is necessary to recognize the initial necessity of concrete learning, of perceptual learning. But, in greater degree in the case of the gifted, the teacher has an obligation to facilitate their moving into abstract learning, to the formation, identification, and utilization of symbols and concepts. This is made possible by encouraging and helping them to identify relationships among things learned, to generalize in terms of such relationships, and to learn, in their own differing ways as much as possible and feasible, the reasons for the things they learn and the phenomena they identify. These are especially realizable by the gifted, since they have superior capabilities to acquire and use symbols. Ward reflects these in his observations: "The theoretical bases should always be given for the facts, opinions, and principles presented" (p. 152) and ". . . the instruction should emphasize the central function and meaning in the acquisition of fact and principle, and the varieties of reflections of meaning in the developed communicative devices of man" (p. 161).

Just as the athlete must develop certain muscle groups if he hopes to engage in his chosen kind of activity, just so must school children acquire certain skills and facts in order to progress in their learning. Because of their impatience to "get on" with what they regard as worthwhile learning, many gifted children find boring the acquisition of some skills—such as handwriting, spelling, and/or the rote mastery of certain facts, as in arithmetic computational drill. In accomplishing such ends when they are necessary, the teacher should recognize that such instrumental learnings can be tolerated by the gifted, or even enjoyed, so long as they are perceived by the child as clearly contributive to and involved in later, more meaningful learning.

Pervading whatever teaching method the teacher may use, at any given time, should be constant awareness of the fact that successes in learning are positively reinforcing not only directly to the learning act itself but also to the psychological processes underlying such learning, as well as indirectly to other desired outcomes of education. Such latter is the case as regards the child's learning to (continuing to) be curious, to sustain (or acquire) the drive to learn, and to be enthusiastic about learning; it applies also to the acquisition of intrinsic motivation and to the development of confidence in his approach behavior to learning. The current enthusiasm regarding the importance of task analysis in education, reflecting discoveries known and acted upon in the 1920s, is attributable fundamentally to the breaking down of a larger learning task into component parts in the hope of assuring successes in those parts—a process helpful to both pupil and teacher.

Often a latent asset in the teacher's helping his/her youngsters learn is the fact that learning can be enjoyed for its own sake. Depending upon the size of the learning task, its meaningfulness, as perceived by the learner, and its identified domain (something that is perceivable by the child as a learning unit—as in a complex payment-interest computational problem, a "nice package" of pros and cons regarding the tax on tea, or on farm support), the child may perceive the learning task as something with respect to which closure, for him, is possible. In contrast with the nongifted, the gifted can so perceive larger units with their more delayed completion and the attendant intangible rewards. This same phenomenon is seen later in the scientist's arriving happily at an esthetically pleasing conceptualization or theory, the poet's reaching a satisfying or tolerable closure on the completion of a poem, or the musician's pleasure on completing a composition.

As was stated, no teaching method is of value uniquely in regard to the gifted. Many methods, adapted appropriately to differing situations, have potential merits in facilitating the learning of all children. Some, however, have a greater potential yield, at times, with the gifted because of the different kinds of learning behaviors they involve. None of these, though, can be generalized as *the* method always to be used with the gifted. Manifestly appropriate to the learning of all children, but often regarded primarily or solely employable with the gifted, is the teacher's operating in terms of individually prescribed instruction. Other methodologies, such as the use of the initial teaching alphabet, the phonetic approach in reading, and programmed instruction, have inherent merits at certain stages for certain kinds of learning for certain kinds of children.

The earlier methodological emphasis, as in the cases of the Morrison, Dalton, and Winnetka plans, had possibilities of wider and longer usage than they enjoyed, but they went by the board when the advocates lost the center of the educational stage and when they were overgeneralized as having equal potentialities at all educational levels and in all (or most) kinds of learning. The Winnetka plan, for instance, had the near-unique characteristics of having broader learning content analyzed into specifics and of requiring practically complete mastery of those specifics at each stage of progression in the learning in a given area. While such could be realizable at certain early grade levels and in the cases of certain kinds of content, it came to be regarded as not feasible at higher grade levels. And there were desirable educational outcomes other than the mastery of a minimal basic content, such as the prevention of an accumulation of lack of mastery. (To allow a child to "pass" on the basis of a "70 percent"—of something—in effect tolerates his not mastering 30 percent of whatever it was that was believed worth learning.)

The revival of this kind of methodological thinking regarding sustained mastery is seen, of course, in the use of programmed instruction. Each of these kinds of mastery approaches contained two very important ingredients: the possibility of a great degree of individualization and the relative mastery (and therefore of experiencing success) in sequential units or stages of learning. However, educational methodologies known to have demonstrable merit at certain grade levels and in certain kinds of content tend to be dropped altogether when it is discovered that they do not have comparable merit at other grade levels and/or in other kinds of content. The phenomenon of panacea-seeking is not confined to the area of health.

Education tends to be permeated with an implicit assumption analogous to the belief that, if one aspirin is good for a person, he should go on a diet of aspirin. Such a phenomenon was evidenced in the enthusiasm shown in educational circles for the "discovery" method and in the stressing of the importance of teaching and nurturing "creativity"— each of which had important educational and social significance which came to be lost or heavily discounted because they were overgeneralized.

The Discovery Approach

The advocacy of the use of the discovery method owed its popularity to the fact that children were being required predominantly to memorize facts or principles without understanding what they were learning and to the fact that chil-

dren were not being taught to "think for themselves." As a result, teachers were urged to present facts to children, or to confront children with situations, in such a way that the youngsters would be caused to discover for themselves other related facts, relationships, or general principles on the basis of which the children could discover that which the teacher wanted them to discover. The basic objective of such an approach was potentially highly relevant to the extent that the pupils would continue to use discovery approaches in their everyday lives. Use of this approach provided an educational holiday for the gifted, since they, in particular, were so constituted that their forte was the recognition of relationships and since they generally had a larger armamentarium of facts by means of which they could do their discovering.

But the fundamental goal of such an approach lay not in the fact of discovery of those things which the teachers wanted them to discover but, rather, in the broader idea or hope that the children could become capable of discovering things or phenomena on their own and of acquiring a recognition that all "facts" and principles are discoverable. The concept and the technique of discovery were generalizable. Obviously, of course, as pointed out earlier, all the facts of mankind could not be discovered by even a generation, and the children differed significantly in their basic capabilities to "discover," to learn the nature of, the pleasure of, the necessity for, the feasibility of, and the importance of the process of discovering. Yet too often one finds the preachments on the merits of this method of teaching disconcertingly devoid of a recognition of such fundamental points.

In a sense, engagement in discovery learning could be contributive to some "liberation of children's minds." The realization that facts are laboriously arrived at and that a multiplicity of related or competing facts or phenomena had to be considered, checked out, and evaluated before the final decision was made could be regarded as contributive to the nurturance of curiosity and to the joy of learning to learn. The identification of a number of potentially relevant facts or conditions also could be contributive to the youngster's getting out of the memorization rut and to his developing a necessary sensitivity to the reality of the existence of multiple possibilities. To a degree, this relatively short-lived methodological agitation, being at least in part a reaction against a normative, "factually" constricted kind of educational outcome, can be regarded as tilling the educational soil in a manner which made even more acceptable the bursting forth of the educational profession's commitment to educate children to be more "creative"—a movement catalyzed by Guilford's identification of the intellectual operation called divergent thinking.

Divergent thinking

Divergent thinking, the psychological basis for the educator's concern with creative thinking or behavior, has inherent in it the demand that, for any given fact or instance, two or more relevant possibilities exist, a condition that attends most acts of discovery. Yet many children were being "educated" in absolutistic fashion—in terms of *the* fact or *the* condition. At this same time, it will be recalled, the social climate was becoming increasingly averse to conformity and regimentation. "Liberation" was the order of the day, and one way to move in that direction was for children to be encouraged or "taught" to be creative. Just as the children who learned through discovery had the possibility of reaping important social and personal psychological gains, just so could children who were nurtured toward or in their divergent or

creative thinking behavior experience the pleasure of exploratory thinking and, in the hopes of educators, be encouraged to develop in a manner that would have later social significance.

Results of creativity in the areas of the arts, music, literature, theater and productive writing were most immediately sought and positively reinforced, partly because the results of such efforts were more tangible, more easily observed, were simpler to identify and, generally, were less personally or socially threatening. Much less encouragement was given to divergent or creative thinking by school children about matters such as curriculum, student government, and other forms of student participation in the educational process, or about the local or national political and economic scene which were both more nebulous and potentially more threatening to the status quo than social phenomena such as Columbus' discovery of America, the Spanish Armada, or the French Revolution. Temporal and psychological distance have insulation value. And then there was the nagging question, for some, as to whether such "teaching" or fostering of creative behavior in children actually would be contributive to similar behavior in them as adults when they became researchers, architects, lawyers, teachers, dentists, electricians, artists, and the like.

Underlying the nurturance of creative thinking in school children, just as was true with respect to the interest in the use of the discovery method, was a psychologically and socially important potential beneficial outcome. Some would construe such efforts to be contributive to the "freeing or liberalizing of the mind." Others, putting such an outcome in behavioral terms, would characterize it as causing or helping the individual to be increasingly sensitive to the probability that there are two or more ways of accomplishing something, two or more reasons for a given personal or group behavior, two or more possible outcomes from a given complex of conditions. The inevitabilities of simplistic thinking would be increasingly challenged and evaluated. Aside from the more apparent results of divergent or creative thinking, a recognition of the reality of possible causation and interpretation and a healthy tolerance of ambiguity could be the more generalized results of such learnings. Such an outcome, as potentially important as it is socially, could be psychologically rewarding to the emotionally secure individual, but it would be—as history has shown repeatedly—threatening to the individual or social order to the extent that he, or it, is insecure.

"Teaching" creative behavior

It is of major importance that the teacher of the gifted so manipulate and capitalize upon the learning experiences of these children so as to cultivate, nurture, and enhance their thinking divergently and creatively. At least four aspects of this area of involvement must be considered. The first is the fact that the gifted tend to have the greatest basic potential for such behavior, differing in degree among themselves, however, and the greatest likelihood of social return in regard to their responding and producing in this manner. The underlying reason for this is their superior capability in discovering and perceiving relationships in combination with their greater possession of and facility in the use of abstract symbols. This is amply illustrated in the cases of persons such as Leonardo da Vinci, Mendel, Einstein, and Land (the developer of the Polaroid camera)—none of whom, in all probability, had been exposed to formal training in "creativity."

Second, divergent thinking or creative behavior must not be simplistically perceived. This kind of behavior is but one in a number of behaviors which take place in varying sequences, in varying combinations, and with such rapidity that they can be differentiated only by means of careful analysis. To create something that is unique—the essence of creating, at least in the experience of the one who does the creating—involves the identification (usually symbolically) of that which is to be created, the checking of experience to see if what is accomplished really is a creation. Within this process of creative behavior, memory and evaluative thinking occur. Divergent thinking or creative behavior can remain the central focus of concern, however, even though other processes are attendant or contributory.

Third, the matter of "teaching" creative behavior requires careful consideration in terms of two problems. In the first place, many gifted youngsters will enter upon their formal schooling out of a background that has not been notably nurturant to such behavior, thus seeming to present a picture of their complete inability or incapacity to behave creatively. Some may present this same picture after having been in school. The teacher has the responsibility to provide such children with whatever variety and amount of learning opportunities he or she can conceive of in order to find out the extent to which such behaviors can be evoked. He or she will need to proceed on the assumption that creative capability is latent in all and with the realization that the learning experiences which are provided can be conducive to varying degrees of such behavior. But the teacher's efforts must be with regard to all the youngsters, even though the quality and amount of creative behaviors are likely to differ among them.

In the second place, even though there are legitimate times and places when youngsters, as a group, can beneficially engage in class experiencing of reacting divergently or creatively, the purpose of such an approach is primarily one of sensitizing them individually to the possibilities of the operation of such behavior. To plan for and carry out a sustained class program of five-days-a-week periods of x minutes each would regiment and reduce to routine a kind of behavior that just doesn't start to function with the ringing of a bell. Rather, stimulating youngsters to engage in and improve in divergent thinking or creative behavior is something that needs to be done at opportune times with individual children. The teacher needs constantly to be ready to capitalize meaningfully upon whatever learning experience the child is engaged in, and which provides legitimate opportunities so to behave, in order to confront the child with the opportunity to engage in such behavior. Such opportunities can occur on the playground as well as in the classroom, and can arise in connection with any school learning area.

The particular kind of behavior evoked will depend upon the composite of the teacher's sensitivities to such possibilities and the nature of the learning situation, and can be manifested in verbal-rational manners (How else might we do this?) as well as expressively in pictures, creative writing, in music, and so on. However, once such possibilities have been identified, they must not become stereotyped or routinized lest important spontaneity be stifled. There is a time for all things, not a thing for all times.

A fourth aspect requiring careful attention has to do with the children's manifesting divergent thinking behavior in particular, and creative behavior to a lesser extent. Granting the importance of positively reinforcing such behaviors, the conditions attending their early appearance and those attending their later manifestations must be understood. When children first engage in such activities, they generally tend to be exuberant, partly because of the differentness of such behaviors from other routine ones in the classroom and partly because of the thrill that attends such self-expression, and partly because of the fact that their differing contributions attract attention from their classmates (and perhaps from the teachers) that they theretofore did not obtain. All of these are "natural" and should be capitalized upon by the teacher.

However, particularly as regards divergent thinking and somewhat as regards the outcomes of creative behavior, on the one hand the fact of deviance must come to be recognized by the child as something that is both an inherent logical necessity of exploring all possibilities and a pleasurable activity that is inherent in behaving in such a manner. He must come, in effect, to be intrinsically motivated as regards such behaviors. On the other hand, some children are, in effect, arrested at an extrinsic motivational level when they behave in such divergent ways. They come up with unusual reasons or unusual creative productions primarily because of their attention-getting value, and this may be reinforcing to their social stimulus values primarily by virtue of their unusualness rather than as a part of the larger process of exploring the totality of a situation. In magnification, we see this latter become the studiously shocking behavior in children (and adults) hungry for attention. The responsibility for the divergent or creative child's progress from an extrinsically motivated to an intrinsically motivated basis for such behaviors necessarily rests primarily with the teacher.

Performance Evaluation

One final component in the teacher's perception of methods is that of the evaluation of the gifted child's performance. Three points are of importance here—

the nature of the information used in making the evaluation, the manner of the evaluation, and the scope of the evaluation. To as great a degree as possible, still recognizing the marked variability in it, the information used in evaluating the gifted child's learning should be objective in nature. Height and weight information, were it of value in this connection, would be about as objective information as one could get; scores earned on well-standardized tests would be quite objective, and teachers' judgmental evaluations would be much less objective.

Information to be used

In getting a reasonably firm picture of the gifted child's performance in academic skills and content areas, the proper use of the scores they have earned on well-standardized, properly administered, and properly scored achievement tests has much merit. (It should be noted, however, that objective tests issued by the publishers of different series of textbooks for use in connection with their texts are open to two serious criticisms: typically, they are not as well standardized as they should be, and they tend, understandably, to be more specifically anchored to the content of the related texts than is educationally desirable.)

Without going into some of the technical problems related to such testing, some of which were mentioned earlier, two points merit consideration here. Performances of children on such tests which suggest that the children have performed much like average first- and second-graders should be examined most critically with respect to their validity. However, a six-year-old who has performed like an average fourth-grader can be regarded with more confidence as having such capability. In the second place, care should be exercised in the use and interpretation of extrapolated scores. A fourth-grader, for instance, who earns a score on a good standardized test (in some specific area) that suggests that he is functioning in that area much like a ninth-grader probably is so depicted in terms of a score which was extrapolated from a form of the test designated as appropriate for fourth-graders. His performance should be verified by having him take an advanced form of the test—one intended for use with ninth-graders. And, of course, all scores earned on even well-standardized tests should be perceived in terms of the magnitude of the error of measurement at the level at which the test was used, and, in most instances, as suggesting the least of which the child was capable.

Such objective information, with all its well-known but less well-understood limitations, provides our best basis for evaluating pupil performance in academic areas. It is presumed, of course, that a professionally qualified person administers such tests, thus enabling the observant teachers to know whether some child skims guessingly through the test, or some child breaks his only pencil and stops too soon, or some child, because of some motor involvement, is unable to make his marks on the test as quickly as he should, or, yet again, some child doesn't have his machine-scorable answer sheet properly lined up with the items to which he is responding. But such possible "slippages," as crucial as they may be in individual instances, occur in only a small percentage of most groups. The matter of whether such tests sample all of the important achievement outcomes must, of course, be taken into consideration.

Contrasting with such objective information, admittedly worth obtaining only once a year (unless retesting is done for checking purposes), are the marks assigned by many teachers, especially as regards performances in academic areas. Whether the teachers' evaluations are denoted by percentages or by letters, they tend too often to reflect some mixture of the teacher's perceptions of the academic adequacy and of intangible, often unidentified, co-related variables such as the teacher's preference for quiet, conforming youngsters, for clean youngsters, for pretty youngsters, or for youngsters who "try hard" even though they don't produce. Still, many teachers do make considered and meaningful judgments, and there is a real need also for separate evaluations by thoughtful and conscientious teachers of the pupils' attentiveness, their citizenship behavior, their cooperativeness, their conformingness, their relations with other children, and the like.

Manner of the evaluation

The manner of the evaluation of the gifted child's learning behavior is of crucial importance. Putting the matter in general terms and recognizing that it is not unique in the case of the gifted, each child's performance should be evaluated both ipsatively and normatively. Both frames of reference should be used consistently and concomitantly, and the child (and his parents) should be helped to understand the nature of each and the importance of both.

The information presented in Figure 4.2 (p. 88) can be perceived in these terms. On the one hand, how the child performed on the academic tests is most clearly depicted in terms of his own basic potential (ipsative). What he does, or has done, can be perceived with reference to his own capability—not in terms of "the Joneses," or of other third-graders. The general failure of school personnel so to evaluate each child has contributed to a very significant degree to concealing the fact and magnitude of the underachievement of gifted children. On the other hand, it is important and necessary that the child, his parents, and other con-

cerned components in society regard his performance in terms of the frame of reference of others (normatively)—that he read comprehendingly much like average fourth-graders, that he reasoned in arithmetic much like average fifth-graders, and so on. It is also apparent in this figure that his basic school learning capability was much like that of average eighth-graders. The levels of both his educational performances and his learning capability are reflected in terms of the averages of specified groups, and not in the lay sense of "normality."

There is no justification in ascribing primary overall importance to the one or the other frame of reference. Each has its time and place; and both are necessary. If we want to know if a given person can read or compute well enough to warrant our encouraging him to apply for some job, we read the job specifications, find that eighth-grade competency is required, find that he scores at or above that level in the specified area, and, in terms of such normative thinking, tell him of his probability of qualifying for the job. If, on the other hand, a child is to be evaluated educationally, there are two clearly recognizable needs —the need to ascertain how well he is doing in terms of his own potential (ipsative) *and* the need to know how well he is doing in terms of grade levels (normative). When his performance is compared with those of his classmates (a normative kind of thinking), if he is well above their real or imagined "average," he may get on the honor roll; if he is well below that point, he may be "retained," or he may be promoted because he "really tried hard," or he may be regarded as needing to be with his "peers." Schools generally have fostered the evaluation of the academic performances of their pupils in terms of the normative frame of reference. Were the schools to operate equally blindly in terms of an ipsative frame of reference, they would show greater sensitivity to each youngster as a person, but this would be socially unrealistic, since children do compete in an open market. Obviously, both frames of reference are important; each must be used as the occasion warrants; and a reconciliation of the results of the two must accommodate both the needs and possibilities of the individual and the differential social requirements involved in going on for further education of one kind or another, or in going into employment.

Scope of the evaluation

The scope or breadth of the evaluation which is made has tended to be less acted upon than talked about. As pointed out earlier, educators contend that they aspire to have their charges emerge from the schooling process with competency or adequacy in four areas—self-realization, effective human relationships, economic self-sufficiency, and civic responsibility. Yet the system of rewards used in connection with the educational process seems to reflect no such breadth of sensitivity. Certainly the evidence of success in the case of the gifted in the area of self-realization is heavily negative. Efforts in the area of effective human relationships have been hampered by the unpsychological use of the concept of peerness and helped by sporadic, and at times misguided, attempts to facilitate the socioemotional adjustment of the gifted. Efforts addressed to the enhancement of economic self-sufficiency have been tempered partly by some of the "realities" of the total economic scene but more by failure to provide socially relevant experiences as regards, for instance, personal budgeting, consumer education, and the like. The area of civic responsibility has been perceived more in terms of good citizenship within the school situation than in terms of extraschool civic realities. The unreality of the schools' evaluating their end products in terms

of such a breadth of professed obligation is reflected in their pervasive practice of according promotional and graduation awards predominantly in terms of conventional evidences of academic performance.

It seems possible, however, to think of the evaluation of gifted children's performances in school in a manner that is somewhat broader than generally is the case and in a manner which, to a degree, tends to reflect at least certain implications of educators' professed goals. Such an approach involves an important consideration of performance in the academic area, the matter of social adjustment, and a recognition of possibilities in the creative area. Greater merit probably would inhere in separate evaluations in these areas, recognizing the probable contributive value of each to the others, rather than in trying to arrive at a single, unitary characterization presumed to incorporate all three.

ACADEMIC PERFORMANCE.   As regards the performance of the gifted in the academic area, it is just as absurd to expect the gifted child consistently to achieve fully to his limit, as suggested by the results of good testing, as it is intolerable for educators to allow or be unaware of the gross degree to which many gifted underachieve. Using the term "disparity" here to denote any difference between the level of measured learning aptitude(s) and the level of measured educational achievement(s), the ideal of zero disparity is unreal primarily because of problems in the measurement area. Further, for measurement, social, and developmental reasons the magnitudes of the disparities would vary among the several achievement areas as well as among different developmental and educational levels. There well may be important skill and substantive areas in a given child's overall learning picture in which he profitably may be intensively involved for a month or even longer which may not be reflected in his measured achievement. Hence, advocacy of zero disparity between achievement and capacity is indefensible. Rather, it would appear justifiable to expect a child's level of educational achievement to approximate that of his learning potential; surely such approximation would represent an improvement over the general picture of underachievement in gifted children.

The determination of the degree of adequacy in a gifted child's learning must be made first in terms of the totality of his behavior over a psychologically meaningful span of time and then in terms of how he performs at any given time. The psychologically unwary may be disconcerted by the fact that a child may seem to be on a plateau in his learning when, in reality, the child may be experiencing an important though unmeasured assimilation of important learnings. Assuming a not-too-great disparity between the level of a gifted child's learning capability and his measured educational achievements in the several academic areas, the nature of the profile for any given child reflecting his performance levels in the several academic areas very well could vary discernibly at different stages in his learning progress as well as at different developmental stages.

SOCIAL ADJUSTMENT. The effectiveness of the interpersonal relationships of the gifted, regarded as reflective of their emotional adjustment, requires careful evaluation. The quality of such relationships must be perceived in terms of its contribution to their necessary communication and cooperation with their classmates and adults and to the legitimacy of their own needs and life styles. This evaluation must reflect a balanced sensitivity to the paradox of each child's need to be alike and the right to be different. Gen-

erally, the objective of helping the gifted to learn to be understanding of and cooperative with others in their social settings is meritorious, just as such an objective for the nongifted is appropriate as regards their relating to the gifted. Yet the "socialization" of no child—gifted or otherwise—should be such that his individuality is negated. And there probably are a few of the gifted who, as Hollingworth pointed out, probably should be accorded the right to progress in their social development in a manner discernibly different form what conventionally is regarded as "normal," barring the presence of pathological conditions. As suggested earlier, the fundamental problem here is that of communication. That there may be accompanying attitudinal and emotional problems of alienation, conceit, or even contempt must be recognized as a possibility, but such would be the results of how those few supragifted are perceived and reacted to by the others in their environments rather than of inherent dispositions in such gifted individuals.

The fact of differentness in individuals is devoid of value—of "goodness" or of "badness." Initially, any value judgments regarding differentness are made by those who perceive it and from the expression of such judgments, overtly or covertly, by the perceivers of the differentness. Those who are different come to perceive their differentness in the light of such expressions. Confidence can be acquired, and inheres in the ably performing individual; he is accorded conceit, or is made conceited, by others. The scope of evaluation must be broad enough to accommodate both such psychologically valid intraindividual and interindividual differences.

CREATIVITY. Certainly if the gifted are expected to be creatively contributive to society, their school learning experiences must be evaluated in terms of the extent to which and the manner in which creative and socially valuable divergent thinking has been manifested in their school behaviors. Helpful as results on some tests of divergent thinking ("creativity") may be in this regard, they in no way should be the sole source of such information. Evidences of originality in art, music, and other forms of artistic and literary expression, novel interpretations of social phenomena (textbook or otherwise), ingenious and unusual explorations of relationships in the quantitative and scientific areas, question-asking and suggestions regarding various procedures in the area of organizational behaviors (the school as an institution, governmental agencies, and the like) are only suggestive of the many kinds of learning situations in connection with which creative thinking can be identified within the school. Of course, such manifestations of creative behavior will tend to occur to the extent that the school, or at least some of its classes, provide a climate which is at least tolerant of, if not nurturant to, such behaviors.

Important in the teachers' helping the gifted to learn is the objective of helping them to progress, as quickly and as fully as possible, from their responding to extrinsic motivation to their being intrinsically motivated. This, of course, must be considered in the light of the level of development of the child, ignoring, for the moment, the reality of the influence of extraschool conditions. One would, for instance, be more tolerant of the need for extrinsic motivation on the part of a child with a mental age of six than one would care to see a child mentally twelve years of age still needing a predominance of extrinsic motivation. The implication of this with respect to the evaluation of their academic and social learning behavior is at once apparent.

Contributive to the child's progress in this manner can be the manner and degree of his own involvement in the evaluation of what he has done and is doing. Rather than totally relieving the teacher of the responsibility for evaluation, it redefines the nature of the relationship between teacher and learner in the evaluation function. Initially, the teacher must identify, or help the child identify, the criteria appropriate to the evaluation to be made. The teacher's role is to help the child understand the nature and appropriateness of the criteria and, perhaps, to enable the child to add some of his own. The standards for the behavior under consideration, initially known and held largely by someone other than the child, become the child's own, become "internalized," and he applies them to what he is evaluating. By virtue of the capacity of the gifted child thus to abstract and generalize, it is particularly appropriate that he can be expected to engage fruitfully in the evaluation process.

THE CURRICULUM
FOR THE GIFTED

As in so many other regards, the matter of the curriculum for the gifted has had meaning primarily in terms of the curriculum for all school children. What has been regarded as good, or at least adequate, for children in general was, therefore, regarded as appropriate for the gifted, although the gifted might be allowed to learn whatever that was more quickly than other youngsters, just as, in reverse, the less capable were allowed to cover the same intellectual terrain at a slower pace. At times, attempts to introduce learning opportunities or demands just for the gifted were rebuffed on the grounds that such special treatment was "undemocratic."

In order more systematically to set the stage for the consideration of the curriculum for the gifted, certain terms will be defined and a general background will be provided in terms of which problems pertaining to the curriculum should be considered. A broadly based psycho-educational definition of curriculum will be suggested, and some considerations of the problems of the curriculum will be explored.

The Concept of Curriculum

Curriculum is taken to be a conceptualization which denotes the total educational rubric which incorporates all learning opportunities. Generally, such learning opportunities tend to be regarded as school-based or school-bound. Within this can be identified one or more programs of study, each of which consists of a cluster of learning opportunities which may or may not involve a structured sequence of learning opportunities. For our purpose here, a program of study is taken generally to incorporate the whole learning scope at the elementary level. At the secondary level it may be so used, but more often is used to denote learning constellations, usually sequenced, which have a dominating major focus, as, for instance, scientific, college preparatory, commercial, industrial, shop, or agricultural. At times, a program of study is characterized as a "course of study," but the term "course," at least as used here, more properly denotes a component within a program of study, such course itself being describable as any constellation of learning opportunities within a structured, or sequenced, or a nonstructured, or non-sequenced program, as in the cases of American History, European History, a foreign language, a science, metal working, typing, and the like.

Like so many concepts in education, that of curriculum can be viewed in terms of a continuum, one end of which represents the situation where the nature of the curriculum is regarded as having been determined by the wise ones in our society. They have determined, in one way or another, the nature of the learnings that are essential or important in society. Such learnings are pickled or packaged, and they are fed to the learners in bits that are to be masticated and assimilated. This essentially adult-oriented perception of what is important to be learned calls for much learning of "fact," for much memoriter learning. Such learnings are anchored primarily in the past and somewhat in the present. They represent, to many, the wisdom of the race.

At the other end of the continuum, advocated by Locke, Rousseau, and others in reaction against going forwards backwards, is the point of view that the child determines, largely on the basis of his felt present needs, what is important for him to learn. The necessary learnings are determined in the light of the pupil's present, the underlying assumption being that such learnings are highly contributive to the pupil's future as an adult. Recent movements toward "free schools," toward the introduction of courses or programs of study of the blacks and other subcultures, and toward the "free universities" exemplify current commitments to this perception of curriculum. Memoriter learning is played down; learning to think in the present and future is regarded as paramount. The "authority" is the child, and the adult is regarded as the facilitator of the pupil's meeting his own needs.

Curricular Revolt

Conceptual revolt has two ingredients: it always has an initial germ of truth or justification, and it quickly tends to come to be overgeneralized, this so often resulting in the dilution or dissipation of its original validity. Usually, that which is revolted against itself has become overgeneralized. The educational demands of excessive rote memorization tended to cause any demands for memoriter learning to be rejected, usually in favor of an educational commitment that, at first at least, involves no such rote learning. Developmentally speaking, such reactions are of a mass character, allowing little if any room for a differentiated kind of thinking that recognizes that some demands can be of one type and others of another. The important need is to arrive at an integrated perception of such a condition—one which involves the recognition of the importance or necessity of which kind of demand, for how long, and in what kind(s) of situation(s).

Current education is involved in an attempt to reconcile the philosophic commitments at the two ends of the continuum with the inevitable interaction between the conceptualizations of curriculum and those of the educational methodologies implicit in each. The educational literature is replete with observations, admonitions, and recommendations regarding the curriculum, many of which are general in nature but applicable in regard to the gifted, and others concerned primarily with the gifted. Mursell (1934), for instance, quotes Dewey: "What the best and wisest parent wants for his own child, that must the community want for all its children." Mursell, although writing generally and a generation ago, made three observations that continue to be of concern to serious educators. Disturbing him then, and reflecting concerns expressed in the 1960s and 1970s, was his point: "From the fact that our present curriculum is largely the product of tradition, rather than constructive, rational insight, comes its two defects. It is a far less effective educational instrument than it might be, first because it is ill chosen, second because it is ill organized" (p. 377). As he saw it, the obstacles to effective learning were the fragmentation of the curriculum into narrowly subdivided courses, the insistence upon standards set in terms of grades and credits rather than of socially significant masteries, and the emphasis upon subject matter for its own sake. He observed, "Our curriculum has developed towards enrichment—which is good. But it has done so in the wrong way—which is bad. We have mountains of food, but few well planned meals. We have a tangled forest, choked with matted thickets, through which lead a few vague trails and wood roads, rather than an orderly and intelligible plantation" (p. 380).

Essentials and Scope

The quality of material on the curriculum for the gifted has ranged from descriptions of gimmicks and games, such as Meredith and Landin's *100 Activities for Gifted Children* (1957), to Fliegler's *Curriculum Planning for the Gifted* (1961), in which he provides both descriptions of curricular possibilities in eleven areas and a philosophical orientation. For our purpose, however, essentially as elaborative of our general emphasis, the following generalizations selected from Ward (1961) are apropos. He advocated that the curriculum for the gifted "should consist of economically chosen experiences designed to promote their civic, social, and personal adequacy" (p. 102), proposing "that a four-fold category of the subject matter of the curriculum should be utilized, the areas being the humanities, the social sciences, the natural sciences and mathematics" (p. 104). Advocating that "there should be considerable emphasis upon intellectual activity" (p. 126), he observed "that the education of the gifted should be designed to promote their tendencies toward creativity" (p. 133), using the term in the broad, rather than the narrow artistic sense. His sensitivity to the "society that was" is reflected in his stating that "the instruction should include content pertaining to the foundations of civilization" (p. 170), elaborating this in the sense "that the history of the various fields of knowledge should be taught as foundational to present concepts within each academic discipline" (p. 172) and "that the classics of the world's history and educational store should be treated as foundational in the development of the thought of man" (p. 175). Extending his thinking more obviously to apply to the secondary school level, he urged "that instruction in the theoretical base of ideal moral behavior and of personal and social adjustments should be an integral part" of the education of the gifted (p. 201). Note that throughout Ward's observations there is an underlying presumption of the capacity of the gifted to do their learning in terms of higher levels of conceptualization.

Historically, at least so far as formal education was concerned, the school was *the* locus of the curriculum. Gradually, educators have been urged to regard the curriculum more broadly—to move out into and to incorporate more the community and other extraschool facilities and experiences. The responsibility for the curriculum still remains within the school structure. Perhaps for reasons of security, the curriculum tends to remain heavily classroom-bound and anchored very heavily in textbooks which are too often limited in socially relevant content. But pupils who are in school do much learning outside the school, some, very importantly, before they enter upon their formal schooling.

For broad psychoeducational and social reasons, therefore, the term curriculum is regarded here as denoting the total gamut of life experiences which are encountered, or are encounterable, in all learning. The curriculum must be regarded as appropriately starting from the immediate, the proximate, and di-

rectly experienced and then coming gradually and necessarily to incorporate the vicarious of both the past and the future. Such a perception of the curriculum implicitly incorporates the possibility, if not the necessity, of the school's capitalizing upon the information and interests of the children, in order to seduce them into becoming interested also in what the educators think the children ought to be interested in. The educational literature teems more with admonitions that teachers should start where the pupils are than with evidence that this is being accomplished. Such seems to be the case especially at levels above the primary grades and, all too often, in regard to gifted children.

The greater capability of the gifted to learn and use verbal symbols and to function conceptually makes it particularly important that their life and learning space be regarded as not just limited to or primarily committed to their learning about the immediate, about the society in which they presently are learning to get along, but also as highly extensible so as to reflect both society as it was and society as it may become. Put more tangibly but still rather globally, the gifted can not only learn of man's present interactions with others but also, because of their greater ease in dealing with abstractions, learn more effectively how man has reacted to man (history, anthropology, literature, and so on) as well as how man may or should in the future react to man (imagination, government, law, philosophy, ethics, and the like). Man extrapolates from the present to the past and to the future by means of symbols and concepts. Such a delineation of the necessary learning experiences in a curriculum has, of course, implications of perspectives and understandings that are appropriate to all children, but their breadth and depth can be greater for the gifted.

Intertwined with considerations about

curriculum are, inescapably, those pertaining to methods of "teaching" and to programs of study. Methods involve the manipulative procedures by which the vast array of learning experiences can be facilitated and enhanced. Areas of study result from the analysis of the learning experiences into component parts or segments which seem—to those who devise them—to constitute logical or functional units, such as reading, arithmetic, or geography; language arts, quantitative thinking, expressive activities; or social studies, the sciences, or the arts.

Responsibility of the Gifted

The extent to which the gifted themselves should be involved in the determination of the nature of the curriculum is a matter jointly of philosophy and psychology. That the gifted should assume full responsibility in this is just as absurd as is the view that only the adults in their environments should do so. The adult curriculum expert, teacher, or parent certainly is in a position to be able to identify those areas in which learning can be socially relevant and productive. Certainly, it is tenable that certain areas can be identified as minimal and that learning in these areas is relatively easy, but this is not the primary problem so far as learning by the gifted is concerned. The greatest latitude should exist as regards the extents and manners of the learnings nurtured—in whatever substantive or social area they may occur. Philosophically, if we want only followers in our society, the gifted will consistently be told what to learn and how they are to do their learning, although they will chafe psychologically under such a regimen. If we want some outcomes other than placid pursuers, the opportunities for self-direction and self-determination will have to be studiously provided, these to be accomplished

within a framework of socially determined limits. Psychologically, if we wish to nurture outgoingness, initiative, curiosity, and creativity as important factors in self-motivated learning, a predominance of opportunities for successful learnings of these natures must be ensured. To this end, a significant input by the gifted in the determination of the curriculum can be an important factor.

ADMINISTERING THE PROGRAM FOR THE GIFTED

This has to be considered in terms of two factors: the chief administrator himself and the characteristics of the program administered. The two, of course, are highly related, the second being inescapably a clear reflection or manifestation of the first. The term administrator is used to denote the chief administrative officer, or superintendent; administration is used to denote both the structure and function—the school operation which, in effect, implements the administrator's educational philosophy.

The Chief Administrator

Two presumptions are made regarding the administrator: that he has attained that status primarily on the basis of sound and adequate professional preparation and experience, and that he is the chief educational officer in the school district—the professional who provides the direction of the educational thrust in the schools. He is not the kind of "leader" who says "Tell me what you want and we'll do it," although he is sensitive and potentially responsive to constructive suggestions. He is not an instrument of the school board—just the "voice of the people"—although he promotes and implements his educational ideas in the light of the realities reflected through his school board. While we shall speak here in terms of local school districts, possible implications having the same focus can be identified in regard to the state level of educational operation.

The acid test of the merits, integrity, and effectiveness of any school program for the gifted is the extent to which the administrator understands and accepts the need for such a program, is basically conversant with its essentials, and is both willing and able to proceed in terms of his conviction. With such an orientation, he would be committed implicitly to the encouragement of educational practices which are more preventive than remedial in nature, thus encouraging the making of provisions for the gifted early in their school lives; yet he would encourage the incorporation of remedial and corrective provisions for those children who come into his schools from situations where they had been overlooked or educationally mistreated as well as for those children with whom the early provisions within his schools had not been effective. Such an administrator no more sees such a program as a "frill" or as an "extra" than he would so regard the fourth wheel on most automobiles. Rather than regarding such a program as a means of "going modern" or keeping up with the Joneses, or as something which must await special funding by the state or federal government, he regards it as an integral part of the total functioning, ongoing educational program.

Such an administrator would be fully sensitive to the fact that the mandating of given administrative structures, such as special classes or groups, does not ensure the operation of the differentiated instructional procedures which they imply. He would be as fully aware of the need for freedom of movement and direction in education as of the dangers of regimentation. He would recognize the need for and inevitability of change in educational methods and content, but in the sense of adapting to changing technological and social needs rather than changing for change's sake. In all of this he would be fully cognizant of his being neither omniscient nor omnipotent; he would seek and welcome the counsel of competent specialists in the area but would not be swept off his feet by them; he would capitalize upon the relevant strengths and capabilities of his staff, evaluating their accomplishments in terms of the objectives of the program.

Administrative structure and function are of major importance, since they make possible the operation of the program in the light of the orientation and commitment of the administrator. Obviously, those employed in second-level administrative and supervisory positions should share the superintendent's philosophy, convictions, and commitment. Being the ones who provide or arrange for the "nuts and bolts" of the program, they need to be more conversant with the specifics of the program operation, even though not necessarily particularly skilled in the techniques of classroom management. Such are the personnel responsible for the presence as well as the effective functioning of the ancillary services of those who provide school social work services, guidance and counseling, school psychological services, and other supportive and remediational functions which are needed, to varying degrees, by many children.

If the teachers of the gifted are to provide for effective democratic participation by their pupils, the administration of the schools must demonstrate a working commitment to such a democratic climate. Again, just as was the case in regard to the youngsters, principals and teachers must be encouraged, or permitted, to function with considerable freedom within the school system's total thrust, as contrasted with the system's being characterized by either a deadening lockstep or a rampant individualism. Deviant and creative thinking on the part of the staff would be encouraged and nurtured just as would be the case with respect to the pupils. Care would be exercised in the selection of properly qualified personnel who are to work in the interests of the gifted. Adequate financial provision would be made for library, laboratory, and other enrichment materials and facilities.

Structure of the Program

The structure of the total school program should be highly permeable and be characterized by great flexibility, care being taken lest such adaptability not deteriorate into gross laxity. As a result of the operation of such a program by such a staff, for instance, groups of bright youngsters from two or more grades may at times engage in learning experiences common to them, a bright fourth-grader may do his learning in arithmetic or science with seventh-graders who have an understanding and adaptive teacher, one or two (or even more, but seldom a class) very capable and interested children may do some of their learning in social studies while working in city, county, or state governmental or business units, some—talented in the arts or music—may work at times with those in their communities who are outstanding in relevant areas, advantage may be taken of college or university classes which are available to advanced high school students, and the like. Learning adjustments such as these—and the list is by no means complete—will vary from short-term situational ones for particular pupils or small groups of pupils to the implementation of policy, as, for instance, in the cases of early admission and capitalizing upon the taking of courses in higher education for advanced

credit. An administrative and supervisory staff that tolerates, makes possible, or encourages such adaptations in the interests of individual pupils, or small groups of pupils, is quite likely to have a viable program for the gifted.

SUMMARY

The implementation of a sound philosophy of education by developing a program which provides appropriate learning opportunities for the gifted involves little, so far as basic educational philosophy is concerned, that is uniquely relevant to the gifted. The primary difference between implementing a philosophically based program for the nongifted and one for the gifted must be related discernibly to the difference between the two groups in their capacities to learn by means of abstractions, generalizations, and conceptualization. And this difference must be recognized as one of degree. Some nongifted learn in such ways, although the scope, depth, and complexity of their abstractions and conceptualizations are more limited than are those of the gifted. And some gifted, of course, do not function in this manner as effectively as they might, owing to intellectual malnutrition and/or attitudinal or emotional factors.

For the gifted, though by no means unique in regard to them, the dominant obligation of education is twofold: to effect the self-fulfillment of the individual and to enable him to make his contribution to society in the manner and to the degree that are in harmony with his potentials. Achievement of the two goals is interactive in nature: the self-fulfilled individual is more likely to be a socially contributive individual, and the act of contributing to society can be self-fulfilling. Contrarily, failure in self-fulfillment results inevitably either in the individual's doing less than his proper bit for society, or in his developing compensatory behaviors which can be of negative social value.

The gifted pupil, with his superior potential for abstract thinking, is both a product of and a promise for the total social milieu of which he is a part. As such, he needs to be able to do his learning with persons who are emotionally secure enough not to be threatened by his honest curiosity and intellectual initiative, who are socially sensitive enough to understand his need for learning in a meaningful social context, and who are of sufficient personal intellectual richness and motivation both to comprehend their pupils' intellectual probings and to provide enticements into greater intellectual breadth and depth. They must understand and be able to act in the light of the difference between helping children to learn and helping them to learn to learn.

While no given teaching method is uniquely appropriate to and generalizable for the gifted, there is an ever-present need for the teacher, at appropriate times, to be familiar with and to make use of any of a large number of means of facilitating learning by the gifted. The curriculum for the gifted, with the millstone of tradition on its neck, needs to be perceived in terms of their total life and experience space, with which the gifted, by virtue of their superior symbolic capability, are especially suited to deal on an expanded scale. Crucial to the integrity and viability of any program for the gifted is the full understanding of and commitment to the focal points in the educational philosophy essential to any program for the gifted. These must be present in the chief administrator and his staff, and must permeate the operation of the whole educational program of which the provisions for the gifted are but an integral part.

7

Educational considerations

Three crucial factors must figure predominantly in the consideration of the merits and feasibility of any program for the gifted child if it is to be viable—the philosophy which undergirds it, the perception of such a program within the school's total commitment, and the characteristics of the personnel directly involved with it.

As has been pointed out, the school administrator and others involved with and related to such a program must incorporate within their total philosophy of education a firm comprehension of and an abiding commitment to the educational and social need for such a program. Given this, it follows, or should follow, that whatever educational provisions are made specifically for the gifted should be regarded as but an integral part of the total educational program, equally as deserving of inclusion

in the total program as the provision of industrial or shop facilities or facilities for those in the commercial area, or provisions for the general education of others, or provisions for the disabled and handicapped.

While the best administrative provision for any program can be made or mandated for any educational undertaking, the educational integrity of any such undertaking depends ultimately upon the functioning of the instructional staff involved in executing the intent of the administration. Even though the cost factor may be regarded by some as of major importance, the position is taken here that it actually is secondary to the others mentioned, since much can be accomplished for the gifted pupil at relatively little extra per capita cost—certainly no more than part of the cost of a band or football uniform.

In this chapter we shall consider two kinds of matters. The first has to do with some background factors that call for recognition and action—a bit of a philosophical reprise, certain important pupil behavioral outcomes, and certain pre-action conditions that may need to be dealt with. The second includes a general orientation regarding program development, important criteria for program development, an examination of the prime mover of the program—the consultant, and the crucial process of identification and assessment.

BACKGROUND AND DEVELOPMENTAL FACTORS

A Philosophical Reprise

All too often, educational efforts to provide for the gifted have been hastily conceived, some little short of whimsical. When such efforts have resulted in initially establishing special classes for the gifted, the results have tended to have the life of gadgets picked up at some passing carnival. Such short-lived undertakings, usually justified on the basis of "at least doing *something* for the gifted," have tended, by virtue of their lack of viability, actually to convince those averse to the idea of providing properly for the gifted that even sound planning and action in the interests of the gifted either had no merit or actually had unfortunate outcomes, or both. Where such hasty and ill-conceived steps have been taken, sound conceptualizations of provisions for the gifted have tended thereby actually to be set back by three to five years—until the educational hangover is cleared up or forgotten. Such ill-fated undertakings result primarily from a lack of a sound grasp of the philosophy that is of paramount importance.

That the school should be regarded as compensatory for the home must be recognized. Even poorly equipped schools are likely to be able to provide learning opportunities that can be superior to those provided in many homes. The role of the school in motivating—or remotivating—the children to learn cannot be minimized, especially in these days of such great concern for the disadvantaged. The responsibility and opportunity of the school in locating the gifted among all segments of our society is of great social import—one that just can't be left to the home. Yet, it must be recognized that many homes provide psychological and educational nurturance superior to that which is likely to happen in many schools, a supportive influence on which too many schools fail properly to capitalize.

That we live in a society that is rapidly changing is not to be denied. But it can be argued that the changes which are observed are, in effect, only superficial, since there remains a continuing need for individuals to function in ways that are important, or essential, in whatever kind of society there is or will be. Regardless of the changes in kinds of work opportunities, in ease of communication, in interactional relationships, there exists a sustained need for at least some members of society to perceive and understand complex causation, to conceptualize, to "think" evaluatively, to reason probabilistically, to be involved in creative thinking. There exists an unending need to know certain facts and principles, but there exists also a constant need to recognize that many such facts and principles are facts and principles only pro tem. Such cognitive capabilities are both important at any given stage in society and necessary in any emergent social situation. And there is an unending need across changing social conditions for the members of society to experience, and to have experienced, valid feelings of self-realization in order that they can engage in socially contributive roles.

Behavioral Outcomes

There has been a persistent tendency to specify the goals of learning which the schools should attain. Some have been stated solely or primarily in terms of what society has been perceived to need. Others, like those of the American Council on Education, have been such as to accommodate both the pupil and society: self-actualization, self-expression, effectiveness in interpersonal relationships, and economic self-sufficiency. However they have been stated, there has been, at least implicitly, an attempt to characterize the nature of the end product of the educational process in terms that would reflect some sort of match between the competencies of the educated and the needs of society as it is and/or as it may be. An attempt at such a match is presented here. While the behavioral outcomes are thought of here primarily as regards the gifted, their applicability in the cases of all youngsters is apparent.

Self-fulfillment

The first of these, understandably, is that of self-fulfillment, roughly analogous to the oft-expressed goal of self-actualization. It is necessary that self-fulfillment be perceived in terms of degree and scope. As has been pointed out, it is necessarily ipsative in nature and is relative, rather than absolute, in nature. While limits may be identified, or presumed, as to the extent of the individual's capability, the probability—or even the desirability—of the individual's achieving literally up to these limits may be somewhat less than 100 percent, yet the extent of self-fulfillment of the gifted cannot be identified in terms of some group average—unless all members

of the group are equally basically capable. And the extent to which it is attained in a given gifted child very well may vary from time to time in his own life. Further, self-fulfillment needs to be perceived broadly so as to encompass his cognitive, emotional, and social behaviors, bearing in mind that individual differences in the emotional and social areas are to be expected and respected.

Substantive adequacy

A second major behavioral outcome is in the substantive area. Regardless of the changing nature of society and of the evanescence of facts, the gifted need the opportunity to become broadly well informed. In a sense, this may seem like saying that people should be allowed to eat, since they will, with considerable likelihood, eat anyway. While the gifted are characterized by an insatiable curiosity and a strong tendency to do much learning on their own, the school is responsible for seeing that they have opportunities at least to sample from a studiously broad intellectual cafeteria.

Communication

A third important kind of behavioral outcome is in the communication area. While necessarily having emotional and social components, which either may be contributive to the need for and effectiveness of their communication or may serve as impediments in the communication process, there is a residual personally and socially important communication function that must be nurtured. Possessed of a literal abundance of verbal symbols, generalizations, and concepts, and the capacity to manipulate these, the gifted themselves can profit from "writing (or talking) to themselves," and the communication interchange between them and others can be socially productive. Just as students can benefit from engaging in "bull sessions" (a communicative process) by coming to state or restate more precisely positions fuzzily taken, just so can the gifted improve their competence in communication by the act of their writing and talking about concepts held and explored as well as by benefiting from the feedback from those with whom they communicate. There is much truth in the statement, "I don't know what I think about that; I haven't written (or talked) about it yet." Recorded scientific history abounds with evidence of the making of notes, the keeping of logs, the written exchanges of notable figures. The fact that Leonardo da Vinci developed a highly idiosyncratic style of note-making well may have been a function of some insecurity on his own part or of a recognition of the fact that he had so few peers with whom to communicate his observations, or some combination of the two. Part of the communicative outcome logically consists of creative writing, but that aspect is incorporated in the behavioral outcome to be discussed next.

Expression

A fourth category of behavioral outcome is termed "expression." Perhaps somewhat incorporated in the "self-actualization" objective, it seems important enough to identify expressive behavior more explicitly. This is taken to incorporate a whole gamut of behaviors —as in the expression that occurs in creative writing (fundamentally an act of communicating concepts and feelings as contrasted with the communication of a major substantive concept, of a theory, or of a critique), or in musical, artistic, and theatrical forms of expression.

The overlap between communicative and expressive behavior is apparent, but the major outcomes are differentiable. Both have heavy self-realization overtones. The creative architect communicates to others through the structure he develops, his conceptalization of an integration between structure, function, and beauty, but he does so more out of an urge to create or express himself than simply to communicate. The youngster who comes up with his own structuring of experiences, facts, or phenomena does so because, we hope, of an intrinsic motivation so to restructure his own perceptions and learnings. To some extent we all behave this way—outside our sleep dreaming—but the gifted, because of their neural dispositions and learning and because of their greater supply of elements with which to work, do so to a greater degree. The fact that this has a higher probability of occurring among the gifted in no way relieves the school of the responsibility of nurturing such behavior.

Attitudes

Probably one of the most important areas in which certain behavioral outcomes are necessary is that of attitudes— the cultivation of the development of certain attitudes in light of which the gifted can function as pupils and will function as adults. This is proposed not in the sense of having the gifted learn these attitudes in some mnemonic manner or by catechetical chattering, but in the sense of their gradually acquiring them in the context of their general learning. Attitudes are themselves generalizations —learned tendencies to react in certain kinds of ways to certain types or classes of situations. Since attitudes are learned, often in unverbalized form, the major responsibility of the school in facilitating their formation must be recognized, although extraschool conditions—the attitudes in homes and in certain other social situations—play important contributive roles.

At least three important categories of desirable attitudes can be identified—

those regarding moral and ethical relationships, those regarding self and social responsibility, and those regarding their cognitive functioning. Without pontificating moralistically, we can make the point not only that certain moral and ethical attitudes constitute a social cement but also, and this is even more important as regards the gifted, that such attitudes have a knowable history of evolution in different societies—a phenomenon that can be discerned in the study of cultural anthropology and comparative religion. Thus, not only are such attitudes understood and accepted in terms of their validity and social relevance, but also an attitude about the nature and evolution of such attitudes is cultivated.

Attitudes towards self and an accompanying social responsibility are crucial. The gifted individual is justified in his feeling confident in his knowledge or in his capability to acquire further knowledge, but he also has a social obligation to put his knowing or capability of knowing to social use. As so much research has shown, his possession of this characteristic is not presumptive of conceit on his part; in fact, the more one knows the more aware he is that he needs to know still more. But the fact that many capable young persons in our society lack such an attitude is reflected in their withdrawal to an essentially parasitic, socially nonproductive existence. The attitude of being a "self" can be more conducive to social contribution than the attitude of being a "cog" in a machine.

As regards the gifted's attitude toward their cognitive functioning, three aspects can be noted:

1. They need to be nurtured toward an awareness of the multifacetedness and ongoingness of man's knowledge. Having finished "the" book, they should experience an ensuing curiosity as to what comes next, what other treatments of the matter would yield.

2. There should be a disposition toward the discoverability of "truth," or of its greater approximation.

3. There should be a sustained predisposition to want to go on learning more, not due to a crippling sense of basic emotional insecurity but because of the attendant enjoyable learning experience.

The gifted do not sit back on their intellectual haunches unless, in effect, they have been taught to do so. There is little need for admonitions such as these for the gifted who have attained a modicum of self-fulfillment, but the widespread tendency of schools to tolerate, if not actually encourage, so much underachievement makes this necessary.

Pre-Action Contributive Conditions

Before formal planning for the introduction of any program for the gifted is undertaken, certain conditions—aversions, attitudes, biases, preconceptions—must be recognized and dealt with. Failure to do so can result easily in the failure of a program to accomplish even a modicum of legitimate aspirations.

Attitudinal apathy

Repeatedly the point has been stressed that, at least among those desiring to accomplish educational adjustments for the gifted, there should be an amenability or susceptibility, if not a strong commitment, to such an undertaking. The main reason for emphasizing this is the unfortunate fact that educators as a group, to say nothing of the parents of school children in general, consistently have tended to be at least apathetic if not averse to manifesting such a susceptibility.

Martinson,[1] in her compilation of in-

[1] One major source of the information compiled by Dr. Ruth Martinson was the *Advocate Survey*. This was a 26-page U.S. Office of Edu-

formation for the Marland (1971) report to the Congress, reported that, in 27 school systems which had been selected from a national sample because of their model programs for children, only five provided (in some way) for the gifted. The summary of regional hearings, held to provide information for the report, showed that 40 of the 50 states had no support personnel responsible in the area of the gifted, and that only three states had three or more such persons. A North Carolina Status Report (1970) revealed that 81.3 percent of the pupils eligible in 1969–1970 to be in programs for the gifted were not so enrolled. Further, 57.5 percent of the administrators stated that they had *no* gifted children (U.S. Office of Education, 1970). Whatever effort was exerted in identifying gifted youngsters was predominantly at the secondary level. Sensitivity to the educational needs of the gifted is at a disturbingly low level among educators in general.

But the professional problem does not stop there. One would expect greater sensitivity on the part of expert personnel. However, Martinson reported that only 3 percent of 104 experts believed the pupil personnel workers showed a "positive attitude" toward the gifted, while 22 percent of them reflected "negative attitudes," other concerns, or apathy and indifference toward the gifted. Weiner (1968), using attitude scales and questionnaires, found that 252 school psychologists and 52 psychometrists were less inclined to favor the gifted than were the 102 less technically involved persons in her study. Those personnel who were working in programs for the

gifted were, understandably, more favorably disposed. Interestingly, personnel with less than 10 and more than 20 years of educational experience were more favorably inclined toward the gifted than were personnel with intermediate amounts of experience. Assuming a continuity of personnel over such a range of experience, one could hypothesize their entering upon professional work with a belief that the gifted deserved special attention, then despairingly becoming resigned, but later developing a conviction as to the merits of doing right by the gifted.

The reality of at least general apathy regarding doing anything special for the gifted on the parts of the parents of school children and other lay experts constitutes no mean social condition which must be recognized and dealt with. Even though public school educators may be presumed to be prepared to be educational leaders, their general record has been one of doing their leading in response to pressures external to the schools.

Professional dispositions

In addition to the pervading attitudinal apathy, there are those tendencies among educators—and among the public who are their products—which must be dealt with in the stage preparatory to program planning for the gifted:

1. The tendency to perceive the problem, or opportunity, too restrictively—a kind of educational tunnel vision
2. The tendency to perceive the problem as involving mainly older pupils
3. The tendency to regard the matters of identifying and assessing the gifted either too simplistically or as defeatingly expensive and cumbersome

USE OF SPECIAL CLASSES. Given the fact that certain youngsters can be clearly or reasonably well identified as deserving

---

cation inquiry sent to 239 persons representing all sections of the nation and chosen for their specialized experience and knowledge on the gifted and talented. Those who completed the 204 forms which were analyzed included state education officials, university professors, education organization representatives, and personnel in school systems.

some kind of educational treatment discernibly different from conventional approaches, there is the initial tendency to assume that there are likely to be several such children, to find out that this is so, and to decide that such differing children can best be provided for by the establishment of special education classes for them. This was the rational underlying the establishment of the "open air" classes in the 1920s and 1930s for physically delicate children and the subsequent establishment of special (autonomous) classes for the emotionally maladjusted or "emotionally disturbed" and for children with "learning disabilities."

Implicit in such reasoning has been the (largely administrative) presumption that classes were the basic units of instruction. Explicitly, such action was based on the following assumptions: one specially qualified teacher more conveniently could help a number of such children; children not so different would not have to compete unfairly with the others; and the teacher of the regular class would not be distracted from her conventional procedures by giving extra help to such youngsters, even assuming that she might be capable of doing so. At times, the contention surfaced that such a "different" child, by being in a class with his "peers," would not be subjected to derogatory remarks by this classmates in regular classes.

It was this kind of thinking and practice, based, it must be noted, upon a modicum of truth and plausibility, that led to the tendency for such classes to be treated and regarded, at least implicitly, as educational and social isolation wards. Again, the educational pendulum began its swing from an all-or-none position to its antithesis—the contention that there should be no special classes—that the "different" really belonged in the regular classroom. Some have not so overreacted,

and are working toward an intermediate position, seeing merit in the use of part-time special-class, or special-situation, arrangements accompanied by positive involvement in regular classes.

Unfortunately, when the matter of doing something educationally special for the gifted has been raised, the initial expressed presumption has tended to be that this will involve only or primarily the establishment of special classes for them. It may have been noted that nothing presented so far has been restricted to the matter of providing special classes for the gifted; rather, the orientation consistently has been in terms of "special provisions" for the gifted. In fact, the point will be made later that a wide variety of desirable provisions can and should be made for the gifted, among which, of course, can be the establishment of special classes or even of special schools.

DELAYING OF PROVISIONS. When there exists a willingness to "do something for the gifted" in a school system, the odds are high that the intended action will be introduced at a higher grade level than is strategically sound. Three possible interacting reasons underlie this disposition:

1. Historically, educational changes have tended more to be introduced from the twelfth grade down rather than from the first grade up—guidance and counseling, "intelligence" testing, visual education, curriculum changes, for instance.
2. The presence of children's educational problems becomes more apparent at the higher grade levels—underachievement becomes more clearly apparent, maladaptive behaviors loom larger, disparities between pupil performances and grade-level expectancies become more easily discernible.
3. Many educators strongly believe that group testing of "intelligence" has little validity below at least the fourth grade.

It is probable that the long-influential post hoc definition of the gifted (as those who already had demonstrated their superior capability) has heavily influenced the late identification of the gifted and, therefore, the delay of doing something for them till later in the school program. There is another possibility: perhaps teachers of pupils in the primary grades just might be doing a better job of working with children of varying degrees of learning aptitude than do those at higher grade levels.

This condition of the introduction of provisions for the gifted at higher grade levels was reflected quite clearly in the highly publicized statewide program for the gifted in which, for its first three years, none of the provisions made in the various localities involved was at the elementary level, and in which only later were a very few "experiments" introduced as low as the sixth-grade level. It is interesting, in discussing the introduction of provisions for the gifted with administrators, that they quickly profess to recognize the merits of starting a program early because of its preventive possibilities, but they generally tend to proceed with the introduction of provisions that are more clearly corrective or remedial in nature, stressing the importance of "dealing with this problem of underachievement" in the gifted. The concept of educational strategy seems to be displaced by ineffective tactics.

IDENTIFICATION AND COSTS OF ASSESSMENT. The identification and assessment of the gifted tend to be perceived either too simplistically or too threateningly. A belief persists that they are easily identifiable—those who are worth identifying —by means of teacher nomination. The results of numerous studies show the danger in this belief. Cornish (1968), for instance, reported that the teachers of 87 pupils nominated 12 of them as gifted,

only five of them correctly, but missed 11 others who could have been so characterized. Routine reliance on the scores earned on group and/or individual tests of learning aptitude can involve error, but not as great as in the case of teacher nomination.

While teacher nomination of the gifted has some value, this approach is too subject to error to justify relying solely on it. Our social definition of the gifted was cast in terms of a Binet IQ of 120 to 125 and above. This can be much more objective than personal judgment. Such characterization is administratively necessary and appropriate with regard to a population so chronologically heterogeneous, ranging as they do from preschool to secondary levels.

But three points are very important in connection with such thinking. In the first place, children who meet this test criterion thus only become eligible to be regarded as gifted, they are only nominated for possible inclusion in the group called gifted. Other evidence must be adduced to strengthen their claim. Some educators seek to accomplish this by specifying that any such candidate also must be found to be superior to some degree in some area, more often than not academic. Doing so, ostensibly as an insurance measure, has two interrelated results: it tends to reduce the number of children who will be regarded by such educators as gifted and it removes from further consideration those children of superior potential who are marked underachievers. The older the school population under consideration, the more this practice tends to be employed.

Second, many educators, acting as though they believed that an IQ is an IQ is an IQ, seek their candidates for the gifted without regard to the nature of the device on which the criterion IQ was obtained. Using IQ 120 as the criterion in connection with a group of disadvantaged elementary school children, the author found that 4 percent of them (all boys) met or exceeded that criterion on one test, 5 percent (again all boys) on a second test, and 8 percent (boys and girls) on a third test. It is in the light of this kind of condition that the primary or basic frame of reference taken in this text is the Binet IQ, or its research-demonstrated psychological (not psychometric) equivalent.

Third, even a satisfactorily high IQ on the Binet, although a psychometrically satisfying number, must be employed psychologically to make certain that it reflects the kinds of behavior that are of primary importance in the gifted —their ability to generalize and deal with abstractions. In terms of this kind of analysis by a competent psychologist, a few children with high enough Binet IQs may not qualify as gifted and a few children with Binet IQs below the criterion can be found to have gifted potential. However, the bulk of those meeting or exceeding that Binet criterion are likely to be found to be legitimately regarded as gifted.

And then there are those who completely reject the Binet IQ as deserving even initial consideration in arriving at a decision regarding giftedness in children, even as it has been defined in this book. During much of the 1960s and into the 1970s, much criticism has been voiced regarding the validity of tests of learning aptitude as indicators of children's learning potential. As pointed out in Chapter 4, no small amount of this criticism has had merit, owing to a number of factors: the use of inappropriate tests; the inappropriate use and interpretation of the results of even the good tests; poor communication of psychoeducationally meaningful information by the examiner; too often only poorly trained psychometrists; and inadequate comprehension on the part of the consumers of such informa-

tion—administrators, teachers, guidance personnel. Most of the valid objections to such testing inhered in the misuse of the results regarding the "disadvantaged." This largely legitimate challenge of the validity of procedures in assessing learning potential, much of it emotionally based and some of it factually founded, has been overgeneralized, and there has occurred another mass reaction where differentiation in perceiving and thinking is called for.

Yet another matter causes "practical" educators to hesitate in instituting special educational provisions for the gifted. Accepting the idea that relevant intellectual capacities can be ascertained meaningfully, and accepting that this necessitates individual assessment by at least properly qualified psychological examiners, they ask how this is to be accomplished. If they are fortunate enough to have on their staffs persons who are so qualified, their psychologists already have more referrals than they can process. If they have no such persons, or only a very few, on their staffs, the problem of accomplishing the assessment procedure looms even larger. They have heard that the going rate for such examinations ranges from \$25 to \$100 per child. They then identify two possible lines of action —either the school can assume this responsibility, or it can be made that of the children's parents. If the school is to assume the responsibility, X amount must be budgeted to cover the costs of N evaluations and, perhaps, the school will have to employ additional staff to make them. In either case, the administrator regards the cost of the possible undertaking as quite threatening.

Some school systems have, most undemocratically, placed on the parents of the children whom they want to be considered for the special program the responsibility for having their children properly assessed. It is argued, in part defensively, that such a practice serves two purposes—those children who are so qualified probably would come from families whose motivation could be helpful to a gifted child in a special program, and the school would be relieved of the expense of evaluating children whose less supportive and psychologically less perceptive parents incorrectly regarded them as candidates for such a program. Of course, the heart of this problem lies in regarding the doing of something for the gifted as something special, something extra, rather than as an integral part of the regular school program.

The problem summarized

In preparing to plan for the introduction of any school program for gifted children, then, it is very important that full consideration be given to predisposing conditions and that, where necessary, ameliorative steps be taken. The reality of apathy, or even aversion, to such action must be recognized. With such attitudes so demonstrably pervasive among those to whom laymen look for educational leadership, it is understandable that they will exist among lay members of society who are, in the last analysis, products of such a system. Professional dispositions to regard the whole matter at a perceptual level—only or primarily in terms of starting special classes, in terms of attacking the problem at later-than-desirable grade levels, of thinking tactically rather than strategically, or of the manner, or even of the feasibility, of properly identifying candidates for such programs, and of thinking, essentially self-defeatingly, of probable costs of even the identification aspect of the programs —all are realities that must be dealt with. To recognize that they exist is to proceed realistically; to regard them as not being correctable or surmountable is unwarranted.

MAJOR PROGRAMMATIC CONSIDERATIONS

Once the idea of providing a program especially geared to the educational needs of gifted children has been accepted on sound philosophical grounds, matters more directly relevant to its implementation require serious exploration, prethinking, and planning. There is a very real need for sound preplanning in terms of which a program is started, but there is also a continuing need to regard it as amenable to subsequent modification. Any such modification, however, must be philosophically and psychologically justifiable. A clear distinction must be made between what has so often been, and sometimes proudly proclaimed to be, an essentially trial-and-error approach and a preplanned soundly based approach within which considered alterations are possible.

Questions such as the following must be answered before any program for the gifted is initiated. What should the general nature of the program be and what initial steps need to be taken? To what extent and in what ways can school systems' procedures for identifying the gifted be utilized, or will they need to be developed? What about the personnel to be involved, and their particular qualifications? In what way(s) should the program be evaluated? What about the extra costs of such a program? And, of course, instructional matters require major consideration: methodological considerations, the problem of interest grouping, the ever-present one of enrichment, and ambiguously regarded acceleration.

In this section we shall examine some of the thinking that must be involved in planning for the development of a program for the gifted. In this connection, we shall pay particular attention to important criteria for program development and to the consultant—who, it will be seen, should be the catalytic heart of the program. Because of its crucial nature in any program for the gifted, we shall consider the identification process, both as it relates to the school's total program and as it pertains specifically to the gifted. In subsequent chapters we shall take up considerations that are basically administrative and those which pertain primarily to instruction—or the more specific aspects of learning facilitation.

Program Development

The necessity of a firm commitment to a sound socially, psychologically, and educationally based philosophy underlying a program for the gifted has been stressed. While this is initially important as far as the central administration of the school system is concerned, it only a little later is every bit as important with respect to both those in the school system who will be involved in the operation of the program and those in the community who will be providing at least financial support for the program. The import of what follows is just as appropriate to a small community as it is to a larger school district.

The time span over which planning and implementation are to take place is very important. Impetuosity is deplored, no matter how well clothed it may be in perfunctory professions of concern for the gifted. It is hardly likely that less than one year will be needed to do the sound planning which is necessary, and two years very well may be more appropriate. Once program implementation is started, the major accomplishments of the first year may be the employment and involvement of the consultant, with, probably, some accompanying adjustments being made for an initially relatively small number of gifted children. To the extent that highly propitious circumstances are present during the first year of implementation, a greater variety of constructive steps can be taken. Other practices can be introduced subsequently to the extent that the work of the consultant is effective.

Let us assume, then, that a philosophically grounded superintendent of schools has come to believe that something should be done in his schools for the gifted. A further, facilitating, assumption is that he enjoys a reasonably harmonious working relationship with his board of education. Being the kind of person he is, he has decided that he wants to move in this direction gradually and firmly, rather than suddenly impose a program on his schools by administrative edict. While the idea of program development is still in the "fetal" stage, he recognizes the nature of probable budgetary problems that have to be faced or avoided. He does not unrealistically presume either that whatever funds might be needed as developments take place will quickly and easily be made available or that initial steps can be taken without some additional funding. He therefore ascertains the nature of the costs to be anticipated. (This aspect will be discussed in the next chapter.)

Such a superintendent will, of course, be at least generally aware of important factors to be taken into consideration in implementing a program for the gifted. He will need to sensitize his board to such factors in order that they more fully can understand the importance of getting the program off well and in order that they not only can participate wisely in the selection of the key person for the program but also can be intelligently critical with respect to any possible extra funding that may be sought. To this end, a set of criteria will be helpful to them in arriving at their decisions. Such criteria can be helpful both in their considering the qualifications of the candidates for the position of consultant and in sensitizing the candidates to the kinds of expectations held for the program.

Criteria for program development

A program for the gifted consists of a synthesis of practices, each of which is known or presumed to be contributive to the facilitation of the effective nurturance of the gifted. Elements or components—practices—are identifiable. Some of these may be inaugurated simultaneously or sequentially, the timing of their introduction being a function of a combination of the philosophy underlying the anticipated program and of local social and administrative factors. The introduction of any practice must be perceived in terms of the nature of its relationships to other existing or anticipated practices. A total strategy must be delineated and any tactic employed within it must be clearly contributive to that strategy.

Such being the case, the establishment of certain criteria for a good program for the gifted is essential. Matters contributive to most of them have already been discussed. Each of the eight—regarded as minimal—will be presented along with relevant implications.

PERSONNEL. The program should start only after identification of the properly qualified personnel who will be involved in implementing it. This is particularly important since, in effect, it provides for a higher likelihood of meeting the subsequent criteria of flexibility, continuity, and interrelatedness. There actually are two components in this criterion: the nature of the personnel involved and the timing of their involvement with the program. The qualifications of the personnel—both staff and teachers—have been discussed generally and will be discussed later in more detail. Those who are to

be working directly in the interests of or with gifted pupils—the teachers—need to be identified one or two years before they are to become actively involved. There is much to be said for choosing such individuals from within the school system in which they are to work: firm judgments as to their manners of working with children can be made, and they will be known for their competence to their staff and fellow teachers. By their being identified early, they can be motivated to take such specialized work as can be contributive to their functioning in their new roles.

If such personnel are identified for their future involvement in the program, they not only can do important "prethinking" about and planning for such work, but, and perhaps more importantly, they can be caused to become involved in planning for the program.

The consultant, being the key person in the program, must be thoroughly versed in the nature of giftedness and highly conversant with the gamut of educational provisions that can be made for the gifted. (This is developed more fully in the consideration of core elements in the preparation of relevant personnel in the next chapter.) He or she (probably she) should have clearly demonstrated individualized teaching competence, preferably at the elementary level. Such being the case, it is likely that she will have demonstrated the operation of the next five educational dispositions.

PREVENTIVE ORIENTATION. The program should be thought about, planned for, and inaugurated with a view to its serving primarily a preventive function. The primary implication is that the program, to be maximally effective, should start at the school-entering age or grade level. But the operation of the program at higher grade levels must so function as to contribute to the prevention of major underachievement on the part of the gifted. As pointed out by Raph, Goldberg, and Passow (1966),

> The bright underachiever is most frequently described as one who "could if he would" or one who "just doesn't seem to be motivated." Such a judgment is commonly followed by admonitions from teachers, guidance counselors, family, and friends to him that he "should buckle down and work," an exhortation which reveals a misinterpretation of the nature of the problem, a problem that is not so simple as to be overcome easily by the will to do better. All too often it is also an oversimplification to expect that an administrative provision, a new device, or a different set of materials alone will obtain different behavior on the part of the learner (pp. 70–71).

The providing of predominantly potentially successful, sequenced learning experiences is regarded as preventive of secondary maladjustment and aversion to schooling, but the possible operation of extraschool conditions inimical to successful school learning must be taken into consideration and dealt with.

SITUATIONAL ADAPTABILITY. The program should be adaptive to but not solely determined by reality factors in the local educational and social scene. Adversive attitudes on the part of the community and of some of the school staff must be anticipated and dealt with, largely in the pre-action stage of program implementation. Publicity regarding the intent to establish such a program, or that attending its inauguration, should be handled most circumspectly. (Some have generalized that too often there is an inverse relationship between the amount of publicity a program receives and the quality of the program publicized.) Of course, to the extent that the making of any special provisions for the gifted is but an integral part of the total ongoing program to that extent it will not be regarded as something unusual.

Certainly, any such program must be adaptive as regards state regulations (although it must be recognized that such regulations were drawn up by man and therefore can be modified by man), characteristics of the local school system's administrative stucture and operation, and the realities of financing. Any attempt to inaugurate a unifaceted program—one consisting solely or primarily of "enrichment," acceleration, special classes, or multiple track organization—would at once be recognized by the discerning as inadequately adaptive to the differing demands in content and skill areas.

FLEXIBILITY.   The program must be flexible—the nature and degree of such flexibility being determined ultimately by the philosophy of the program for the gifted and immediately by the needs of particular gifted children or groups of gifted children. What is regarded as essential education in general can be perceived on a time dimension or on a content dimension, or in terms of some accommodation of the two. The former is evidenced by those educators who hold that x years—usually 12—are needed for children to be "educated." Those holding this view presume the identification of some specified content, or combinations of differing kinds of content, which children require the specified length of time to master.

This kind of normative thinking becomes sticky with respect to slow learners and fast learners: should the former be released at the end of their educational sentence even though they have not learned twelve years' worth? And should the latter be kept in for their full sentence even though they may have done their twelve years' worth of learning in nine, ten, or eleven years? To some, this may seem to be an absurd position to take regarding the fast learners, but a number of high school principals, with the support of their superintendents, maintain adamantly that no child is to be graduated from high school before he has reached, or closely approached, "the" age of graduation. Such school personnel tend to favor "enrichment" as a means of making the serving of the full term tolerable. On the other hand, it is possible to regard the amount of learning to be accomplished as constant, and the time needed to accomplish such learning as variable. That the average youngster will accomplish this in twelve years still can be granted, but slow learners are allowed longer learning periods and the fast learners are allowed to go on to greener educational pastures at whatever age they have completed the specified learning. Educators of the former persuasion tend to see great dangers of social and emotional maladjustment in the latter conception, but manifest little concern about the possibility of such maladjustment in connection with their time-served orientation.

Obviously, flexibility is much more feasible under the content-constant arrangement. But even with this, still greater flexibility of learning situations is possible. To some extent flexible educational adjustments are becoming increasingly a part of our educational picture. It is no longer a novelty for certain advanced pupils to work with those in higher grades in certain subject-matter areas. One fourth-grader, having demonstrated to his teacher's satisfaction that he already knew the kinds of learnings in arithmetic expected of fourth-graders (or even of fifth-graders), undertook, with only a modicum of help, a year's work in sixth-grade arithmetic which was a part of a new mathematics program. One bright sixth-grader, having demonstrated clearly that he was performing well

above the average for ninth-graders, went directly into the ninth grade without having to submit to the intellectual regurgitation of junior high school. (He was on the honor role all through high school, made the National Honor Society, engaged in numerous extracurricular activities, and planned to enter college "early" to prepare to enter law.) By the mid 1950s there was a healthy incidence of relationships between high schools and colleges and universities whereby certain advanced pupils were enabled to take certain college courses for credit before they were formally graduated from high school.

But the concept of flexibility has some broader implications. One of major importance is the possibility of allowing adequately qualified children below the conventional school-entering age to enter school. The too-simply handled matter of grade placement calls for more flexibility. Two kinds of situations arise here: that of the proper placement of a child who has been within the school system for a year or more, and that of the proper placement of children just coming into a school system from another one. The conventional rule of thumb of age minus five equals grade level, challengeable as it is for many children, is particularly devoid of merit in the case of gifted children. As long as we have had schools with conventional grade levels, the practice of placing a given child with those he most resembles in school achievement, ease of learning, and social maturity is more admired than practiced. Decision making in this matter about bright children with respect to school transfers (even within the system) is a case in point: one too often encounters instances where bright children have had to wait six to eight or more months before being properly placed with their academic peers. Martinson, in assembling information for use in the U.S. Office of Education report on the education of the gifted and talented (Marland, 1971) observed:

> Such arrangements as flexible scheduling, independence of mobility in learning, decision making and planning by pupils, the planning of curriculum based on pupil interests, use of community specialists, special pupils teaching others with similar interests, research seminars, flexible and individually planned curriculum requirements, and flexible time blocks all have been used successfully in lessening the rigidity of the school structure for the gifted (Section IV, p. 1).

CONTINUITY.   The program must provide for continuity. As used here, the term continuity has a restricted meaning—denoting a condition such that any gifted child whose needs ostensibly are being well met at one grade level should progress into whatever level is next for him in the expectation that he will encounter comparably favorable learning conditions at that new grade level. A child properly admitted early to the first grade does very well because the teacher in that room not only provides the kind of learning opportunities particularly appropriate to him but also is not prejudiced against him because he is "under age." Too often, when such a child goes into his next grade placement (second or higher), he encounters a teacher who may be different in both respects from his first-grade teacher. One boy, who had completed his elementary work in four years, was placed for half a day in a junior high school, because there were believed to be some potentially valuable learning opportunities for him at that level, and then went to a high school for the other half day. Frequently, the junior high school principal, who was less than enthusiastic about the arrangement, complained that this boy "belonged back with his peers" and noted every minor deviation in the boy's behavior as indicative of his "immaturity." However, in the senior high school setting, he quickly became assimilated into that group, scored third in a state Latin contest, earned high marks, and entered successfully into extracurricular activities. Half of that boy's school year was wasted, to say the least.

Looking at the matter of continuity in terms of another kind of situation, consider the case of the bright child who has spent the first two or three years of his school life in classrooms not noteworthy for their effectiveness in meeting the needs of gifted children and who then goes into, say, a fourth grade where sound provisions are being made for the gifted. Unless great care is taken with such a child in helping him adapt to learning and life styles that probably are quite new to him, he can fail miserably to benefit even moderately in a potentially highly favorable situation. Of course, the later such changes are made—whether by promotion within a given school system or by transfer from another one—the less likely there are to be adequate educational and psychological returns even under superior conditions.

Only a program that provides philosophical and educational continuity can be expected to be effective with the gifted. Ignoring for the moment possible effects of extraschool impingements, the lack or inadequacy of continuity can be apparent with respect to three components in the educational milieu: attitudinal disharmony among educational personnel successively encountered by the gifted; a disjointedness among the kinds and levels of content being encountered by the gifted; and a probably inescapable variation in the educational methodologies used with the gifted. Given properly qualified teachers, the last is probably the least serious potential problem. To provide effectively for the education of the gifted, it is necessary not only to know about and be able to adjust to what the gifted have experienced before entering upon any rung of the educational ladder but also to know about and provide properly for what will occur at the next level into which each will progress. Such considerations must figure prominently in the necessary successive reevaluations of each gifted child receiving special consideration—a matter of particular importance at the elementary level.

Meeker (1968) provided some evidence of the importance of continuity. She followed up on the high school performances of 67 gifted youngsters (34 boys, 33 girls) who had been among the 197 in a special elementary school program for the gifted years earlier. She found that those earning A's in high school came almost wholly from the Binet IQ range of 130–136, whereas those above 141 made most of the C's the group had received. Particularly relevant is her observation that those in the elementary level program did less well in high school, owing to the later poor educational nurturance they received.

INTERRELATEDNESS OF LEARNING. The program must incorporate provisions for interrelating learnings both as regards the content and process components of learning and as regards the cognitive, social, and emotional aspects of the learner. Including an admonition regarding the importance of the potential interrelatedness of children's learnings may seem to some to be purposeless pedaguese, but the fact remains that compartmentalization, fragmentation, and social sterility still can be found in excess.

Lacks of sensitivity to the interlockingness of learning experiences are more easily described than their antitheses. The school district that decided to strike a swift blow for modernity inaugurated the teaching of a foreign language to all of its fourth-graders, using the first twenty minutes of specified school days

for that purpose. Supplementary teaching staff were employed. The undertaking was, of course, officially regarded to be successful, even though in not a single instance was any effort exerted to provide for any carryover whatsoever into the regular classwork of the children —as, for instance, related literary, historical, cultural, or geographic learnings regarding the cultures speaking the language being taught so assiduously. Unusual would be the school district which does not have at least one elementary school principal who has flatly required his teachers to use only the textbooks officially designated for specific grade levels in order not to encroach upon the professional domains of teachers in the next higher grades. Departmentalization, seen in its extreme form at the secondary level but coming increasingly to be used at lower grade levels, tends to mitigate against teachers' capitalizing on possibilities to help pupils benefit from areas "taught" in isolation. A group of "socially maladjusted" pupils were being "prepared" to take jobs in the community by, in part, having them add just large sets of numbers instead of having them figure out bills for food, parts, services, and the like. A group of children of migrant workers were being similarly drilled on adding, subtracting, multiplying, and dividing masses of numbers which could better have been dealt with in terms of their everyday experiences. Particularly for the gifted, the possibilities for discovering and understanding relatable learning experiences in highly varying areas are limited only by the initiative, insight, and breadth of learning and social sensitivities of their teachers.

For a while, in the late 1950s and early 1960s, the idea of the education of the "whole child" was a matter of much ridicule, chiefly on the part of noneducators. But the movement to educate the whole child was in large part a recognition by educators that they had been concerning themselves excessively with the academic learnings of their charges. The reaction against this was typically extreme, just as was at times the pattern of education against which the reaction was directed. That the reaction against educating the whole child was so short-lived was due in large part to a residual relatedness: maladjustment in the social and emotional areas mitigated against effective learning in the academic areas. Frustration in academic learning has its emotional components, just as do successes in learning. True, children were expected to learn, but what they were to learn was not only in the academic area but also in the social and emotional areas, and possibilities existed for academic learnings to be accompanied by social and emotional learnings. Children should do their academic learnings in ways that enhance mutual social sensitivities and respect. Social understanding not only should result from learnings in geography, history, economics, and literature, but also should be an essential component in such learning. Understanding of others can be facilitative to self-understanding with the attendant thoughtful nurturance provided to that end by the teachers. Here, too, the possibilities for the gifted are greater by virtue of their greater ease in perceiving relationships and in acquiring more inclusive conceptualizations.

IDENTIFICATION PROCEDURES. The program should be started only after sound identification procedures, preferably relevant to all pupils, have been at least planned, if not actually put into operation. Earlier we have discussed some important factors to be taken into consideration in identifying the gifted; later we shall consider this matter more systematically. Here, the primary focus is that the identification process should be

an integral part of the school's total procedures in meaningfully ascertaining the learning capabilities of all of its children. The same fundamental procedures apply as well to the retarded and the "average" as to the gifted, certain specific emphases being important in the cases of the gifted. Just as the making of proper educational provisions for the gifted should be regarded as but a part of at least the implicitly mandated educational program for all the children, just so should the assessment of their learning capabilities be regarded.

EVALUATION. The program should be started with a full and firm anticipation that it will involve meaningful evaluation both of what happens to the pupils in the program and of general aspects of the program per se—the extents to which criteria such as have been mentioned have been met or realized. Any meaningful evaluation, whether of pupil outcomes or of program aspects, entails at first the specification of the variables which are to figure in that evaluation. While, in the planning stage, some consideration must be given to the manner in which such variables are to be measured, specific decisions regarding the measurement of certain of these variables may need to be made later, probably with the help of broadly perceptive experts.

Often, there is a tendency first to consider possible variables which could figure in the evaluation, to try to anticipate how they can be measured, and, if certain measurements do not at that time seem feasible or possible, to drop such variables from consideration. Too often this results fundamentally in creating only self-fulfilling prophecies, thus impairing the value of any such evaluation. Hard-to-get-at variables—pupil or programmatic, if they are deemed philosophically important, should be retained on the assumption that ways subsequently known or developed can later be found.

Two factors should be borne in mind: the evaluation procedure must not be perceived only in terms of extant tests, questionnaires, or other convenient devices and procedures, and the concept of evaluation must incorporate both short-term and long-term time spans. Too many evaluations tend to be made as of the end of a given year, thereby failing to yield important and necessary information about the stability or permanence of behavioral outcomes. Evaluation will be considered more fully in a later chapter.

Williams (1958) has listed thirteen characteristics in terms of which programs for the gifted should be evaluated. Essentially, they can be incorporated in the eight criteria which have been stated, but three of them might be seen as going beyond what has been proposed. His characteristic number two—"The objectives for the development of talented youth are clearly defined. These should include the general objectives of the school or district-wide programs for the gifted and the goals for individual children."—might be regarded as having been presumed in the underlying philosophy of the program. He specifies "The school system needs to provide continuous training for teachers in improved methods of instructing gifted children." This has merit in that it places upon the school district a responsibility for helping its qualified personnel keep au courant. This probably is quite important from the standpoint of the school's providing financial assistance or encouragement and schedule flexibility for its relevant personnel insofar as their visiting demonstration centers and professional meetings is concerned, but might be more limited if interpreted in the sense of only an intraschool training

program. His twelfth characteristic— "The school system fixes the responsibility for a program for the gifted on one or more persons and budgets specific funds for personnel and supplies."—well may be added, although such action was largely implied in the earlier discussion of the roles of relevant administrative and supervisory staff.

In the light of these conditions, our superintendent proceeds to seek either to bring into his schools a qualified person who will devote himself fully to the program or to so capitalize upon a member of his present staff—administrative, supervisory, or instructional—who already may be adequate (or who reasonably shortly can become so) in working in the interests of the gifted. He therefore proposes to his board of education that the district employ a consultant who is qualified to do the kinds of things he has heard such consultants do. The board approves after being assured of the budgetary feasibility of the development, a search committee is appointed to identify likely candidates for the position, and the most promising ones are evaluatively interviewed.

But such interviews should be regarded as two-way affairs. Not only must the candidates be interviewed and evaluated, but they will need also to ascertain the nature of the situation into which they might be moving. The candidate will need to evaluate the kind of educational climate in which she might be working—both the general educational climate and that which pertains more directly to work with the gifted. The candidate needs to find out if the administrative perception of doing something for the gifted was hastily or thoughtfully arrived at, whether clearly apparent "results" were expected "yesterday," or whether, while certain observable evidences could be discerned toward the end of the first year, more tangible evidence of the consultant's work would become increasingly apparent from the second year onward. The candidate would need to know how realistically the budgetary needs for the program-to-be had been anticipated: Were the consultant's salary and hierarchical position in the system comparable to that of, say, the supervisor of curriculum or at least that of the supervisor of elementary instruction? Were adequate provisions made for the psychological evaluation of the children who might be helped? Was the proper provision made for the consultant's travel among the schools? for special curriculum needs? and the like?

The consultant

The discussion of program development must focus heavily upon the consultant, because the primary responsibility must be centered in that individual who has the necessary total perspective. (Her preparation and competencies will be discussed in the next chapter.) The nature of certain of her functions necessarily will anticipate provisions and problems which later will be dealt with more fully.

Whereas the classroom teacher can be expected to work directly in the interests of the gifted pupils in her classroom, the consultant would work in their interests within the whole school system. The number of such individuals ultimately needed in a given school situation would, of course, depend in large part upon the size of the school system. Certainly, as it will become apparent after we have examined her functions more closely, there should be such a consultant for not more than 5000 school children— which would involve her concern with the educational interests of between 300 and 500 gifted youngsters.

In larger school systems, there may be a need for a program director, who will have one or more consultants. In such situations, whether the program for the gifted should be started with a large "superstructure" or in a more limited manner would have to depend upon a number of factors. Serious consideration should be given to the merits of starting the program off gradually and letting it build up as its merits come to be recognized throughout the system. As we shall see later when this person's functions are described, the need for such a person cannot be determined solely in terms of the probable number of gifted pupils whose learning situations are to be enhanced. Administratively speaking, the consultant would function as a line rather than as a staff person. In the case of a larger school system, the director of the program would have staff functions, essentially of an administrative nature, and his one or more consultants would have line functions.

The consultant would have six kinds of major responsibility:

1. Assuming that nothing yet has been done toward the actual implementation of the program, there would be certain preparatory steps to be taken within the school and community, following, hopefully, those pre-action steps described in the preceding chapter.

2. Teachers would be helped in effecting appropriate adjustments for gifted children in their rooms.

3. Movement would be started toward the establishment and operation of class or school interest groups.

4. Steps would be taken to effect sound acceleration-enrichment provisions for the gifted.

Incidental to these four would be such things as being involved in the identification process, working with educational personnel in the larger problem area of assessment, helping parents—and perhaps some educational personnel—to understand the nature of educational adjustments being recommended or made for specific children, making recommendations for obtaining extra instructional materials, and providing liaison with community facilities and individuals as well as with higher education facilities.

5. Effort would be exerted continuously to create and sustain a predominantly strategic perception of the whole undertaking without sacrificing certain tactical necessities.
6. Research on outcomes of the program would be carried out or caused to be done.

While each of these will be elaborated, it must not be assumed that they will take place sequentially or that they are one-time matters; some necessarily will be essentially concurrent, some will figure more prominently at certain times than at others, and some will be a matter of sustained concern.

PREPARATORY STEPS. The consultant would have the responsibility for further cultivating, among the educational staff and the parents of all children, an understanding of the nature of the educational, psychological, and social characteristics and needs of gifted children and of the social and educational philosophy that should undergird efforts to provide effectively for them. Particularly helpful in this regard would be the early use of actual, though unidentified, case presentations, which should be at different educational levels, as illustrative of the magnitude of individual differences and the different kinds of needs to be met.

Of primary importance, at this stage, is her planning to assess the situation in which she will be working. She will need to ascertain the attitudinal climate. What do the other supervisors, the various school principals, the teachers, and the parents think about the idea of helping the gifted learn more effectively? What points of view must she cultivate

and capitalize upon in order that she can work in a cooperative—or at least a tolerant—school environment? While she will need to work constantly toward sensitizing all to the strategy of what is anticipated, she will need also to make clear that certain immediate specifics are, in large part, feasible within the present structure. She will need to reflect a sensitivity to the fact that, probably, many teachers already are doing or wanting to do some things that she can help them with.

Consideration will need to be given to the nature of the pupil evaluation procedures (marking, promotion) being employed, with a view particularly to their meaningfulness in regard to the gifted. As partially contributive to this, the consultant will need to ascertain the pattern of group testing—of both educational achievement and "intelligence" —and the philosophy that underlies such practices. At what grades are such tests routinely administered? What tests are used? What use or uses are made of the test results? Since, so often, "intelligence" testing starts at only the third or fourth grade and since the consultant is committed to early identification, there may be a need for her to cause such testing to be inaugurated at the kindergarten or first-grade level. By virtue of her (presumed) orientation in this area, she may be particularly helpful in assisting in the planning of appropriate testing and sound interpretation of the results of such testing. Because of her having been sensitized to the relative importance of process and product, she will, of course, prefer to recommend, at the early levels, tests which appropriately sample both process and product—thus not only getting crucial information on the capabilities of children, but also avoiding legitimate challenges of results obtained only on product-dominated tests. She must do this, of course, with an abiding awareness of the educational importance of attendant evidence of product. She will need, also, to be constantly cognizant of the difficulties inherent in achievement testing at these early levels.

The consultant will need to familiarize herself with the nature of the services available within the school system, and even in the environs, for effective individual psychoeducational examination and assessment of children. How many psychological examiners and/or school psychologists are there available? What is the extent of the demand for their services? What are the school personnel's perceptions of their roles? How are the school children referred for examination or evaluation? Once candidates for the consultant's help are identified by group testing screening procedures, the consultant will need competent individual assessment of such children, if necessary helping those concerned to recognize that such must involve considerably more than just individual testing. The consultant can, by having the school psychologist work also with bright children, help break down pupils' and teachers' perceptions of him as one who works only with slow and/or emotionally maladjusted youngsters.

The consultant will need to find out how the system and different teachers evaluate the educational performance of the children. In case these practices are perfunctory and essentially group oriented—each child described in terms of his "peers"—the consultant will have a longer row to hoe than if children's performances are considered in the light of their respective capacities to learn. Since the consultant will be perceiving the youngsters in whose interests she will be working in terms of individual profiles of performance and capability, as reflected in Figure 4.2, the understanding and tolerance by others of such an approach may be matters that would have to be dealt with. As her work gets under way, she very well can prepare for her own files such a profile for each pupil in whose interest she has worked. This will be of value as her interest in each child continues, and it can provide information by means of which she later can evaluate one aspect of her work.

Because the consultant will be working with teachers in order to facilitate learning by the gifted, she will need to know what exists within the school system in the way of instructional aids, curriculum materials, and library facilities. She will need to know the extents to which different teachers have made use of such materials. Are such materials maintained in administrative or supervisory museums, or are they made easily available to individual teachers who actually make use of them? Are adequate provisions made for replacement of consumable portions of the material, and are they selectively kept up to date? To what extent are the teachers involved in the selection of materials? Depending upon the extent to which the school's budget restricts the purchase of such materials, the consultant may find it necessary to enlist the cooperation of the PTA or other groups to help the schools obtain them. One PTA, for example, assumed the long-term responsibility for placing a set of encyclopedias in each room in its elementary school.

The consultant will need to be well informed regarding community facilities that may be of value in helping teachers with some of their gifted pupils. To what extent are there in the community individuals—parents or otherwise—who can be brought in to work with groups of bright youngsters who have special interests in common, or with whom certain bright youngsters can work for varying lengths of time? What possibilities exist with respect to libraries that are accessible to the youngsters? How sensitive and how informed are the librarians with respect to particular needs of differing bright children? The consultant can do much to effect a fruitful liaison that will be helpful not only to certain bright children but also to others. If junior college, college, or university facilities exist in or near the community, to what extent can such helpful relationships be cultivated? While the possibilities for advanced-credit arrangements can figure largely in such considerations, other possibilities of intervisitation not involving former school credit should not be overlooked.

It is particularly important that the consultant give thought early to the strategy of her impact upon the school system. Public school personnel are disposed to think of working with the gifted, or for providing for them, relatively later in the school program. Sound strategy calls for the consultant to simplify her target rather than at first to diffuse her efforts over a broad range or to concentrate her efforts on children who already have had two, three, or four years of learning to be underachievers. Rather than letting bright children early succumb and therefore need educational and psychological resuscitation, sound preventive action is needed. It therefore is necessary for the initial efforts of the consultant to be directed in the interests of bright children in the very early stages of their educational careers.

More specifically put, the consultant would be wise to devote her attention during her first year to those bright children who are in kindergarten—or in the first grade if there is no kindergarten. This is fundamentally important from the standpoint of total strategy, and it also simplifies the consultant's task because fewer teachers and fewer subject-matter problems initially have to be dealt with. Such strategy would be reflected in the following manner. Let us say that during her first year, the consultant works only with the teachers who

have bright children in the kindergarten (or in the first grade). The next year, the consultant would work with those teachers in the next higher grade, and "pick up" those new teachers and their bright pupils entering the schools at the level just worked with. (Some of the teachers still at that level may need some continuing help with their entering bright children.) If the work of the consultant has been effective, the teachers with whom she already has worked will tend to need decreasing help, thus enabling her to work with additional teachers. A comparable progression of effort can be envisioned with respect to succeeding grade levels. This type of operation makes it possible for the consultant to work in the interests of gifted children in terms of a longitudinal perspective, thus enabling her to help teachers provide a continuing and integrated educational growth for the children. The effort per child already worked with thus should decrease as the number of teachers worked with increases and as the children progress in school. In many school systems, much preparatory work will be needed in order that such a strategic approach will be accepted.

Obviously, the effectiveness with which the consultant will be able to work in the interests of different gifted children will be affected by the attitudes, temperaments, personal commitments, and professional competencies of the principals in whose buildings she will work and of the teachers with whom she will be working. The condition of individual differences is not limited to children; they are found also among principals and teachers (as well as among parents). Building principals differ markedly in how they believe children should learn and how teachers should "teach." Some are forthrightly committed to maintaining quite rigid programs in which children are perceived as needing to be "educated" with their "peers," in which third-graders, for instance, are just that, and in which only "tried and true" methods are tolerated. And there are teachers who hold similar views and therefore work comfortably only in such a setting. On the other hand, there are principals who subscribe heartily to the idea of individualized instruction and who encourage and help the teachers in their buildings to modify conventional educational procedures in whatever ways may seem appropriate in order effectively to create truly individualized learning opportunities for their children. And there is, of course, the inevitable mix of the latter kind of principal with the former type of teacher and the former kind of principal with the latter type of teacher.

Since the consultant's efforts will be in the direction of effecting individualized adaptations of educational practice in the interests of particular gifted children, strategy would dictate that she plan to initiate her classroom efforts in those school settings which already show at least some probable tolerance of what she hopes to accomplish. The underlying assumption is that the consultant owes it to the good of the developing program to seek to get favorable results first in those situations in which there are least likely to be negative factors and then progressively to direct her efforts to those schools or teachers whose opposition or inflexibility may be something less than total. In those instances where the yield from the consultant's efforts is highly likely to be zero, or near zero, the possibility of transferring bright children to more likely nurturant settings—buildings or classrooms—must be kept in mind. Thus, before specific efforts are exerted in the interests of specific children the consultant would need find out in what buildings and with what teachers her efforts would be most likely to be productive.

TEACHER HELP.   Much of the consultant's work in the interest of gifted children will be in the form of direct assistance to their teachers—not only helping teachers know about and get access to things and activities that can be helpful, but also cultivating support, among other teachers, other school personnel, and even parents, for those kinds of adjustments for particular children which appear indicated.

Many teachers truly want to do things for children but, for one reason or another, just don't know how to proceed. The consultant can help such teachers find out about supplementary learning materials that can be obtained—many of them made available without charge by a wide variety of national firms. While many of the commercialized learning materials that increasingly are being made available have been developed for children who have difficulty learning, there are some which have potential value for bright children. (A few firms are showing in their catalogs the mental levels to which some materials are suited.) Many games have been marketed which can be directly facilitative to concept development; others may be justified in connection with learning activities only up to that point.

Most importantly, the consultant, because of her experience and special preparation, can be of great assistance in helping the teacher find out about and get access to reading materials—at the school, community, state, and national levels—which can add significantly to the children's learning resources. Many teachers do not know about the availability, at modest costs, of what are, in effect, enrichment kits in the areas of art, music, science, and social studies. The consultant can help teachers match such kits to the needs of particular children, seeing to it that such kits later become part of the school system's supplies and hence available subsequently for use by other teachers. The consultant can alert the teachers, and probably others within the school system, to the merits of gifted children's being provided with added learning opportunities by means of their being enrolled in approved correspondence courses. The consultant may need not only to arrange for the school district's paying for such courses but also to help the teachers carry on such work within the school schedule. By virtue of the breadth of familiarity and contact with persons and facilities in the total community, the consultant can help the teachers of the gifted children in whose interest they are working to find out about and utilize such potential resources.

Since the consultant and teacher will be working out jointly the differing kinds of modifications in the educational program for the children and since the consultant will be operating in terms of a larger perspective of the educational situation, there inevitably will arise situations which involve modifications which must be worked out with other teachers, principals, supervisors, and, not infrequently, parents. The consultant is in a position to do this more effectively than is the teacher. All too many teachers are hesitant to do with and for their children certain very desirable things because they fear (or have been told!) that such departures from the conventional are not tolerated by their principals. And no small number of other teachers are hesitant to make modifications or adjustments because they unjustifiably believe that their principals would not look with favor upon such attempts. While this type of intervention is more likely to be needed in instances where a given gifted youngster can benefit from going to a different school for part of the day, or where he would do better by "taking part of his work" with some

teacher other than his regular class teacher, sometimes such intervention is necessary when the anticipated modifications can be accomplished, with the help of the consultant, just in the regular class.

Of course, as the consultant works with teachers in the interests of specific children, she will need to be able to act in the light of her perceptions of enrichment and acceleration. More crucial is the fact that she will need to preplan and execute a sound strategy aimed at helping the teacher, the principal, the parents, and sometimes the child, to understand the educational and psychological merits and limitations of each at any given point in the child's educational progress. In this regard, the consultant's wise introduction of relevant research evidence can be quite helpful. In the case of the acceleration of any bright youngster within a given elementary school, as well as from an elementary level to some secondary level, much of the contribution of the consultant will be with respect to the teachers into whose rooms the child is being advanced. In fact, much of this will need to occur prior to the child's transfer. Enrichment and acceleration, with their attendant possibilities and problems, will be discussed later.

INTEREST GROUPINGS. Emerging naturally from the kinds of adjustments that have been discussed is the creation of children's special interest groups. In this regard, the consultant can serve as more than a motivator to, or facilitator of, such developments; she can serve two other important roles. She can help the teacher to be more fully receptive to the educational soundness (in terms of conceptualization possibilities) and to the importance of the relative stability or continuity of special interest-group activity in whatever area or areas may be chosen. Interest-group activity of the "seven-day wonder" variety can have some value as a distraction or escape from humdrum learning and may, at times, awaken some interests of a more desirable nature, but too often this kind of activity is of limited significant educational value. Second, and just as important, the consultant can help insure educationally meaningful feedback to their classmates by those children so engaged. This can do much to forestall the arousal of negative feelings on the part of those children who are not in the special interest groups and to prevent the creation of an undesirable kind and amount of social distance between those not in the group and those who are enjoying such opportunities. The consultant also can be helpful to the teacher who may not know that some adult or group in the community can be asked to participate, at least at some stage, in the activity of a given special interest group.

Looking at the work of the consultant a bit differently, we can perceive her accomplishments as taking steps that will be contributive to the development, within the school system, of a progression in adjustment. At first, her efforts will be in the interests of specified children, perhaps a matter of helping *a* child in *a* class. Depending, of course upon the nature of the school community and neighborhood, there may be only one such child in a given room, or even in a given grade. The consultant will, then, be on the alert for situations where two or more bright children of comparable capabilities and interests can be helped to form special interest groups. She can facilitate their functioning as such, for whatever time may be appropriate. This functioning can be either within the regular class times or, busing and teacher hours permitting, after school. As such groups proliferate, the beginning of a Colfax pattern can be identified and worked out. After a year

or two, from one or more afternoons a week, the operation of such groups well may provide the basis for establishing a special class or so. Such classes will have more viability and general acceptance since they have emerged in a gradual, understandable situation rather than having been imposed suddenly by administrative fiat.

PUPIL ASSISTS. The consultant can be instrumental in the establishment of an early admissions program and in facilitating the adjustment of youngsters so admitted. The matter of early admissions will be discussed more fully later, but the responsibility of the consultant both to the early-admitted child and his teachers merits consideration here. Providing for a bright child to be admitted properly to school earlier than the conventional age is a relatively simple thing; what happens to him after he is admitted is much more complex. It is therefore very important that the consultant properly prepare the teacher with whom such a child initially is placed. If at all possible, the consultant will exercise great care to see that he is placed with a teacher who is not the conventional grade-one-age-six, grade-two-age-seven stereotype. While such stereotypy is more characteristic of school administrators, no small percentage of teachers also believe firmly that "peerness" is basically a function of chronological age.

The point that has been made regarding the importance of certain preconceptions of teachers as determiners of effectiveness of children's learnings is but part of a larger matter regarding the consultant's role in assisting gifted pupils in their educational adjustment. Time and again, situations have been encountered where a bright child has truly blossomed under an understanding and effective teacher in one grade and was promoted to a higher grade only to become a sullen, withdrawn, or overtly aggressive maladjusted, "underachiev-ing" child under a distressingly less competent and sensitive teacher. The child thereupon entered further train-ing to become an underachiever.

The consultant, as the facilitator of educational adjustments for the gifted, if she is working in a school system with an ungraded primary program for in-stance, may need not only to make sure that gifted children progress through that level in accord with the purpose of such a program but also to help the teachers within it, as well as those into whose grades children come from such a program, fully to understand the phi-losophy of such a provision, to accept understandingly those children who pass through the ungraded primary level at faster rates than conventionally might be expected, and to make any adjustments in curriculum or method that may be appropriate for different gifted children.

The consultant can work to effect smooth transitions of the gifted from the elementary level to the junior high school level, from the junior high school level to the senior high school level, or, in certain cases, from the elementary level to the senior high school level when the junior high school level is skipped. In like vein, the consultant, with whatever assistance of the high school counselors is appropriate, can help the gifted to plan their transition to higher education facilities, whether it be in respect to the high school pupils' getting started on and pursuing advanced credit college courses or in making the full-time shift to college.

In contrast with the responsibilities and opportunities of the consultant at the earlier grade levels in facilitating identification, in helping in curricular and methodological matters, in evaluat-ing, and the like, her work with and for the older gifted children will be concerned more with program planning. All along the line, there well may be a continuing need for the consultant to work with administrators and teachers in helping them recognize and be will-ing to make educational adjustments for the gifted.

STRATEGY ORIENTATION. Initially, the consultant may need to emphasize the importance of strategic thinking about doing things for the gifted, as contrasted with the tactics of a program—the ac-complishing of any of the many specific things that may be contributive to such a program. In effect, the consultant will need to work assiduously to try to effect a sound comprehension, among all con-cerned, of the philosophical basis, the psychological appropriateness, and the attendant educational needs in terms of which specific actions are to be taken. Such understanding before any specific provisions are made for the gifted must be the foundation of the program, rather than the even-well-intentioned promo-tion or initiation of certain provisions primarily because of some truly periph-eral situation. Even once such an under-standing has been achieved in a school system and community and even after certain specific steps have been taken to facilitate learning by the gifted pupils in it, there remains a continuing, though somewhat lessened, need to work in such a manner because new teachers and new parents are constantly coming into the community.

RESEARCH. The consultant has a major responsibility either to conduct research on the effectiveness of the various steps that she has caused to be taken or to cause such research to be done. The gen-eral increasing sensitivity to the matter of educational accountability should be helpful in this regard. Procedures al-ready are at hand, or quite easily can be developed, by means of which such research can be conducted. The study and evaluation of the various facets of the outcome of work by the consultant which not only lend themselves easily to objective study but also are educationally and socially important are limited only by the degree of concern, curiosity, and ingenuity of the consultant or her research surrogate.

Certain aspects can be identified as illustrative, though in no sense as restrictive. An ongoing type of "research" should consist of the ascertainment of pupil, parent, and educator reactions to the various adjustments being made for the gifted. Certainly, research on the degree of underachievement before and at various times after certain of the provisions were inaugurated would be very important. Since one objective of the consultant will be to help the teachers work with their gifted children such that they will be achieving educationally reasonably in accord with their potentials for such work, the disparities between performance levels and capability levels should be less in the cases of those children in whose interests the consultant has worked than in the cases of those, of comparable capability, not so helped. Objective data of this sort are relatively easily obtained, and the results should throw meaningful light on the functioning of the consultant and the effectiveness of the program. The description of the extent and manner of pupil participation in school and community affairs would be important to know, both in order to reveal the variety and extent of such activity and in order to serve as a basis on which to identify new and untypical possibilities. Very important would be the collection of objective information—on a before-and-after basis—regarding the total adjustment of the gifted children in whose interests the consultant has worked. In the early stages of a program, objective educational achievement and adjustmental information can be collected and analyzed on children who have had the services of

the consultant and on comparables who have not. Comparative data can be collected, also, on the holding power of educational adjustments effected at the secondary level.

While implementation of the various educational adjustments accomplished by the consultant can have beneficial outcomes for those specific children in whose interests she has worked, the concepts, methodologies, and sensitivities which the teachers acquire or enlarge upon tend also to affect how the teachers, with whom the consultant has worked, perceive and work with children not directly in the purview of the consultant. The extent of such side effects, or the results of an "educational osmosis," can be ascertained quite objectively and the possible larger impact of the consultant program thus learned.

In regard to the gifted in the schools, two things have happened. The implicit assumption that the regular school program adequately meets their (and society's) needs widely has been challenged. Regarding programs for the gifted as an educational "extra" has put them in need of special funding. The provision of such funding consistently came as a result of the special efforts of a few persons whose motivation was based primarily either in a philosophical and psychological commitment to the needs of both the gifted and society or in a desire to capitalize upon some event, such as Sputnik. In either event, the persons responsible for the development of special funding for programs for the gifted tended to be ones whose tenures in such positions of influence were disconcertingly short. As a result, the programs that were thereby made possible tended to be so short-lived that whatever was to be done for the gifted had to be quickly realizable and quite apparent. Clearly, the consultant approach described here is not of this nature. As in the building of a home, it involves the assessment of the terrain and of the soil, the construction of a sound foundation, and the building of the home brick by brick. Even the erection of prefabricated houses necessitates some of these steps and has to be furthered by the adding of unit rooms or walls, but even these have a functional relationship to the anticipated total product.

It is in the light of the total context that planning for the introduction of a program for the gifted and the inauguration of such a program must be regarded. In all school districts, and particularly those using the services of a consultant on the gifted, there are assets that can be capitalized upon. In many school districts, liabilities loom and difficulties will be encountered, but they can either be dealt with wisely and positively or, if necessary, circumvented.

Identification

Some concepts of major importance in the identification of the gifted already have been discussed because they shed light upon the nature of the giftedness with which we are primarily concerned—the capacity to learn and function verbally symbolically. The most fundamental of these concepts concerned the nature of the test evidence which is most clearly suggestive of superior basic capacity to learn—evidence regarding the psychological operations which make learning possible (process), the extent to which the child has learned in the total act of living (product), and the comprehension of the nature of the interaction between process and product. While this is of importance in regard to all children, it is of particular significance with respect to children in middle and lower socioeconomic classes. Relevant, too, has been the illustrative evidence regarding the effectiveness of teacher identification of gifted youngsters. To only a limited extent will such matters be considered

in this section. Our primary concern here will be more with the gross structure or procedure necessary to the identification of the gifted than with the more highly specific details of such a procedure. The fundamental orientation here will be in terms of a procedure which, rather than being regarded as errorless, can result in less error than generally might be expected. To deny the presence of a knowable amount of error in such a measurement would be just as unwarranted as to overgeneralize regarding it.

The point has been emphasized that the making of provisions for the gifted should be regarded as but an integral part of the whole, well-functioning educational program for all children—the slow, the average, and the gifted. Implicit in such thinking is the assumption that there is, or should be, a sound learning aptitude group screening testing program which is intended fundamentally not only to provide teachers with valid objective information regarding the school learning aptitudes of all their children (within the limitations that already have been discussed) but also to help in the early and systematic identification of children who may need to be considered as candidates for special attention—whether as slow learners, as fast learners, or as possible learning disabled children.

Resistance to testing

At this point it would seem well to examine the phenomenon of resistance to actions based upon such assumptions. This resistance—not confined to those directly involved with children's learning—has been due to two factors, each of which has a discernible degree of validity yet each of which has, unfortunately, been magnified. The resistance to such testing of school children has been based upon the way or ways in which some teachers, and others, have used the information yielded by such testing. Valid criticisms of this testing have been based upon at least the facts that (1) tests of limited validity have been used, (2) those doing the testing have inadequately comprehended the information yielded by even valid tests, and (3) those doing the testing have, partly as a result of (2), ineffectively communicated to the teacher, or others, the findings from the tests they used. Fortunately, conditions such as these are by no means universal, but they have existed to such an extent as to cause legitimate concern, as reflected in formal aversive reactions from Boston to San Francisco.

Negative reactions to teachers' uses of the results of such testing have, in fact, been due to the three factors that have been identified but have involved another component. If the ways in which teachers tended to use the results of testing are taken as evidence of the adequacy of how they were "trained" in the process of becoming qualified to be teachers, such preparation must be regarded as ineffective. This is a major complaint of many administrators who, interestingly, generally do relatively little to help their teachers learn how to do better in this regard after they are employed. The other negative component, not unrelated to the one just mentioned, is based upon the contention that teachers are prejudiced toward their pupils by the test scores which they receive as a result of testing, being disposed thereby to expect more and to press for more from those pupils who earn high scores (usually IQs) and to expect less of and to press less with those who have earned low scores. Research, varying considerably in adequacy, tends to support this contention, usually in the cases of those teachers who have had inadequate orientation on the merits and limitations of such test scores.

But the presumption here is that such limitations need not exist. They can be minimized, if teachers

1. are adequately sensitized regarding the nature of the behavior samplings made in such testing and regarding the relevance of such samplings to the kinds of school learning which are involved.
2. use mental (or developmental) level rather than IQ as the focal frame of reference in their thinking about and planning for their pupils.
3. are adequately informed regarding the qualitative—and not just the quantitative—nature of the children's performances in test situations in order to relate this to school learning.
4. are properly sensitive to and informed about the matter of measurement error in such testing.
5. are responsive to the admonition that children's performances on such tests generally should be regarded as minimal reflections of their learning potentials.

Optimal use of testing

Assuming that the screening procedures are psychoeducationally valid, two important points need to be considered. If the results of such a procedure are to be of maximal (preventive) value, the testing should be started early. While it is true that certain widely used group learning aptitude tests are not well suited to yield helpful information on the younger children, others, especially some of the newer (and still well-standardized) tests can provide educationally relevant information on children from the kindergarten up. In the case of bright children in particular the early obtaining and use of such information is necessary to help prevent their getting an early start in learning to be underachievers. A subsequent round or so of proper group testing of learning aptitude during the first three or four years of schooling—kindergarten and up—can be important in picking up "late starters" and in checking on earlier-obtained scores. Late entrants and transfers can be screened by means of good group tests.

PROCESS AND PRODUCT TESTING. The importance of using group tests which have samplings of both verbal or language, and nonverbal or nonlanguage, areas should be recognized, since the nonverbal portions of certain of the tests can throw light upon the presence of process aspects of learning potential when a child's performance in the product area has been discernibly lower. This is particularly crucial in the cases of those children who come from less-than-average acculturation backgrounds. Care must be exercised not to equate the psychological information yielded by such nonlanguage or nonverbal portions of most current group tests of "intelligence" with that on "performance" tests. Generally, the former reflect educationally relevant process more clearly than do the latter.

It always must be recognized that different "intelligence" tests yield different kinds of information about the children tested. Seven-year-old José, for instance, earned three different IQs on as many different tests—71, 102, and 131, all carefully given within a two-week interval, and all properly scored. He earned the 71 on the Peabody Picture Vocabulary Test, which reflected his limited acculturation (product). (He was the son of a migrant worker.) The 102 was earned on the Kuhlmann-Anderson (group) test, and sampled a mixture of what he had learned (product) and of the psychological operations he had with which to do his learning (process). However, he earned the 131 on the Cattell Culture-Fair Test, which reflected primarily the amount of process with which he could learn. Obviously, his teacher's perceptions of, and her expectations for, him could have been different had only one of these tests been used. Teachers' perceptions of their youngsters in terms

of how they perform on such tests are fundamentally a function of the quality of the teachers' preparation to deal with such information—what they understand that information to mean and how they then interact with their youngsters in the light of such information.

The use of such a group testing screening approach makes it possible to identify two kinds of children who need to be educated as gifted. On the one hand, there will be those whose combined scores on the two kinds of sampling—process and product—meet the criterion being used. On the other hand, there will be those youngsters whose performances on the nonverbal, or nonlanguage, portion of the test suggest that basically they have at least superior capability but whose performances on the verbal portion will be perceptibly lower. The latter group will need, at least for a time, special educational treatments addressed to helping them build up what their limited acculturation has deprived them of.

PSYCHOLOGICAL EXAMINATION OF CANDIDATES. Once children have been so identified as candidates, it is customary to have them psychologically examined individually by means of the Stanford-Binet or some other equally valid instrument. When a good group test has been used, this is less for the purpose of "validating" the IQ obtained on the group screening device than for the purpose of getting a fuller picture of the characteristics and manner of the child's cognitive functioning.[2] The practice of individual psychological examining of children as

---

[2] If the WISC is used for such a purpose, it should be clearly recognized that the Verbal portion on it much more nearly yields the same kind of educationally relevant information as the Binet than do either the Performance portions and the Full Scale IQ. Actually, the Binet makes a much more diversified sampling of behaviors relevant to children's school learnings than does even the WISC Verbal.

candidates for being educated as gifted therefore serves three potentially important purposes—a fuller understanding of each child's intellectual operations is thus made possible, insurance is taken out against the possibility of faulty leads from group testing results, and children who have taken no prior tests and/or whom teachers or parents may regard as gifted can be carefully evaluated.

Such a procedure presumes that the school district has on its staff, or can bring in, competent school psychologists—persons who, as a result of their assessment of a child, can supply his teacher with a psychoeducationally meaningful description of how the child operates intellectually and not just a report of the child's "IQ." Such service can be definitely helpful to the teacher and contributive to the child's effective learning, and should be an integral part in any program for the gifted.

Yet there are schools and school districts where such special service is not provided or cannot be obtained, as in the cases of certain schools in some rural or economically disadvantaged areas. And the odds are that there are some gifted youngsters in such situations. Such being the case, it would be justifiable to locate those children by means of a sound group testing procedure, *provided* that (1) the tests used were psychologically soundly selected and properly administrated and scored, and (2) the results of the tests were very carefully analyzed and effectively related to the pupils' anticipated learnings. In view of the alarmingly limited competency of some who are doing sanctioned individual psychological testing of school children, certain school districts would be better off if they employed two good group screening learning aptitude tets in order to identify their gifted youngsters.

ACHIEVEMENT-TEST DATA. Thus far, we have considered the process of identifying gifted youngsters in terms of only one variable—tested learning aptitude—a procedure which involves reduced probable error. We then need to expand our approach by using other procedures that are known or believed to be contributive. Keeping for the moment within a testing frame of reference, many advocate using also achievement-test data in deciding whether children qualify for consideration as gifted. When achievement-test performance is used, some criterion is needed—say a performance at least one standard deviation above the child's agemates, or a performance that is describable in terms of its being some number of years above his age- or grademates (depending upon the child's age or grade). Either of these may still be such as to indicate that such a gifted child is actually underachieving—in terms of his own capability. Neither of these criteria should be used alone, and they are of limited value even when used along with a learning aptitude criterion.

When this part of the procedure is used, three possible kinds of conditions may appear:

1. There are those children who test sufficiently high on both "intelligence" and achievement tests to meet the criterion. Little ambiguity is likely to exist in such instances.

2. There are those children who test sufficiently high in "intelligence" but not in achievement. Too often, such children are passed up as gifted and allowed to continue in their underachieving educational lives.

3. There are those children who test sufficiently high on achievement to qualify but not high enough in "intelligence." Some such children may be considered to have "blown it" when taking the learning aptitude test and can be recognized as plausible candidates for a program for the gifted. In some instances, they are illogically regarded as "overachievers" and may or may not be regarded as eligible.

The children in the last two categories need careful individual evaluation, the odds being high that they would be found to be bona fide gifted candidates, assuming that the achievement tests have been properly used.

Some have contended that it is justifiable to decide primarily on the basis of achievement-test results which children should be in a program for the gifted. Their explicit reasoning takes one of two forms: (1) Since, they say, "intelligence" tests are, after all, essentially achievement tests, why not do the identifying of the gifted in terms of high performance on regular achievement tests? (2) Or, since the scores children obtain on "intelligence" tests correlate so highly with those obtained on general achievement tests, why not identify the gifted by means of the scores earned on achievement tests? Assuming that there could be identified a cutoff score on such achievement tests above which children would need to score if they were thus to be regarded as gifted, the chances are six or seven out of ten that such a procedure would identify children who would, in terms of the scores earned on valid learning aptitude tests, be reasonable candidates for placement in a program for the gifted. While somewhat better than chance, and probably a bit better than teacher nomination, such a procedure would be unjustifiable for two major reasons: (1) It would, in effect, provide only a seemingly plausible basis for operating under the post hoc perception of the gifted—as those who had shown by their superior performance that they are gifted—a position challenged earlier in this book. Such an approach could involve the use of achievement tests with children in the first two grades, a level at which such measurement is precarious. More importantly, it would contribute to the identification of the gifted at later levels than is desirable. (2) It would fail to identify those basically bright children who, for any number of reasons, had failed to learn to the extent or degree which their basic learning potential could make possible. Children high in process but low in product would tend to be missed—a socially wasteful condition.

If those planning or operating a program for the gifted are strongly committed to the nurturance of "creativity" and if they are not satisfied with nurturing creative behaviors in those children who have been identified by the approaches described, they may want to try to locate children who have creative possibilities and who may not otherwise have been identified. Such educators may decide to use some combination of the various tests which have been developed for this purpose. Those who do this, however, need to be aware of the limited validation of such devices.

Teacher nomination

Moving from the frame of reference of test-based information in the identification of gifted children, the practice of having teachers nominate candidates for a program must be recognized. Published findings rather consistently have shown that teachers tend both to nominate as gifted many youngsters who, on more careful assessment, do not qualify and to fail to nominate some who, on more careful assessment, could qualify. In large part, such studies have asked teachers to characterize their nominees only grossly as "gifted." In one illustrative study of the validity of this practice, Pegnato and Birch (1959) asked junior high school teachers to identify those youngsters who were "mentally gifted." A total of 91 children, out of the total of 1400, were known to have earned Stanford-Binet IQs of 136 or higher. The teachers nominated a total of 154, only 41 of whom had earned such scores. Interestingly, 72 of the 91 were found to have earned

Metropolitan Achievement Test scores (reading and arithmetic averaged) two or more years above grade, but 236 others, below the 136 Binet IQ, scored equally well. Findings of this nature are typical, teachers being found to identify many children who fail to qualify and missing as many as 50 percent of those who could qualify on the basis of individual psychological examination.

However, such a nomination procedure can be sharpened somewhat if the teachers are provided with a behavioral check list in terms of which they can make their selections. Instead of being asked to identify children in terms of some nebulous term such as "gifted" or "mentally gifted"—a population which the nominator can define as broadly or as narrowly as he chooses—the teacher is asked to name those youngsters who have been observed to behave in certain ways. Illustratively, such a list, in a publication by Kough and De Haan (1955), includes characteristics such as "Reasons things out, thinks clearly, recognizes relationships, comprehends meanings," "Retains what he has heard or read without much rote drill," "Knows about many things of which other children are unaware," "Uses a large number of words easily and accurately," and the like. While there clearly is merit in having teachers thus participate in the identification process, the children so identified should be further evaluated in terms of their properly measured learning aptitudes. And one must always be concerned about gifted pupils who, for one reason or other, were not nominated.

Emotional and social aspects

The identification of those pupils who, by virtue of scoring high enough on group or individual tests of learning aptitude and achievement, might be found appropriate for a program for the gifted requires consideration also of the emotional and social aspects of the potential participants. The magnitude of the importance of these aspects may vary with the age at which the identification takes place: the older they are, the more likely problems in these areas are likely to be observed and the more habituated such maladaptive behavior patterns are likely to have become.

More specifically, given a youngster who, in terms of total capability, is eligible for such a program but whose emotional and/or social behavior appears likely to impair his working out in it, questions may arise as to whether he should be admitted on the assumption that such difficulties will dissipate or whether he should be "cleaned up" before he enters upon such a program. If he is a first- or second-grader, the chances are very high that his situation is quite different than if he were a fifth- or sixth-grader. Obviously, no single type of adjustment procedure or program can be recommended for all such children, but probably in more cases than not such a child's maladjustment can be traced to his not having received intellectual nurturance appropriate to his high capability. Some children bring this kind of "unhappiness" into the school; more acquire it in the school. Generally, when there is "emotional flak" in children at the early elementary grade level, proper educational adjustments—bringing educational opportunities and expectations more in harmony with learning potentials—will contribute largely if not entirely to the dissipation of such difficulties; the later in the child's educational career this occurs, the more likely that help of other kinds will be necessary, either before he enters the program or while he is in it.

Other behavioral evidences

While the odds are fairly high that the major portion of those youngsters in a given school district who would qualify as gifted would be identified by a psychologically sound group screening procedure, especially if cognitive learning is to be the main focus of concern, other behavioral evidences of superior performance and promise should be examined. The children's activities outside of school can be indicative. Keeping in mind the educational levels of the children, certain classroom behaviors can be suggestive of superior potential: generalized and sustained curiosity—when it is intellectually rather than emotionally motivated—and certain unusual, rather than grossly bizarre, cognitive behavior may be suggestive. Participation in any of the whole gamut of school activities should be considered.

The kind of behavior which children manifest, of course, is to some extent a function of the nature of the educational settings in which gifted children are being identified. The extent to which children, at any grade level, are likely to be manifesting curiosity or may be able to volunteer " 'way out" responses to learning problems depends upon the extent to which the classroom setting is conducive to evoking such responses. Some educational settings are so thoroughly lock-step in nature that curiosity and divergent responses are not tolerated, let alone nurtured. It is not idly contended that many school operations actually negatively reinforce curiosity and original behavior, predisposing the youngsters in them to learn "the" answers rather than learn how to learn.

And it must be recognized that some youngsters get on honor rolls and get elected or involved in extracurricular activities for reasons other than high intellectual promise. The extent to which such is the case often depends as much upon the philosophical orientation of the educational program as upon the intellectual or academic characteristics of the children so recognized. The degree of the school staff's familiarity with the activities of their children outside the school is a function of the staff's perception of the school's extraschool responsibilities and opportunities. Broadly sensitive educators, on the other hand, are disturbed by the fact that so many bright children have compensated for unchallenging class work by pursuing intellectually challenging extraschool activities, and they take some comfort in the realization that such youngsters have thus taken steps on their own to attain some degree of self-realization outside the formal educational structure. Since the noting of such pupil behavioral clues of intellectual promise is done, for the most part, by teachers, it is important to bear in mind that teachers' perceptions of pupils' noteworthy behaviors often are a function more of the teachers' than of the pupils' behaviors per se. Emotionally secure teachers tend more to see positive behaviors in their pupils than do insecure ones.

Grossly to screen out youngsters who possibly can be regarded as gifted and later more precisely to check individually on the amount and kinds of potential they may have are necessary components in the identification of those youngsters who can do their learning more effectively in some kind or kinds of program for gifted pupils. The identification process is but an initial step. After the eligible gifted children have been identified and provided for educationally, subsequent checking on both the characteristics of each child and of his program require systematic reevaluation. Depending upon conditions, this will involve either reassessment of the child's capabilities, exploration by means of more specialized tests, or an essentially routine rechecking in order to make sure that an appropriate match is being made between the child's capabilities and his educational program. The younger the child when he is initially identified and assessed psychoeducationally, the more likely intensive reevaluation should be made at, or near, the end of each of the early school years. The need for such reevaluation will tend to decrease as the child attains higher educational status. The concept of reevaluation should not be regarded as inevitably necessitating the retesting of learning aptitudes or the further exploration of learning potential by different devices, although periodic measurement of educational achievement would be essential. The matter of evaluating the broader psychoeducational picture of each gifted youngster will be discussed later.

SUMMARY

The creating of a public school program for the gifted must be perceived as a thoughtfully deliberate and socially important undertaking. As such, it requires the philosophical anchorage which has been stressed, a clear specification of socially and psychologically important behavioral outcomes to be effected in the pupils involved, and a practical aware-

ness and understanding of professional predispositions in the light of which such action is to be taken. The program needs to be established on the basis of important criteria pertaining to the personnel to be involved, major educational dispositions regarding the nature of the educational needs of the pupils, and the matter of evaluation. Strategy calls for the inauguration of the program with a carefully selected person—the consultant—whose responsibilities range from early cultivation of the educational and social soil preparatory for the program to the conducting of research on both the pupils and the program. The soundness of the whole undertaking can be determined by the quality of the identification procedures utilized. The fact that such a program so often has to be regarded as something "extra," rather than as an integral part of the regular education of all pupils, makes doubly necessary its sound preplanning and early implementation.

8

Administrative
considerations: I

The nature of the consultant's functioning and the matter of identification have been discussed to clarify the major initial and more tangible aspects of a program. Even though the appointment of the consultant and the authorization of identification procedures are administrative matters, just how these are to operate depends heavily on the qualifications of those who are to render such services. The delineation of personnel competencies and of subsequent actions in the light of them are administrative functions. The costs of a program are, of course, of major concern. While the instructional staff needs at least a general orientation regarding costs, the administrator will need to anticipate and provide for evaluation—both of the pupils and of the program; it is on the basis of his policy statement in this regard that his staff will proceed.

PERSONNEL

The key to any program is the quality of the personnel involved in it, both in its general encouragement and support and in its implementation. No program will become effective unless there is deep and firm commitment to it and full comprehension of its purpose and procedures. This is true with respect both to the higher-level educational staff and to those on the front line—those who are helping the pupils in it to acquire those behaviors identified in its objectives.

Education in particular has seen more than its share of program failures when either of the two essential and interacting elements was lacking. Potentially fruitful educational programs, well conceived by "front office" personnel, have been essentially unproductive when they have been poorly or inadequately comprehended by teachers. Promising practices which could have led to programs have been introduced by individual teachers, or even small groups of teachers, only to fail abjectly, if not actually create antagonism to the objectives focal to them, because their possible merit in the total educational and social picture has not been recognized by school personnel in controlling positions in supervision or administration. This has been true particularly as regards programs for improving the quality of education of the gifted, perhaps largely because the evidence of the poor quality of much education has not been apparent to the uncritical observer or because the large amount of evidence that has existed has been so consistently ignored.

We shall discuss first some factors that need to be taken into consideration as we think of the adequacy of the personnel involved. We shall then identify the kinds of personnel with whom we are concerned. Elements important in their preparation will be considered, and then we shall seek to identify the extents to which these elements should figure in the identification and preparation of the personnel essential to a good program for the gifted.

Training vs. Preparation

First, we should distinguish between "training" the personnel and "preparing" them. Perhaps to many such a distinction may appear academic, but the difference actually is one between thinking perceptually and thinking conceptually. The term *training* connotes the establishing of rather specific habits, as when one trains a dog to come when called, or perhaps even as a teacher is trained to make lesson plans. *Preparation,* on the other hand, means the identification and establishment of the underlying general principles on the basis of which certain habits may be formed.

Obviously, the preparation needed to get a program started differs from that needed to maintain it. Much more preparation, and of a different kind, must take place before a program can get started, and even in its early stages. In a sense, personnel preparation must precede program initiation, whereas training can occur early in or during a program (although certain preprogram training has its place). Even though teachers may understand the kinds of outcomes desired, they early need to know different kinds of ways to facilitate learning by their pupils. Once a program is under way, such "methods" can be elaborated and adapted.

It is crucial that those who are to be involved in an effective program for the gifted give evidence before they become involved in it, or quite early in their preparation for it, of not only accepting but also being deeply committed to the fundamental objectives of any such program—the bona fide self-realization of the gifted and their achievement of effective social participation. And this implies not just a passing genuflection to such ideals but a persisting evaluation of what and how the gifted are learning to those ends. This further implies that those involved in the program think to a marked degree, although not exclusively, in terms of how individual children are doing and only secondarily in terms of "class averages." Their competence to grasp the concepts essential to the unique learning needs of the gifted is of major importance.

Provisions must be made for the preparation of all educational personnel who will be involved in mounting and maintaining the program, with the recognition that their needs for such preparation will vary in kind and amount. Those in administrative positions may need preparation both as to the philosophical and psychological concepts underlying the program and as to the numerous functional interrelationships between the provisions for the gifted and the other aspects of the larger educational operation. Those in supervisory positions will need this kind of preparation but will need also to be more conversant with the different kinds of practices the teachers will be employing. As indicated earlier, the consultant will need the most thorough preparation, since she will be not only the intermediary between the administrative and supervisory staffs and those in lower educational echelons but also the one who will be rendering assistance directly to the teachers. Ancillary personnel will need certain preparation as to the major objectives and as to specific ways in which they can contribute in the light of the concepts underlying the education of the gifted. This applies not only to teacher aides (if they are to be part of the program) but also to school and city librarians, the teachers of children not in the program, and parents of all the children in the school.

Core Elements
in Preparation

Without limiting the scope of the preparation to these points, at least six matters should be dealt with adequately. It is overridingly necessary that the first of these be the delineation of the *philosophy* undergirding such a program. The nature of this philosophy already has been discussed. Contributive to its implementation are five fundamental concepts. To say that such a program should focus primarily on *prevention* and only secondarily on remediation can be regarded as speaking philosophically, yet such an emphasis has important psychological overtones in regard to education's being a self-realization type of experience, with attendant personal feelings of accomplishment, joy of learning, and just downright personal happiness and adjustment.

Related to this is the importance of a persistent but still soundly rational effort, in the case of each child, directed toward the *rapprochement of his achievement and his capability to achieve.* Important as this ongoing individual evaluation is and as significant as it should be in the academic or cognitive area, it must be perceived broadly to include social, emotional, and creative areas of behavior.

Fundamental to adequate preparation, necessarily differing for differing kinds of personnel, is a sound orientation regarding the nature of the psychological process of *conceptualization* and the nature of concepts. Since the outstanding cognitive characteristic of the gifted is their ability to generalize and conceptualize, it is particularly important that those working with, and in the interests of, the gifted should understand just what is involved. While it may be stated philosophically that such "higher mental level" behavior should be nurtured and capitalized upon, it is necessary that the psychological nature of that behavior be understood. Many personnel will need help to be able to realize that some bright children need, first, the bits and pieces of information (percepts) on the basis of which they can generalize and conceptualize. Even though many bright children do much generalizing and conceptualizing on their own, some will need nurturance in the processes, especially in certain situations. Given certain generalizations, they may need help in arriving at higher-order conceptualizations as well as in engaging in extrapolations from what they have attained to something not yet experienced. Teachers need to know when pupil behavior called conceptualization occurs or could occur in order that it can be reinforced or nurtured.

The matter of the breadth and the *variability of the intraindividual behavior* of the gifted has been clearly demonstrated in research. In preparing those who would work in a program for the gifted this is of importance for two reasons: (1) When such phenomena occur, they must be understood and reasonably nurtured, not merely tolerated. (2) When they do not occur, the possibility that they may be caused to occur should be actively explored. In the latter case, however, only the possibility of their occurring in response to some environmental manipulation should be explored; the necessity of their occurring should not be imposed.

Whereas the consideration of *teaching methods* figures largely in training programs for teachers of the gifted, the exploration of the characteristics of methods of facilitating learning by the gifted, the consideration of the supporting philosophical and psychological justification for them, and the identification of the potential wide range of appropriate content should characterize the initial phase of preparation. In a sense, a deductive approach to this area is indicated. After the characteristics or criteria of desirable procedures for facilitating learning are identified and understood, methods which have those characteristics or meet those criteria can be examined in terms of the extent to which they appear, or are known by research, to contribute to the desired learning outcomes. Much literature on the education of the gifted describes "tricks of the trade" which have only limited value in meaningfully educating the gifted. At best, they provide for a widening of experience, admittedly of possible value in the education of all children and perhaps initially contributing to learning by the gifted, but many of them are devoid of possibilities of nurturing those kinds of learning most noted in the gifted: their moving more quickly from the concrete to the abstract, their typically exploring for causal or other relationships, their progression up the hierarchy of concepts, their extrapolating to anticipated or unknown situations, interpretations, and evaluations. Lest the education of the nongifted be perceived in too limiting a manner as a result of

such a listing, it should be noted that all children are capable, to varying degrees, of such behavior, but the education of the gifted has tended too often to be limited to the extents observed in the nongifted.

Just as the preparation should include a broad sensitization to the numerous ways of facilitating the wide range of learning behaviors of the gifted, just so should there be an effort to sensitize all personnel to a broader conception of the *content* with respect to which such methods could be employed. In addition to a toleration of much current content, serious consideration should be given to areas not conventionally incorporated, such as social and cultural anthropology, semantics, elementary logic, consumer economics, international relationships, social psychology, ecology, philosophy, and the like, recognizing the while the necessary interrelationships among these.

Granting, then, the importance of such elements in the preparation of personnel, to what extent is each necessary to the different kinds of personnel? Table 8.1 summarizes the varying degrees of presumed need. The frequencies with which the plus marks appear in the different columns indicate the relative importance attached to the differing elements for the different categories of personnel. The purposes of the preparation will vary for the different kinds of personnel, in some instances being conducive either to tolerance and general understanding or to a sensitivity to the elements, and in others being regarded as heavily contributive to effective implementation in the classroom.

It is presumptive even to imply that the foregoing analysis is complete or exhaustive. It is intended, rather, to suggest an approach to a fruitful breakdown of what should be accomplished in preparing personnel for mounting, and to some extent maintaining, a program.

Table 8.1. Relative importance of elements of preparation program
for different categories of involved personnel.

Element	Administrators	Supervisors	Consultant	Teachers	Others
General philosophy	++	++	++	++	++
Preventive emphasis	+	+	++	++	+
Achievement-capacity rapprochement	+	+	++	++	+
Nature of concept behavior	+	+	+++	+++	+
Behavior variability	+	+	++	++	+
Methods and content	+	++	++	++	+

COSTS

Decisions have to be reached and recommendations have to be made by the administrator pertaining to the costs of the program. We shall consider this matter of costs only in terms of the local school district. However, the variables considered can suggest certain components for which state-level funding should be anticipated. After describing some conditions which can affect the anticipation of costs of a program and noting illustrative cost descriptions and predictions, we shall consider categories of costs that must be anticipated.

The introduction and maintenance of any special program for the gifted will entail some extra cost. Those antagonistic to the idea of such a program tend to magnify the possible costs involved; those supportive of the idea tend to maintain that an acceptable, or even good, program for the gifted need cost no more than the extra costs involved in providing for a football team, a shop program, or even a band. Attempts to justify extra expenditures on the gifted often are ill-considered. A school that provides football-team facilities for its students, for instance, not only provides direct participation opportunities for the players, ticket sellers, cheerleaders, and managers but also provides opportunities for vicarious, projected involvement of much of the student body and for the parents' identification and pride in the involvement of the youngsters who are

actively participating in the sport, or sport-related activity. Even though the number of participants in the sport may be significantly smaller than the number of gifted children in the school, the number of those who "benefit" from the special activity probably can be discernibly larger. Further, the act of such participation is much more tangible and understandable than is a gifted youngster's discovering the relationship between ontogeny and phylogeny. Further, such comparisons involve thinking more at the secondary level than at the elementary level. But the attempt to justify extra expenditures for the gifted on the grounds that there are extra expenditures on sports, shop, or music too often implies an inappropriate derogation of such activities, and tends completely to ignore the matters of justifiable self-realization of the gifted and of their possible social contributions. Doing what needs to be done for the gifted should stand on its own feet as a legitimate part of the total educational commitment.

Anticipation of Costs

It would seem as simple a matter to specify how much a program for the gifted costs a school district that has such a program in operation, or to specify how much it would cost to start a program, as it would be to state how much it costs a family to have a baby. The magnitude of any firm figure or estimate stated by experienced or expectant parents, however, would differ from that of inexperienced or uninformed parents not only in terms of the level of their prior health practices but also in terms of the variables which they regarded as relevant. Although itself a variable, the delivery and immediate postnatal costs would be included. But to what extent would other variables be included by cost-conscious parents? The mother's prenatal examination and care (when they are not included in the delivery costs)? The postnatal medical care of the infant/child—physical checkup, inoculations, minor treatments—these of course varying markedly among differing socioeconomic levels? The toys? The costs of baby sitters? And economically hardheaded parents would take into consideration whether the infant/child would share a room with one or more siblings or would have a room to himself, the latter case making his "space costs" as attributable to the total costs as was the father's separate study or home-office. An analogous problem exists with respect to anticipating costs of programs for the gifted in the public schools. The costs involved in starting a local program very well could differ as between the initial phase of the program and its subsequent operation. The scope of the program can vary from a minimal, ice-breaking one to a full-fledged one. As with so many matters, that which seems superficially simple can become quite complex on fuller analysis.

The extent of special financing of a program for the gifted in any school district depends upon the nature of the educational operation that is under way and the kind of operation that is anticipated. A school program that already includes a good (total system) pupil testing program, a good library and an abundance of supplementary learning materials and equipment, an effectively functioning guidance and counseling program, and has teachers already dis-

posed to individualize their instructional procedures will necessitate relatively little extra funding to make possible certain desirable adjustments for its gifted youngsters. Albeit of little merit, should those planning to start off a program for the gifted be thinking primarily in terms of establishing special classes for such pupils, both the initial and operating costs could be discernibly greater, especially if the school pays for transporting the youngsters from a number of different school buildings to those in which the special classes are to be located.

Whereas the specialized individual psychoeducational determination of eligibility and assessment of children for the gifted program may legitimately be charged to such programs, all children need library and laboratory facilities. While any special efforts, or expenditures, which may be made to enhance such practices may, at least to some extent, be chargeable to programs for the gifted, it must be realized that improvements in such facilities which are so effected also contribute to richer educational opportunities for many children who may not be regarded as gifted. In a similar manner, when a consultant is employed to work with teachers in the interest of the gifted, many of the nongifted stand to benefit from the resulting improvement in the attitudes and procedures of the teachers with whom the consultant has worked. To some unmeasured degree, numerous educational provisions made in the name of the gifted, while initially charged to a program for the gifted, have potential generalizable benefits for other pupils.

School districts which already have programs for the gifted and which are in areas where colleges or universities provide no relevant course or institutes may have a need to furnish their own in-service training. If the school districts are large, they may have enough personnel working in the interests of the gifted to provide their own institutes, which would involve bringing in specialists. Since most districts would not be large enough for this, they would need to join with others and operate regional or area in-service activities. These would involve both a sharing of expenses of the invited specialists and necessary interdistrict travel cost. Financial encouragement could be provided, for instance, to relevant public school personnel to attend regional programs run by The Association for the Gifted and the National Association for Gifted Children. Budgeting is possible for all such kinds of professional sustenance.

Certain costs can be anticipated easily and quite specifically. Transportation costs, for instance, whether for transporting youngsters to special classes or special activities, or for a consultant to get to those teachers with whom she will be working in effecting appropriate educational adjustments, can be reasonably accurately foreseen. The salaries, or portions of salaries, of those who will be working directly with gifted pupils can be reasonably clearly specified. But other necessary expenditures also must be anticipated, although they generally have to be thought of categorically rather than in terms of nicely specified items. The following quotation from the Marland report (1971) both sets the stage and identifies certain kinds of anticipatable needs:

In urban communities where libraries and laboratories are available, educators have made special arrangements for individuals to use materials and to experiment under supervision. Good library and laboratory space in schools are highly desirable, with open areas for special projects and study. Even with good libraries and adequately stocked laboratories, it is necessary to use auxiliary resources and materials, if the interests of the gifted are to be met. Special programs have been restricted in their success because of limited facilities. Pro-

visions should be made so that gifted students, whether urban or rural, have access to resources and space.

Special transportation funds should be available for needed study and research opportunities. These should not be categorically limited, but should be documented and justified. These funds may be required for widely varying and sometimes unpredictable purposes, ranging from archeological studies by special interest groups, to gathering research specimens for marine, botanical, or biological research, to visits to specialized libraries and museums, to special contacts with artists; from individual studies of political process, to documentary studies, to recording of interview or photographic data, to acquisition of unaccessible materials.

Media and material needs are also unpredictable in advance. Funds should be made available for purchase of standard equipment and expendable supplies so that students who wish to function in areas of creative expression may do so. The young painter or musician should not be restricted by the nonavailability of supplies, equipment, musical scores, or suitable instruments. Similarly, the young person who wishes to report his research findings creatively should have access to the necessary photographic or graphic source materials and media. Ready availability of materials and encouragement to use them enhance interest in learning and extend talents (Section IV, pp. 6–8).

Caution must of course be exercised in deciding just how "extra" instructional costs are determined. Viewing the matter from an administrative point of view, if the average annual per pupil expenditure at the elementary level is, say, $800, each gifted child in the regular class already is "costing" the district $800. To create a special class of 30 gifted pupils may be regarded as "costing" the district $24,000, when in reality such a total expenditure would have occurred if no such class had been created. It is the *extra* cost that must be considered.

Even though the matter of the costs of

a program for the gifted should not be the primary basis on which a decision is made, it must be given major consideration. Certainly, planning must not proceed in such a limited manner as to cripple the inauguration of such a program from the start. Nor need it proceed in such a manner as to cause the proposed program to be perceived as financially megalomaniacal. It should be neither too little from the standpoint of the legitimate good of the pupils nor too lush from the standpoint of the taxpayer. Surely, it is not unrealistic to expect that, on the average, at least 5 percent of a school district's budget should be specifically utilized in the interests of some 8 percent of its children.

Cost Descriptions

Meaningful bases on which to predict what a program for the gifted might cost are difficult to cite from the literature. On the one hand, when costs have been reported on programs, the components sometimes have not been identified, and sometimes when identified have suggested definitely limited perceptions of what such a program should include. On the other hand, reported figures generally have represented actual annual or excess costs, usually with the natures of the programs unspecified, and such dollar characterizations have very limited value over time. Recognizing that we don't know the components making up the different programs used here illustratively, we shall examine cost descriptions in terms of dollar characterizations and in terms of a ratio, or index, characterization. Actually, dollar characterizations have quite limited merit over time. However, the ones cited are historically interesting because they were reported so globally and noninformatively regarding the nature of the programs on which they were based, and at times reflected relative costs for different

kinds of exceptional children within a given time period.

Dollar characterizations

Although most textbooks on the education of the gifted don't have "costs" even as an entry in their indexes, a few have presented cost information. De Haan and Havighurst (1957) stated, "Programs for educating gifted children cost approximately 1 to 3 percent of the total school budget. . . . Smaller classes, special administration and supervision and materials and facilities for the program all add to the expense" (p. 70). They presented the figures shown in Table 8.2 for Cleveland expenses. Note that if these costs were characterized in terms of cost ratios or indexes, that for the gifted would be 1.41 as contrasted with 2.33 for the mentally retarded and 4.01 for the deaf.

Williams (1958) reported costs of gifted special class programs in Cleveland, San Diego, and Portland. (The absolute figures were for the 1950s.) In the Cleveland major work classes, for 1954–55, the annual per pupil cost was $275.53 (differing from the $376 cited by De Haan and Havighurst, above), as contrasted with $265.98 for pupils in the

Table 8.2. Cost of educating children in Cleveland, Ohio, 1944-45.

Type of program	Cost per pupil
Elementary grade classroom	$ 266
Major work classes	376
Boys' occupational school	434
Mentally retarded	436
Hard of hearing	619
Trade school for girls	639
Blind	933
Crippled	1026
Deaf	1067

Source: DeHaan and Havighurst, *Educating Gifted Children,* 1957, Table 4, p. 70. ©1957 by The University of Chicago. Published 1957. Reprinted with permission of The University of Chicago Press.

regular elementary grades; with $435.64 for the mentally retarded; with $619.19 for the hearing impaired; and with $932.95 for the blind. In San Diego, for 1955–56, the annual excess cost to the district was $96.75, in contrast with $174 for the "severely retarded," while in Portland (1957–58) the added annual per pupil cost was $58.65. Approximately 90 percent of the San Diego and Portland costs were for instructional and administrative purposes.

Whereas figures such as those just cited reflect essentially a special-class program for the gifted, cost projections supplied the California state legislation in the early 1960s were arrived at by including per pupil screening and identification, complete pupil studies, preservice and in-service preparation of teachers and other school personnel, instructional costs, consultant services, and evaluation costs. While the annual per pupil excess cost was estimated to be close to $250, it must be recognized that costs of pre-program preparations of relevant personnel were included, and this would constitute no small portion of the per pupil cost.

With a view to helping in anticipating costs of a "program" for the gifted, and essentially in terms of establishing special classes for them, Williams (1958, pp. 410–412) posited an elementary school of 500 pupils, of whom some 10 to 20 percent would be "more capable," and included cost items for a half-time teacher ($2500), special books and supplies ($250), teacher training procedures ($250), and capital outlay and maintenance ($250). On this basis he indicated that the per pupil annual extra cost would be between $35 and $70. Incorporating the same components and presuming a high school total population of 1100 pupils, he found the possible annual per pupil excess cost to run between $31 and $62. Presuming a school district with 4500 children in grades K–VI, 2100 at the junior

high level, and 1400 at the senior high school level and including also a half-time supervisor ($4000), a full-time consultant ($6500), and a half-time psychologist ($3000), he figured the per pupil annual excess cost would be $40 to $80, and that the total annual outlay would constitute approximately 3–5 percent of the district's total annual budget. Comparative figures for other kinds of exceptional children were not provided, so no cost indexes were obtainable.

Ratio characterization

When estimates are made specifically in terms of dollars, constantly changing costs cause ambiguity and uncertainty. A much more usable characterization is an index, or ratio, of cost—an indication of how much more or less it costs to "educate" a gifted child in comparison with the "average" child. While the study now to be considered provides much gross dollar information, one of its major purposes was to characterize costs relatively in terms of an "index," or ratio.

Frohreich (1973) reported a school administrator-oriented intensive study of selected school programs directed toward (1) establishing "relative costs of various exceptional child programs compared with regular child programs," (2) identifying "those components, elements, and conditions which seem to have the most pronounced effect on" programs and costs, and (3) "determin[ing] the criteria employed in identifying the various categories of exceptional children and obtain[ing] an estimate of the prevalence of each category." On the basis of expert evaluation, 24 school districts in five states (California, Florida, New York, Texas, and Wisconsin) were chosen to provide data for the study. The data were collected by means of six data forms, and at least one member of the research team "visited and interviewed a teacher of at least one typical classroom for each category of exceptionality operated by the district." Expenditure components on which data were sought included: "administration, teachers and teacher aides, clerical and secretarial, guidance and counseling, health services, food services, transportation, other supporting services, fringe benefits, instructional supplies and equipment, operation and maintenance, other costs of current operation, debt service, and capital outlay" (p. 519). Shown in Table 8.3 are certain of the overall data in the study.

Two things in these data are particularly interesting. Only five of the 24 highly recommended school districts had programs for the gifted, and, even taking into consideration all of the expenditure components of the study, the per pupil expenditures for the gifted were relatively low. (Of course, we don't know anything about the quality of their programs for the gifted.) In the analysis of the expenditure categories that contributed most to cost differentials between exceptional and regular programs, it is striking that only the administrative category was found to figure in the case

of the gifted. Only one other category—the speech handicapped—was found to have a single dominant expenditure category, and that was "other instructional support." Since Frohreich had only five districts with programs for the gifted, he didn't present the cost index for them, but he did present such information for the multiply handicapped, of which he had only four samples: 2.73. (The index for the gifted turned out to be 1.14.) Certainly, the use of an index for this purpose is much more communicative than are absolute costs.

Reimbursement Practices

No school administrator needs to be told that the state augments the funds of the local school districts for the operation of approved programs, but some teachers and numerous teachers-to-be are not aware of that fact. The intent here is only to indicate that, in a few states, the administrator anticipating the district's cost for a program for the gifted can take into consideration the possibility of some degree of special reimbursement. The manner and the extent of

Table 8.3. Frequencies, costs, and prevalences in exceptional programs studied.

Category of exceptional program	Number of programs reported	Expenditure per pupil				Percentage prevalence
		Lowest	Mean	Median	Highest	
Intellectually gifted*	5	$ 548	$ 759	$ 809	$ 872	2.00
Educable mentally retarded	22	708	1316	1316	2358	1.30
Trainable mentally retarded	22	562	1532	1627	2657	.24
Auditorily handicapped	18	533	2067	2103	4671	.10
Visually handicapped	17	852	2448	2197	9105	.05
Physically handicapped	15	713	2197	2113	4210	.21
Speech handicapped	21	541	794	709	1027	3.60
Special learning disorders	20	850	1703	1757	2874	1.12
Emotionally disturbed	14	804	2510	1683	6982	2.00
Multiply handicapped*	4	1339	2013	1941	2830	.07
Homebound hospital	—	—	—	—	—	.22

Source: Adapted from Frohreich, 1973, Tables 1, 3, and 4.

*Discretion should be used in making inferences about or in using the data presented for the intellectually gifted or multiply handicapped programs. Data for these programs were gathered from too small a sample of school districts from which to base future program and fiscal planning.

such reimbursement vary among states as well as within states from time to time.

Although some local school districts have been known to introduce certain practices facilitative to learning by the gifted without extra outside financial assistance, most school districts depend upon special funding from the state even for practices, let alone programs. Such expectations have long been reinforced: extra funding by the state of special education provisions for the handicapped dates from the early part of the century. Such extra funding has been in addition to state payments to local districts to supplement the funds raised by local taxes for the basic educational program—reflecting, perhaps, persisting local failure to recognize special education as an integral part of the basic educational responsibility.

Historically, states reimbursed local school districts for their special education efforts on the basis of specified amounts for different kinds of special classes. In Pennsylvania in the late 1930s, for instance, the operation of approved special classes for the mentally superior entitled the district to $200 for each class. Later, the amounts to which the districts were entitled tended to be determined by formulae which involved factors such as attendance and cost differentials. In some instances, reimbursement is made on a per capita basis; in others on a per capita basis with practices specified. In still other instances, extra funds are provided the local districts for projects or programs for which an accounting has been provided, the local district being required to contribute some specified portion of the costs. In a few instances, federal funding is channeled to the district through the state educational office. The earlier practice of giving such supplementary funds to the local district after the educational services have been rendered is giving way to that of award-

ing funds on the basis of formal statements of intent and assurance that such services would be provided. The wide diversity of special reimbursement practices clearly reflects the exploratory stage of funding provisions for the gifted.

Merely as crudely illustrative, in the early 1960s the funded average annual excess per gifted pupil expenditure was $28 in Illinois and $65 in California. In California, for instance, special funding is provided for two educational functions: the evaluation of pupils for participation in the local program and additional instructional needs. On this basis, local school districts with approved programs were reimbursed up to $40 for excess costs of initial identification (raised to $50 in 1972) and up to $60 per pupil for excess instructional costs (raised to $70 for 1972–73; $80 for 1973–74; $90 for 1974–75; and intended to be $100 thereafter).

Cost Elements

In anticipating the costs of a new program or in accounting for related expenditures in an ongoing program, certain categories of costs should be considered. We shall consider six which should figure in determining the extra costs incurred in educating the gifted at the local district level. The costs within some of these categories can range from those needed for a minimal program to those appropriate to a full program for the gifted.

Administration

Two administrative roles warrant consideration: that of the "central office"—the superintendent of the school district—and that of the building principals. The extent to which each should be chargeable to the gifted program will differ as between the planning and initial implementation stage of the program and the later stage after the program has been gotten under way. The extent to which the central administrative officer will be involved, more in the first stage than in the second, will depend upon a combination of his philosophy and the adequacy of his administrative and supervisory staff. Even granting this, it is doubtful that more than 5 to 10 percent of the costs of central administration could be attributed to the first stage and perhaps not more than 2 to 3 percent afterward. (It could be reasonably contended that no time of the central office administrator properly should be charged to the gifted program, since his involvement in introducing or running such a program is but an essential part of his total professional responsibility.) As far as the costs of the principals' involvement are concerned, the percentages, in the buildings in which the program operates, could be 20 and 10, respectively. Where a qualified consultant for the program would be involved, these percentages should be materially reduced.

Supervision

Here, too, there are two supervisory components to consider. First, the direct involvement of persons designated as general supervisors, curriculum consultants, or special area supervisors will vary with the formal definitions of their roles, their perceptions of their roles, the nature of the teacher-supervisor interactions, the varying natures of the provisions for the gifted, and the stages of the program. Overall, it would seem plausible that the percentages, for the two stages, would approximate 10 and 5, respectively. Second, the principals of most schools have supervisory as well as administrative responsibilities. Depending, as always, upon the pattern of supervision operative in the district, it is reasonable to anticipate that, for the

two stages, not more than 10 and 5 percent, respectively, of the principals' time would be chargeable to the gifted program. Obviously, this will vary further depending upon the nature of the provisions made for the gifted in the particular school. Here again, in the supervisory area, such responsibility well might be significantly reduced if a qualified consultant on the gifted program were involved.

The consultant

Obviously, all of the cost of the consultant—at least her salary and her travel in the district—is chargeable to the program. As has been pointed out, her involvement would, or should, materially reduce the extents to which costs of others could justifiably be attributed to the program.

Teaching

The costs of educating the gifted must be carefully determined, care being taken not to ascribe to the program for the gifted those costs which would be involved in the regular program. It is the *extra* costs which have to be considered. The total costs of a special class for the gifted are not extra costs, since the children in that class would have been in the regular classes if there were no such provision. If the size of the special class is less than that for the district (and if more than customary supplies and equipment are provided), the per pupil cost would be greater for the gifted both in terms of actual teaching costs and in terms of greater space costs per pupil. Therefore, some portion of teaching costs is ascribable to the program.

The costs of outright half-day special classes are easily ascertainable and attributable, although any attempt so to ascribe teaching costs for such children when they became parts of the regular classes would not be. When a regular class teacher establishes special study groups of gifted youngsters within or along with the regular class, some percentage of the teaching costs might seem attributable to the program. At first blush, it would seem appropriate to use some percentage figure (five such children in a class of 25 might thus be regarded as representing 20 percent of the teaching costs), but such interest groups seldom act as such for entire school days. Bookkeeping legerdemain might be able to reflect the number of minutes or hours per school week on a percentage basis. However, such an attempt at accounting rigor borders on the frantic; assuming a teacher who is reasonably sensitized to and prepared to work with individual pupils, the teacher makes adaptations and adjustments for the more capable pupils as a part of her regular class teaching. The costs of basically good teaching hardly should be attributed to a program for the gifted.

Other extra costs are relevant:

1. The costs of special in-service institutes and of contributive extension courses, to the extent that they are paid for by the district
2. District expenditures for tuition and scholarships for teachers for summer and regular year on-campus specified preparation
3. District reimbursement to the program teachers for travel to demonstration centers, special conferences and workshops, and the like

Instructional facilitation

The primary criterion for including the provisions in this category is that they be quite directly contributive to enhancing the learning experiences of the gifted in the classroom. The costs of teacher aides, either in connection with special classes for the gifted or as uniquely adjunctive to regular class teachers who use their services in activities individualized for the gifted in such classes, are clearly program relevant. Associated with such would be expenses incurred in bringing in specialists or consultants for the purpose of providing supportive or elaborative learning opportunities. Expenses incurred in providing correspondence courses for certain of the bright youngsters would be chargeable to the program. The subcategory of special learning materials—library book additions, special learning aids, programmed learning equipment and materials, science and art kits, and the like—all can be regarded as facilitative to learning by the gifted. However, only the extent to which they are uniquely relevant to and used in the program should they be charged to the program. Introducing a program for the gifted into a school system very well may be the precipitating stimulus for the school to add such things for all, or many, of its children, even though such additions may at first be used mostly by the gifted. The extent to which such additions are chargeable, then, to a program for the gifted, well may call for more than superficial consideration. Relative frequency or extent of such special use would seem to be the most defensible basis for including such costs. As such facilitative materials and equipment came to be used by the nongifted—as they will—their costs should be increasingly included in only regular instructional costs.

Certainly any school expenditures made for transporting individual gifted youngsters, or groups of such youngsters, on visits or trips to sites or events that directly bear upon the learnings of those gifted children should be considered in ascertaining excess per pupil costs. Also includable should be tuition costs paid by the district for bright pupils working, under proper supervision, for advanced credit in higher education and/or in special workshops. In fact, this subcategory might better be captioned "scholar-ships," taking care to include in it the granting of funds both directly to care-fully selected, economically hard-pressed gifted youngsters, and indirectly in their specific interests to their parents for the purpose of enabling them to complete their high school education—a point that was developed earlier.

Pupil identification, assessment, evaluation, and counseling

The determination of gifted per pupil excess costs for services such as these will vary in the light of the nature of the gifted program to be inaugurated and the nature of the basic education pro-gram of the district. If the program to be initiated involves only one or two of the early grade levels (strategically desirable), the costs will be somewhat less than in the case of a program involving all the elementary grades. Certain of these costs will decrease a bit after the program has been under way for a couple of years. If the basic program into which the gifted program is introduced includes no practices of group testing of children in learning aptitude and achievement, either major changes therein will be needed or extra, compensatory efforts to make up for this lack will be needed. If, on the other hand, such group test-ing already is an integral part of the basic program, the initial costs of the gifted program will be less. Such costs will vary, then, with two conditions: (1) they will be highest in initiating and maintaining a gifted program in a dis-trict that has no, or little, relevant group testing; and (2) they will be least in initiating and maintaining a gifted pro-gram in a district that has relevant and contributory group testing. The use of teacher nomination in identifying the gifted child will be less expensive than such testing, but will be also less efficient.

But the identification of candidates for a gifted program is only a first step. Each candidate needs to be assessed psy-choeducationally in order to ascertain if he qualifies for inclusion in the pro-gram. To too many, this involves only finding out if the candidate's IQ is high enough. But, as has been pointed out, much more than this is needed: the magnitudes of his particular strengths and of his relative (intraindividual) weaknesses must be ascertained, both his potentials for learning and the levels of his achievement. Not only is this initial assessment necessary, but subsequent an-nual or biennial assessments often are needed also, especially in the cases of children in the lower elementary grades.

The extent to which the costs of ser-vices such as these should be chargeable to a district's program for the gifted is the point at issue. If a school district soundly and systematically obtained and made educational use of the results of good group testing of capacity and achievement, such results could help materially in both identifying and de-termining eligibility of candidates, thus decreasing somewhat the demands on the psychologist's time. When school dis-tricts do not engage in such practices, the costs of their introduction, as a means of helping get a gifted program started, would not justifiably be charge-able to the gifted program, since the values of such practices, provided they are sound, could redound to the benefit of all the children as a part of what a good basic program should be. The too-prevalent assumption that psychological assessment and evaluation of gifted chil-dren in a program is a one-time thing is limiting in determining the cost of such services. While it is administratively con-venient for a portion of a state's reim-bursement to a district maintaining a program for the gifted be specified on a per capita basis, whether only for initial assessment or for necessary successive ones, the district must realistically determine its costs for such services in terms of the percentage of the psychologist's time that is involved directly in the program.

The costs of the staff's involvement in the evaluation of pupil performance should be anticipated even if fine approximation may not be possible. Again, the extent to which such activity would (or should) positively affect pupil evaluation in general would need to be recognized.

The costs for counseling services would need to be determined in terms of the proportion of time specifically devoted to the gifted, although the extent to which there would be a need for them probably would be generally less than in the case of the services of the psychologist. Whereas the need for psychological assessment service would be greater at the elementary grade level and decrease at the secondary level, the need for counseling service would have the reverse pattern. Counseling services would be needed for only a small percentage of the gifted at the elementary level and, particularly if sound occupational guidance functions were included, to varying degrees individually for most of the gifted at the junior-senior high school level. The essentially adjustmental counseling at the elementary level would, or should, be less at the secondary level where occupational counseling and guidance would dominate. The earlier the level at which the gifted program was introduced, the more likely this would be true.

Presuming that any program for the gifted would include a part-time or full-time qualified consultant, the manner in which and extent to which there would be need for her involvement in connection with such services could depend upon the extent to which the

consultant worked with such personnel and with the teachers. Given a consultant with limited background and competency in the areas of such services, greater involvement of the specialized personnel would be needed. Certainly, in evaluating the youngsters, for instance, the competent consultant could figure most importantly and prominently.

Notice that Williams (discussed above, p. 215) gave only superficial attention to the costs of services such as these. As has been indicated, the costs for these services in relation to a program for the gifted should be determined first in terms of the extent to which the specialized personnel are directly involved. In order to illustrate the kind of thinking and planning called for, let us take the elementary school population of 4500 which Williams posited. If, in terms of our definition, we took only 5 percent as a conservative estimate for the gifted, we have 225 probable candidates. (It is likely, though, that more than this number would be regarded as eligible for consideration.) What does this mean in terms of likely demand on the time of a psychologist? Since in many instances more than the administration of a single individual test would be necessary, if an assessment is to be made, it is doubtful that more than six children a week can be properly processed. (Absurd figures of four or more children examined per day by a psychologist clearly reflect only the crudest psychometric testing, rather than sound assessment.) This number of children and this rate of assessment would mean that the candidates would need to be assessed the year before the program was formally started. And this assumes, further, either no or a very limited early admission consideration. In any event, a full-time (competent) psychologist would be needed just for this population. The counseling costs might constitute about one-fifth of a counselor's salary at this level. If the program were initiated at later grade levels, the counselors would be involved to a greater extent, since remedial and other adjustmental efforts would be necessary.

Program evaluation

In these days of educational accountability, and since most states require it when they fund special programs, the administrator should anticipate the costs of evaluating the program. Whether needs should be anticipated specifically for research on the program or whether the evaluation should be regarded as at least part of the research could affect the magnitude of this item. Probably, at first, this category should be conservatively determined. While few school districts use the figure prevalent in industry, this category very properly should represent at least 3 percent of the total estimated cost of the program.

The responsibility of the administrator, with the help of his staff, to anticipate soundly—neither too niggardly nor too expansively—the costs of a program for the gifted is a major one. Cost anticipation for ongoing programs can differ from that for programs which are to be introduced, although the same categories of costs must be considered. What a district is doing, or ought to be doing, for all its children, some of whom are bright, should be differentiated from what is to be, or is being done uniquely for the gifted. Of course, this generalization, if pressed to the ultimate, could mean that added provisions for the gifted would only slightly exceed the per pupil costs in the regular program.

PUPIL AND PROGRAM EVALUATION

The administrator needs to anticipate an evaluation of the program which is to be initiated and to take an anticipating stand regarding the fact of evaluation and, in at least a general sense, the nature of it. While such action is necessary at both the state and local levels, we shall be concerned primarily with the local level. Since some of the concepts involved in pupil evaluation are highly relevant to program evaluation, we shall consider first the matter of the evaluation of pupil performance. In light of a reawakening and legitimate concern for accountability in education, proper anticipation of evaluation is important.

Any teacher who perceives any pupil's performance in terms of its adequacy or correctness evaluates the pupil. In doing so, he may characterize the pupil's performance as "perfect," "satisfactory," "unsatisfactory," and the like. At the end of a given grading period, an overall characterization may be stated in such terms, in letter-grade equivalents, or in some kind of percentage equivalents. The pupil who is regarded as "passing" or "failing" a given grade is evaluated. The according of some kind of honors status at the end, say, of high school is an act of evaluation. Regardless of the great variability among the standards which are used, implicitly or explicitly, the determination of goodness or poorness constitutes an evaluation of the pupil's educational behavior.

The principal or superintendent who studies compilations of age-grade data depictions of the numbers of pupils "at grade," "below grade," and "above grade" does so with a view to evaluating the progress of the pupils in his unit. While the tabulations of such data are themselves only descriptive, the administrator reacts to them evaluatively. In doing so, he may infer from such tabulations that schools or teachers are doing their work well or poorly. If an excessively large percentage of pupils is below grade, he may draw inferences regarding the adequacy of the "teaching" being done. He may do as many administrators did in the generation now mostly past and introduce the practice of promoting all pupils annually, in the belief that such will be psychologically beneficial to the pupils. Or he may, as one major city superintendent did, issue an edict that no child should be failed because he had found that the added cost to the district for failed pupils was very large. (Having thus "saved" the district some $400,000, determined on this basis, he was reappointed the following year at a substantial increase in salary for his "economy move.") Any evaluation of such age-grade data pertains to teachers, schools, or districts—as contrasted with evaluation of pupils' performances.

The person who compiles the results of objective testing of educational achievement is only describing. The median achievement of this grade is so-and-so; of that, so much. There are such-and-such changes over specified grade levels. Evaluation does not occur until the data are characterized as indicating "good," "average," or "poor" performances.

Such practices make little sense in the case of the gifted. In fact, they make little if any sense regarding all pupils, since they all tend to involve standards which are only secondarily relevant as regards the pupils themselves. They merely show what "the Joneses" or the "Smiths" are doing and throw no light upon how any pupil is performing in terms of his own capacity. In the case of teachers' characterizations of pupils, the standards may be those of differing teachers' presumptions of the ideal or of the adequate, or they may be generalized standards of the averages of groups. In the case of administrators and their age-grade analyses, the assumed standard is a grade a year. At least for the gifted and for the slow-learning pupils such normative standards are psychologically less than desirable, and the idealized standards of perfection are both unreal and elusive.

In recent years, the idea of the accountability of education has been increasingly talked about. Central to this issue has been the question raised, at first more often from without the educational system, as to whether the schools are effectively educating their children. The idea is, of course, not new. At least from the beginning of this century, surveys were made in specific school systems and in statewide studies, the results of which provided the basis for raising such a question. Surveys recurring since early in this century in the New York City schools, for instance, reflected a 90 percent commonality between the results of successive evaluations and the ensuing recommendations for improvement. From the first quarter of this century, studies of the educational status of the gifted by Terman and others consistently revealed the short shrift being given the gifted. More generally, the most recent concern being voiced regarding Johnny's poor reading and computing has disposed toward a greater recognition of the importance of accountability. Actually, some form of evaluation has been in operation as long as there have been efforts to educate, but the climate of accountability is a more recent development, brought about by a number of conditions in the social milieu—the post-school performances of the "products" of education, the rising costs of education, the characteristics and demands of the labor market, and the like.

Having considered much that generally is relevant to accountability, we shall now focus on certain major aspects of the problem of evaluation with respect to the education of the gifted. Rather than review studies of an evaluative nature, we shall consider two major areas in which evaluation is important— the conceptual problems important in the evaluation of gifted pupils and those regarding the evaluation of programs for them. In connection with this, as well as with many other points which have been considered, it is important to recognize that most phenomena do not exist as specific points or even as dichotomies. Satisfactory and unsatisfactory performances and good programs and poor programs are never absolute conditions that are completely discretely separable. Most of the concepts, characteristics, and conditions exist as variables, each ranging from some point of lessness to some point of moreness, and thinking in terms of phenomena that exist on such progressions, or continua, is always more difficult than is thinking in terms of oversimplified absolutes or in terms of simple dichotomies. This latter kind of thinking is more perceptual than conceptual in nature.

Pupil Evalution

Two initial clarifications are necessary. First, pupil evaluation and pupil assessment, as these terms are used here, should be clearly differentiated. What has been presented earlier in this book has had to do largely with assessing children to determine whether they qualify and can function as gifted. It is true that the ascertainment of the extent to which a gifted child is achieving academically in terms of his capacity for learning has an element of evaluation in it, but the intent here is to consider the larger problem of pupil evaluation. Second, while we shall be concerned primarily with the gifted, the underlying concepts are basically applicable with respect to all school children. This only further illustrates the point that the basic philosophy and fundamental psychology of educating the gifted actually should undergird the education of all children—the main differences being in regard to the spread, complexity, and, perhaps, the scope of the learnings involved.

Put most succinctly, evaluation of gifted pupils must be broad, deep, and long, and each of these must be educationally, psychologically, and socially meaningful.

Breadth

The gamut of potential behavior of the gifted long has been shown to be very wide. Even though many of the gifted and talented have been recognized as outstanding primarily in one area of behavior, they generally have been at least above average in other areas of behavior. (Correlation, not compensation, is the rule.) Those whose superiority has been of particular note in the academic or verbal area have tended to be highly visible in social leadership, in emotional stability, and in esthetic areas. Those who have tended to stand out primarily because of their creative behavior tend to have academic potential and sophistication superior to the average. Those who have been recognized as particularly outstanding in one or another area of behavior and who have seemed to the less perceptive to be only average or below in other areas have tended to be publicized more than have those who have clearly demonstrated overall superiority. This has tended to be true of the gifted and talented in their later educational stages and in their postschool lives.

But for the educator whose responsibility it is to identify the gifted and talented in their early lives, there is a very great need to "cover all fronts" in order that potential superiority can be nurtured early in whatever areas it can be discovered. Both for this purpose and also in order to provide a basis for broadly sensitive research, evaluation of the gifted must ascertain potentiality of performance in the verbal area (which is crucial to so many subareas), in the quantitative area (which is crucial to many subareas), in the creative area (which itself is quite broad), in the esthetic area (in the broadest sense of artistic production and participation), and in the social-emotional area (important as regards both social leadership and adjustment).

The performances of the gifted in schools have tended to be characterized primarily in terms of academic achievement largely because of historical inclination in that direction, heavily because of the increasing availability of objective measuring devices in that area, and probably partly because of the tendency of so many to regard education simplistically. The long reliance upon school grades as evidence of such performances has been attended by an equally long recognition of their limitations—subjectivity being the primary one—and an increasing social aversion to the implied precision of depiction which they connoted. This and other factors in our social climate have produced an increasing tendency to characterize academic achievement or performance in pass-fail terms—a typical reaction from implied preciseness to excessively gross depictions. As so often happens in such reactionary periods, the pass-fail practice presents the danger of being overgeneralized—lacking sensitivity to the fact that there are certain kinds of learning/performance situations for certain individuals at certain times when such gross characterizations have social, psychological, and educational merit, and that there are other times when the loss of more precise information is truly crucial and vital. Most evaluations in the academic area should serve two purposes: to provide the pupil with information that will be helpful to him, as an individual, in a diagnostic and potential remedial sense, in better achieving more in harmony with his capacity to achieve in the area in which he has been evaluated, and to inform the pupil where he stands, in a social framework, so far as such achievement is concerned.

Depth

Whether breadth and depth in evaluation can be truly differentiated might well be argued, but in contrast to the need to be broadly sensitive to the many important kinds of behavior, there is a need to evaluate each of them in considerable detail. For illustrative purposes, let us start off most simply with the evaluation of pupils in the educational achievement area. Many studies both of the gifted and of total school populations have reported such achievement in terms of all-encompassing grade-point averages or in terms of scores that reflected some kind of total performance on standardized tests. The child is "on the honor roll" or "has an EGS of 6.4"; he performed on the Stanford Achievement Test (itself consisting of five or more subtests) like an average child in the fourth month of the sixth grade. Such molar characterizations have some value, perhaps, to the administrator and to the layman. More precise information is communicated when achievement is characterized in terms of reading, arithmetic, spelling, social studies, and the like. These, however, still are rather "lumpy." It is better to go more deeply into the matter and characterize reading in terms of reading comprehension and word knowledge, or arithmetic in terms of problem solving, quantitative concepts, and computation, or social studies in terms of knowledge, comprehension, application, inference, and the like. Evaluation of "cognitive" behavior, as such, would be so gross as to be nearly meaningless; the payoff comes with the evaluation of the components which make it up. In like manner, classroom behavior of both pupils and teachers can be analyzed in depth by a variety of approaches and devices, such as the Steele-House-Kerins Class Activities Questionnaire (p. 306).

In the same sense, evaluations in depth

are possible in each of the other areas of behavior. Social leadership, for instance, can be depicted in terms of its presence in dyadic relationships, in small-group relationships, and in large-group relationships, as well as in terms of intraschool and extraschool situations. Creative behaviors admit of comparable breakdowns into factors such as the need for an initiating stimulation, the medium employed (both input and output), the degree of anchorage in the proximal, volume of creations, social relevance, and the like. In fine, evaluation in depth involves the analysis of behaviors, in whatever area, into their component elements as well as for varying kinds of situations.

Length

Many of the evaluations of the behaviors of the gifted have been made while the children were in experimental or demonstration settings. The fact of such settings itself plays an important part in influencing the motivation, attitudes, and performances of both the youngsters and the educational staff involved in them. This is but one of many instances illustrating the generalization that the act of measurement or evaluating affects the performances being measured or evaluated. Evaluation always is a matter of the moment and of the setting in which it is done, and it has value as of that time and place. Such evaluation has informational value, but the fundamental problem is not whether the children in question can be momentarily intellectually enlivened or resuscitated by given manipulations, important as that may be, but whether they continue to thrive in like manner in ensuing educational and/or social climates. The greater the time span over which sound evaluation is made, the more significant it will be educationally and socially. Information must be ob-

tained to throw light not only on how the gifted who were provided special learning facilities, say in the early elementary grades, perform at later educational levels but also on how they perform after they left school. Such has been true of the Terman studies; the last published study was a 40-year follow-up (Oden, 1968). (Cronbach and Sears are reported to be making a 60-year follow-up study.)

But such evaluations, even though they may be desirably longitudinal in nature, must be regarded with caution. In large part, they have involved either of two biases: On the one hand, some of them have consisted only of descriptions of how the gifted under study have performed, as in the Terman studies. On the other hand, they have involved the descriptions of how the gifted in experimentally treated groups have performed in comparison with ostensibly comparable youngsters in control groups. Since the control groups usually are identified within the same milieu as the experimental groups, the question of the typicality of the findings can be raised. While much information already is at hand regarding how the gifted in the average, essentially unprovided-for conditions have performed, it has not been compiled longitudinally for the purpose of being compared directly with parallel information on comparable gifted in varied treatment conditions.

Meaningfulness

Granted the adequacy of evaluation in terms of the breadth, the depth, and the length of concern, whatever evaluation is made must be meaningful in a further sense. Perhaps the factor of convenience has figured most largely in contributing to the tendency to ascribe primarily educational meaning to most evaluations of the gifted. While the social importance of educational adequacy can not be denied, there are other considerations of great importance. The extent to which the gifted have been able to capitalize socially upon their superior potentials and achievements and the extent to which they have experienced a sense of self-actualization are psychologically meaningful, both to the individuals themselves and to society in general. The extent to which the gifted have been enabled to play socially contributive roles is socially meaningful. The pattern of the Terman studies has well reflected this broad conceptualization of evaluation.

Program Evaluation

There is a very real distinction that should be recognized between the establishment and operation of a program for the gifted and the introduction of practices which are known or presumed to be helpful in their learning. Inaugurating a practice of individually prescriptive teaching, even when it involves more than one teacher or grade level, does not constitute establishing a program for the gifted, even though such an educational approach may have some results that may be beneficial to some or many gifted children. Providing only for the establishment of special classes or special work or study groups of gifted children is not programmatic, although such may be facilitative to learning by some bright children. Making it possible for gifted children to enter school early and arranging for bright youngsters to take courses for advanced credit must be regarded as only practices. These and other kinds of practices may serve as component parts of a program, but they do not become meaningful parts of a program until their functioning as integral parts of a total school program is realized.

A program is something more than an amalgamation of practices, however good those practices may be known or be-lieved to be. A program requires a major conceptualization of what is to be accomplished and how it is to be accomplished. Fundamental, obviously, is an explicit statement of the philosophy of the undertaking. Given this, the undertaking must be analyzed into its component parts, with specific planning as to when and how such parts are to be introduced. Overall, a program must have conceptual and philosophical integrity, it must be coherent, and it must have continuity throughout the grades. All such planning must provide for effective interaction with other parts of the total ongoing functioning of the school system. Obviously, it must have firm administrative support—not just acceptance or tolerance. It must involve the working of effective relevant school personnel—teachers, supervisor, the consultant, and others—whose special competencies and commitment in this area are recognized within the school and community. Since any such program has both administrative and instructional aspects, these two must complement each other. Sustained, periodic, and well-planned evaluation of at least parts or aspects of the program should occur in order that effectiveness can be ascertained and needed modifications can be made.

The program evaluation with which we are concerned here has two aspects—the evaluation of the program as program, and the evaluation of pupil outcomes which can be attributed to the program. With respect to the latter, the points developed regarding pupil evaluation are relevant. The important thing to keep in mind is that we need to be concerned with pupil behaviors—are the achievements, adjustments, and attitudes of the children taken into consideration broadly and deeply enough and over socially and psychologically significant lengths of time? The matter of program evaluation can, of course, be considered either in connection with state programs or with regard to local school district programs. At first, we shall concern ourselves primarily with the latter and then, because at least certain of the fundamental elements are in common to them, consider briefly the evaluation of state programs.

To be aware of its limitations and difficulties as well as to recognize its possibilities, we should perceive program evaluation in the light of certain measurement concepts. Certainly, it lacks the precision of weighing a baby on valid scales, of ascertaining the miles per gallon an automobile delivers when its load, route, driving speed, and so on are specified, or even of ascertaining the educational achievements of pupils on well-standardized tests. While it may involve a qualified observer who may use a checklist in order to insure coverage of important points, it lacks the precision possible in recording the numbers of times pupils leave their seats, the frequency with which they manifest adaptive or maladaptive behaviors, or the attendance of teachers at demonstration centers. Each of these actually is a measurement function in terms of which judgments are made as to goodness or adequacy. Underlying all such activities is the premise that generalities are demonstrable through specificities.

Program evaluation requires such specification, but still is complex. There are two essential aspects in such evaluation. First, to what extent are there specific conditions present which would make possible the mounting of a program? Second, and most important, do the conditions actually function in contributing to the desired outcomes? Structure is relatively easy to specify and to identify, being essentially a " 'tis or 'tain't" matter: Is there a stated philosophy of the program? Are special educational materials present? Are the personnel adequate in number and quality?

Is there adequate funding?—and the like. Function, on the other hand, tends to be much less precisely discernible. All the factors mentioned, as well as others, well may be present but not functioning well or just not functioning. Functioning, especially, has to be perceived in terms of continua. Instructional use of supportive materials can range from zero or only occasional and highly incidental use, to "normal," educationally sound use, to intense use to the extent that the materials become the primary focus of learning activities rather than contributive to specified educational ends. Funding provisions may range from the barest minimum of one or two activities, say testing and extra materials, to a wide range of appropriate activities, such as pupil travel, teacher aides, scholarship support, and the like.

Local

The evaluation of local programs can be carried out in one of three ways:

1. Outside experts can be brought in, thus increasing the probability of the evaluation's being broadly and objectively accomplished.
2. Personnel within the school system can make the evaluation, thus providing for the much-touted self-study values of such an approach. To some, the self-study approach can be sensitive to local "realities" of which the outsider may be unaware; to others, the recognition of and accession to such realities may be the very factor which mitigates against the development of a sound program.
3. A combination of the two approaches probably is preferable, providing that they are well balanced.

As either contributive to the evaluation or integral to it, two contrasting procedures will be described. The first is a detailed self-inquiry form intended for use in a district's identification of its practices, the overall impact of which might be regarded as a kind of program evaluation, and which also could be used as a survey form across districts. The second procedure, considerably more molar in nature but still specifying essential components, more clearly reflects what the larger components of a good program for the gifted should be.

In 1959, the author prepared for the Illinois Council on Educational Administration a survey form which could elicit rather general information on a district's identification practices of the gifted and rather highly specified information regarding elements in the district's practices. Provision was made for the persons using this inventory to indicate, separately for the elementary, junior high school, and senior high school grade levels, when the practices named were "little or none—not frequent enough to report," "moderate—present but spotty," and "extensive—essential part of our program." Four categories of practices were identified: enrichment (19 specific activities), acceleration (8 practices), special grouping (9 practices), and other provisions (11 practices). The inventory called also for the checking of one or more of six evaluative statements regarding the programmatic quality of the provisions identified. The inventory could serve as a means not only of identifying what was being done—at what level and to what extent—but also of suggesting adaptations that could be made.

Considerably more encompassing and reflecting a distillation of the opinions of experts in the field of the gifted is Renzulli's evaluative structure, *Diagnostic and Evaluative Scales for Differentiated Education of the Gifted* (DESEG) (1968). The fifteen components are divided among five categories: philosophy and objectives (existence and adequacy of a document, application of the document), student identification and placement (validity of conception and adequacy of procedure, appropriateness of relationship between capacity and curriculum), the curriculum (relevance of conception, comprehensiveness, articulation, adequacy of instructional facilities), the teachers (selection, training), and program organization and operation (general staff orientation, administrative responsibility and leadership, functional adequacy of the organization, financial allocation, provision for evaluation). The evaluation of the fifteen components, each characterized as a "program requirement," provides for consideration of both structure and function. No small amount of judgment is involved in evaluations of the components which are worded in terms of "adequacy," and a confusion has arisen in the minds of some users of the instrument regarding the relationship between adequacy and appropriateness—it being argued that certain practices may be appropriate for certain situations but would be regarded as inadequate in some ideal sense. Nevertheless, the scales can be of considerable value in a district's self-evaluation, or in its use by qualified outsider, in that the crucial components of a sound program are thus delineated.

Evaluation necessarily consists of doing two things. If a good program should consist of a given number of specified components, it is necessary first to ascertain which of these components are present in the program being evaluated. This phase is fundamentally one of description. Once the components, whatever they are, are found to be present, a determination must be made as to whether they are functioning in the intended manner. This is a judgmental process, and such judgments must be made in the light of a comprehension of the fundamental philosophy of the program. If, for instance, individualization of instruction be a desirable component of a program, and if a teacher gives one pupil 20 problems to work out and others only

10, this may be regarded as evidence that individualizing is taking place. But this is only descriptive. Whether such action on the part of the teacher is "good" or appropriate must be decided in terms of whether the first child really needs that much extra drill or practice (when, in reality, if he is gifted, he actually may need fewer), whether he needs a greater variety of experiences on the basis of which she will help him more meaningfully to generalize, or whether she wants just to keep him busy for the same length of time it takes the others to complete the 10. Any judgment regarding the appropriateness of such a practice is made primarily on philosophical grounds and secondarily on psychoeducational grounds.

Evaluation, then, involves the descriptive act of stating what essential components are present or absent in a given program and then the making of judgments as to whether such components are functioning appropriately. If certain important components are found to be absent, the discovery can serve as the stimulus for their being considered for incorporation, but an evaluation approach such as the Renzulli structure can serve yet another purpose: it can be of value to a school district that is planning to establish a program in that it specifies components which should be included in it.

State

While the specifics of program evaluation at the state level are quite likely to vary from state to state, and even from time to time within a given state, certain major elements are common to both local and state program evaluation. The policy which is to be implemented in a state program very well may incorporate certain elements of a philosophy of a program for the gifted but may just as well fail to be broad-based. The Illinois program, for instance, reflected only little and late consideration for the early identification of the gifted, for early admission (administrators generally were against it), and for providing for the gifted in the early elementary grades even though such would be called for in an adequate philosophy of educating gifted children. On the other hand, it recognized the importance and necessity of doing something (demonstration centers, scholarships for teachers-to-be-of-the-gifted, in-service education of educational personnel, summer institutes) toward helping teachers work more effectively with the gifted. Contrasting somewhat with the development and evaluation of a program within a specific school district, the state program has to be developed and evaluated in terms of school districts that can be anticipated to differ widely among themselves as to sensitivity to the problem, willingness to start doing something for the gifted, and ability to take appropriate action.

Before considering the facets of a state program that must be evaluated, it is important that the role of the department in the development of education in a state be recognized. First, it is at least highly probable that the educational thinking at the top level is in the educational vanguard of the state. It is so high a probability as to be a fact that, within any given state, there is a small number of local school districts the quality of whose educational thinking far surpasses that at the state level. (A parallel exists with respect to the national level vis-a-vis state and local levels.) This condition maintains even when state-level educational personnel are appointed solely or primarily on grounds of professional competence as contrasted with appointments that are heavily politically influenced. And yet, in spite of this inevitable condition, educational thinking at the state level generally tends to be in advance of that in the local districts. And, obviously, state-level educational thinking tends to be so far in advance of that in certain local school districts that communication between them is rendered almost impossible. This whole matter is but a particular instance of the generalization that, while any regulatory agency tends to be "behind" certain components in the domain of regulation, it also is "ahead" of the majority of the components in its domain and therefore is generally capable of exerting a leadership influence in the total domain. This generalization holds at the national level, at the state level, at the local school district level, and even at the school building level.

Recognition of this is of particular significance when we consider the matter of state-level programs for the gifted. Not only are there marked "individual differences" among states but also among the school districts within any given state. Even though the components to be evaluated in state programs may be generalizable across states and school districts, at least certain of the components must be recognized as varying in extents of realizability in different states and at different times.

Although they have not been empirically derived and validated, at least five components appear to be paramount:

1. There must be a clear policy statement for the program, and it should incorporate, or clearly be based upon, a sound philosophy of the education of the gifted.

2. Administrative and instructional facets of program operation must be implementable.

3. Financial support must be realistically anticipated.

4. Immediate competent personnel needs must be met, and future personnel needs within the state must be realistically anticipated.

5. The local programs which the state is intended to stimulate must be conducive to discernible changes in the behaviors of both pupils and educational personnel.

Each of these will be elaborated.

POLICY/PHILOSOPHY. The objectives of a state program need to be clearly stated. These objectives result from a statement of the policy of the state program, and this, in turn, must reflect a sound philosophy of the education of gifted children. The essentials of this philosophy already have been identified, but certainly aggressive early identification, early education, a preventive rather than a remedial perception of the educational process, and breadth of perception of giftedness and talent should be reflected clearly.

IMPLEMENTABILITY. What is sought to be accomplished must result from the blend of two things: the fundamental objectives of the program and a recognition of the realities of local situations in which movement toward the objectives must take place. In a very few districts, merely a furtherance of what already is under way may be appropriate. In many others, what may be perceived locally as taking a major step may need to be facilitated. Adaptations to local administrative and supervisory realities may be needed, recognizing that in some districts "realities" may be more fictional than real. Differing degrees of readiness, both administrative and instructional, will need to be nurtured and capitalized upon. A wide gamut of educationally relevant variables will need to be dealt with—staff, parental and pupil attitudes, pupil evaluation practices, curricular matters, pupil promotional policies, library facilities, and the like. And in a few districts, where only a modicum of motivation and sensitivity exists or can be cultivated, very small first steps will need to be taken. The range of needs parallels that of teachers working with bright youngsters: some should be helped rather quickly to undertake major evaluative or conceptual learning experiences, some should be helped in undertaking relatively simple cognitive tasks, and some should be provided at first with very basic experiential nurturance. But underlying whatever situation, a major perception of the larger goal should exist in the light of which such adaptive steps are taken.

FINANCIAL SUPPORT. This has two aspects—support for the operation of the program at the state level and support to be provided to the local school districts. Funds are needed both for the administrative functions of the staff in charge of the state program and for providing a variety of services to the local school districts in connection with the programs which are being started or operated: informational and promotional activities (not the end-all, but an important initial phase), consultant services (by far the largest state staff activities so long as they are functional rather than fictional), and assistance for the evaluation of and research on and in the state program. At the local level there can be needs for either primary or supplementary funds, depending upon the nature of the local program being assisted, for such as the following: pupil instructional facilitation (pupil travel, the acquiring of extraschool expertise for work with the pupils, appropriate correspondence course supplementation, and so on); broadly conceived pupil scholarship help; facilitation of pupil assessment, evaluation, and counseling; possible local library development or improvement; partial funding of directly involved staff (for a program director, if needed, and certainly for the consultant); improvement of relevant staff competency; and additional per pupil reimbursement, especially if the mandated class size is less than the average class size in the district.

In days of financial stress in the public schools, this may seem as if great additional funding is called for, but much can be accomplished by redirecting the use of funds already available. Certain of the funding by the state should be provided with view to its progressively being reduced, say over a period of five years, as the local district increasingly makes the program for the gifted an integral part of its regular educational program.

PERSONNEL ANTICIPATION. This too has two aspects. On the one hand, there is the overriding need for competently prepared top-level state staff personnel who are soundly committed to and versed in the philosophy of educating the gifted. This applies almost equally to those at secondary and tertiary levels within the state staff, since they are the ones who actually will be working in the field with local district school personnel. Given this adequacy, there is the other major problem of finding or creating a pool of personnel who actually will implement the state program within the local districts. There is a widespread tendency for enthusiasts—not all of them lay persons —to cause a program to be mandated when there are inadequate competent personnel to carry out the program. In recent years, for instance, the school laws of many states have been changed to require that all exceptional children of one kind or other—the handicapped, the retarded, those with learning disabilities, and the like—be provided with education appropriate to their particular needs without at the same time assuring that there will be enough teachers properly prepared to provide such education. This results in either of two conditions— ill-prepared teachers are employed to provide such education, resulting in low-quality operation, or the practical absurdity of the legal requirement is recognized and the responsibility is essentially ignored.

To avoid such a condition, the state program must provide not only for the cultivation, often de novo, of both administrative and instructional personnel who will be competent to initiate the local programs, but also for the educational embellishment of those educational personnel who have given evidence of having made a start toward being so qualified and who are involved in programs just getting started. To this end provisions must be made for funding scholarships or other financial inducements that will enable experienced teachers or teachers-to-be to obtain the preparation (not "training") which can enable them meaningfully to take part in educating the gifted children. For those teachers who have given evidence of having moved soundly toward this goal but who still need further preparation, in-service and other institutes are needed.

Three conditions need to be recognized in regard to planning to staff the local district operations which are to be parts of the state program. First, since the Sputnik spurt of concern for educating the gifted when a number of new teacher preparation programs came into being, the number of such programs has materially decreased, thus making it necessary for state programs either to provide for the establishment of such preparatory programs or to plan for their personnel to go outside the state to acquire such preparation. Second, the tendency is to regard the matter of preparing teachers primarily as one involving more specialized work in methods of teaching. While it is important that teachers of the gifted know a variety of ways of facilitating learning by the gifted, it is much more important that they be well grounded in the philosophy which should underlie all such methods. A philosophically well-grounded teacher

is likely to work out for herself effective "methods," given the appropriate educational climate in which she can do so. But the frequency with which teachers well versed only in "methods" have failed soundly to facilitate learning is most distracting. Third, such a recognition of the importance of having competent educational personnel in order to mount a sound program for the gifted necessarily will delay the implementation of the program in many districts. Castles in the sand have been erected by many administrators who did not recognize that the development of a sound program for the gifted is a deliberate process that may take two or more years. This is a point which funders of state programs and/or the administrators of such funds often fail to recognize adequately.

BEHAVIORAL CHANGE. State programs should be mounted to effect changes in behavior—a change in the educational practices in local school districts, and hopefully significant improvements in the behavior of the children who have been in the programs. This generalization holds whether the new program is for driver education, for vocational education, for the mentally retarded, for the learning disabled, for the gifted, or for any other purpose or group. The driver education program (because of its tangibility) was regarded as being so effective that its products receive favorable consideration in regard to insurance rates; the programs for the gifted (because of their intangibility?) have had difficulty in receiving even sustained acceptance among educators. Just as a parent hopes to educate his child to behave in certain ways even though the parent is not around to see that he does so, just so should a state program seek to motivate local school districts to continue to educate their gifted after the impetus of the state program has lessened or disappeared. For local school districts to do things to improve the quality of education for the gifted only so long as there is state-level financial motivation for them to do so probably is somewhat beneficial for the gifted who are involved in such activities, but this does not constitute a sound program for the gifted.

Granting the appropriateness, and often the need, for state departments' helping local school districts get started in providing more adequately for the education of their gifted children, the real value of such state assistance is manifested in the continued educational behavior of the local school district after the original dollar impetus no longer exists. Numerous educational practices have been introduced into school systems by means of special funding and they have seemed sound and highly acclaimed, but many of them have been unhesitatingly dropped or abandoned when the special funds no longer were made available, suggesting strongly that such schools have failed to recognize that the philosophy underlying the special efforts was but an integral part of the fundamental philosophy of education. When local programs for the gifted have been started under the aegis of a funding state program and then dropped, the fundamental contribution of the state program is negligible at best. An analogy between this situation and that of the extrinsic-extrinsic motivation of the individual is apropos here. If the local district doesn't make such provisions on its own, it hasn't learned to "want" to do so.

A second aspect involves the behavior of the gifted children who have been involved in whatever the state program has been promoting. After all, such programs are instituted for the fundamental purpose of effecting changes in the behaviors of the children and not just to give professional personnel something more dignified or au courant to do. The importance of the breadth and depth of such

behavioral changes already has been dealt with in some detail, but certainly evidence must be adduced regarding such aspects as the adequacy of provision for the whole variety of giftedness and talent, the extent to which both the latent bright and the manifestly bright perform within plausible reach of their potentials, the school-holding power for both of these kinds of youngsters, their present and postschool learning, their emotional and social adjustment, and their subsequent involvement in and contribution to societal affairs. Accountability in terms of such behavioral breadth and such time span can do much to reflect upon the educational and social value of state programs.

SUMMARY

Given the understanding and commitment of the central administration—both local and state—to the necessity of a program for the gifted, the attendant responsibilities are apparent. Central among these, of course, is the recognition of the appropriate preparation of those to be involved in such a program, ranging from the major orientation of the central administrative staff to that of the teaching and ancillary personnel. The necessary consideration of costs should be neither niggardly perceived nor unrealistically expansive. In a typical population, the allocation of 3 to 5 percent of an instructional budget for 5 to 8 percent of a school population should be logically defensible. Many regular school programs have components that need only to be extended more specifically for the gifted; many others, lacking these, will need added components. Common to both conditions would be the planning for a consultant whose responsibility it would be to work in the interests of the gifted.

The administrator's obligation to plan

for the evaluation of the operation of his schools and to delineate at least the major dimensions of that evaluation is clear-cut. The evaluation of pupil outcomes—broadly conceived—is of primary importance at the local school level but still of significance in a state program perspective. Programs need to be evaluated, both as to whether they provide adequately for the components which are necessary to them and as to whether they are functioning effectively. This is true at both the state and local levels. State programs are effective to the extent that the local programs which they seek to promote contain an integral part of the total local program after the enticement of additional funding ceases.

9

Administrative considerations: II

Clearly enunciated administrative decisions or policy statements are needed also in regard to matters which relate more directly to facilitating learning by the gifted. In this light, we shall consider early admission and other aspects of acceleration, tracking, and special classes. Bear in mind that the administrative stances we are considering only set the stage on which learning is expected to take place. What happens on the stage—how the teachers (and others) help the children learn on that stage—is instructional in nature and will be considered in the next chapter.

EARLY ADMISSION

Given the premise that prevention of underachievement and of an aversive attitude toward learning in the gifted is of primary importance, it would seem to follow inescapably that the gifted should be helped to continue in the kinds of

cognitive learning which many of them manifest before being allowed to enter conventionally upon their formal schooling. In the cases of those who, for one reason or other, have been growing up in situations that were not conducive to this, society has an obligation to seek them out and to see to it that they are provided the nurturance to which they are entitled. Even most of this latter group will have given behavioral evidence which those of appropriate perceptive ability can discern as suggestive of high intellectual promise during the preschool years. Early admission is important in respect to both those in whom promise is manifest and those in whom it is latent.

Kinds of "Early Admission"

The term "early admission" has been used to denote three different kinds of situations. One is that in which children are allowed to enter upon their public schooling—either at the kindergarten or the first-grade level—at earlier chronological ages than specified as the "proper" or legal school-entering age, without regard to their measured learning capacities. Understandably, a few studies involving this orientation have yielded ambiguous findings. A second, which appears in much of the literature on the gifted and which logically includes the first, denotes pupils' or students' entering upon some portion of the educational sequence at a chronological age that is less than that at which such entrance "normally" occurs. For the most part, in the literature on the gifted, this has pertained to early entrance at the college or university level. To a lesser extent, this usage has pertained to letting bright pupils enter upon high school courses or year levels "beyond their years." At the elementary level, such a practice has been called acceleration. A combination of prior superior academic achievement and/or present superior capacity to achieve academically serves as the primary basis for making this kind of educational decision.

The third usage—the one with which we are concerned here—pertains to allowing children to enter upon their formal public schooling at chronological ages less than the conventional entering age, but only if they are regarded, by competent specialists, as having a capability that suggests a high probability of succeeding in the formal learning situation. This necessitates, of course, a sound psychological assessment of each child, a major component in which (but by no means the sole one) is evidence that the child has matured mentally to such an extent that he is likely to be able to meet the learning demands of the schools. Often, when the possibilities of early admission are hotly argued, one side argues in terms of the first usage and the other in terms of the third usage.

Early admission is not to be confused with the various "head start" provisions, which became quite visible in the 1960s. The major thrust of the head start efforts was to compensate for the limited acculturation experienced by different kinds of "disadvantaged" children. However, it must be recognized that, within this population, there can be some bright youngsters who could benefit from a special kind of psychological nurturance and who could thereby become legitimate candidates for early admission.

Interestingly, the provision of early admission has received scant consideration in formal literature on the gifted. In some texts it is dealt with only passingly in spite of its fundamental psychological and social importance. Other major texts ignore it completely, even though Hobson (1948) had published significant longitudinal findings on at least the lack of deleterious effects of such a practice at the school-entering level.

Early admission is but one way of accelerating gifted children. While the larger concept of acceleration and its many ramifications will be taken up later, early admission is regarded as of sufficient importance to require consideration in and of itself. The fact that it has been given such little consideration in the literature strongly suggests that the practice has been overtly or covertly opposed, owing undoubtedly to the failure to consider seriously both its psychological and social aspects and the related research. Many educators paradoxically have professed their commitment to "meeting the needs of individual children" and to the importance of preventing underachievement in the gifted but have been averse to, or uninterested in, admitting gifted children earlier than the conventional time. Generally, such aversion on the part of educators has been contributed to by the wording of school laws, ignorance of the results of sound research, experiences with ill-conceived instances of early admission, experiences with parents of ineligible children, and unwillingness or inability to deviate from a traditional lock-step perception of "education." Some parents oppose early admission until they are given an opportunity to study the facts.

Before we consider the underlying rationale, a sharper delineation of early admission is in order. While it is always important, in making adequate educational provision for a gifted child, to take such steps in terms of an understanding of all the important factors in his situation, this is particularly necessary in deciding whether a bright child should be admitted early to school. The school-entering period is one of the major landmarks in the child's life. For almost every child it involves an impingement on his life style of a whole pattern of forces that are discernibly different from those of his home and/or neighborhood. For the bright child from an advantaged home, the initial encountering of school experiences can mean an opportunity for him to continue fruitfully those learning experiences which well may have been highly intellectually satisfying in the home. For the school-entering bright child from a disadvantaged home, the school can provide learning opportunities than can challenge and satisfy him in new and fruitful ways, or it may constitute a cultural contrast that may be highly distracting or threatening. While both kinds of youngsters can and should be admitted early, given the presence of other factors suggesting high probability of success, they would need to be provided with quite different learning opportunities. The shift from home to school involves differing kinds of emotional demands and adequacies for children coming from different kinds of emotional climates. Related to this are possible differing social demands resulting from the child's encountering new significant others in the new setting.

Contributive to adjustment to the expanded and more diversified demands are, of course, health and physical factors.

It is especially necessary, then, that, when deciding whether a bright child should be admitted early, his total psychological picture must be the initial basis for decision. And this is only a part of the total assessment: the nature of the educational situation into which he may be admitted is equally critical. Of course, on the one hand one could consider the admitting of a bright youngster early to *any* kind of educational program, where he would just have to sink or swim like all the rest of the pupils, or one could consider such action with a view to his being reasonably assured of encountering a studied continuity in his learning growth. In the former, the bright child might still "make a go" of it; in the latter, the chances of successful early admission should be markedly higher.

Rationale

Much of the nature of the rationale of early admission has been implied in what has just been suggested. The underlying premise would be that, given a child who is bright and who is known or believed to have other factors in his favor (or at least not strongly contraindicative) and who already has started on his accelerated learning before the conventional age for entering school, society—through the school—should make it possible for him to contine in his learning at the pace he already has manifested, instead of, in effect, causing him to suspend such activity and growth for one, two, or three years until he becomes "old enough" formally to enter school. In the highly important strategic sense, permitting a properly evaluated bright youngster to enter upon his schooling can prevent—

or at least can delay—his early learning to become an underachiever. This generalization holds for either the child coming from an advantaged home, where much conventional learning already may have started, or the child coming from a disadvantaged home or neighborhood, where early learning, though possibly not of an academic nature, has been clearly in evidence. Early admission is seen as a means of contributing to the furthering of learning already started, and as preventive of the arrest or suspension of early learning.

Early admission is not for any child who is believed to be bright. It is, rather, for the bright child of preschool age whose total psychological picture warrants it, and it must be perceived in terms of the kind of educational program into which he is to be admitted. Analogously, it is preferable that a patient be admitted, not to just any hospital, but to one known to have facilities appropriate to his condition.

Criteria

It is psychologically unsound to specify a single criterion in terms of which an early admission decision should be made. It is, however, justifiable to make specific statements about the criteria and then to arrive at such a decision on the basis of the pattern of interrelationship that exists, or is believed to exist, among them. We shall consider the various factors that, at minimum, should be considered.

Bear in mind the fact that at no time has any allusion been made to the grade level to which the child should be early-admitted. Depending on the child and the nature of the educational program available, this could be kindergarten or some higher grade level. In order to simplify our consideration of these fac-

tors, we shall assume that we are considering the possibility of early admission at least to a first grade for which conventional educational objectives are professed.

Learning aptitude

First, it is necessary to ascertain the child's learning capability. We must recognize here that, while generally we can say a child is likely to be gifted if his IQ is of a certain magnitude or greater, the IQ should not be the primary basis on which eligibility for early admission is to be established. A child with a valid Binet IQ of 150, for instance, could not receive serious consideration for early admission to the first grade if he were three years old; his mental level would be comparable to that of an average child four and a half years old—an intellectual capability suggesting a reasonable chance of succeeding on conventional reading readiness tasks. But most generally, the early-admission candidate should have a Binet mental age (or its psychological, not its psychometric, equivalent) at least equal to and preferably a bit higher than that of the average child in the grade for which early admission is being considered. If early admission to the conventional first grade is being considered, then the candidate should have a valid Binet mental age of at least six to six and a half years. By like reasoning, a valid Binet mental age of at least five and one-half years would suggest a plausible candidate for early admission to the conventional kindergarten.

Allusion has been made to the "conventional" first grade and kindergarten. Even though it may be difficult to specify just what is meant by "conventional," some attempt is necessary because any decision regarding early admission must take into consideration not only the child's relevant characteristics but also the nature of the milieu into which he may be admitted early. While very few conditions are completely devoid of intellectual stimulus value, they differ in the extent to which they forthrightly evoke or demand the kinds of cognitive functioning in which we are primarily interested. This is particularly true of kindergartens; the first-grade level generally is taken to be the first stage in the formal educational process, where children usually are expected to get started on their verbal and quantitative learning, thus making demands of symbol acquisition and use. The criterion suggested for early admission to kindergarten presumes a program of activities nurturant primarily in the motor, social, and emotional areas and only secondarily in the more formal cognitive area; for this a somewhat lower mental maturity level well may be appropriate. Some kindergartens, however, are perceived essentially as early, or educationally preparatory, first grades and forthrightly involve their youngsters in the early stages of formal school learning. For these, the suggested mental-level criterion may be a bit low.

It is highly probable that an initial criterion for consideration such as this would be sound for some 80 percent of the children who are being evaluated for early admission. The other 20 percent or so, those from culturally nonnurturant environments, those who are physically impaired, and even some who are emotionally maladjusted, must have their eligibility ascertained by means of their performances on tests predominantly tapping process. For candidates in this latter group, a six-to-seven year level performance on tests such as the Columbia Mental Maturity Scale, the Leiter International Performance Scale, the French Pictorial Test of Intelligence, and the Cattell Culture Fair Test probably

would be adequate. In rare instances, where there are unusual characteristics in the children or in their environments, it would be desirable either to consider as eligible for further consideration youngsters falling somewhat below the minimum or to require others to manifest a somewhat higher mental age.

In the process of assessing the child, the school psychologist will be looking for information and cues, both from the parents during the initial interview with them and in the different behaviors of the child while he is taking the tests, which will suggest the possibility of the child's having special aptitudes in areas such as science, art, and quantitative and linguistic functioning that can be capitalized upon if the child is admitted early. Many such candidates already have demonstrated in their preschool behavior strong interests and considerable competencies in one or more of these areas. Others will be found to have the potential but not to have had the nurturance that would cause them so to function, as in the case of one five-year-old boy who earned a Binet IQ of 160 but who also showed a lack in the quantitative area. On the advice of the psychologist, the kindergarten teacher created situations involving opportunity for quantitative learning, and the child almost avidly progressed in that area. (He was one kind of "disadvantaged" child: he had been reared in a professional-level home in which the incidental nurturance was entirely verbal rather than to any discernible degree quantitative.)

It must be clearly recognized that, while the child's mental level (his MA, not his IQ) should be the criterion of primary importance—the characteristic first to be considered—other characteristics of each child also must be carefully ascertained and assessed. Such other characteristics may be supportive to an overall psychological picture predisposing toward early admission; or some may contribute so negatively that special conditions would be attached to his early admission, or even contraindicate it.

Educational achievement

Probably to an extent not expected by many, an interestingly large percentage of the strong candidates for early admission will be found to perform effectively at the first-, second-, or third-grade level in reading comprehension (a more crucial area than reading vocabulary or word recognition) or in arithmetic reasoning (more definitive than arithmetic computation). It is well to ascertain the extent to which the candidate's preschool learning has taken place, particularly in the verbal and quantitative areas. This can be done best by means of properly standardized achievement tests, taking due precaution with respect to the problem of measurement error at this lower level. Standardized tests used for this purpose must be selected with great care. The Wide Range Achievement Test, for instance, yields scores in "reading" and "arithmetic," but only word recognition (not reading comprehension) and arithmetic computation (not arithmetic reasoning) are the aspects really sampled.

Properly standardized reading readiness tests can be used meaningfully with less clearly plausible candidates. The experienced evaluator can obtain comparable information by observing the child's reading behavior which may be involved in or incidental to the psychological examination, by means of having the child read, from his own books if appropriate, and by observing the kind and amount of his self-initiated quantitative functioning. The parents can report the reading and arithmetic behaviors of their children, but it is well to make sure what they mean by such terms. Reading, whether supervised or independent, must be more than reciting the alphabet or only looking at pictures

in newspapers, magazines, or books, and arithmetic must be something more than only reciting multiplication tables, even though such behaviors can have some positive suggestive value.

Since bright youngsters, on their own, often engage in learning activities and so capitalize upon what appears to be incidental learning experiences during the preschool period, it is essential to ascertain the kind and amounts of such learning which have taken place. The bright youngster who, for one reason or other, already has made discernible progress in either or both the verbal and quantitative areas has one pattern of educational need if he is admitted early. The youngster who is bright enough to be admitted early but who has not done so, for one reason or other, will require a discernibly different kind of school program; but he still should be admitted early (other factors being favorable) in order that he can get started on legitimate and socially important self-fulfillment.

Emotionality

As we have noted, the early-admitted child may need to adapt to a somewhat different emotional climate than he has been used to. One such child may feel as if he were being liberated for further learning; another may perceive the newness of the school setting—perhaps with the "help" of significant others in his environment—as quite threatening. It is essential, therefore, that the child's emotional capability to perform in the anticipated new situation be assessed. Has the dependency behavior of the child in his home and neighborhood been such that his dependency needs in the new school situation will impair his learning efficiency? What is the probability that the child's positively responding to the learning opportunities in the new situation will, in effect, constitute a diversion from, or substitution for, his (learned) need to be dependent? Has the manner in which his "bright" preschool behavior been regarded by others in the home or neighborhood environment been such that his behavior in the new school situation is likely to have a negative impact upon his new teachers and classmates? (Here it is necessary to differentiate between behavior that is generally obnoxious or grossly egocentric and behavior that reflects a justifiable degree of self-confidence and to recognize that the difference well may be in the eyes of the perceiver.) What is the probability that such emotional inflation can be effectively attenuated? Other behaviors of the child must be considered because of their possible emotional ramifications: the child's eating habits, his sleeping pattern, the possibility of bedwetting, behavior that is passively or actively aggressive, and the like. While it is highly probable that adjustmental problems of these kinds and magnitudes will be found in only a small percentage of candidates for early admission, the emotional strength and resiliency and possible weaknesses of all likely candidates should be taken into consideration.

The assessment of the quality of the emotional adjustment of the early entrance candidate will not be discussed here in any depth, since that would necessitate a rather intensive clinical digression. Suffice it to point out that some young bright children behave in a way called emotional maladjustment primarily because they have experienced intellectual starvation and/or there is a misperceived communication gap between them and others in their environment, and their maladaptive behavior is an expression of the attending frustration. In such instances, and given, of course, insightful educational placement, the maladaptive behaviors tend to disappear reasonably shortly after proper early admission.

Social behavior

The lay person has little difficulty in seeing a difference between how a child (or any person) "gets along with himself" and how he "gets along with others" —regarding the one as emotional adjustment and the other as social adjustment. However, how the child "gets along with himself" is a condition that at least largely has been learned in a social context. With the possible exception of a very small percentage of cases, where physiological or neurological pathology is known to contribute to social maladaptation, emotional adjustment is a function of the quality of the social interactions which the child has experienced. Even in these relatively few exceptions there is a learned "emotional overlay" which well may play the larger role in social adjustment.

The quality and extent of the candidate's social interaction must receive careful evaluation, since he may be entering upon situations that may make quite different demands for social interaction. Some such youngsters come from situations in which they understandably have been "loners"—where there either were very few or no other children in the home or neighborhood with whom they could, or were allowed to, interact— especially children of reasonably comparable interests or capabilities. Others may come from situations in which there were numbers of other youngsters with whom they could interact but with whom social communication was limited because of a disparity between them due to differing levels of conceptual functioning. Here again, because of the generally greater adaptive ability of bright children, conditions of this kind are likely to be in the minority. When they do exist, the history of the child's social behavior and a careful assessment of the probability of his making the essentially new social adjustment are necessary.

Some bright preschoolers have been known to "prefer" to be alone and to play or do things by themselves because of a considerable degree of self-sufficiency. Others have been "loners" because of the nature of their total social situations. The fact of the child's being such an isolate should not be taken as an automatic minus in the area of social behavior. The quality of his imaginative play and other improvisations well could mark him as a most likely early-entrance candidate.

*Physical and health
conditions*

Even though bright youngsters generally are better off in these regards, such factors call for attention. The retiring short child could present a different adjustment problem than would an outgoing, healthily confident short child. No adequately bright child who is cerebral palsied, or who is deaf, or who is blind, or who is otherwise physically impaired should be denied early admission solely on such grounds—other factors being essentially favorable. But he would need to be evaluated also in terms of the appropriateness of (possibly adapted) educational facilities into which he could be admitted. In like manner, candidates with special health conditions require careful assessment in order to decide, with the assistance of a properly competent medical authority, whether the demands resulting from early admission would be excessive or whether being admitted early would have probable habilitative or rehabilitative benefits— taking care to ascertain, if at all possible, whether the health condition may be related to some psychological factor.[1] For

an occasional child having one or more of these serious problems, there is no justification for failing to consider the possibility of the school's providing home-school telephonic facilities as a legitimate kind of early admission.

Reynolds (1962) observed,

Actually, there is no evidence that physical development is a relevant variable in determining whether or not children should enter school early. It may be more important to ascertain that the child is in good general health than to learn whether he is tall or short, stocky or thin, well-coordinated or awkward (p. 11).

The total psychological picture remains the determining factor, with, of course, a recognition of the possible need in some instances for adaptive physical education, some possible adaptation to classroom and playground demands in terms of both fine and gross motor coordination problems, and the like.

Attitudes

The importance of parent, teacher, and pupil attitudes toward early admission must be recognized. Parents who seek to have their bright children admitted early understandably favor the practice, generally for sound psychological and educational reasons. However, the school or some other social agency may seek out or accidentally discover a child for whom such a provision might be made. In such instances, the parents may need to be helped to recognize the merits of admitting their children early. While the practice of early admission may be tolerated or approved officially by a school district, particular teachers or principals within such districts may be strongly averse to such

---

[1] In assessing children with physical impairments, it must be recognized that most medical doctors, perhaps even more so than conventional educators, generally may not be favorably disposed toward early admission. Their expertise

in the medical/physical area must be differentiated from that appropriate to the psychoeducational area.

action. In those instances where they can be persuaded to "try it and see," most careful follow-up of the child and the school is necessary. In those instances where school personnel aversion is too strong, the possibility of the child's being entered in another building, or with another teacher, should be considered. Generally, when a bright child has been carefully and soundly evaluated and found to have good probabilities for success and where the nature of the educational situation into which he is placed has been well prepared and followed up, the justification for such action becomes increasingly apparent, and others— parents and educators—come to recognize the desirability of the practice of early admission.

There may be times when a child is apprehensive about entering school early. Again, with proper evaluation of the child—especially of his dependency needs—and a careful preparation and cultivation of the "educational soil," he can be persuaded, rather than forced, to give it a try. Given such conditions, the probability of his coming to like the new arrangement is quite high.

Throughout this discussion, no consideration has been given to the chronological age of candidates for early admission. The reason is that the factors or aspects demanding primary consideration are psychological. If a first-grade teacher is shocked by the idea of having a four-year-old in her class, this is a reflection on the nature of the teacher's concept of education rather than on the age of the child, and ignores what has been taking place in and around that child during his four years of living. In extreme and rare instances, say where a three-year-old has a mental level of five or more, very insightful assessment and planning are called for. Special tutoring, rather than regular school placement, may be indicated until more develop-

ment in the social and motor areas is attained.

Pervading this discussion, too, has been an assumption that competent and adequate psychological services are available for the proper assessment of the children. "The IQ" as a criterion has been absent from the discussion because, so far as learning capability is concerned, the mental age (preferably of the Binet type) is the crucial variable. Beyond this, the psychologist who is competent can identify the cognitive styles and areas in which the child is presently or potentially effective in terms of the kinds of newly extended learning opportunities which he may encounter. With respect to the disadvantaged child, the psychologist should be able to discern, within the child's test performance and in much of the child's other behavior, evidences of superior basic learning potential, or process, when performance in the product area is limited. He is able to see, integratively, the nature and effects of interactions among basic capacity, acculturation, emotional, social, and physical factors and conditions.

Even though the school psychologist would be the person primarily responsible for assessing the child and should be involved in ensuing discussions of his suitability for early admission, the consultant should enter the picture at least before the final decision is made. The consultant would be involved in at least three ways:

1. She would need to understand the child, since she would play a major role in helping the teacher with whom the child would be placed.

2. She would be in the best position to recommend specific placement of the child, since she would know the suitabilities of the principals under whom and the teachers with whom the child could be placed.

3. She would be the effective liaison person who could bring in the parents and the

concerned educational personnel who should be actively involved in the planning for the child.

Administrative Matters

Early admission such as has been discussed will, in some instances, pertain only to entrance into kindergarten or the first grade. But in other instances the early admittee very well can be placed directly in the second or third grade, depending, as always, on the total picture of the child and the nature of the educational milieu. All such early entrants should be reassessed, annually for at least two years, with a view to deciding on the next appropriate grade-level placement. Some will, in certain years, need to be placed at the next higher grade level (educational conditions being favorable); others very properly should be placed at higher grade levels if conditions warrant that.

Many school administrators, when discussing the possibility of admitting bright children to school before they reach the conventional school-entering age, become very disturbed because they fear that such candidates would be so numerous as to create a very large problem. However, if one recognizes that there are likely to be only some ten bona fide eligibles in every 500 about-to-enter children, the potential evaluation task is not overwhelming. This, of course, will vary with the type of community; and there are bound to be some parents (even of truly retarded children) who will seek to have their children admitted early.

If the practice of early admission were to be introduced conscientiously in a school system, it could be done systematically and with limited demand on the school's psychological staff. Once those children who are to be considered for evaluation are known, they could be tested in groups of three to five by means of carefully selected group devices, taking care to use also the Cattell Culture Fair Test (or a known equivalent) for the children coming from disadvantaged situations. The consultant, or other qualified person, could administer and score the group tests and interpret the results of such testing in terms of probable eligibility. Out of such a screening would come those whose performances were regarded as warranting their further individual psychological assessment.

The decision as to whether a bright child should be admitted early to school, then, must be made in terms of the total psychological picture of the child. No single positive factor will suffice. And the initial disposition to recommend for early admission can result only from this total psychological picture. Highly relevant are the nature of the educational situation into which the child may be admitted early and the attitudinal milieu of the child's total situation. The varying degrees of significance attached to each of the relevant factors can vary as educational conditions vary among themselves and as they come to be in the future.

Research

Early admission, as defined here, is one of the better researched practices in the education of the gifted. More studies have been made of more relevant variables over longer periods of time than for other aspects of their education. The results of such research have been as consistently positive as they seem to have been consistently ignored.

Research standards

Offhand, it would seem a relatively simple task to ascertain whether early-admitted youngsters benefited from the practice. In view of the apparent general aversion of educators to the practice, clear and strong evidence regarding the merits or dangers would seem highly necessary. Actually, in view of the fact that there has been a limited implementation of early admission, the amount of research on it has been relatively extensive. Since the quality of this research has varied considerably, it is well that we consider, at least in a rather gross sense, certain components of acceptability of such research. The strengths of the research reports to be discussed later can be evaluated in terms of such variables.

There should be a clear definition of the procedure, this to include a clear statement of the criterion, as well as of the related assessment procedures employed in deciding whether the children qualify as early entrants. The nature of the educational setting into which the children are admitted should be described clearly—was it the run-of-the-mill educational condition or did it involve adaptive adjustments? If the latter, what was the precise nature of such adaptations? There should be objective, or near-objective, measures of the later behaviors of the early entrants. Most obviously, this would include measures in the educational achievement or performance area, but there also should be evidences of other kinds of behavior, such as social and emotional adjustment, acceptance by classmates, participation in nonacademic activities, relative college entrance and performance, and the like. It is apparent, in such a listing of behaviors to be checked, that the greater the time span covered the more meaningful the picture obtained. Other facets of the practice could be measured or judged, such as the matter of the possible extra costs and demands upon staff time, the nature of the impact of such a provision upon other components in the total educational situation, and, perhaps,

implications as to the possible benefit, both to the individual and to society, of the operation of the procedure.

Evidence and findings

With remarkable consistency, although the research has varied considerably in rigor, the research findings have been favorable to early admission, as defined here. Two kinds of studies would seem to the unwary reader to suggest negative results. In one type, the term "early admission" was used with respect to admitting children who were chronologically younger than the prescribed entering age, without regard to their "intelligence." In the other type, decisions regarding early admission were made only in terms of IQ. Neither of these is relevant to the practice as described here. For the most part, early entrance decisions in the research have been made in terms of Binet mental age. (Recent increasing use of the WPSSI and WISC can contaminate the picture, but for known, or knowable, psychological reasons.) Unfortunately, research on early admission generally has not involved the use of well-planned control groups which would make possible the comparison of well-defined early entrants with other children equally qualified for early admission but not admitted early. In a few instances, crude comparison groups have been identified; in these cases the results have not reflected negatively on those admitted early and functioning under comparable educational conditions. Probably of greater overall importance is the fact that even though children have been admitted early to highly likely diverse educational settings, their educational performances have been consistently superior across them.

The evidence varies from that which is essentially observational in nature to that which is elaborately supported by quantified data. Reynolds (1962) cited Cutts and Moseley (1953) as describing an experiment in early admission, begun in New Haven, Connecticut, in 1922, in which eight children, so assigned to the first grade, "completed the work satisfactorily and moved on to higher grades with increasing success" (p. 16). Miller, in the Reynolds overview of early admission, described the practice in the Evanston, Illinois, schools as having been initiated as early as 1925. She reported that the relative standing of the early entrants improved as they advanced in grade level, a condition which seems generally to maintain among the various studies.

Marshall S. Hiskey summarized the research on "Twelve Years of Early Admission in Nebraska" in Reynold's monograph (1962, pp. 43–50). He concluded: "All studies made to date reveal that the early entrants, as a group, rate as well as or better than the children who enter on the basis of chronological age" (p. 50). He cited a statistical analysis by R. E. Stake of data on early entrants to kindergarten. Stake found 473 children who had taken nationally normed achievement tests in the third grade and who had been admitted early to school on the basis of Binet mental age. He found that entering children who had a preschool Binet mental age of 5–8 were, on the average, over a half-year above the national norm on the achievement test at the end of the third grade; those with a Binet mental age of 6–7 were, on the average, over a year above the national mean. More specifically, Stake found that 64 percent of the former group fell in the top fourth of third-graders and 82 percent of those in the latter group fell in the top fourth of national third-graders. This would appear to lend objective support to the Binet mental-age criterion for early admission proposed herein.

By far the largest single study of the relative performance of early entrants has been that by James R. Hobson (1948, 1956). In 1933, the Brookline, Massachusetts, schools started the practice of admitting children early to the kindergarten on the basis of results of physical and psychological examination. The minimal psychometric criterion was a Binet mental age of five years no months. His study followed ten of the classes through high school graduation (1946–1955). Shown in Table 9.1 are data on those admitted early and those admitted at age. It will be noted that the percentages graduating with honor and

Table 9.1. Performances of under-age and at-age Brookline admittees.

	Under-age		At-age	
	Boys	Girls	Boys	Girls
Percentage graduating with honor (1946-55)	18.75	25.46	8.43	15.04
Percentage elected to Alpha Phi* (1946-55)	12.95	18.71	5.83	8.68
Four-year high school academic average				
Class of 1946	2.432	2.519	2.224	2.330
Class of 1947	2.534	2.730	2.185	2.380
Frequency of extracurricular participation, classes of				
1946 and 1947	11.53	22.89	8.69	15.24
Percentage admitted to college, classes of 1946 and 1947	59.4	54.8	36.8	25.8

Source: Adapted from Hobson, 1956.

*Election to Alpha Phi, an undergraduate high school honor society, was based on participation and prominence in extracurricular activities as well as on scholarship.

membership in Alpha Phi pertain to the full ten-year period. The data for the high school averages, frequency of participation in extracurricular activities, and admission to college are for only the graduating classes of 1946 and 1947. In his earlier study, Hobson had noted that under-age children originally admitted by test not only exceeded their fellows scholastically on the average but were referred less often for emotional, social, and other personality maladjustments.

Monderer (1953) followed through the first five grades those children who had been admitted early in the Fairbury, Nebraska, schools. The early entrants surpassed those regularly admitted in school marks, teachers' ratings of social adjustment, and performance on the Stanford Achievement Test. Mueller (1955) had the teachers of different urban and rural Nebraska schools rate their 4275 pupils in kindergarten through the fifth grade, some of whom were early entrants, on achievement, health, coordination, acceptance by other children, leadership, attitude towards school, and emotional adjustment. While those admitted early were given the largest percentages of high ratings on all seven traits, they stood out particularly on acceptance and emotional adjustment.

Clearly, the determination of the merits and limitations must be made over some meaningful time span and in terms of a variety of factors. To obtain only academic performance information during or just after only one year of school experience could result in grossly misleading conclusions, either for or against the practice. A number of the studies cited have reflected time perspective and psychological breadth—even to the point of yielding evidence on the attitudes of classmates toward early entrants. The importance of a Binet mental age (or its demonstrated equivalent) as the pri-

mary determining factor, though not the sole one, is clearly supported.

Implementation

While it is not mandatory that the practice of early admission be carried out only under the supervision of the consultant for the gifted, it would be highly desirable. The consultant most appropriately could be the one in the school system to whom candidates for early admission would first become known, whether they may have been learned about informally as possible candidates, or may have been initially screened in order to reduce the likely number of "false positives." The consultant, on her own or with the help of the school social workers, can do much to prepare the parent for such action or to counsel the parents if such action is not indicated. The consultant can do much to identify that point in the educational scale—teacher or grade level—for which the child's placement is being considered. The teacher with whom such a child is likely to be placed can benefit from the counsel of the consultant as how to proceed if she has not had prior experience with this kind of educational provision. Later, the child's progress into and through later grades may be facilitated through wise checking and suggestions by the consultant.

It is possible that it may not be feasible, for one reason or another, for a child who well qualifies for early admission to the first grade to be so admitted. In some such instances, the child may be placed in a good private school or with a good private tutor in order that he can, in effect, bide his time chronologically but continue with his learning. Two factors are of importance here: the psychoeducational adequacy of such placement and the capability of the parents, or some interested person, to pay for the arrangement. When such an arrangement has worked effectively, the child then can be entered directly into the second or third grade, providing the other relevant conditions are appropriate.

The practice of early admission is no more to be universally and hastily employed than it is to be categorically opposed. Just like any other possible provision for the gifted, it is a practice toward which those interested in the gifted should be favorably disposed whenever a full consideration of all the relevant factors warrants it. Since the first few instances of early admission in a school system always are the most crucial, it is especially necessary to make certain that there is a high probability of success, since the school personnel involved will be more favorably impressed by clear-cut local positive results than by what research long has told us positively about it. Were it a matter only of logic and analogy, early admission, as Worcester (1956) pointed out, is a "provision for an individual to progress comfortably at a speed for which he is built. To drive a car in low gear in order to stay with slow-moving traffic may result in an overheated engine" (p. 12).

ACCELERATION

Obviously, if early admission of the gifted is to be implemented and if other kinds of acceleration are to be employed, some administrative stance should be taken, preferably reflected in a policy statement, which manifests either a tolerance of or the advocacy of such provisions. However, it must be kept clearly in mind that even though administrators may authorize such essentially structural adaptations, this by no means assures that the desirable attendant instructional adaptations automatically will follow. The administrator can provide the stage, but the supervisors and the teachers are the ones who determine the nature of the play that takes place on that stage.

"Acceleration" vs. "Enrichment"

Some who have considered the enrichment of educational programs for the gifted have sought to differentiate between "horizontal enrichment" and "vertical enrichment," the former denoting learning more at a given conceptual level, the latter denoting added learning believed to be directly contributive to the child's progressing to a higher conceptual level. At first blush, the latter may be hastily regarded as a means of accelerating the child's learning or development. The term "accelerating" clearly requires analysis.

Let us consider, for example, a child who is chronologically six years old and who is capable of learning much like an average eight year old. Does providing him with learning opportunities known to be appropriate for eight-year-olds constitute accelerating him? Administratively yes, but psychologically no, since such a provision is merely giving him learning opportunities appropriate to his capability. The rate at which he is developing is pretty much determined by the child's own developmental disposition, assuming the operation of no detrimental factors. Developmental rate per se is not such that it likely can be speeded up in the schools, although it can be deterred. Allowing this child to learn at his mental level, rather than at his chronological level, is merely facilitating the operation of a capability that has come about naturally; it is not accelerative to his mental growth, although it does (or can) contribute to his not withering on the mental vine. While suitably adapted psychological nurturance is not accelerative of the individual's biologically determined pattern of development, its results may seem to be so because of lower prior expectations of the individual; it is, however, significantly contributive to sustaining that rate of development which is fundamentally characteristic of the individual. Acceleration, then, is not a "speeding up" of growth; it is, rather, an educational adjustment to the individual's higher than average level of learning capability.

Whereas enrichment is instructionally oriented, acceleration generally has meaning in terms of an administrative frame of reference. In the age-grade analyses of administrators, children who are at the grade level generally expected in terms of their chronological ages are regarded as being "at grade"; those a year or more younger than their conventional grademates are regarded as being "accelerated" a year or more; and those a year or more older than their conventional grademates are accordingly regarded as "retarded." By virtue of this, accelerated children generally are those in grades with children who typically are older than they are. As we explore the acceleration of the gifted—putting them in grades with older children— we shall see that certain modifications and near-circumventions are made for the gifted that are, basically, accelerative in nature.

The Educational Backdrop

Before we consider accelerative practices and possibilities, two aspects of the "educational backdrop" will help provide perspective. In the first place, we distinguished earlier between learnings in the skill areas and those in the content areas. The point was made that enrichment was particularly appropriate in regard to the content areas. Acceleration, on the other hand, is particularly appropriate in the skill areas. As the child acquires skills—in writing, computing, reading, and the like—he goes on, or should go on, to the acquisition of more, or more refined, skills in that area. After all, if he has learned well that four and four are eight, further work on that, outside of a moderate degree of review and reinforcement, is both a misuse of his time and boring to him. The attainment of skills being relatively easily observed and measured, the fact of acquisition is easily ascertained, thus making it reasonably safe to push along in the acquisition. This would seem to make quite plausible the possibilities for acceleration, particularly at the elementary school level. In the second place, the tolerance of accelerative practices is determined heavily by what the educator regards "an education" to be. If the educator (or parent) regards "education" to be the putting in of 12 (or 13) years at the precollege level, administratively perceived acceleration is a fiction. If, on the other hand, "education" is believed to consist of the acquisition (or "mastery") of a given amount of knowledge, regardless of the amount of time required for such learning, the possibility of utilizing accelerative practice exists.

There are two important points to recognize in considering the possibility of accelerating a gifted child. The first is that the decision must be based upon the careful consideration of what already has been referred to as the "total psychological picture" of the child. While the matter of primary importance is the child's mental level (to what grade level in school is his mental level most suited?), all the other factors that go into a total psychoeducational assessment of the child must be considered and duly weighted. At one level, mental level and emotional adjustment will very much dominate the picture; at another level, the extent and nature of his educational achievement in one or more areas will come to play an increasing role in the determination. The second point is that deciding whether to accelerate a given gifted child, and if so how much, must be regarded as a recurring theme—a matter that calls for careful consideration at successive points in the child's educational progress. Generally, the need for such reconsideration decreases in frequency from the elementary to the high school level. At the elementary level, this assessment will be not only to the child but also of the teachers with whom he may be working. At the secondary level, the assessment will tend to be tempered more in terms of the course or subject-matter areas into which the child may be accelerated. In larger high schools, it may be possible and necessary also to take into consideration the teachers of such courses or in such areas. Acceleration, whatever its intrinsic merits in a generalized sense, never occurs in a social vacuum. Acceleration, no matter how favorably regarded, should not be perceived as inevitably disposing toward fruitful educational outcomes. Unfortunately, there exist teachers under whom an accelerate actually could be harmed psychologically and educationally. Fortunately, there are others under whom an accelerate can blossom.

The term acceleration will be used here in the sense that any decision to employ it for a given child will have been reached on the basis of a full consideration of all of the important relevant factors. No absolute amount of acceleration can be specified as desirable. It may vary from a half-year—where a try-out or an adjustive, transitional period is regarded as desirable—to as much as three or four years. For the most part, however, a one- or two-year acceleration is likely to be appropriate. While the act of deciding on any of these amounts of acceleration may take place at one point in a child's educational life, it is more likely to be called for at different times in the child's later educational experience. The probability of its properly being a "one-time-thing" for gifted children in general is quite low.

Kinds of Acceleration

It is desirable to think in terms of three types of accelerative practices. The more conventional—that of placing or moving the child to some grade level where older children conventionally are working—will be designated as "gross acceleration." In this type, the full evaluation of the child and his situation will, of course, have been made before such acceleration is effected. The "grossness" denotes only the fact that the child is moved from the learnings at one point to all, or practically all, of the learnings at some higher level. Illustrative would be the early admission of the child into school, later transferring him from, say, a second grade to a fourth grade, advancing him from, say, the seventh grade to the ninth grade, or subsequently enabling the pupil to enter college "early." The term "selective acceleration" will be used to denote enabling a child who is in, say, the third grade to do his arithmetic with fifth-graders, letting a sixth-grader take general science with eighth- or ninth-graders, or enabling a high school junior to take, in a nearby college, a course in English, history, chemistry, and the like. Making it possible for a bright child to take some special correspondence course, generally appropriate to older youngsters, would be an instance of selective acceleration. There is also a practice that can be called "adaptive acceleration," in which a child's regular class teacher provides him with learning materials and learning opportunities which "normally" are encountered by or expected of older or higher-grade youngsters. For instance, a second-grade teacher may enable a bright child to engage in learning opportunities in her room in arithmetic or reading which are standard fourth-grade fare. While these kinds of accelerative practices can be differentiated logically, they may be appropriate in a number of combinations within the educational life of a given bright child. We shall consider these kinds of accelerative possibilities a bit more fully.

Gross acceleration

The underlying rationale of and the steps preparatory to early admission have been discussed. In most instances of appropriate early admission, the action to be taken will consist of letting the child enter upon his formal schooling at the kindergarten or first-grade level at some earlier-than-conventional age. However, there are bright children who very properly, and safely, can be placed directly in the second or third grade.

SOME EXAMPLES. Consider the facts regarding Paul. At the age of five years, six months, he very clearly manifested the academic performances of an average child eight years ten months of age. Life for him was thoroughly enjoyable. He played vigorously and happily with the children in his neighborhood, although every chance he got he played with eight- and nine-year-olds rather than with five- or six-year-olds. While he was generally quite active, ate well, and slept well, he had his quiet moments when he read (as well as he could) the newspaper, magazines, and books that were in his home, drew imaginatively, and tinkered with construction toys. His parents reported that he "pestered" them with "why" and "how" questions, and they reasonably consistently gave him help in what seemed to them to be an insatiable desire to do his own reading. On the Stanford Achievement Test, his

reading comprehension score was like that of an average child in the fifth month of the third grade (3.5), his vocabulary performance was 3.7, his performance in arithmetic reasoning was 3.1, and his score on computation was about that of an average second-grader.

Paul had had no kindergarten experience, and there was none in his school district. His whole picture was such that the possibility of merely entering him early in the usual first grade was unrealistic. Should he be entered in the second or the third grade? It was judged that he would adjust well emotionally and socially in either. A second-grade teacher in the school to which he would be going was highly regarded because she had already shown that she liked children and did a number of extra things to help different youngsters in her class, yet her pupils were consistently recognized as "being well grounded in the fundamentals." Both third-grade teachers were "lock-steppers"—their pupils all had the same assignments and were given the same texts; they were regarded as "firm" and quite "democratic."

While Paul was placed with the second-grade teacher who has been described, she started him working with third-grade materials, after checking him out to see if he had the essential second-grade competencies; she observed, after Paul had been with her a month, that he probably would be doing fourth-grade work before much of the year had passed. He did so well that next he went into the room of a good fourth-grade teacher. More than two years after being admitted early, Paul was continuing to be an achieving, happy, well-liked, and healthily motivated youngster.

In contrast, there was Ralph, a five-year-old in another community whose preschool picture was practically identical to that presented by Paul. At first, the school "authorities"—in this case the principal of the building in Ralph's district—insisted that children learned best when they were with their "peers" and that, since Ralph would, if entered early, be with older children, "he would feel out of place and become emotionally upset because he would feel that he was being pushed ahead." The possibility of his being entered at the second- or third-grade level, hopefully with a sensitive and cooperative teacher, was completely out of the question, since that would only make worse what was feared in regard to first-grade placement. On the parent's insistence (and since the father was a person of some influence in the community), Ralph was grudgingly accepted for the first grade and placed with the more promising first-grade teacher in that school. Although she had been provided with information about Ralph's reading capability, it was her belief that first-graders should read material specified for the first grade and that, even though both Ralph and his mother told her he already had read those materials, she had Ralph confine himself to them, in order that he "could read them real good" (sic!). When she believed that he could do that "real good," she said, he then could read to children in the kindergarten. Since she didn't believe in allowing first-graders to go to the school library, that avenue of escape was denied Ralph.

Within three months Ralph had become a "problem." His teacher said he "couldn't" read even first-grade material, was sulky, and was mean at times with the children with whom he had at first nicely played. Ralph's behavior at home changed too. The once happy, gregarious, inquisitive youngster became moping, withdrawn, and uninterested. The chores he had formerly done willingly around the house now were being neg-

lected; the parents got the impression that he was being intentionally messy. The parents, the teacher, and the principal believed Ralph should be kept in the first grade for the rest of the year on the assumption, or hope, that he would "adjust." When the matter became only worse, the parents decided to move to another part of the community where Ralph could be in a school where there was a different kind of principal and where at least some of the teachers could help him do his learning in a better psychoeducational climate. They moved, and a more fitting placement was effected, this time with a second-grade teacher who employed accelerative practices. Four months after this Ralph manifested a renewed interest in life in general and in school in particular. Had he remained in the original school situation, the probability would have been high that he could have become a quiet, skillful underachiever about whom some teachers later might have become very concerned.

Gross acceleration often is effected rather perfunctorily, a child being "jumped" a grade without full consideration of the psychoeducational appropriateness of the move. Such acceleration tends more to be a concession to the fact that the child is more capable than his classmates than an effective adjustment to the facts in the case of a given child. What happened in Roger's case illustrates both the magnitude of ramifications that can be encountered and a kind of return that can be accomplished. Roger first was brought to the attention of the psychologist by a teacher, who asked if he could help with a bright child not in her class but in her small school. A meeting was arranged with the boy's mother and the principal, who brought with him a rather full and informative cumulative folder on the boy. Roger then was in the sixth grade, and the principal was concerned that their junior high school, and perhaps even their small senior high school, would not have a rich enough offering for a youngster as bright as he appeared to be.

During his school history there, Roger had performed in a very superior manner on good group "intelligence" tests, at all times in the 130s and above. His achievement had been tested at three different times by means of a good achievement test. At the first testing, Roger scored on all the crucial sections of the test at least two years above the norm for the grade he was in. The last testing, in the sixth grade, showed no performance below the ninth grade, and most were at least at the tenth grade. Roger's social, emotional, and health histories were explored carefully, and it appeared that he was a buoyant, well-liked, very interested, and highly motivated youngster. The mother, a working widow, had a healthily strong interest in her son's welfare. The impressions gathered in the conference were checked with the peripherally involved teachers and fully supported. The information was regarded as of such validity that further, individual, testing was not needed.

The mother commuted daily to a city some fifteen miles distant for her work. Since it happened that the psychologist previously had worked effectively with one high school principal and some of his guidance personnel in the interests of another bright youngster, he recommended that Roger be entered the following year directly into the four-year high school—skipping the junior high school entirely. After the possibility of Roger's entering there was fully explored with the principal, the mother moved into the district served by that high school. While Roger did not address himself specifically to that end, he quickly earned a place on the honor roll, staying on it throughout his four years. He engaged in from one to three extracurric-

ular activities each year during his high school experience. He expressed a number of varying interests, the area of law becoming increasingly the focus. At the psychologist's suggestion, Roger established contact with a group of lawyers, and, during his last year of high school, was allowed to become increasingly involved in doing chores about the office of one of them without pay. His increasingly close association with one of the members of the law firm—who happened to be a state's attorney—did much to sharpen his interest in that area. He entered college two years "early" and was doing very well in the first year of a liberal arts program.

The use of gross acceleration can, of course, be a boon to the gifted child, a pleasure to his teacher, and of ultimate benefit to society. Relieved of the boredom attending educational repression, the properly accelerated child can be a pleasure to his teacher(s) because he is happily engaged in learnings appropriate to his capabilities. If he is allowed to work in and with advanced group(s) in the manner of any child who rightfully belongs at that level, being regarded by the teacher, and therefore by the other pupils in his group, as just another legitimate member of his new group, and if his teacher fosters only the normal relations of interactive learning, neither is the accelerate caused to feel that he is "different" nor are his classmates caused to perceive him as "different." Under such conditions the properly accelerated gifted youngster quickly assumes, and is granted by his classmates, his properly contributive role in the class. When such conditions do not exist, the accelerate quickly comes to be perceived as different and he responds to their perceptions by becoming or being different. In such a situation, the attitudes and perceptions of the classmates reflect primarily the consciously or unconsciously manifested attitude of the teacher.

HOW MUCH ACCELERATION? At times it is asked how much gifted children should be accelerated. Often implicit in such a question is an oversimplified perception of the gifted, an assumption that they constitute a more homogeneous group than they really do. Even when only the variable of their learning capability is considered, they are a highly varied group. They also present a large array of differences in their educational competencies and in their interests or special bents. The magnitude of appropriate acceleration is a function also of the grade levels with respect to which it is being considered. Acceleration must be a carefully considered individual matter. We go back inescapably to the importance of the total psychoeducational picture of each child. Some should not be accelerated at all, at least at the particular time such a possibility is being considered; many very properly can be considered in terms of an acceleration of one to two years; probably 10 percent of them should be considered for greater acceleration. Even such thinking must take into consideration the nature of the educational setting within which acceleration is being considered.

Only one generalization seems justified: assuming other factors to be suggestive of the desirability of acceleration, the child should be considered acceleratable only up to that level just below the composite of his objectively and validly demonstrated level of learning capability and his demonstrated educational competency in crucial educational skill areas and/or in substantive areas. Primary concern is seldom called for with regard to certain routinized educational performances, such as rote spelling, simple arithmetic computation, and cursive handwriting—contributive though they may be—since spelling and arithmetic computation can be markedly improved in surprisingly short times under proper motivation and compensatory typing can

be developed and probably have greater functional value later in the child's life.

HIGH SCHOOL TO COLLEGE. When administrators, supervisors, and teachers are acceptant of the idea of acceleration and when they are understandingly cooperative in its implementation, gross accelerative practices are relatively easy to implement at all grade levels in the schools. However, accelerating pupils from high school into college often presents a different kind of problem, owing largely to the fact that integration of adaptive efforts at the college level may be more difficult to effect. Whereas the consultant in the schools can help facilitate the child's total adjustment at the level to which he has been accelerated, such follow-through is much less possible when the pupil has been entered in college "early," especially if the college is in another town. Educational and social factors in the higher-education situation make demands on the early entrant which may differ markedly from those which he may have met quite well in the relatively simpler structure of the high school. This means that the characteristics in the milieu of the potential accelerate, those of the social and educational situation out of which he will be coming, and those of the total situation into which he may be going necessitate careful consideration. In no sense should this call for care suggest any limited educational and social merit and need for acceleration into higher education. Quite the contrary. The practice probably is grossly underutilized.

While our consideration of educational provisions for the gifted focuses primarily below the higher education level, accelerative possibilities both within and above the high school level require at least the recognition of the major kinds of higher education accommodations possible for the high school accelerate. Isolated instances of bright children's entering college at early ages long have been on record. The most noted, and, unfortunately, certainly one of the most disappointing, was William James Sidis, the son of the psychologist Boris Sidis, who had passed the Harvard entrance examination at the age of nine but was not allowed to enter until two years later. (See, for instance, Hauck and Freehill, 1972, pp. 76–85.) Opponents of the idea of educational acceleration, usually with only a meager comprehension of the facts in even Sidis' case, have uninhibitedly overgeneralized on this and a few similar instances in their strongly voiced opposition. Yet, over the years, many other bright youngsters have been quietly accelerated, even as much as four or five years, and have gone on to be well-adjusted, socially contributive individuals. But such actions have been only sporadic in nature, resulting from some highly favorable combinations of factors in their situations rather than results of even a germinal educational and social philosophy which could make possible such an opportunity for the relatively many who need and could benefit from such a practice.

Efforts of the Ford Foundation, through its establishment of the Fund for the Advancement of Education, did much in a major way to sensitize both high schools and higher education to educational and social possibilities and values in gross acceleration from high school (1953, 1957). Its Program for Early Admission to College, later called the Advanced Placement Program, was started in 1951. Funds were made available both for full and partial scholarships and for financial assistance to the participating colleges and universities. By 1956, a total of 1229 students from 110 secondary schools throughout the country took examinations and entered 138 colleges in September of that year, nearly half of them enrolling in Harvard, Yale, Princeton, Cornell, and Massa-

chusetts Institute of Technology. The Program for Early Admission to College recognized "that many American high schools are not equipped to offer their ablest students college-level work, and that even in high schools that are so equipped, some students who have demonstrated a capacity for work can profit more by entering college earlier than usual than by remaining in high school" (1951, p. 5).

The 1957 report was written after two entering groups of scholars had graduated from college. It is interesting to consider certain of the summary observations in the report in the light of the procedure that has been discussed for grossly accelerating a bright child below the higher education level and in regard to possible problems in transition from high school to college.

In a few cases, some of the colleges made mistakes in the selection of their first group of Scholars, and some were overprotective in their handling of the Scholars during the first year of the experiment, but by and large these difficulties were overcome in the selection and handling of subsequent Scholar groups.

Academically, all four groups of Scholars have outperformed their classes as a whole and their Comparison students.

The Scholars encountered more initial difficulties in adjusting to campus life than their older Comparison students, but most of those difficulties were minor and were soon overcome.

There is some evidence that in many cases early admission to college freed Scholars from the boredom and frustration of an unchallenging high school environment, gave them new intellectual momentum, and enhanced their social and emotional maturation.

Among the first two groups of Scholars who graduated, the proportion planning to go on to graduate school was substantially higher than among their Comparison students.

In all but a few cases where such data are available, the parents of the Scholars and the principals of the high schools from which they came have expressed themselves as favorably disposed toward the results of the experiment.

The evidence gathered thus far already suggests that high school academic aptitude and the ability to handle the responsibilities of college life are the *sine qua non* of early admission, and that colleges should not be overprotective in the handling of early admission students (pp. 9–10, reprinted by permission of the Ford Foundation).

The gross acceleration program thus implemented contributed to a later development—that of making it possible for bright high school students to take certain college courses while still in high school, generally characterized as advanced credit programs. We shall consider this provision in our next section.

Selective acceleration

The essential characteristic of this kind of accelerative provision is the fact that the child probably retains his "basic" educational placement for most of his academic work but is enabled to take certain subjects or courses with classes or groups at higher designated grade levels. Generally, the child's educational base tends to be regarded, by age-oriented educators, as that which is appropriate to his chronological age. In selective acceleration, the child who is "in" the second grade may be allowed to work in, say, arithmetic, or to "take" his reading with third- or fourth-graders. The sixth-grader who studied general science in the junior high school across the street would be a case in point. A bright tenth-grader could "take" his English, physics, or chemistry with eleventh- or twelfth-graders.

Obviously, where the academic work is departmentalized, or where certain teachers handle quantitative learning and others handle verbal learning, such adjustments can have definite merit. However, in the case, say, of a third-grade teacher who works with her children in all the academic areas, a very real question can be raised regarding the use of selective acceleration. The potential problem is analogous to the learning "disjointedness" mentioned in connection with some attempts to operate under the early Colfax plan: the problem of sustaining communication between the children in the regular class and those who go from it to other classes or interest groups for other substantive learning, and the importance, if not the necessity, of such a teacher's helping her children to integrate their learnings—to see relationships between and among subject-matter areas. Some teachers just cause the bright children so provided for to live, in effect, two separate educational lives, ignoring the importance of the interrelatedness of learnings and neglecting important interacting feedback by the brighter students to the students in the regular class. Such can be conducive to the alienation of the gifted from the regular pupils. Selective acceleration has certain potential values, but it must be employed judiciously.

At first, gross acceleration and selective acceleration may seem to be clearly separate and discrete provisions. Yet, for certain bright children, a combination of them may be quite appropriate, as in the case of the boy who was promoted from the first to the third grade. Certain of his educational competencies were quite appropriate to the third-grade level. His reading, however, was such that he could work more productively with sixth-graders. In such a situation, having accepted the appropriateness of his third-grade placement, the problem would be whether to employ selective acceleration in reading or to provide what later will be discussed as adaptive acceleration. Again, while adaptive educational procedures may be thought about logically separately, there well may be times when they should be used along with one of the other forms.

Arrangements whereby high school students are enabled to take certain college courses (or even advanced correspondence courses, under proper supervision) constitute one kind of selective acceleration. Their performances in such situations are evaluated on the same lines as are those of regular college students. In some localities, certain high school students have been able to spend half of their school day in high school and the other half attending college classes. A few students have been able even to go directly into sophomore college standing upon their graduation from high school. Such arrangements are characterized as advanced credit provisions, in contrast with the Advanced Placement Program, which the College Entrance Examination Board inaugurated in 1954. Two possibilities exist in regard to this: The student, while still in high school, can take examinations in specific college areas and, if he passes them according to college standards, can earn college credits for such courses and be able to take more advanced courses or take other courses when he fully enters his college program. The other possibility involves only a different timing of the examinations—usually taking them after graduating from high school and before entering college. Often colleges and universities, in their testing programs for entrants, provide for students to take special examinations, the passing of which entitles them to take more advanced courses in certain areas or to be excused from taking certain introductory courses.

There are two other possible adjustments providing for selective acceleration, though they are not widespread. In communities where populations are large enough and college facilities (and dispositions) exist, certain colleges have of-fered college-level courses in the high schools. The use of TV courses offered by colleges for college credit opens up possibilities for bright high school pupils not in large cities.

While such selective acceleration practices bridging the gap between high school and college definitely have merit, in that they enable more capable high school students to get on more quickly with their college work and thereby become socially productive at earlier ages, their role in furthering intellectual growth, in sustaining healthy intellectual curiosity, and in enabling the brighter students to enjoy and succeed in productive intellectual endeavor must be recognized as their greater fundamental returns. Perhaps almost perfunctorily at times, capitalizing upon such provisions enables gifted pupils to demonstrate early and quickly their adequate orientation in introductory courses in areas, and thus use their time for more advanced work. Early acquisition of college course credits, a kind of academic currency, has some value and much convenience; but the sustained nurturance of conceptual growth is much more valuable both to the gifted themselves and, ultimately, to society.

Adaptive acceleration

The term "adaptive acceleration" is used to denote a teacher's letting a child in her class do learning in her classroom which is associated with that of a higher grade level. Such instances have been alluded to earlier. Although usually thought of with respect to the elementary school level, this kind of adjustment can be, and is, used at higher educational levels. The junior high school general science teacher, for example, can enable some brighter pupils to read about and work on more advanced materials and projects associated with the basic content of the course. The results of such activities, when reported to the regular class, can be enriching to the listeners and reinforcing to the reporters. Such work can be regarded as "enrichment" or "vertical enrichment" insofar as the regular class members are concerned, but it is (or can be) accelerative as regards the brighter youngsters involved in it. Because of the greater possibility of integrating the selectively accelerated work with the child's learnings in other areas taught by the same teachers and because the use of such a provision may not be so likely to contribute to increasing the social distance between the gifted and the nongifted, there would appear to be considerable merit in selective acceleration in instances where gross acceleration was neither possible nor desirable—at least at some given point in the child's educational life.

Many who oppose the idea of accelerating the gifted presume that it involves promoting the child to a level for which he may not have the prerequisite skills or knowledge. Certainly, such apprehension is legitimate, but the presumption often is unwarranted. Any sound evaluation of a pupil who is a candidate for acceleration would require, of course, that the extent to which he is academically prepared to engage in any such higher-level learning be taken into consideration. Important and necessary as this is, the fact of intraindividual differences among subject-matter areas must be recognized. The decision to accelerate, grossly or selectively, should be made in terms of the relationship between the competencies of the child and the learning area which will constitute the primary demand.

For instance, a bright fourth-grader may appear to be a candidate for gross acceleration to a sixth grade but may be only at fourth- (or even third-) grade level in arithmetic computation. Since the bulk of the educational demand at the sixth-grade level is verbal in nature

and relative weakness in arithmetic computation tends to be quickly remediable in the gifted under meaningful motivation, such a child very well might be so advanced (other factors being favorable) to work with a sixth-grade teacher who could help him recognize the contribution which computation skills can make to his learning. Under such a condition bright youngsters have been known to "improve" in the routine computational areas as much as three grade levels in as little as four to six months. As has been pointed out, the gifted can master certain content and skills at a surprisingly rapid rate when they see the relationship between what they are expected to learn and what they are interested in learning. Of course, the fundamental idea here is highly relevant to learning by all children, but the rate of such compensatory learning tends to be considerably greater in the brighter children. However, it is important to keep in mind that the later such compensatory efforts are exerted, the less rapid will be the favorable response to them, since earlier-established nonlearning habits will have had longer to become strongly rooted.

It is an unfortunate "fact of life" that failures in accelerative practice are more talked about than are successes. That such failures have occurred cannot be denied. Usually, they have resulted from one of two conditions. Either the accelerate has been inadequately assessed and he should not have been accelerated at that time, or he has been found to be suitably qualified for acceleration at that time but he has been put forward into a situation that is more contributive to his failure to make the adjustment than it is properly facilitative to his learning. It still is true that a discouragingly large percentage of teachers and administrators oppose the use of accelerative practices. Such being the case, the aversive and hypercritical attitudes of such persons make difficult or impossible the accelerate's effective educational adjustment. (Some parents oppose the idea of acceleration, largely because they are products of a system that generally opposed it and, at times, because they have heard of its misuse.)

In many situations the accelerate is perceived as an unfortunate "lone wolf" —a situation that is a function of two conditions. First, the strangeness or differentness of the accelerate is initially and primarily a function of the way in which others perceive him. He is regarded by others as strange or "different" and thereby is disposed to regard himself in that manner and, perhaps, to play the role thus accorded him. Contributive to this is the fact, changing slightly over recent years, that accelerates have been so few that numerically they have been lone wolves. The facts are such, however, that there could be considerably more of them, thus both reducing their novelty and providing for more social, intellectual, and educational exchange among themselves. If professionals and laymen were to understand more fully the psychological characteristics of accelerates, misconceptions of them would at least lessen if not disappear.

Research on Acceleration

As hotly argued as acceleration has been and as studiously avoided by educators as it seems to have been, one might assume that the practice has been the focus of little, if any, research. Since educators generally have favored "enrichment" over acceleration and have used acceleration so sparingly, one might guess that their strong commitment to keep the gifted with their "peers" would be based upon extensive and firm research findings. However, such is by no means the case. Since the adults in our society have so little experienced or heard favorably about sound accelerative practices, they, themselves, as products of an educational

system run by persons who have been averse to the effective use of acceleration, have tended to be hesitant in accepting the acceleration of their children.

While the research evidence may not seem to be massive in its amount, it has been remarkably consistent in that those who have been accelerated, one way or another, have tended to do well later. The overall favorable evidence should be all the more impressive since it pertains to such a variety of accelerative procedures in such a wide range of educational situations. In the bulk of the situations, acceleration has been effected without serious consideration of the nature of the educational conditions from which pupils and students have been moved, without a full psychoeducational assessment of the youngster who was accelerated, and without much consideration of the nature of the educational condition into which the accelerate moved—all important factors in desirable acceleration. Little, if any, research has involved the comparison of the children's behaviors before acceleration with their successful behavior after acceleration. It is quite possible that the results of studies of this nature could even enhance the already favorable picture of acceleration.

The evaluation of the performances of accelerates has a long history. A study of nearly six thousand Harvard undergraduates from 1901 through 1912 showed that the younger, and presumably accelerated, students had better academic records, were accorded more honors, and had fewer disciplinary involvements than did their older classmates (Pressey, 1949). A twenty-year study at Dartmouth revealed that those who had entered at or before the age of sixteen received two and a half times as many honors as did their older classmates. Terman found that those in his group who were accelerated a half-year or more tended more frequently to graduate from college, to do graduate work, to earn higher marks, and to receive more graduate honors. Later in life they tended more than the nonaccelerate to earn the highest ratings in occupational success and to be better in physical health and adjustment (Terman and Oden, 1947). Pressey (1949) reported his own highly confirmatory findings and urged the consideration of greater degrees of acceleration at the college level than Terman, in the early days, had discovered. The National Association of Secondary School Principals, presumably basing their stand on the results of a 1940 National Education Association inquiry which showed that only 12 to 15 percent of junior and senior high school principals favored acceleration, at first opposed the Ford Foundation plan for admitting students to college early, which, as has been noted, was regarded as both successful and relatively feasible.

Evidence at the precollege level is equally convincing. Not only are the findings on early admission undeniably favorable, but the research evidence on varying kinds and amounts of acceleration at different educational levels after conventional admission and before graduation from high school consistently has been favorable to the use of acceleration (Elwood, 1958; Justman, 1953, 1954; Klausmeier, 1963; Martinson, 1961, 1972; Mirman, 1962; Morgan, 1959; Ripple, 1961; Schwartz, 1942).

Even though there is consistent evidence that accelerates tend as a group to do better academically than do their older and higher grade-level classmates, if this were not the case—if they did only as well as their higher-level classmates—there still could be merit in acceleration. Academic achievement per se reflects only one facet of educational and social adequacy. Other advantages inhere in acceleration. The sustaining of interest in things academic by means of acceleration as contrasted with the stifling of strong curiosity by being held back with repetitious and boring school work can itself be a large positive factor. The importance of better social and emotional adjustment resulting from sound accelerative practices, owing to the gifted child's not becoming frustrated by unproductive intellectual endeavor, must be recognized.

From the standpoint of the rights of the gifted (or of any) child to enjoy at least a close approximation of self-fulfillment and to become a socially contributive individual, the possibility of acceleration—along with other types of facilitating learning—seems to be studiously ignored or blindly rejected. Lehman (1953) has stressed that the most productive years in the gifted have been the early years, and the direction of this implication remains valid, even though factors in present-day society suggest that these years are being extended somewhat later than reflected in his data. Pressey (1959) has made much of the importance, if not the necessity, of enabling the gifted to finish their formal schooling early in order more quickly to become socially productive (and more self-realized). In the manner of Passow (1955), one might argue that, if there were some 2,700,000 high school graduates in 1967–1968, and if only one percent of them had been accelerated one year, society would have had available some 27,000 man-years of earlier, socially important social productivity. But the pervading aversion to the use of acceleration on the part of public school personnel remains, in spite of the underlying philosophy, psychology, and research evidence. As Gallagher (1966) observed, "When negative attitudes still persist in the face of strong evidence, some more persuasive emotional factor would seem to be present and needs to be identified if these procedures are to be put into operation in our public schools" (p. 100).

Regardless of the kind of acceleration which is administratively authorized, it must be accompanied by suitable instructional facilitation of the pupil's learning. Whatever the kind of acceleration employed and at whatever time(s) in the gifted child's educational career, the decision to use it must be based on a full consideration of the nature of the educational situation from which the child is to be accelerated, a full and integrated understanding of the child's characteristics, and thoughtful consideration of and planning for the kind of educational situation into which he is being considered for acceleration. If a pupil who has been accelerated does not benefit from the adjustment, the failure can be attributed with confidence to one or more of three reasons:

1. The basis on which the decision was made to accelerate him was ill-considered; he and his total interests were not adequately assessed.
2. Instructional methodologies were not appropriate to the acceleration.
3. Negative attitudinal factors were operative.

TRACKING

Logically includable, but not crucial in thinking about effectively educating the gifted, is the administrative provision for the "tracking" of pupils. Tracking, or multiple tracking, is a form of educational organization in which pupils, usually of the same grade level, are assigned to three or more ability sections—fast, average, and slow learning, or further fractionations of these—with a view to facilitating their learning. The concept of tracking properly can be construed to incorporate not only the kind of educational organization just mentioned but also special classes and even, to some extent, interest groups within classes. However, special class provisions have legal authorizations either in the wording of the school law or in the procedures ad-

ministratively established for the purpose of implementing the law. Such authorizations usually specify standards for the special classes regarding at least pupil eligibility, class size, and special certification of the teachers, and generally have attending provisions regarding special reimbursement for approved classes. No such legal regulations or provisions authorize tracking; such authorization is a local administrative matter. The fundamental reason is that tracking, at least originally, was introduced to facilitate the learning of all pupils, whereas special educational provisions are tailored for specific kinds of pupils—the retarded, the physically impaired, the emotionally maladjusted, the learning disabled, and the gifted. We shall consider special classes for the gifted in the next section.

Sauvain (1934) pointed out that Harris quoted from the annual report for 1873–74 of Superintendent Stevenson of Columbus, Ohio, regarding the operation of a multiple track program. Shearer (1898) described a grouping plan that had been in operation for ten years, stating his rationale thus: "Instead of having pupils roughly sorted into large, loosely graded classes, in which the classification must grow more and more unsatisfactory as time passes, those of very nearly equal ability are placed together in a room. In the essential branches the classes are still more accurately graded, according to ability, into small divisions" (p. 443). With an idea having such face validity, expansion of the practice was inevitable. Findley and Bryan (1971) report that the NEA Research Division, sampling school systems in 1966, found 43.2 percent to be specially grouping some children but not most, and 27.5 percent carefully grouping all children. Understandably, the heaviest emphasis on careful grouping was reported by school systems with enrollment of 100,000 or more children (45.8 percent).

It is interesting that, from the time of

the very early uses of the practice, such grouping was taken to be quite simplistic —the same grouping was assumed to be equally potentially effective for whatever learnings the child had to acquire— whereas later others recognized that one grouping might be helpful for learning in one subject-matter area but that different groupings would have to be made to facilitate learning in other areas. Some who early opposed such "homogeneous" grouping contended that children in one track would be deprived of the stimulus of working with pupils with other competencies. Otis (1932) countered this claim: "There is plenty of range of ability even within a so-called homogeneous group to afford all the stimulation necessary to a slow pupil, and plenty of opportunities for certain pupils to help others" (p. 118). At first, the educational goal was primarily educational achievement; later, and more particularly as illustrated by the Findley-Bryan report, the social and cultural outcomes came to receive more intensive consideration.

Problems in Tracking

There are, however, a number of annoying problems involved in the practice of tracking. They vary from those which are essentially educational in nature to those which have social overtones, and from the factual to the attitudinal. Even though these problems exist both at the elementary and secondary levels, we shall consider them primarily in terms of the elementary level; the greater frequency of departmentalization at the secondary level somewhat tempers some of the problems.

Administrative-instructional compatibility

Tracking is but one instance of a pervading problem—the possibility of a disparity between the administrative crea-

tion of a structure intended to facilitate learning and the modification of instructional practices as a result of such an arrangement. Administratively, groupings of fast, average, and slow learners are introduced on the assumption that the educational procedures employed within such groups will be modified such that the learnings by the children will be differentially helpful to the children within the groups—that the educational methods, and perhaps even the educational content, will differ according to the capabilities and needs of the children in the different tracks. Too often, differently adaptive teaching procedures do not occur; less often are there modifications in the content expected to be mastered by the different groups. The administrative authorization and implementation of tracking is relatively simple, assuming that the school board and the community accept the idea. However, what the teachers do within the different tracks is another matter. If the instructional staff has not been properly prepared for the procedure, not only do the tracking procedures tend not to differ in ways appropriate to the different tracks, but also manifest or covert teacher attitudes toward the pupils in the different tracks often are inimical. Since special preparation of the teachers to deal properly with the pupils in the "fast" and "slow" tracks seldom is provided or required, conventional "teaching" habits tend to operate at all levels, thus mitigating against the presumed educational benefits of tracking.

Educational outcomes

Some perceive such structuring as contributing only to facilitating the achievement of children in the basic educational areas, whereas others strive not only for more effective learning in such areas but also for the enhancement of the personal adjustment and the social perceptions and attitudes of the youngsters—and this disparity complicates the picture with respect to not only the matter of appropriate educational methodology but also the doing of research on the yield of tracking and the meaningful communication and synthesis of the results of research. Unfortunately, academic achievement generally is the sole focus of concern.

Placement criteria

There is considerable variation and ambiguity in the criterion employed in placing children in the different tracks, some decisions being made only on the basis of judged or measured learning aptitude, some only in terms of judged or measured educational achievement, some in terms of some combination of these two variables, and some taking still other factors into consideration. When the results of learning aptitude tests are used as a basis for the sectioning, such action usually is taken in terms of IQ rather than MA—a practice that can have psychoeducational merit only to the extent that the group being so divided is chronologically homogeneous, and one which becomes decreasingly valid as one goes up the elementary grade ladder. At times, the cutoff points are determined, whether for measured learning aptitude or for measured or judged educational achievement, more in terms of the desire to have groups of reasonably comparable size than in terms of relatively homogeneous educational expectations.

Pupil performance evaluation

A fourth problem is that of pupil evaluation, or marking, practices. In some systems which have a three-track arrangement, the youngsters in the fast section are expected to earn (or receive) primarily A's, those in the average section are expected to receive perhaps, a few B's, but mainly C's, and, while few

of those in the slow section are expected to receive C's, most would be expected to receive D's or lower. At times, such a practice is forthrightly promulgated. In other instances, the whole range of marks may be given to the pupils in the differing tracks, but they have subscripts which indicate the track in which the mark was earned. In a few school systems, more than three tracks may be established.

So long as basically conventional marking systems are employed, the evaluation of pupil performance within a track program can, at best, be ambiguous and confusing. When the marks which pupils receive are determined in the light of how the whole grade has been seen to perform—a social rather than an individual frame of reference—pupils often seek to get placed in slower tracks in order that their performances will be more favorably perceived. This tends to occur more at the secondary than at the elementary level. And then there are principals who alter the marks which teachers have given in order that they will be more in accord with marks presumed to be appropriate for the different tracks.

Teacher allocation

Teachers differ in their willingness to "teach" the different tracks. Generally, teachers tend to prefer fast sections and not to want to be assigned to slow groups. In order to be "fair," some administrators rotate the teachers among the tracks—the implicit assumption being that differing methods and special preparation are not needed for the differing kinds of educational responsibilities. At times, the attitudes of the teachers toward their roles and/or toward the youngsters in their sections contribute toward lowered morale as well as toward socially unfortunate attitudes among the children of one track toward those in other tracks. That such conditions have existed and can exist reflects upon the inappropriate philosophical and psychological orientation of the staff implementing even a tracking practice.

Research

A sixth problem exists with respect to research on the effectiveness of tracking practices. In view of the highly varying conditions that have been mentioned, let alone variations known to exist among the educational, social, and economic climates of the schools within which tracking has been employed, it is quite understandable that no clear-cut generalizable findings have indicated either an overall desirability or undesirability of the practice, at least so far as its value for the gifted is concerned. After reviewing the evidence, such as it was, from 1910 to the late 1960s, Findley and Bryan (1971) concluded:

Ability grouping, as practiced, produced conflicting evidence of usefulness in producing improved scholastic improvement in superior groups, and almost uniformly unfavorable evidence for promoting scholastic achievement in average or low-achievement groups. Put another way, some studies offer positive evidence of effectiveness of ability grouping in promoting scholastic achievement in high-achieving groups; studies seldom show improved achievement in average or low-achieving groups.

The effect of ability grouping on the affective development of children is to reinforce (inflate?) favorable self-concepts of those assigned to high achievement groups, but also to reinforce unfavorable self-concepts in those assigned to low achievement groups (p. 3).

Social implications

This leads into an aspect of tracking concerning which attitudes are more plentiful than sound research evidence, but one having broad implications with respect to both educational and broad social considerations. This aspect came to receive increasing attention in the late 1950s. Because of the nature of most aptitude testing, based heavily on product rather than on process, because of the school's failure to individualize teaching procedures, and because of the gap between pupils' needs and the nature of the curriculum provided for them, the pupils who were assigned to the slow track tended, in many school districts, to be predominantly those who were of minority ethnic extraction and/or those who were in the lower socioeconomic classes. Thus, tracking came to be perceived as contributive to segregation, regardless of whatever possible face validity it might have from a psychoeducational point of view.

This concatenation of conditions, taken in terms of a presumption that children should have equal opportunity (the Washington, D.C., lower trails were for the "blue collar" students, according to the superintendent of schools), led to Judge Wright's decision that the track system in the Washington schools be abolished, since it contributed to racial and economic discrimination in the public school system, and that a new, nondiscriminating plan be filed with the district court by October 2, 1967 (*Hobson* v. *Hanson;* Garber and Seitz, 1969). While the national impact of this decision is yet to be determined, the legal and socioeconomic implications of the practice of tracking, even though it may have certain, though limited, merits in regard to the brighter pupils, must be considered most cautiously.

In fact, tracking as a means of facilitating the education of the gifted is open to serious question. First, it is at least highly likely that bright youngsters would be placed in the fast section(s) without having had adequate psychoeducational assessment. Second, once a child is placed in a fast section, especially at the elementary level, the odds are high that he will have a teacher who is not properly prepared to help him learn the way he should. A third factor is one of attitudinal risk. Even granting a proper assessment of pupils before placement in the fast section, and the presence of a duly competent teacher for that track, a much more than typical philosophical and psychological orientation of the other staff members would be needed in order to preclude the manifestation of negative attitudes toward those in the track by those—pupils and teachers—not in a fast section. Due consideration also would have to be given to the import of the Wright decision and associated legal pronouncements.

Even though tracking is not looked upon with favor as an effective means of improving the education of the gifted, it should not be assumed that a properly implemented tracking practice is beyond the realm of possibility. As generally employed, tracking has been too simplistically, hastily, and administratively perceived and implemented to serve the purpose for which it originally was intended.

SPECIAL CLASSES

Too often if a school system operates one or more special classes for the gifted, this has been taken to be a "program" for the gifted. At times, such classes have been only isolated fragmentations of educational activity, often constituting attempts that, in the larger sense, actually have been inimical to the educational welfare of the gifted. Generally, such classes have not resulted from careful planning and tend to be short-lived. Too often, they have been the result of some administrative whim, often placatingly authorized and implemented, and seldom grounded in sound educational philosophy.

Organizationally, the establishment of special classes for the gifted is first of all an administrative matter. Such local action usually is taken in the light of existing public school legal provisions, although a local district can take such steps even though no relevant state regulations exist if the district does not look to the state for extra funding for that purpose. As with the other practices that result from administrative authorization, the fact of such authorization does not assure appropriate quality instruction in the classes which are established.

Special classes differ in that those at the elementary level tend more to involve all the areas of academic learning, whereas, by virtue of the departmentalized nature of the secondary school, those at the secondary level involve different groupings of youngsters for the different subject-matter areas. Depending upon the size of the secondary school—junior or senior high school—there may be special groupings in certain areas but not in others. Further, such groupings may be constituted of differing constellations of pupils. In fact, something approaching a tracking system thus tends to be operative at the secondary level. The establishment of special classes for the gifted at the elementary level involves more radical departures from the conventional teaching structures than at the secondary school level. Our discussion will proceed primarily in terms of the elementary level.

We shall glance only briefly at the history of such classes, noting particularly how early efforts were made to establish them. Like so many attempts at educational improvement, many were very short-lived because they were so much manifestations of a few highly motivated individuals, and, more fundamentally, they were not an integral part of a total, philosophically based educational program. Special classes can be established at the start of or very early in a program for the gifted, or they can be established (but in either case only as a part of a program) only after certain preparatory or contributive steps are taken, thus in effect emerging meaningfully. Special-interest groupings of gifted youngsters, which do not require formal administrative authorization, can, but need not, constitute initial steps toward formally authorized special classes.

A Bit of History

The history of the establishment and operation of special classes for the gifted is a long one, and it is not reviewed here fully. An early overview is provided in the Twenty-third Yearbook of the National Society for the Study of Education (Whipple, 1924) and later ones in sources such as Hildreth (1966). Over a significantly wide geographic scope and within a time span of only a few years, special classes for the gifted appeared on the educational scene, predominantly at the elementary level. Race (1918) had started a class in Cincinnati in 1916. In that same year Stedman (1924) started such classes in the Los Angeles schools. Whipple motivated the establishment of a class for gifted children in Leal School, Urbana, Illinois, in 1919. Leta S. Hollingworth (1926), of Teachers College, Columbia, was responsible for the creation of special classes in Public School 165, Manhattan, by 1922. The first class in Cleveland was started in the Denison school, with Henry H. Goddard (1928) as consultant. Interestingly, Goddard observed:

> Rarely has this work been carried below the fifth grade. In the Cleveland schools, while the work began in the fourth and fifth grades, gifted children are now often picked from the first grade. *Thus these bright children do not wait for recognition until they have learned habits of idleness by being forced to mark time for three,*

four, or five years; rather, they are given their opportunity at the very beginning (p. 4). [Emphasis added.]

Yet, according to Freehill (1961), in 1948 only fifteen of 3203 cities reported such classes. There was, of course, a spurt after Sputnik, but three trends were discernible:

1. The making of special provisions for the gifted was coming to be perceived as including more than the establishment of special classes.
2. Special class (and other), provisions occurred increasingly at the secondary level and, relatively, decreasingly at the elementary level.
3. Increasing concern was being evidenced regarding learnings in areas other than academic—social, emotional, and creative.

In school systems that are large enough, that have appropriate pupil population distribution or facilities to move the pupils around within the system, and where special classes for the gifted are in operation, constellations of such classes, or special schools, are possible. Probably the oldest and most widely known example of this type of structure is the Bronx High School of Science (Meister chapter, pp. 210–234, in Witty, *The Gifted Child*, 1951). In Cleveland there developed centers for two or more special classes for the gifted—at both elementary and junior high school levels. In some instances colleges or universities have cooperated with the public schools in providing special classes or special schools for the gifted—the Hunter College Elementary School (started in 1941), with a later development at the secondary level, being the best known example. The possibility of the establishment of such special schools to serve larger population areas must be recognized in view of the movement to establish larger educational administrative units in order that richer total educational programs can be provided.

Interest Groups as Contributory

While special classes can be part of a total program for the gifted, and, wisely managed, contributive to the total program for all pupils, educational strategy dictates that they should emerge out of a carefully developed conceptual background and after the need for them and their probable merits have been fully demonstrated and recognized—by the educational staff and the parents—as a logical sequel to other efforts and provisions made in the interests of the gifted. They thus emerge in an atmosphere of understanding rather than one of smoldering resentment.

Provisions for interest groups

The regular classroom teacher can contribute importantly to this end by making it possible for certain pupils in her class to do some of their learning in interest groups. Such an interest-group approach has merit, of course, with respect to youngsters of all ability levels, even though we are concerned here with only the gifted. And it must be borne in mind that interest grouping has merit even though it may not be regarded as ultimately contributing to the emergence of special classes for the gifted. In its simplest form, it is nothing more than teachers acting in the light of what they have been expected to read about in many education courses, but the gap between knowing and doing often is great. Given two or more youngsters in a room who learn very quickly what is expected of the class as a whole—or who already have done such learning—and given the not unlikely condition that they are interested, or can be lured into

being interested, in some common activity related to their learning, they can be allowed or encouraged jointly to explore further that interest—instead of just being given "10 more problems," or "20 more words" to work on. The identification of differing foci of cognitive interest in the capable youngsters who can be involved in related activities is necessarily a function primarily of the substantive awareness and sensitivity of the teacher.

A fourth-grade teacher, for instance, had a very bright boy in her room (he was eight years old and achieving much as a sixth-grader) who was very interested in maps and map-making and two other bright youngsters who also had considerable interest and capability in that area. They agreed that they could form a "company" to make special maps for the whole school. After completing the regular work of the class, they worked in their "shop" in a corner of the classroom, which the teacher had assigned to them. They examined maps in a wide variety of sources and managed to arrange for an informing tour of a plant which printed atlases. They obtained closure in this interest, after a couple of months, by finally developing a composite map with a series of seven transparent overlays which showed the progressive emergence of European countries over seven centuries.

The idea of interest-group activity exists, of course, beyond that in the single classroom. Illustrative is the development which occurred in the Colfax elementary school in Pittsburgh (Pregler, 1954). Initially, bright children from more than one grade were allowed to engage in "club" activities for two hours a week, during the regularly scheduled program, and under the direction of competent and motivated teachers. In time, this grew to a whole afternoon each week. The children maintained contact with their regular classmates, often taking back to their regular classes certain extra information and ideas they had acquired or developed in the "club" activities. In another school, an elementary school science teacher learned that two of his more capable youngsters were quite interested in and curious about the area of aviation. At first he worked with them one afternoon a week after school. He gradually involved a friend of his, from a nearby air base, in their activity. The word got around that such an interest group was meeting after school, and the size of the group increased. Much of their activity was relatable to work in other classes, and feedback opportunities were capitalized upon by their regular teachers. The activity grew in numbers and the range of interests expanded such that, in a year, the activity became an integral part of the regular school program—which speaks well, of course, of the educational sensitivity of the principal.

Largely, interests are nurtured, cultivated, created, or capitalized upon by or in the school. Provisions within the school for the operation of interest groups are therefore most feasible and effective by virtue of the possible relationships between the learnings and experiences gained therein and the other learning activities in the school. But there are legitimate curricular areas for which the school is inadequately staffed or equipped to provide appropriate explorations and developments. A few schools may, for instance, have personnel who are highly competent or outstanding in areas such as music, art, the theater, and/or various substantive areas, but such is often not the case. For the most part, teachers interested in nurturing and capitalizing upon highly specialized interests can, and should, avail themselves of whatever compensatory expert assistance there may be in the community, whether it be a local artist, musician, theater group, city or county

official, or librarian, or a neighboring junior college, college, or university. In some instances, the initiative to establish interest groups which could be of educational merit can come (or be caused to come) from persons or groups having no formal relationships to the public school program—the staff of a museum, a church, the League of Women Voters, youth organizations, and the like. Illustrative descriptions of such developments can be found, for instance, in the Fifty-seventh Yearbook of the National Society for the Study of Education (N.B. Henry, ed., 1958) and in De Haan and Havighurst's *Educating Gifted Children* (1957).

Criteria for special-interest activity

Whatever approach may be used to stimulate and cultivate the intensive or extensive interests of the gifted (as well as of all pupils), that which is used must meet at least two major criteria—the special-interest activity should be at least adjunctive to the regular school program, and it must provide for or contribute to conceptual growth. While, ideally, such activities must be regarded as but parts of the broadly perceived curriculum of the school, in many instances they will function in addition to or as a simple elaboration of the regular school learnings.

Granting this range of relatability to the program for which the school is responsible, three conditions are necessary in any case. First, that which is engaged in, as a special-interest activity, needs to be regarded and dealt with in terms of its relationship to the conventional content learning to which the school is committed. (In one large community, a group of well-intentioned women decided to run a series of Saturday morning art museum sessions for the public school children, the women taking turns showing and talking about their specialities. Attendance was very good and the interest well sustained. Yet the art departments of the public schools were in no way involved and there was no evidence of feedback and coordination with the efforts of the schools in the areas of art, history, or geography. Without denying the possibility of some worthwhile social returns from the project, the educational fruitfulness of the undertaking, even for children of average capability, was limited.) Further, time for involvement in such interest activity should be incorporated within the formal school time of the children so engaged. With the increasing need to transport children to educational facilities, gifted children cannot, in effect, be deprived of such educationally broadening experiences if interest groups meet after the bus has left. In many schools, this will necessitate a reconsideration of educationally effective uses of the pupils' time.

Second, there must be a reasonable expectation that either the intra- or para-school interest groups will not be superficial or merely escapist in nature. Some interest activities start off at essentially a perceptual level. If they remain there, they tend to be short-lived. Some, however, by virtue of the substantive adequacy of the teachers involved, blossom and grow into conceptually productive activities. Still others start at a conceptual level and therefore have a greater probability of being sustained.

Third, the perception of the possibilities of the uses of special-interest groups should encompass all grade levels, recognizing the differing conceptual capabilities of youngsters of differing ages. Possible special-interest activities for first-graders associated with Thanksgiving (not just cutting out paper pumpkins!) would have different potential conceptual and time spans than would such activities focused on tenth-graders' interest in say, astronomy, or local government, or local ecology. Some interest groupings can involve pupils in more than one grade level.

Especially with respect to the gifted, the interest activity should provide for conceptual growth. Many interest activities in which the gifted are encouraged to become involved may, for the moment, intrigue them as skills to be acquired or as isolated bits of learning but end just there. The gifted child does learn easily the elements involved in many special areas of concern, but it is his discovery of the relationships among the elements that is the major educational payoff.

This separate consideration of some possibilities of the utilization of special-interest groups for gifted children is in no way intended to suggest that a generalized practice along such lines would constitute a program for the gifted. Such a practice can, and should, occur in regular classes, in a tracking program, or even in special classes. When the practice of interest grouping is effectively utilized, doubting Thomases discover that those gifted who are involved not only lose nothing in the way of conventional learning but also progress rapidly in it because interest in learning has been both sustained and reinforced. Not only the utilization of interest grouping but also the transition to the establishment of special classes can be facilitated by the consultant.

Some Problems

Two kinds of problems exist with regard to the establishment of special classes for the gifted. (Unfortunately, they can exist with respect to any special classes.) One of these arises when the establishment of such classes is being considered and can extend into the early stages of their operation. The other can come about while the classes are in operation.

Unfortunate social attitudes

Other than the problem of too-hasty and ill-conceived establishment of special classes, with the attendant and inevitable problems associated with such action, the major aspect requiring most careful consideration is the possibility of contributing to unfortunate social attitudes among teachers, pupils, and parents prior to, during, and after their establishment. The best intended, most positively sincerely motivated line of social action can be rendered totally ineffective, or actually harmful, if the attitudes of those involved in or related to that action have been or are caused to become negatively critical to the undertaking. To the extent that the interpretations and definitions of "equal opportunity" vary and to the extent that populations or subpopulations are hypersensitive about socioeconomic group differences, to those extents must sound and deliberate planning for the establishment of special classes for the gifted be jointly and forthrightly engaged in.

One of the major fears of or aversions to the idea of having special classes for the gifted—particularly at the elementary level, since the curriculum of the high school so often practically dictates the establishment of special classes in certain of the subject-matter areas—is based upon the apprehension and contention that such a grouping of the bright children will cause the nongifted to regard the gifted negatively, resentfully, or hypercritically, and that the gifted, by virtue of being in separate groups, will come to look disdainfully or contemptuously upon the nongifted. That some such situations have existed must be recognized; however, that such a condition is true generally has been shown by no research. When such a deplorable condition has existed, it must be attributed primarily to overt or covert manifestations of attitudes on the part of adults—teachers and parents—from whom the children involved learn these attitudes, either directly or indirectly. That such attitudes are held by the adults can be attributed in large part to faulty preparation for the making of such provisions—the failure to help those concerned to understand the philosophical, psychological, and educational bases for such action and the failure to familiarize them with the mass of research findings showing that such adverse outcomes are neither inevitable nor probable. Further contributive to resistance is the fact that many of the parents of public school children are products of schools which had no such provisions, and they tend to be apprehensive about or totally aversive to educational practices with which they have had no experience. It is largely for these reasons that so much consideration has been given thus far in this book to the importance of providing a good foundation for the inauguration of practices. When sound preparatory steps are taken and when communication channels between the gifted and nongifted are made functional, good special classes for the gifted can have the rich personal and social yield for which they are intended.

Isolation
from the mainstream

Once special classes for the gifted are established, preferably after aversive attitudes have been at least tempered, a condition can obtain which will present a problem; in fact it can cause a regression to aversive attitudes on the parts of both adults and children. The condition definitely is avoidable; if it arises, it is correctable.

Initially, and continuing to some extent even now, special classes for the gifted were perceived as clearly separate groupings of children of specified but limited age or grade ranges, with some specified lower "IQ" limit, in which the children did all their school learning. Later, it became recognized that there were certain school activities in which academic learning potential was not the crucial variable and from which other learnings could result. In the light of this recognition the gifted who did their academic learning in special classes were included with the other children in social, physical education, music, and art activities.

It is doubtful that the trend thus to get special-class gifted pupils at least partly back into "the mainstream" of education resulted directly from any attempt at differentiating among learning aptitudes. The aim was to forestall or break down the alienation that was regarded as possible or likely between those in special classes and those in regular classes, and it was believed that this could be accomplished by having the special-class youngsters commingle with the others in the "non-book-learning" areas. (The popular cliché was "a part of, not apart from.") Regardless of what brings them together, skillful teachers can capitalize upon opportunities to effect fruitful interaction between the two kinds of pupils even in cognitive areas.

SUMMARY

A program for the gifted must be inaugurated on the basis of formal administrative policy commitment and decisions which bear directly upon instructional aspects of the educational undertaking. Such stands should be based upon a full comprehension of the underlying philosophy and should include a full recognition of the preventive value of thoughtfully executed early admission. Whereas school administrators typically have been little concerned

about the gifted at the elementary level —especially in the lower elementary grades—they, as well as many who have written in the area, appear to have been remarkably unresponsive to favorable research findings on admitting the gifted to school prior to the conventional school-entering age—practices in Nebraska and the state program in the 1960s in Minnesota notwithstanding.

The research evidence on acceleration, of which early admission is one manifestation, has been consistently positive, especially when one recognizes the wide range of educational levels at which it has been employed and the varying conditions attending the practice. While the use of accelerative practices within the gifted's classroom needs no formal administrative pronouncement, as one moves to selective acceleration, which involves the use of classes other than the pupil's "regular" one, to gross acceleration, the "skipping of grades," the need for evidence of at least a tolerant administrative stance becomes apparent. Whatever the form of acceleration practiced, a full assessment of both the pupil and his milieu is necessary.

Tracking, requiring at least tacit administrative approval, has a long history of practice with ostensible good intent. However, it has been one of the glaring examples of the gap between administrative good intent and the attainment of expected instructional outcomes, due largely to the involvement of inadequately prepared teachers. Concern for pupil outcomes in areas other than educational achievement has made it additionally suspect, even to the point of evoking an adverse judicial pronouncement. Especially at the elementary level, its value in regard to the gifted is at best marginal.

The establishment of special classes for the gifted clearly requires administrative authorization, especially when this constitutes a departure from the established educational program. Such classes, or even centers, often misperceived as constituting a program for the gifted, well may be a part of such a program but are not necessary to it. When they do exist, especially at the elementary level, it is better that they emerge out of a pattern of meaningful interest groups of the gifted and that they function as integral parts of the total school program.

10

Instructional
considerations

Just as the rules of the game must be made clear before play starts, just so must fundamental administrative policies be promulgated for the inauguration or operation of a program for the gifted. Just as the game is played within these rules—whether clumsily or skillfully—just so is the "education" of the gifted carried out—whether ineffectively or effectively. Just as the presence of well-intentioned and clearly delineated rules of the game does not assure skillful play, just so the existence of clearly stated, philosophically well-grounded, and potentially contributive administrative policies does not guarantee effective facilitation of learning by the gifted.

The problem of implementation is broader than the consideration of this or that method. The field of education teems with advocacies and practitioners of methods—many of them having highly valid nuclei, and many of these having been overgeneralized into pana-

ceas or fetishes. Rather than present at any length one or more potentially promising instructional approaches, this chapter will discuss facets of instruction which must be considered in deciding how and when to do what. Important perspectives have significance across methods but can be highly determinative of the uses of particular instructional approaches at different stages in children's learnings. In this light we shall consider some perceptions of objectives, some perceptions of program values, the relationship between skill and content, the matter of enrichment and instructional acceleration, illustrative materials and resources, and method per se.

OBJECTIVES

The nature of instruction should be determined in the light of major overall objectives, to which the school's general task and the classroom's specific strategies should be committed. Three kinds of these will be identified—more or less conventionally stated objectives, psychologically based objectives, and more formal taxonomies of objectives. That they are being considered separately does not mean that they are mutually exclusive.

Conventional Objectives

A twofold objective has been posited for this book: that each child has a right to self-fulfillment appropriate to his capabilities and that each child has an ultimate right and obligation to attain status as a meaningfully contributive member of society. These are particularly cogent as regards the gifted, since society must look to them for major conceptual contributions. In like manner, other statements of major aims of education have value in identifying ultimate objectives and should serve to give direction to more specific contributive activities, but they do not delineate enough those almost-atomistic learning behaviors which are necessary to the attainment of those objectives. The four major objectives stated by the American Council on Education, and considered earlier, are a case in point. In and of themselves, there is nothing "wrong" with these kinds of major objectives, but there is an annoying gap between the aspirations reflected in such global statements and the "products" of education. Decisions on classroom strategies require more specific delineation of behaviors that are contributive to such major goals.

Psychologically Based Objectives

In one sense, the objective of self-fulfillment is psychologically based, but it is molar and largely admonitory in nature. Its justification has been determined largely by evidence indicating that unfulfilled individuals tend to be malad-

justed in society and that fulfilled ones tend to be not only happily and effectively adjusted but also socially contributive. Numerous psychologists for some time have identified different patterns of developmental levels, the implications of their findings and postulations being that children should be given opportunities to learn by confronting tasks which are appropriate to their developmental levels—neither "insulted" by tasks below their attained stages nor frustrated by tasks discernibly above their levels. More recently, educators have made much of Piaget's essentially organically determined developmental levels in light of which learning materials and instruction are being adapted (Phillips, 1969; Piaget, 1971).

Quickly after Guilford published his perception of the structure of intellect in 1956, educators identified "creativity" as an important goal in education. But his analysis came gradually to have a broader impact in that attention was called, again, to other kinds of intellectual operation. In addition to his cognitive operation, which had come to be taken for granted, at least in a holistic manner, his operation called memory, which had tended to play such a dominant role in school learning, his divergent thinking, the basis for educators' concern about creativity, and his convergent thinking, which was being deplored by so many critics of education, he identified evaluation as a differentiable kind of intellectual operation. This latter was, of course, not new to educators. It long had been identified as an objective, at least by a few, as an important kind of educational outcome, but it had been so difficult to evoke, identify, tolerate, and evaluate that it figured little in most classrooms. However, probably because Guilford delivered such a well-packaged and objectively based analysis of intellective behaviors and because of a socioeducational readiness for such an analysis of educational outcomes—at least so far as the kinds of operations that were involved—educators were stimulated to raise questions regarding the extent to which such behaviors were being evoked in their pupils. To what extent, for instance, were children engaging in divergent thinking and in evaluative thinking?

Getting meaningful answers to questions such as these requires something more than passing out questionnaires or administering objective tests. Once the classes and teachers to be involved were identified, the content to be involved had to be determined, the kinds of teacher behavior had to be clearly specified, recording equipment had to be provided and the pupils given time to adapt to its presence. After the data were thus laboriously collected, what took place had to be transcribed and then the teacher stimuli and pupil responses had to be analyzed. Crucial research of this kind takes much careful planning, usually requires a trial run in order to refine the methodology and to see if the data yielded are analyzable in terms of the purpose of the study, is tedious, and is relatively quite expensive, to say nothing of the conceptual demand made on the researchers themselves.

One such fruitful study was made of the "productive thinking" of gifted youngsters in the social studies area by Gallagher, Ashner, and Jenne (1967), who found that the pupils not only tended to give divergent and evaluative responses when the teachers' questioning was appropriately structured but also appeared to enjoy the different approach and to understand better the convergent thinking reflected in tests on the topics under consideration. While the study was conducted in a highly favorable setting, and an understandably few subsequent studies have essentially confirmed the "discovery" that pupils tend to respond, or to learn to

respond, in ways that are directly related to the kinds of questions which teachers ask, the major yield of the Gallagher-Ashner-Jenne study was in the delineation of a procedure for analyzing pupil responses in terms of a conceptual structure of thinking. Unfortunately, relatively few studies of this nature—valuable in regard to all pupils and not just to the gifted—have been made. Even though they tend to make clear what long should have been obvious, the act of such researching on the nature of teacher-pupil interaction has much potential value in sensitizing teachers to one of the crucial roles they play.

Taxonomies of Objectives

We have moved from the consideration of the statement of educational objectives in a very gross, molar sense, which have value in suggesting the general direction in which education should strive, to a consideration of more specific objectives, this time in terms of psychological factors. Even more specific objectives are identifiable, but it is helpful if such specifically stated objectives are perceived in terms of some logical or conceptual structure. The term "taxonomy" is used, as Plowman (1968) states, to denote "a system of classifying objectives, principles, and facts in a manner consistent with their natural or logical interrelationships" (p. 2). In this sense, the different psychological depictions of progressive developmental levels is taxonomic in nature. So, too, is Guilford's analysis of psychological operations, the kinds of stimuli to which the "intellect" responds (contents), and the results of those operations on those contents—his "products."

Interestingly, the most publicized development of a taxonomy of educational objectives started with a consideration of the problem at the higher education level. However, the results of work along this line are applicable down at least into the elementary grades. At the 1948 Boston Convention of the American Psychological Association an informal group identified three general categories of objectives—cognitive, affective, and motor skill. Subsequently, a committee of five tackled the job of identifying those objectives in the cognitive realm. Out of this came education's most widely used taxonomy of educational objectives (Bloom, 1956). Later Krathwohl and his group developed a taxonomy for the affective realm (1965). The analysis of the motor-skill area has been undertaken by Cratty (1967). The teacher and the curriculum specialist for the gifted would do well to regard their responsibilities for the education of the gifted in terms of Bloom's taxonomy of educational objectives in the cognitive domain. (They could benefit from an attempt to relate them to Guilford's "products.") For this reason, a rather gross outline of Bloom's taxonomy is presented.

Knowing and remembering. This incorporates knowledge of specifics, knowledge of ways and means of dealing with specifics, and knowledge of the universals and abstractions of a field. The knowledges under this range from knowledge of terminology and knowledge of specific facts to knowledge of theories and structures.

Comprehending. This involves translation (taking an idea or event and communicating it in a new form), interpretation (seeing relationships among ideas, events, or physical, social, economic, or political structures) and, extrapolation (the projection of the effects of certain behaviors or conditions).

Applying—using information from a number of subject-matter areas or sources to solve a problem.

Analyzing—breaking down into its component parts a mathematical problem, an instance of human behavior, a social situation, a physical phenomenon, or a chemical reaction.

Synthesizing—putting analyzed elements together, perhaps in new structures or relationships.

Evaluating—the making of judgments about conditions, objects, events, or ideas on the basis of external criteria and/or on the basis of value judgments.

These different ways of behaving need to be perceived in terms of the mental levels of gifted children. Some would be quite appropriate to Binet mental levels of 6, 7, or 8; others much more attainable and productive with mental levels of 10 to 12 and up.

Two points are noteworthy regarding any such taxonomy. First, while the different kinds of behaviors are identified and described as though they were mutually exclusive—the risk always inherent in any logical analysis—they are very definitely interactive. A child needs to know and remember things in order to apply them, in order to analyze them, and in order to evaluate them. Evaluation requires comprehension and analysis. A parallel condition existed with respect to Guilford's depiction of interactive operations. Second, such a breakdown of learning behaviors is necessary in order that each of the different learnings can be nurtured, and, in order to ascertain the effectiveness of the educational process, the manifestation of those behaviors must be measured not only to see if they have occurred in the specific situations but also to ascertain the extent to which they have generalized beyond those specific situations.

The very existence of a multiplicity of taxonomies (there are others, less well developed than Bloom's) suggests either that taxonomies are needed for separate perceptions of the learning process—the cognitive, affective, and motor skill, for instance—or that we have yet properly to see the problem as a whole. We may not yet have arrived at an adequate synthesis of our varied perceptions. Williams (1969) endeavored to describe one such, although he did so in terms of encouraging "creativity." Seeking to incorporate Piaget's perception of behavior development, Bloom's taxonomy of the cognitive domain, Krathwohl's taxonomy of the affective domain, and Guilford's structure of the intellect, he suggested an interaction between the teacher and the curriculum in order to effect these pupil behaviors (1) in the cognitive domain—"fluent thinking, flexible thinking, original thinking, and elaborative thinking," and (2) in the affective domain—"curiosity" (which he equates with "willingness"), "risk taking" (to him, "courage"), "complexity" (which he regards as "challenge"), and "imagination" (which he calls "intuition"). The extent to which this attempted synthesis will be helpful to teachers of the gifted remains to be seen.

PROGRAM PERCEPTIONS

Margaret Mead (1954), addressing herself more to the importance of scope in a given program than to the matter of differences among programs, observed, "The more diversified, the more complex the activities within which children are encouraged to play a role, the better chance for the superlatively, discontinuously gifted child to exercise his or her special talent" (p. 214).

On casual consideration, the need for such diversification may seem incongruent with the heavy emphasis in this book on symbolic learning and conceptualization in and by the gifted. But it must be recognized that such cognitive capabilities play major parts in meaningful social contributions not only in the arts, sciences, and professions but also in advanced technologies.

Whether there is such diversification among descriptions and operations of programs for the gifted is difficult to determine. The writers of such descrip-

tions may regard their statements as having more commonality than do their readers. And the extents to which the behaviors of children in programs actually approximate program aspirations may be not at all clear. Arn and Fierson (1964) examined the literature on ten programs for the gifted: the Bronx High School of Science, the Cleveland Major Works Program, the Colfax Elementary School (Pittsburgh), the Evanston Township High School, the Hunter College Elementary School, the Indianapolis Public Schools, the Lewis County (N.Y.) Seminar, the Palo Alto Unified School District, the Portland Public Schools, and the Quincy Youth Development Program. They perceived these descriptions as reflecting 117 values, which they reduced to ten, and they indicated the percentages of the procedures as contributive to those ten values. (Table 10.1). Rather than capitalize upon analyses such as this one or attempt some new structuring, we shall concern ourselves with content and methodological consid-

Table 10.1.   Arn and Fierson program values and emphasis.

Program value	Percentage of emphasis (rounded off)
Increased opportunity for academic growth	75
More extensive development of academic skills	52
Advanced development of work and study habits	50
More productivity due to improved learning climate	36
Increased motivation	30
Better personal and emotional development	21
Fuller social development	19
Increased opportunity for individual rate of growth	11
Expansion of interests	9
Development of aesthetic values	7

Source: Adapted from Arn and Fierson, 1964.

erations of a somewhat more molar nature. Their interrelatedness will become apparent.

SKILL AND CONTENT

Ignoring for the moment the school's responsibility to foster the social and emotional adjustment of its charges, the more formal learning by children can be regarded as consisting of the acquisition of certain skills and the mastering of certain content. The relationship between the two kinds of learning can be represented in graphic form as in Figure 10.1, limiting our perception to the precollege level. On entrance into school, the bulk of the learning demand is in the skill-acquisition area, although some content mastery is hoped for. As the child progresses through school, the emphasis on skill acquisition lessens, but never disappears, and the emphasis on content mastery increases. The relevance of this to the education of the gifted will appear later when we consider the matter of enrichment and acceleration.

The area about which there is the greatest contention is that of content. Is there a specified amount and kind of content that must be mastered in order for one to be "educated"? On the one hand, there are those who believe firmly that such can be clearly and specifically identified, and that mastery of such content is a necessary preparation for life. Others contend, equally vigorously, that the act of living itself provides the content, and that successfully coping with everyday

Figure 10.1. Relationship between skill and content in formal education.

life experiences in itself serves better the purpose of preparing for living. Those who maintain that education is life would subscribe to this position, but with a different end in view. Generally, the public schools have held to the former position.

Historically, the determination of the content of public school learning has been dominated by the consideration of what was needed for later learning at the higher education level. Only very slowly has the public high school adjusted to the fact that the majority of its graduates did not go into higher learning. Granted that there is *a* content, the assumption has been made that it can be adequately mastered in the conventional twelve years of schooling. It was on this assumption that bright pupils were required to serve their time. This led to the creation of a dilemma for educators: is the "education" of a child to be perceived in terms of his having mastered a constant content, or is it to be perceived in terms of his being required to put in a constant amount of time in order to be "educated"? In the light of such conceptions, the problems of enrichment and acceleration arose with respect to the education of the gifted. If "the" content were mastered in less than the conventional amount of time, acceleration was inevitable; if the amount of time put in were the primary consideration, enrichment (of some kind) was a possibility. To an unfortunate extent, neither of these kinds of educational adjustments adequately involved a primary consideration of the crucial psychological characteristics and needs of the gifted pupil.

Before examining more intensively the matters of enrichment and acceleration, it is important to examine what the schools have tended to regard as essential content. Historically, the task of each educational level was to prepare the pupil for learning at the next higher level.

In reverse order, this meant that what the college or university expected influenced what the content was to be at the secondary level, and this in turn heavily influenced the nature of the content at the elementary level. This condition has, of course, affected to a major degree what public school educators regarded as appropriate content and has, in fact, served to limit their perception. As a result, they have striven, almost desperately, to construct new educational houses out of the odds and ends they have had available. At the impact of Sputnik, for instance, the courses at hand (foreign language, mathematics, the conventional sciences) were reworked and extended further down the educational ladder. Only the most innovative educators sought to institute new courses or areas of learning activity such as cultural anthropology, consumer education, general language, logic, sociology, and the like—adapted, of course, to the educational level at which they were, or could be, introduced. While innovations such as these could be of value to most pupils, they could be of particular value to the gifted.

ACCELERATION AND ENRICHMENT

As earlier, the term "acceleration" will refer to those practices of teachers which enable pupils to undertake learning activities usually engaged in by pupils who are older than they are. Such practices could be denoted better by the term "instructional acceleration" in order to differentiate them from administratively perceived acceleration, as discussed earlier.

The more thoughtfully one considers what is involved in enrichment and in instructional acceleration, the more elusive and superficial their differences become. Given the administrative authori-zation, or even tolerance of acceleration, there are things of a sound accelerative nature which the teacher, probably with the help of the consultant, can do for her gifted. As has been pointed out, gross acceleration or selective acceleration of a gifted youngster necessarily involves something more than just permitting the child to work all or part of the time with another teacher at some higher grade level; the teacher receiving the accelerate must be anticipated to be able to help such a child learn effectively at the new level and even may need to help the accelerate make minor catch-up adjustments in certain relevant skill learnings. Not only can the consultant be highly contributive to the adjustments of both the youngster and the receiving teacher in such kinds of acceleration, but she can be of considerable help when the teacher employs adaptive acceleration in her own room, especially if she needs materials other than those conventionally used for her regular grade. (The possibilities of and research on acceleration have been discussed in the preceding chapters.)

Horizontal and Vertical

Enrichment and accelerative provisions for the gifted tend to be regarded as discrete ways of making educational adjustments for them. While logically they can be differentiated, a relationship between them may be overlooked. In large part, each can imply that there is a basic pattern of experience which constitutes "education." Enrichment implies the introduction of some amount of an extra something which amplifies, or makes more meaningful and/or interesting, that part of "education" which is regarded as essential. Acceleration, in its more common usage, implies that the essential core of education is acquired at a rate faster than the average. In this sense, a child is said to be educationally accelerated if he demonstrates at point A in his life a mastery or adequacy that "normally" is not expected until he reaches point B or point C in his life. The thinking thus is essentially chronological in its orientation. A child's program is regarded as "enriched" when that something extra which he is allowed or encouraged to experience is appropriate to the level at which the child is known or believed to be working successfully, or at which he is expected to be working. This has caused some to regard enrichment as horizontal (something added at his present level) and vertical (something added above his present level), the latter suggesting a content acceleration. More specifically, horizontal enrichment would consist of giving, say, a child learning effectively at fourth-grade level more material known or presumed to be appropriate for fourth-graders. In vertical enrichment, he would be given access to learning experiences at some grade level above that in which his adequacy was observed.

However, it is characteristic of gifted youngsters that they not only can learn easily material with which they are appropriately confronted but also that they tend to generalize from such learnings and, more importantly, that they tend, by virtue of such generalization, to extrapolate beyond their immediate learnings. This means that a fourth-grader, having mastered the "essentials" (of a given subject-matter area), and having been provided with Enrichment 1, Enrichment 2, and Enrichment 3—all of fourth-grade-level "difficulty"—will tend to integrate these (perhaps with some help) into a "broader meaning" and from that will tend, on his own, to extrapolate to a higher level of understanding, thus manifesting a readiness for enrichment called vertical. In other words, he is so constituted that he makes seemingly inevitable progress toward fifth-grade (or higher) level functioning. Whether this status be regarded in terms

of his being "ready" for fifth grade (or higher) placement is an administrative matter; whether it be regarded as a condition to which the fourth-grade teacher should adjust (by "vertical" enrichment) is a matter which has to be dealt with on the basis of teacher skills and/or administrative disposition toward or against acceleration. Thus, we have terms which are logically differentiable but seemingly inevitably psychoeducationally interwoven, at least for the gifted. However, enrichment and acceleration do call for separate consideration.

Enrichment and Content

Enrichment is a type of educational provision that is particularly appropriate for the content aspects of the school task. In terms of the relationship roughly depicted in Figure 10.1, opportunities for employing it increase as the child's involvement of content increases, although they are by no means absent from the beginning of schooling. Taking enrichment to mean the provision of learning opportunities for children in addition to "the" content of education, it at once becomes apparent that enrichment can refer to anything from the passingly informative (that Calcutta and Burma are at about the same latitude as Miami, Florida, or that the Panama Canal is due south of Pittsburgh) to the deeply penetrating or broadly exploratory (from the blasting of hillsides in the construction of highways to the "digging" of a new Panama Canal by atomic explosion, with its historic, economic, ecological, cultural, and political ramifications). Having bright children help in school office work, assist their less capable classmates in their learning, look up meanings of auxiliary lists of words, and the like can serve enrichment purposes, but only to certain extents and in certain limited ways. It has been the face validity of so many kinds of such activities that has caused educators so generally, so quickly, and so misleadingly to claim that they meet the needs of the gifted by means of "enrichment." (That such extra activities serve also to help keep brighter youngsters busy longer helps, too.) The fact that such provisions have constituted an educational half-truth has caused most serious educators of the gifted to look twice at all such activities and try to ascertain the extent to which they are truly enriching, rather than entertaining or diversionary.

The literature on the gifted abounds with suggestions as to how their education can be enriched—with descriptions of approaches, devices, and materials intended to make dreary, largely rote learning of "the" content a bit more palatable. In order that their enrichment merits may be evaluated, they should be regarded in the light of three factors or conditions which, although they are logically differentiable, are psychoeducationally interactive.

Relativity of Enrichment

Enrichment is relative, not absolute, in nature. Whether an activity is enriching must be determined in the light of the learner's psychological and educational characteristics and of his cultural and social milieu. This being the case, it is primarily an individual matter, rather than a class activity.

The fact that a child's surname may have been derived from the occupation of a major ancestor may be enriching to one child and "old hat" to another. "Sesame Street" can be enriching to some youngsters but only diversionary or entertaining to others. While it is true that a movie on adaptive animal behavior or a rerun of the TV series, "America," may be of value to a whole class, enrichment, at least as it is used here, is a matter of providing the individual child, or maybe two or three of them working together,

with additional broadening and concept-enhancing learning opportunities.

Even though enrichment should be individually determined, this does not mean that two or three bright youngsters, to each of whom such adaptation has been made, cannot engage in a common enriching activity. Some social or cultural period, for instance, can be the major focus of an enriching activity, but the cooperating children can address themselves to different facets of that period, such as economic, cultural, historical, literary, and artistic areas of intensive exploration. A child with a Binet mental age of 10 might well flounder and fail to be "enriched" if expected to deal with conceptual complexities appropriate to one with a Binet mental age of 15 or 16; in reverse, the latter probably would be only bored with involvement at a lower conceptual level. An enriching exploration of the economics of strikes could be beyond the comprehension of a child with a Binet mental age of 8. Related to this, of course, is the necessity of a match, or near-match, between the substantive aspects of the enriching activity and the extent of the child's prior and current educational experiences and adequacy. This match must involve consideration of the fact that different learning activities have different enrichment possibilities for different mental levels.

Concept-Contributiveness

The enriching activity must be contributive to the child's conceptual growth. It must be psychologically contributive, not a drill activity in and of itself. A child may need to acquire some skill, say, in computing percentages (which he will do most quickly under proper motivation), but only as a means of studying scoring procedures in sports, or family budgeting, or economics, or population growth, and the like. A child may need to learn the alphabet, not as an end in itself, but as a means of facilitating his use of a dictionary, a telephone book, a directory, or an index. If a child knows what a Ouija Board is, it may be of only informational value to him to learn that it is a "Yes-Yes" Board, unless such information is cast in a context of general language and the French-German background of the name is identified. Learning that some birds dig worms out of trees with tools can be an interesting bit of new information in and of itself, but it should be a stepping stone to the study of the use of tools by lower animals. The bits and pieces of enrichment appropriate to the lower grades, which well may contribute to the development of low-level concepts, need to be succeeded by larger content and concept structures in the upper grades.

Substantive Adequacy of the Teacher

The extent to which enrichment can be effective is determined by the substantive breadth and insight of the teacher who seeks to use it. The teacher who "knows" only her subject is grossly limited, like a sightseer traveling through Yellowstone Park wearing blinders. The teacher of English who lacks a knowledge and comprehension of the historical, political, and geographical concomitants of a given period in language development or literature is in a poor position to help her gifted pupils have enriching learning experiences.

As a means of checking on the scope of explorable enrichment, the teacher would do well to mark, on the perimeter of a circle, the major substantive areas and then to connect those points with lines. Each line, in effect, can represent the question: "What possible relationships exist between A and B?" Single lines would suggest relatively simple relationships—as, for instance, one between geography and economics. (What role did geography play in determining the economic development of certain places, or certain areas?) More complex explorable relationships can be denoted by having the line from geography bifurcate and go to economics and to government. (Given the condition that the development of certain economic patterns, say barter and monetary exchange, may have been heavily influenced by geographic conditions, what was the attendant nature of local and national governmental structure and function?)

Assignment of activities

Many different kinds of activities have been regarded as "enriching." Few of them are truly enriching, at least as far as we are concerned with the gifted. Let us look at some of them in terms of one or more of the criteria proposed for enrichment. Having gifted pupils help the teacher score papers, help slower pupils in their learning, do clerical work in the classroom or in the school office, and even participate in student activities such as student council, the school paper, and the like tend to be primarily occupational in nature—they keep gifted pupils busy during the time they have left over after they have "done their school work," and generally contribute little to concept enhancement, although they may have social values. The introduction of arithmetic and mathematical tricks, puzzles, short-cuts, and the like are diversionary and entertaining (so long as the pupil is successful in them) but generally fall short in concept nurturance and enhancement. Having bright pupils engage in "extra" reading and arithmetic, when that is all that is involved, may be conducive to the improvement of those skills, but the interest factor must be given serious consideration here. At times, extra skill-enhancement work can result in the acquiring of additional information, but so often it is only that.

To be truly enriching for the gifted, whatever is engaged in must be clearly contributive to and ultimately (and forthrightly so as far as the teacher is concerned) involve concept development and growth. "Things are learned"—and all children can do much learning—but for the gifted the important factor is their deriving relationships, or being helped to discover such relationships, among the elements and/or structures they are newly encountering. Such new learnings must be assimilated and integrated meaningfully into larger structures or conceptualizations. Such is the forte of the gifted and it needs nurturance.

The possibilities available for enrichment are as limitless as the active fruitful curiosity and imagination of a well-informed teacher. Such a teacher can be sensitive to and capitalize upon gifted children's capabilities for exploring relationships between arithmetic and mathematics in the quantification of simple objects and phenomena, sports data, travel, production costs, economic conditions and phenomena, the use of formulae for purposes of precise description and communication; between geography and history, politics, economics, literature and music; between varying art forms and musical styles and individual and social psychological conditions and phenomena; between life styles and cultures and geography, history, and economics; and the like. Relationships of such a nature are explorable throughout all the grades of school, appropriate adjustments in complexity and depth being made, of course, to the mental and achievement levels of the children involved.

Materials and facilities

Contributive to such enrichment, of course, is the availability of materials and facilities—the bricks, mortar, and even minor schemata out of which concepts are made. Most obviously important are classroom and school libraries. In 1955, the American Association for the Advancement of Science initiated a Traveling High School Science Library Program which provided a rotating lending library of 200 science books. This resulted both in many of the more capable pupils' getting temporary access to enriching materials and in high schools' being helped in the selection of books for the purpose of improving their libraries. Over the period 1955–1962 nearly 6000 high schools took advantage of this. From 1959 to 1964 such an arrangement was made for elementary schools, giving some 3000 schools access to the 160 books circulated in that program. Out of this experience, Deason (1963) compiled a list of more than 900 paperback books on science, many of which have been added to school libraries.

Many teachers of the gifted have helped their youngsters get access to added books, records, and experimental materials that were made available by formal and informal consultants in their communities who were interested in helping with the gifted. Martinson, however, reported that less than 2 percent of the gifted were given opportunities to work with specialists or in other group settings (Marland, 1971). Certain book clubs put on the market packaged seminars on art and music. Originally started on a limited scale, but now relatively widely available, are computer and science kits which can be put in school libraries where single or small groups of gifted pupils can gain access to them. For many children in the United States, the use of television has been little explored with a view to enrichment possibilities. While some commercial programs have this kind of potential value, the increasing use of cable TV and of closed TV circuits (within cities and counties) can be effectively capitalized upon. Lecture series and classes offered by radio by more and more colleges and universities can provide enrichment opportunities. Apparently little explored, however, has been the use of correspondence courses for enrichment purposes. Such could be of particular value where facilities are limited. The Accrediting Commission of the National Home Study Council, 1601 18th Street N.W., Washington, D.C. 20009, issues a brochure on the accreditation procedure and criteria for correspondence schools and periodically issues a directory of accredited private home study schools.

Whatever the facilities available for enrichment, they are not synonymous with enrichment. Mere use of them may not constitute enrichment. The teacher plays the crucial role in determining whether any learning opportunities or facilities will be contributive to the focal phenomenon of enrichment—the evocation, nurturance, and enhancement of increasingly higher levels of conceptualization. It is understandable why little, if any, research has been done on the effectiveness of enrichment.

The question often is asked: "Which is better for the gifted—acceleration or enrichment?" The very asking reflects unfavorably upon the asker's perceptions of the total educational, psychological, and social needs of the gifted. In a roughly analogous manner, asking "What is needed for life—air or water?" would suggest a limited perception of the nature of life. It is not a matter of which; it is, rather, a matter of how much of which and when. Neither should be perceived as a one-time thing. While efforts to facilitate learning by enrichment rather consistently should characterize the educational climate of the gifted, there very well may be times when enrichment should be of special concern—as when a child, having been accelerated, then needs added input in order to effect

conceptual consolidation, integration, or "mental packaging" at the new and higher level. There well can be situations in which the child can more appropriately be accelerated one year or more at two different times rather than two years or more at one time. The nature of the tactics of acceleration and enrichment must be dictated by the strategy of the total social and psychoeducational consideration of the child. And the relative weights of the variables which interact to create this complex will vary at different stages in his educational life.

METHODOLOGICAL CONSIDERATIONS

In material written about the gifted, the term "methods" has varied connotations. At times it is concerned with procedures used to identify the gifted. At other times it deals with matters such as enrichment, acceleration, special classes, or counseling. Even matters such as special financing, administrative provisions, and library expansion have been considered under the rubric of "methods." The term is taken here to denote teacher-initiated procedures which can range from classroom-based activities to the capitalization upon a wide variety of extraclassroom facilities. *Method* should be regarded as denoting classroom strategy.

Notes on Learning

Two points bear reemphasizing. First, the position has been taken that teachers don't teach, in the popular sense of the term. Their primary function is to manipulate children's environments so as to facilitate learning by their pupils. Different pupils require differing kinds of learning nurturance. Some need more "drill"; usually the gifted need less. Some need more tangible and obvious learning activities; the gifted need some of these, but the bulk of their learnings tends to be less tangible. The teacher can play a significant role in the child's learning by being constantly cognizant of and adaptive to his unique experiences and capability, by so manipulating his learning confrontations that he is assured of success in his learnings, by making sure that the child well habituates his learnings, by making sure that he moves on to more advanced learnings, and by helping the child recognize and integrate the relevance of what he has learned. The teacher also can help the gifted child learn not to learn, either by confronting the child with learning demands which he is not yet prepared to meet or, more often, by confronting the gifted child with learning demands which he already has met and which he therefore finds unchallenging. In any case, the child learns, and he learns in terms of the nature of the nurturant environment which the teacher provides.

Second, the same psychological principles operate in regard to the learning of all children. All children have a need for self-realization, a need to be successful in their learning, a need to see the personal and social relevance of what they are learning or have learned. Understanding and success are reinforcing to the learning activity.

In a fundamental sense, there would appear to be little merit in describing any method of facilitating learning by the gifted as unique to this group of children. Little, if any, case can be made for a claim that there is *a* method uniquely appropriate to the gifted. Any method must be based upon the fundamental psychological principles which apply to all children, although certain adaptations need to be made in the light of the different levels and rates of learning aptitude of different children. Even if there were a method regarded as uniquely appropriate to some gifted, its general applicability, even for the gifted,

would be questionable. Adaptations would be necessary to at least three variables in the learning situation:

1. The characteristics of the teacher—his or her personality, substantive orientation, and prior teaching habits
2. The characteristics of the gifted child—his level of mental maturity, degree of giftedness (a child with a Binet IQ of 130 as contrasted with one of a Binet IQ 165), his social milieu, his profile of strengths and relative weaknesses, and his interests
3. The nature of the area of learning—art, literature, music, natural sciences, physical sciences, and so on

In addition, adaptations may need to be made in terms of the scope of facilities in the school and in the community, as well as in terms of the pervading philosophy of the school and community.

Curriculum

It is important to recognize the inescapable interaction between content and method. Learning facilitative procedures will differ markedly as between expressive activities in art, music, and theater and areas of substantive learnings such as literature, social studies, mathematics, and the sciences. The literature on the gifted has literally teemed with content-oriented studies of the curriculum which had varying degrees of relevance to how to facilitate learning by the gifted.

The most sustained and systematic work along this line has been done in California. By means of a grant from the U.S. Office of Education, Plowman (1969) initiated in 1963, for the Department of Public Instruction, a three and one-half year program called "California Project Talent" within the state's program for the gifted, which had been legislated in 1961. While it was concerned with the full spectrum of problems in developing programs for the gifted and while the interim reports (on counseling-interactional programs—1966; on acceleration programs—1968; on special class programs—1968; and on enrichment programs—1969) dealt with major relevant topics, much having methodological import pervades the general report. As Plowman stated, "Crucial aspects of this project were the demonstration and discussion of ways of organizing content and learning experiences, of providing flexible progression through content, learning experiences, and grade levels; and of counseling and instructing gifted children and youth" (1969, p. 1).

A major influence in California's sustained and effective interest in the education of the gifted has been the work done by Martinson and her students. Her sensitivity to the interrelatedness of pupil characteristics, content, and method is reflected generally in her 1961 reports and, more specifically, in her report of the use of a study-seminar approach in the San Diego schools.

Literature on Teaching Methods

Much already has appeared in the literature on "teaching" methods for the gifted—most of it with respect to content-appropriate method. Table 10.2 gives a representative sampling of relatively recent texts. This information by no means should be regarded as reflecting even reasonably adequately the extent to which teaching methodology for the gifted has been dealt with in the literature. Publications bearing directly upon this area, especially in the wake of Sputnik, have been issued from the U.S. Office of Education, from national organizations, from state departments of education, from members of public school staffs, from specialists in colleges and universities, and even from lay persons. The percentages presented should not be taken as absolutely precise; in a gross sense, though, they do reflect the

variation in the extent to which differing authors or reading compilers have seen fit to address themselves specifically to the matter of method. The close relationship between content and methodology is clearly apparent, suggesting, perhaps, the difficulty or futility of considering a "teaching" method uniquely appropriate to the gifted. Further, methodological considerations tend quite often to be incidental to or implicit in general material written about educating the gifted. This is most clearly evident in Ward's book (1961) on the philosophy fundamental to educating the gifted, "method" per se being so inextricable from that content that it isn't even included as a topic in the book's index.

Much that has been published on methods for the gifted has been addressed to "enrichment," usually with respect to the different subject-matter areas, but often reflecting a sensitivity to the fact that enrichment in one area quite often can and should involve relatable areas. Illustrative of this kind of methodological help is Gibbony's "Enrichment—Classroom Challenge" (1967), issued by the Ohio State Board of Education. In addition to suggestions regarding the uses of community resources, letter exchanges, instructional media, and the library, the bulk of the booklet provides lists of enrichment cues separately appropriate to the elementary and secondary levels. These in turn are subdivided into subject-matter areas. The 1368 leads (745 for the elementary level, 524 for the secondary level, 71 on community resources, and 28 on the library) are distributed among seven subject-matter areas at each level, ranging from 223 for elementary science to 40 each for music and art. Here, again, the possible value of these to all pupils, and not to just the gifted, is apparent.

As mentioned earlier, much attention has been paid to creativity in gifted children—its existence, importance, and fur-

Table 10.2. Method-relevant content in recent representative texts on the gifted.

Author(s)	Title	Date of publication	Percentage of method-relevant content	Nature of method-relevant coverage
		TEXTBOOKS		
Hildreth	*Educating Gifted Children*	1952	30-35	General, in the Hunter College elementary school setting
DeHaan and Havighurst	*Educating Gifted Children*	1957	40-50	Includes a chapter on community factors and resources
Sumption and Luecking	*Education of the Gifted*	1960	20-30	General
Durr	*The Gifted Student*	1964	20-30	General
Gallagher	*Teaching the Gifted*	1964	50-55	Includes chapters on arithmetic, science, and social studies
Hildreth	*Introduction to the Gifted*	1966	20-30	General
		INVITED COMPILATIONS		
Shertzer	*Working with Superior Students*	1960	10-20	Includes a section on community involvement and reports on four programs: Phoenix (Arizona) Union High School; McKinley High School (Canton, Ohio); Marshall (Michigan) High School; and Central High School (Springfield, Missouri)
Everett	*Programs for the Gifted*	1961	80-85	Includes suggestions from secondary education in the U.S.S.R., from German gymnasia, and from English grammar schools. Programs described: Lewis County, New York (enrichment for talented rural youth); Germantown (Pennsylvania) Friends School (enrichment in a small high school); Ohio State University High School (a core-centered program); Portland, Oregon (a high school program in a medium-sized city); Evanston (Illinois) Township High School (program in a large comprehensive high school); and the Bronx High School of Science
Fliegler	*Curriculum Planning for the Gifted*	1961	85-90	Includes chapters on social studies, arithmetic, creative mathematics, elementary and secondary science, creative writing, reading, foreign languages, creative art, music, creative dramatics
French	*Educating the Gifted*	1964	10-15	General
Gowan and Torrance	*Educating the Ablest*	1971		Includes parts on individually prescribed instruction, the Talcott Mountain (Connecticut) Science Center, and creativity

therance. The fundamental problem here, in contrast with learning always to respond in some prescribed manner—an essentially rote kind of learning—is in keeping alive, or even reviving, the child's realization that two or more responses can be made to any stimulus or situation with his attendant evaluation of the different identified responses for the purpose of selecting the response appropriate to the given situation. The fundamental psychological return from nurturing creative behavior is that the "spirit is freed," resulting in the child's considering more than one possible line of responding, exploring other than narrowly prescribed relationships, discovering constellations of experiences that—to him—are new and rewarding. Specific classroom strategies addressed to this end are effectively described by Torrance (1962).

Some Overall Characteristics

Quite appropriately, it has been stated that methods do not a teacher make. Given those qualities that are important in a teacher of the gifted—substantive competency, a love of learning, emotional adequacy, and the like—teaching competency can be enhanced by some fundamental "tricks of the trade." The intangible nature of the products of learning by the gifted makes the teacher's task much more demanding than is true in the case of the learnings by many nongifted. The finished bookend is manipulable, tangible, and easily measured to see if it meets specifications. On the other hand, the major educational outcomes of the gifted—their growth in ability to see relationships and to conceptualize—often are frustratingly intangible and difficult to observe, measure, and, to many, even to understand. Perhaps it is in part the nature of the outcome that makes it so difficult to de-

scribe satisfyingly any teaching method or methods as uniquely relevant to the gifted.

Prethinking

Certain kinds of things which the teachers of the gifted can do in order more effectively to facilitate their learning may sound like professional housekeeping suggestions which would be appropriate for all teachers. Certainly, the reader can find many good books on teaching methods which would cover this area much more adequately than will be attempted here. Only three major characteristics will be dealt with here—those that must characterize the classroom strategies contributive to learning by the gifted—and we note that brighter youngsters, probably more than the others, quickly will sense the absence of one or more of them.

In the first place, the teacher must prethink the job of facilitating the learnings of the youngsters. This means that both the distant and immediate goals must be identified, preferably in written form, and this is done best in behavioral terms rather than in abstract philosophical terms. The distant goals, once stated for the year or for the semester, will bear reexamination and sharpened specification within shorter periods of time. Immediate goals, whether they be for the month, week, or day, should be accorded the same treatment. Especially for the less experienced teacher, unwritten aspirations of this sort tend to be nebulous and elusive; in written form, they can be healthily confronting and demanding. The general and specific objectives conducive to these goals should be identified, always in behavioral terms. In this connection, help can be gotten from one or more of the relevant taxonomies. Once this is done, the basis is laid for the identification of discernible achievement on the parts of the pupils, and reinforcement tactics can be applied as appropriate. Identification of facilities—materials and situations—must be an integral part of such preplanning.

While it is always well to do such anticipating as specifically as possible, keeping a second line of action in mind if the first is unexpectedly inappropriate or not feasible, it serves its purpose much as does a speaker's outline of his talk, as contrasted with his reading a formal paper before a group. Further, the teacher must be able to table or discard certain advance plans in order to capitalize upon unexpected developments such as a school-relevant local movie, some local or national development, some child's new experience, and the like.

*Matching
the child's level*

Second, the learning experiences expected of the child should be appropriate to his level. This has three ramifications, first and foremost of which is the effective matching of the learning expectancy to the child's properly ascertained mental level. Sensitivity to a sound taxonomy of developmental level is in part incorporated in this. Equally important is the necessity of making sure that the child has acquired those basic facts, skills, and concepts that must be contributive to his more advanced learning. It must be recognized that no child just fails in a general sense to achieve. His inadequacy is due to a lack of quite knowable specifics—the failure to have acquired contributive basic facts, the failure to have adequately habituated certainly highly specific knowledge or skill components, the failure to integrate such components.

Social factors

Third, the "methods" used by the teacher must reflect a sensitivity to the social factors in the situation—to the so-cial milieu of the child. The child's learning must be situationally appropriate. This calls for the teacher's taking cognizance of the social interactions among the learners, adjustmental factors in the situation, and the possible interplay of contrasting cultural value systems. But this sensitivity also must extend beyond the immediate social situation; at times the pupils will need help in recognizing the ultimate social relevance of their present learnings, though not in the sense of naggingly reminding them of such things as the claim that those who graduate from high school earn more than do those who don't. The use of such extrinsic motivation on the gifted would indicate clearly that the teacher using it just didn't understand gifted pupils and the social importance of intrinsically motivated behavior.

SUMMARY

To maintain that children learn rather than that they are taught does not relieve adults—parents and teachers—of the responsibility of anticipating what the outcomes of that learning should be or of seeking out and employing strategies that can be facilitative to learning by children. Statements of the objectives of such learnings have tended to vary in nature from the general philosophical, to the general psychological, to the more sharply delineated taxonomic, reflecting a tendency toward objectives that are characterized increasingly in terms of both the actual behaviors to be nurtured and the developmental realities of the learner.

The total domain of children's learnings would seem to consist of the acquisition of simple habituated skills and the acquisition of content. Yet, especially as regards the gifted, thinking in terms of content can be restrictive if it is regarded simply as information to be garnered. Conceivably, a child could amass a large amount of content—a mass of information—without its being structured in cognitively more powerful manners. While the gifted are disposed, by virtue of the nature of their intellectual potential, to acquire easily a voluminous amount of the bits and pieces of content and are disposed also to discover for themselves increasingly complex relationships among those data and to develop resulting concepts in that process, a primary cognitive goal in their education must be the assiduous nurturance of conceptualization. By virtue of such thinking, accelerative practices would seem more appropriate in the skill area of learning, and enriching practices more productive in the content area thus broadly perceived. Both acceleration and enrichment are important in the education of the gifted, the extent and manner of the employment of each being determined by the particular social, psychological, and educational needs of a given child at a given moment and reflecting sensitivity to the child's total milieu.

It can no more be contended that one teaching method should be uniquely effective for the gifted than that one is universally effective with all children. Whatever aspect or component of any teaching method is effective must be recognized as varying from teacher to teacher, from child to child, from time to time, from learning area to learning area, and from one social milieu to another. If there be a dominant crucial variable, it is the teacher—and, particularly for the gifted, the teacher must be broadly substantively competent, emotionally secure, insatiably curious, equally capable of working with individual children and with groups of children, and fully socially sensitive.

11

Rural and compensatory aspects

If, as has been indicated, the educational needs of the gifted in the larger population centers have been neglected, this is doubly true as regards those of the gifted in population centers of 2500 and less— for a number of reasons. Generally, the educational facilities in rural areas tend to be less adequate than in the larger communities; this is one reason for the national trend toward the merging of small school districts and the establishment of intracounty and multicounty school administrative units. Although the provision of good or superior educational facilities does not necessarily assure commensurate improvement in the quality of education, differences in salary scales tend to attract both teachers and administrative personnel away from smaller units to larger units. Urban salaries tend also to attract the parents of school children and the children themselves after they finish their formal

school learning. Not only are there believed to be better employment possibilities in larger centers of population, but the kinds and degrees of intellectual challenges in those employment opportunities appeal to the school-leaver. This by no means is to be construed to imply that only the intellectually inadequate remain in the rural areas; fortunately, enough of the competent remain to keep things running. But the fact of the "brain drain" remains with us, and for much the same kinds of reasons as it occurs between countries.

THE GIFTED
IN RURAL AREAS

This general condition seems to have been little studied, especially as regards what happens to the gifted in the small community. Lee and Newland (1966) made such a study in an unusual small Illinois community—unusual because its children had been tested over a nine-year period by means of the Kuhlmann-Anderson and the Kuhlmann-Finch Intelligence Tests and the records were intact. The data are shown in Table 11.1. It can be seen that, over the nine-year period, nine of the ten children with Kuhlmann IQs of 130 and higher had left the community, only six of them having graduated from college. Some of the ten who completed high school had left the community to attend high school elsewhere. One of these, a boy with the highest IQ in the nine years to have attended the local school, had entered college, dropped out after a "fight," had wrecked several cars, lost a series of jobs, spent most of the fall and winter of 1963–64 in a New York jail charged with rape, and returned home after the charges were dropped, where he has held only occasional odd jobs. His mother died in a "mental" hospital during his early boyhood, and his father, usually unemployed, was a chronic drinker.

The account that follows, concerning a gifted boy's problems more than a generation ago, presents elements that continue to characterize problems of the gifted in rural areas: the presence of high potential, limited educational facilities, the underachievement picture, and the potential social contribution that can be salvaged.

In the early 1930s, ten-year-old *Tom* in a community of less than 500 was found to have a reasonably valid Binet IQ of 185. At that time he was sitting in the seventh grade of his local elementary school. While the level of his measured educational achievement was nowhere near his high learning potential level of 18 years six months, he was achieving much like an average tenth-grader. Accelerated enrichment materials were informally provided for him and his teacher by the psychologist working in the boy's interests, and he was enabled to acquire skills in the use of a rented typewriter. (When he turned in typewritten reviews of his ten extra readings in order to obtain a special certificate for such extra work, they were turned down because they were not in his handwriting!) An attempt was made to enter him in a high school in a community of some 15,000, some three miles away. Unfortunately, at that time the state had no provisions for reimbursement for transportation and tuition costs. His economically marginal family could not provide such transportation. Further, his own school dis-

Table 11.1. What happened to Slumption Junction's eighth-grade graduates.

School year	Eighth-grade graduates		High school graduates		Attended college		College graduates		Left community	
	Boys	Girls	Boys	Girls	Boys	Girls	Boys	Girls	Boys	Girls
1950-51	7(1)	10	6(1)	5	—	—	—	—	5(1)	8
1951-52	8(2)	10(1)	7(2)	6(1)	2(2)	1(1)	1(1)	1(1)	5(2)	10(1)
1952-53	5	11(1)	1	2(1)	1	1(1)	1	1(1)	4	10(1)
1953-54	6(3)	9	5(3)	6	5(3)	—	2(2)	—	5(3)	9
1954-55	7	8	2	3	1	—	—	—	5	7
1955-56	14	14(1)	5	9(1)	2	1(1)	—	1(1)	8	11(1)
1956-57	11(1)	7	7(1)	6	2(1)	2	—	—	9	5
1957-58	12	6	7	5	2	—	—	—	5	5
1958-59	7	9	4	7	1	1	—	—	3	7
TOTAL	77(7)	84(3)	44(7)	49(3)	16(6)	6(3)	4(3)	3(3)	49(6)	72(3)

Source: Lee and Newland, 1966. Used by permission of Kappa Delta Pi, An Honor Society in Education.

Note: Figures in parentheses indicate children with Kuhlmann IQs of 130 or higher.

trict could not, or would not, pay for his tuition in the neighboring district, and no "patron saint" was found to assume financial responsibility. He stayed three years in the five-teacher high school with its meager offerings, which were augmented somewhat by the psychologist in a nearby college.

An attempt was made to find a college or university that would provide a full scholarship for him and assure him of the opportunity to work to pay for his room and board. Equally importantly, the school that took him had to recognize that, while Tom was very bright, he was a gross underachiever, although, fortunately, he had good residual motivation to learn, and much "educational repair" work would be needed for the first year or so. The psychologist, by virtue of his being quite involved then in national college personnel and guidance activities and having only recently extensively surveyed the literature on higher education, was familiar with the claims and intents being expressed in the literature with regard to helping bright students enter higher education. As a result a canvas was made of 17 such institutions in regard to their willingness and ability to meet this boy's needs. Only four encouraging replies were received, and the most promising of these, on learning that the boy would be only 15 years old at entrance, decided not to accept him. He went to the nearby college where his program was closely watched over by the psychologist.

As had been predicted in the letters earlier sent out in the canvass of the colleges and universities, his academic marks during the first year were of only high C quality. (He left college unexpectedly toward the end of the first semester in an unsuccessful attempt to find work, but was helped to get reinstated.) The quality of his academic work gradually improved such that he was given part-time employment as a student assistant in mathematics during his senior year. While residual elements of his poor study habits continued to plague him, he finally earned a Ph.D. in mathematics at a major institution. He later participated in one of the advanced institutes, co-authored at least one text in

higher mathematics, and became the chief statistician in one of the country's major atomic centers. He took a major part in running a state science fair and, at last report, was endeavoring to help some bright students in his state.

There are gifted youngsters in the rural areas. Even though their concentrations are not as great, their educational and psychological needs are every bit as great as in the urban areas. And society's need to have them become significant social contributors is important. Within our changing social picture, with the decrease in the number of small farms and the attendant increase in the number of large farms, with the advances in technology learnings in agriculture, cattle raising, and poultry production, and with the attendant interactive factors in the economics of rural living, producing, and marketing, there are very significant social roles to be played by the rural most able. After all, some 15,000,000 of our public school children live in rural areas, and probably some 500,000 to 750,000 of them are gifted.

So far as the gifted are concerned, the fundamental problem in the rural areas is much the same as in the urban areas—recognizing that there *are* gifted youngsters who have at least special educational needs and providing properly for them. While the possibility of using, for instance, correspondence courses as supplementary educational diets must be recognized as promising for the urban gifted child, this would seem even more so in the case of rural gifted children. A real factor in such a practice is the added cost, thereby incurred by the local district, which probably already is hard-pressed financially. This, however, need not be an insurmountable obstacle if a state funding program for the gifted is perceived as being obligated to assist children in rural as well as in urban districts, if funding practices are broadly enough perceived so as to include all or part of the extra costs necessary for the provision of such courses, and if state, regional, or county supervisors (or a consultant on the gifted) help the teachers get access to and use such materials.

While, in the last analysis, the teacher is the focal person in determining the adequacy of efforts properly to educate the gifted, the effectiveness of the teacher's functioning can be increased by the proper functioning of other school personnel just as it can be impaired by the lack of such supportive activities or by their failure to function properly. Understandably, the literature on the education of the gifted has been dominated by descriptions of programs in large or reasonably large school situations. However, such descriptions of large-based operations may tend to cause the administrator and teacher in smaller or rural schools to see little that is applicable to their situations. Undoubtedly contributive is the fact that such descriptions have tended to provide information more about the form of such efforts than about the fundamental substance in effectively educating the gifted. Form without substance tends to be more comprehensible by virtue of its relative tangible nature; for the same reason the general public tends to react primarily to the appearance of uniforms and marching cadence of the school band rather than to the quality of the music produced. In contrast, the fundamental substance, or essence, of properly educating the gifted is intangible, often little comprehended by the majority, and perhaps even threatening to some.

Role of the Teacher

Even in large school systems, when at least reasonably adequate facilities are provided to help teachers operate effectively, the teacher, in the last analysis, is the crucial and basically contributive person. Some teachers, working without the benefits of a "program" but deeply committed to the profession of teaching and therefore keenly interested in their youngsters as individuals, have worked quite effectively with bright pupils, keeping alive their joy of learning and helping them discover and explore expanded intellectual horizons. It is especially to this kind of teacher that we must look for help in meeting the needs of the gifted in the smaller and rural school districts. This type of teacher seeks to increase the adequacy of her preparation at least as much because of her own still-alive desire to learn as because of her desire to progress up the salary scale, by taking extension and summer school courses. Intent and desire are admirable, but they are better implemented with relevant preparation. With view to helping the teacher in situations lacking the program facilities that have been described, the following suggestions are offered. We shall think first in terms of the teacher in what has been a relatively highly decentralized situation and then in terms of possibilities attending the more recent trend toward the development of larger administrative units in less populous areas.

The teacher
as individualist

The practical problem boils down to the identification of those kinds of things which the teacher may attempt to do for her bright pupil(s) which usually are done by the kinds of specialists involved in a major program for gifted pupils—the consultant, with or without the help of the curriculum supervisor or specialist, the school psychologist, the counseling and guidance personnel, and ancillary personnel. Certainly, she should not expect to do all the varied things for which these kinds of personnel are responsible, but she can do much that reflects the essence of their possible contributions. Such personnel do not have exclusive rights to or knowledge of the concepts which are fundamental to their effective operation.

We start out with two contributive elements in the situation. First and most importantly, there is a teacher who already believes she has a pupil whom she regards as bright and whom she wants to help. The teacher for whom the following suggestions are intended is not the one who regards her class only as a class; she is committed to trying to individualize her "teaching" and probably believes also that a few of her pupils need special help because they do not seem to learn as easily as do most of the others in the class. Second, if she has read thus far in this book, she will have encountered facts, concepts, and general principles that are essential to the effective education of bright children and will have read how different kinds of school personnel should perform in the light of such information. At least general directional cues thus may have been picked up, and these can be amplified and adapted by following up relevant references which can be accessible through interlibrary loans.

Given the initial disposition to do something appropriate for the child and this general orientation, the teacher may want to check on the adequacy of her basic preparation for doing what she wants to do by noting the areas of preparation recommended in Table 8.1. Chances are that she will need refurbishment in the vital area of the nature of conceptualization. Borrowable books contributive to this area, to mention only some representative ones, range from Russell's (1956) readable book on children's thinking, to portions of Ausubel's (1968) educational psychology, to Piaget's (1971) on the development of children's intellectual processes, to Bru-

ner's (1973) on the psychoeducational process.

STUDYING THE CHILD. Assuming that our teacher has a pupil who seems to learn much more easily than do the other members of her class, she needs to know more precisely what the child's learning capability level is in order properly to adapt learning possibilities to the child. Ideally, of course, this would involve having the child psychoeducationally assessed by one adequately prepared for that task, but many teachers, especially in small towns or rural areas, do not have access to such specialized help. If the teacher, with, of course, the cooperation of the child's parents, cannot arrange for such assessment with a psychologist in a neighboring school district or community clinic, she may be able to have it made by a competent person in a reasonably near college or university.

Lacking these avenues of help, she justifiably can resort to testing the child herself by means of one or two good group tests of "intelligence." If necessary, help in this regard can be obtained by writing an appropriate staff member of her college or university for information about the tests and how to go about obtaining them. When she proceeds in the light of this advice, she must be as certain as she can be of at least two things: the group tests must be (1) good and (2) appropriate to her needs. (The use of two good tests would be desirable, and their results must be considered as reflecting at least a minimal picture of the child's capability.) It must be established by her observation of the child's test-taking behavior that he addressed himself seriously and cooperatively to the task. The type of teacher under consideration here is of above-average quality and can learn much regarding the manner of the child's intellectual functioning by noting the kinds of behavior manifested by the child in the test situation. This teacher may need to purchase a package of each test to be used (even plumbers and carpenters buy some of the tools they use), but she can use them also with other bright children whom she will discover, and may want even to use some of them in order better to understand some of her slower learning pupils. If the school does not engage in group testing of educational achievement, she will need also to provide for this. She would do well to assemble her findings on each child formally on a chart such as that shown in Figure 4.2 in order to sharpen her perception of the youngster in terms of the rapprochement between capability and achievement.

Whereas the consultant would be concerned with programmatic matters of locating and providing for gifted pupils in a school district, our teacher already has identified a youngster whom she believes to be at least above average, and her concern, as the teacher, is to discover or work out some added ways of helping him learn. To this end, her earlier professional preparation probably included exposure to the plethora of "methods" courses available, and her state and national educational journals tend to contain much "how to" material. Much uninvited professional advertising material professes to constitute or contribute to teaching method. In all this, she will encounter "gimmicks" galore, and she must recognize their values and limitations. As used here, the term "gimmick" denotes either some assemblage of materials, usually something other than those available in the customary educational armamentarium, or a combination of such materials with instructions regarding their recommended use. She must realize that they can have either or both of two values. By virtue of their being different from conventional materials they can have initial

interest or diversion stimulus value, sometimes as much to the teacher as to the pupils. Following the instructions for their use can involve the pupil for a period of time in one or more activities that well can have some educational value. Yet such gimmicks can have as much sustained intellectual nurturance value as mastering the manipulation of a Hoola Hoop or of a baton. However, in one way or other and to varying extents, any gimmick can be used by a knowledgeable teacher to institute or contribute to the kind of learning so important to the gifted in concept development. But the teacher must know what that concept development is like and must be able to perceive and use the gimmick to that end. The teacher is focal in the activity, and her comprehension of the nature of concept development is fundamental.

ENRICHMENT AND ACCELERATION. If the teacher in the small school district finds a more promising youngster in her class or school, she can do much to provide, or cause to be provided, educational experiences that can be enriching and/or accelerative in nature. She can capitalize upon, or cause to be introduced, the services of a traveling library or of interlibrary loans. As mentioned earlier, a wide variety of kits are available in, for instance, the areas of science, mathematics (statistics, computer construction and use), music, and art. Some correspondence courses can be used in the upper elementary level grades, and a larger number of them can be used at the secondary level. Given adequate sentience to surrounding phenomena and an understanding of the nature of conceptualization, the opportunities for the nurturance of concept development are as great in rural areas as in urban areas.

The costs of such "extras" usually is a problem, yet it has been a matter of continuing admiration that so many teachers in economically limited school situations have been able, one way or other, to find ways to have such things provided by means of fund-raising class or school activities, getting individual parents or other adults interested in providing some facilitative learning materials or experiences, involving the PTA in raising funds (not all the money so raised has to be spent on a projector, an encyclopedia, or a bicycle stand), and persuading educational administrators to purchase kits for the school library or pay for extension courses as legitimate instructional expenses.

ANTICIPATING THE FUTURE. Such a teacher will, almost inescapably, become involved with helping this kind of child think ahead about his future academic and occupational goals. She may need to bring into the picture early the high school counselor or guidance person. If there is none, she will—whether she is an elementary level or secondary level teacher—need to have available, or be able to get access to, information on suitable colleges and universities. In this regard she will need to have, or have access to, the most recent governmental, professional, or commercial compilation of information on scholarships and other higher education financial aid. She very well may need to make sure that her bright youngster becomes known to the principal or other administrator in order that he or she can participate in national scholarship contests.

In the cases of physically disabled bright youngsters, the teacher can help both the children and their parents set meaningful socially productive goals that can result in at least partial economic adequacy as well as some sense of self-fulfillment. Had the teachers of that quite bright blind girl been properly concerned and informed and so directed their efforts, even to the point of bring-

ing, or having her parents bring, the girl to the attention of competent vocational rehabilitation personnel, she could have undertaken at least paraprofessional training and become self-supporting (and self-respecting) rather than just a marginal broom-maker.

THE HOME BACKGROUND. In order adequately to understand her bright youngsters, the teacher will need also to know about their economic backgrounds, the emotional climate of their homes, and the value systems under which the children are growing up. The lack of motivation and attitudes of despair and seeming total resignation in the homes of disadvantaged rural children must be ascertained and dealt with, or in some way compensated for. Possibilities along this line are shown by some of the results of the "higher horizons" efforts which involved working with both pupils and their parents who were disadvantaged (Schreiber, 1962).

OTHER SOURCES OF HELP. The school librarian can be extremely helpful to both pupils and teachers by making available, or even helping find, related reading materials, or possibly ordering added materials. But many elementary schools have neither libraries nor librarians. Some interested teachers develop modest libraries in their classrooms, often getting help from their parent-teacher organizations to build up general reference materials and/or selected materials in specified subject-matter areas. Such teachers tend also to know pretty well about the availability of appropriate reading materials in the state or nearby local library or bookmobile. While interest and willingness of this sort are of particular value in the cases of bright youngsters—whether rural or urban—there is considerable potential value for many of the other children.

Although most teachers for whom this portion is intended are not likely to be in states which have funds which can be used for the gifted—especially those not in special classes or in some kind of formal program—there is no significant reason why they should not seek such funds or other assistance from their state departments of education in their attempts to provide better for their promising pupils. Strategically, of course, such an approach should proceed through the proper local administrative authorities. In the absence of local willingness to seek such assistance, "innocent" inquiries or desperate appeals directly to the proper person at the state level could serve as drops of water on the granite. The expression of such needs tends to have a better chance of being effective if it is channeled through a state organization, such as the state chapter of The Association for the Gifted, or through some outstanding and highly influential person in the state's educational structure. The needs of individual teachers such as have been discussed here are grossly inadequately recognized and badly need to be met.

The teaching profession is not without members who take justifiable pride in having helped promising youngsters attain goals appropriate to their superior potentials. The teacher cannot do everything for all her bright children all the time, but he or she can do some things for some of the gifted children some of the time. The teacher gains a significant sense of self-fulfillment in going such "extra miles." More importantly, it is often true that when teachers do well things such as these, they can thus be influential in causing their school administrative superiors to recognize the merits of such activities and thereby become more disposed to provide such services as integral parts of the regular school program.

The teacher
in a centralized program

In contrast to the teacher striving, in a kind of educational isolation, to do something more appropriate for her particularly capable pupil(s), such a teacher working in some type of larger educational structure has better opportunities. Generally, under such an arrangement, certain services are provided within the larger instructional and administrative unit which can help her be more effective. The kinds of services thus provided vary, of course, with the stated purposes of such coordinated efforts and, most importantly, with the philosophy which sets the stage for their actions.

With the increasing tendency of schools to merge, for intracounty and multicounty units of school administration to come into being, structures are being created which more and more warrant the incorporating of regular staff members who will provide these kinds of necessary assists to the educational process. It is interesting to all and distressing to some that special educational personnel, for instance, have been added so relatively easily to such school units to augment the efforts for the mentally retarded, whereas the gifted, who constitute an equally large portion of the total school population, do not have their needs equally seriously considered and met.

Two kinds of merging have occurred. First, two or more school districts have formed "cooperatives" which render for the districts involved educational services of a particular kind, such as the educating of the handicapped. Such cooperating districts tend to maintain their respective basic administrative autonomy but are able, by means of such cooperative effort, to provide services (classes, specialized instruction, psychological services, supervision, and others) which they, individually, had not found or re-garded as feasible. For our kind of teacher there are two possible pluses in such an arrangement: the possible avail-ability of the services of psychologists (hopefully competent), and the poten-tiality of access to a wider variety of educational milieus within which to operate. Second, larger administrative units are being mandated, usually in terms of larger-size minimal pupil popu-lation areas. Thus a school district with, say, 75 pupils becomes an integral part of a larger one of, say, 10,000 pupils.

While the oft-criticized one-room school may have had unusual possibili-ties for intuitively based individualized instruction and personal attention, the financial base upon which it was oper-ated was such that only meager facilities could be provided. (Many school districts in the country have more members on their school boards than there are pupils in their schools.) The consolidated dis-trict, by having a larger financial base and a less topheavy administrative load-ing, is regarded as capable of providing a larger variety of educational offerings for groups of similar pupils. The con-solidation of districts could entail a greater likelihood of sensitivity to educa-tional problems and needs and thus a greater likelihood for the provision of expanded kinds and amounts of teacher advisory and technical assistance. There would also be the possibility for greater pupil fluidity within the larger district, thus enabling one or more pupils in one part of the expanded district to take advantage of more suitable facili-ties elsewhere in the district, assuming that the necessarily expanded transpor-tation facilities in the new district could be made available for such a purpose. The extent to which such educational deployment would be utilized could de-pend, of course, upon the educational philosophy operational within the dis-trict.

In the light of this general condition, the chances of this kind of teacher's get-ting assistance in identifying and work-ing out suitable educational adjustments for her gifted youngsters would be in-creased. A consolidated district having from five to ten thousand pupils would be at least theoretically able to provide for use throughout the district the dif-ferent kinds of supportive personnel we have discussed. Psychological and super-visory services tend early to be provided, counseling and guidance functions tend soon to be systematically provided for, and the concept of library needs tends to be broadened. In fact, school con-solidations of such size well could de-velop a program for the gifted pretty much as has been discussed, at least so far as providing consultants for the gifted, although the fact of geographic spread in some districts well might call for adaptations of such a program.

However, even though cooperatives and consolidated school districts are emerging on the educational scene, there are gifted youngsters in many school settings in which joint efforts such as we have described are not present. The gifted in such limited settings are as much disadvantaged youngsters as are those gifted among ethnically different and economically limited groups. For state programs for the gifted to be truly balanced and properly encompassing, they must provide forthrightly for the gifted youngsters who are in the less populous and educationally limited areas.

COMPENSATORY EDUCATIONAL EFFORTS

Motivation to provide more adequately for the gifted has been both sporadic and sparse. Terman's early work on and in the interests of the gifted caused a wave of related efforts which soon subsided into a ripple of consideration, although a few of his co-workers, while continuing to be committed, unfortunately had relatively little sustained impact upon public school operations. The shock of Sputnik resulted in analyses of our high-level manpower needs and helped provide a social climate in which The Association for the Gifted and The National Association for Gifted Children emerged. There followed an arousal of some state and federal interest, which resulted in some spotty funding of activities regarded as helpful to the gifted, and a reaffirmation of concern at the national level for the gifted (Marland, 1971). Ephemeral interests and professional commitment tend to follow federal and state funding of research and educational tinkering. Some, who were temporary "authorities" on brain-injured children, became equally quickly "authorities" on the gifted, when that was where the money was; and some of those later became equally publicized "authorities" in the more recently specified areas of the emotionally disturbed and of the learning disabled. Nationally, the number of persons who are knowledgeable regarding the gifted and who have remained committed over the years to their interests is disappointingly small.

In this section we shall consider kinds of representative efforts in the interests of gifted school children which, in effect, have been directed toward the stimulation of and compensation for local school programs. By special arrangement, some of these have been carried out as temporary parts of the regular public school programs, largely in the hope that they would come thereafter to be integral components in those programs. Some have been supplementary or ancillary to the regular school programs. And some have taken place because local school systems were either unwilling or unable to take steps to provide more meaningfully for the gifted.

State Programs

Excluded from consideration here are those legislative changes made at the state level which authorized or established components within departments of instruction charged with responsibility in the area of the gifted—many of which have turned out to be only paper gestures.[1] Nor shall we consider state department regulation changes which provided for early entrance into school and/or for the mounting of local programs for the gifted, often without adequate funding of them. Rather, we shall consider certain state programs which provided for the funding of state-motivated but locally implemented instructional efforts that were to be regarded as demonstrational or "experimental" in nature. Some of these programs provided also for funding of necessary specialized personnel and of scholarships—more often than not in higher education.

California Project Talent

Two state programs have resulted in considerable contribution to the recent literature on the gifted. Mention already has been made of them. While the California Project Talent program basically was funded by the U.S. Office of Education with added financial support being

[1] Pennsylvania appears to have pioneered in wording its school laws to provide for the inclusion of the gifted. Originally, its special education legal provision was for only the "handicapped." In the early 1940s the wording was changed to "exceptional," this term having been legally defined as including the mentally superior—for whom special classes already were in operation. Subsequently, under pressures by those specially interested in the mentally retarded and emotionally disturbed, the wording "regressed"; then, in 1961, it was again worded in terms of "exceptional," and it was announced that Pennsylvania was able legally to provide for the education of the gifted as a part of its special education program (Pennsylvania Department of Public Instruction Proceedings, 1963).

supplied by the cooperating school districts, its design and implementation were the responsibilities of the California State Department of Education. It was specifically characterized as a "demonstration of differential programming in enrichment, acceleration, counseling and special classes for gifted pupils in grades 1–9." The fact that the California program was specified to apply from the first grade up is noteworthy, as contrasted with the Illinois program, which showed less sensitivity to the lower grade levels. The California program was under the direction of Plowman, helped significantly by Martinson (1961), who directed the California State Study of needs, existing programs, and costs. The districts which cooperated in the project were identified in terms of geography (three north, three south) and their interest in and ability to be involved in the designated facets of the study. Plowman (1969) summarized the undertaking as follows:

> California Project Talent, as coordinated with the California Mentally Gifted Minor Program, promoted the following practical results: (a) pupil enrollment in the mentally gifted minor programs expanded from approximately 38,000 in 1962 to approximately 90,000 in 1966; (b) as a result of the visitations to Project Talent demonstration centers, the program prototypes that were developed have influenced the educational programs in well over half of the districts in California offering mentally gifted minor programs and in a number of school districts in other states; (c) all of the school districts in California have developed and submitted to the State Department of Education acceptable "written plans" describing their mentally gifted minor programs; the vast majority of these written plans demonstrate clear evidence of the incorporation of theoretical models for curriculum developments advocated by the CPT demonstration centers; and (d) teacher, student, parent, and administrative evaluations of the four program pro-

totypes and the summer workshops have resulted in unequivocal commendations for the goals and accomplishments of these programs (p. 88).

The written plans were submitted and generally reflected an initial sensitivity to what was needed, but some 80 percent of them were returned to the local districts with suggestions for further refinement.

The Illinois Program

The Illinois State program was an interesting contrast to that of California. In 1959 a Special Study Project for Gifted Children was initiated in the state Department of Public Instruction. By means of $300,000 appropriated over a four-year period by the state for that purpose, 44 study projects were completed by school districts and universities, the findings were collated, and the proposal for the Illinois Plan for Gifted Children was drawn up. By 1963 a biennial appropriation of $6.75 million was provided to implement it. Of this total, $4.9 million was allocated for support to local school districts for the provision of special services, $1.2 million was designated for the establishment of demonstration centers, $550,000 was specified for research on curriculum and evaluation, $750,000 was earmarked for summer workshops, in-service training programs, and year-round fellowships and scholarships for improving professional competence, and the balance was used for administrative costs. It was estimated at that time that the contributions of the participating local school districts would amount to some five million dollars.

The commitment of the State of Illinois to providing special funds for educational programs for the gifted is reflected in the amounts of money appropriated specifically for that purpose. Subsequent biennial and annual budget reports reflect a surprisingly sustained commitment. One million dollars more was appropriated for the 1965–67 biennium. Owing to changing accounting and reporting practices and shifting state-level personnel, precise statements of subsequent appropriations and expenditures are hard to come by. However, keeping in mind the fact that Illinois had the fifth largest elementary school enrollment in the nation in 1965, Table 11.2 gives rough indications of the amounts appropriated by the legislature to help local school districts provide more adequate educational programs for their gifted children.

Thus, from 1963 through 1974 the State of Illinois appropriated nearly $40,-000,000 in the educational interests of the gifted children in its public schools. Under continued financing in 1973, for instance, were 20 "demonstration centers," nine of them in Cook County, which has some 49 percent of the state population. Ten of the centers were in communities with total populations of 28,000 or less—five of these in Cook County. Two were in communities having populations of 10,000 or less. (Personal communication from Sidney J. Slyman of the Illinois Department of Public Instruction, April 12, 1973.)

The contrast between the California and Illinois efforts is interesting. The California program was conceived in terms of an overall conceptual structure in light of which the participating school districts implemented identifiable components. Throughout its operation, there was a discernible, pervading philosophical and theoretical commitment in terms of which the local districts would seek to contribute specified kinds of outcomes. In Illinois, however, the interests and predelications of the local districts themselves were the primary determinants of what was to be explored or determined. As a result of this, for instance, it was only considerably after the inauguration of the program that even limited commitments involving lower elementary level pupils became a part of the program.

Program backers

The purpose of the funding of special programs by federal or state agencies can be regarded in two lights: as a means of helping local districts defray costs of ongoing programs that make above-average financial demands on the districts, or as a means of inducing local districts to introduce new programs. Many administrators regard the provision of such extra monies just as a way of helping local public school districts to defray the extra and relatively heavier costs of those types of services and materials which already are regarded by local school officials as needed or appropriate. The current supplemental funding of basic educational programs is a case in point.

However, in large part, many extensions of what originally was regarded as adequate basic educational programs have come about because certain extra-school interest groups believed that certain deficiencies existed in the current educational programs. Such groups took actions which served to make many educators aware of needs that either were

Table 11.2 Illinois annual appropriations for the gifted in public school programs.

Fiscal year	Amount
1968	$3,842,000
1969	3,133,000
1970	3,550,000
1971	3,550,000
1972	4,000,000
1973	4,400,000
1974	4,000,000

Source: Illinois state budget reports.

being ignored or that seemed unmeetable. Besides serving this sensitizing function, such groups tended to be influential in causing special funds to be made available in order that at least a start could be made in meeting the newly identified needs. Such has been the case with respect to areas such as vocational education, driver's education, and special education.

For instance, the impact of special interest groups generally was primarily instrumental in making educational administrators aware that different kinds of disabled children existed and had legitimate educational needs which were not being met. At the same time, such interest groups influenced state legislatures (or other governmental bodies) to provide extra funds which could assist the local schools in providing the desired kinds of education. Often, the extra financial assistance which was thus provided the local districts only partly defrayed the extra costs, but such funds did constitute an extra impetus to the provision of local educational facilities—often sufficient to cause such newly introduced services to become integral parts of the ongoing local programs. In a sense, while such extra funding in part sensitized local school officials to needs of which they may have been unaware, they, perhaps more importantly, served a "pump priming" function, helping get local schools started in doing something the value of which they would come increasingly to recognize and for which the local schools could assume increasing financial responsibility. Historically, this kind of development has been true as regards the visually impaired, the acoustically impaired, the speech impaired, the "crippled," the educable mentally retarded, the trainable, and more recently the emotionally maladjusted and disturbed, the gifted, the educationally handicapped, and the "learning disabled."

Generally, federal and state funding of public school programs for the gifted has been intended to contribute to at least some combination of the following objectives:

1. To provide or increase a sensitization to particular problems or needs
2. To provide demonstrations of approaches to meet those needs
3. To encourage experimental evaluations of such approaches
4. To facilitate the development of local programs which incorporate such practices or approaches which have been found to be contributive to or productive of the outcomes which initially were deemed important

(Not included in this list but generally included in statements of intent for such fundings are objectives relevant to the initial preparation of teachers, in-service "training" of teachers and supervisors, and the like.) Especially as regards the fourth objective stated above, there is the implicit if not explicit intent, or desire, to help get started certain practices or programs which the local schools will continue after the "pump priming" funds cease to be available.

Program effectiveness

In an attempt to get some specific information regarding the extent to which the Illinois program, for instance, had been effective under such substantial funding, the following questions were asked of the Department of Public Instruction:

1. How many experimental/demonstration programs have been started as a result of the financial/consultative nurturance by the state?
2. How many local programs that were initiated on an experimental/demonstration basis continued after special funding/consultation was eliminated or substantially reduced?

3. How many special programs
   a. involved specifically identified grade levels (and what were those grade levels)?
   b. were addressed, rather, to subject-matter or activity areas—social studies, mathematics, science, literature, creativity, etc. as vs. fourth-grade, sixth-grade, etc. designations?
   c. were focused upon or addressed to major educational strategies or practices which would (should) permeate an entire school system, such as early admission, acceleration, enrichment, individually prescribed instruction, school library development and usage, and the like?

However, such information could not be supplied (Slyman, *op. cit.*).

One can speculate that gifted children benefited to some degree from the nearly 40-million-dollar Illinois investment. Some teachers probably either were given the opportunity to do more of what they wanted to do for their gifted youngsters or were helped to learn some things that would facilitate learning by their bright pupils. And some supervisory and administrative personnel were given the opportunity to inaugurate, or learn about, some educational practices appropriate to the gifted. Owing to the persisting problem of local personnel turnover, some educational professionals who had had the opportunity to learn about and try provisions appropriate to the education of the gifted could carry to their new educational employment locales at least a heightened sensitivity to and optimism about the gifted. But the absence of programmatic research data suggests a limited sense of accountability. Perhaps even more significantly, the fostering of practices rather than the development of sound programs had a limiting value in soundly meeting the educational needs of the gifted.

In spite of the professed lack of specific information regarding the strategic impact of the Illinois program on the gifted children in the public schools, the program was interesting in several respects. It certainly was one of the more highly publicized, financially successful programs, its director, David M. Jackson, becoming an international consultant on state and national programs for the gifted and being primarily responsible for the establishment of the National/State Leadership Training Institutes on the Gifted and the Talented. House, Kerins, and Steele (1970) pointed out:

In its final form the Illinois Program consisted of five complementary approaches to improving the local programs for the gifted: (1) partial reimbursement to local schools for the extra costs of operating programs for the gifted; (2) establishment of approximately twenty regional demonstration centers to provide operating models of various approaches to the education of gifted children; (3) state support of experimental projects to advance knowledge of education for the gifted; (4) establishment of a small state staff to coordinate the entire program and to render consultant service; (5) the creation of several training programs, including summer institutes and in-service workshops, to increase the number of specially trained personnel who could work in the gifted programs (p. 3).

The spinoff from the experimental facet of the program was extensive both in formally published and informally released reports of research. Gallagher (1966) discussed specifically the findings of seven such Illinois studies and reported 22 funded but uncompleted research projects. In harmony with the permissive policy of the Illinois program, these studies were individually prompted rather than planned parts of a larger research design.

As House, Kerins, and Steele pointed out, the demonstration centers were the focus of the Illinois Plan, intended to serve "as the main instruments of change." Colton (1968) stated the objectives of this aspect of the program:

> The Illinois Plan includes demonstration centers which are intended: first, to provide for Illinois educators and other citizens, convincing and readily available demonstrations in operating situations of a number of approaches to the education of gifted children; and second, to help schools which are similar in characteristics or geographically near to develop their own programs.

Two things happened. First, while it was intended that the demonstration centers would put themselves out of business after a few years by disseminating their programs, their directors developed into a cohesive and powerful group nearly equal in policy determination with the state staff and Advisory Council. Second, an extensive study of the extent to which the centers had been contributive to helping or influencing other schools to introduce the practices being demonstrated revealed that, while the centers attracted 6000 visitors in 1968–69 (including 3500 teachers and administrators), of whom 79 percent professed attitude changes from neutral to positive, the 29 percent who did try something new which they had observed in the demonstration centers were of a population already committed to change. In view of the investment in this aspect of the total program, the conclusions of the evaluation of the demonstration center approach were:

1. "Only about 2 percent of the target reimbursement centers had adopted a demonstration program *in toto*—the original goal of the centers."
2. "At best, districts seldom adopted new programs from demonstration centers, although some attempted to."
3. "When the quality of gifted programs in these districts was related to other variables, there was no relationship between quality of program and visits to the dem-

onstration centers or visits from demonstration personnel."
4. "Changes directly attributable to the demonstration centers tended to be not very far-reaching" (House, Kerins, and Steele, 1970, pp. 27–28).

A shift, therefore, was recommended from the operation of demonstration centers to the establishment of Area Service Centers.

Three factors merit consideration as we think of operations such as the Illinois and California programs. First, and paramount: only to the extent that local school district personnel incorporate in their philosophy of education a full sensitivity to the special needs of the gifted is the establishment and operation of demonstration centers, or even of "service centers," likely to be of value. Both state departments had statements of a philosophy of educating gifted children, although they differed discernibly. Whatever the philosophy professes, it must be reflected in the inauguration and operation of local district programs.

Second (and particularly apparent in connection with the Illinois program), research in such matters as evaluating the impact of the demonstration centers leads to the development of procedures and devices that can be used in connection with other educational efforts. Illustrative was the instrument developed for the purpose of evaluating classroom behavior (Steele, House, and Kerins, 1971). Their 25-item Class Activities Questionnaire purports to reflect lower thought processes (memory, translation, interpretation), higher thought processes (application, analysis, synthesis, evaluation), classroom focus (discussion, test/grade stress, lecture), and classroom climate (enthusiasm, independence, divergence, humor, teacher talk, homework). (Comparisons of behavior in average and gifted classes yielded results in the directions one would expect.)

The third condition, by no means limited to these programs, has two aspects. On the one hand, as is often true of research in education, much was done with a seemingly studied unawareness of the availability of relevant approaches and procedures of others. That the Illinois researchers well might prefer to evaluate aspects of their program by means other than, say, Renzulli's Diagnostic and Evaluation Scales of Differential Education for the Gifted (1968), could be understood if the existence of such scales had been recognized and logically rejected as inappropriate, since researchers tend either to want to validate their own approaches against others known to exist or just prefer to do things in their own ways. This is not meant to imply that the Illinois evaluation of the demonstration centers approach was invalid. But when research is either highly idiosyncratic or provincial, communication and conceptualization are made difficult, if not impossible. On the other hand, much of this research on the gifted has been tantamount to the rediscovery of the wheel, or it seems to have emanated from Gallagher's (1966) Department of Redundant Research.

The planning, funding, and execution of only two state programs for the education of the gifted have been rather briefly described. The Illinois program is noteworthy because it was so heavily state-financed, with, of course, certain attendant local school financial involvement. The California program, while planned at the state level, initially involved federal funding which later was assumed by the state, plus the related local financing.

Federal Provisions

Federal funding of efforts in the interests of the gifted, prompted by patterns of pressure quite comparable to those which had operated within the state, consisted of grant funds for the purpose of enabling state departments of education, universities, and colleges to pursue lines of endeavor which such local agencies had identified and which were regarded by the U.S. Office of Education as appropriate within the wording of the law which made money available to it for that purpose. Thus state departments of education obtained funds which were used in conceptually integrated programs executed by the state, as was the case in California, or which were then allocated to universities and/or local school districts which carried out projects deemed by them to be relevant to the state's commitment, as largely was the case in Illinois. Also, federal funds were granted directly to universities and colleges for the implementation of programs involving research on the gifted and efforts to improve the quality of public school education of the gifted by developing or adapting curricula more suited to the unique needs of the gifted. There were, also, two other major thrusts—the funding of efforts to educate, de novo, teachers and others who later would work in the interests of the gifted and the funding of institutes intended to improve the competencies of teachers already on the job, either to continue in their work with the gifted or to prepare to undertake such work.

A major departure from this pattern was the establishment, by means of funds administered by the U.S. Office of Education, of the National/State Leadership Training Institute on the Gifted and the Talented (N/S-LTI-G/T). This came about as a result of a recommendation in the USOE Commissioner's Report (Marland, 1971) that national leadership training institutes be held "to upgrade supervisory personnel and program planning for the gifted at the state level." According to an undated release describing the endeavor (personal communication, Irving S. Sato, Project Director,

N/S-LTI-G/T, October 13, 1972), the federal funds for this undertaking were allocated to the Office of the Superintendent of Public Instruction of the State of Illinois, and the project headquarters (financially administered by the Office of the Superintendent of Public Instruction of Ventura County) was established in Los Angeles. "As a major means of accomplishing [the objectives of the Institute], three multiweek Leadership Training Institutes (LTI) will be held during three successive summers beginning in FY 1974. Each LTI will train at least three persons from each of the 10–16 participating states each summer." The first such LTI was held in the summer of 1973.

A Kentucky Effort

In 1966, the Kentucky legislature authorized the establishment and operation of the Lincoln School, a residential high school "for the education of the exceptionally talented but culturally and economically deprived children of the Commonwealth of Kentucky" (Gold, 1970). Officially sponsored by Governor Breathitt, it was funded by the state and fiscally administered by the University of Kentucky. With its candidates expected to come from highly divergent and generally limited backgrounds, conventional criteria of intellectual giftedness and talent were regarded as of dubious merit. While achievement and learning capacity were tested, primary emphasis in selection was placed upon teacher nominations in terms of pupil promise and need. In the first year of the school's operation, 1967, there were 62 pupils. The second year's enrollment of 98 was made up of 51 percent male, 42 percent blacks, and 60 percent urban pupils; of these, 99 percent expressed the desire to attain one of the school's major aims—college entrance. The school had to close after the third year because the legisla-

ture failed to fund its operation. During the third year of operation, nearly half of the graduating seniors had received scholarship and other financial assistance ranging from $750 to $4000 per year, by means of which they were enabled at least to start their college work in a variety of institutions. Contributive, at least in part, to the demise of this promising educational endeavor was the fact that "the state's educational community maintained an almost universal aloofness" (Gold, 1970).

Emphasis on Teacher Learning

The mounting of special programs and projects directly addressed to the improvement of the education of the gifted consistently has been concerned with two facets of the problem—the specific and direct employment of procedures which are believed to promise or assure improved learning by the gifted and the capitalization upon such efforts as a means of improving teacher competencies and supervisory sensitivities. While, generally, both of these interests have been involved, the relative emphasis upon the one or the other has varied either among the programs and projects and/or over time within any one of them. When the thrust of any such special effort is the advancement of learning by the gifted who are involved, those children and their teachers very well may be helped. However, better educational strategy has been widely believed to necessitate the inclusion—by visitation, observation, or other secondary involvement of demonstration sites—of educational personnel other than those working directly with the children in whose particular interests the projects may have been initiated. The nature and extent of such perspective was reflected, for instance, in Plowman's allusion to the visitations and their believed contribution to practice in the school districts not directly involved in Project Talent. Such "spread" is the aspiration of most mounters of programs and projects. Whether the Illinois finding of the low yield of visitation at demonstration centers is generalizable or unique to the operation of the program must be considered.

It may help if such special efforts are regarded in terms of the following structure. In the first place, there are special efforts which are made integral parts of the ongoing public school operation. Such is clearly illustrated by the Bronx High School of Science, the California project, and the Illinois program. Second, there are efforts that are formally related to but are discernibly elaborative of the regular public school educational program. Such would be illustrated by the Hunter School program and the Lincoln School attempt. And then there are those special efforts which are clearly adjunctive to the regular public school program. Illustrative of this category are, of course, the private schools established specifically for the gifted, and the special summer science and mathematics institutes funded by the National Science Foundation and usually administered by colleges and universities. Different foundations also have funded locally run programs and projects.

The Governor's School in North Carolina

Interestingly illustrative of efforts of the last kind is the Governor's School of North Carolina. Initiated in the office of Governor Sanford, and fiscally administered by the office of the state superintendent of public instruction, this undertaking initially was funded, during the years 1963, 1964, and 1965, by a substantial grant from the Carnegie Foundation of New York and other grants from business and foundation leaders in Winston-Salem, North Carolina. Financial

responsibility for the school then was assumed by the state department of public instruction, and the school has been part of North Carolina's program for the gifted at least through the summer of 1975. No federal monies have been used for the school.

Operating on the campus of Salem College, the eight-week summer program was intended for some 400 boys and girls from rising junior and senior high school classes who were selected on the basis of superior ability in some academic area or a high degree of talent in some area—art, dance, drama, or music. State-level screening and audition teams selected participants from local, quota-determined nominees. Tuition, room, board, instructional supplies, and books were provided; only travel and personal costs were defrayed by the pupils. In 1973 there were 77 nonwhite pupils in the group.

The dual aspiration to be of help not only to the pupils involved but also to teachers of the gifted is reflected in the statement of objectives for the Governor's School (undated promotional leaflet):

1. "To provide for selected students distinctive and properly functional educational experiences that relate to their promising talents, hoping thereby to obtain both increased self-realization for the individuals, and gain for society through the fruits of their distinctive labor."

2. "To search for and establish in this unrestricted setting curriculum substance and instructional procedures which will provide a training ground for prospective teachers of the gifted, and stimulate local school personnel to provide more adequately for these young people in the general school program."

Formal attainment of units of credit was not intended, although the local school districts of the pupils attending the school could so credit their participants.

Nor was conventional public school acceleration in the areas of study intended, although performances in the academic areas were describable in terms of measures on standardized achievement tests.

The selection of participants in terms of either superior ability in some academic area or high degree of talent in one of the arts clearly reflected the intent of the school to provide a balance of opportunities. The school was committed to provide three main areas of learning activity, as described by Dr. H. Michael Lewis, the school's coordinator of curriculum (1970):

> *Area I: Special Aptitude Development.* This is the Area where lies the pupil's special talent or giftedness, on the basis of which he or she was chosen to attend the Governor's School: Dance, Drama English, French, Mathematics, Music (choral, instrumental), Natural Science, Painting, Social Science.
>
> About two-thirds of a pupil's class time is devoted to Area I. Teaching materials used in this area are chosen with a view to acquainting pupils with the latest developments in the field of the specialty, and pupils are encouraged to anticipate and to speculate concerning possible solutions of problems and developments likely to arise in their field of specialty in the future.
>
> *Area II: General Conceptual Development.* In this Area the pupil is expected to expand interests and knowledge beyond his own concentrated specialty to include the whole spectrum of advancing knowledge. Here are emphasized integrative principles of knowledge, by which narrow specialties are transcended and seen as incomplete parts of a larger whole. A course in the "logic of the sciences and the humanities" forms the nucleus of study in this Area, supplemented by selected readings from the *Great Books of the Western World* series.
>
> About one-sixth of the pupil's time at the GS is devoted to Area II. F. S. C. Northrop's *The Logic of the Sciences and the Humanities* (New York, 1947) was used

as a unifying text during the summer sessions of 1967 and 1968, and Dr. Northrop himself spent three days in July 1968 on the campus as lecturer and consultant.

> *Area III: Personal and Social Development.* Gifted persons and leaders, by definition, are outstanding, and, consequently, are many times looked upon as being eccentric. . . . If a person so dubbed does not understand the motives of such dubbing, or does not otherwise have psychological insight into the meaning of this social phenomenon, he may be caused, by pressure of fear of being rejected by his social peers, to suppress development of his giftedness. Much creativity and leadership is lost to society by reason of this vicious treatment of our creative and innovative talent.
>
> Through study of the psychological problems involved in being gifted, and by becoming acquainted, through reading the biographies of talented people of the past, with methods that others have used for solving such problems, gifted pupils are prepared to strengthen their personalities through the resulting insights, so as to free them for fullest development of their capacities (pp. 3–4, reprinted by permission of the Governor's School of North Carolina).

Special seminars, study groups, projects, displays, and dramatic, vocal, and orchestral performances were provided for. Not only were superior staff selected for all the areas, but outstanding specialists also were brought in to promote and evaluate performances in all areas. No evidence has been published regarding any effect the Governor's School may have had on public school provisions for the gifted.

Private Schools

In considering the total problem of educating the gifted, it is logical to recognize the role, or possible role, played by private schools. Yet, generally, private schools operated for only the gifted are an ephemeral phenomenon. While incidental in the description of G's education, in Appendix A, the conditions attending the establishment and operation of the private school which she attended probably were near-typical.

The reader might routinely expect to be able to find in the appendix a listing of private schools for the gifted. If such a list were to be compiled and if it were to be meaningful, there would have to be two kinds of assurance—that the schools would be of such quality that they merited serious consideration, and that they were, as of this reading, still in operation. The absence of adequate accreditation standards and a systematic procedure for applying them make the compiling of such a list an exercise in futility. Certain preparatory schools that have a long history of educational quality have had programs heavily geared to more capable pupils, but they have catered to more than the gifted and they have rendered educational service primarily to families in the upper income brackets.

Seven limiting factors

It is well to consider major factors which contribute both to the low prevalence of private schools only for the gifted and to the fact that, when attempts have been made to establish them, they have been so short-lived. At least seven kinds of factors are identifiable. Perhaps most significant has been the fact that attempts to establish such schools have tended to be based more on the perception of the special educational needs of certain specific children than on a conceptualization of the educational needs of the gifted in relation to society's needs. The parents of one or more gifted children have seen a need for their children and have sought to meet it, usually because of inadequate provisions for their youngsters in their local schools. Undoubtedly more parents recognize such needs than have the conviction that there ought to be such schools and/or the competence, time, energy, influence, and money needed to establish and maintain them.

Second, any attempt to establish such schools would occur in a social milieu in which there are bound to be at least two attitudes antagonistic to the idea: lay opinion is not generally supportive of such thinking because of an all-too-pervading fear of elitism, and even professional opinion would not be supportive, either because of the lack of a general conviction that such efforts would be either educationally or socially productive or because public school personnel would regard the undertaking both as educationally divisive and as likely to pull out of the regular school population certain of the pupils in whom educators long have taken pride. The contention would be voiced that the nongifted would thus be deprived of the opportunity to share their learning experiences with and benefit osmotically from the learning experiences of the gifted.

Third, in many states the local school districts are held accountable for all children of legal school attendance age within their jurisdiction. This means that children who are not attending the regular schools in the district must be attending other schools which are state-approved. This, in turn, would make necessary the state approval, or accreditation, of private schools for only the gifted. Generally, standards for such accreditation are lacking.

Fourth, and more obviously, a very real factor is the financing of such schools. Barring the availability of some major funded endowment, such schools would have to depend very heavily upon funds raised mainly through tuition—a factor that limits their accessibility so far as lower, or even medium, economic level groups are concerned—a condition manifestly unfair to the gifted among the economically disadvantaged. The economic factor tends to dispose toward the operation of such private schools at the elementary level, since educational provisions at this level are less expensive than at the secondary level. Even when private schools for the gifted operate effectively at the elementary level, there can be problems related to the pupils' transfer into public secondary schools when there are marked contrasts in the philosophy and methods between the two kinds of school settings.

It could be argued that the relatively low prevalence of gifted children among the total school-age population would mitigate against the establishment of private schools just for them. If prevalence were a major determining factor, we would need to recognize that, in terms of our definition of the gifted in terms of social need, some 6 to 8 percent of our general school population would be the population to be considered. This contrasts sharply with the 1 to 3 percent of school-age children who are disturbingly emotionally maladjusted, with some 3 percent who are seriously retarded in learning aptitude, with some 1 percent who require special consideration because of impaired orthopedic or sensory conditions, or with the three-tenths of 1 percent who have received considerable attention—the trainable—because of their severe impairment in learning aptitude. Private schools have existed, and do exist, for many of these kinds of children. Mere prevalence is not logically the crucial variable.

A sixth limiting factor is that society tends to react much more to the tangible than to the intangible, and to impairment rather than to adequacy or superiority of functioning. On the one hand, society has made certain attempts at providing educational and other compensatory facilities for the disabled and handicapped because their sporadically perceived needs have been apparent. In the case of the gifted, on the other hand, more of the gifted have been able to learn to accommodate themselves to their failure to attain self-realization and society seems to have been able to get by with the contributions of those few gifted who have managed—largely without formal help by society—to become at least nominally productive. In other words, the "crying need" of the gifted has not been as apparent as have the needs of the less fortunate.

Whether population mobility may be a major factor limiting the establishment or continued operation of private schools for only the gifted merits consideration. It would be interesting to ascertain the extent to which the parents of children in different learning aptitude categories, such as those with Binet IQs below 80, those between 80 and 120, and those above 120, change their residences. Both length of stay and magnitude of move would need to be considered. One might suspect that population mobility would be greater among the extremes of the normal distribution than among the central portion of the range. The brighter segment of the population probably both would be more likely to seek fields more suited to their capabilities and also would be affected by changing social needs which often call for redeployment of high potential. (This should not be regarded as identical to the kind of "intellectual erosion" reflected in the Lee-Newland study, 1966.) If such greater mobility were a fact, it could make increasingly difficult the establishment and continued operation of private schools for the gifted.

Private schools for the gifted do not appear to be a viable alternative in the effective education of the gifted. They are of a stop-gap, compensatory nature, born primarily of the failure of public school education to meet its full social responsibility. The much more stable, democratic, and potentially fruitful approach would be for the public schools to provide adequately for the education of the gifted as an integral part of their total educational responsibility and commitment.

SUMMARY

If effective education is highly contributive, if not necessary, both to the welfare of society and to the psychologically healthy self-realization of the individual and if these ultimate major objectives have a particular meaning as regards the gifted, serious consideration needs to be given to the social, psychological, and educational needs of the more than 500,-000 probable gifted youngsters in rural settings. It probably is a matter of convenience that major state programs mounted for the gifted have been so grossly addressed to the gifted in the larger population centers. In an era so concerned with equality of opportunity and with the disadvantaged, the rural gifted deserve more consideration than they have received. Whether these gifted are in scattered small districts or in larger consolidated school districts, very real educational adjustments can be made for them. The changing economics and technology impinging upon productive rural life call for very real social contributions by the rural gifted.

The implications of the kinds of activities essentially outside the pale of the regular school program merit consideration. That such efforts have been made, and others of like nature probably will be made, must be regarded as a plus, so far as the total social-psychological picture is concerned. That educational situations exist such that efforts of these sorts appear to be needed well can be regarded as at least a zero, if not a minus, so far as the education program in general is concerned. We can't get away from the facts that 57.5 percent of the

administrators in the U.S. schools canvassed in the School Staffing Survey of 1969–70 were shown as indicating that they had *no* gifted children and that, among those recognizing the existence of the gifted, at least a third or more received no special consideration. Further supportive of this impoverished picture was the fact that of the 27 school systems which were chosen from a national sample because of their model programs for children with exceptional learning needs only five included some kind of program for the gifted. Further sharpening the nature of the need is the fact that public schools, when they do provide something facilitative to learning by the gifted, tend to do so at the higher rather than at the lower grade levels.

The compensatory efforts which have been made outside the regular public school structure certainly have some residual social value in that they have enabled at least some few gifted children better to realize their capabilities and thus, presumably, to become more fruitful contributors to our society. But these, again, seem to be more biased toward the upper grade levels—as witness the various "prep" schools, the Lincoln School attempt, and even the Governor's School in North Carolina. But much more important than this condition is the fact that they came about because the public schools have so widely failed to regard providing adequately for the gifted as an integral part of their total educational function. The fundamental danger in regular public school educators' formally or informally recognizing the contributions of meritorious extrapublic school services and operations is that such may be encouraged to continue as separate facilities rather than constituting valid functions within the basic educational program.

However, the merits and limitations of any such extrapublic school provisions cannot be considered simplistically as all good versus all bad. Often extrapublic school educational or psychoeducational services are developed first outside the public school situation with a view to their later becoming regular school operations. The value of such peripheral services thus can come to be recognized and then be more easily incorporated within the regular school operation. Further, especially as regards certain small schools, they may provide valuable and necessary services which the small school districts are not financially capable of providing. Such has been the case with school psychological services, special clinical services, special programs for the markedly disabled, and the like. But even in such instances there is a major need for integration between any such extraschool services and the regular educational functioning of the school. The need for such integration has been more professed and admitted than met.

Evaluation of educational services provided the gifted outside the regular public school program must be made in terms of two fundamental criteria. Each assumes a probable impact of the extraschool effort upon the ongoing regular educational program. First, the extraschool endeavor will be valuable to the extent that it is conceptually conceived and implemented as contrasted with being only perceptually evolved. Conceptually conceived efforts are much more likely to be of strategic value, whereas perceptually based efforts are much more likely to be of only tactical value. The former provides for sound growth; the latter, more just for expansion; and these are by no means synonymous. The contrast pointed out between the California and Illinois state program is a case in point. The second criterion well could be regarded as subsumable under the first, but it calls for attention in its own right.

To the extent that the effort has a major preventive commitment, it will be basically contributive. There are two aspects to this. As legitimately important as it may be, effort at remedial education of the gifted is less fundamentally contributive. Also, efforts which are addressed solely or primarily to furthering the education and self-realization of those gifted youngsters who already have demonstrated their ability to withstand or benefit considerably from extant educational programs may have social and psychological value for such children but contribute nothing directly to the uncovering and nurturing of those young bright children who have not manifested their abilities to withstand or profit from conventional educational winters. As noteworthy and meritorious as the Governor's School of North Carolina has been, this would be a major shortcoming in it. As delectable as the various crumbs of special extrapublic school efforts may have been, the overall picture calls for regular, well-balanced public school provisions by means of which the needs of the gifted can be nurtured and the needs of society more fully met.

12

Research

This chapter is addressed chiefly to the consumer of the results of research. However, he who is planning research on the gifted would do well to give careful consideration to consumer criteria.

It is not the intent here to review research on the gifted, although a few studies will be used illustratively. Periodically, *The Review of Educational Research* includes issues summarizing research on exceptional children, in each of which there has appeared a chapter on the gifted.

RESEARCH APPROACH
TO THE GIFTED

Some could contend that research on the gifted and the need to educate them is not called for, because all children in society need to be "educated." The question as to whether society actually needs

the gifted might be raised by some whose primary concern is the "common man," especially in time of social quiescence, but times of heightened social concern (as, for instance, after the appearance of Sputnik) create at least a temporary awareness of the need for high-level personnel, especially in the technological and scientific areas.

Concern for the "proper" education of the gifted is an even more esoteric matter, since society has seemed to many to have muddled through pretty well under whatever educational practices have been in operation. Accountability for the adequate education of the gifted has in no way approached that of the teaching of typing or the coaching of football. In fact, the rising challenge of the 1960s and 70s of the adequacy or contributive value of all education has caused some to wonder if the schooling period isn't, after all, more a time for the unhampered maturing of individuals, with perhaps the provision of a nonnegative nurturance, rather than a period of pupils' and students' learning prescribed things at specified times.

The time was, and still is to a considerable extent, when the textbook was a compendium of "truth" in a presumed absolute sense. Even today, in certain parts of the world, the teacher is the only one who has a textbook: he reads from it, his pupils copy down what they hear and memorize it. This absolutistic, mass-level perception of the textbook is giving way, with more substantively oriented teachers, to a differentiated perception that reflects sensitivity to the fact that many "facts" are ephemeral, that "truths" often are relative, that at least certain values are functions of social conditions which themselves change, and that the views expressed by authors of textbooks are functions of their differing theoretical positions.

It is hoped that this text will be perceived in this latter sense. Some values have been posited—that self-realization is both psychologically and socially essential and that the gifted should be educated such that they can assume contributive roles in society. Some "truths," or at least near-truths, have been identified. But many statements in this book need research substantiation or disproof. It is hoped that the reader, neither lulled into an intellectual placidity not frustrated into blind attack, will seek out affirming or negating evidence regarding such matters. Those whose "teaching" has consisted of giving their pupils "the" answers may succumb to the belief that this book has given "the" answers. Yet, while what has been presented often has been stated quite affirmatively, much objective validation still is needed. (Some suggestions for inquiry have been interspersed throughout, and some provocations to this end appear in Chapter 14.) The fundamental tenet of the researcher

—that whatever exists is its own best argument for its not existing—can be tempered for the educator: the fact that some educational condition (content or method) has been created should serve as the stimulus to finding a better one. This admonition is addressed to the prompting of restless inquiry rather than to just itchy dissatisfaction or blind challenge.

Recent Studies, 1927–1965

From 1927 through 1965, slightly more than 500 formally published articles, chapters, and books reported in *Psychological Abstracts* had titles directly relatable to gifted children and the condition of giftedness. (Somewhat more than 600 others dealt clearly and primarily with creativity.) Ninety percent of these 500 or so references had publication dates subsequent to 1950. More than half appeared over the years 1959–65, 59 of them appearing in 1959 and 62 in 1962. An average of some six such publications per year appeared before Sputnik, as contrasted with slightly more than 40 per year for the period 1959–65. While data such as these must be regarded most critically, since a six-page article or a small study is counted as heavily as is a monograph or a book, they do reflect an early limited research concern for the gifted; and there has been a later, post-Sputnik, subsidence—20 per year even for 1963, 64, and 65.

It is interesting that, while Catherine Cox Miles wrote an outstanding summary of research on gifted children for Carmichael's *Manual of Child Psychology* and wrote an updating revision for his 1954 edition, the third edition of the manual (1970), compiled by Paul H. Mussen, contains no such chapter. Not included even in the subject index are references to the gifted or mentally superior, whereas mental retardation is accorded a full chapter. Only five research citations, out of several hundred in the various chapters which clearly deal with psychological concepts having major potential relevance to the gifted, carried in their titles specific reference to the gifted or to giftedness. On the other hand, the numerous specific citations which related to the mentally retarded, the disadvantaged, the deaf, and even the autistic reflect both the scope of sensitivity of the authors of the several chapters and the direction of social concern—a function of special-interest funding of research, which in turn reflects commitment of individuals or groups to the areas.

At first blush, this may suggest that the gifted are being given short shrift. In considering this state of affairs, it is necessary to recognize that research efforts regarding the gifted have been more of a technological and professional rather than of a scientific nature. The gifted were found to be physically superior to the nongifted, to learn many things earlier than do other children, to be no more maladjusted than the nongifted, to have important differences among themselves just as in other subpopulations, to become frustrated, often to underachieve, to tend to do well in society after school, to tend to be creative, to benefit or not to benefit from different educational treatments, and the like. All such things are well worth knowing, but they too often are just isolated bits or clusters of information. Too often they are unrelated to general principles which have scientific significance.

Stages
of Research Study

The scientific study of man, or of any subgroup such as the gifted, follows a discernible progression. First, molar man is studied, from one point of view or other. Then subgroups are studied as groups, as in the cases of the mentally retarded, the gifted, the autistic, the disadvantaged. Their characteristics are ascertained, at first in and of themselves. Later, and often far too slowly, the findings about the subgroups are perceived in the light of, or serve as a means to suggest, general psychological principles. The gifted, the retarded, the disadvantaged become frustrated and either withdraw or compensate by behaving aggressively, just as do all other members of the total group. They acquire attitudes according to the general principles of learning. From the mass stage of studying groups as groups, man progresses to the stage of learning certain things about the groups or the individuals who constitute them, and then to the stage, if he is lucky, of understanding the behavior of groups, and their members, in terms of general principles.

It well may be that we are moving into the third stage; hence there are fewer scientific studies of the gifted per se and more concern regarding the general principles which make their behavior more understandable and which can make more effective any action taken in their interests. In large part, after all, the gifted differ from the nongifted more in degree than in the kinds of behavior which they manifest.

To regard the bulk of the research on the gifted as falling in the second category is not to regard it disparagingly. While there have been many minor, pinpointed studies of the gifted, the following statement (Newland, 1957) provides a larger perspective of what has been accomplished—keeping in mind the fact that it appeared two decades ago:

> He who would compare systematically the research literature on the gifted with that on other kinds of exceptional children would come inescapably to some interesting conclusions. For no less than 35 years, the results of the largest single study of any type of exceptional children have been available for use in the identification

of the gifted, in delineating quite objectively their needs, and in suggesting kinds of educational adjustments for them (Terman *et al.*, 1925, 1926, 1930, 1947). The largest single follow-up study of any kind of exceptional children was done on bright children admitted prior to the conventional school-entering age, restudied in high school, and further studied at college entrance (Hobson, 1948). Major studies of the Cleveland major work class program have been made (Sumption, 1941), and a ten-year follow-up study has been made of a single special school program for the gifted (Hildreth, 1952). Major objective evaluations of educational and social outcomes of college acceleration programs over seven years have been published (Pressey, 1949). Three systematic statewide studies of educational mortality among high school potential college material were made nearly 20 years ago. Objective evidence on the educational retardation of the gifted has been adduced for over 35 years, and can be simply and easily checked by any school teacher or administrator who would but analyze his test data. While many more studies of other types of exceptional children and of programs for them have been made than there have been for the gifted, few, if any, of them have had the psychological breadth, geographic scope, time span, or social orientation which characterize the studies mentioned for the gifted. Surely, the extent and the nature which characterize the provisions for the gifted, and the information on the various possible provisions for the gifted are "on the record" for him who would but read (p. 3, reprinted by permission of the superintendent of schools, Cook County).

Miles (1954) had this to say about Terman's work:

The major study of the gifted, Terman's 50-year project, reached its halfway mark at midcentury. The "composite picture" which emerged from study over a 25-year period of some 1500 gifted children by Terman and his associates stands as a monument to intelligent planning and the devotion of an investigator to an important psychological and educational problem (p. 984).

In large part, the major essence of Terman's findings has been found and refound, but, with changes in the scientific and social milieu, sharper and broader research on the gifted has become possible. Guilford's development of his theory of the structure of intellect, for instance, gave rebirth and scientific justification of the educator's concern for creativity—something that our educational philosophers had urged since the beginning of the century. The improvement of measuring devices and the development of new ones, having added to a better potential psychological grounding of the testers and assessors, have helped us not only to obtain a more meaningful picture of the capabilities of the gifted but also better to seek out the gifted among the disadvantaged. A broadened social perspective of education-in-society has contributed to more concern for the disadvantaged, especially the gifted among them, and for the social relevance of the curriculum. Social psychology has emerged as an embryonic science, thus opening the way for sounder consideration of the social learning of the gifted and their roles in society. And education itself has new possibilities: a growing acceptance of earlier educational responsibility for children, the ungraded primary (and even ungraded schools), the improved quality and increased amount and variety of audiovisual facilities, programmed instruction, the use of individualized instruction, and meeting the valid and increasing demand for educational accountability. And each of these is researchable.

RESEARCH TECHNIQUE

Since this is written chiefly for the consumer of research findings, the details of research design will not be considered intensively as such; a course or a few books on research methodology would much better serve that purpose. Yet, one needs some general orientation on methodology in order better to understand and evaluate the findings of research. The fact that a report of a research study has been given some kind of formal publication exposure cannot be taken as evidence that the research was well done or well described or even warrants the author's generalizations or implications. It is to help the consumer develop and use a healthily critical rather than an impulsively rejecting attitude that the present discussion is written.

Studies vs. Experiments

It is well to distinguish between a "study" and an "experiment." Each has its values and limitations. A study is intended to ascertain the status or condition of something that exists or is presumed to exist. It can range in scope from just finding out simple things (such as the breakfast-eating practices of the children in a given first grade or the extent of national teacher training facilities for a given group) to the identification and description of major conditions. The meaning or implications of the findings of a study become more cogent when they are compared with the findings of a comparable study of another group—as for instance, learning that the average height of a large random sample of gifted ten-year-olds is greater than the average height of a comparable population of nongifted ten-year-olds.

Good studies can identify conditions but they cannot establish causes for those conditions. (Nor can experiments firmly establish causes, for that matter, as will be indicated later.) Studies can contribute to the conducting of experiments in either of two ways. Having identified some condition, they may thus arouse curiosity as to why the condition exists, and this may lead to the experimental exploration of the relationships between or among possible causes. Also, pilot studies can be made preparatory to the conducting of experiments—for the development, tryout, and refinement of procedures and devices which subsequently will be used in experiments, or even in miniature, exploratory-type experiments conducted to make clearer the variables to be studied in subsequent, more definitive experiments.

The tendency in much educational literature to call innovations "experiments" can be misleading. Experiments are conducted in order to sharpen the picture, as precisely as possible, regarding possible or probable causes of conditions. Actually, especially in the area of education, experiments do not establish causes. At best, they can show the closeness of relationships between or among variables or conditions. Finding or establishing this closeness of relationship does not constitute the establishment of causation. This is inferred from the experimental evidence. Finding that condition B varies as condition A is operative does not establish condition A as the cause of change in B. Correlation does not establish causal relation. If, for instance, children's learning is found to be better when a given teaching procedure is employed and not to be any better in the absence of that procedure, the difference in the pupils' behavior may be as attributable to the attitudes of the teachers and the pupils involved in the experiment or to some other unidentified and unmeasured variables as to the teaching procedure under study.

The essence of any experiment is control of the variable or variables under study. The whole experimental procedure must be so meticulously described that it can be exactly replicated. The variable or variables being considered must be precisely defined. The criterion, or standard against which the outcome is to be evaluated, must be clearly identified. Generally, there are one or more control or comparison groups which are directly comparable to the group(s) under study, the treatment or educational procedure being employed with the experimental group(s) but not with the control group(s). The variables under study are measured in both groups as precisely as possible, after-treatment comparisons are made between the results on the two kinds of groups, and the results are evaluated. There also are hybrid study-experiments in which the subjects studied act as their own "controls."

Many studies of and experiments on the gifted have been inadequate because of failure to meet one or more of the conditions thus far identified. Good experiments with the gifted are very difficult to execute. Historically, the idea of the experiment in social sciences has come from the physical sciences, where controls were relatively easily shielded from known or suspected possible extraneous influences, the situation being relatively experimentally "sterile." Conducting an experiment on gifted children in a given school or school district is quite a different matter. Especially without precautions to the contrary, teachers of experimental and control groups talk among themselves about what is going on, or the teachers of control classes observe something different going on in the experimental classes and may modify their procedures along similar lines. The talking of the youngsters involved can have a contaminating effect. And both teachers' and youngsters' knowing the kinds of outcomes expected, or under study, can affect the results. The necessary condition of experimental sterility in the physical sciences is most difficult even to approximate in education.

Only a very small percentage of the consumers of the results of research can be expected to comprehend adequately the more involved statistical procedures which are used to describe (and indirectly to imply the evaluation of) the quantitative yield of experiments. They can, however, with a modicum of common sense evaluate the findings in terms of the total study or experiment. For example, a study was conducted to ascertain whether a Colfax-type of plan for elementary level gifted pupils was beneficial to them. Statistically, the study yielded negative, or at least nonpositive, findings. However, when the children involved were transported from different schools to a school situation in which the Colfax-type approach was to be attempted, neither they nor their teachers were adequately informed as to the educational purpose of the manipulation— perhaps on the assumption that this was a kind of control. The fact that there was no feedback to the youngsters' regular classes from their special group experiences, itself an important component in the Colfax idea, contributed to the resulting psychoeducational alienation of the pupils participating in the study. No statistical analyses of the results of this study, no matter how "refined" they may have been, could compensate for the failure adequately to consider the contaminating variables that were involved. Good research is a tedious, demanding undertaking. Whether a study or an experiment is contemplated, one-third to one-half of the total task consists of properly identifying and stating the problem and deciding on the appropriate methodology.

Nature of Current Research

Considering the almost-incidental attention which the gifted have received, the rate of formal publication during the 1960s and 70s cannot be regarded as grossly disappointing. However, its nature generally has shifted from large studies, such as those by Terman, Oden,

Hobson, and Hildreth, to studies of lesser scope. The "bits and pieces" of research in this area have tended largely to come from studies done for master's and doctor's degrees, and these are necessarily more restricted. Factors in the current socioeducational scene tend to mitigate against monolithic or programmatic research concerned with the gifted —the manner and extent of the funding of such research, the failure of so many who would be capable of such research to manifest an encompassing, abiding, and intense commitment to it, and the reluctance of local and state level personnel to carry out undramatic research that could be at least contributive to a larger understanding of the problems in the field. Perhaps three other factors contribute to this lack of intensive research effort:

1. There is a general lack of social concern for the gifted and an apparent belief that the gifted and their adequate education present no "crying need" as compared with the more obvious ones of the disabled and the disadvantaged.
2. Many may believe that the bulk of the basic needed information about the gifted already is at hand.
3. The complexity of adequately educating the gifted may be regarded as so great as to preclude definitive research on it.

The lack of funds for research often is blamed for the paucity and poor quality of research on the gifted. This is less a cause than a result of a lack, on the part of those working in the area of the gifted, of a firm commitment to the importance of research and of relevant research competence wherewith to convince certain fund grantors of the necessity to commit part of the funds to research.

As the foregoing implies, it is helpful to differentiate between research on the gifted and research on their education. There is, however, another area basic to these two: research pertaining to society's need for the gifted.

RESEARCH ON SOCIAL NEED

Emergence of Social Leaders

Any society or social group tends to have its leader. The more primitive the society, the more likely all leadership responsibilities tend to be ascribed to a single individual; the less primitive the society, the more the leadership responsibilities tend to be shared—either on a horizontal basis or in a hierarchical structure. The more primitive the society and the more the threats to its survival tend to be physical in nature, the more its leader tends to be selected, and even trained for, on a physical basis, closely paralleling the condition at the infrahuman level. While the primitive leader tends to attain his status through physical prowess, he tends—at least in the early social evolutionary stage—to be accorded also primary roles in decision making outside the physical realm. After the emergence of this type of leadership at the mass level, differentiation tends to appear, resulting in leadership status being accorded to the "wise man" and the medicine man. As the governance function further evolves, a council is constituted and performs an essentially integrative function among differentiated leadership components.

This progression is identifiable not only as regards primitive social group evolution but also in our more complex society. The college or university president was initially all things—the educational policy maker, the fund raiser, the business administrator, and the public relations person for the institution; only very slowly have certain of these functions have delegated to specific others within the unit and their integration developed. This manner of leadership evolution is discernible in any emerging and developing social group—in unions, in professional organizations, in school districts, in PTAs, in the church, in gang behavior, in playground behavior.

Identification
of Leadership Needs

Generally, leadership roles tend to emerge in response to emergencies or quasi-emergencies which serve to sharpen the social group's perception of a need of this sort. In addition to such social role determination by emergencies, social observers—philosophers, anthropologists, and the like—identify needs for leaders. They tend to do so in terms of "the long view" rather than in terms of sporadically confronting demands.

Such quietly arrived-at perceptions of society's need for leadership by the gifted have existed at least since the early Greeks and have been restated by many philosophers and other social observers over subsequent centuries. Early in this century, such observations were voiced by Terman and his followers and in part buttressed with many of the data from the series of studies he started. Sputnik, of course, was part of an emergency situation that reawakened a social awareness of the need for leaders especially in the scientific and technological area.

This actually was but a revival of an awareness that World War II had heightened. As Wolfle pointed out in *America's Resources in Specialized Talent* (1954), "By the end of the war each of the councils (American Council of Learned Societies, American Council on Education, National Research Council, and Social Science Research Council) had become impressed by serious shortages of personnel in its own area and by the peculiarly important role played in the

national defense effort by this selected group of highly trained individuals" (p. xi). Prior to the appearance of his book, Wolfle, singly and jointly with others, had thirteen publications bearing on this matter over the years 1951–53. His book threw definitive light upon the needs of society and reflected on the extent to which education was meeting that need. His book *The Uses of Talent* (1971) depicted the post-Sputnik picture. Chronologically paralleling Wolfle's significant earlier contributions was the publication of *Encouraging Scientific Talent* (Cole, 1956), which similarly identified society's needs and also reported data on a national sample of 32,750 high school seniors' college-attending intentions and plans. The recommendations made on the basis of these findings pertained more to educational strategy than to classroom tactics.

The heavy emphasis in these studies, as well as in the rather large percentage of related studies made during the immediate post-Sputnik period, was on needs in relatively tangible and clearly observable areas. Needs in the less tangible areas were identified or acknowledged, but such attention was less effective in prompting social action to meet them. If corrective action resulted in the areas of psychology and education, for instance, such action was perceived more in terms of contributing to the turning out of more and better scientists and technologists than in terms of directly meeting needs in the area of social relationships. With the consideration of the needs of the dependent, of the maladjusted, and of the disadvantaged coming more to the fore (themselves building up to an economic emergency), the needs for high-level personnel to work in the social area are receiving slowly increasing attention.

The need for research on the leadership roles which the gifted can and should play in society continues. While studies of society's needs have tended to be more concerned with those which are clearly apparent—science, technology, and health—there has been some sensitivity to other, less tangible, areas. But studies of needs in the less grossly apparent areas are badly needed. In fact, both replication and extension of the studies of social needs must be made, especially in light of the fact that, even within a decade, certain former needs tend to become obsolescent and other new ones arise. Along with this condition, the actual needs in continuing areas tend to vary with social conditions. The need of teachers, for instance, was very great during the late 50s and the 60s, but fears of an oversupply of certifiable teachers characterized the early 70s. National data have to be interpreted in terms of varying and shifting geographical needs—as, for instance, in regard to the problem of the delivery of health and medical services to rural areas and the mobility seemingly characteristic of commerce and industry. Society's perception of its needs for the contributions of high-level personnel, while continuing to include needs in the production area—science, industry, and agriculture, for instance—is coming slowly to incorporate needs in the area of special services, as in welfare, community mental health, legal services to the disadvantaged, services to the aged, utilization of natural resources, the growing services involving data processing, and a variety of governmental functions.

What Leadership Research Must Do

Research on society's leadership needs must have two characteristics. It must depict the total national picture, both immediate and soundly projected, but it must be increasingly sensitive to ris-

ing needs in generally unrecognized areas. The part which local educators can play in or benefit from such studies must be recognized in the light of an increasingly mobile population, but the local schools can, and should, ascertain much more clearly than they thus far have the roles which their gifted can play locally. Such studies, the results of which could have definite implications regarding the curricula they offer, could help stem somewhat the intellectual erosion which many smaller communities experience.

The results of such research at both the national and local levels can be capitalized upon wisely if three factors are properly considered:

1. The mobility of our population must be recognized and adjusted to with a view to meeting both local and national needs.
2. The shifting sands of social needs make ever more questionable the goals of "training" future high-level personnel for highly specific kinds of social involvements in society. There is a growing need for an initial, relatively wide-based fundamental preparation on the basis of which later, perhaps presently unrecognized kinds of more specialized preparation can follow.
3. The primary characteristic of the gifted is such that they are uniquely susceptible to this pattern of preparation. Their learning potential is of such a nature that they in particular can benefit from the broad, general learning which would be involved.

RESEARCH ON THE GIFTED

Criticisms of Terman

The generalizability of Terman's stage-setting findings on the gifted has been challenged by some. The contention that he had a highly selected population cannot be ignored. His primary basis of identification could be regarded as a circuitous, self-fulfilling one: he selected those who already had, in effect, demonstrated that they had learned quickly; they, therefore, were likely to continue to learn quickly. Given the status of "intelligence" testing in his time, this was inescapable, but he, like any researcher, had the right to select the population he wanted to study. Actually, by virtue of the psychological nature of the behavior samplings of even the early Binet, he was tapping process to such an extent that this criticism is greatly weakened.

It has been observed by some close to Terman and his research that he may have affected certain of the outcomes of his study by personally counseling and motivating some of his subjects, and even by facilitating their education. The fact that he maintained a surprisingly sustained contact with his subjects over the years could be supportive to such an observation. However, that such a condition could have been a primary factor in determining the nature of the overall yield of his studies and/or that of his close co-workers seems highly unlikely in view of the fact that subsequent, less personally committed studies have produced findings essentially corroborative of his.

More importantly, criticisms of his findings regarding their physical characteristics, their health conditions, and their socioemotional adjustments call for more serious consideration. Most replication studies in these areas have themselves been made on populations that have been almost equally open to question with respect to their being "typical." Certainly, this would be true to the extent that the post hoc definition of giftedness prevailed. Generally, though, Terman's research-based characterization of the gifted appear to have been substantiated. Later we shall suggest the merit of more broadly validating his findings or of more soundly restricting them.

Personality of the Gifted

First, however, we shall consider the area of personality characteristics. The research evidence in this area already has been touched upon in relation to other matters. Using essentially the results of a single study, the intent here is to suggest a psychological basis for the consistency of the general direction of the findings and to suggest further research which could both broaden the scope and strengthen the nature of such findings.

In 1971, a syndicated newspaper column in which a recent book on the "psychopath" was reviewed carried the large-type heading, "Gifted Young Person Often Psychopath." The reverse was what the author of the book had said, but the caption writer reflected a kind of thinking about the gifted that has been surprisingly persistent at least among laymen over the years. It is not uncommon to encounter the observations of novelists, artists, and musicians to the effect that major maladjustments are the necessary or highly frequent accompaniments of exceptional creativity. That such conditions or phenomena have occurred together is recognized. Even that some creating has served a compensatory purpose in the lives of some can be accepted as plausible. But to generalize in this vein is to attach undue significance to incidental, and perhaps even selective, observations, and to ignore the importance of basing generalizations upon the results of systematic ascertainment of the facts of the matter. The fundamental issue is whether, given a large representative sample of a population which has been identified as gifted and another large representative sample of the general population, there will be discernibly significant differences between the populations in their effective emotional adjustment or in their personality characteristics. Personal observations yield, at best, impressions; systematic objective study yields a much closer approximation to the "truth." In all probability some man has been observed, or known, somewhere to have bitten a dog, but men do not bite dogs.

From the early 1920s, research-based reports on the personality characteristics of the gifted have demonstrated remarkably consistently their superiority to the nongifted. That this research literature has been so repetitive in this regard, even though the representativeness of the populations studied may be questioned, is not surprising when the psychological reasons for such differences are examined and understood. While we shall consider the differences which have been reported (without reviewing all the studies that are on record), we shall be more concerned with the reasons—the psychological inevitability, as it were—for the pattern of differences, recognizing certain possible biasing factors.

In order to be meaningful, a consideration of the personality characteristics of the gifted must include more than the conventional enumeration of their traits per se. It makes matters much more easily understood to examine such traits in contrast to those of other children. An early study by Lightfoot (1951) serves this purpose illustratively, though we recognize that her data were collected in 1939–1940 and in a special setting.

Using a variety of approaches—collecting information on home backgrounds, interviews, the Maller Personality Sketches, ratings on personality variables, a projective technique results, and case studies—she studied bright and dull children who were in special classes in the Speyer School (PS 500 in New York City). One group, the "Terman" group, consisted of 48 children with Binet IQs of 135 and above, ranging in chrono-

logical age from 10 years 1 month to 12 years 10 months. The other group, the "Binet" group, consisted of 56 children with Binet IQs in the 75 to 90 range (with a few from a "slow learner" class who ranged as high as 100), ranging in age from 10 years 1 month to 13 years 5 months. In all, there were 38 girls and 66 boys. Where appropriate, the evaluators of her clinical data made their judgments without knowing whether the data were on the bright or on the dull. Ratings of the personality traits were provided by the different teachers who had worked with the children being studied, although they were advised to make their ratings in terms of "the average child of all children of the same age" they had known. These behavior checkings were in terms of what the children had been observed doing (*having* many friends, *acting* withdrawn, *helping* others, and so on) as contrasted with making judgments or drawing inferences about the children (*feeling* insecure, *feeling* competitive, and the like).

Lightfoot synthesized her overall findings in terms of Murray's "needs"; Table 12.1 sums up the results. Contrasting the overall picture of the characteristics of the bright with those of the dull children, it is easily apparent that the bright youngsters presented a picture of being outgoing, sociable, independent, curious, and creative, whereas the dull youngsters were perceived, in terms of the composite of the information obtained on them, as withdrawn, dependent, and highly self-protective.

The picture is sharpened a bit when the ratings which both kinds of children received on 40 attributes of personality are considered. These ratings were secured from administrators, teachers, and psychologists in the school. The number of raters involved varied from three (for seven children) to nine (for 11 children), 61 of the children being rated by four

Table 12.1. "Needs" characterizing bright and dull pupils.

The bright	The dull

MOST CLEARLY

Achievement—to overcome obstacles, exercise power, strive to do something difficult as well and as quickly as possible.	*Dependence*—to seek aid, protection, or sympathy; to cry for help; to plead for mercy; to adhere to an affectionate, nurturant parent; to be dependent.
Affiliation—to form friendships and associations; to greet, join, and live with others; to cooperate and converse socially with others; to join groups.	*Seclusion*—to exhibit isolation, reticence, self-concealment (the opposite of exhibition).
Autonomy—to resist influence or coercion; to defy an authority or seek freedom in a new place; to strive for independence.	
Cognizance—to explore (moving and touching); to ask questions; to satisfy curiosity; to look, listen, and inspect; to read and seek knowledge.	
Creativity—to produce and develop original ideas; to devise new methods, construct hypotheses, offer novel explanations, create a work of beauty.	
Dominance—to influence others; to persuade, prohibit, dictate; to lead and direct; to restrain; to organize the behavior of a group.	

NEXT MOST CLEARLY

Appearance—physical beauty, looks, attention to clothing and one's person.	*Defendance*—to defend oneself against blame or belittlement; to offer extenuations, explanations, and excuses; to resist "probing."
Protectiveness—to nourish and/or protect the helpless; to express sympathy; to "mother" a child.	*Deference*—to admire and willingly follow a superior individual; to cooperate with leaders; to serve gladly.
Recognition—to excite praise and commendation; to demand respect; to boast and exhibit one's accomplishments; to seek distinction, social prestige, honors, or high office.	*Placidity*—calmness, passivity, or a well-controlled emotional system (the opposite of emotionality).
	Rejection—to snub, ignore, or exclude another person, animal, or thing.

Source: Adapted from Lightfoot, 1951.

or more. The following observations are based upon the differences between the averages of ratings assigned the two groups of children:

1. The most extreme ratings reflected the cooperative behavior and the curiosity of the bright children. Most of the other averages, for both groups, hovered close to the midpoints of the ranges of behavior. Where there were discernible differences, they were in favor of the bright youngsters, though the averages for the dull fell at or near the midpoints.

2. The behavior of the bright children was regarded more favorably in 34 of the categories. In three instances, the averages were a bit above the midpoint (favorable), but the slower youngsters didn't "show off," didn't manifest physical aggression, and responded to authority a bit "better" than did the bright ones. In three other instances, both groups being essentially at midpoint, the slower ones were a bit less selfish, a bit more submissive, and slightly less likely to "seek commendation." Actually, the differences between the groups were quite small on all six of these personality traits.

3. The most marked differences reflected the bright children as being perceived as much more often showing originality, manifesting self-confidence, concentrating on their own activities, getting much more enjoyment from mastery problems, and being discernibly self-sufficient.

Here, too, the same contrasting overall picture is apparent. Of course, this latter rating information was part of the total synthesized picture, but it could have been "washed out" if the other four sources of information had been contrarily consistent enough to do so.

Before examining the fundamental psychological picture here, we must recognize that these children had been and were in special classes in a school that in all probability was not typical of even New York City schools. Whether the behavioral contrasts of these two groups of children were a result of having been in special classes, or even in a nontypical school, cannot be determined. Did these groups of children differ, even somewhat, before they entered the special class/school situation? Or did they enter upon the school experience quite alike and then encounter experiences, attitudes, and expectations which caused or helped bring about such differences? Those who oppose the provision of special classes for such exceptional children would maintain that the differences found were the inevitable consequences of such differentiated treatment. Those of contrary conviction would maintain that these children had manifested such contrasting behavior pictures prior to their special class experiences. And a third group wisely would observe that the findings warrant neither interpretation or inference. Before any such inference could properly be drawn, some other kinds of information would be needed. Data of a similar kind, though, of course, differently obtained, would be needed on these children before they entered upon their schooling. This kind of baseline information is missing from

most research on the gifted, because so few researchers in the area are committed to the longitudinal research required to obtain it. If one were to think only in terms of the New York City situation, one would need, also, comparable information, preferably longitudinal in nature, on children who were directly comparable to those in the study in Binet IQ, sex, and ethnic/socioeconomic characteristics and who were in different schools with and without special class provisions. If one were to seek to make interpretations more broadly, comparable information would be needed as well from other school systems.

Lightfoot's research has been considered here rather intensively as illustrative of relative breadth and depth in a given situation and also as a stage-setter for a consideration of why the gifted so consistently have been found to possess such characteristics. In this discussion the primary locus of concern will be the school, although many of the phenomena which can be contributive in the school will operate in like manner in children's extraschool lives.

How the Gifted Adjust

The greater ease with which the gifted learn, generalize, and abstract disposes toward a greater likelihood of success in school. By contrast, the slower children more frequently experience failure or nonsuccess. Self-confidence, with its frequent accompaniment of outgoingness, tends to be associated with successful experiences; insecurity and withdrawingness tend to be associated with the absence of successful experiences. There are, of course, exceptions to the overall generality, which weaken but do not destroy it—the quiet, seemingly retiring behavior of the very competent and succeeding child (possibly reinforced by his near-unique social communication situation?), and the compensatory outgoingness of the child who, though not particularly successful in certain areas, finds some sort of tolerable expression and social acceptance in some kind of behavior peripheral to the school task of "book learning." But these, it must be remembered, are the exceptions and not the generality.

Keep in mind, too, that, to varying degrees, both the gifted and the nongifted generalize. The gifted, experiencing successes in a few learning situations —in school and out of school—generalize in anticipating success in subsequent learning demands (they generalize also when they underachieve); slow-learning children, experiencing a dominance of failure over success, come to expect that they will not be successful in subsequent learning situations. Both kinds of children, like all of us, do such generalizing "unconsciously." In this sense, the cards appear to be stacked in favor of the gifted child's becoming happier, more outgoing, more self-confident. Mark May's early findings that bright children cheated less (they didn't have to) than less capable children and that they tended more to respond to delayed and less tangible rewards were but threads in the total comprehensible pattern. The generality, "Unto every one that hath shall be given, and he shall have abundance; but from him that hath not shall be taken away even that which he hath" (Matt. 25, 29), or "Correlation, not compensation, is the law of nature," is operable here.

The predominance of research on the personality characteristics and adjustment of the gifted can be attributed to at least two conditions: (1) perhaps an apprehension, on the parts of the less gifted and of the nongifted, regarding these areas, and (2) certainly the zeitgeist of general interest in personality and adjustment and the growing development of procedures for measurement in these areas. Second only to this in volume of research was the exploration of the cognitive styles of the gifted, with

particular reference to their divergent, or creative, thinking. Studies of these, essentially elaborative of an already presumably established condition of giftedness, seem to have been as much concerned with the evaluation of hopefully relevant testing instruments as with the extension or refinement of the picture of the nature of the gifted.

Studies of the prevalence of the gifted among the general population, as contrasted with those in populations of high concentration and convenience, have not been at all systematic. And studies of inter- and intraindividual differences among the gifted have been only incidental, as have been studies of the achievements of the adult gifted. (Explorations of the areas of achievement and underachievement of gifted children are considered in connection with their education.)

Research Needed

It hardly can be denied that educational and social practices fall far short of the clear implications of the reasonably firm research findings on the gifted. Yet the researcher is insatiable in his desire for more and better information. In any field, the researcher's perception of needed research is a function first of his knowledge of the field and second of the extent to which his curiosity is broad, deep, and active. Nose-counting and trait enumeration and description may be quite broad but can lack depth of psychological anchorage and integration. The following identification of areas needing further research is by no means exhaustive; their breadth and depth are only hinted at.

Widely based studies

As has been suggested, there is a definite need for a more widely based study of the gifted population. The clearly restricted samples of the gifted that have been studied have contributed to essentially unsupported contentions that the gifted are relatively equally prevalent among the different socioeconomic strata of our society. The very few reports of the frequency of gifted children among the disadvantaged populations are of limited significance both because of the limited scope of the populations sampled and by virtue of their often-varying and ambiguous definitions. Retrospective studies such as Bond's (1967) of Negro doctorates indicate that some bright Negro children managed to emerge but throw no light on the prevalence of high capability in that group at early school ages. The fact that research of this kind must include studied samples of varied socioeconomic levels, of differing ethnic groups, and of the disadvantaged determines that it should be truly broadly based. In order for such a study to have psychological, rather than just psychometric, merit, the testing would need to be done (preferably on children 5 to 12 years of age) by means of a variety of tests ranging from process-dominant to product-dominant, on a variety of widely differing socioeconomic levels and ethnic groups, and with due consideration for the operation of widely differing motivational patterns. (The use of "protest" tests of "intelligence" for this purpose which have been developed as "culture-relevant" and are heavily weighted in esoteric product will be much less soundly productive than the use of tests which sample fundamental psychological operations.) Such a highly worthwhile study would require at least five years and probably would cost not less than $750,000.

Longitudinal studies covering life-spans of not less than 30 years and similar to those of Terman, Bayley, and the Antioch studies but even more comprehensive and more sensitive to the gifted are badly needed. They could be particularly enlightening if they included, and the results were analyzed in terms of, gifted children who had spent at least some of their educational lives working under some kinds of special educational provisions as well as those who had had no such educational experience.

Comparative studies

Comparative studies of the gifted and nongifted would be most fruitful if they were of greater behavioral scope and psychological depth than they have been thus far. In all such studies there is a need for data collected in a wide variety of ways:

1. From all available objective records of performance
2. From autobiography and from biography
3. From interviews both with the subjects themselves and with significant others in their lives, the information so yielded to be analyzed on the basis of preestablished procedures
4. From controlled observations periodically executed in terms of clearly specified behaviors
5. From a well-conceptualized program of testing.

Such a program, largely reflected in the Terman studies, would entail the sustained commitment of one or more organizations and/or individuals.

Studies of shorter duration and concerned with populations from birth to, say, ten years of age could be most productive if they included large, representative populations within which those who are gifted would appear. Comparative studies of the gifted and nongifted, each by sex, could be quite fruitful as regards the objective delineation of the early varied manifestations (observed and measured) of a diversity of giftedness and talent. Considerable information of this general nature already exists, but most of it has not been analyzed in terms of giftedness.

Environmental influence

Lest the impression be gained that the kinds of studies so far proposed should be perceived in a social vacuum, they should incorporate the examination of the influences of factors in the social milieu of the gifted—the nature and extent of the attitudinal environment in which the gifted are growing up, the nature of their communication with both other children and the significant adults in their environs, and the development of their value systems. Relatively isolated, small-scale findings exist in each of these areas, but they lack depth and psychological packaging. Exploration of questions such as the following could be rewarding: What characteristics of conditions attract the gifted to certain goals and repel them from others? To what extent are these and certain types of social relationships soundly relatable to their superior capacity to conceptualize? What are the significant parameters of social communication—both verbal and nonverbal—among the gifted and between the gifted and the nongifted? Do these differ as between the less gifted and the highly gifted? What intellectual, social, and emotional effects, if any, are discernible in the gifted's being obliged or compelled to associate with the less gifted? And primarily or solely with only their chronological peers? And what are the effects of such in the case of the nongifted? The whole area of the relationships between the gifted and their social milieus, particularly as regards communication, is important for both intellectual and social reasons, and to both the gifted and the nongifted.[1] This is admittedly a most complex area for research, but it is an educationally and socially important one.

Mobility of the gifted

As has been pointed out, we know far too little about the mobility of the gifted and their parents. What are the factors or conditions which cause them to leave some situations and attract them to others? What are the accommodation demands and opportunities for compensation for which the gifted, as children, should be prepared so as both to effect good or adequate personal adjustment and to meet effectively the demands of a constantly changing society? Current agriculture, for instance, makes quite different demands on the mentally superior than in our earlier agrarian picture. To what characteristics unique to or typical of the gifted, and on which society should capitalize, do differing social demands appeal? What factors operate, and how do they operate, in high-level personnel who change their areas of scientific and professional involvement? Certainly, the raising and answering of questions such as these imply thinking in terms of social engineering, the major components of which must include broad-based preparation of the gifted for future social involvement and the inculcation of attitudes in them that will facilitate their adjustment in a changing society.

Indicator behaviors

When people encounter or hear about a highly gifted or truly talented adult, questions seem inevitably to arise. "What was he/she like as a child?" "Did he/she do things during early childhood that

---

[1] The personal and social importance of communication has been noted frequently in this book. The fundamental phenomena involved in communication operate in all persons. Happily, in the case of the gifted, the problems are relatively simple, even though they require conscious recognition and adjustment. A greater awareness of the problems can be obtained by reading about the admittedly extreme conditions

of two deaf mutes being tried for murder: *The Brute* by des Cars (1952), a fictionalized detective-type story, and *Dummy* by Tidyman (1974), a factual and insightful account of an illiterate.

suggested the presence of the brightness or talent?" Such questioning by a layman suggests the following line of reasoning (though not thus formally put): "If behavior A, B, or C were present in this unusual person as a child, and if my child manifests this behavior, perhaps I have a gifted or talented person in the making." Eventually, the same manner of thinking characterizes the researcher in this area—but the concern here is less oriented to a particular child and concerns children generally. While the literature on the gifted contains studies of precursors of genius and talent, the methodologies, largely retrospective in nature, have been so varied that this area still must be regarded as in need of systematic research. It is informative to learn that certain behaviors have been identified in the early childhood of persons who later attained recognition as very bright or talented, but the researcher is left with some unanswered questions: Was such behavior observed, or observable, in young children who later did not attain such recognition? If so, what happened in such instances, as contrasted with what happened in the cases of those attaining recognition?

More fundamentally, the researcher of this condition would have to raise and try to answer this type of question: What systematically derived array of behaviors, not restricted to the cognitive area, in quite young children must be observed and measured which validly would suggest the presence of particularly high promise? Having identified and looked for those behaviors, the researcher must answer two other questions: (1) When certain promising behavior precursors have been observed, to what extent and in what ways can they be nurtured? (2) Having identified latent precursors of promising behavior, to what extent and in what ways should society attempt to evoke and nurture them? The fact that the asking and answering of questions such as these must be done in the light of highly varying social conditions can make this important undertaking seem overwhelming.

Potential for creativity

The potential for creativity, a facet differentiable from high-level learning aptitude but apparently at least in part related to it, awaits more penetrating research. Some research needs in this area have been identified earlier, the primary

"Mary! Mary!"

(Drawing by C. Barsotti; © 1972 The New Yorker Magazine, Inc.)

one being the need to validate in adult behavior the suspicions of creativity that have been aroused by performances in childhood on tests essentially presumed to measure "creativity." This problem is particularly complex for at least two reasons. First, assuming for the sake of argument that such tests for children are valid, a child may be found by means of them to manifest at, say, age eight, high creativity potential only to have things happen (or not happen) to him subsequent to that time which completely thwart the manifestation of this behavior when he becomes an adult. (The extent to which such a sequence of events is generalizable for children so identified itself needs to be established by research.) Second, it is psychologically highly plausible that thinking divergently, the psychological essence of creativity, is a function of the conjoint operation of two variables—some above-average capability to function cognitively in the manner called creating plus the existence of a psychological condition that is conducive to such behavior, this latter being a function of two conditions: the sense of psychological well-being that enables the individual to tolerate the possibility of two or more lines of action instead of being so emotionally constricted that only one line of action is tolerable, and the effect of nurturing the individual such that he is further disposed to seek out and explore the possibilities of two or more possible lines of action or thought.

The complexity of anything more than superficial research on the divergent thinking and creative thinking behaviors of the gifted is apparent in the listing of even the more apparent problem areas: (1) the development of valid tests of divergent thinking—by far the simplest problem; (2) the development of valid tests of creative thinking—a truly difficult problem so long as the two kinds of behavior are differentiated; (3)

the development of sound principles and valid procedures for the nurturance of the two kinds of behavior; and, as essentially contributive to this, (4) the identification of factors and conditions which are peripheral to the formal educational process but which may either facilitate or impair evocative and nurturant conditions. Problems such as these must be studied not only in the light of the varying social contexts in which they operate but also in terms of the fact of the heterogeneity of the gifted group—those of less than Binet 150 probably presenting less complex problems than those of above, say, 170.

Precursors of talent

Bearing in mind the distinction which has been made earlier between talent and skill, much research is needed in the area of the talented. The potentially more fruitful area would appear to be that of the precursors of talented behavior. Much has appeared in the serious literature on the talented about the grossly observable early behaviors of adults recognized as talented. They have been reported as being manifested at quite early ages through performing on musical instruments, composing music, drawing and painting, miming, and role playing. To the researcher, though, the question arises as to which kinds of behavior might be observable before such grossly apparent evidences are noted. To what ranges and patterns of sound stimuli are such children responsive during their very early years? What is the evidence on early manual and bodily agility, on color and form discrimination, on projections and identifications with different roles in interpersonal relationships? And light is needed on what happens to very young children who showed such propensities but who, in adult life, failed to continue to manifest them.

Demonstration research

Research on the gifted is undertaken primarily to uncover new descriptive information on them. There is, however, another kind of research activity that can contribute to their more effective education and more fruitful social contribution. Essentially in the sense of bringing coal to Newcastle, there can be state and local needs that should be met by means of what may be called demonstration research. For decades, information has been amassed which depicted clearly the extent to which the gifted are educationally retarded in light of their respective capacities. No condition is more clearly recognized by those conversant with the field of the gifted; some even have sought to play down the importance of the deplorable condition partly because concern with the problem has diverted attention from other problems in the area of the gifted and, perhaps, partly because of the seeming futility in the attempts at ameliorating the condition. The consumers of such retardation research information have tended either just to acknowledge its general presence or to shrug it off as "just too bad" without seeming to recognize its social and educational significance. For this reason, in spite of its "I-told-you-so" nature, there can be a need for admittedly duplicative research to be carried out at state and local school district levels in order to make more apparent, especially to lay significant others, the nature and magnitude of needs and (more germane to this section) the repercussions of such under-achievement on the personality characteristics and adjustments of the under-achieving gifted. Systematically collected objective information on this and other characteristics of the gifted can serve as a tangible basis for eliciting constructive action on the part of both the lay public and many professional educators. This is the general strategy which has charac-terized the initial steps in states which have mounted programs for the gifted.

Correlating subprojects

Much of the foregoing is directed toward sharpening a picture of the gifted, the general nature of which already is pretty well known. Most of the research proposed here have been monolithic in nature—undertakings perhaps too encompassing for an individual to accomplish and certainly too broad in themselves to be accomplished by means of master's and doctoral research. However, if such undertakings were perceived in terms of programmatic research, it could be structured such that specific subprojects, which were clearly identified as directly contributive to the total thrust of the research, could be quite productive. The financing of such research always is regarded as a major problem, but this problem tends to be met when the need for such research is clearly voiced and firmly pressed with the conviction which such research warrants. Unfortunately, once such fundamental funding is accomplished, camp followers spring up by the dozens and attempt to "do research" that is only hastily and superficially perceived. Whether fortunately or unfortunately, the attention spans of such researchers tend to be only as long as the time for which their projects are funded.

RESEARCH ON THE EDUCATION OF THE GIFTED

Again, bear in mind that this section is not intended to summarize research in this area. Rather, it is intended to consider matters that are of importance in research on the education of the gifted and to suggest that the consumer of research findings should regard reported research as significant to the extent that the researcher has shown adequate sensitivity to them. To this end, a set of consumer criteria is proposed. These criteria can, of course, be helpful to the producer of sound research.

Only one who is little concerned with precise research and who ignores or is insensitive to the wide variety of potentially significant variables involved would presume to summarize integratively the results of the many formally published studies of the education of the gifted. At best, he could report the findings in the differing terminologies of the various researchers, taking care to differentiate between those studies purporting to throw light upon relationships between educational procedures presumably employed and the outcomes that seemed attributable to them and those studies dealing with the development of content and curricula deemed appropriate for the gifted. Yet, in an overall sense, the highly varied kinds of educational treatment,[2] when they actually have varied in ways appropriate to the greater aptitudes of the gifted, seem to have produced or to be related to at least no negative or, more consistently, generally positive results with the gifted. That there has been this general consistency of favorable outcomes or sequels may be attributable to any one or a combination of factors: The treatments have been appropriate and the outcomes really resulted from them. The gifted have such intellectual resiliency that they tend to respond favorably to whatever educational treatment they receive. With marked consistency, "experimenters"

---

[2] The term "treatment" is used to denote any of the whole variety of educational provisions, singly or in combination, that have been employed in the interests of the gifted—ranging from early admission, different "teaching" approaches, special nurturance of creativity, advanced accreditation, to the use of (but not the development of) specially adapted or developed materials and/or content.

tend to get the results they anticipate. And formal publishers of research tend to prefer to publish only studies that have yielded positive results.

If serious educational researchers forthrightly refrain from undertaking what, to many, seems like quite simple research that could differentiate good from poor teachers because of the difficulty in establishing an adequate criterion of goodness of teaching and on account of the number and complex interaction of potentially contributing variables involved, it would be understandable if serious students hesitated to conduct experiments intended to throw light on the merits or limitations of different educational treatments of the gifted. Generalizations on the outcomes by both the producers and the consumers of such research should, for the same reasons, be made with considerable critical restraint.

Major Variables

Note the following major variables that should be recognized and controlled for, assuming that the researcher has clearly defined the kind of educational treatment which is under primary consideration. At least these variables must be regarded as capable of affecting the nature of the outcomes and the generalizability of the results and implications. While their relevance to anticipated research is apparent, they will, for convenience, be discussed with respect to only completed research. The list is suggestive, not exhaustive.

What was the nature of the population involved? Were they the once popular top sixth of any class? Those of IQ of 125 and up? Those of IQ 150 and up? Or those above IQ 175 or 185? On what test or tests? At what age(s) or grade level(s) were they? Socioeconomically and/or ethnically, what was the nature of the population? Was the population such that analysis of outcomes for sex differences was possible?

What was known or required of the teachers involved? Was the sex of the teacher(s) a factor? What were the prior teaching experiences of the teacher(s)? What were the special qualifications of the teacher(s)—specifically certified for teaching the gifted, specifically prepared for the undertaking, or run of the mill? What were the substantive adequacies of the teacher(s) in the study? What were their adjustment pictures? What were their attitudes toward the study, toward research in education, toward the approach under study? Did the analysis of the results of the study give evidence of a sensitivity to the operation of the teacher variable?

Was the nature of the curriculum which was intentionally or unintentionally involved in the treatment under study clearly delineated? If the study was directed toward the evaluation of the curriculum, rather than toward the evaluation of the treatment within the curriculum, to what extent was it adequately described? What was the relationship between the curriculum involved in the study and the curriculum of the school/system? If the educational treatment under study involved more extensive though incidental one-to-one teacher-to-pupil or pupil-to-pupil relationships than is typical in most classrooms, or in those used for control, what steps were taken to make sure that the outcomes of the treatment were attributable to the treatment per se rather than to the fact of increased interpersonal relationships, which usually are themselves rewarding and motivational in their effect?

What was the social and educational climate of the setting in which the research was carried out? What were the socioeconomic and ethnic natures of the setting of the study? What was the administrative philosophy of the system in which the study was done—its possible facilitating or inhibiting effect? To what extent was communication among the participating, and between the participating and nonparticipating, teachers controlled? To what extent was the teachers' awareness of the nature of the hoped-for outcomes controlled for?

And what were the measures obtained? Were they clearly relevant to the variable under study? Were legitimate secondary outcomes measured? Were the outcomes both educationally and socially relevant? Were they gross or detailed? If data were obtained observationally, were the behaviors observed clearly behaviorally defined? Were observations made or inferences drawn regarding important behaviors? If data were obtained by means of tests, were they of acceptable merit and relevance?

Control of Variables

Usually the researcher seeks to have one or a smaller number of clearly defined variables, the operations of which he seeks to ascertain. If he limits the situation such that only one variable is clearly under study, he runs the risk of having to study its "effect" in an unrealistic, psychoeducational vacuum. If he does not do so, he runs the risk of having a clouded picture in which he is unable clearly to ascribe whatever outcomes he observes to the variable he seeks to study. One way to resolve this dilemma, at least in part, is for him to study the operation of his variable in a large variety of situations in which the possible contaminating variables are known or believed to be present, assuming or hoping that the possible side effects of the secondary variables will be randomly distributed and will cancel out, yielding a resultant picture of "normality." Little research on the education of the gifted has been of this latter sort because it is beyond the capability and facilities of most researchers in the area.

Two kinds of approaches generally are used. One involves the creation or identification of one or more groups in which the treatment under study operates—usually called the experimental group. There then is created or identified one or more groups in which that variable is not provided for, steps being taken to make the latter, or comparison, groups as nearly as possible comparable to the experimental group. Usually, this equating of the two kinds of groups is attempted in terms of at least learning capability (somehow defined and measured), sex, and socioeconomic status. Often little attention is given to the variables about which questions such as those above have been raised.

Attempts to equate the two kinds of groups are of three sorts:

1. The averages of the variables regarded as crucial in the experimental and comparison groups are established as essentially equal, which by no means assures their equivalence.
2. The averages and the dispersions, or scatters of the individuals around the averages, are established as essentially equal, providing for a closer approximation to equivalence.
3. Each individual in the one kind of group is matched on a one-to-one basis with an individual in the other kind of group on the variables regarded as important, much more sharply approximating the equivalence of the two kinds of groups.

Another kind of approach involves the study of specific individuals over time and conditions, each of whom, it is contended, "serves as his own control."

In each approach, observations and/or measurements are made at a specified time and repeated at one or more subsequent times, and the amount(s) of change noted and evaluated. The evaluation usually involves statistical analysis aimed at discovering the extents to which the change or changes may be attributed to experimental and chance factors. The consumer would do well to note that when the producer states that his findings are "significant at the .05 level," or at some other level, he is indicating only that, other conditions being equal, a change of the specified magnitude or greater is likely to happen due to chance only five times out of a hundred. Whether a change of that statistical significance is educationally or socially significant is a decision which the consumer must then make.

While most consumers of the findings of research in this area are not sufficiently sophisticated statistically to make highly technical evaluations of the data treatment, they can and must examine closely the research procedures employed, finding out if the researcher has provided sufficient information that questions at least such as those which have been presented for illustrative purposes can be answered. If this is not possible, perhaps the researcher did his research as fuzzily as he wrote it up. Studies of an exploratory nature do not call for quite the same kind of intensive examination and criticism as do those of a more definitive research nature; their "yield" is the identification of a problem to be studied more rigorously and the identification of potentially fruitful procedures to be employed in doing so. When the research purports to yield firm information, the consumer needs to evaluate such information most critically.

Consumer's Criteria

Overlapping somewhat a few of the points that already have been made but having broader applicability, the following major points must be considered in evaluating research in this area. These are, in effect, consumer's criteria and they can serve to sharpen his response to the tone of caveat emptor that has been implicit in our discussion. Nine such factors or facets should be taken into consideration:

1. The research design
2. The nature of the population involved in the study
3. The nature of the educational treatment studied
4. The kinds of behaviors sampled
5. The measures of the kinds of behaviors involved
6. The milieu of the study
7. The scope of the study
8. The duration of the study
9. The generalizability of the findings

In order to maintain a stable frame of reference, we shall think illustratively only in terms of research on tracking, ignoring for the moment what impact legal opinions on the use of tracking may have. We shall concern ourselves with the kinds of questions that must be raised in trying to decide on the extent to which research results on tracking have validity. (The discussion will be particularly meaningful if Findley and Bryan's 1970 report on ability grouping has been read.) A similar type of thinking should be employed with regard to research on other kinds of educational provisions for the gifted.

The research design

To a large degree, the answering of the crucial questions regarding research design bears upon certain points to be discussed later. Was thoughtful planning of the research evidenced in the report of the study, or was the report cluttered with casual, incidental observations regarding some of the suspected, and not researched, contributing factors? While certain points and questions pertaining to this already have been raised, two would seem to warrant being repeated because of their overall importance. (1) Just how specifically was the primary

variable under study defined? Was it only grossly characterized as an administrative redistribution of pupils among the tracks? Or was there included with that the explicit assurance that there were accompanying, appropriately differentiated instructional procedures employed? (2) Were the variables sufficiently well defined and the procedures precisely enough described so that others could duplicate, or replicate, the research without first-hand knowledge of what had been done? Disappointingly few studies of the education of the gifted meet this criterion.

The population

At what age or grade level(s) was the study made? How large was (were) the group(s) studied? Was there a single class studied, or several classes at a given grade level, or one class at each of several levels, or several classes at more than one level? For a variety of reasons, the outcomes could differ among primary level, elementary level, junior high level, and senior high school level.

The size of the population is not the crucial variable: how representative was the population, as to socioeconomic, ethnic, and even as to giftedness? Findings could differ distractingly among black, Indian, Puerto Rican, Jewish, deep south, north, highly urban, essentially rural, and middle- and upper-class white children, as well as between the just-gifted and the highly gifted. Or was a systematically stratified mix used? How wide a range of "giftedness" was involved—from some kind of IQ of 125 up, from 135 up, or from 150 up? Was provision made for the consideration of possible sex differences? After all, there are important differences between boys and girls in both maturation rates and levels at different times, as well as in social attitudes and value systems. The nature of the population involved, among other variables, has a definite bearing upon the generalizability of the findings.

The treatment

Keeping in mind that the introduction of a multiple track program is first and foremost an administrative matter, just how was it inaugurated—solely on the basis of top-level decision, or with the active cooperation of the instructional staff and even of parents? Just what were the essential characteristics of the instructional procedures employed with the bright youngsters as compared with those employed in the other tracks? Or in heterogeneous groups? Were the teachers of the bright pupils given, or required to obtain, any special preparation that would help them to accomplish properly their particular instructional tasks? Did the teachers actually do the kind of "teaching" appropriate to helping bright children learn effectively? Against what were the performances of the gifted in the track program compared—against their own earlier performances (an always convenient but sometimes misleading procedure) or against the performances of comparable children in nontrack programs in comparable schools?

The behaviors sampled

How specifically and objectively were the different kinds of relevant behaviors defined and considered? Granting that this kind of question can be answered relatively clearly as regards the pupils involved, how adequately were teacher behaviors considered? And the interaction between the behaviors of the teachers and those of the pupils? If certain behaviors of both teachers and pupils were given due consideration, were there other, and possibly influencing, behaviors involved that should have been taken into consideration—those of the noninvolved teachers, of the administrative staff, of the parents? All such behaviors would be but parts of the total primary variable under study.

Measures

Given the fact that the relevant behaviors have been well specified, how were the behaviors measured and/or observed? What measuring devices or procedures were used (1) in identifying those children who were to be in the "fast" and comparison groups and (2) in ascertaining the outcomes of the learnings? As has been pointed out, there is a wide variety of group and individual tests of "intelligence," and the same lower IQ limit, say of 125, can yield quite differing populations on different tests. (In one school building, 75 first-graders were found who had earned IQs of 125 or more on a group test and were being treated educationally as "gifted." However, a retest a year later of that same total first-grade population by means of the same test turned up only 58 of those 75 as meeting not just the criterion of 125 but the criterion of 120!) Most studies of outcomes use either standardized achievement tests and/or teachers' judgments of academic proficiency. Again, there is a plethora of achievement tests of varying validity and relevance. If teachers' judgments were used, were the teachers provided with criteria (behavioral descriptions) in terms of which to make their judgments, and how clearly and how specifically were the criteria stated in terms of those pupil behaviors? The nature of pupil classroom responses is heavily influenced by the nature of the teacher's questioning and expectations. How objectively was each of these defined and ascertained and how well was the pupil-teacher interaction of each of them ascertained? Whether an attempt to answer questions such as these is made, of course, goes back to the way(s) in which the problem was set up and the educational treatments delineated.

The milieu

Often ignored in regard to such studies is the fact that they are carried out in a larger social context which could have some bearing on the outcomes. No small number of such studies on or about the gifted have yielded findings that were taken to be the result of the experimental treatment when, in reality, they resulted from, or were heavily influenced by, social milieu factors. The climate of the school itself is important—a school that is highly favorably disposed toward "experimentation," a school that already has done things in the interests of the gifted, a school that is just getting started in doing something for its gifted, a school community that is strongly committed to staying with "the tried and the true," a community that generally is heavily committed to "education," or one that is essentially indifferent to it. The question has to be raised—what was the nature and possible contributive effect of school and social factors in both the school and the nonschool lives of gifted children before they were exposed to the educational tracking experience? [On the basis of their study of 20 boys and 15 girls in grades two to five, with Binet IQs of 150 and above, Gallagher and Crowder (1957) observed: "Children in the present group coming from schools where there were few bright children showed more motivational problems than (did) the children coming from schools where there were many other bright children" (p. 318).]

Further, when educators introduce special provisions for the gifted at the fourth- or sixth-grade level, usually overlooked is the fact that the gifted already have had three or five years of study- and learning-habit formation before being exposed to the different treatment. (One elementary school principal, who suddenly "got the word," at midsemester transferred a bright youngster to a higher grade in another school where provisions reportedly were being made for gifted children, totally ignoring the social relationships which the child already had established and the matter of his establishing new ones!) Some children, some of them gifted, come into the school environment out of social situations which have involved the cultivation and operation of systems of values that are discernibly at variance with those which schools generally are expected to inculcate. What some of these children aspire to may differ considerably from what the school may regard as appropriate. Some subcultures are not as "achievement-oriented" as our larger culture tends to be. Culture patterns, value systems, "motivation"—all these are parts of the social milieu in which preschoolers have lived and learned, and which continue to be influential during their school lives.

There also is a need for concern regarding the attitudes of the parents toward the tracking (or any other arrangement) into which their children have gone. To what extent had the school administration worked out this problem of helping the parents to understand and accept (or at least tolerate) the idea of tracking—through the PTA and/or conferences with concerned individual parents? Equally important is the need for considering the extent to which and the manner in which the instructional staff has been prepared to accept, cooperate with, and otherwise assist in implementing such a program? Even though the teachers as a group overtly may have accepted the practice of tracking, certain teachers may subtly manifest their aversion in ways which sap any educational or social values which the practice of tracking may have had. Even certain teachers who work with their tracked bright pupils can affect the educational climate in a school system, thus impairing (or enhancing) any potential values of tracking. Another pervasive phenomenon that needs to be taken into consideration with regard to the total social milieu is the general practice employed in evaluating pupil performances; more than one headache has been caused by the marking system employed in a tracking program.

The scope

What was the breadth of pupil performance evaluation after involvement in the multiple track condition—whether immediately afterward or some time after such experience? More than academic outcomes should be studied. Illustratively, what about the emotional adjustments of the gifted who were in the tracking program? Are the gifted "happier" because their superior potentials are being or have been more effectively challenged in their track? What about the social adjustments of the gifted in such a program—their social reactions among themselves, with the other children in other tracks, and as contrasted with the social interactions of comparable gifted in nontracked, otherwise comparable situations?

What about their social attitudes during the period of the study (or during their tracking experience if that be longer)—are they more snobbish toward or more acceptant of the nongifted? What were the interpersonal attitudes of *all* the gifted children in the school system—not only those who were tracked —a year or so *before* the experimental group(s) had been identified? let alone while they were in their section(s)? And afterward? How did such attitudes compare with those of the nongifted? [Though not in regard to the tracking problem but fundamentally suggestive,

Silverstein (1962) sought to ascertain not only how some New York City children perceived their classmates in terms of liking to have them as friends but also how they themselves expected to be so perceived. Using 350 fifth-graders in 13 classes in 11 schools, he found that the 66 children with Otis Quick Scoring IQs of 130 and above rated the other children more favorably than they expected themselves to be rated. But this was not unique to the supra-130 youngsters; the same kind of relationship was found in the lower IQ groups.] Was due consideration given to the time of the pupils' introduction into the tracking program, as well as to the length of time they were in it? Was objective information obtained on the nature and possible impacts of the aspects of the social context mentioned above? To what extent were post-public school aspirations and performances relatable to involvement and noninvolvement with tracking experiences?

The duration

The period of time over which the possible effects of an educational program are studied is very important, as suggested to some extent by the foregoing. The length of time the children were exposed to tracking experiences becomes shorter the later the practice is introduced at the elementary level. When it is used at junior and senior high school levels, it becomes contaminated both by the operation of earlier established learning habits and by the departmentalization that is present at those levels. The research question at the higher levels can be: "What are the effects of tracking in Subject A, Subject B, . . . ?" although some attempts at generalizing the results may be made. But the term duration as used here applies more to the point or points in time at which the possible effects are measured—whether just at the termination of the tracking experience or at a point or points materially subsequent to the experience. In other words, the question should be not only what are the pupils' behaviors like at or near the end of their participating in a tracking program but also one, two, or more years afterward. The measurement of sustained effects, while usually regarded as essential in the area of educational achievement, should reflect a broad sensitivity to behaviors in the adjustment area, the social area, and emotional area, as has been suggested.

The generalizability of findings

Many researchers with varying degrees of research sophistication quite legitimately make studies to try to find out what the facts are in their particular situations. Some of them properly report their findings only in terms of the settings in which their studies were made; others exercise no such restraint, uninhibitedly generalizing the implications of their findings—like one researcher who made a rather careful study of the deaf in two residential schools in one state and then proceeded to generalize about "the" education of "the" deaf. The consumer has the obligation not only to ascertain whether the researcher exercised restraint in generalizing from his findings but also to be equally cautious in drawing his own inferences from circumscribed studies.[3]

But the consumer of research findings

tends quite properly to ask: to what extent are the findings of a particular study generalizable? Seldom are research studies of the education of the gifted sufficiently encompassing and controlled to yield "the truth." This being the case, the "true" picture of or about tracking, for instance, must be constituted like a mosaic out of bits and pieces, each of which must have research integrity and each of which should incorporate adequate sensitivity to the factors which have been identified. But even mosaics have patterns, some conceptual structure. The consumer, then, must balance his desire to understand the larger picture against the quality of the findings of (largely) highly individual pieces of research. The results of a study of some particular educational treatment of the gifted in a class can be suggestive, but only that; other comparable or elaborative studies of the same variables or phenomena are needed to yield corroborating results before even embryonic generalizations can be drawn.

So, the little educational plant—tracking of the gifted—has to be studied not only in terms of the nature of the plant, which misleadingly seems so easily observable, but also in terms of the nature of the complex and probably varying soil in which it grows, in terms of its complex root system, in terms of the climate in which it is expected to grow, and in terms of what it produces. Such is true of studied practice in the education of the gifted; it should make one hesitant to accept placidly and uncritically the findings reported.

But the problem of the education of gifted youngsters is much broader than the highly garbled provision of tracking. Any of the other kinds of provisions— early admission and other forms of acceleration, enrichment in all of its elusive manifestations, special classes, underachievement as a product of their learning, and even the evaluation of

[3] One educator, apparently seeking to demonstrate that he was well informed, insisted that the results of Test A correlated .85 with those on the Binet, either forgetting or being unaware of the facts that (1) the correlation was found in only one study, and that on a special group of children, and (2) a correlation reflects only the degree of similarity between the relative positions of the members of a given group on the two variables under study.

consultants as key personnel—very well could have been used to illustrate the importance of the nine criteria which consumers of research information should use.

In no small number of studies, curiosity has been directed toward the presumed effect of different kinds of educational treatment upon characteristics of the gifted. Illustrative are summarizing statements prepared by Martinson for the Marland (1971) report: "Conclusions derived from the studies generally agreed that participants (in special class programs) did not develop personality or social problems, did not become conceited, or did not suffer health problems because of pressures; rather, participants showed improvement, not only in academic areas but also in personal and social areas," and, on the basis of her 1961 study of gifted pupils in a variety of school situations and having other educational provisions: "All of the evidence from the assessment of personal, social, and psychological factors indicated that gifted pupils participate in special programs without damage." [4]

The Domain of Research

Even when one unjustifiably ignores the milieu in which research is done and

[4] Logically, two kinds of questions arise in regard to this typical conclusion. One is concerned with the possible effects (sequelae or covariants) of, say, special class placement upon the personal and social characteristics of the gifted. Such placement may have a negative effect, no effect, or a positive effect. This effect may be perceived either as bringing to light latent characteristics or enhancing characteristics already manifested. The second question is, perhaps, even more fundamental: If Condition B is found to occur after Condition A, with what degree of justification can one infer that Condition A caused Condition B? This type of post hoc ergo propter hoc reasoning has caused some researchers to attribute the changes they found to the unique character of the treatment under study, when the mere fact of being singled out for special study could have been the major contributing factor.

when one assumes that the pupil population in the study is clearly defined and appropriate as to degree of learning aptitude, grade level, sex, and socioeconomic/ethnic composition, there are three remaining variables in terms of which research findings should be considered. Figure 12.1 suggests not only the complexity of each of those variables but the range of inevitable interaction among them.

For convenience the three parameters are presumed to be orthogonal to each other. Thinking in terms of this kind of structure can be helpful in grossly conceptualizing the total possible research undertaking on educating the gifted (or any other group), each possible substructure being a study or a category of studies. Treatment 1 could be early admission, which could be studied in regard to Behaviors 1 and 2 (say educational and social adjustment), over Time Span 1 (say one year). A conceptual scheme such as this could be of help also to the consumer in sorting out and correlating the findings of many studies.

SUMMARY

In spite of the marked variability in the amount and quality of research on the gifted, the research base of information on society's need for them, on their essential characteristics, and on some of their educational performances, is much greater than is the evidence that society, through its primary agent of education, is providing adequately for them. Society's provisions to assure them of a reasonable degree of self-fulfillment and to nurture them as potential contributors to society reflect much more than the oft-observed lag of one generation between the availability of relevant research evidence and the taking of action in terms of those findings.

Society's need for the contributions of

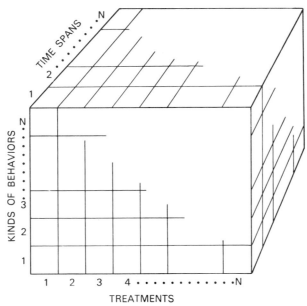

Figure 12.1. *A three-dimensional structure of the research domain of the education of the gifted.*

well-grounded, well-adjusted, creative individuals has been well documented by research. But awareness of this has been prompted largely by the existence of emergency conditions. There is a sustained albeit at times seemingly unrecognized need for high-level personnel in scientific, technological, and social areas. Social change is so accelerating that the earlier statements of highly specific occupational goals for such individuals is giving way to the necessity of thinking and planning in terms of classes of goals —of areas of involvement rather than the performing of highly specified functions.

Research evidence on the characteristics of the gifted points clearly to their being capable of benefitting from the broad-based preparation for their possible roles in an emerging society. That they can acquire such competencies at no threat to their social and emotional well-being seems reasonably clearly indicated. Further research on the gifted per se is needed more to sharpen the picture

of them than to establish the basic picture.

While research on the education of the gifted has varied markedly in quality, the overall yield suggests strongly that they have benefitted discernibly from the wide variety of educational provisions used with them. Whether their thus benefitting has resulted from the different kinds of special educational treatment or from their basic potential to benefit from almost any treatment, or from some combination of the two, is not at all clear. Whether the gifted actually need some or any of the more observable kinds of educational provisions in order properly to come to fruition or whether they could benefit equally or better from the provision of more subtle, but still very real, nurturant educational climates in which they are allowed to grow and mature largely on their own is a question that awaits study. Such a nurturant educational climate still would require that they be identified early and that they have in their educational environs significant adults who are sensitive to them as individuals, who are conceptually oriented as to the nature of giftedness and the needs of the gifted, and who are of superior substantive competence.

It is, of course, true that the producer of research information is obligated to be clearly sensitive to the limitations of and generalizability from his study, but it is doubly incumbent on the consumer of such information to be highly critical of all such findings. The suggested criteria can be helpful in this regard. But a disposition toward tolerance also must exist. Any researcher has the unchallengeable right to define his problem, his population, and his treatment(s) in whatever way he chooses, but his conclusions must be drawn in the light of those conditions, and the consumer of such information must make his interpretation of any such research with similar restraint. The consumer who perceives the generalized gifted in the light of the findings of research on only those above Binet IQ of 150, or above 185, or

who perceives the matter of early admission in terms of research based only on a calendar definition of school readiness, is a victim of his own unsophisticated orientation. Contrarily, ardent advocates of providing more adequately for the gifted can be guilty of faulty extrapolation or generalization in citing only research favorable to their bias.

It is trite but true to observe that more research is needed. But it must be good and improved research. The researcher is obligated to familiarize himself with and assimilate relevant findings of others in order properly to cast his problem in terms of what has been done and what needs to be done. It is necessary also that the consumer of research information perceive that information in perspective—in terms of some conceptual structure. A suggestion believed to be helpful to this end has been offered. To the extent that the results of research are thus perceived in an integrated manner the taking of social and educational steps on the basis of such information is warranted.

13

Summary

This consideration of the gifted has focused primarily upon their capability in the cognitive area—more specifically their capability to function symbolically. This capability is regarded as a resultant of the interaction of two conditions. The fundamental one is the individual's neurological constitution, which is essentially genetic in nature. This is taken as the given with which and in the light of which society, largely through its schools, must work. The second condition is the total amalgam of influences which impinge upon the organic condition which constitutes the potential for superior cognitive behavior. The consideration of these influences is limited primarily to their informal social and formal educational natures. They can be depressive, retarding if not actually impairing the development of latent potential for superior functioning. They can be neutral, neither arresting or depressing nor facilitating the functioning of individuals. Or they can be nurturant, stimulative to the neurological promise and evocative of and reinforcing to the kinds of responses of which the individual basically is capable. It is the second condition with which this book has been concerned, particularly as regards the part played by schools—but always within the total social context.

The 1969–70 School Staffing Survey revealed that 57.5 percent of public school administrators reported *no* gifted children in their schools and that only a minor portion of the effort expended in their interests occurred at the elementary school level. Yet all of the administrators queried were products of professional "training" institutions in which a large percentage of them probably had read and heard about individual differences, and perhaps an even larger percentage had encountered admonitions regarding the importance of "meeting individual needs." Such persons are employed by society to provide professional direction and guidance for its educational programs. But it must be recognized that the majority of those who approve of and employ such administrators themselves are products of public school programs, such as those administered by the respondents in the survey.

THE PREACHING-PRACTICE GAP

The gap between preaching and practice, so far as making educational adjustments in the light of individual differences is concerned, is due to a number of factors. What amounts to hypocrisy is implicitly or explicitly accepted; talks about meeting individual pupil needs are splendid public relations gestures even though implementation tends so largely to be ignored. Implementation is difficult to effect because of "the public," many of whom did their learning under educationally limited conditions, or because the "training" institutions just preached and did not follow through in showing how such adjustments could be accomplished. The anticipated costs of making such adjustments were regarded as excessive, although funds for other equally costly, or even more expensive, undertakings were relatively easy to obtain. Or old habit patterns are hard to change.

Illustrative of this gap is the case of a state university college of education, evaluated more than once as among the top five in the nation. (The extent to which this kind of situation is generalizable is, of course, not known.) Its staff long has stressed the importance of "meeting individual needs." Over the past thirty years it has provided no left-hand seats or chairs for its students. Within the past ten years the person in charge of elementary education, when asked to identify two or three nearby elementary schools where students in a course on mental hygiene could observe exemplary teachers who really were individualizing the work of their pupils, was unable to do so. A teacher in a local school, who just recently had received her master's degree in elementary education from the college, continued routinely to assign "the next 15 problems in the book" to all the pupils in her class. In an elementary school over which it has exerted major influence, a father of a first-grader who was three inches taller than her classmates found it necessary, after his requests for suitable adjustments had been perfunctorily acknowledged and ignored, to go into the classroom and adjust his daughter's seat and desk to a more appropriate height. And a staff member who played the major consulting role in the development of a state program for the gifted, and who himself had studied gifted underachievers, helped the state department be proud of a program which during its first three years involved no systematic attempts at providing for gifted pupils below the sixth-grade level.

Educators as a group long have professed an awareness of society's need for the contributions of the gifted, but this seems to have been more an acknowledgement of the roles the gifted have played than any reflection of a firm commitment to doing things to facilitate their becoming effective members of society. Educators seem not as much to have provided for the proper education of their gifted as to have taken credit for their accomplishments. If the gifted are to play the roles in society of which they are capable, they need the kind of education that is conducive to that end.

If, as Wolfle (1957) reported, each 3 percent of increase in the gross national product requires a 5 percent increase in scientific manpower, the schools have a very real social need to meet. President de Kiewiet, of the University of Rochester, put the matter succinctly before the 79th Congress: "We can no longer afford to waste or neglect available resources of human skill. It has suddenly become clear that as a nation we are still too casual, too inexpert, too wasteful in our attitude towards brains and ability."

IN RETROSPECT— HITS AND MISSES

Intentionally not a text on methods of teaching the gifted, of which many are advocated, the present book has sought to identify and provide a rationale for factors that should loom large in providing appropriate learning opportunities for the gifted. A formal review of research on the gifted and their education has by no means been attempted, but research illustrative of and relevant to that rationale has been utilized. Certain needs and possibilities for research in both areas have become evident—one need being the importance of the reader's challenging statements in the text and in the field with view to ascertaining the extent of their validity.

There have been eight major thrusts in this book. Some of them are little in evidence in most texts in the field; others are so "old hat" as to seem trite. These emphases will be reviewed briefly.

Major Concern with the Social Milieu

For educators to think about and plan for the gifted essentially in only a formal educational context is unrealistic. The determination of whom to regard as gifted must be based primarily upon the needs of society. The fundamental attitudes of the gifted toward learning are socially determined. Just what and how they should learn must be recognized as a reflection of the society in which they have lived, in which they are living, and in which they will live. Their postschooling participation in society must be anticipated effectively in what and how they learn in school. Research on and about the gifted must be socially sensitive.

This is easily said and not often provided for. To some, it involves social perceptions that have been relevant to the maintenance of a static society—the society in which educators and school children's parents have grown up; to others, it involves trying to anticipate what a constantly emerging and changing society will be—the specifics of which cannot be sharply perceived but the major dimensions of which can be anticipated through an assessment of both immediate and later needs and in terms of history and philosophy. While the perception of society in a molar sense is necessary, it must incorporate also perceptions of subgroups and interpersonal relationships. The communication aspect of these is important—both among the gifted themselves and between the gifted and the nongifted.

It cannot be gainsaid that society has managed pretty well to get along and progress with the participation and contributions of those gifted who have managed to emerge from a condition of educational neglect. On the other hand, it cannot be disproven that society might be better off if the gifted had been more adequately nurtured and their superior potentials more fully capitalized upon. This contrast between a laissez faire attitude and one disposed toward a planned society is, of course, not unique to the field of education. Some deplore the former; others regard the latter in terms of its extreme, implicitly regimenting form. Sporadic crises tend to be disruptive to the former; ameliorative perceptions tend to reduce the threat seen fearfully in the latter. Either position, it seems, necessitates a serious consideration of the roles which the gifted are to play and how they can best be prepared to play them.

The Role of Philosophy

Although it is probably not a true dichotomy, man either reacts almost blindly from moment to moment, succumbing to immediate pressures, or he behaves in the light of some major orientation. Provisions for the gifted (this book contends) have been made more in the former way than in the latter. It seems probable that the intangibility of giftedness—its nature, its manifestations, and its "products"—has been largely contributive to society's actions, through its agency of education, and that society has tended to respond to threats to its security rather than to plan and respond, even to threats, in terms of an overall consideration of the potential role of the gifted in society. Many of society's actions in the interests of the disadvantaged, for instance (and the gifted well might be regarded as such, since so many of them have learned to be under-achievers), have been responses to issues as issues instead of responses in terms of the underlying major concepts. Such major orientations, regarded here as philosophies, have not been wanting. For the most part, they have to a discernible degree reflected a general sensitivity which, either implicitly or explicitly, has included the gifted as among those whose individual needs should be met.

While a philosophy of educating the gifted is, after all, an integral part of that of educating all children, it must incorporate those psychologically relevant facts and principles which sharpen it in terms of the gifted. Two essential emphases have been stressed: that the gifted should be educated such that their reasonable self-fulfillment, or self-actualization, was assured, and that the gifted should be educated with view to their becoming contributing members of society. Lest the unwary regard the top-level gangster as bright and self-fulfilled (which he probably is), he is not likely to be regarded by most as socially contributive (unless his existence and operations are regarded as the cause of the employment of more law enforcement personnel, thus providing jobs for more people).

But the existence of a supportive philosophy is not enough, as the history of education so well has shown. Again and again, the point has been made that those in charge of education must have not only a full comprehension of the philosophy but also a sustained and firm commitment to it and the capability of implementing it. Only in such light can any sound educational program for the gifted—national, state, or local—be mounted and maintained.

Definition of the Gifted

Generally, the responsibility for defining the gifted has imposed little restraint on authors in this field, one even deigning to define the gifted population on which he wrote a book. The post hoc view—regarding as gifted those children who already had manifested superiority in performance—long has limited action to meet their needs, in that they thus tended to be identified late, relatively insensitive educational screening was involved, and latent and disadvantaged gifted tended to be overlooked. The relatively short-lived defining of them as constituting the top sixth of the general population came more from a temporary sense of social need than from psychological and educational understanding, and it was, at times, construed unwisely in terms of the top sixth of any class rather than in terms of the total population of children. Defining them as the top 2 or 3 percent of the general school population may have been more a matter of administrative convenience than of a grasp of the essential nature of giftedness or social need. Terman's defining of his gifted group in terms of Binet IQ of 125 or more reflected a sensitivity to the importance of the ability to generalize and abstract.

And yet even Terman's definition was fundamentally an arbitrary one, since all children, and even some lower animals, manifest this kind of behavior. It therefore seemed necessary independently to turn to some social criterion which then could be stated in (admittedly oversimplified) psychometric terms. The definition proposed herein was so developed. It appeared that some 5 or 6 percent of our adult population was engaged in occupations that required at least a discernibly high degree of ability to deal with generalizations and abstractions. Adding to this percentage an arbitrary "insurance" factor of 2 or 3 percent for error and loss in the system, and relating this to the distribution of Binet IQs, it appears that the schools should anticipate that at least those of Binet IQ of 125 and above (or equivalent) would be needed to carry on the major functions of society—science, law, medicine, education, architecture, engineering, and the like. It should be noted that this definition is as of the current status of society; later studies of like nature would be needed to ascertain if the needs of society have changed. But the primary anchorage, or criterion, of this uniquely arrived-at definition is one of social need, with a secondary translation in terms of objective test results.

Incidental to this, it should be realized that the psychometric criterion of a Binet IQ has been used because the Binet yields evidence more sharply relatable to school-learning behavior and to the capacity to think abstractly than do many other individual tests. While both the Binet and the increasingly widely used Wechsler Intelligence Scale for Children (WISC) can yield such IQs, the same number from the two tests does not "say" the same thing psychoeducationally. This is particularly true as regards the use of the Binet and the WISC Full Scale IQ; the WISC Verbal IQ, as contrasted with its Performance IQ and the Full Scale IQ, most nearly "says" the same thing as the Binet IQ about a child in terms of his capacity to generalize and think abstractly in ways directly relevant to the most crucial aspects of school learning. When used properly in terms of soundly validated research on children, the WISC does have other potential psychological descriptive values.

Such a definition obviously is a gross one, but it provides a rational basis for the necessary first step in identifying the gifted. The necessity for a full psychological assessment, rather than only psychometric characterization, of such children has been stressed. The residual heterogeneity of the population thus identified still must be recognized. Not only are there quite large differences among those in this group in the core characteristic of capacity to think abstractly—to acquire and use symbols—but there are other important differences among them. There are those who, along with superior capacity in this area, have marked aptitudes in the area to which the term "talent" is applied. The position taken in this book has been that truly talented individuals are high also in basic capacity to think abstractly and to conceptualize. The distinction between those who are truly talented and those who are only, or primarily, highly skilled is made on this basis. While this position appears rational, in terms of the psychological characteristics of the behaviors of the talented, it may be regarded by some as arbitrary. But arbitrariness can be equally validly ascribed to those who perceive "talent" more expansively.

Within this group, too, there will tend to be some who can be regarded as "creative." If the capacity to create, as the term generally is used, is regarded as a psychological trait, then it must be assumed that it exists among all individuals, differing in degree among them. While the objective measurement of this capacity to create is not nearly as well validated as is the measurement of the capacity to function symbolically, the relationship between the two appears reasonably highly positive. The fact that this kind of relationship appears more clearly to be rather high among adults who have been socially evaluated as creative than among children suggests the probable importance of appropriate nurturance of this capability in gifted children. The position has been taken that divergent thinking in children, which most of the tests of "creativity" most plausibly sample, is regarded as differentiable from thinking creatively in that the latter entails social communication which, in effect, involves a social evaluation, or validation, of the products of divergent thinking. It is the nurturance of divergent thinking in children, then, that is educationally and socially important.

The position taken has been that the capacity to function symbolically, denoted as "learning aptitude" because of its educational connotation as contrasted with the more broadly perceived "intelligence," is basically genetically determined. This, however, is by no means the whole picture. While this potentiality often seems to be self-manifesting, it must have the opportunity to do so, probably often should be nurtured, and certainly can be depressed. This condition has particular significance regarding the gifted who are among the socioeconomically disadvantaged. In this regard, the all-too-slowly recognized distinction between the disposition to function symbolically and achieved functioning in that area is of very real potential value in identifying the gifted among the disadvantaged—a matter of no mean social importance.[1] To this end, identification of such gifted more in terms of the author's "process" than in terms of "product" seems particularly promising.

Emphasis on the Individual

Regarding the performances of gifted pupils in the light of the average of their classes or of their grade norms has contributed in no small degree to their being, in fact, the most retarded children in school. The fact that gifted pupils so often are perceived, albeit correctly, as performing academically better than their classmates has done much to lull parents and educators into accepting or tolerating performances that generally have been well below psychologically based expectations. Particularly important with respect to the gifted, but a concept in fact applicable in regard to all children, their academic performances should be evaluated in the light of their respective capabilities. Over the long haul, though varying at certain times, the educational achievements of the gifted should closely approximate their individual learning aptitudes.

In the case, for instance, of a gifted youngster who is sitting in the third grade, whose level of capability (MA) has been adequately ascertained and whose educational achievements have been properly measured, he should not be per-

---

[1] In September 1973 a national conference was held on the "culturally different gifted." Reports from the conference are available from The Foundation for Exceptional Children, 1920 Association Drive, Reston, Va., 22091.

ceived as just doing better than his classmates but, rather, in terms of how closely his level of educational achievement approximates his own mental level. Care must be taken not to oversimplify this by expecting all levels of his achievement thus to approximate his mental level, because performances in different educational areas involve different degrees of operation of the potential reflected in the MA. There are discernible intraindividual differences in educational performances, and the pattern of each child's differences will vary from time to time depending upon the nature of his educational exposure and motivation. Proposed for this purpose was a chart, which could be used probably not more often than once a year, on which an elementary school child's capability and achievement levels can be plotted in order that the teacher, the child, and the child's parents can reasonably precisely perceive his status; a comparable characterization of a pupil's potential and performance by the use of centiles or stanines is possible at the secondary level.

Again, this matter has been put quite simplistically, since only educational achievements have been considered. Even properly ascertained mental levels, not just IQs, should be regarded as minima. But the importance of regarding other behaviors of gifted children—or of all children—in terms of their mental levels should be recognized. Is our bright third-grader expected to behave socially like his classmates, or is it properly recognized that his interpersonal relationships could be more rewarding and meaningful to him and comprehensible to others when he is given opportunities, at least part of the time, to interact with others whose mental levels approximate his? Since curiosities and interests tend to be related more to mental level than to chronological age, although these may be attenuated by the stage of motor development and social conditions, is his

plausible boredom with those interests manifested by his classmates perceived in terms of the possible challenge and reward in areas more suited to his level of mental development?

Important as it is to regard the different kinds of performances of the gifted child in the light of his own capability to perform, there still is a need for his performances to be perceived in terms of a social frame of reference. Regarding him as being capable of performing at some higher level involves a comprehension of how others, generally, at those levels have performed. The determination of levels necessarily is a social process and is only descriptive in nature. When it is said that ten-year-olds (or sophomores, or any other group) do thus and so, it logically means that the average performance of ten-year-olds (or of any other group) was found to be thus and so. When the behavior of a gifted six-year-old or of a retarded fourteen-year-old is observed to be similar to that of the average ten-year-old it is descriptively put in terms of a social frame of reference when it is said that he behaves like a ten-year-old. Given a six-year-old or a fourteen-year-old child who is observed to have ten-year-old capabilities, he is perceived in terms of a social frame of reference when it is inferred that he should be able to perform, at least academically, much like all average ten-year-olds.

Regarding gifted youngsters as "ready" for advanced placement examination or work requires a knowledge of what generally is involved. Deciding whether a pupil's performance adequately approximates his capability level is a matter of evaluating the individual in terms of himself (although social norms are used to this end); deciding whether the individual, in terms of basic capacity or achievement, can perform well enough to qualify for certain kinds of group membership or games involves the use of social frames of reference. Both are necessary.

The pupil, his teacher, and his parents, need to know how he is doing with what he has; he, and they, need to know whether what he has in the way of capability or achievement is adequate to different kinds of social demands.

Educational Orientation

In the belief that the preciseness of people's speech reflects the preciseness of their thinking, the connotation of "training" is deplored. The implication of the general use of "teaching" is rejected, and the illogicality of "overachievement" is so apparent as to preclude its use in thoughtful communication. It is suspected that the prevalence of the use of the first two terms reflects, more than many might wish, a drillmaster perception both of the preparation of the professional personnel for working with children in school and of the procedures employed in connection with pupils' learnings. It hardly seems to be academic quibbling to observe that training school personnel to teach children denotes quite a different perception of the educational process than does preparing school personnel to facilitate the learning of children. More likely to be associated with the former are regimentation and rote learning; with the latter, individualization and nurturance. It is believed that this distinction is of particular importance in regard to the education of gifted children. For them especially it is more important that the educational personnel in their lives be substantively steeped than that they be made adept in some particular teaching method. We cannot so easily dispense with the term "teacher," but the person in that role should be regarded as the one specifically charged with the responsibility of so manipulating pupils' environments as to facilitate their learning.

This is but prelude to the focal point of view that there is no "method"—administrative or instructional—that is uniquely appropriate to or totally effective with the gifted. (It is believed that this and following statements are applicable to varying degrees in regard to all children, but we shall proceed only in terms of the gifted.) While differences among approaches are discernible—administrative provisions such as acceleration, early admission, tracking, and special classes, and instructional approaches such as the use of interest groups, individually prescribed instruction, enrichment, the "discovery" method, and others—arguments as to which is best or better are just that, and even discussions about their relative merits are of limited fruitfulness when there is an underlying premise that any one of them is "the" answer. In the educational life of a gifted youngster, it is possible that all of them may, at one time or other, be put to good use.

Even though claims of the desirability of no single approach can be justified, the educational nurturance that is needed has certain clearly identifiable characteristics. Indicating the order of their relative importance is unwarranted, since they are essentially equipotential. The nurturance should be substantively rich, both as regards materials in and related to the school and as regards the scholarly adequacy of the teacher. To a marked degree, it should evoke "reasoning" behaviors—discovery, generalization, evaluation, exploration, extrapolation, and divergent and creative thinking—but it must involve also a sensitivity to rote learning in its secondary and purely contributive role. It should be highly adaptable to situations such as the kinds of learning expected—both immediate and remote, in quantitative, verbal, and social situations. It should always be adaptable to the natures of individual learners—their levels of development and their social milieus. It should be sensitive to the fact of concept hierarchy, providing for each child's acquisition of concepts appropriate to his immediate capability and facilitative to his acquiring more advanced concepts, ensuring his acquiring the perceptions and the low-level concepts that will be contributive to such advancement. It should provide for each child's seeking out new conditions and new relationships, and it should provide for a degree of intellectual abandon which will nurture his thinking divergently. It should provide for success in the learning endeavor, thereby inculcating a joy in the act of learning and thus contributing to learning to learn. Given at least these in a tolerant social and educational climate, his emotional well-being and social adjustment are practically assured.

Underachievement in the gifted

The condition of underachievement in the gifted should be regarded as a result of learning. The term typically denotes the fact that a pupil is performing, usually academically, at a level that is lower than his level of capability for such learning. Either or both of these two levels may have been arrived at intuitively or by means of objective measurement. Necessarily, it is perceived in an individual frame of reference—the pupil is doing less well than *his* capacity suggests is possible; the use of a social frame of reference—that he is doing less well than the average of his class—can be psychoeducationally cluttered. More often than not, the condition comes about when the child is performing at a suspected or known subpotential level and this performance is tolerated, encouraged, or otherwise reinforced by significant others in his milieu—his teachers, his parents, and/or his social peers. In such situations, some impression or knowledge exists regarding his level of capability, and the disparity between performance and potential exists even though its presence may, on provocation, be deplored and even adjusted to.

Another, more pernicious, possibility exists: the child's performance may arouse no curiosity or concern, or it even may be perceived with the accompanying belief that he lacks even average capability, and the performance, whatever it is, may be accepted (reinforced) because "He's at least trying." In such instances latent high capability and the fact of underachievement both can be missed —a condition that easily could exist among the disadvantaged.

In both kinds of situations, underachieving behavior has been learned. Such learning starts early and, by the time its presence becomes grossly observable, the habit pattern is so strongly established that conventional corrective efforts tend to be of little avail. For some reason, however, certain educators have gone on record as refusing to regard underachievement as a major problem in the area of the gifted, thus, in effect, further contributing to what amounts to a very real social loss.

That underachievement by the gifted represents a less-than-adequate return on their intellectual capital and thereby represents an educational short-changing of society becomes a source of deep personal dissatisfaction when certain of them undertake more advanced work and fail in it both because of their poor habits of application and the lack of relevant substantive preparation. The possibility cannot be ignored that, inherent in the periodic unrest of youth, there is a mixture of protest against the limited apparent social relevance of prescribed curricula and of the underlying frustration resulting from the condition of underachievement—whether such protest is forthrightly aimed at the institution of education or is displaced toward current issues. But such extrapolations, even if valid, are not sufficient to make a case against underachievement; the attending individual malaise and the ensuing social loss also are very important.

A sound perception of educational underachievement must incorporate a recognition of four points:

1. The presumption of absolute efficiency—of each child's achievement levels always being in perfect harmony with his capability to achieve—is not implied. Neither level is that precisely measurable and there are times when there can be legitimate lags, which, however, later can be lessened.

2. The condition of underachievement, as thus tolerantly described, is neither universal nor of uniform magnitude, but it is discouragingly prevalent.

3. The condition per se is not formally, institutionally encouraged; it is unwittingly nurtured, in large part by the manner in which the achievements of the gifted are so often faultily observed.

4. The earlier in the child's school life the possibility of the occurrence of underachievement is recognized, the more likely its development can be avoided; and when it does occur, the earlier its presence is discovered, the greater the probability of success in correcting the condition.

Divergence and creativity

Divergent thinking and creative behavior in the gifted merit serious consideration. As was pointed out, the scientific delineation of divergent thinking provided psychological support for a concern with creativity which educators long had recognized philosophically but had pretty generally ignored. To some this awakened concern constituted a welcome escape from an increasing emphasis on rote learning and what was being perceived increasingly as a movement toward intellectual and social regimentation. To others it was, of course, a threat, since it invited departures, even though

in most instances only temporary, from what they regarded as important: basic learning of "the" answers.

Whether it was regarded as "liberating the mind" or as a plausible educational excursion, for many divergent thinking became an educational fad. To some it became even a fetish, an all-consuming endeavor believed to be beneficial primarily in its own right. Others came to believe it should be incorporated into the larger gamut of cognitive behaviors that could be of value both to the individual and, ultimately, to society. To some the tangibility of its outcomes was paramount, as in art, the theater, and in music. To others, not denying the importance of such, its major benefits inhered in an increased disposition to explore other-than-conventional, stereotyped approaches to problems, to additional facts and phenomena, to new structurings of relationships, to conceptualizations other than the most obvious or the longest-accepted. To some, it was a new frontier that became too quickly and narrowly generalized; to others, it was an awakened recognition, elaborative of and enriching to the picture of major educational outcomes, of the importance of revitalizing and capitalizing upon children's early disposition to be untrammeled by the limiting effects of "reality." And to some, it was another educational activity to which only specified school periods should be devoted for all children at the same time, whereas others more appropriately sought to encourage it and cultivate it whenever opportunities presented themselves with individual children.

The educator is obligated to capitalize upon tendencies of children to think divergently or creatively. To do this, it is necessary, first, that he be aware that such a disposition exists and know what its characteristics are. He himself must be sufficiently emotionally secure that he can at least tolerate such divergent behavior, just as the child must be emotionally secure enough to engage in such behavior. Beyond tolerance, the educator must nurture such behavior, perhaps starting with class activities directed to that end but quickly proceeding predominantly in terms of the events and readiness of each child. This nurturance has two important aspects: the readiness to capitalize upon such manifestations and, if necessary, to create situations which will evoke them, and the reinforcement of such behaviors when they do occur, spontaneously or in response to stimulation. In doing so, the educator must realize that, as in the cases of other behaviors, children manifest the behavior as a means of satisfying significant others in their environs—extrinsic motivation, but that they can come increasingly to behave in such a manner as a result of demands inherent in the situation—intrinsic motivation, and that the latter condition is the ultimate goal of such nurturance. Since the gifted have both more components with which to "create" (facts, elementary relationships, and so on) and a greater capability for seeing quickly and accurately more relationships among those components than do the nongifted, the probability of their being more "creative" than the nongifted is one of the givens in the total situation.

Tactics and Strategy

Those educators who take comfort in doing "at least something for the gifted" very well might be doing something inimical to the interests of gifted school children. Initiating "programs" for the gifted by providing for them, in some way or other, from the sixth grade up, a practice probably based upon the operation of the post hoc definition of the gifted, is a case in point. Such a tactical approach may, in fact, be helpful to certain of the gifted at that level and may correctly be regarded as trying to meet

a need that is narrowly perceived and defined, but it cannot be regarded as a program. Tactics is the taking of action in the here and now; probably, as often as not, it contributes little to the solution of the overall problem of which the specific need of the moment is but a part. However, when tactical steps are taken knowingly as a part of a larger strategy, they not only help to meet the needs in the particular situation, or kind of situation, but also contribute to the accomplishment of the larger goal for which the strategy has been drawn up. Tactics tend to be issue- or situation-oriented rather than concept-oriented. Such is true whether one is thinking in terms of action at the national, state, or local level.

In contrast with acting tactically, thinking and acting strategically involves the comprehension of the problem in its total, or at least much larger, ramifications and a conceptualization of a wide-ranging attack on the problem in the light of a broad philosophy which incorporates an integration of all, or as many as possible, of the facts relevant to the problem. While thinking, planning, and acting strategically in the interests of the gifted necessarily will involve a recognition that some gifted school children will need some corrective and remedial provisions, the major thrust must be preventive. To this end, the competent program consultant starts at least the major portion of her program (tactics-within-strategy, rather than just tactics) with the youngest gifted children in the school and builds it progressively up the educational ladder, capitalizing tactically upon the varying degrees of readiness among the school personnel with whom she is working. Like an orchestra director, she brings into action at proper times whatever components are appropriate to the total performance.

Strategy dictates that planning and acting in the interests of the gifted must be primarily programmatic in nature and only incidentally in terms of specific practices. The specifics of such strategy will differ somewhat as regards planning at the national, state, and local level. Essential at all these levels, of course, would be the delineation of the socially relevant and psychologically sound philosophy in terms of which the program is to be developed. At the local level in particular, at least the following program features should figure prominently:

1. There should be a socially and psychologically defensible definition of the gifted.
2. The program should provide for appropriate entry and placement of pupils into the schools and grade levels.
3. It should be characterized by fluidity of individualized scheduling and work, thus making for adaptive and readaptive provisions for each child over his educational life span.
4. It should reflect a sustained sensitivity to the interrelatedness of the content to be learned and of the processes to be cultivated and nurtured.
5. The advance planning should provide for continuity—both as regards the educational life of each pupil and as regards the maintenance and further development of the program.

The importance of other factors such as pupil assessment and evaluation, financing, and research must also be recognized.

Research

No area of exceptionality among school children has been more broadly researched than that of the gifted. This is true particularly as regards the longitudinal and essentially validating study of the gifted. Research on the education of the gifted, while having all the complications and contaminations of all the research on educational approaches and procedures, generally has reflected beneficial results both educationally and so-cially. The study of society's need for high-level personnel consistently has shown a wastage of high potential and the importance of providing systematically for their adequate education. The facts about and needs of the gifted, remarkably established from the time of Terman in the 20s, far exceed education's systematic efforts to provide for them. Those who have opposed special efforts to educate the gifted have tended either to ignore facts at hand or to distort them by taking out of context certain of the findings.

While research has reasonably well delineated the characteristics, needs, and possibilities of the gifted, more definitive research remains to be done. More research is needed, for instance, on the nature and extent of the inter- and intra-individual heterogeneity among them, on the extent of their presence among the disadvantaged, on the nature of creative behavior and the validation of instruments purporting to measure "creativity," on communication and other social phenomena in relationships both between the gifted and the nongifted and among the gifted themselves, on their geographic mobility, on their occupational adaptability, and on the gifted who have not had the opportunity to benefit from special educational provisions. Owing to the psychological nature of the phenomenon of giftedness, it seems likely that such research would not alter significantly the basic picture of needs and possibilities, but could do much to sharpen the picture and enhance their social contributions.

Status

Certainly the facts we have on the gifted, and on society's need for the contributions of the gifted, far exceed the actions that have been taken in their light. Epitomizing the total situation is the fact that a majority of formally canvassed educational administrators maintained that they had no gifted children in their school systems. We know that when the gifted are properly provided for educationally, they are better educated and more socially sensitive and contributive, yet relatively little is provided to that end. We have convictions resulting in both omission and commission that have not been affirmed or refuted. Unfounded fears of a generalized elitism often undergird failure to take constructive action. And there probably are convictions supportive to the implementation of efforts in the interests of the gifted—on particular educational practices, on creativity, on prevalence among the disadvantaged, for instance, which themselves still need validation. And we have fundamental needs that are not being well met —the enhancement of self-fulfillment through legitimately expectable achievement rather than the derogation of self-respect through underachievement and the wasteful failure to plan to capitalize upon and utilize high potential in socially important roles.

IN PROSPECT— NEEDS AND POSSIBILITIES

It makes no sense to be concerned for the gifted as though they were an isolated and encapsulated group functioning in a purely compartmentalized situation called the school. They have come out of a social context which has affected them, they are doing their school learning in a context which itself has major social components within its own structure and in relation to others, and they will go out from their formal educational setting into a society that is complex and constantly changing. Perforce, they must do their learning so as to accommodate the seeming paradox between the fact that the only thing that is constant is change and the reality that the more things change the more they are the same. They must do their learning in

terms of what things are at the moment and at the same time be ready and able to learn things as they will become. They in particular are capable of learning that while the specifics of society change, there are generalizations, principles, and ethical and moral value systems that can be conducive to the understanding, acceptance, and adjustment to inevitable social change, even though some of them may be subject to modification due to continuing scientific discoveries and altering social conditions.

While all children are subject to the immediate and ultimate demands of this changing-though-constant society, the gifted, by virtue of their greater ability to function symbolically, can be expected to be able to understand and adjust to the complexities of their immediate situations and to profit from the kinds of learning that will facilitate their subsequent adjustment to evolving social demands. If, during their formal schooling, they have learned to learn and have been enabled to be successful in learning to enjoy the challenge of having to learn more, and if their disposition to seek new perceptions and conceive of new principles and relationships has been nurtured, their being able to assume major socially contributive roles is enhanced, if not assured.

In this section we shall review some illustrative major social changes and constancies and explore certain related educational needs and possibilities, especially as regards the gifted. Although identified separately, the different variables must be recognized as highly interactive and highly interdependent. Single causation is a very low-level concept; no response, personal or social, results from a single stimulus.

Facets of the Milieu

The focus of concern and the nature of interpersonal involvement have been expanding from what was essentially local even a century ago to state, national, and international perspectives. While matters that are essentially local still have to be dealt with in terms of local realities, increasingly the manners in which they are dealt with are coming to be worked out in terms of state and/or national conditions and regulations, and, at times, in terms of international realities, as, for instance, in the case of the utilization of natural resources. The values of goods and services are less and less determined locally and more and more influenced by union efforts, federal governmental regulations, and by the value of the dollar on the international currency market. Heavily contributive to this change has been the role played by communication—increased facilities for travel and for the exchange of information.

Changes
in the population

The population disposition within the United States has shifted from predominantly rural to very heavily urban, and the high concentrations of population are beginning to spread out into the suburbs, giving rise to the concept of the megalopolis as a constellation of cities, suburbs, and neighboring small towns and communities as an economic entity. The identification of school districts, once such a relatively simple matter, now is in a state of flux.

The age constitution of our population is changing. The adolescent and youth group, increasing both in relative numbers and affluence, is being given greater attention with regard to the marketing of goods. By virtue of improved health and work conditions, a much larger portion of our society is made up of older persons, whose needs—physical, social, and psychological—are only beginning to be recognized, let alone met. Their presence is helping to influence

the growing realization that there is an increasing need for services, as contrasted with earlier primary concern with providing materials. Some are trying to reconcile the effects of enforced retirement and its presumed lack of social production with the possible productivity of "senior citizens." Pressey (1967), for instance, has pointed out that Michelangelo was chief architect of St. Peter's from age 72 until 89, Voltaire published a tragedy at 83, Benjamin Franklin began his autobiography at 65 and finished it at 82, and at 70 helped draft the Declaration of Independence. Goethe completed *Faust* at 82, and Churchill was Prime Minister of England from 77 to 81.

More than ever before, our population is mobile, both geographically and occupationally. As Wolfle (1971) pointed out, "From Herodotus to Adam Smith to the Bureau of the Census there is evidence for what can be called the first principle of occupational specialization: As a society advances economically and culturally, the number of occupational specialities increases" (p. 11). He revealed that in an average recent year, one professional man in ten has made a geographic move and one in twenty has changed from one kind of occupation to another. A study by the National Academy of Sciences of the period 1958–1966 revealed, for instance, that of one class of Massachusetts Institute of Technology graduates, half had left their first jobs within three years, two-thirds within four years, and three-fourths within five years after graduation. Of the 1894 solid-state physicists identified in the 1964 National Register of Scientists and Engineers, 1388 had their Ph.D.s in other branches of physics, 318 in chemistry, 109 in engineering, and 33 in a variety of other disciplines. The continuous emergence of new specialties has significant implications regarding the education of the gifted.

Transition to adulthood

In the light of the generalization that the more primitive the society the more clearly identified and defined is the age at which its members make the transition from carefree childhood to responsible adulthood, such transition in the United States has become increasingly delayed and obscured. Partly ameliorative has been the passage of laws concerning child labor, marriage, voting rights, property rights, driving rights, and criminal responsibility. The overlap with these of laws pertaining to compulsory school attendance and child dependency has contributed to an ambiguity of the social status of the adolescent, who is paradoxically confronted by the statements, "You are old enough to know better" and "Remember, you are not an adult yet." The fact that such points in life necessarily are defined in terms of chronological age rather than mental level helps to make difficult certain adjustments by the gifted. The very capable twelve-year-old finds difficulty in engaging in even part-time work experience in an office or laboratory that could be both intellectually and financially rewarding to him, whereas a much less capable person of legal age can be so employed. The superior capability of the gifted to understand the concepts underlying the multiplicity of changing criteria of appropriate ageness and the possible contributive value of extraschool learning experiences call for the educator's full comprehension of both, and the ensuing attempts to effect productive matches between them.

Trade unionism

Increasingly, professional and paraprofessional groups are becoming infused with the concepts and procedures of trade unionism. While certain factors ostensibly contribute to this development

—mere size of an organization which increases the distance between employer and employee, improved communication which facilitates learning of the effectiveness of the use of organized pressures, and changing financial conditions which make added demands on both employer and employee—an important question must be raised: to what extent has the pervasive regard of professional preparation as "training" been contributive to regarding the profession of teaching by administrators as subject to regimentation and time-clock-punching and by teachers as a time-spent-on-the-job type of involvement? This is, of course, both an exaggeration and an oversimplification of the situation, but there does appear to have been a movement away from perceiving education as a profession requiring sound substantive preparation and deep personal commitment toward perceiving it as a trade for which workers are trained and at which they will put in the required time. To the extent that such is the case, implications regarding the proper education of the gifted can be of major import. While we are fortunate to have, perhaps, a predominance of professionally committed teachers, the inroads of the trade union toiler are all too discernible.

Changing attitudes toward education

Certain attitudes toward education also are changing. Some which have been relatively dormant have become manifest; others are emerging as a function of the current social situation. Only five of them will be identified here. The value of education probably always has been criticized by some members of society. Highly regarded and strongly advocated at times of emergencies, whether because of its presumed directly contributive values or possible transfer of training values, the adequacy of education's meeting social needs was increasingly questioned during the 1960s and 70s. This criticism was not only voiced by many adults who had been "educated" but also manifested by those still involved in the educational process. In spite of oases in the educational desert, the frames of reference of the many who were critical of education were highly diverse, and gaps between promise and performance were widely identified and deplored. Contentions regarding the inadequate education of the gifted were but a small part of the total picture of dissatisfaction.

STARTING EARLIER. The growing conviction that the educational process should be started earlier in children's lives has been conducive to the lowering of the age of social responsibility for education. The actions taken in the light of this conviction have been based not only on a belief in the value of more and earlier education but also on the emergence of a socioeconomic condition—the need to provide for the young children of an increasingly large number of working mothers. Increasing attention was paid to similar efforts in Israel, Russia, and China. Possible attendant psychological and health benefits were increasingly recognized. Even though kindergartens slowly became integral parts of public education programs, both nursery schools and kindergartens had been accessible generally to the more economically advantaged in our society and had tended to operate as paraschool activities. While both kinds of private and public efforts could be beneficial to some gifted children, this was not regarded as the primary basis for justifying them.

CONCERN FOR THE DISADVANTAGED. Considerably contributive to this changing attitude was the burgeoning concern for the disadvantaged. A combination of hu-

manitarian and economic motivations, helped by a growing dissatisfaction with the extent to which much education was regarded as lacking social viability and the increasing discovery of the seeming importance of early and socially relevant nurturance, created a sensitivity to the disadvantaged unparalleled in our history. There being some chronological overlap between this and the impact of the Sputnik era, the prevalence and problems of the gifted among the disadvantaged received increased attention. The relative roles played by ethnicity, socioeconomic status, and learning aptitude in the education of the disadvantaged are by no means clear. Socioeconomic status appears to be more crucial than ethnicity. Among those who have managed to reach college, Sewall and Shah (1967) have observed, "If other factors are allowed to vary as they will, young people of most minority groups— Negro, Spanish-American, Indian—are less likely to enter college than are young people of the Caucasian majority, but if ability scores and socioeconomic status are held constant, there is very little difference in college attendance that can be attributed to race per se."

ACCOUNTABILITY. The growing belief that education should accomplish what it claimed and the varied evidence that it was falling far shorter than many had hoped or realized provided fertile soil for the growing attitude that it should be held accountable. Contributive to this were the development and use of systems accounting in business and government, improvements in educational measurement and research, and the growing problem of paying for education. To a limited degree, this attitude was not new with respect to the education of the gifted; it long had been demonstrated (although only sporadically) that the gifted were underachievers—that the schools tended not to help them learn to legitimately expectable extents.

AVERSION TO REGIMENTATION. Orwell's satirical *1984* and Whyte's *The Organization Man* were both timely manifestations of and powerful stimuli to a growing attitude against regimentation. Largely contributed to by increasing misuse and abuse of testing procedures, the growing identification of social stereotypes, and, perhaps, increasing mechanization in society, there thus developed in our society an aversion to practices long inherent, although essentially futilely objected to, in education. Such a development was conducive to the reawakening of at least two long-held educational aspirations—both of particular relevance to the gifted. Support was provided for the view that what was called education should incorporate, in addition to the too-pervasive commitment to factual, or rote learning, learning experiences involving the nurturance and cultivation of "reasoning"—seeing relationships, extrapolating, generalizing, conceptualizing, and evaluating. Support was provided also for the view that educators should capitalize upon and nurture the long-ignored, nascent divergent thinking and creative behavior of children.

Important Constancies

With all of these, and other, changes, there are major constancies. The overriding one, of course, is the constancy, the inevitability, of change itself. Along with this, society always will have a continuing need for and belief in some kind of education of its members, probably not only for the young ones in it, in order that the society can be perpetuated. The form and content of that education will need to vary with the kind of society and the total context within which the society exists.

Psychological constancies

And there are important psychological constancies. The fact of the existence of a wide variety of individual differences among the members of society is a given. While refinements in the understanding of the nature of the process of learning and of its important facilitating and deterring accompaniments will continue to be discovered and the ways in which the act and manner of nurturance of learning will be "newly" described in varying ways, the fundamentals of the learning act and of its nurturance remain. The essence of behavior modification, for instance, is as old as man's—and animal's—learning; current formal recognition of it has involved mainly a systematization of what has been knowable about it and refinements in its intentional use, although seemingly inevitable overgeneralizations regarding its use and value are appearing. Success always has been essential to learning, although its definition and implementation still call for greater understanding and use.

Role of the schools

Just what and how the schools should do for and with children in order that the needs of society will be met has been a matter of constant concern. Granting the constancy of society's belief that its members should be educated, this constancy has involved the continuing dilemma of opting for skill training versus broader preparation. Rather than totally accepting either position, the continuing question has been how much of which, when, and for whom? Paralleling this is the continuing question as to whether education is preparation for life or whether education is life.

To what extent should formal education be responsible for providing the training needed by skilled workers? For providing a broader preparation for those who would work in science and the professions? Should education attempt to serve both purposes—by providing the skill training first for all and then the broader preparation later for those who remained within the system, by attempting to provide both kinds of education essentially simultaneously for all from the start, or by being committed solely to the one or the other? Should education be regarded as specifically preparatory for adult life, or should the schools provide an education as essentially an enhancement of children's lives on the assumption that, in living such enriched lives, the children thereby become prepared for adult life? Or, as some have believed, should perhaps the school years be regarded primarily or solely as a time situation during which maturation would be allowed to take place naturally, perhaps with a bit of nurturance but definitely not dominated by any challengeable presumption that conventional "teaching" would take place during that interval? The history of education is replete with advocacies of each of these views and with the reports of organized educational efforts along each of these lines of thought. Each of these positions abounds in implications regarding the nature of the education of the gifted.

The phenomenon of protest

It would seem appropriate to identify also the constancy of the phenomenon of protest, limiting it here to protest against education by those still within the system. (The press for accountability in education, regardable as protest in nature, is not of this sort, since it has come primarily from those of postschool age.)

This phenomenon of protest should be perceived in terms of three frames of reference—the complexity of its causation, the observability of its manifestations, and the nature of its productivity. Usually, there are two or more conditions contributive to protest, although one condition serves as the precipitating cause. The manifestation of the protest may vary from a quiet, subtle, though always mounting aversion to the condition protested against to explosive social action, which may be either quite clearly directed against the aversive condition or directed toward some other social condition or organization (displacement). The protest usually is productive, although its fruits may be highly varied—from only relieving tension in the protestors to effecting changes in the condition against which the protest is directed. These changes may be directly socially contributive, or only secondary benefits may accrue.

In spite of some sincere and well-founded, though sporadic, attempts to try to improve educational practices, no small number of critics regard our educational system as essentially having gone forward backward over the past two centuries. Many activities which now are integral parts of the regular school curriculum appeared first as extracurricular activities which were instituted and engaged in by pupils, although coming later to be tolerated and even encouraged by some school personnel. Such activities were subtle and productive protests compensatory for the lack of social relevance of the basic curriculum. Edison and Lindberg protested by withdrawing from the formal educational picture.

A part of the protest movement of students in higher education in the 1960s was clearly directed against the educational structure. With the exception of the complete, selfish withdrawal of some from the educational and social scene, attempts were made to establish "free universities" and efforts were at least partially fruitful in causing the introduction of a broader range of social content into college and university offerings. Without integration being the issue, some protesting adults sought to establish "free schools" for their children. Much of this was attributable to the lack of fit between the nature of educational endeavors and the realities of extraschool society. That such protests were not minor adolescent gestures is reflected in the following comment made in *Youth Transition to Adulthood,* the report of the Panel on Youth of the President's Science Advisory Committee (1974):

> Every society must somehow solve the problem of transforming children into adults, for its very survival depends upon that solution. In every society there is established some kind of institutional setting within which the process of transition is to occur, in directions predicted by societal needs and values. In our view, the institutional framework for maturation in the United States is now in need of serious examination.

Again, while the tenor of this comment and the varied kinds of protest have not been presented in terms of the gifted, their relevance to the effective education of the gifted seems apparent.

Current Needs and Opportunities

The fact of a general need for providing more adequately for the effective education of the gifted seems well established. Certain quite specific needs have been considered: The performances of the gifted—academic and otherwise—must be evaluated in terms of each individual's capability as well as in terms of social norms. Correspondence course work seems little used for either enrichment or acceleration; there probably is a need for the development of such courses addressed more specifically to the needs of the gifted. That the PTA, theoretically a potentially vital force in education, could be of value in exerting part of its efforts in the interests of the gifted has been suggested. In some states, compensatory efforts by other groups of parents and by citizens' advisory committees have worked both for the gifted and for the general improvement of educational operation. Other factors warrant fuller consideration.

As regards education in general, at least four kinds of needs merit examination—the need for new thinking and action in regard to the content of education, the need for uninhibited critical thinking about methodological approaches, the need for sound thinking regarding the financing of educating the gifted, and the further consideration of the goals of educating the gifted. While each of these could warrant extended disquisition, they will be dealt with only briefly.

The content of education

The justification of old content and the identification of new content of education must be thought of in two ways —as contributive to the better education of all children and as particularly contributive to the effective education of the gifted. Developments over the 1960s and 70s in the areas of science and mathematics, for instance, have rather clearly reflected this difference—the improvements in science being more contributive to general education, although adding much of information value for the gifted, and the developments in mathematics being for the most part perceived by not a few as particularly contributive to the gifted. In fact, in the 70s, the general educator's enthusiasm over the new developments in the area of mathematics has begun to wane. Yet, for the gifted these developments contributed to their thinking mathematically. If there is a reversion to the older mathematics, a development probably quite meaningful for the masses, it is to be hoped that certain values for the gifted will not be sacrificed. New developments in the social studies and language areas, only flirted with so far, have promise both in broadening the awareness and understanding of the nongifted and in further contributing to higher conceptualizations in these areas by the gifted.

Methodological approaches

Methodological developments await both rediscovery and pioneering. Approaches involving one-to-one learning relationships, early capitalized upon as a means of facilitating education of the masses, are coming again to be recognized as having value not only to the tutor but also to the tutored. Such an approach can be of very real value to many gifted so long as the practice is not reduced to a sterile, time-saving, overgeneralized addiction. Generally, we continue to be committed to the classroom as the only locus of learning. While the sporadic excursions into the community, as a part of school-based learning, have merit, their use has been unduly circumscribed. England's "School of the Sea" involves an escape from provincial settings for a few weeks, but falls short of, say, a year's guided (learning) tour of a country or of the world. Bus-based efforts of this sort in our country have been so unusual as to be regarded as newsworthy. Land-based bus or railroad schools and internationally planned airplane schools are not beyond the realm of possibility. The TV with cable and closed-circuit arrangements serves mainly a base-broadening function but has great potential for some of the learning by the gifted. Programmed learning operations understandably are addressed more to the en-

hancement of general learning than to meeting the particular needs of the gifted, although developments in the nurturance of cognitive processes can be particularly contributive to learning by the gifted.

Financing programs

As legitimately serious as financial problems are in regard to education in general, the costs entailed by making special provisions for the adequate education of the gifted must be perceived in reasonable perspective. Many things can be done by insightful and committed teachers to enhance the education of the gifted that necessitate no extra, or relatively no major, expenditures. The everyday world teems with too-often unrecognized relationships, with many relatable phenomena, with possibilities of formulation of nurturing and stimulating conceptualizations for those who have the sensitivity, initiative, and substantive background to help children capitalize upon them. However, mounting programs with program consultants, added learning materials, and ancillary personnel call for expenditures that, in the last analysis, may be more properly regardable as "extra" costs. But, as only a casual consideration of change and improvement in education will show, what is to be regarded as "extra" is a function of just how the educational program itself is perceived, of the philosophy underlying education. Sound practices which at one time were introduced and were then perceived as costing "extra" tend to become integral parts of the ongoing program and not then to be regarded as extra. And what is regarded as essential and as extra depends upon overall societal values. As Cartter (1971) observed, "A nation that spends $17 billion on federal research and development but cannot find the $100 or $200 million to bolster the major institutions that produce trained intelligence to maintain our scientific effort will not long prosper." While his statement applies to scientific preparation in higher education, the attitude underlying it applies in thinking about the gifted in the public schools. Probably idiosyncratic value systems determine the uses to which we put our money more than do social needs.

Goals for the gifted

The position has been maintained that three fundamental objectives should be stressed in regard to educating the gifted: (1) that they be educated such that they become self-fulfilled, (2) that they be enabled to learn to function within a reasonable degree of their capability, and (3) that they be helped to learn such that they can contribute to society in harmony with their superior capability. The latter objective admits of two interpretations. One involves the assumption that the gifted, once they are early identified, are to be educated for the specific occupations for which they are believed to be suited. As a student said in his valedictory address, "What we resent is feeling that we are being educated only to fulfill some predetermined role in society." The other interpretation—that they should be educated for participation in more general kinds of roles rather than for immediately anticipatable, highly specifiable roles— is much the better for two reasons. First, such predetermination implies that society is static—that which has existed and does exist will exist—a position quite at variance with the reality of a constantly changing, emerging society. Second, high-level social roles exist today that weren't even generally thought of ten or twenty years ago. The essential nature of giftedness is such that this generalization appears tenable: barring early personal (not imposed) commitments to

some area of interest (the exception rather than the rule), the brighter the child the broader should be his substantive learning—both factual and conceptual—and the later he properly can be expected to concentrate on any given area of learning and possible later social involvement. The emphasis is on the gifted's learning to learn rather than just learning.

Instead of thinking about the education of the gifted in terms of specific individuals' being earmarked for specific future roles in society, it is better to regard them in terms of possible later matches between their capabilities and categories of social involvement and contribution. In 1962 Fritz Machlup, of New York University, identified knowledge industries and knowledge occupations which included education, research and development, communications media, information machines, and information services. This kind of thinking is relatable to Hollingworth's observation (1936): "It seems highly probable that *conservation* of knowledge in the learned professions depends mainly on intellects between (Binet) 130 and 160 IQ; while actual *advancement* of knowledge requires a degree of intelligence above 160 IQ." Certainly in the later stages of education there should begin to appear differential adaptation in the education of the gifted.

The schools should be properly concerned with the creative possibilities and the creative behavior of the gifted, giving critical thought to the extent to which extant content and methods are, or can be, made meaningfully nurturant to such behavior. Certainly of at least equal importance, educators themselves ought to be as committed to creative thinking on their own part as they are to causing it to occur in the children under their jurisdiction. In contrast with the products of divergent thinking in children, those of adults face a test of social relevance—whether immediate or ultimate. In the case of divergent thinking, or creative behavior, in the area of the arts, this criterion is employed later than in the cognitive area.

Creative thinking by educators

The need for creative thinking by educators probably is greater in the content area of education than in the methods area. Certain possibilities along this line have been suggested which have merit. The more obvious public school developments in the areas of science and mathematics came about largely under a threat stimulus to society. But there are less obvious, and perhaps equally fundamental, needs for the introduction and development of content areas that can both enlighten the masses and challenge the highest potentials of the gifted, as, for example, economics, from consumer economics to more substantive economics; law and government, from local to national and international, and from services to substantive perspectives; semantics, from elementary precision in communication and thought to the complexities of communication processes; anthropology and psychology, from the facts of relatively simple behavior to the dynamics of personal and group behavior; and logic, from elementary reasoning to formal logic and the logic of science. Creative developments along any such lines will, of course, meet resistance by those who favor the "tried and true" and will make major strategic demands to facilitate their introduction.

A broadened perception of the nature of financial assistance to the economically disadvantaged gifted is badly needed. While conventional assistance by means of scholarships is important and probably will continue to be necessary, supportive funding is required by some as compensatory to the gifted child's family for the money he might have earned had he dropped out of school instead of completing his public education. Even transportation funding may be needed by some of the more isolated and disadvantaged gifted. The source or sources of such funding and the responsible and sensitive administration of such assistance are important problems in this connection.

Too easily and uncritically, both professional and lay persons interested in effecting educational change in the interests of the gifted tend to think and plan to act in terms of establishing special classes for them. Without in any way implying that there is no place for such classes, or even for special schools, in a full program for the gifted, especially in large centers of population, we must regard such an initial step as impetuous, as tactical rather than strategic, and as potentially limiting to the school district's perception of how the needs of the gifted can or should be met. Even though, in long-range strategical planning, a special class program may soundly be anticipated, earlier prior steps and fruitful action can be taken.

If any single, formal first step can be safely identified, it would be the district's employment of a qualified consultant on the gifted, granting that due preparation for such action has been made. The consultant, acting along lines that have been suggested in the text, particularly in working with individual teachers in the interests of their gifted pupils, can accomplish what is needed to help teachers, other educational personnel, parents, and the pupils to realize that effective adjustments can be made —first for individual gifted children, then with small groups of them, and later probably with some type of Colfax adaptation. Out of such, a sound awareness of the potential benefits of special class arrangements can evolve. Of at least equal importance would be the continuation and extension of a kind of adaptive education in the cases of other gifted youngsters who, for one reason or other, may not be able to participate in the special class provision(s).

Seeking out the gifted

Education's finding and providing for the gifted can be thought of crudely as analogous to a strip-mining operation. Those gifted who have been easily accessible or clearly apparent, under the post hoc definition of the gifted, have been somewhat provided for or tolerated. Serious mining for high-grade intellectual ore is difficult and therefore not generally practiced. The geographic distribution of our population has contributed heavily to this condition. 1970 Census Bureau data showed that 73.5 percent of our population lived in population centers of 2500 or more, as contrasted with 69.9 percent ten years earlier. Some 80 percent of our population was in cities of 50,000 or more, whereas only 12.4 percent lived in places of 1000 to 2500 persons. Whereas California, New Jersey, and New York had 85.5 percent of their populations living in towns or cities, Vermont had 67.8 percent living in places under 2500, followed by Virginia (61 percent), South Dakota (44.6 percent), Mississippi (44.5 percent), and North Dakota (44.3 percent). Just how prevalent gifted school children are in such rural areas is not known, but untapped resources in all probability are there. The trend toward the establishment of larger consolidated school districts in rural areas can contribute to locating and providing for their gifted, but inherent in the operation of such units is the problem of the delivery of adequate educational services for the gifted. Specific consideration of the gifted in rural areas is essential not only from the standpoint of their adequate self-fulfillment but also in terms of stemming, at least somewhat, the brain drain that can threaten rural integrity and adequacy. We must not lose sight of the fact that some portion of our gifted population, those in rural areas, are geographically disadvantaged.

Even though the problem of meeting the needs of the gifted has been better delineated by research than it has been handled in educational practice, the need for more definitive and integratable research on them and about their education remains. The educator, as the consumer of research findings, must realize that even well-executed research in this area does not provide "the" answers; at best it provides more definite approximations in the description of situations on the basis of which action can be taken in the light of an underlying philosophy and value system. However, any failure more precisely to delineate reasons and lines of action should not be taken by educators as sufficient reason for not taking steps thus far reasonably clearly supported by research.

Attitudes of the gifted

The gifted are both products of and shapers of social influences. Figuring largely in this condition are the attitudes of significant others toward them and the attitudes which they themselves acquire and manifest. However, insufficient attention has been paid to the development in them of attitudes that could be socially contributive. That it was important, both to them and to society, that they be helped to acquire positive attitudes regarding their capabilities and the rewarding fact of learning was stressed, and research was cited which showed that the gifted had positive attitudes toward others. But the latter kind of educational and social outcomes was largely ascribed, almost incidentally, to their superior capability to grasp and deal with abstractions and generalizations rather than specifically identified as a conscious goal in helping them to learn. Yet such must be an integral part in helping them to become adjusted contributing members of our society.

The listing of a series of attitudes which the gifted should be helped to develop properly could be regarded as highly presumptive. The appropriateness of attitudes is a function of historical perspective and of individual life space. However, it seems possible to identify the major characteristics of certain desirable attitudes to be held by the gifted—again recognizing that such characteristics can apply as well to the attitudes of all children.

It would seem reasonable that the attitudes of the gifted should both reflect a sensitivity to reality and be tempered by idealism. They should reflect both a sense of personal worth or integrity and of social being. Certainly their being aware of their greater capability is not to be denied any more than one's awareness of his height, but this can be the basis of a feeling of legitimate confidence rather than of conceit. Educational provisions by means of which the gifted are given the opportunity to work both with their intellectual peers and with the nongifted have been found to be contributive to such confidence tempered with modesty. It would seem that this attitude toward self in relation to others should be accompanied by an attitude toward others in relation to their situations, the hoped-for result being at least an understanding, though not necessarily an acceptance, of the behavior of others. Understanding at least tempers rejection and can be contributive to cooperative behavior. Of at least equal importance is the development in the gifted of an attitude of social responsibility—a sense of positively contributing to the society of which they are a part. During the 1960s and 70s, the active revolts against and the passive withdrawal from

components in society were a function largely of what was perceived as a lack of social relevance of much of what and how they were being required to learn. The development of a blend of personal worth and of social responsibility and opportunity has been a major focus in this book.

REPRISE

The position has been taken herein that there are children who can be identified early as gifted, although they constitute a surprisingly heterogeneous group. They are individually entitled to self-fulfillment in the light of their particular patterns of superior capability. This is important to their psychological well-being, but it is facilitative also to their assuming contributive roles in adult society. Society depends greatly upon the gifted both for its immediate effective action and for its inevitable growth. The focus has been heavily upon educational provisions with these ends in view.

Disappointingly constant in our society has been the general absence of any systematic educational provision for the gifted as an integral part of the total educational program. Those provisions during our first century which were of benefit to some of the gifted were a function of education's being provided largely for the select few—for the professions—rather than of any attempt to seek out and to provide for the gifted as such. In the current century, the impact of the potential impetus of the work of Terman and his students, while truly preparatory and potentially facilitative, was negligible so far as its evoking major educational activity for the gifted was concerned. Only what was perceived as a major threat to our national security precipitated the taking of any major steps in the interests of the gifted, as evidenced in a temporarily heightened sense of needs for scholarship assistance at the higher educational levels, a short-lived expansion of facilities for preparing workers in the field, and the mounting of a few national, state, and local programs for the gifted. However, the quality of a mandated program, for any category of children or adults, is realizable only to the extent that there are fully committed, philosophically and psychologically well grounded, and professionally qualified personnel available to implement it.

Society tends to react rather than to act. To a few who long had been deeply committed philosophically to educational movement in this direction, the post-Sputnik spurt of interest in the gifted seemed to provide an opportunity to take steps which could be socially contributive; to many, this was but an opportunity for new kinds of educational employment by means of which they could "try something new," constituting

a kind of educational fungus growth. As is true with such developments—both promising and futile—financial aspects loomed large, and such was the basis on which failure to act was rationalized. The basic question is whether failure to act in the interests of the gifted was due to lack of funds or a lack of understanding commitment. A consideration of developments in our society leads to the conviction that where there is firm commitment, funds usually are found.

Social and educational movement in the interests of the gifted should not have to come about on the basis of emotional appeal or reaction, as has been true in the case of the handicapped; it must come about as a result of logical consideration and planning for an increasingly effective society. The growing problems associated with the effective uses of our natural resources make ever more important the shepherding of our intellectual resources.

14

Topics
for consideration

Even though the acquisition of facts and concepts is essential to the understanding of any area of concern, such acquisition alone constitutes a relatively limited educational outcome. In order to press the reader beyond this point, the following topics for consideration are presented. They are a varied lot, ranging from a challenge for a critical reading of the book, to the consideration of issues and contentions that have logical pros and cons, to the acquisition of facts that reflect the reader's local and state situations.

Some items explicitly call for positive and negative criticism or the citation of evidences of validity or invalidity; in others such a demand is implicit. In some instances where the facts are to be obtained, evaluation and inference are implicitly called for. Obviously, more than the reading of this book will be contributive.

1. Many factually unsupported statements have appeared in this book. Identify at least five such statements and marshall facts and/or opinions that bear on their validity *and* invalidity.

2. The making of special educational provisions for the gifted is not justifiable in a democracy such as ours.

3. Providing special educational opportunities for the gifted causes them to "lose the common touch."

4. The real test of whether school children are gifted is the extent to which they satisfy the post hoc definition of the gifted.

5. Contrast the post hoc and the social need definition of the gifted in terms of their relative merits and limitations.

6. To what extent is the following valid? The social definition of the gifted proposed in this book may be defensible nationally at a given time in our society, but is of little, if any, educational relevance to my community.

7. If the specialists on the gifted themselves don't agree on the definition of the gifted, general educators cannot be expected to proceed with making educational provisions for them.

8. The fact that more gifted appear among the upper socioeconomic classes clearly supports the contention that giftedness is primarily a function of such nurturance.

9. The problem of providing properly for the gifted rests, or should continue to rest, with the regular classroom teacher.

10. Until "authorities" on the gifted can agree on what is best for the gifted, we are not justified in setting up any special educational provisions for such children.

11. Since we can't at once do everything that we believe is needed for the gifted, we'll just do a bit at a time.

12. The introduction of any single educational practice which is known or strongly believed to be good for the gifted is better than just not doing anything in their interests.

13. It is indefensible to maintain that no single provision is adequate for meeting the educational needs of the gifted.

14. "Real" improvement in the education of the gifted will come about through improving the perceptions and skills of established, generally experienced educators rather than through the introduction into the educational system of well-prepared, though less experienced, educational personnel.

15. The assertion that the gifted should be helped, or caused, to work up to, or more nearly up to, the levels of their respective potentials is indefensible, since if this were accomplished the gifted would have no reserve with which they could engage in other activities essential to their development and/or to their potential contribution to society.

16. The schools can do little about the underachievement of the gifted, since such underachievement is more socially than educationally determined.

17. Taking a specified frame of reference such as everyday facts and phenomena, some area of social studies, mathematics, or science, identify a hierarchy of concepts within that area, showing how those of given levels contribute to the development of those at the next higher levels.

18. Observations have been made regarding the phenomenon of "brain drain" and that of shift in scientific and professional roles in society. What are the facts in these regards with respect to your community? What factors have contributed to the situation which you have identified? (There may be a dominance of "drain" from some communities and one of "influx" into others. Either condition merits this kind of consideration.)

19. Show the validity or invalidity of the following: advocates for the gifted, such as the author of this book, would have us believe that the social need for contributions by the gifted is greater than it really is.

20. Considering the high school dropout population in your community, what percentage of it would fall in the category of gifted as defined herein? Identifying them specifically by name if possible (and dealing with the whole matter in an ethically responsible, confidential manner), what have been the facts in their educational history (regarding underachievement, for instance), in their socioeconomic backgrounds, and in the attitudes of their parents and social peers toward education? If possible, get personally acquainted with some of them and get their side of the story, forgetting as well as you can the fact that you are a teacher/parent.

21. To the extent that educators have a socially and psychologically sound philosophy of education and to the extent that they understand the psychological characteristics of children they will not need to be told what to do for the gifted.

22. Consistently the position has been stated that learning expectations for the gifted should be set in terms of their respective learning aptitudes, which have been ascertained by means of competent psycho-educational assessment and with the proviso that such indications are in many cases minimal. On the other hand, much is written to the effect that the setting of

educational expectations in terms of the results of "intelligence" testing is negatively prejudicial to the interests of children. If this is not just a " 'tis-and-tain't" argument, wherein lies the resolution of the different points of view? What factor or factors mitigate against that resolution?

23. Assume that you have been officially appointed chairman of the committee in your local school district which is charged with the responsibility for

   a. recommending for official apointment other necessary members of the committee,

   b. ascertaining what, if anything, is needed in your schools in the interests of the gifted, and

   c. recommending, in order of implementation, whatever steps may need to be taken.

   Describe how you would go about this, assuming that your committee has been given a year's time to accomplish the task. You may assume that your present role in the community is that of a PTA member, that of an elementary or secondary level teacher, or that of a school administrative staff member.

24. Some "get acquainted" questions—

   In terms of your local situation:

   a. Is there a PTA committee appointed in the interests of the gifted? Is it active? What has it accomplished? What should it be doing?

   b. What percentage of the time of the psychologist(s) is involved with the gifted? In what way(s)?

   c. Taking the newspaper coverage for, say, a month (preferably including Education Week), what percentage of space was given to the gifted per se (not just to "individual differences")?

   d. What official administrative provisions regarding the gifted are "on the books"? Is action in harmony with them?

   e. What are the policy and practice regarding early admission?

   f. Is there a local committee, or branch, of the Association for the Gifted? Of the National Association for Gifted Children? If so, to what extent is it active and productive?

In terms of your state situation:

   a. What legal provisions regarding the gifted per se exist? In what ways are they implemented?

   b. If there are personnel with defined responsibilities in this area

   (1) What are those responsibilities?

   (2) What is the nature of the preparation and qualifications of such personnel with regard to this work?

   (3) What has been the history of personnel turnover within this staff?

   (4) In what ways and to what extent have the services of such state personnel been contributive to local efforts in the interests of the gifted?

   (5) What has been the nature of their research on the gifted?

   c. Over at least a six-month period during the last school year, what percentage of the noncommercial content of your state educational journal has pertained specifically to the gifted?

   d. Is there a state chapter of the Association for the Gifted? Of the National Association for Gifted Children? In what way(s) has it been active and productive?

These questions are only suggestive. If you cannot ask more and better ones, *you* aren't being "creative"!

APPENDIX A

A pupil-school case history

The following account is presented in order to illustrate kinds of problems—and opportunities—that can arise as effective education of the gifted is sought by strongly motivated and perceptive parents of a gifted child. In one sense this situation is not typical, in that these parents, having a bright child, wanting her needs to be met and not finding appropriate facilities in their public schools, undertook to start and run a private school for gifted children. Yet the kinds of problems which they encountered, both in the operation of their school and, later, in their child's transition into the public schools and colleges, reflect educational attitudes and conditions essentially inimical to legitimate expectations of the self-realization of a gifted youngster.

This approved account consists of information taken from correspondence with the child's mother over a span of some 15 years. The parents are professional people. The father had functioned as a public school psychologist and then, more recently, as a technical consultant to aerospace firms. The mother had prepared as a psychometrist to at least the master's level, had worked as a public school psychologist, had taught a class of educationally retarded children, one of severely mentally retarded children, and one of gifted, and had taught at the college level. She had worked as a psychologist, taking referrals from a psychiatrist. The child with whom we are concerned will be denoted as "G." She lived in at least two western states; the southeastern state in which she lived, briefly, will be denoted as "X." The schools involved were the private school which was started

373

and run for the gifted, two western public high schools, and one western private high school. One western college figured most prominently in G's education.

In illustrating certain problems involved in attempts to provide educationally for the gifted outside the regular public school situation and depicting G's parents' quest for her self-fulfillment, the private school and some of its problems will be described, G's problems and progress will be described, and certain educational observations germane to the thrust of this book will be discussed.

THE PRIVATE SCHOOL

The private school came into existence primarily because two psychoeducationally sensitive parents wanted their four-year-old bright child to benefit from educational experiences not available in the public schools of their community. This felt need was generalized, the cooperation of like-minded parents was obtained, and the school was started. As so often is true in such an undertaking, the key person found it necessary to assume many responsibilities. G's mother wrote, in 1958, "I try to function as a psychologist on this job, but also as teacher, principal, psychometrist, purchasing agent, public relations director, fund drive organizer, and property accountant (plus housewife and mother)." Such a concentration of responsibilities probably was necessary in the initial stages, but may have been, at least in part, contributive to the termination of the enterprise seven years later (1964).

Philosophically, the educational efforts were directed toward ensuring the establishment of a good foundation in the academic fundamentals and keeping alive in the youngsters an interest in learning. The pervading interpersonal and intellectual atmosphere sought was informal, personal, friendly, happy, and exploring.

In the words of the mother, the teachers sought to "inculcate a rational skepticism, not cynicism, but a questioning attitude toward life." With a pupil population that initially was chronologically and intellectually relatively homogeneous, the interests expressed by the youngsters—broadened at times by teacher-identified possibilities—constituted the primary points of departure in the learnings. As the youngsters grew older, discussion groups, seminars, and larger foci of intellectual concern came to be typical components of the learning experiences encountered. Such learnings by such children did not at all lend themselves to formal structuring into fixed specific time periods for the several subject-matter areas, such as arithmetic, social studies, language, science, and the like. The importance of the disparity between an educational operation such as this and that of conventional educators—especially teacher-trainers—will be seen later.

The establishment of this private school was well intentioned, particularly as regards the major concern for the adequate intellectual nurturance of the bright youngsters. However, the operation of the school presented very real problems. The local public school superintendent regarded such an effort as "educationally divisive." For the most part, parents of children in the school constituted the school's board of trustees. G's father, then serving as public school psychologist in the local system, was president of the board, a precarious dual role to say the least. Some members of the board became expansive, wanting to develop a chain of such schools; others became dissatisfied with the policy of rigorously selecting pupils. Later in the school's operation G's parents became the targets of obscene telephone calls. There was evidence that the brakes on their car were tampered with, resulting in a miraculously avoided serious accident involving G and her mother. The parents were threatened by lawsuits. They were reported to the Internal Revenue Service for investigation, although the agent making the investigation termed the situation as a "most disgraceful bit of misrepresentation." Trustees or trustee's wives saw their children's being in the school as contributive to their social aspirations. There were problems regarding the physical facilities for the school. There were seemingly inevitable financial and funding problems; G's mother reported that, counting cash and unpaid salaries, the parents had put some $70,000 into the school.

Assuming that the teachers could be properly paid, their selection and retention presented real difficulties. Some who were highly recommended for work in the school were so out of tune with its philosophy and procedures that they either just couldn't adjust or they needed to be helped for a year or more in order to work effectively. Teachers who functioned superbly in the private school later became dismal "failures" when they went into public school teaching. The professional dissonance between the two situations seemed to defy accommodation.

The matter of evaluating the school was a problem area. Even though the youngsters in the school consistently scored two to six grade levels above their chronological age "expectancies" and those who left tended to do well, or at least acceptably, in conventional school situations, key "professional educators" were most critical. For instance, one teacher trainer in a nearby university brought one of his classes to visit the school (without orienting his students as to its philosophy and nature). In his subsequent feedback to the principal he expressed great concern regarding the lack of systematic planning of the educational program for the children. Another, who maintained that each child's school day should be systematically scheduled such that x percent of the time would be devoted to reading, y percent to arithmetic, z percent to social studies, and the like, regarded the private school program as most inappropriate.

But our primary concern here is with G, and we shall turn to her now. We shall consider what she was like, her educational experiences, her adjustments, and achievements.

G AND HER ROCKY ROAD

The fact of Eskimo parentage was apparent in G when steps initially were taken to adopt her at the age of one and a half years. At that time she was reported by the agency psychologist to have a Binet IQ of 101. This same psychologist retested her a year later, at which time formal adoption was completed. Because of implications relating to appropriate psychological evaluation of the gifted, the following excerpt is given from the mother's account of the examination:

We [G and her potential adoptive mother] were sent into a playroom where there were a low table, two children's chairs, a rocking horse, a doll house, and some blocks. We took the two chairs and waited a considerable length of time. The psychologist came in, frowning, lifted G without a word from her chair and plopped her side-saddle onto the rocking horse, jerked up the table beside her, and sat herself on the chair. She opened her kit, took out the protocol form and shot questions at me about name, birthdate, etc., and filled it out. Then she looked at me a long and meaningful glance and said, "I'm told you are a psychologist. Undertrained but acting like one. I suppose you've tested this child over and over until she has memorized all the answers?" I murmured that G had taken only the agency's test the year before. She snapped out the Binet equipment onto the table and snapped questions at G. Once G looked around at me, troubled, and I smiled and said, "Answer the lady, Sweet Puddin," and the psychologist said, "If you can't keep out of this, you must leave the room." G shrugged and grinned at me, and turned back to the test. Several times she had already almost fallen off the tottery rocking horse when reaching for a block or something, and finally she started saying "No! No!" and refusing to answer. The psychologist stood up, swept the equipment into her kit, and said, "A very ordinary child," and left the room.

The agency caseworker later told the mother that G had "tested between 115 and 125." There had been some concern, on the part of the agency staff, lest there be too great a disparity between G's intelligence and that of her highly professional parents, but the adoption finally was approved because of the quality of the relationship that had been observed to exist between them and G.

G was, in all probability, excessively tested, since her early behavior clearly gave evidence that she was at least a bright child. Her mother reported, "At $2\frac{1}{2}$ she had started 'acting' parts that she specially liked from TV shows, demanding that the family take parts too and stay in character all day," and "She was one of those very verbal children who doesn't stop talking from the time she wakes until she goes to sleep, constantly asking about generalizations which she had conceived and wanting our opinion." Only a bit later, G commented, "My mother says when I read better so I can read cookbooks, I can do all the cooking." At age 5 she was reading fourth-grade books with pleasure and ease. Subsequent IQs were reported to be WISC Full Scale 139, Binet 155, Goodenough (Draw A Man) 189, and a public high school group-administered Otis of 119. G's mother was moved to comment, "What bothered us most was that her IQ

took off like a 1929 stock market graph and kept climbing—140s at age 4, a freak 200-plus at 5, 160 at 12, and 190s at 17." There doesn't seem, however, to be evidence that G herself had become too IQ-sensitive.

At age 3, G reportedly was "picking out and composing little melodies" on the piano. When piano lessons were started when she was eight years old, her teacher thought she was highly talented and sought to push her along. G rebelled and stopped taking lessons. During nursery school G was urged to take tap and modern dancing lessons, but G observed, "Dey not nice. Dey wiggle." However, when she shifted to pre-ballet dancing lessons, she became enchanted and continued for eight years. When G was in the fifth grade in the private school, she was reading Shakespeare, Hogben, Thomas Jefferson's letters to Hamilton, and Nancy Drew mysteries. She scored at the eighth- and ninth-grade levels on the Stanford Achievement Test, even in arithmetic, although she later seemed to forget the arithmetic. As her mother observed, "No subject seems hard for her; she soaks up knowledge like a blotter soaking up ink. She seems to understand (and love) anything in the humanities. She is at home with and enjoys the arts—all of them, with an emphasis on music. She hates science and mathematics yet can get As in them for the moment." (Later she wrote a paper for a regular public high school course in biology, on which she received a C—, that a publisher offered to publish as a juvenile book if she would write an introduction appropriate for it.)

But G's educational problems were yet to come. Anticipating the probability of G's later attending college, her parents decided that she should enter a large public high school. As her mother tells it, "I called everyone the Board of Education would tell me about, called colleges and universities and heads of psychology departments and directors and child clinics and experimental classes, and you name them." (She even called Terman.) Some inquired suspiciously, questioning G's brightness, and "Don't you think a normal life and good interpersonal relations might be the first area to explore?"

G's mother heard of one theoretically accessible high school that made special provisions for gifted youngsters. She was told that G could be entered in the ninth or tenth grade. The program was individualized; it was possible to plan a six-year program, with a tie-in with an Advanced Placement Examination program. However, they did not live in the district served by that high school. The fact that G's father (now in the aviation industry) was anticipating his being transferred precluded their moving into this most promising school district.

In exploring public junior high school placement possibilities, G's mother encountered the pervading contention that G should be "educated" with her age peers. She was, after all, only 10 and "seventh-graders should be 12½." (This type of contention was later to be heard in other educational settings—both in high school and in college.) *If* the local junior high school accepted her, she could not continue either Latin or French, which were not offered at that level and could not continue with her Spanish until the ninth grade. She could not take algebra until the ninth or tenth grade. Social studies would involve repetition. Placement examination results in English showed her to be at ninth- to tenth-grade level. While the teachers there observed that she probably could do the work "very well," she still was "a little girl."

It finally was decided that G should be entered into the tenth grade of a large public high school. Intending to spread G's high school learning over a period of four or five years, the parents asked that she be given a light academic sched-

ule in order that she would be able to continue with dance, voice, and drama outside of school. But G, at age 11, was scheduled for driver's education (since all 15-year-old tenth graders took it). She "took" vocational guidance and study habits (including how to outline lessons —something she had been doing for at least three years). She was required to take physical education even though she already was taking four hours per week of professional-level dance, two hours of horseback riding, plus one to two hours' daily swimming. Her Spanish consisted of literally memorizing page after page of conversation, and if she used a word or phrase not on a given page she was given an F for the day.

She brought home an English test on which she had received the grade of 20 percent. Because G's mother checked the paper and thought it should have been marked 96 percent, she took the paper to G's English teacher in order to find out what the problem was. G's mother thereby learned four things: (1) The pupils in the class were not allowed to take their test papers home. (2) G's paper had been scored by means of the wrong key; using the appropriate key, the teacher also found that it should have been marked 96 percent. (3) The teacher refused to correct the recorded grade; after all, only one test didn't count that much. And (4) G ought to be in the fifth or sixth grade where she could be getting straight As and would be happy and well adjusted. The D which G received in Spanish was assigned by the guidance counselor, and not by her teacher, because he believed G was too immature for second year Spanish and ought to repeat Spanish I.

It was understandable that the quality of G's academic performance would be highly variable, shifting without seeming reason from A or B to D or F. Even the English teacher, who was most openly critical of the parents' belief that G could do tenth-grade work, admitted that G was not too immature to handle the work. However, she observed that G seemed to have a vivid and charming way of expressing herself—far better than many of the others in her class. G clearly had, the teacher said, both superior understanding and empathy for the characters in Julius Caesar. But the parents were ruining her socially by not having her placed with her "peers" (agemates).

The attitudinal climate in which G was expected to be learning was a problem. Three of G's six regular teachers openly expressed resistance to her not being with her "peers." Her mother was directly accused of being a cruel and unnatural parent who wanted to exploit and shove her child through school. Both G and her mother were told that high school was a place where children experimented in boy-girl relationships in preparation for marriage. In view of that aim and G's age, she was out of place. The three teachers also consistently told G, before her classmates, that her parents were stupid, cruel, callous, and most unwise in letting her be in senior high school. Consistently, her mother was told that G should be in the sixth, or even the fifth, grade where she would be "happier." Even though this climate was excessively demanding on G, she, in describing the situation to her parents, expressed the view that she could make the teachers accept her a little the next year and that she should "have it made" by the third year.

G's parents decided to place her in a private high school which was operated on an individualized basis. After a semester here, her parents thought she should have public high school experience. However, after a frustrating semester in the public high school, she was transferred back to the private high school. The C average which she brought with her did not suggest that she was bright.

Her performance in this new educational setting quickly corrected that impression; she even earned 100 percent on a 40-minute algebra assignment. Although during the last year of this high school program her father was transferred to a southeastern state, State X, she was able to complete it—one course being handled essentially by correspondence. She graduated from high school in 1966, completing the six years of junior-senior high school work in two years.

Her mother had been advised to get in touch with the person in the State X department of education who was officially concerned with the education of the gifted. This person made a number of potentially helpful suggestions—place G in a school which provided an independent, periodically supervised study course, put her in a program that provided for Advanced Placement Examinations, explore the possibilities of a correspondence program offered by the University of Nebraska, and the like. However, since the parents did not live in a school district that had any of those provisions and since the transportation and tuition problems involved in sending G to other possible school districts seemed unsolvable, it was decided that G should finish the western private high school program by mail and that she would be kept out of school for a year, except for a two-month period when she attended the local high school as a "guest," during which time she was elected cheerleader. During this year she acted in a professional theater, modeled a bit, and became interested in and "good" at cooking, dress designing, and housekeeping. During this time, at age 13, she wrote an article and sold it to a national magazine for $500. It was during this year too, that she was one of 18 chosen out of more than 75 auditioned to participate in making records for a children's choir. She had, in the meantime, auditioned for other recording companies, for TV, and for radio. She also won a part in *The King and I,* which was staged by the local Theater Under the Stars, putting in 10 to 14 hours a day on this project. Her mother reported, "While doing this, she read more about Asia than a lot of college majors do. While playing in *Carousel,* she read voraciously on New England and Colonial days. In connection with a part in *Caesar and Cleopatra,* she read a lot of Bernard Shaw, the history of Egypt and Rome, and some psychology which the director had mentioned."

Attempting to enter college in State X also presented problems. State schools accepted no one under age 16. Freshman classes in all colleges were full, and it was not possible for G to enter at the sophomore level in the absence of adequate performances on advanced placement examinations. However, her father's work was such that he was again transferred, this time back to the western state where she was to encounter additional problems at the college level.

Since at least at the age of 12 G had expressed a strong interest in becoming an actress, and so she undertook a major in theater arts and a minor in dance. By virtue of her enthusiasm over the opportunities available, she quickly became involved in a 14- to 16-hour-a-day schedule, and the pace began to tell on her both physically and academically. Concerned with what was happening, G's mother went to her daughter's counselor. Again, the mother encountered attitudes that varied from accusatory to resistant to adjustive. The head counselor advised the mother that the parents should obtain psychiatric help for themselves, since they must be "sick" to allow G to be in college at such an early age. G's own counselor commented, "Anyone who is smart enough to be in college at the age of 15 should be earning As rather than just fairly strong Bs." The head of theater arts observed, "She is highly tal-

ented, but if she has taken more than she can handle, it's her problem." He admitted that she had taken over, on a relatively short notice, a major part in a scheduled production, thus enabling them to proceed with its presentation and benefitting financially from doing so. But he firmly took the position that if she was old enough to be in college, she was old enough to be able to judge what she could do. He advised having her drop one course and take an F in it. The stagecraft teacher, when told of the total situation, said, "I hadn't realized it, but her time card shows that she has put in 120 hours backstage, with a third of the term to go, and only 80 are required." He gave her an A in that course and excused her from it for the rest of the semester. She pulled her average up to B plus the next term and made essentially As after that.

Her adequacy in the college program was not confined to the academic area. She became a varsity cheerleader and was one of three, out of a sizable group, to be nominated best actress of the year, best director of the year, and most valuable student of the year. More than one of her teachers characterized her as the "department dynamo." The head of the department later described her as the most rewarding student he had had in 20 years. She obtained her A.B. at the age of 17. In the spring of 1969 she was elected to a college National Honorary Society.

Accounts of the extents to which gifted youngsters attain self-fulfillment too often reflect only or primarily academic and/or technical or professional achievement. Always playing a significant part in the total developmental picture are social and emotional factors. There were such factors in G's situation. The following descriptions of three of them reveal her emotional buoyancy, which helped her no end to ride the emotionally troubled waters, and show that she demonstrated a social-emotional maturity much more in harmony with her mental level than with her chronological age. That she had this buoyancy, or ego strength, is undoubtedly due in large part to the healthy emotional nurturance under which she grew up. As her mother observed, "Actually, part of G's happy learning was her preschool home life. G was not 'trained' consciously. We enjoyed her so much that she was part of our entire life 24 hours a day. It wasn't training-on-purpose; it was enjoying a cute baby."

As early as age two, G had to deal with a social problem which stemmed largely from the fact that, by virtue of her Eskimo heritage, her skin was darker than that of other children. After an Easter brunch a little boy came to her home with some children to show their Easter baskets, and he snarled, "I ain't goin' in there. My daddy shoots Gooks when they don't stay in Korea where they belong, and I ain't playin' with no Gooks, either." (He was six years old and had been in the kindergarten three years without being regarded as capable of going into first grade, whereas G, although only two years old, had started to read.) Neighborhood tension existed between the two children for two years when the relation between them was climaxed and terminated by her telling him, "I'm adopted and your mother's stuck with you!"

Essentially the same kind of problem arose when the family was living in State X. At first, the 25 or so children in the apartment village where they lived accepted G with delight and apparent affection, but after report cards came out (after the period when G had been a "guest" pupil in the school), one boy, two years older than G and six grades behind her, started calling her a nigger, and another boy took it up. The first boy said she might think she was pretty smart but his father and mother thought she

was a freak. Saying that they shoot niggers in State Y and drown them in State X, they tried to throw her into a lake. "We're going to stick you in the mud, you nigger, and see how you feel." When G gave one of the boys a bloody nose and kicked the other in the groin, they let her go and went home. After the episode, G's playmates accepted her more and their relationship was on a firmer basis. While G handled the situation self-sufficiently and with considerable maturity, it was quite stressful for her. Later, when she was in college, one of her (married) instructors tried consistently to date her even though she was much younger than her classmates. Since she was, in effect, "beholden" to him in order not to fail the course, she cleverly maintained her distance, telling her parents, "I mean to get the A I'm earning in his course before I 'trash' him."

As G's mother describes the total situation in college, G was very well accepted by her classmates, many of the regular high school boys seeking in vain to date her in spite of her being only 11 years old. She was popular at the high school dances to which her parents took her. By the age of 16, when she was in college, she was socially very well accepted by her classmates, going on numerous dates to dances, concerts, and the like. Always enjoying social relationships, she seemed to be a social chameleon, enjoying friendships with 5-year-olds, 12- and 13-year-olds, college students, and up to 80-year-olds. She seemed capable of adapting enjoyingly to the social demands of whatever ages her friends were.

Her activities, strong interest, and successes in highly varied kinds of situations, both in State X and later in the western state, were contributed to heavily by her high visibility. On graduation from college she immediately wanted and got an apartment of her own. She ushered in theaters and soon took a job in a department store. In three and a half weeks she was made a department manager in the store. She then became a local representative for one of the manufacturers of the cosmetics she was selling. With salary and commissions, she became financially self-sufficient at the age of 19.

In the meantime, with the help of an agent, she had received three offers of motion picture parts. These ranged from one for three days to one for 10 to 14 weeks. She then accepted one for seven years with the understanding that she would play a part in one movie and take varied kinds of training thereafter. She was assigned to a teacher to learn to speak Eskimo and to an anthropologist to learn Eskimo culture, and she was given three months to live with an Eskimo family on Baffin Island, to wear Eskimo clothing, to prepare and eat Eskimo food, and to practice the language in situ—in which time the film authorities expected her to acquire fluency. If this first picture is the success expected, she is to be provided a full-star buildup.

G'S EDUCATIONAL-PHILOSOPHICAL ATMOSPHERE

Because of their relevance to points made in this book regarding the effective education of the gifted, certain of G's mother's observations have been presented here, either paraphrased or in direct quotation. Written incidentally in the course of conventional correspondence, her observations and contentions differ from much educational pedaguese.

In spite of the educational inanities, administrative roadblocks, and faulty psychological premises encountered in the course of G's attempted public "education," G's mother believed her to have been effectively educated both in the narrow sense of acquiring the necessary academic proficiencies and in the larger nurturant sense: "She is a good student. She has a broad and hungry curiosity, a desire to learn every new thing that comes along so long as it is not concerned with science or mathematics. But she is far from the popular idea of the 'brain'." G's mother believed that her daughter's "education" was chiefly extracurricular and "rooted in an intellectual curiosity and love of learning that her one semester of public high school cancelled for four or five years and that college didn't do much for or against. It was in her senior year in college that she showed the same desire-to-learn that had been typical of her, and even then it seemed that college offered little. It was only after she had been out of college a bit over a year that she was really hungry to learn again."

Two aspects of this situation must be viewed critically lest they lead to too-sweeping generalizations. G's interests were different from those of many gifted youngsters who are more focused on the academic areas of mathematics, science, or even the humanities; G could become "interested" in such areas, but only as she perceived them as contributive to her primary interest in the theater. The second aspect probably is psychologically more crucial: the keeping alive and the sustained nurturing of her desire to learn. In this latter regard G's mother's observation is apropos: "If the school's business is the development of the child, it has *one* problem—how to inspire or feed this need-to-learn, this hunger-to-learn."

Since G's mother was speaking out of a broad background of actual classroom experience, her contention regarding the necessity and the feasibility of individualizing instruction is most relevant. "The teacher *must* teach each child. She cannot file them like a key-sort operator as if they were cards and treat them accordingly. What works for John may be a failure for James, and the teaching of James may make a failure of John. The yipping about the size of classes is unneeded and false; some teachers would teach a class of 5 or 10 by a mass education approach; some teachers can and do teach 50 kids as 50 *individual* kids. I doubt that the process can be taught in college, though methods and teaching techniques can be. Teaching is an art that can be smoothed and widened and developed." Inherent in "teaching" is the something-else—a personal and professional commitment. As she observes, "I think the methods I used were less methods as such than teacher attitude and a conscientious regard for the individual learner. I have never had a class so large that the problems of every individual in it were not a matter of concern, and as long as the pupil feels that concern, he'll learn. I used the 'love 'em and learn 'em' approach, using 'love' to mean 'concern.' It is the personal concern that is vital."

AN OVERVIEW

There are several reasons why this account is provided in such detail. The private school involved was only one of many that have been established, some for even shorter periods and a few for longer ones. Others with comparable life spans will appear in the attempt to do for gifted youngsters what so many public schools are failing to do. Many of its problems were indigenous; some of them could have been either avoided or moderated. Such an operation necessitates the involvement of particular kinds of "teachers" and supporting staff.

The perceptions of conventional educationists of the functioning of such a school illustrate all to clearly certain reasons why so many public schools fail to provide adequately for the education of the gifted. Success in "teaching" is not an absolute phenomenon; it is always relative to the situation in which "teachers" work. As was apparent in this account and as has been developed in this book, some teachers, perhaps a few of them with extra help, can work effectively with gifted children—they are the ones who truly are effective in individualizing the learning experiences of bright youngsters; others, the "lock-steppers," have no place in attempting to provide adequate education for the gifted. Certainly, G's being in a school such as the private one (and perhaps in large part owing to the sensitivities of her parents) was facilitative to her intellectual growth. The situation only enabled G to learn what she basically was capable of learning.

In a fundamental sense, G was typical of gifted youngsters—she had superior basic symbolic learning capability and she had a strong drive-to-learn that, fortunately, was not snuffed out. She was superior in her basic outgoingness which, for her, had a large social component, as contrasted with the superior outgoingness of others which finds its realization in the "quiet" learning of primarily cognitive behavior. G, with her superior basic learning potential, had, however, a primary focus that was different from that of many gifted youngsters whose accounts appear in the literature, nicely illustrative of the heterogeneity one finds among the gifted. As her mother reports, "Teachers kept saying she is not a genius —just a bright little girl. Don't push her. Geniuses are mathematical and science prodigies only." Without quibbling regarding the meaning of "genius," G quite probably is among the top 1 percent of the general population, and failing to regard her as a genius was no excuse for failing adequately to provide for her education as a gifted child.

This rather full description of G's experiences in the system provides an account of the not unusual educational flak which many bright children encounter. As is apparent, G was fortunate enough essentially to benefit from a considerable amount and quality of emotional and intellectual nurturance which sustained her through quite discernible vicissitudes. And yet she manifested repeatedly a healthy self-sufficiency. It should be remembered that G's situation was reported as seen by her mother; a competent "outside" professional psychologist might have seen certain aspects of G's situation somewhat differently.

APPENDIX B

One of the ships
that passed
in the night

Those who are actively working with or in the interests of the gifted receive numerous inquiries from parents and teachers about what can be done for their bright children. In some instances, appropriate and feasible recommendations can be made and facilitative action relatively easily taken. In all too many instances, however, feelings of futility are only aggravated because it seems either that nothing constructive is possible or that only some stopgap, palliative provision, rather than a conceptually based program, is accessible. At times, the result is only a temporizing commiseration with the parent or teacher by the "expert."

In the literature, accounts of educational adjustments for the gifted which have turned out well tend to predominate. (And may they increase!) Such accounts certainly make clear that, under given conditions, effective adjustments are at least possible. However, accounts of pseudo-solutions, failures, or very limited, partial adjustments can illustrate harsher realities—the difficulties of getting something appropriate done for the gifted, particularly at the elementary level, in public schools whose administrators typically either deny that they have gifted youngsters in their schools or else regard it as appropriate to make limited provisions only at higher grade levels.

The following account is based upon correspondence with a well-motivated and thoughtful parent who learned he had a bright youngster for whom the public schools in his community lacked adequate educational provisions. It reflects the breadth of consideration which must be given in helping the parent work out the problem of his child's effective education. There is no evidence of a "happy ending"—only a beginning and some intermediate steps. A solution may later have been worked out.

Our account starts out with a letter from the father, at the suggestion of the Ford Foundation for the Advancement of Education, to the president of the Association for the Gifted. (The father was a professional person; his wife was a college graduate.) The father stated his case:

My six-year-old son has been given a battery of tests, and we are advised that he falls into the highly gifted category with an IQ of "well above 150." The small (midwestern) town in which we live (population under 10,000) has no provision of any sort for the education of above-average children. I am investigating the possibilities of relocating if it is necessary to insure that my son will receive an education adequate for his capabilities.

At present, I need to know specific locations of public schools which have elementary programs for gifted children. I should therefore very much appreciate any lists, references or other information which you might be able to give me.

The letter suggested an interested, businesslike, sensitive parent who was willing to go to considerable lengths to obtain appropriate education for his son. Usually mothers are the ones who make such written inquiries. Later, the possible significance of the father's writing the letter will become apparent.

A perfunctory, reference-to-sources reply could have been made, but the president of the Association wanted to tailor a reply to the total situation of the child and of the family. His response, one week later, is presented essentially in its entirety. Not only was relevant information sought, but an attempt was made to provide the parent with programmatic concepts which he might later use, if and when he reached the point of evaluating two or more possibilities that might present themselves.

I have your letter inquiring about school systems in which you would be likely to find provisions appropriate to your son's superior academic potential. This thoroughly legitimate and seemingly easily answerable question is, in fact, rather difficult to answer as precisely as both of us should like.

Not infrequently, school districts which have received or presently receive considerable publicity for their provisions for bright children have only spotty or actually grossly inadequate programs. Some have practices at one level which are not integrated with practices at other levels. Others have practices or programs which were initiated by a given school administrator and which will continue only so long as that administrator is in that school system. Some school districts mistake practices for programs.

Your being willing to move to any community in which sound provisions are being made for children such as yours is commendable. I might well be able to suggest communities lying literally at any point on the compass from you; and they would range from essentially rural to highly industrialized communities. Rather, then, than name indiscriminately all the communities which we may know of (and still be likely to miss some deserving mention), wouldn't it be better if you told me the direction in which you would be most likely to move, the distance you would be willing to go, and the kind of community in which you would prefer to obtain employment, and, perhaps, even the type of employment which would suit your experiences, competencies, and aspirations? This would help us think in terms of a better "fit."

Cleveland, for instance, has had, for nearly forty years, special provisions for bright children in the elementary schools. Special facilities have been in operation for a long time in certain schools in New York City. Similar large-city identifications could be made for highly publicized programs in other large communities in other parts of the country. But near here there is a small, almost-rural community that has a little-publicized program for its bright children that is very good. And from another nearby community some bright children and their parents are being brought in by their teachers and principals and we are jointly working out educational provisions appropriate to the children's needs. This community has no publicized "program," but the particular teachers and principals involved in these "cases" are doing a superb job for these children.

May I ask you, then, in return, to give me more specific information about yourselves, your own occupational needs and competencies, and more specific (test) data on your son (when he was tested, the name(s) of the test(s) used, and the specific test results). Maybe I can then best refer you to some physically more convenient competent person for the kind of help I know you want and need.

In the meantime, may I suggest that you read, if you already have not done so, the book by Ruth Strang, *Helping Your Gifted Child,* published last year by Dutton. In case you should be interested in reading more, I'm sending along, also, a list of readings.

In a bit over two weeks the father replied with a two-and-a-half page, single-spaced typed letter. Somewhat excerpted and with specific identifying information modified in order to protect those involved, his reply follows.

Thank you so much for your letter concerning the location of school systems with special programs for gifted children. My wife and I sincerely appreciate your interest and desire to help. Although we have been seeking information for several months and have written many organizations and agencies concerned with gifted children, your letter is the first personal answer we have received and it has encouraged us greatly.

I will endeavor to outline specific information in answer to your questions, and will be glad to supply any further information you may wish.

Testing. M was first tested last year when he was about 5½. The Stanford-Binet was administered by a teacher connected with the local school system. She was ex-

perienced in such testing although not a licensed tester. The results were in the 160–180 range. M also scored at the fourth-grade level on scholastic achievement tests.

Both to check the original evaluation with a more officially qualified person and to obtain counseling, we then took M to Dr. H at a nearby university. Dr. H administered the Wechsler Intelligence Scale for Children among others. The results tended to modify the original I.Q. evaluation to the 150–160 range, and he reevaluated the results obtained on the original Binet test which had been sent to him. I have arranged for Dr. H to send you the complete test results and the evaluation made of M which, properly, are not available to us. Dr. H's counseling has been of great help to us, and it was he who stressed the need to place M in a school system which could better develop his potential. Perhaps I should mention one small factor which may not be contained in the report you will receive. Dr. H's test results are probably somewhat affected by the fact that he speaks with a slight European accent, and M told me after the tests that he "couldn't understand his speech" part of the time. In all probability, however, the effect of this is small. As we understand it, the I.Q. measurement is best treated as a general indicator of intelligence and potential, and the range that he falls into, regardless of the specific I.Q. numbers obtained by various methods, indicates the need for a school system which offers him a more adequate opportunity.

Present School Situation. M is now in the first grade of the local school. The school system itself does not recognize individual differences, and classes are divided alphabetically without reference to degree of ability. M's teacher is interested in him and has some understanding of his needs. However, her class contains 40 pupils and she is neither trained nor has the time to give him any effective help. His abilities have already been noticed by the other children, and the personal problem of feeling "different" is already developing for M. However, the school experience has helped his social adjustment and his ability to make friends seems to be improving. Fortunately, in spite of the lack of any challenge or stimulation, he has been kept "busy" enough that he is not yet too bored and seems to like school. He had already had two terms of nursery school and a year of kindergarten.

The teacher has already suggested that, although she may be able to cope with him for the remainder of the year, she feels that he should be placed in at least the third grade next year. His ability, particularly reading ability, seems to be about the fifth-grade level of the local school. This acceleration is the only step possible here, and even this may not be permitted by the school officials. Although M is physically large for his age, his emotions and physical abilities are those of a six-year-old. His social relationships with children his own age have been difficult. I wonder how you view this type of acceleration, and whether or not you feel it could be a temporary solution if I am unable to relocate by next September.

Background. A short biographical note may help answer your questions about my own occupational needs and competencies —I am 36, my wife 32. We both attended X University where my wife obtained her A.B. I continued my education at Y University where I received a B.S. degree. In addition to M, now 6½, we have another son 2½. We originally lived in [an eastern state] where I worked in the area of economics. We later moved to [a midwestern state] where I am similarly involved, at a modest professional-level salary. Although one of the units of my basic company is located in a western state where I understand there is a special program for the gifted, there is almost no possibility of my being able to relocate there while remaining with my present company.

I am very happy in my present job, my career prospects with this company are excellent, and we like living in this small community very much. I certainly prefer my present life to that of my previous suburbanite-commuter existence. However, we recognize the responsibility we have to ensure M a good education and a chance to develop his potential. Naturally, relocation will depend primarily on my ability to obtain a satisfactory position with another company in an area which offers an adequate school system. [He goes on to discuss the very real difficulties inherent in looking for another position without jeopardizing his present harmonious relationship with his company.] The problem of relocation is also complicated by the fact that many people in the business community neither understand nor appreciate the need for special education of the gifted child, and thus I probably cannot express this motivation in investigating job opportunities. . . . Perhaps the only alternative is to begin to seek another position and to hope that among those available, one will be in an area in which you would recommend a specific school.

Private Schools. There is one other question on which I should greatly value your opinion. We have both considered the possibility of locating where M could attend a private day school. Are there many such schools with really good programs for gifted children? (We definitely would not consider a boarding school since we feel that the home environment is essential for a young child.) We gave thought in terms of only public schools both because we believe they provide a more natural and realistic environment and because of the financial considerations. The financing of college educations for both our boys must take precedence. However, we would like your comments on this possibility.

I can say only that we have a sincere desire to do all we can to give our child the educational opportunity that he deserves. Doing this and at the same time fulfilling the economic responsibility for providing a full and pleasant life for all my family presents problems which are difficult. Your letter has made me feel that it can be done, and my thanks for your personal interest is heartfelt.

Five weeks later the father received an answer, in part, as follows:

I have delayed replying to your last letter because I was waiting to receive the report which you said Dr. H was going to send me. This has not yet been received. Also, I was checking with a person in your field whom I know about placement possibilities for you. . . . He suggested that you could get in touch with the central office of your professional association and they could help you without your company being aware of your considering moving.

The report from the psychologist arrived three weeks after this letter was sent. It is interesting in a psychometric sense as well as in a psychological sense, in that it suggests something of the nature of the relationship between M and his mother.

M was brought to my attention for the first time when an ex-student of mine, an elementary school teacher, sent in the results of a Stanford-Binet (1960) which she had administered to M. This teacher was not an experienced psychometrician and in checking over the test it was found that she had overscored several items. Her results of this test was an extrapolated I.Q. of 197. The same teacher also had administered a Metropolitan Achievement Test: Primary 1 Battery Form R. On this test, M achieved an average reading grade equivalent of 3.4 and a number grade equivalent of 3.8. M at that time was five years and seven months old.

M's mother brought him for an evaluation a year ago. M is a completely delightful child. He is a robust healthy little boy, with excellent color and bright blue eyes. He looked forward to the testing like other children anticipate a visit to the circus. . . . Rapport was established instantaneously. The child was eager, spontaneous and paid close attention. There was no sign of anxiety, however, he was excited. M was then five years and eight months old.

His WISC Pattern was as follows:

Verbal Tests	Scaled Scores
Information	16
Comprehension	13
Arithmetic	20
Similarities	17
Vocabulary	16
(Digit Span)	(15)

Performance Tests

Picture Completion	14
Picture Arrangement	12
Block Design	14
Object Assembly	11
Coding (A)	18

This test pattern on the WISC earned M a verbal I.Q. of 140, a performance I.Q. of 127, and a full-scale I.A. of 137. [Two matters are of particular interest in these test results. While the Binet IQ probably was invalidly high, owing to the errors in scoring that were mentioned in the report, the "correct" Binet IQ probably was higher than the Verbal IQ of the WISC. Second, certain characteristics of M's pattern of WISC Scaled Scores, particularly on the Verbal tests (product) should be noted. His performance on the Information and Vocabulary tests place him in the top 2 percent of his age group, and his Comprehension score places him above 84 percent of his age group. After all, he was from a superior home which could be nurturant in these areas. His Similarities score (process) also is strongly suggestive of definite superiority, probably in the top 1 percent. While there was considerable variability among all the scaled scores, all were at least somewhat above the average scaled score of 10.]

I would like to add a few descriptive comments. After the second item on "Information" I hastened to screen the booklet from M, because he read the questions upside down before I could read them to him. Before instructions were completed for "Coding" he exclaimed, "Oh, I know what you want me to do." His responses came quickly and he realized himself if his answers were correct or not.

In addition to the WISC, I administered a DAP [Draw a Person] and a CAT [Children's Apperception Test—a projective test]. The DAP was strongly primitive for such a sophisticated child. Considering the lower score in the performance on the WISC, as well, it seemed to me that M's stronger areas are in the verbal, number, and abstract areas. The CAT showed high vocabulary level, rich imagination, and quite a sense of humor. It also indicated strong demand for the mother's exclusive attention as well as conflict with the mother.

Finally, I took M to the Reading Laboratory and asked him to select books to read to me. The books he selected were high second and low third grade readers. He read fluently, without mistake, good inflection and apparent enjoyment and comprehension.

Shortly afterwards M's parents came to see me without the child. They are poised, well-educated people representing the picture of upper-middle class parents. His mother was rather tense and distraught about the problem young M caused her. She was quite ambivalent when confronted with the possibility of having an unusually able child. She was concerned about nonacceptance among the peer group, at the same time she indicated personal difficulties in accepting the child. The father seemed much less threatened by the whole issue, more relaxed and more flexible as a person. . . . During the final interview with the parents we discussed the limited facilities and educational opportunities which the small midwestern community had to offer a child like M. Therefore the parents are considering relocation to a community where the child could find adequate stimulation, teachers who understand and foster ability in students and other children who have comparable abilities.

At the present I understand they are considering moving M from the first grade to third grade in the local schools. This might be an adequate temporary expedient, but can hardly be considered adequate.

A bit more than three years later, the father wrote:

During much of the past three years, my being moved to another location, on the initiative of the company, seems to have been under sustained consideration. During that time, the problem of M's progress in school was temporarily helped by skipping him one grade. At 9½, he is in the fifth grade, and until this year has seemed to find the work interesting.

My company has finally announced that the executive offices will be moved to [a large city in a southern state]. In view of our prior correspondence and your offer to suggest possibilities to me, I would appreciate your appraisal of the various educational opportunities in this new location. Shortly my wife and I will be going there to look for a home and your counsel would be most helpful in determining what sections of the city we should consider.

Five weeks later, the president of the Association wrote the father (1) saying that the files for the Association yielded no information regarding any persons or programs in the community that would be likely to help him in finding adequate educational facilities for his son, (2) suggesting that the father write the state department of public instruction for information on any program(s) or provision(s) for the gifted in or near his new location, and (3) wishing him "the best of luck" in getting something satisfactory worked out for M.

In a sense, this account comes nearer being realistic than do the more conventional success stories about something having been done for gifted youngsters. The relative dearth around the country of appropriate educational facilities for the gifted results in frustration both in those who would help parents such as this one and on the part of parents seeking such help. In those few instances where parents of bright children have reasonable access to established good programs for the gifted, the inquiring parents can be referred with confidence to those in charge of such programs. But, as has been pointed out, many programs, or attempts at programs, are so evanescent in nature that one can refer such parents only with his fingers crossed since the program may have disappeared, and probably did, when the key figure in its development went to another school system.

What, then, logically and realistically are the possibilities of helping parents such as M's father? Ideally, yet of very low probability, the parent can be referred to competent persons in communities which have established programs of good quality for the gifted. They can be referred to persons known to be competent and effective in school districts that do not have formal or major programs for the gifted, confident in the knowledge that such individuals will work out for the parents and the children particular, often highly individualized adjustments for such children with those teachers and supervisory personnel whom they know to be effective. And there will be some instances in which youngsters who have been found validly to have much promise can be placed with effective teachers and their educational needs thus met for at least a short time. What can and will be done for such youngsters in succeeding years may be quite a different matter. Optimistically, if bright children can be identified and helped during their early school years, they may experience enough self-fulfillment and successful learning experiences that they will develop motivation sufficiently strong to enable them to weather later educational vicissitudes with reduced damage.

Bibliography

ABRAHAM, WILLARD. *Common Sense about Gifted Children.* New York: Harper & Brothers, 1958.

Administration Procedures and School Practices for the Academically Talented Student. Washington, D.C.: National Education Association, 1960.

Advocate Survey—*A Survey of Leadership in Education of Gifted and Talented Children and Youth.* Silver Spring, Md.: Operations Research, 1971.

ALBERT, ROBERT S. "Genius: Present-day Status of the Concept and Its Implications for the Study of Creativity and Giftedness." *Amer. Psychologist* (1969), **24,** 743–753.

ANASTASI, ANNE, and R. F. LEVEE. "Intellectual Defect and Musical Talent: A Case Report." *Amer. J. Ment. Defic.* (1960), **64,** 695–703.

ARN, WILLIAM, and EDWARD FIERSON. "An Analysis of Programs for the Gifted." *Gifted Child Quarterly* (1964), **8,** 4–8.

AUSUBEL, DAVID P. *Educational Psychology: A Cognitive View.* New York: Holt, Rinehart and Winston, 1968.

BACHTOLD, LOUISE M. "Interpersonal Values of Gifted Junior High School Students." *Psychology in the Schools* (1968), **5,** 368–370.

———, and EMMY E. WERNER. "An Evaluation of Teaching Creative Skills to Gifted Students in Grades 5 and 6." *J. Educ. Research* (1970), **63,** 253–256.

BARBE, WALTER B. "A Study of the Family Background of the Gifted." *J. Educ. Psych.* (1956), **47,** 302–309.

———. *One in a Thousand: A Comparative Study of Moderately and Highly Gifted Elementary School Children.* Columbus, Ohio: State Department of Education, 1964.

BARRETT, HARRY O. "The Intensive Study of Thirty-Two Gifted Children." *Pers. and Guid. J.* (1957), **36,** 192–194.

BARRON, FRANK. *Creativity and Personal*

Freedom. New York: D. Van Nostrand Co., 1968.

———. *Creative Person and Creative Process.* New York: Holt, Rinehart and Winston, 1969.

BARTLETT, F. C. *Thinking: An Experimental and Social Study.* New York: Basic Books, 1958.

BAYLEY, NANCY. "Development of Mental Abilities" in Paul H. Musson, ed., *Manual of Child Psychology* (3d ed.). New York: John Wiley & Sons, 1970, pp. 1163–1209.

BELL, MARY E. "A Comparative Study of Mentally Gifted Children Heterogeneously and Homogeneously Grouped." Doctoral dissertation, Indiana University, 1958.

BENNIS, WARREN G. "A Funny Thing Happened on the Way to the Future." *Amer. Psychologist* (1970), **25,** 595–608.

BENTLEY, JOHN E. *Superior Children.* New York: W. W. Norton & Co., 1937.

BERELSON, BERNARD, and GARY A. STEINER. *Human Behavior.* New York: Harcourt Brace Jovanovich, 1964.

BIRCH, JACK W. "Early School Admission for Mentally Advanced Children." *Exceptional Children* (1954), **21,** 84–87.

BISHOP, WILLIAM E. "Successful Teachers of the Gifted." *Exceptional Children* (1968), **34,** 317–325.

BLOOM, BENJAMIN S., ed. *Taxonomy of Educational Objectives—The Classification of Educational Goals Handbook: Cognitive Domain.* New York: David McKay Co., 1956.

BOND, HORACE MANN. *A Study of Factors Involved in the Identification and Encouragement of Unusual Talent among Disadvantaged Populations* (Report on USOE Project No. 5-1859). Atlanta: Atlanta University, Jan. 1967.

BOYD, HERBERT F. "Peer Group Perception of Mentally Superior Children in Grades One through Four." Doctoral dissertation, University of Illinois, 1958.

BRUNER, JEROME S., *et al. Beyond the Information Given.* New York: W. W. Norton & Co., 1973.

BURTON, WILLIAM H. *Introduction to Education.* New York: D. Appleton-Century Co., 1934.

CARMICHAEL, LEONARD, ed. *Manual of Child Psychology,* 2d ed. New York: John Wiley & Sons, 1954.

CARTLEDGE, C. J., and E. L. KRAUSER. "Training First-grade Children in Creative Thinking under Quantitative and Qualitative Motivation." *J. Educ. Psych.* (1963), **54,** 295–299

CARTTER, ALLAN M. "Scientific Manpower for 1970–1985." *Science* (1971), **172,** 132–140.

CLARK, RONALD W. *Einstein: The Life and Times.* New York: World Publishing Co., 1971.

CLEVELAND, ELIZABETH. "Detroit's Experiment with Gifted Children." *School and Society* (1920), **12,** 179–183.

COBB, MARGARET R., and GRACE A. TAYLOR. "Stanford Achievement Test with a Group of Gifted Children." *1924 Yearbook* (Part 1), *National Society for the Study of Education,* **23,** 275–289.

COLE, CHARLES C., JR. *Encouraging Scientific Talent.* New York: College Entrance Examination Board, 1956.

COLTON, DAVID L. *Policies of the Illinois Plan for Program Development for Gifted Children.* St. Louis: Center for Educational Field Studies, Washington University, August 1968.

CONANT, JAMES B. *The American High School Today.* New York: McGraw-Hill Book Co., 1959.

CORNISH, ROBERT L. "Parents', Teachers', and Pupils' Perception of the Gifted Child's Ability." *The Gifted Child Quarterly* (1968), **12,** 14–17.

Council for Exceptional Children. "Professional Standards for Personnel in the Education of Exceptional Children." *Professional Standards Project Report.* Washington, D.C.: The Council, 1966.

Council of Chief State School Officers. *Gifted Children and Youth.* Washington, D.C.: The Council, 1962.

COX, CATHERINE M., *et al. The Early Mental Traits of Three Hundred Geniuses.* Vol. II, Genetic Studies of Genius. Stanford, Calif.: Stanford University Press, 1926.

CRATTY, BRYANT J. *Movement Behavior and Motor Learning.* Philadelphia: Lea and Febiger, 1967.

CUBBERLEY, ELLWOOD P. *A Brief History of Education.* New York: Houghton Mifflin Co., 1922.

CUTTS, NORMA E., and NICHOLAS MOSELEY. *Bright Children: A Guide for Parents.* New York: G. P. Putnam's Sons, 1953.

DEASON, HILARY J., ed. *A Guide to Science Reading.* New York: New American Library, 1963.

DEHAAN, ROBERT F., and R. J. HAVIGHURST. *Educating Gifted Children.* Chicago: University of Chicago Press, 1957.

DES CARS, GUY (trans. Michael Luke). *The Brute.* New York: Greenberg, 1952.

DEUTSCH, MARTIN, and BERT R. BROWN. "Social Influences in Negro-White Intelligence Differences." *J. Social Issues* (1964), **20**, 24–35.

DEWEY, JOHN. *Democracy and Education.* New York: Macmillan Co., 1916.

DOMINO, GEORGE. "Identification of Potentially Creative Persons from the Adjective Checklist." *J. Consulting and Clinical Psych.* (1970), **35**, 48–51.

DUNLAP, JAMES M. "The Education of Children with High Mental Ability," chap. IV, pp. 147–188, in William M. Cruickshank, and G. Orville Johnson, eds., *Education of Exceptional Children and Youth.* Englewood Cliffs, N.J.: Prentice-Hall, 1958.

DURR, WILLIAM K. *The Gifted Student.* New York: Oxford University Press, 1964.

EDGERTON, HAROLD A., and STEWART H. BRITT. "The First Annual Science Talent Search." *The American Scientist* (1943), **31**, 55–68.

Educational Policies Commission. *The Purposes of Education in America.* Washington, D.C.: The National Education Association, 1938.

EICHENWALD, HEINZ F., and PEGGY C. FRY. "Nutrition and Learning." *Science* (1969), **163**, 644–648.

ELWOOD, CLARENCE. "Acceleration of the Gifted." *Gifted Child Quarterly* (1958), **2**, 21–23.

EVERETT, SAMUEL, ed. *Programs for the Gifted: A Case Book in Secondary Education.* New York: Harper & Brothers, 1961.

FINDLEY, WARREN G., and MIRIAM M. BRYAN. *Ability Grouping: 1970. Status, Import, and Alternatives.* Athens: Center for Educational Improvement, University of Georgia, 1971.

FINNEY, BEN C., and ELIZABETH VAN DALSEM. "Group Counseling for Gifted Underachieving High School Students." *J. Counseling Psych.* (1969), **16**, 87–94.

FLANAGAN, JOHN C., *et al. The American High School Student.* Cooperative Research Project No. 635 (1964). Pittsburgh: University of Pittsburgh, Project TALENT Office.

FLIEGLER, LOUIS A. *Curriculum Planning for the Gifted.* Englewood Cliffs, N. J.: Prentice-Hall, 1961.

———, and C. E. BISH. "The Gifted and Talented." *Review of Educational Research* (1959), **29**, 408–450.

FOGARTY, JOHN E. "Stimulating Special Education through Federal Legislation." *Exceptional Children* (1964), **31**, 1–4.

FREEHILL, MAURICE F. *Gifted Children.* New York: Macmillan Co., 1961.

FRENCH, JOSEPH L., ed. *Educating the Gifted* (revised). New York: Holt, Rinehart and Winston, 1964.

FRIEDENBERG, EDGAR Z. "The Gifted Student and His Enemies." *Commentary* (1962), **33**, 410–419.

FRIERSON, EDWARD C. "Upper and Lower Class Status Gifted Children: A Study of Differences." *Exceptional Children* (1965), **32**, 83–90.

FROHREICH, LLOYD E. "Costing Programs for Exceptional Children: Dimensions and Indices." *Exceptional Children* (1973), **39**, 317–324.

The Fund for the Advancement of Education. *Bridging the Gap between School and College.* New York: The Fund, 1953.

———. *They Went to College Early.* New York: The Fund, 1957.

GALLAGHER, JAMES J. "Peer Acceptance of Highly Gifted Children in Elementary School." *Elementary School J.* (1958), **58**, 465–470.

———. *Teaching the Gifted Child.* Boston: Allyn & Bacon, 1964.

———. *Research Summary on Gifted Child Education.* Springfield, Ill.: Office of the

Superintendent of Public Instruction, 1966.

————. *Analyses of Teacher Classroom Strategies Associated with Student Cognitive and Affective Performance.* Urbana: University of Illinois, 1968.

————, MARY J. ASCHNER, and WILLIAM JENNE. *Productive Thinking of Gifted Children.* Washington, D.C.: Council for Exceptional Children, 1967.

————, and THORA CROWDER. "The Adjustment of Gifted Children in the Regular Classroom." *Exceptional Children* (1957), **23**, 306–312, 317–319.

GARBER, L. O., and R. C. SEITZ. *The Yearbook of School Law 1969.* Danville, Ill.: Printers and Publishers, 1969.

GIBBONY, HAZEL L. *Enrichment-Classroom Challenge* (revised). Columbus, Ohio: State Board of Education, 1967.

GODDARD, HENRY H. *School Training of Gifted Children.* New York: Harcourt Brace Jovanovich, 1928.

GETZELS, J. W., and P. W. JACKSON. *Creativity and Intelligence.* New York: John Wiley & Sons, 1961.

GOLD, MARVIN J. *The Lincoln School: Its Rise and Demise.* Paper presented at the 48th Annual International Convention of the Council for Exceptional Children, 1970.

GOSLING, THOMAS W. "A Special Academic Class in the Junior High School." *School Review* (1919), **27**, 241–255.

GOWAN, JOHN C. *An Annotated Bibliography on the Academically Talented.* Washington, D.C.: National Education Association of the United States, 1961.

————, and E. PAUL TORRANCE, eds. *Educating the Ablest.* Itasca, Ill.: F. E. Peacock Publishers, 1971.

GREEN, DONALD A. "A Study of Talented High School Drop-outs." *Vocational Guidance Quarterly* (Spring, 1962), **10**, 171–172.

GROTH, NORMA J., and PRISCILLA HOLBERT. "Hierarchial Needs of Gifted Boys and Girls in the Affective Domain." *Gifted Child Quarterly* (1969), **13**, 129–133.

GRUBB, RICHARD D. "Disparities in Elementary School Children among Reported Adjustment and Psychoeducational Characteristics." Master's thesis, University of Illinois, 1969.

GRUPE, AUDREY J. "Adjustment and Acceptance of Mentally Superior Children in Regular and Special Fifth Grade Classes in a Public School System." Doctoral dissertation, University of Illinois, 1961.

GUILFORD, JOY PAUL. "The Structure of Intellect." *Psychological Bulletin* (1956), **53**, 267–293.

————. *The Nature of Human Intelligence.* New York: McGraw-Hill Book Co., 1967.

HAGGARD, ERNEST A. "Socialization, Personality and Academic Achievement in Gifted Children." *School Review* (1957), **65**, 388–414.

HALL, THEODORE. *Gifted Children: The Cleveland Story.* New York: World Publishing Co., 1956.

HARRIS, WILLIAM T. *Classification in Graded Schools. Report of the United States Commissioner of Education for 1891–2,* Vol. 1, pp. 601–636.

HAUCK, BARBARA B., and MAURICE F. FREHILL, *The Gifted—Case Studies.* Dubuque, Iowa: Wm. C. Brown Co., 1972.

HELSON, RAVENNA, and RICHARD S. CRUTCHFIELD. "Mathematicians: The Creative Researcher and the Average Ph.D." *J. Consulting and Clinical Psych.* (1970), **34**, 250–257.

HENRY, NELSON B., ed. *Education for the Gifted.* Chicago: University of Chicago Press. The Fifty-Seventh Yearbook of the National Society for the Study of Education, Part II, 1958.

HILDRETH, GERTRUDE H. *Educating Gifted Children.* New York: Harper & Brothers, 1952.

————. *Introduction to the Gifted.* New York: McGraw-Hill Book Co., 1966.

HOBSON, JAMES R. "Mental Age as a Workable Criterion for School Admission." *Elementary School J.* (1948), **48**, 312–321.

————. "Scholastic Standing and Activity Participation of Underage High School Pupils Originally Admitted to Kindergarten on the Basis of Physical and Psychological Examination," Pres. Address, APA Div. 16, Sept. 1956 (mimeo.).

Hobson v. *Hanson,* 269 F.Supp. 401 (Originating in D.C.)

HOLLINGSWORTH, LETA S. *Gifted Children: Their Nature and Their Nurture.* New York: Macmillan Co., 1926.

———. "The Terman Classes and Public School 500." *J. Educ. Soc.* (1936), **10**, 86–90.

———. *Children above 180 IQ Stanford-Binet.* New York: Harcourt Brace Jovanovich, 1942.

———, and M. M. RUST. "Application of the Bernreuter Inventory of Personality to Highly Intelligent Adolescents." *J. Psych.* (1937), **4**, 287–293.

HOUSE, ERNEST R., THOMAS KERINS, and JOE M. STEELE. *The Demonstration Center: An Appraisal of the Illinois Experience.* Urbana Ill.: University of Illinois, Center for Instructional Research and Curriculum Development, Dec. 1970.

Illinois Council on Educational Administration. Information Inventory on Provisions for Gifted Pupils in Illinois Schools. *The Illinois Council on Educational Administration* (1959), **4**, 51–56.

JANSON, VERNA G., and JAMES J. GALLAGHER. "The Social Choices of Students in Socially Integrated Classes for the Culturally Disadvantaged." *Exceptional Children* (1966), **33**, 221–226.

JENSEN, ARTHUR R. "How Much Can We Boost IQ and Scholastic Achievement?" *Harvard Educational Review* (1969) **39**, 1–123.

JOHN, VERA P. "The Intellectual Development of Slum Children: Some Preliminary Findings." *Amer. J. Orthopsychiatry* (1963), **33**, 813–822.

JOHNSON, CAROLYN M. "The Creative Thinking, Verbal Intelligence, and Creative Writing Ability of Young Gifted Children." *Diss. Abstracts* (1969), **29**, 4187.

JUSTMAN, JOSEPH. "Personal and Social Adjustment of Intellectually Gifted Accelerants and Non-accelerants in Junior High Schools." *The School Review* (1953), **61**, 468–478.

———. "Academic Achievement of Intellectually Gifted Accelerants and Non-accelerants in Junior High School." *The School Review* (1954), **62**, 142–150.

KINCAID, DONALD. "A Study of Highly Gifted Elementary Pupils." *Gifted Child Quarterly* (1969), **13**, 264–267.

KLAUSMEIER, HERBERT J. "Effects of Accelerating Bright Older Elementary Pupils: A Follow-up." *J. Educ. Psych.* (1963), **54**, 165–171.

———, WILLIAM L. GOODWIN, and TEKLA RONDA. "Effects of Accelerating Bright, Older Elementary Pupils: A Second Follow-up." *J. Educ. Psych.* (1968), **59**, 53–58.

KOUGH, J., and R. DeHAAN. *Teachers' Guidance Handbook, Part I: Identifying Children Who Need Help.* Chicago: Science Research Associates, 1955.

KRATHWOHL, DAVID R., BENJAMIN S. BLOOM, and BERTRAM B. MASIA. *Taxonomy of Educational Objectives—The Classification of Educational Goals Handbook 2: Affective Domain.* New York: David McKay Co., 1965.

LAYCOCK, FRANK, and JOHN S. CAYLOR. "Physiques of Gifted Children and Their Less Gifted Siblings." *Child Development* (1964), **35**, 63–74.

LEARY, TIMOTHY. *Multilevel Measurement of Interpersonal Behavior: A Manual for the Use of the Interpersonal System.* Berkeley, Calif.: Psychological Consulation Service, 1957.

LEE, RAYMOND E., and T. ERNEST NEWLAND. "A Small Community and Its Gifted School Children." *The Educational Forum* (1966), **30**, 363–368.

LEHMAN, HARVEY C. *Age and Achievement.* Princeton, N.J.: Princeton University Press, 1953.

LESSINGER, LEON M., and RUTH A. MARTINSON. "The Use of the California Psychological Inventory with Gifted Pupils." *Pers. and Guid. J.* (1961), **39**, 572–575.

LEWIS, H. MICHAEL. *Opening Windows onto the Future.* Winston-Salem, N.C.: The Governor's School of North Carolina, 1970.

LIDDLE, GORDON. "Overlap among Desirable and Undesirable Characteristics in Gifted Children." *J. Educ. Psych.* (1958), **49**, 219–223.

LIGHTFOOT, GEORGIA F. *Personality Characteristics of Bright and Dull Children.* Teachers College Contributions to Education #969. New York: Bureau of Publications, Teachers College, Columbia University, 1951.

MANN, H. "How Real Are Friendships of Gifted and Typical Children in a Program of Partial Segregation?" *Exceptional Children* (1957), **23**, 199–201, 206.

MARLAND, S. P., JR. *Education of the Gifted and Talented.* Vol. I: Report to the Congress of the United States by the U.S. Commissioner of Education, 1971.

MARTIN, W. E. *Children's Body Measurements.* Washington, D.C.: U. S. Government Printing Office, U.S. Office of Education, Special Publication No. 5, 1955.

MARTINSON, RUTH A. *Educational Programs for Gifted Pupils.* Sacramento: State Dept. of Education, 1961.

——, and MAY V. SEAGOE. *The Abilities of Young Children.* Research Monograph Series B, No. 13-4. Washington, D.C.: The Council for Exceptional Children, 1969.

——, DAVID HERMANSON, and GEORGE BANKS. "An Independent Study-Seminar Program for the Gifted," *Exceptional Children* (1972), **38**, 421–426.

MAYER, MARTIN. "The Good Slum Schools." *Harpers,* April 1961, 46–52.

McCLELLAND, DAVID C., *et al. The Achievement Motive.* New York: Appleton-Century-Crofts, 1953.

MEAD, MARGARET. "The Gifted Child in the American Culture of Today." *J. Teacher Educ.* (1954), **5**, 211–214.

MEEKER, MARY. "Differential Syndromes of Giftedness and Curriculum Planning: A Four-Year Follow-up." *J. Spec. Educ.* (1968), **2**, 185–196.

MEREDITH, PAUL, and LESLIE LANDIN. *100 Activities for Gifted Children.* San Francisco: Fearn Publishers, 1957.

MILES, CATHERINE C. "Gifted Children." Chapter 16 in Leonard Carmichael, ed., *Manual of Child Psychology.* New York: John Wiley & Sons, 1954, pp. 984–1063.

MILLER, VERA. "Academic Achievement and Social Adjustment of Children Young for Their Grade Placement." *Elementary School J.* (1957), **57**, 257–263.

MINER, JOHN B. *Intelligence in the United States.* New York: Springer Publishing Co., 1957.

MIRMAN, N. "Are Accelerated Students Socially Maladjusted?" *Elementary School J.* (1962), **62**, 273–276.

MONDERER, J. H. "An Evaluation of the Nebraska Program of Early Entrance to Elementary School." Doctoral dissertation, University of Nebraska, 1953.

MORGAN, ANTONIA BELL. "Critical Factors in the Academic Acceleration of Gifted Children: A Follow-up Study." *Psychological Reports* (1959), **5**, 649–653.

MUELLER, KARL. "Success of Elementary Students Admitted to Public Schools under the Requirements of the Nebraska Program of Early Entrance." Doctoral dissertation, University of Nebraska, 1955.

MUELLER, WILLIAM J., and J. W. ROTHNEY. "Comparisons of Selected Descriptive and Predictive Statements of Superior Students, Their Parents, and Their Teachers." *Pers. and Guid. J.* (1960), **38**, 621–625.

MURSELL, JAMES L. *Principles of Education.* New York: W. W. Norton & Co., 1934.

MUSSEN, PAUL H., ed. *Carmichael's Manual of Child Psychology,* 3d ed. New York: John Wiley & Sons, 1970.

NEWLAND, T. ERNEST. "Something *Can* Be Done for the Gifted." *Cook County Educational Digest* (1957), **20**, 3–4, 8.

——. "Some Observations on Essential Qualifications of Teachers of the Mentally Superior." *Exceptional Children* (1962), **29**, 111–114.

——. "On Defining the Mentally Superior in Terms of Social Need." *Exceptional Children* (1963), **29**, 237–240.

——. "Psychological Assessment of Exceptional Children and Youth." Chapter 3 in W. M. Cruickshank, *The Psychology of Exceptional Children and Youth,* 3d ed., pp. 115–172. Englewood Cliffs, N.J.: Prentice-Hall, 1971.

——. "Assessing the Cognitive Capability of Exceptional Children." In Don L. Walker and Douglas P. Howard, eds., *Special Education—Instrument of Change in Education for the '70s.* Selected papers from the University of Virginia Lecture Series, 1970–71, pp. 25–43. Charlottesville: University of Virginia, 1972.

NICHOLS, ROBERT C., and J. A. DAVIS. "Characteristics of Students of High Academic Aptitude." *Pers. and Guid. J.* (1964), **42**, 794–800.

North Carolina. *A Status Report, Program for the Education of Exceptionally Talented Children.* Raleigh, N. C.: State Department of Public Instruction, 1970.

National Academy of Science. *Doctorate Recipients from United States Universities, 1958–1966.* Publication 1489. Washington, D.C.: National Academy of Science, 1967.

ODEN, MELITA H. "The Fulfillment of Promise: 40-year Follow-up of the Terman Gifted Group." *Genetic Psychology Monographs* (1968), **77**, (first half) 3–93.

O'ROURKE, RICHARD H. "A Study of the Creative Thinking Abilities, Attitudes, and Achievement of Academically Talented Students in the Honors Programs and Regular Classes at Cooley H.S. 1962–1965." *Diss. Abstracts* (1969), **30**, 962.

ORWELL, GEORGE. *Nineteen Eighty-Four.* New York: Harcourt Brace Jovanovich, 1949.

OTIS, A. S. "Ability Grouping: Replies to L. B. Brink, T. M. Center." *School and Society* (1932), **35**, 798–800; **36**, 116–118.

PACE, WARREN J. "The Academic Effects of Assigned Gifted Students to Special Centers in the Fairfax County Schools." *Diss. Abstracts, Inter.* (1970), **31**, 936.

PARKYN, GEORGE W. *Children of High Intelligence: A New Zealand Study.* New York: Oxford University Press, 1948.

PASSOW, A. HARRY, et al. *Planning for Talented Youth.* New York: Bureau of Publications, Teachers College, Columbia University, 1955.

PEGNATO, CARL W., and JACK W. BIRCH. "Locating Gifted Children in Junior High Schools: A Comparison of Methods." *Exceptional Children* (1959), **25**, 300–304.

Pennsylvania Department of Public Instruction *et al. Proceedings of a Conference on Planning Better Services for Emotionally Disturbed Children of School Age.* Harrisburgh, Pa., 1963 (mimeo).

PETER, L. J., and R. HALL. *The Peter Principle.* New York: William Morrow and Co., 1969.

PHILLIPS, JOHN L., JR. *The Origins of Intellect: Piaget's Theory.* San Francisco: W. H. Freeman and Co., 1969.

PIAGET, JEAN. *The Construction of Reality in the Child.* New York: Ballantine Books, 1971.

PIELSTICK, NORVAL L. "Perception of Mentally Superior Children by Their Classmates in Fourth, Fifth, and Sixth Grades." Doctoral dissertation, University of Illinois, 1958, and in *Perceptual and Motor Skills* (1963), **77**, 47–53.

PLOWMAN, PAUL D. *An Interpretation of the Taxonomy of Educational Objectives.* Sacramento: the author, 1968.

———, and JOSEPH P. RICE, JR. *Final Report: California Project Talent.* Sacramento: California Department of Public Instruction, 1969.

PREGLER, HEDWIG. "The Colfax Plan." *Exceptional Children* (1954), **20**, 198–201, 222.

President's Science Advisory Committee, Panel on Youth, *Youth: Transition to Adulthood.* Chicago: University of Chicago Press, 1974.

PRESSEY, SIDNEY L. *Educational Acceleration: Appraisal and Basic Problems.* Columbus: Ohio State University, Bureau of Educ. Research and Monographs, No. 31, 1949.

———. "Concerning the Nature and Nurture of Genius." *Science* (1955), **68**, 123–129.

———. "A New Look at Acceleration," in *Acceleration and the Gifted.* Columbus: Ohio State Department of Education, 1963, pp. 1–4.

———, and ALICE PRESSEY. "Genius at 80, and Other Oldsters." *The Gerontologist* (1967), **7**, Part 1, 183–187.

PRINGLE, M. L. KELLMER. *Able Misfits.* London: Longman, 1970.

RACE, HENRIETTA V. "A Study of a Class of Superior Intelligence." *J. Educ. Psych.* (1918), **9**, 91–98.

RAPH, JANE, MIRIAM GOLDBERG, and A. HARRY PASSOW. *Bright Underachievers.* New York: Teachers College Press, Teachers College, Columbia University, 1966.

RENOTSKY, ALVIN, and JONS GREEN. *Standard Education Almanac.* Los Angeles: Academic Media, 1970.

RENZULLI, JOSEPH S. "Identifying Key Factors in Programs for the Gifted." *Exceptional Children* (1968), **35**, 217–221.

————, ROBERT K. HARTMAN, and CAROLYN M. CALLAHAN. "Teacher Identification of Superior Students." *Exceptional Children* (1971), **38**, 211–214, 243–248.

REYNOLDS, MAYNARD C., ed. *Early School Admission for Mentally Advanced Children.* Washington, D.C.: The Council for Exceptional Children, 1962.

RIPPLE, RICHARD E. "A Controlled Experiment in Acceleration from the Second to the Fourth Grade." *Gifted Child Quarterly* (1961), **5**, 119–120.

ROE, ANNE. "The Psychologist Examines 64 Eminent Scientists." *Sci. Amer.* (1952), **187**, 21–25.

————. *The Making of a Scientist.* New York: Dodd, Mead & Co., 1953.

RUSCH, R. R., D. A. DENNY, and S. IVES. "Fostering Creativity in Sixth Grade." *Elementary School Journal* (1965), **65**, 262–268.

RUSSELL, DAVID H. *Children's Thinking.* Boston: Ginn & Co., 1956.

SAUVAIN, WALTER H. *A Study of the Opinions of Certain Professional and Non-Professional Groups Regarding Homogeneous or Ability Grouping,* Teachers College Contributions to Education No. 596. New York: Bureau of Publications, Teachers College, Columbia University, 1934.

SCHREIBER, DANIEL. "The Higher Horizons Program." *New York State School Boards Association Research Bulletin* (1962), **4**, 1–10.

SCHWARTZ, W. P. "The Effects of Homogeneous Classification on the Scholastic Achievement and Personality Development of Gifted Pupils." Doctoral dissertation, New York University, 1942.

SCRIBNER, SYLVIA, and MICHAEL COLE. "Cognitive Consequences of Formal and Informal Education." *Science* (1973), **182**, 553–559.

SEWELL, WILLIAM H., and VIMAL P. SHAH. "Socioeconomic Status, Intelligence, and the Attainment of Higher Education." *Sociology of Education* (1967), **40**, 1–23.

SHAFFER, L. F. *The Psychology of Adjustment.* Boston: Houghton Mifflin Co., 1936.

SHAW, MELVILLE C., and JOHN T. McCUEN. "The Onset of Academic Underachievement in Bright Children." *J. Educ. Psych.* (1960), **51**, 103–108.

SHEARER, W. J. "The Elizabeth Plan of Grading." *Addresses and Proceedings of the National Education Association, 1898,* Vol. 37, 441–448.

SHERTZER, BRUCE, ed. *Working with Superior Students.* Chicago: Science Research Associates, 1960.

SHUTTLEWORTH, FRANK K. "The Nature versus Nurture Problem II: The Contributions of Nature and Nurture to Individual Differences in Intelligence." *J. Educ. Psych.* (1935), **26**, 655–681.

SILVERSTEIN, SAMUEL. "How Snobbish Are the Gifted in Regular Classes?" *Exceptional Children* (1962), **28**, 323–324.

SMITH, DONALD C. *Personal and Social Adjustment of Gifted Adolescents,* CEC Research Monograph Series A, No. 4, Washington, D.C.: Council for Exceptional Children, 1962.

SPEARMAN, C. *The Abilities of Man.* New York: Macmillan Co., 1927.

SPECHT, LOUISE F. "A Terman Class in Public School No. 64, Manhattan." *School and Society* (1919), **9**, 393–398.

STEDMAN, LULU M. *Education of Gifted Children.* New York: Harcourt Brace Jovanovich, 1924.

STEELE, JOE M., ERNEST R. HOUSE, and THOMAS KERINS. "An Instrument for Assessing Instructional Climate through Low-Inference Student Judgments." *American Journal of Educational Research* (1971), **8**, 447–466.

STEWART, LAWRENCE H. "Interest Patterns of a Group of High-Ability, High-Achieving Students." *J. Counseling Psych.* (1959), **6**, 132–139.

SUMPTION, MERLE R. *Three Hundred Gifted Children.* New York: Harcourt Brace Jovanovich, 1941.

————, and EVELYN M. LUECKING. *Education of the Gifted.* New York: Ronald Press Co., 1960.

SUSSER, MERVYN, ZENA STEIN, GERHART SAENGER, and FRANCIS MARCELLA. *Famine and Human Development: Birth, Death, Health and Mental Competence after the Dutch Hunger Winter 1944/45.* New York: Oxford University Press, 1974.

TAUBMAN, PAUL, and TERENCE WALES. *Mental Ability and Higher Educational Attain-*

ment in the 20th Century. Berkeley, Calif.: Carnegie Commission on Higher Education, 1972.

TERMAN, LEWIS M., *et al. Genetic Studies of Genius.* Stanford, Calif.: Stanford University Press.

    I—Terman, L. M., *et al. The Mental and Physical Traits of a Thousand Gifted Children.* 1925.

    II—Cox, Catherine M. *The Early Mental Traits of Three Hundred Geniuses.* 1926.

    III—Burks, Barbara S., Dortha Jensen, and L. M. Terman. *The Promise of Youth.* 1930.

    IV—Terman, Lewis M., and Melita H. Oden. *The Gifted Child Grows Up.* 1947.

    V—Terman, Lewis M., and Melita H. Oden. *The Gifted Group at Mid-Life.* 1959.

    (*See also* Melita H. Oden. "The Fulfillment of Promise: 40-year Follow-up of the Terman Gifted Group.")

———. "Status of the California Gifted Group at the End of Sixteen Years." National Society for the Study of Education, *Intelligence: Its Nature and Nurture,* Thirty-Ninth Yearbook, Part II. Bloomington, Ill.: Public School Publishing Co., 1940, pp. 67–84.

———. "The Discovery and Encouragement of Exceptional Talent." *Amer. Psychologist* (1954), **9,** 221–230.

TIDYMAN, ERNEST. *Dummy.* Boston: Little, Brown and Co., 1974.

TORRANCE, E. P., *et al. Rewarding Creative Thinking.* Minneapolis: University of Minnesota, 1960.

———. *Guiding Creative Talent.* Englewood Cliffs, N.J.: Prentice-Hall, 1962.

———, and DEAN C. DAUW. "Attitude Patterns of Creatively Gifted High School Seniors." *The Gifted Child Quarterly* (1966), **10,** 53–58.

———. "Creative Young Women in Today's World." *Exceptional Children* (1972), **38,** 597–603.

U.S. Bureau of the Census. *Statistical Abstract of the United States 1966* (87th ed.). Washington, D.C., 1966.

U.S. Department of Commerce. *Projections of School and College Enrollment: 1970 to 2000.* Series P-25, No. 473. Washington, D.C., Jan. 1972.

U.S. Office of Education. *School Staffing Survey, 1969–1970.* Washington, D.C.: Department of Health, Education, and Welfare, 1970.

VERNON, PHILIP E. *Intelligence and Cultural Environment.* London: Metheun & Co., 1969.

WALLACH, MICHAEL A. "Creativity," in Paul H. Musson, ed., *Manual of Child Psychology,* 3d ed. New York: John Wiley & Sons, 1970, pp. 1211–1272.

———, and NATHAN KOGAN. *Modes of Thinking in Young Children: A Study of the Creativity-Intelligence Distinction.* New York: Holt, Rinehart and Winston, 1965.

WARD, VIRGIL S. *Educating the Gifted.* Columbus, Ohio: Charles E. Merrill Books, 1961.

WARREN, JONATHAN R., and PAUL A. HEIST. "Personality Attributes of Gifted College Students." *Science* (1960), **132,** 330–337.

WEINER, JEAN. "Attitudes of Psychologists and Psychometrists toward Gifted Children and Programs for the Gifted." *Exceptional Children* (1968), **34,** 354.

WELCH, L. "Recombinations of Ideas in Thinking." *J. Appl. Psych.* (1946), **30,** 638–643.

WHIPPLE, GUY M., ed. "Report of the Society's Committee on the Education of Gifted Children." *Twenty-Third Yearbook of the National Society for the Study of Education,* Part I, Section 2: Special Studies. Bloomington, Ill.: Public School Publishing Co., 1924.

WHITEHURST, MARTHA F. "Reported Behavior Problems and Discrepancy between Mental Age and Grade Placement." Master's thesis, University of Illinois, 1968.

WHYTE, WILLIAM H., JR. *The Organization Man.* Garden City, N.Y.: Simon and Schuster, 1956.

WILLIAMS, CLIFFORD W. "Organizing a School Program for the Gifted." Chapter XVIII, pp. 395–413, in *Education for the Gifted,* 57th Yearbook of the National Society for the Study of Education. Chicago: University of Chicago Press, 1958.

——. "Characteristics and the Objectives of a Program for the Gifted." Chapter VIII, pp. 147–165, in *Education for the Gifted,* 57th Yearbook of the National Society for the Study of Education. Chicago: University of Chicago Press, 1958.

WILLIAMS, FRANK E. "Models for Encouraging Creativity in the Classroom by Integrating, Cognitive and Affective Behaviors." *Educational Technology* (1969), **9,** 7–13.

WITKIN, H. A., R. B. DYK, H. F. FATERSON, D. R. GOODENOUGH, and S. A. KARP. *Psychological Differentiation: Studies of Mental Development.* New York: John Wiley & Sons, 1962.

WITTY, PAUL A. "A Genetic Study of Fifty Gifted Children." *Intelligence: Its Nature and Nurture.* Thirty-ninth Yearbook of the National Society for the Study of Education, Part II. Bloomington, Ill.: Public School Publishing Co., 1940, pp. 401–409.

——, ed. *The Gifted Child.* Boston: D. C. Heath and Co., 1951.

——. "Gifted Children—Our Greatest Resource." *Nursing Outlook* (1955), **3,** 498–500.

WOLFLE, DAEL. *America's Resources of Specialized Talent.* New York: Harper & Brothers, 1954.

——. *The Uses of Talent.* Princeton, N.J.: Princeton University Press, 1971.

WORCESTER, D. A. *The Education of Children of Above-Average Ability.* Lincoln: University of Nebraska Press, 1956.

WRIGHT, JUDGE J. S. *Hobson* v. *Hansen* (U.S. Court of Appeals Decision on the District of Columbia's Track System), Civil Action No. 82–66. Washington, D.C.: U.S. Court of Appeals, 1967.

Index

401